The Content of Faith

Karl Rahner

THE
CONTENT
OF FAITH

*The Best of Karl Rahner's
Theological Writings*

*Edited by Karl Lehmann and Albert Raffelt
Translation edited by Harvey D. Egan, S.J.*

CROSSROAD • NEW YORK

1992

The Crossroad Publishing Company
370 Lexington Avenue, New York, NY 10017

Originally published as *Rechenschaft des Glaubens. Karl Rahner-Lesebuch*
© Verlag Herder Freiburg im Breisgau
Benziger Verlag Zurich 1979.

English translation © 1993 by The Crossroad Publishing Company.

Printed in the United States of America

Library of Congress Cataloging-in-Publication Data
Rahner, Karl, 1904–1984
    [Rechenschaft des Glaubens. English]
    The content of faith : the best of Karl Rahner's theological
writings / edited by Karl Lehmann and Albert Raffelt ; translation
edited by Harvey D. Egan.
       p.   cm.
    Translation of: Rechenschaft des Glaubens.
    Includes bibliographical references and index.
    ISBN 0-8245-1221-9 (cloth)
    1. Theology.   I. Lehmann, Karl, 1936–   . II. Raffelt, Albert.
III. Egan, Harvey D.   IV. Title.
BX891.R35213   1993
230'.2 — dc20   92-27765
                                               CIP

Contents

Translation Editor's Preface   xi

Introduction
Karl Rahner: A Portrait, by Karl Lehmann   1

WHAT IS CHRISTIANITY?

1. A Short Formula of the Christian Faith   45
2. The Sacramental Structure of the Christian Salvation-Reality   49
3. Christianity and World Religions   51
4. Christianity Is Not an Ideology 55
5. Jesus Christ: The Synthesis   63
6. Why Remain a Christian?   66

THE MYSTERY OF EXISTENCE

7. The Mystery of the Human Person   73
8. Nature as Creation   82
9. Life   85
10. The Human Person as God's Creature   89
11. The Human Spirit   90
12. "You Are Dust!"   92
13. Freedom Received from and Directed toward God   96
14. Freedom as the Total and Finalizing Self-Mastery
    of the Subject   100
15. Freedom and Ensnarement in Guilt   103
16. Love: The Basic Human Act   107
17. Propositional Knowledge and Primordial Consciousness   114
18. Intellectual Honesty and Human Decision   116
19. The Divided and Enigmatic Nature of Humanity   118
20. Individuality and Community   121
21. The Child   123

22. The Challenge of Growing Old 129
23. The Pilgrimage of Life 131
24. Human Death 135
25. On Work 137
26. Patience 138
27. On Illness 141
28. Renunciation and Self-Realization 144
29. Laughter 148
30. On Getting About 152
31. Seeing and Hearing 154
32. Primordial Words 159
33. Hearer of the Word 164
34. The Contemporary Inner Threat to Truth 169
35. "Freedom": A Contemporary Slogan 174
36. Christian Faith and Secularization 177
37. When Are We Peace-Loving? 179
38. Creative Hope for Peace 180
39. The World and the Angels I 182
40. The World and the Angels II 188
41. The World and History as the Event of God's
    Self-Communication 193
42. Evil and the Devil 196
43. The Need of Redemption 199

ON THE LIVING GOD

44. The Word "God" 205
45. Images of God 211
46. Troubled Atheism? 213
47. God Is Far from Us 216
48. Natural Knowledge of God? 220
49. Experience of Self and Experience of God 222
50. God Is No Scientific Formula 227
51. The True God 230
52. God in the Old Testament 232
53. God in the New Testament 233
54. The Uniqueness of God in the New Testament 237
55. God as Person in the New Testament 240
56. On the Personal Being of God 247
57. God Is Love 250
58. God, Our Father 257
59. Non-Christian and Christian Conceptions of God 259

132. Pray Daily Life! 510
133. The Prayer of Petition I 513
134. The Prayer of Petition II 518
135. Love of God 520
136. Baptism and Confirmation 524
137. Original Sin 526
138. Sin and Guilt 531
139. Venial Sin 535
140. Morality without Moralizing 537
141. Existential Ethics 543
142. Penance and the Anointing of the Sick 544
143. The Eucharist 547
144. The Meal of Pilgrims 550
145. The Mystery of Christian Marriage 553
146. The Sobriety of Christian Life 556
147. Calm Readiness for God 560
148. Christian Flight from the World 562
149. Christian Joy in the World 566
150. Grace and Dying with Christ 568
151. To the Greater Glory of God 571
152. The Unity of Love of God and Neighbor 579
153. Internal Threat to the Faith 587
154. The Christian in the World 588
155. The Missionary Task of the Christian 592
156. Christianity and Literature 597
157. Faith and Culture 599
158. A Prayer to the Lord Who Is Present 604

HOPE IN GOD

159. Utopia and Reality 609
160. Christian Pessimism 612
161. The Advent Person 616
162. The Real Future 619
163. The Christian Understanding of Death 625
164. The Intermediate State 631
165. Judgment 632
166. Purgatory 633
167. Eternal Damnation? 634
168. Eternity in Time 637
169. Hope of Eternal Life 641
170. The Beatific Vision 649

171. Heaven   651
172. Resurrection of the Flesh   652
173. Christian Optimism   657
174. Prayer for Hope   658

Selected Bibliography   663

Translation Editor's Preface

Karl Rahner was a Jesuit for sixty-two years, a priest for fifty-two years, and he led a "theological life" for almost forty-five years. He taught theology at Innsbruck, Munich, and Münster, and he lectured all over the world. Four thousand written works, paperbacks in excess of one million copies, numerous entries in multivolume theological encyclopedias and reference works, as well as several volumes of television, radio, and newspaper interviews make up his bibliography.

Not only did Rahner write on almost every significant theological topic, but he also entered into dialogue with atheistic, Buddhist, Jewish, Marxist, Muslim, Protestant, and scientific thinkers the world over. His unanswered questions have provided fresh points of departure for a host of theological thinkers. Add to this his significant impact upon the Second Vatican Council, his fourteen honorary doctoral degrees, and the large number of doctoral students he directed, and one can see why he is aptly called "the quiet mover of the Roman Catholic Church" and "the Father of the Catholic Church in the twentieth century."

So prolific and variegated is his work that one should speak of the "many Rahners." He enjoyed the sobriquet "theological atomic physicist," endured the often-misunderstood label "transcendental Thomist," and eschewed the epithet "Denzinger theologian." He considered it essential to wrest the hidden vitality remaining in the often-desiccated school theology of his time and to transpose for the contemporary person the traditional wisdom he had mastered. Those who dismiss Rahner as an abstract and convoluted thinker overlook the "mysticism of everyday life," which runs throughout his writings. Rahner the *pastor,* the *homilist,* the *spiritual director,* and the *teacher of prayer* is never very far from the surface of even his most difficult works.

Rahner not only explained critically and precisely what the Christian faith is, but he also sought to *unite* people with it. To Rahner, theology is more than faith seeking understanding; it is as well a mystagogy that gives the people of God experiential union with the faith by leading them into their own deepest mystery. Thus, he was more a "sapiential" than an "academic" theologian.

I have been reading Karl Rahner for almost thirty years and teaching his thought for over fifteen. I consider this anthology to be the best point of entry into the life's work of this remarkable theologian. No anthology can substitute for reading all the works of this theological titan. Nonetheless, as the best cross-section of Rahner's theological writings available, I consider it the "Norton's" of all the anthologies of his work.

With a view to an English-speaking audience, I slightly emended Lehmann's introduction, eliminated extensive German footnotes, and added others. I altered verb tenses in the Lehmann "portrait" of Rahner, because Rahner died on 30 March 1984. Footnotes were substituted for the awkward "list of sources" section of the German text. Corrections, but not major retranslations, of already existing English translations, were made. Subheadings within individual selections were eliminated.

Numbers 39 and 40, "The World and the Angels," were added, not only because they illustrate Rahner's fascinating angelology, but also because they explicate his notion of evolutionary creation as "created self-transcendence" that is not only becoming, but also becoming *more.* Number 92, "The Triune God," focuses upon the most creative theological reflections on *the* Christian mystery to occur in hundreds of years.

Number 106, "Women and the Priesthood," addresses not only a timely topic, but also illustrates how Rahner approached authoritative declarations of the magisterium with critical reverence. One of the most daring approaches to ecumenical dialogue may be seen in number 119, "Theses for the Unity of the Churches." Number 126, "A Letter from the Pope in the Year 2020," is a masterpiece of Rahner's view on the papacy and on a more vitally spiritual church. Number 129, "What the People Actually Believe," underscores a frequent Rahnerian theme: the need for the magisterium to listen to the "catechism of the heart" of the faithful.

Number 141, "Existential Ethics," offers a critical corrective to the essentialistic ethics that dominated Catholic theology for so long. To Rahner, the human person not only shares a common human nature with others, but is also *unique.* Ethics must reflect this anthropological fact. This entry also indicates the influence of St. Ignatius of Loyola on Rahner, especially Ignatius's spirituality of the discernment of spirits.

Number 159 illustrates Rahner's emphasis on a spirituality that loves the world, maintains its hope in *eternal* life, and never reduces God to an element in this world. Number 160, "Christian Pessimism," underscores Rahner's conviction that human finitude and sin will never permit an intraworldly utopia, that everything must pass through death, and that *God alone* must be a Christian's true utopia. Numbers 164, 166, 170, and 171 bring his rich eschatology into sharper relief. Finally, number 173, "Christian Optimism," illustrates his strong conviction that no matter what life may bring, everything "ultimately ends in the arms of an eternally good, eternally powerful God."

Harvey D. Egan, S.J.
Boston College

INTRODUCTION

Karl Rahner: A Portrait[1]

by Karl Lehmann

I. HIS LIFE AND THE HISTORY OF HIS WORK

Karl Rahner was born on 5 March 1904 in Freiburg im Breisgau. His parents, Professor Karl Rahner (1868–1934) and Luise Rahner, whose maiden name was Trescher (1875–1976), came from the Freiburg area. Just like their parents, the seven brothers and sisters (Karl was in the middle) were true descendents of the Alemanni tribe: a bit reserved and brooding, but quite reflective and with a somewhat melancholy humor.

Karl Rahner grew up in the city from 1908, when the family came to Freiburg, until 1922. His father was a respected *Gymnasium* professor in Pfullendorf and Emmendingen, and later active in the training of teachers in Freiburg. His father's ancestors came from Tirol. His mother was uncomplicated and brave, but very intelligent and devout. The soul of the home, she created the family's Catholic and open atmosphere. All seven children passed the matriculation examination (*Arbitur*) which admitted them to university studies, and they did go on to study.

Hugo, who was about four years older than Karl, entered the Jesuit order in 1919. Both Karl and Hugo had great praise for Professor Meinrad Vogelbacher, the religion teacher who taught them both. Karl Rahner did not have much to say about his school days. He received the usual schooling "with good, but completely ordinary results," and obtained his *Arbitur.*

In April 1922 he told his brother Hugo that he, too, was going to enter the Jesuit order, but that Hugo had in no way influenced him to do so. Then came two years in the novitiate at Feldkirch (in the Voralberg).

---

1. Slightly emended for an English-speaking audience. —Translation editor.

1

After three months of further humanistic education, he studied philosophy for the usual three years at Feldkirch and at Pullach, near Munich (1924–27). According to Jesuit custom, Rahner taught Latin in the juniorate at Feldkirch for two years (1927–29), and studied theology at Valkenburg (Holland) from 1929 to 1933. Cardinal Faulhaber ordained Rahner at St. Michael's Church in Munich, on 26 July 1932. His religious superiors decided that he should pursue a scholarly career in the history of philosophy. Accordingly, in 1934, after the so-called tertianship (the final year of spiritual training), he was sent to his home-city of Freiburg for doctoral studies in philosophy at the university there.

1. Beginnings and Influences

For more than forty years Karl Rahner has been a towering figure in theology. His early philosophical publications, *Spirit in the World* (1939)[2] and *Hearers of the Word* (1941),[3] placed him in the front ranks of the young and gifted shock-troops of Catholic philosophers, who broke out of the narrow confines of the *neoscholastic school philosophy* in the 1930s by bringing into prominence, again, the original Thomistic intellectual heritage through confrontation with post-Kantian, modern philosophy. Joseph Maréchal — and, perhaps to a less explicit degree, Erich Przywara — were his clearly identifiable mentors.

Among his philosophical companions were, above all, his friends J. B. Lotz, G. Siewert, M. Müller, and B. Welte. In Martin Heidegger's seminars at the University of Freiburg they all learned the art of philosophical questioning, the meditative penetration of incessant thinking, and the mastery of alert interpretation.

But to Freiburg the young Karl Rahner brought with him other, and no less essential, experiences. His first publications[4] bear witness to an intense reading of Origen, the fathers of the church, and the great mystics of the high Middle Ages, and the ever-present influence of his older brother Hugo. His reworking in German of M. Viller's 1930 book, *Aszese und Mystik in der Väterzeit* (Freiburg i. Br.: Herder, 1989, new unchanged edition), published in 1939, is a result of these concerns.

Very early on, the education and training in the Society of Jesus developed that triad of his tension-filled spirituality that dominated Rahner's thinking and action to the day he died: (1) the restrained passion

---

2. Trans. William V. Dych (New York: Herder and Herder, 1968). For practical purposes, I have eliminated Lehmann's extensive German footnotes and added some of my own. —Translation Editor.
3. Trans. Michael Richards (New York: Herder and Herder, 1969). This seriously flawed translation is soon to be replaced by one done by Joseph Donceel.
4. See, for example, nos. 6–7, *Theological Investigations XVI*, trans. David Moreland (New York: Seabury Press, 1979), 81–134.

of a deep personal piety; (2) the constant struggle with objective forms in the church, theology, and obsolete forms of life; and (3) finding God in all things.[5] The collection of meditations *Encounters with Silence*,[6] which came into being — not by accident, and not without an inner connection — with the work on his projected dissertation, *Spirit in the World*, is a helpful book for many to this day. It offers a good insight into the depth of the spiritual forces and dynamics at work in his theological thinking.

At the same time, it is from this vantage point that one can appreciate what has been Rahner's hallmark from the start: his concrete concern for the believer. Although he never explicitly associated himself with the proponents of the "kerygmatic theology" of his day, this proclamation-related approach to theology, in Innsbruck during the 1930s, involved the intense effort of his closest Jesuit colleagues and was well-known to him. Also in everything, in his philosophical, patristic, spiritual, and pastoral writings, there lay hidden a secret revolt of his vital and original faith against the bland and desiccated scholastic philosophy and theology given to him during his studies, according to the long tradition of his religious order.

Granted that Rahner, the young student and teacher, may have been skeptically reserved toward this "Scholasticism stuff," still it is clear that, in almost every area, he certainly mastered this immense mass of learning in the church's tradition. It is also obvious that he quietly came to terms with it repeatedly and sought to make it fruitful by formulating it in a different way.

The many years of activity in this school "of hard knocks" did not rob this bright spirit of the desire to think, as it had so many others. Rather, it gave him wings, disciplined his "objective" reflection, and required him again and again to bring his new vision into contact with the church's tradition. Later, Rahner said of himself: "But if I'm going to sing my praises here I should say that this didn't happen by presenting a thought-system different from scholastic theology.... I tried to ferret out the inner power and dynamism which is hidden within scholastic theology. Scholastic theology offers so many problems, and is so dynamic, that it can develop within itself, and then, by means of a certain qualitative leap, can surpass itself. As a result, even as a simple scholastic theologian, one can make considerable progress."[7]

---

5. See *Theological Investigations III*, trans. Karl H. Kruger and Boniface Kruger (Baltimore: Helicon Press, 1967).

6. Trans. James M. Demske (Westminster, Md.: Newman Press, 1960).

7. "Grace as the Heart of Human Existence," *Faith in a Wintry Season*, ed. Paul Imhof and Hubert Biallowons, trans. ed. Harvey D. Egan (New York: Crossroad Publishing Company, 1990), 17.

2. Basic Studies and Breakthrough

The irony of history and a Catholic philosophy professor did not want Karl Rahner to teach philosophy, as his religious order had originally intended. The incident is well known. Martin Honecker, Karl Rahner's dissertation director at Freiburg, did not accept his dissertation *Spirit in the World* (*TI XVII*, 243, "my philosophical thesis for M. Honegger [*sic*] was turned down"). After so long a preparation, the switch to theology happened very quickly, due primarily to the shortage of teachers. Soon Rahner received his doctorate in theology at Innsbruck. His still-unpublished dissertation of 136 pages was "*E latere Christi:* The Origin of the Church as the Second Eve out of the Side of Christ, the Second Adam: An Investigation into the typological Meaning of John 19:34" (1936). In 1937 he received his *Habilitation* (postdoctoral degree) and was appointed to the faculty as a professor of Catholic dogma on the basis of his earlier works in patristics and the history of dogma. He taught at Innsbruck from 1937 until the spring of 1964, except for the interruption brought on by the Nazis and the war.

The following years gave birth, in addition to the already mentioned more comprehensive books, to his first great scholastically formulated articles on uncreated grace, to writings on the theological question of "concupiscence," and to his only biblical-theologically oriented article, "*Theos* in the New Testament."[8]

From the very beginning the Rahnerian aspect of his theology stamped his specific teaching assignment. Above all, his intensive work on grace and on the history and systematic theology of the sacrament of penance determine the essential structure and the hermeneutical profile of this doctrinal theologian to this very day. His patristic and historical-dogmatic interest now turned its attention to more precise research in the early history of the sacrament of penance, which resulted in numerous articles published between 1948 and 1958.[9]

In addition to his theology on the sacrament of penance, the focal points of his teaching at Innsbruck were: creation, the primordial human condition, and grace. Extensive and frequently hectographed manuscripts of those lectures in doctrinal theology are an important source for the unfolding of Rahner's theology.

Shortly after he began to teach at Innsbruck, he was interrupted for almost ten years. In 1938 the National Socialists dissolved the theological faculty. But it continued, in part, in Sitten/Wallis, where Hugo Rahner worked. Karl Rahner lived in Vienna from 1939 to 1944, where

---

8. These articles are in *Theological Investigations I*, trans. Cornelius Ernst, O.P. (Baltimore: Helicon Press, 1961).

9. *Theological Investigations XV*, trans. Lionel Swain (New York: Crossroad Publishing Company, 1982).

he collaborated in numerous ways — preaching, lecturing, giving re-
treats, teaching courses, and providing theological expertise — in the
pastoral institute directed by the prelate K. Rudolf. After a brief inter-
lude spent in the pastoral care of the local residents and displaced
persons in lower Bavaria toward the end of the war in 1944 to 1945,
Rahner taught theology at Berchmanskolleg in Pullach near Munich
until 1948, a period he called a kind of "emergency theology." Rahner
often emphasized that this unpropitious period left almost no time for
real scholarly work.

Prolific publication in the area of spiritual theology took place right
after the war. More than one hundred thousand copies of his Lenten
sermons *On Prayer,*[10] which were delivered in bombed-out Munich
in 1946, circulated in the German language alone. This book is certainly one of Rahner's most read and most helpful publications. Two
other aspects of his theological interest appeared during these years:
his explicit attention to the church's pastoral and pastoral-theological
situation and questions of church reform.

3. Difficulties and Obstacles

Despite all sorts of criticism, Rahner engaged, cautiously, in a positive
discussion with situation ethics. The thunderstorms caused by the encyclical *Humani generis* (1950) bypassed Rahner for the time being.
The penetrating essay on the problem of the relationship between nature and grace shows his independent creative power as applied to
timely questions.[11]

An almost five-hundred page, comprehensive study — from the
perspective of the history of dogma and systematic theology — of the
"new" Marian dogma of 1950 was not published because of disagree-
ments, which reached Rome, among the censors within his religious
order. This study, unpublished even to this day, would have been the
only serious theological work written in German on Mary's bodily
assumption into heaven. One can only guess what its *ecumenical* contribution to this dogma would have been. This often-mimeographed
manuscript, which appeared in many editions, is the source of his
extensive treatise on death, and the essay on the development of
dogma.[12]

In a 1954 address, Pius XII publicly rejected a portion of Rahner's

---

10. No translator named (New York: Paulist Deus Books, 1968).
11. "Concerning the Relationship between Nature and Grace," *Theological Investigations I,* 297–317.
12. *On the Theology of Death,* trans. C. H. Henkey, revised by W. J. O'Hara, 2d edition (New York: Herder and Herder, 1967); "The Development of Dogma," *Theological
Investigations I,* 39–77.

courageous theological reflections in his *The Celebration of the Eucharist,*[13] quoted out of context, of course, and imprecisely interpreted, but without mentioning anyone's name. The "quotation" was given to the pope in such a way that he suspected nothing about the hidden target of his address, for this had been concealed by Father Robert Leiber, S.J., the pope's private secretary.

A far greater conflict occurred in 1962, just before the start of the Second Vatican Council. There is no doubt that a certain circle wanted to limit Rahner's publicity and activity in view of the address "Do Not Stifle the Spirit,"[14] given at the Austrian Catholic Congress on 1 June 1962. This lecture seemed to be the suitable excuse for imposing on Rahner a kind of watered-down "prohibition to publish" without previous Roman censorship. The Paulusgesellschaft,[15] comprised of an overwhelming number of German-speaking Catholic academicians and chaired by the then German chancellor, Konrad Adenauer, gathered signatures on Rahner's behalf. Archbishop Herman Shäufele of Freiburg im Breisgau also intervened because he was the "protector" of the multi-volume *Lexikon für Theologie und Kirche* and feared work on this project would stop, because Rahner was the key editor. These, along with other initiatives, persuaded Pope John XXIII not to enforce the prohibition, but it was never lifted. Characteristic until the day he died was Rahner's attitude toward such difficulties.[16]

4. Theological Investigations

What only the limited and specialized world of theological experts knew about Rahner's widely diverse works — published in such varied ways — became available for a wider audience when the collected

---

13. With Angelus Häussling, trans. W. J. O'Hara (New York: Herder and Herder, 1968).

14. *Theological Investigations VII,* trans. David Bourke (New York: Herder and Herder, 1971), 72–87.

15. See Rahner's laudatory remarks concerning the Paulusgesellschaft in his preface to *Theological Investigations V,* trans. Karl Kruger (Baltimore: Helicon Press, 1966).

16. In *I Remember: An Autobiographical Interview* (trans. Harvey D. Egan [New York: Crossroad Publishing Company, 1985]), 63, Rahner says about this episode: "First, I would say that all the things that happened did not affect me as terribly as they might affect young theologians today. You see, if a person is a member of a religious order, a Jesuit, and really takes into account that his religious superior can send him to India or to the African bush — and that can happen without further ado — then one does not get so frightfully worked up about getting into occasional difficulties with Rome over one's theological work. When the Congregation of Faith in Rome under Cardinal Ottaviani once said that I could write only in conjunction with a special Roman censor, then I said to myself: 'Well, I just won't write anymore, and then the matter is over and done with, right?' But nothing came of it because the council arrived. And according to Roman methods, such instructions are then silently forgotten. But you see from this that in the old days a Catholic theologian didn't get as worked up about this sort of thing as one does today."

articles appeared in 1954 to 1955 as the first two volumes of *Theological Investigations*.[17] Here was one of the few theologians capable of rethinking the church's tradition freshly and radically. Rahner intended through this collection of essays to "confirm young theologians in the conviction that Catholic theology has no reason to rest on its laurels, fine though those may be; that on the contrary it can and must advance, and precisely, so that it may remain true to its own laws and its tradition."[18] Perhaps it was precisely this unusual viewpoint that was fascinating. Here was a representative of Catholic theology honestly confessing that there were many stones, and not much bread, in the centuries-old cupboard of church tradition. But this was no superficial move to accommodate the "spirit of the times," nor a self-forgetful sneering at the highly significant questions posed by Protestant theology. It was clear that precisely here one did *Catholic* theology in an unquestioning, unpretentious, "obvious," unhampered encounter with the problems posed by modern philosophy, exegesis, and the natural sciences. Rahner's view came to fruition in the collection of essays in the first two volumes of the *Theological Investigations*. The third volume, which appeared in 1956 and was subtitled *The Theology of the Spiritual Life,* made it immediately and absolutely clear that a Christian could really live with, and even die with, this theological giant as a mentor.

Karl Rahner's reputation grew extraordinarily in those years. It seemed as if the great success and the ready acceptance of these certainly difficult to read volumes now opened all the previously closed sources of his thinking. All his energy seemed unleashed. He felt himself entitled to speak and to fight. In an unusually short space of time, one important theological contribution followed another. They were collected especially in volumes IV (1960) and V (1962) of the *Theological Investigations,* and translated into many languages. When Rahner died in 1984, there were sixteen German volumes.

5. Contributions to Theology and Participation at the Second Vatican Council

During this period he also began the long years of work on the second edition of the monumental *Lexikon für Theologie und Kirche* (1957–65) and on the *Quaestiones Disputatae* series (1958ff.), which he coedited with Heinrich Fries. The collection of pastoral theological es-

---

17. *Theological Investigations I; Theological Investigations II,* trans. Karl H. Kruger (Baltimore: Helicon Press, 1963).
18. *Theological Investigations I,* xxii.

says *Sendung und Gnade* (1959) followed.[19] Soon thereafter came the scientific-theoretical plan for *Handbuch der Pastoraltheologie*, which appeared in four volumes from 1964 to 1969.

These were unimaginably productive years. If Rahner had withdrawn from real life and from the church's spontaneous needs during these years, then one assumes that he certainly could have written a great "Catholic systematic theology" in the seclusion of his study. But he decided otherwise. This became especially evident when he took over the chief responsibility for publishing along with J. Höfer the *Lexikon für Theologie und Kirche*. For Rahner the best of theology should not just remain stuck in a few elite heads, but should be made available for the use of *all* those with responsibility in the church. He was invited to speak or to lecture in almost every major middle-European city and university. Translations of his books — including the formidable *Theological Investigations* — spread abroad in all major languages.

His success undercut the untrue claims that Rahner spoke with teutonic obscurity and that he was all but impossible to understand. Perhaps the starting point for many of his reflectio s — "school theology" — is the reason his way of thinking attained international acclaim and acceptance. Every theologian knew the state of the question from his or her own study of the traditional theology, and thus could more easily follow its further development. And the success of his mature systematic synthesis, *Foundations of Christian Faith* (1976; ten German editions and translations into all major and many minor languages)[20] underscores his continuing appeal in international circles.

In 1960, before the Second Vatican Council, Rahner was named an advisor to the commission on the sacraments, although it never made use of his expertise. As we have already seen, ultraconservatives attempted to have Rahner disqualified just before the council. However, Cardinal König of Vienna made Rahner his advisor, thus opening up the possibility for him to collaborate, from the beginning, as a *peritus* (expert) on the theological commission. Soon he was officially named a *peritus.*

Only now can the history of Rahner's influence on the Second Vatican Council be written. In so doirg one must not think first of the individual sentences he wrote in the conciliar documents. Rahner collaborated wholeheartedly in the teamwork of the many who put

---

19. Published in three English volumes as: *The Christian Commitment: Essays in Pastoral Theology,* trans. Cecily Hastings (New York: Sheed and Ward, 1963); *Christian in the Market Place,* trans. Cecily Hastings (New York: Sheed and Ward, 1966); *Theology for Renewal: Bishops, Priests, Laity,* trans. Cecily Hastings and Richard Strachan (New York: Sheed and Ward, 1964).

20. Trans. William V. Dych (New York: Seabury Press, 1978).

together the final drafts. He never considered any document to be the product of a single author. But the nature of the situation demanded that Rahner defend one position rather than another.

Rahner's influence, however, came not only from his collaboration during the council, but also from the international preconciliar acceptance of his theological ideas whose conciliar spirit paved the way for this council. In virtue of his "authority" Rahner succeeded, with Y. Congar, E. Schillebeeckx, J. Ratzinger, C. Moeller, G. Philips, H. Küng, and others, in supporting those forces that wanted to reject the prepackaged and already prepared schemata, and to break through into freer theological territory.

Cardinal Döpfner also made Rahner his theological advisor. In this way Rahner participated indirectly in some of the council's critical moments in the autumn of 1962 when the German-speaking, French, and Dutch bishops were able to influence important preliminary issues: for example, the selection of the episcopal members of the various conciliar commissions and the withdrawal of the schema on the "sources of revelation."

Rahner attached great importance to the statement that the collaboration among bishops and theologians was in no way "organized" — that it was not, as some claimed, a conspiracy of theologians from the Rhine's right and left banks — but rather something that arose spontaneously. His numerous lectures to the various bishops' conferences on conciliar themes made him an unpretentious but important advisor to many council fathers. Here his brilliant mastery of Latin served him well. His coediting of the documents and the commentaries on the texts of the Second Vatican Council (three supplementary volumes of *Lexikon für Theologie und Kirche* and the *Kleines Konzilkompendium* [with H. Vorgrimler]), and his numerous interpretations of conciliar statements, have made Rahner, to our day, a trailblazer who made this council a living reality.

6. In the Postconciliar Situation

On 1 April 1964, shortly after his sixtieth birthday, Rahner succeeded Romano Guardini as the holder of the chair for Christian "world view" and the philosophy of religion at the University of Munich. His many obligations connected with the council burdened him while he held this chair. Ultimately Rahner wanted to rejoin a theological faculty in the postconciliar period. Besides, the time for "professors of world views" was over. Because the theology faculty at the University of Munich could not fulfill his wish to direct doctoral and postdoctoral dissertations, Rahner accepted a call to the Catholic theological faculty at the University of Münster, which had conferred on him an honorary doctorate in 1964.

There he taught dogma and the history of dogma from 1 April 1967 to 1 October 1971.

The overall postconciliar situation in the church soon made theological work difficult. Camps, which before were rather easily discerned as "conservative" or "liberal," separated. Previous allies now defended propositions, either from the right or from the left, which Rahner would not accept without opposition. His two-year discussion with Hans Küng about the latter's book *Infallible? An Inquiry* (1970)[21] is the most prominent example. The situation grew murkier, the way even more burdensome. At the same time Rahner became concerned that the will to reform initiated by the Second Vatican Council was weakening. Rahner had often delineated the perspectives of the postconciliar church.[22] Now he believed that he was obliged to brand regressive tendencies.

This branding probably began in Munich in March of 1970, with the lecture "Freedom and Manipulation in Society and the Church," the occasion being the conferral on Rahner of the Guardini prize of the Catholic Academy in Bavaria.[23] The position on issues taken by the joint synod in Germany in 1972 prompted him to make many statements about church reform in his *The Shape of the Church to Come*.[24] Quite a few of his former supporters found some of these ideas hard to accept. The suspension of the weekly newspaper *Publik* was, to Rahner, symptomatic of the German Catholic church's "march into the ghetto."[25] Rahner's position in this regard became especially evident at the plenary sessions of the joint synod of West German dioceses from 1971 to 1975, above all in his disagreement with Cardinal Höffner. When the international theological commission established by the Holy See did not meet his expectations, he resigned before the end of his five-year appointment (1969–74).[26]

It cannot be denied that Rahner lost many friends in those years. Of course he also won new ones. One may certainly have differences of opinion about this or that statement from Rahner. Much is an expression of a certain resignation, a deliberate acidity, or an intentional one-sidedness, "because otherwise no one will listen." Perhaps many of his ideas in earlier publications were more nuanced and less easily mis-

---

21. Trans. Edward Quinn (Garden City, N.J.: Doubleday, 1972).

22. See *The Church after the Council*, trans. Davis C. Herron and Rodeline Albrecht (New York: Herder and Herder, 1966).

23. In *Meditations on Freedom and the Spirit*, trans. Rosaleen Ockenden, David Smith, and Cecily Bennett (New York: Seabury Press, 1978), 33–71.

24. Trans. Edward Quinn (New York: Seabury Press, 1974).

25. See "Open Church," *The Shape of the Church to Come*, 93–101.

26. On this matter, see "The Congregation of the Faith and the Commission of Theologians," *Theological Investigations XIV*, trans. David Bourke (New York: Seabury Press, 1976), 98–115.

understood. Now his ideas — often oversimplified and juxtaposed — caused more excitement. Perhaps people had not really taken notice of what he had actually said and repeated, again and again.

Yet it seems to be patently unfair to judge all of Rahner's work on the basis of these isolated, and mostly negative, outcries about the church's situation. Without attempting to trivialize those provocations, one must still try to understand and judge them in the total context and in the total meaning of his work up until now. Perhaps we are still too close to these events to be able to make a balanced judgment.

One thing is certain, however: his energetic objections and complaints about a repeated lack of readiness for conversion of the church's system came from a wounded heart, which loved even the church of his day with the same passionate zeal as before. Frequently one gets the impression that those in the church who often spoke against Rahner — some from rather high watchtowers — became so forgetful that they hardly remember anymore his almost invaluable achievements for, and service to, the church. In order to maintain the power of the Christian promise against all forms of defeatism, time and again Rahner purposely waxed almost utopian. Will people hear this call?

II. BASIC STRUCTURE AND PROFILE OF HIS THEOLOGY

The basic structure of Rahner's theological thinking is hard to summarize. To separate out — from a multidimensionally interwoven and highly complex life's achievement — individual, discrete "elements" would be transparently wrong. All too easily *one* aspect of his theology considered *without* the other becomes false. Radical immediacy to God, speculative ingenuity, pastoral concerns, sensitivity to the importance of the theological tradition — one would have to be able to say all this and many other things *at the same time* in order to articulate the origin and clarity of his theology.

1. A Theology That Knows History
Rahner's main achievement — along with other theologians of course — was to bring a doctrinal theology trapped in its own tradition slowly back to its sources again. One must be perfectly clear about the conditions under which a reform of the traditional school theology was at all possible. Except perhaps for the theology at German universities, the firmly established and highly uniform state of the question, structure, and content of traditional dogmatic theology offered no other possibility for deepening and widening its scope than for talking to itself. To be sure, there were always important theologians — such as Romano Guardini and Hans Urs von Balthasar — who simply set up

shop *alongside* the marketable scholastic theology. But their thinking was more often than not unrelated to it. These undoubtedly influential thinkers, therefore, did not have a transformative effect precisely where dogmatic theology was translated into the church's lived life, in the day-in and day-out theology of the schools.

Because of his studies in the Jesuit order, Rahner was thoroughly immersed in this theology, usually taught by intelligent scholastic theologians, especially by H. Lange and F. Hürth. Only a few of them knew all the branches of the traditional school theology as well as Rahner. He had truly mastered it, knew it from within, and was comfortable with it. Many were just "trained" in it, and simply "passed it on." This is the main reason for their sterility. Rahner often fiercely combated this petrification of thought and empty formalism. Rather early in his career he was reproached for this. Overlooked in this reproach was the fact that here was someone who spoke in this way from an intimate and penetrating grasp of this way of thinking. He clearly perceived the ambiguity in what was assumed to be conceptually "precise." He also saw the sterility of worn-out methods of making "distinctions." But he also recognized its healthy drive toward relentless intellectual discipline. Despite all the concrete subjectivity present in the process of handing on this theology, he mastered the objectivity and universality of theological reflection. He smiled at the many fastidious sophistries, but by no means did he laugh at the sometimes hidden clarity and the penetrating power of the essential and fundamental experience of the faith — even if this was occasionally distorted almost beyond recognition.

From the viewpoint of the history of ideas and church politics, Rahner had no choice but to enter into this "milieu." This took courage, because many had dried up in an endless conceptual wasteland or, at best, erected a few of their own curious, but mostly, irrelevant opinions. The self-assurance of his thought, which did not drown in the endless, dead mass of material, reminds one of what Hegel says in his *Phenomenology of Spirit:* "the life of the spirit is not the life that is afraid of death, or keeps clear of devastation, but the life that endures death and maintains itself in the midst of death." In fact, at first, Rahner took up very precise individual problems in scholastic theology,[27] a theology whose inner power to change and whose systematic consistency become apparent, perhaps, only slowly. The concepts "supernatural existential" and "anonymous Christian" are born in the context of a

---

27. See "Concerning the Relationship between Nature and Grace" and "Some Implications on the Scholastic Concept of Uncreated Grace," *Theological Investigations I*, 297–346.

more precise interpretation of the encyclical *Mystici corporis,*[28] and out of the accompanying tension-filled circumstances, although they were developed very early and fully developed later on. The new theologoumena proved their inner necessity and their functional worth in this confrontation with already existing categories.

Karl Rahner would never have been able to decipher the theses of scholastic theology if he had not been thoroughly familiar with the writings of the great fathers of the church and of medieval theology. Scholastic theology was, after all, derived from the great fundamental theological experiences. One cannot understand Rahner's theological achievement if one does do not take into account, and constantly presuppose, his decades-long, intensive, mainly hidden wrestling with the great tradition.

Rahner's often all-too-modest self-characterization conceals somewhat the richness he gained through association with the tradition. After all, the "speculator," as his colleagues who were more expert in history often dubbed him, did receive his doctorate and teaching appointment because of his patristic and scholastic investigations. More than one-thousand additional pages of patristic and dogmatic-historical studies clearly document that Karl Rahner also understood, or, as the case may be, learned something about, subtle historical study and its virtues. If one has only come to know the Rahner of the late 1950s, '60s, '70s, and '80s, one would almost miss the richness and mastery of his historical thinking, which is the very foundation on which his thought stands. This would be the case, in part, because precisely these historical works were only published later, or never in any comprehensive way (this is especially true of his studies on Mary).

2. Against Positivism

Very little of this vast knowledge is directly discernible in his publications over the last twenty years [1959–79]. It is not particularly emphasized, but it is "at work," nonetheless. Many individual details may no longer be explicitly present in the wealth of this learning, but the enduring basic experiences are silently at work. When needed they are suddenly there, as if it were the most obvious thing in the world to know all about them: his vast knowledge of scripture, the history of Montanism, the baptismal theory of Gregory of Nyssa, the basic ecclesiological problems of Augustine, the decisions about semi-Pelagianism, the *theologia negativa* of Thomas Aquinas, the mystical experiences

---

28. See "Membership of the Church according to the Teaching of Pius XII's Encyclical 'Mystici corporis Christi,' " *Theological Investigations II,* 1–88.

of John Ruusbroec, the subtleties of late scholastic theology (Molina, Suarez, Ripalda).

Of course, to Rahner historical work was never an end in itself. Complaints about how fruitless many historical works are for dogmatic and systematic theology grew louder and louder. "What is it that makes the properly historical in studies like those of de Lubac or de la Taille so stimulating and to the point? Surely it is the art of reading texts in such a way that they become not just votes cast in favor of, or against, our positions (positions taken up long ago), but that they say something to us which *we* in our time have not considered at all, or not closely enough, about reality itself. This is not to say that we should study the history of theology in order to justify our own private innovations, although this sort of culpable silliness is by no means unknown; but we should enter into association with a thinker of the past, not only to become acquainted with his views, but in the final analysis to learn something about reality. It is because historical theology is too much lecture-room disquisition . . . that we learn from it only about that part of the past which is, in any case, already preserved in modern theology, but not about that part which shapes our future from our past. It is no wonder, then, that the great work of historical theology, one which deserves our constant praise for our positive gains from it, has so far been able to exert so little pressure toward overcoming the deficiencies of the textbooks."[29]

We need not waste words in stating that tradition here does not mean merely recognizing what exists or glorifying the past. Rahner is familiar with the classic power of the "theology of distinctions," in order to develop with its help an inner, critical sensitivity to the value of the actual tradition. Conceptual thinking is necessary, but definitions alone are just a poor beginning, nothing more. Tradition is important because it can activate, expand, and perhaps even correct, contemporary reflection on the faith.

Above all Rahner hates sterile positivism that carries on in a bombastic way. However, the deeper impulses of positivistic "thinking" are thoroughly at work in him: inexorable confrontation with reality, sensitivity for a theological "advance" achieved (no matter how this is expressed conceptually), and the creative confirmation of what has been achieved. Critical trust in a refined tradition of faith knows that such insights have come about throughout the history of the church. "No real achievement is ever lost to the church. But theologians are never spared the task of prompt renewal. Anything which is merely conserved, or which is merely handed down, without a fresh, personal

---

29. *Theological Investigations I*, 9–10.

exertion beginning at the very sources of revelation, rots as the manna did."[30]

It is precisely his immediate familiarity with the sources of the faith which gives birth to the daring and candor of his theological thought. Again and again his thought has an extraordinary reliability because of his awareness of the complex historical experiences connected with the subject, because aspects of the faith — some essential, some not — surface (the analogy of faith), because he senses warning signals and limitations, and all this in the context of the freedom of his own historically sensitive theology.

It is only the truly multidimensional knowledge of a great expert which enables this often uncannily sure-footed theologian to walk along the edge. The path to such certitude had its own share of danger, doubt, and dead-ends, of course. This multidimensional knowledge is also the source of his unerring sense of theological "tact," which hardly any of his "followers" (this does not mean "students"!) have, because they cling to him literally (e.g., the various interpretations of the "anonymous Christian"), or fixate on individual trains of thought, rather than focus on the nuanced context as a whole, and thus construct a problematic "system."

Because Karl Rahner placed himself squarely on the historical path of theological thought when dealing with familiar theological questions, his thought gained an astonishing world-wide power to communicate, to transcend many languages and mind-sets, and apparently to overcome difficulties of expression effortlessly (without thereby failing to recognize the achievement of good translators, and without, at the same time, overestimating the lasting, profound effect of such an influence).

The dry ideas passed on in the theological schools were known almost everywhere. Virtually every theologian on the face of the earth had learned them and put up with them. There is no doubt that before, during, and after Vatican II Rahner could show the "Roman" theology its limits from the inside, and that it was not just disdained "from above." His universal and profoundly understanding way of thinking, despite all disputes, gained him great respect during the council even among many conservative theologians.

Again and again, his sophisticated knowledge of church history and theology gave Rahner a surprising trustworthiness, and this allowed him to exercise a certain recklessness in his theological thinking on the most difficult questions (nature and grace, the development of dogma, the basis for christology), and in the most dangerous of times (and these

---

30. Ibid., 10.

go back to the years before World War II!). We can hardly evaluate, directly, the importance of such vast knowledge today; we can only surmise its importance in a sort of "historical" retrospective glance.

3. Faith Seeking Insight

Although a direct insistence upon "positive facts" is far from Rahner's way of thinking, nonetheless it does not undervalue the important and emphatic nature of the "factual." Rahner's basic formula, "spirit-in-world," is still valid, and shows his recognition of the importance of "matter," the world, and history right from the start. This is, ultimately, why Rahner could never accept the kind of thinking that revolves in a closed circle, or that is content with being turned in on itself. Thus he has critical reservations not only vis-à-vis classic, formal logic, but also concerning certain forms of modern hermeneutics. Yet an infinite passion for questioning is characteristic of his theological thought. "Hard, sober *questioning* — drilling when necessary — really is an act of piety incumbent upon the Christian who is intellectually alive."[31] He answers everything conscientiously, in strict confrontation with the way contemporary men and women understand existence and the world; everything is thoroughly exposed and subjected to realistic testing.

Everyone knows the movement so characteristic of Rahner's questioning and searching spirit. The thought surfaces slowly, often self-consciously and shyly. And so many of his essays are a bit uneven and tiresome to read, because of the long "preliminary remarks." First, the subject to be investigated is carefully circumscribed. Then the state of the question, and the position of the one questioning, as well as the problem, are carefully delineated. Traditional categories and ways of thinking are tested for their ability to give information about, and answers to, current questions. At the same time, as a sort of "tutorial," Rahner reminds his reader of the traditional material dealing with the subject.

This is the unmistakable hallmark of his unique, experimental style of thinking. He tries to arrive at a deeper determination of the essence of the matter by coming at it from all possible angles. He critically evaluates the traditional answers and tries as many fresh approaches as possible. This "method" of investigation is not a pedagogical whim intended to train, or to win over the reader. It is the lively movement of his thinking itself. When Rahner writes, his thought is both experiment and accomplishment. Although much reflection has already taken place, a "result" is just not simply presented.

In a peculiar kind of dialectic that can be traced back to Plato, Rah-

---

31. *Ich Glaube an Jesus Christus* (Einsiedeln: Benziger Verlag, 1968), 8.

ner's thought visibly ignites itself out of its own inner necessity. Then the *one* liberating thought appears — always a bit suddenly, although prepared for — and he pursues this thought to its ultimate practical consequences. The "preliminary remarks" create space, so that beyond the information currently available the full reality can be revealed in all its aspects.

Once the key word that delivers the insight is found, then the thought can evolve precisely because the complexity of the reality, which has been thoroughly preserved, is carried forward and is made fruitful in the multidimensionality of theological thought. For this reason Karl Rahner's writing style and individual sentences in so many of his works appear at first so "boxed-in." But *one* thought remains which runs like a powerful leitmotif throughout, and yet hesitates to shut out completely the areas that are connected with it.

It is clear that inherently such a way of thinking has limitless possibilities. No question is too "stupid," no scholarly knowledge too removed, no labor spared. Again and again, he approaches problems in new ways. The gospel is constantly made more fruitful by productive conflict.

Yet his thought never smacks of placing everything in question. Whoever accuses Rahner of this has totally misunderstood him. His passionate probing spirit has no formal apriorisms. His thinking is never a self-satisfying "glass-bead game." His treatment of a topic never lets his reader go with a soothing answer, but no one ends up in just empty questioning either. He always demands something substantial. He never revels in any sort of hollow, pathetic "intellectual honesty" that in the end would consist of impotent, subjective demands that have nothing to do with the real issue of faith and thought.

Nor can this kind of thinking simply be separated into "method" and "content." Rahner never uses these two for their own sake. His theological work always has something worthwhile to say, because his own concrete theological thinking handles the given, unavoidable questions smoothly. His new-born insight — often written down right after he has come to it — may often be awkward stylistically, but it is almost always a *clear thought* that breaks new ground. For this reason Rahner may be hard for some people to understand, but he is always intelligible to those who make the effort to think along with him.

Rahner's importance for *ecumenical theology* is based on this same kind of thought process. There is very little expressly ecumenical or "controversy-oriented" in the first half of this creative theological work. Rahner's impact on ecumenical theology is primarily the result of his precise, self-critical, and carefully nuanced presentation of Catholic theology. And this theology is always presented with the sensitivity of a man who is thoroughly knowledgeable in the field of Protestant theology.

Rahner gained this kind of global knowledge as a member of the ecumenical working-group of Protestant and Catholic theologians (the Jaeger-Staehlin group), to which he belonged beginning in 1948. The early Rahner offered an essentially indirect ecumenical theology. His basic tendency continues later on, and here one discerns a more focused and immediate engagement with the questions of ecumenical theology.[32] The basic problems common to the great Christian churches vis-à-vis the contemporary social situation captured Rahner's interest, as many of the essays in the *Theological Investigations* attest.

The dialogue with the reformed churches was more natural for him, and, therefore, one finds relatively little material on the theology of the Eastern churches. But these particular writings of Rahner should not obscure the fact that his theology is ecumenical from the outset. The method he used most often, namely, indirect ecumenical theology, reaches its limit where Rahner has not explored his partner's position enough, and yet he draws far-reaching conclusions out of his own reflection. This is especially true in the case of his *Vorfragen zu einem ökumenischen Amtverständnis* (Freiburg i. Br.: Herder, 1974). Yet this undeservedly neglected text is an important example as a "test" of how far the Catholic understanding of office in the church seems able to be modified. *Foundations of Christian Faith* presents a beautiful example of a natural relationship to what is Catholic, in the original sense of the word, and for an on-going ecumenical dialogue, even if it often occurs only implicitly.

4. Spiritual Inexhaustibility

Karl Rahner was no rationalist. From the very beginning he insisted upon his inability to exhaust his own thinking. The thinking subject, even in its own infinite inner space, understands itself to be a *question*, which, in its own finitude, exists in reference to the other which is not itself. This essential self-limitation of thought does not hinder the thought, but gives it an inner legitimacy.

The ultimate theological ground of such a state of being-in-reference-to-the-other, which the thinking spirit experiences, reveals itself as that which we call "God." This is the source of the deep certitude of his thought. Its entire dynamic and its inexhaustible ability to renew itself are found here. The ever-greater-God dimension of his theological thinking paves the way for the infinite search, without dis-

---

32. See Karl Rahner and Heinrich Fries, *Unity of the Churches: An Actual Possibility*, trans. Ruth C. L. Gritsch and Eric W. Gritsch (Ramsey, N.J.: Paulist Press, 1985).

solving into despair or pessimism.[33] This radical breakthrough to the ever-greater God gives his theology an alert, critical sense for the concepts it develops. With every fiber of its being his theology wants to avoid simply putting a label on God, or to allow all-too-human depictions of God. Again and again, he asks whether there could not be something greater and more suitable for God.

Nourished and made wise by a deep awareness of transcendence, this skepticism vis-à-vis what is currently offered and available is present, basically, only in order to allow God alone to have the last word. Such a basic point of view also results in the fact that Rahner, despite his critical affirmation of tradition, does not lose himself in external history or in the abundance of an indifferent positivism. Nor does he go astray in the aimless, formless, incessant going-beyond-everything that is characteristic of the transcendental movement of the finite spirit.

The ever-freshly revealed originality of the faith, presented meditatively in *Encounters with Silence,* and powerfully developed later on in "Science as a 'Confession,' "[34] gives rise to that self-critical instrumentality which spiritual tradition calls the gift of the "discernment of spirits." It is no accident that in Rahner such considerations almost naturally flow into the spiritual dimension of concrete faith, where they ultimately become the most evident.

But this means that transcendence gained in this way is, at the deepest level, already mediated, because — precisely as experienced — such transcendence has already become to some degree "immanent." The power of transcendental experience shows its true depth precisely in this: it rediscovers itself in thousands of ways in the concrete experience of the world. This does not mean that the experiences of the world are too quickly made into something theological. For example, work remains work, and the unavoidable fear of death cannot be denied.

Rahner allows the human to express itself. Precisely in doing so human beings prove that they cannot avoid themselves as a total question. The accompanying phenomena — for example, unconditional personal love, absolute obedience to one's conscience, an experience of the insurmountable finitude of one's own existence experienced in guilt, pain, and death — reveal, once they have been accepted (perhaps with resistance and pain, but nonetheless joyously), the secret call of that most radical, protecting, and forgiving *nearness* of the mystery of God. We are not talking about some sort of eccentric theological concept, but rather about that truth regarding human beings and things that brings their undisguised reality into true consciousness for the very

33. See "Being Open to God as Ever Greater," *Theological Investigations VII,* 25–46.
34. *Theological Investigations III,* 385–400.

first time. A particularly successful example of this seems to be the little
book "Everyday Things."[35]

The reason Karl Rahner has become a gentle spiritual teacher for
so many companions on the way is because of his enduring ability to
mediate the distance and the nearness of God as a presence, hidden
in faith, for all the situations of human life. The power of Christian
faith is present not in the realm of the purely "supernatural," but rather
right in the daily existence of real people. This faith shows itself to be
fraternal, in the best sense of the word, precisely because it is ready
to tackle all human questions courageously, and because it does not
seek excuses for avoiding any genuine need. Such an attitude makes
the offer of faith arising out of these situations not only attractive, but, in
the midst of all complex reflections, it uncovers the "pastoral" roots and
the missionary solidarity of such faith. Rahner's pastoral or pastoral-
theological "interest" is not something extraneous, the "application" of
an unmediated theological theory. Rather, his pastoral concern arises
out of *one* and the same basic direction, that of seeking and finding
in faith.

III. PHILOSOPHICAL-THEOLOGICAL STARTING POINTS

This basic pattern translates into the concrete form suited to it in contemporary thinking, namely, philosophy and theology. This brief portrait
cannot touch upon the full scope of the themes which Karl Rahner has
dealt with in his voluminous works. We are going to limit ourselves to
the philosophical and theological *starting points* from which the individual categorical developments take their origin, and to which they
keep returning.

1. The Transcendental Posing of the Question
It is not easy to make this starting point clear, because it lies on a
multilayered level of contemplation that is hard to comprehend. The
transcendental posing of the question means especially that Rahner's
thinking does not simply accept "the given" without examining it. He
sees an advantage in the intensified inclusion of concrete subjectivity
for the articulation of the faith (formally and materially), an advantage
which he will not do without. For this reason, with modern philosophy
(from Descartes to Heidegger) he asks, expressly, about the conditions
of possibility for the facts of a case, to the extent that these can be

---

35. Found in *Belief Today*, trans. M. H. Heelan, Rosaleen and Ray Ockenden and
William Whitman (New York: Sheed and Ward, 1967), 1–43.

made clear from human subjectivity, and by going back to it through an analysis of the constitutive "moments."

The use of such a way of thinking in the theological field is easily suspected of being primarily an a priori construction, which attempts to deduce what cannot be deduced by "natural reason," namely, the objective-historical dimension and Christianity's absolutely graced dimension. In reality this suspicion is unfounded. Without a doubt the early Rahner — at least in *Spirit in World* — begins with a metaphysics of finite knowledge without anchoring himself directly in a theological foundation for this kind of thinking. This way of proceeding is only fair and reasonable for a philosophical treatise.

But as early as *Hearers of the Word,* his basic approach clearly changed: to begin with, the *reality* and *actuality* of Christian revelation is *presupposed,* and from there he asks about the subjective, anthropological, and religious-philosophical conditions *why* a human being, as knowing and freely acting, is able, and allowed from his own "nature," to have anything to do with something such as "revelation." One can rightly call such a manner of thinking a "transcendental" explication that presupposes the "facticity" of a reality and simultaneously — in a sort of suspension of its positing character (= positivity) — makes an inquiry before the bar of reason into the ground of legitimacy of its being thus [*Sosein*].

Of course, such a consideration cannot be called "a philosophy of revelation," especially since the starting point in this case is already a fact of *Christian theology,* which then, on its own, seeks after the "natural" and with that the humanly accountable presuppositions of revelation. Such a starting point, at the heart of theology, poses a transcendental retrospective question about the conditions necessary for the valid reception of revelation by a human subject. And, basically, this already transcends a general "philosophy of religion."

But theological "facts" are not accepted ideologically and uncritically; rather, they are subjected to transcendental verification "from below," inasmuch as this is possible. The dimension of the transcendental positing of the question is, above all, the realm of human subjectivity whose own multidimensionality and living depths may remain hidden. The answer must be elicited, in the first place, from the questioned content of the correlative conditions within human subjectivity. Transcendental method is "critical" precisely in this way: namely, it avoids "flying over" immediately into the "transcendental" realm.

Of course, this is where the various transcendental philosophies part company. In contrast to Kant and neo-Kantianism, Rahner builds on P. Rousselot and J. Maréchal in presupposing that there is an ultimate identity between reality and the transcendental structures which have been shown, a oneness of knowing and being (in the classical sense). Along with the concept of "spirit" in German idealism (not only!), "reality" is interpreted as being present-to-itself, especially as this manifests itself in the execution of reflective thinking, and in the mediation that occurs in this reflective thinking (*reditio completa in seipsum* = complete return to oneself).

Rahner avoids idealism's latent danger with help from Heidegger's philosophy and from the theological concept of creatureliness, by radically maintaining the finitude of human existence — and without detriment to the inner limitlessness of the human spirit with all its potential. He stresses that finite knowledge is dependent on taking in objects, and that finite reflection cannot grasp itself by itself.

A metaphysics of limited knowledge, mediated by Heidegger's 1929 book, *Kant and the Problem of Metaphysics,* and the Thomistic *conversio ad phantasma* (turning to sense appearances), a central motif in *Spirit in World,* play a large role in the first moment. The second element in Rahner's thinking comes from a global criticism of idealism and of Heidegger's notion of "ontological disposition" (*Befindlichkeit*) and perhaps, even if less significantly, from M. Blondel's *Action.* Rahner's knowledge of these is partly filtered through French-Belgian Jesuit theology. Ignatius of Loyola often contributes.

Rahner's own philosophy of life plays a certain role, yet not one to be overestimated. The unique field that arose between traditional "realism" and the modern "transcendental" way of thinking became a sort of hard-to-determine philosophical middle ground *between* the two usual philosophical fronts. This kind of thinking is relatively foreign to both traditional scholastic philosophy and modern transcendental philosophical reflection. In this sense Rahner consciously uses a pedestrian concept of "transcendental," which proves its worth more in concrete theological practice than in methodological reflection as such. The immediate effectiveness of this kind of thinking is clearly beyond doubt. Thus Rahner quite correctly sees traces of "transcendental" thinking, already in transcendental form, in Plato, Thomas of Aquinas, and so on — in any case before Kant. But the fact of the matter is not expressly proven philosophically.

With this in mind, two other points of view become clear, namely, the relationship of Rahner's thought to Heidegger's and the omission of certain philosophical perspectives, or themes, in the way the young Rahner thought. That Rahner was a pupil of Heidegger is beyond dispute — and Rahner himself often admitted this. Yet Rahner's remarks indicate a deep uncertainty about the relationship itself.[36] In any case,

---

36. See Karl Rahner, *Faith in a Wintry Season,* 15–16.

Rahner's work cannot be labeled "dependent" on Heidegger, or hardly so. Rahner is too much of a thinker oriented to *theological* issues to reflect much about such a "historical" connection. The essential points of contact with Heidegger have already been noted. But it is evident, despite very important reference points (e.g., the concept of *Befindlichkeit, existential,* and so on), that basically Rahner's thought does not pursue Heidegger's basic concern, namely, the question about the meaning of Being and the problem of a fundamental ontology. There are hardly any common formulations of the question in these areas.

For example, Rahner never mentions the difference between Heidegger's concept of *Dasein,* in the specific sense of the word, and the general concept of modern "subjectivity." This is not a reproach but merely a hint that the relationship, which has been vastly overestimated, should be put back in its proper perspective. Many of the same concepts in the writings of both men are used in very difference senses: "existential," for example. In my opinion only one strong similarity exists: between Rahner's reflections on a theology of mystery and Heidegger's 1943 work, *Vom Wesen der Wahrheit,* given in lectures and heard by Rahner in 1935.

Of late, Rahner had to contend with the criticism that his philosophical starting point, at least in *Hearers of the Word,* was simply based on the model of nonhuman, material beings, and hardly on intersubjective, personal coexistence. Upon closer examination this criticism is unfounded. It also seriously overlooks what was philosophically feasible in the prewar years, and underestimates the position he took in comparison to the other attempts of his contemporaries. The prewar period could not develop a "transcendental philosophy" (which one?) and a fully developed personalism, or a philosophy of intersubjectivity. To this day this has not been done sufficiently well.

Because of Thomas Aquinas's authoritative influence, Rahner's early concepts of "historicity" and "personality" can be traced back very clearly to the old scholastic philosophy, and that means an orientation to material beings. In criticizing this, one forgets — apart from the circumstances already mentioned — that to a great extent Rahner tried very quickly to close this loophole in his theological works.[37] It is, after all, characteristic that precisely the earlier critics of *Hearers of the Word* (for example, B. K. Primm and E. Quinn) emphasized the working out of the personal aspect of the revelation-event and its reception. But this really does not get to the heart of the matter. What has to happen is a

---

37. A striking example of this is his now famous essay, "Reflections on the Unity of the Love of Neighbor and the Love of God," *Theological Investigations VI,* trans. Karl-H. and Boniface Kruger (Baltimore: Helicon Press, 1969), 231–49.

renewed reflection on the relationship of philosophy and theology in Rahner's thought.

2. The Role of Philosophy in Theology

We need not waste any words about Rahner's philosophical talent. But this is not to say that he first developed a philosophical system which he then imposed, from outside, on theological questions. In fact, one cannot distill a pure philosophical structure out of his theology. In the beginning, as long as Rahner was still working extensively in the field of philosophy, one would be more likely to get such an impression, although this would not be true for *Hearers of The Word*. His transition from philosophy to theology soon brought a noteworthy change of orientation, even if this new direction would only be worked out thoroughly, much later.

To Rahner, in the realm of Catholic theology there was no longer a "pure" philosophy that could be isolated or clearly demarcated. Rather, there was primarily a transcendental posing of questions *within* theological experience and statements. The considerations about the "supernatural existential" and about the relationship of nature and grace strengthened this conviction in him. It is from within theology that he asks about the conditions of possibility why, for example, one of us, a human, could become God.[38] This is not a transcendental deduction in the idealistic sense, but rather presupposes, in faith, the event of revelation. Of course Rahner does not deny the autonomy of philosophical thinking, but his efforts as a thinker are in the service of theology right from the start.[39] The goal-orientation of Rahner's thinking is incontestable. Still P. Eicher's 1970 book, *Die anthropologischer Wende: Karl Rahners philosophischer Weg vom Wesen des Menschen zur personalen Existenz*, shows how fruitful a philosophically oriented examination of Rahner's thought can be. In many ways Rahner offers more thoughtful reflection on the riddles of God, humankind, and the world than many a professional philosopher.

There is not much to say at this point about his transcendental way of beginning "from below." It is clear that his fundamental approach, namely, to take the starting point of transcendental thinking into his theology, became increasingly greater in the course of time.[40] As a result, Rahner became more and more skeptical of a closed system of thought

---

38. "On the Theology of the Incarnation," *Theological Investigations IV*, trans. Kevin Smyth (Baltimore: Helicon Press, 1966), 105–20.

39. See "Some clarifying Remarks about my own Work," *Theological Investigations XVII*, trans. Margaret Kohl (New York: Crossroad Publishing Company, 1981), 243–48.

40. See "Philosophy and Theology," *Theological Investigations VI*, 71–81, and "Phi-

that is prior to, and independent of, all theology. The scholastic system of thinking, which he himself further developed and handled masterfully, can no longer demand this degree of binding power. Several philosophical ways of thinking have gained entrance in Catholic theology (even officially in the documents of Vatican II; see the theological anthropology found in *Gaudium et spes,* for example).

Noteworthy considerations regarding theology surface in different philosophies, each in its own right (hermeneutics, linguistic philosophies with a metaphysical and analytical stamp, the philosophy of society, of history, etc.) without necessarily leading to a new philosophical synthesis. Thus the philosophical *praeamubula fidei* (preconditions for believing) dissolve in their own apologetical clarity, and so, in part, lose their own immediate power to convince. Does this mean the end of philosophy in theology?

The end of a particular, uniform, ready-made, presupposed philosophical system is not the end of thinking in theology. Rahner included transcendental thinking more and more forcefully in his theology. This is the source of his critical formulation of questions in the last fifteen years ([1964–79] for example, in "transcendental christology"). There are, of course, checks and balances, especially in christology, which have not been thoroughly examined. The increasing pluralism of philosophies is forcing theology to its own reflections in the matter of faith. And theology can get impulses and help for theological reflection from many ways of thinking, even from those it does not, at first, suspect.

In his later years Rahner had a basic "skepticism" against *one* philosophy (just look at his reflections regarding plans for the study of Catholic theology). In this matter Rahner, the theologian, had primarily a missionary motive; he had the ability to hold fast to faith's ultimate universality, in all its radicality, that goes beyond the necessary generality of a philosophical system. Faith may not make itself dependent upon specific philosophical concepts, otherwise it loses its *own* explosive power, which can be made visible through many philosophies, and yet transcends all of them.

It is probably for this reason, also, that in his later years Karl Rahner no longer used "isolated," basic philosophical considerations to deepen his "philosophical" starting point. One may regret this, but it is appropriate, at least from a theological point of view, at least if one takes into account the missionary-pastoral dimension of all theological investigation. His withdrawal from the purely philosophical field

---

losophy and Philosophizing in Theology," *Theological Investigations IX,* trans. Graham Harrison (New York: Herder and Herder, 1972), 46–63.

happened as planned, and is in no way a kind of self-chosen virtue in the midst of distress or resignation, because it produced an immense heightening and tightening of theological questioning and thinking, as such. At the same time the theological concern of this thinker became, of itself, ever "more direct."[41]

3. Anthropologically Oriented Dogmatic Theology

The transcendental way of thinking that unfolds at the core of his theology remains, essentially, in the area of the question about the human person. For this reason people have often misunderstood the anthropological focus of his theology as an anthropological abbreviation of theology, because they have interpreted the human as a separate theme "alongside" God, matter, and the angels.

But Rahner understands the human person as, by nature, a being of transcendence toward the world and toward God. Thus this very determination, which means that human beings at the very core of their being are open to *all* existence, in and of itself rules out any naive anthropocentric narrowness. The true essence of the human person as being "somehow" *everything* (as, for example, Aristotle and Thomas Aquinas formulate it) does not at all permit a simplistic anthropological reduction. Such a reduction would destroy the uniqueness of the human person.

From this point of view, because a human being is essentially drawn to God (which we do not want to prove now), and, in addition, because a human being cannot speak about this God without having a possible relationship to him, then "anthropocentric" and "theocentric," properly understood, are not in opposition. Rahner develops three principle reasons for the necessity of an anthropological "turn" in theology.[42]

1) The question about a particular object is, from a philosophical and theological point of view, only possible, basically, when the question about the knowing subject is also raised, because a priori the subject must include the horizon of the possibility for such objective knowledge. This means theologically, then, that revelation, which is given primarily for the *salvation of human persons*, encounters human beings, inasmuch as they are capable of receiving it, in their transcendental being, even if, in fact, they resist it.

2) Contemporary philosophy and theology cannot and may not lag behind the transcendental-anthropological way of posing problems

---

41. See, for example, "The Current Relationship between Philosophy and Theology," *Theological Investigations XIII,* trans. David Bourke (New York: Crossroad Publishing Company, 1975), 61–79.

42. See "Philosophy and Philosophizing in Theology," *Theological Investigations IX,* 46–63.

found in modern philosophy (from Descartes, Kant, through German idealism to the fundamental ontology of Heidegger).

3) Every responsible theology has to consider the connection between the human person's experience of self in the world and the content of strict theological truth. On the basis of what has been said so far, this cannot present, primarily, merely a formal-logical context for deduction or explanation, but demands the illumination of the correlative meaning (which does not mean merely a "continuity" of *human* knowledge and experience) between the human questions about the world and existence, and divine revelation.

The working out of such connections is not only of a religious-pedagogical and didactic kind, but rather forms the precise task of systematic theology. It must formulate the gospel challenge for contemporary persons in such a way that latent misunderstandings, skewed ideas, and meaningless conclusions remain removed from the truth of the faith. This fundamental-theological-apologetical determination of all theology is best realized with the help of the transcendental-anthropological method in theology.[43]

4. Rahner's Basic Theological Starting Point

In addition to these formal determinations and foundations, we have to ask where the formal and material theological starting point is to be found, which makes the systematic filling-out of such an anthropological-transcendental theology possible. In 1970, when the theological literature hardly raised the question (to say nothing of giving an answer), I suggested that the fundamental theological experience — which corresponds to the methodological demands already mentioned, and which did not mean a material-theological abbreviation, and which contained in itself a genuine systematic potency for development — was to be found in the *experience of grace.*

Then I noted that a more precise study of Karl Rahner's writings could surely offer several basic constellations. Meanwhile, several other attempts at an answer have been actually undertaken, and these can only be welcomed. Karl Neufeld proposed the thesis, and made it intelligible to a certain extent, that the central idea of Rahner's theology is *sin as the loss of grace* (including thoughts on the sacrament of penance). As Neufeld's 1974 article in *Stimmen der Zeit* says, "The notion of sin as the loss of grace unlocks the substantial unity in Rahner's theology and philosophy, in his sermons and in his spiritual advice. All

---

43. See "Reflections on Methodology in Theology," *Theological Investigations XI*, trans. David Bourke (New York: Seabury Press, 1974), 68–114; "Reflections of a New Task for Fundamental Theology," *Theological Investigations XVI*, 156–66.

the important theological questions intersect at this point: the question about God, about the human person, the human being's knowing and deciding, about revelation and salvation, about the church and the world. This is where the experience of faith and scientific work, traditional teaching and new hypotheses, theology and spirituality meet. And so everything is contained in this seed."

As the person who worked on Rahner's collected works on penance,[44] Neufeld certainly uncovered an important vein in Rahner's thinking, as I also mentioned above about the importance of Rahner's historical and systematic theology of the sacrament of penance. And yet one can show historically that long before the studies on penance, which were first published between 1948 and 1955, the central structure of Rahner's theology can be recognized. The formula "sin as the loss of grace" seems to me, however, to be too little developed with regard to content. This formula presupposes the reality of grace as a more fundamental dimension.

Johannes B. Metz made an impressive attempt to examine the creative mediation of dogmatic theology and personal life-history in Rahner's entire theological corpus.[45] Rahner placed the "subject" squarely into the consciousness of traditional dogmatic theology. But here it is not a matter of a transcendental subject, but rather the "subject is the human person enmeshed in his own experiences and histories, and out of these identifying himself ever anew" (Metz, 307).

With that, the human person in his history of religious experience is again the objective theme of dogmatic theology. And so Rahner's theology is dogmatic theology applied to life-history, combining the biographical and one's religious denomination, that is, *theology as mystical biography of a Christian person today*. "Rahner's theology should be called biographical, because the mystical biography of religious experience, of life-history before the veiled countenance of God, is written into the doxography of faith. And it should be called biographical in order to point out that Rahner's so-called transcendental theology is not a high-handed deducted theology, which gains its correctness and irrefutability at the price of tautology, but rather a conceptually shortened and condensed story of life lived in the presence of God" (Metz, 308).

To be sure, Metz does not mean a "new theological subjectivism." In fact, he is quite accurate about Rahner's style. Metz knows that this "life-history dogmatic theology," without prejudice to its biographical

44. See *Theological Investigations XV: Penance in the Church*.
45. Johannes B. Metz, "Karl Rahner — ein theologisches Leben. Theologie als mystische Biographie eines Christenmenschen heute," *Stimmen der Zeit* 99 (1974): 305–16.

and denominational nature, "is applied in everything, as in no other theology, to that which is objectively teachable" (Metz, 308). I think that this element of emptying and "revealing," of mission and communication, at one with the new ecclesiological dimension of his theology, ought to claim a still greater place of importance.

In the meantime, the investigations, particularly of Klaus Fischer and of T. Mannermaa from Finland, have confirmed the earlier suggestion about seeing a central crystallization of Rahner's theology in the experience of grace. An enormous amount of material has unfolded and further developed this insight considerably, in its many individual dimensions. Basically, the first larger historical and systematic works deal with determining the relationship of human existence, God, and grace. The *experience* of grace is the point where this relationship crystallizes. Here grace is not primarily created grace, but God in God's own self-communication.

Viewed anthropologically, "grace," precisely as communicated, is not a thinglike reality in the human person, but rather a determination of the spiritual subject, who by grace comes into immediate contact with God. The only reason grace is not understood mythologically, or as if it were a thing, is because grace is understood from the point of view of the subject.

We do not particularly need to describe the phenomenon itself at this point. Rahner himself tried to do this again and again.[46] He was particularly successful in the two works "Everyday Things" and "Experiencing the Spirit."[47] He mentions the theological background of this "experience," in a preliminary way, in his works about the relationship of nature and grace, as well as in his works about the supernatural existential.

Rahner achieved something decisive by using this starting point. The "most objective" dimensions of the reality of salvation, namely, God and his grace, simultaneously appear as the human person's most subjective dimension, namely, the immediacy of the spiritual subject to God through God himself. The transcendence of the human spirit, which by its nature is already unlimited and, as such, cannot be totally distinguished from its supernatural finalization by simple conceptual reflection, implies a multitude of levels of such an experience.

With this point of view Rahner uses a scholastic theological thesis, namely, that with the existence of a supernatural, grace-elevated salvific act, eo ipso, an a priori formal object is given, which as *formal*

---

46. See, for example, "Reflections on the Experience of Grace," *Theological Investigations III*, 86–90.

47. In *The Spirit in the Church,* trans. John Griffiths (New York: Seabury Press, 1979), 1–31.

cannot be attained by any natural act (traces in scripture: the experience of the working of the Spirit, "the grace of enlightenment," "the light of faith"). Thus Rahner finds in the classic "analysis of the act of faith" the earliest statements that correspond to a transcendental-theological method, because in the analysis of faith the question is explicitly raised about the a priori conditions for the possibility of the knowledge of a particular reality. Also, this makes evident that such a formulation of the question is itself only possible when the respective subject area, as such, is already known.

This kind of transcendental theology knows, essentially, about the real irreducibility of history. This basic relationship is made evident with an analysis of the act of faith: Why is revelation that is heard and accepted, that, as such, appears in the first place only in the human person's knowing and willing (and thus in a certain way must correspond to the a priori structures of the human spirit), why is such revelation not just a human word — even if it is also a word caused by God *about* God — but rather God's very own word, even though it has entered into the human horizon of understanding? Answer: the hearing of God's revelation as the very word of God (in the sense just explained) presupposes as a condition of possibility in the human subject that God, as coprinciple, is supporting the hearer's act through God's own self-communication.

In focusing on the experience of grace Rahner first proceeds with the phenomena that are closest to ordinary human existence, or which gradually root them in their ultimate ground. Because he understands the human person, right from the outset, as "spirit-*in-world*," this experience of grace does not mean a description of introverted, subjective "events." Thus he uses as examples of these experiences of grace such things as sleeping, eating, standing, laughing, and so on. At this point, at the latest, it becomes clear how much Ignatian spirituality and his own original spiritual experiences, with the already mentioned elements, coincide in his starting point.

Rahner also uses this starting point for a more profound analysis for understanding revelation.[48] In this context the task arises of bringing the transcendental relationship with God, as just mentioned, into contact with the *history* of revelation. The revelation-event exhibits two aspects: the constitution of the grace-elevated transcendence of the human person as an enduring, even when denied, always effective, grace-filled existential, and therein the resulting, already mentioned, experience of God's absolute and forgiving nearness.

---

48. See Karl Rahner and Joseph Ratzinger, *Revelation and Tradition*, trans. W. J. O'Hara (New York: Herder and Herder, 1966).

However, because all human transcendence fulfills itself *in* history and is historically mediated, the historical-categorical self-interpretation of revelation also belongs to this moment which we have just mentioned. The thematic objectification of this supernatural transcendental experience occurs in it. The transcendental, a priori opening-up of the human person to the triune God, and the God of grace, does not occur in an individualistic and unhistorical introspection. "It is necessarily accomplished in the history of the action and thought of humankind, and may be so very explicitly or quite anonymously. Consequently, there is never a history of transcendental revelation in isolation. History in the concrete, both individually and collectively, is the history of God's transcendental revelation."[49]

God's self-communication in grace is certainly a "transcendental" existential of the human person, but it comes to itself, and to the individual, only as mediated in salvation and revelation history. The transcendental and the historical-categorical moment are not side-by-side, but rather form a unity, and are characterized by their own reciprocal relationship of conditioning each other.

This basic point of departure runs through Rahner's entire theology. Again and again, this fundamental insight is reflected in different variations and communicated concretely down to the final concrete formulations of the question.

Under certain conditions one can discern *three* phases in the unfolding of his "transcendental theology." In the first phase, which lasted until the mid-fifties, his transcendental thinking, for the most part, occurred only in a few especially suitable problem areas and within the given, basic structures of classical theology. The second phase takes up, more explicitly and comprehensively, the transcendental leitmotif within theology. Now the concept of "transcendental theology" appears programmatically. At this time Rahner was mainly working out a "transcendental christology."[50]

His efforts in this direction systematically simplified the area of the historical-categorical and, in a certain way, left it "abstractly" behind. It was, perhaps, mainly for this reason that criticism of his transcendental starting point mounted. The criticism has to do, mainly, with arguing that Rahner's transcendental starting point neglected the intersubjective, personal, and, especially, the sacramental dimensions. He is also criticized for leaving out of his considerations the brutally real, the political, and more comprehensive social relationships.

In more recent years (the end of the sixties) a *third, more inten-*

---

49. Ibid., 17.
50. See *Foundations of Christian Faith,* 206–12.

sive, effort began which thematized more clearly the a priori elements in theology, above all, the concrete, nondeductible dimension of history, and the fact that faith ultimately cannot be captured by reflection. Transcendental theology remains primary, but he broadened the area of the transcendental; above all, the limits of transcendental theology are made clear.

And so the christology of this third phase achieves a new emphasis, in that the historical Jesus comes into sharper relief. This is evident in the book he wrote with Wilhelm Thüsing, *A New Christology*.[51] Without a doubt, from a completely different angle, his conversations with Johannes B. Metz contributed to the nuancing of his transcendental starting point.

And so it is clear that he worked very hard at resolving the relationship between the transcendental and the categorical-historical. For many reasons, and with some justification, the transcendental dimension predominates from volume eleven through nineteen in his *Theological Investigations.*

This is not the final word, of course since important investigations are still going on. Thus, for example, too little attention has been paid to the very extensive "On the Theology of Symbol,"[52] where he offers such a resolution. The span of his efforts reaches from his theological dissertation to the essays on the theology of the Sacred Heart, and on the Ignatian *Exercises* to the already-mentioned third phase.

In this context a comment by his brother Hugo is worth mentioning because of its importance for the comprehensive interpretation of Rahner's theological thought. Hugo thinks that the treatise "On the Theology of Symbol" embodies the whole direction of Karl's theology. In this context his extensive theology about things, the body, everyday virtues, and secular accomplishments — based to a great extent on the Ignatian spirituality of "finding God in all things" — has not yet received proper attention.

The above-mentioned third phase is connected with the work of his early years (*Investigations I–III*). The unity and nuancing of these same efforts are a good example of the fact that, on the whole, there are no radical changes in Rahner's theology, although there are decisive and powerful shifts of emphasis within it, and questions are approached, again and again, in new ways. In several individual problems, as, for example, the matter of monogenism and the "intermediate state," Rahner expressly changed his earlier opinion, which was connected to classical theology, and proposed new hypotheses.

---

51. Trans. David Smith and Verdant Green (New York: Seabury Press, 1980).
52. *Theological Investigations IV*, 221–52.

Difficulties in understanding arise now and then when statements from several phases are put together in one text, as, for example, in the brief section on christology in *Foundations of Christian Faith*. Moreover the question remains whether his transcendental starting point does not often make itself independent of the richness of its own dimensions.

5. The Concrete Development of His Basic Thought

One always creates the impression of being a schoolmaster in trying to reduce the manifold themes and theses of such rich reflection to *one* basic thought. Yet it is still necessary, in all truly systematic thinking, to grasp the many disparate movements of such a thought-process at their center of origin. An exhaustive presentation would have to show how the basic starting point which we have sketched is reflected repeatedly in Rahner's numerous individual treatises, and how it always achieves concrete clarity and nuanced confirmation. Since this kind of compartmentalizing excerpted from the fullness of the basic experience cannot be presented here, I may be permitted to touch upon just a few basic themes as they originate from this constructive center. Moreover, this is the time to point people quite simply to Rahner's work itself. No "portrait" can substitute for the requisite working with the sources.

His interpretation of revelation-history, in the above-mentioned sense, brings with it a totally new conception of the relationship between world-history and revelation-history.[53] Properly understood, salvation history is, on the whole, coextensive with human intellectual history. Of course, concrete history is never simply the history of revelation. "The latter takes place in the former, always in an indissoluble unity, with error, misinterpretation, guilt, abuses; it is a history both just and sinful. . . . "[54] It is also here that Rahner's efforts at a theology of non-Christian religions and of the "anonymous Christian" occur. Christians ultimately achieve their diacritical possibility for discerning a genuine revelation history in the whole of human history only from Christ; he, himself, is the unique climax of revelation history, which, carried by God's grace, moves in the world's constant self-transcendence toward this omega point.[55] The transcendentally understood relationship between (graced) spirit and (revelation) history implies the absolute savior, the Godman," as the climax of the history of grace in the world. He is the historical, unsurpassable, irreversible, and thus eschatological

---

53. See "History of the World and Salvation-History," *Theological Investigations V,* trans. Karl Kruger (Baltimore: Helicon Press, 1966), 97–114.

54. *Revelation and Tradition,* 17–18.

55. See "The Secret of Life," *Theological Investigations VI,* 149.

manifestation of God's victorious self-communication to the world.[56] From this starting point one could easily show the inner connection to Rahner's sacramental theology and his ecclesiology.[57]

In this context we can point out that Rahner himself presented a glimpse into the inner structure of his theological thought in the different sketches for "The Need for a 'Short Formula' of Christian Faith."[58]

These reflections would be incomplete without always keeping in mind the addresse of theology which Rahner always kept before him: the contemporary person's need for and understanding of faith. It is only here that theology can gain entrance.

6. Concern for Pastoral and Practical Theology

From the very beginning Rahner's theology has a sense for pastoral questions and a concern for the faith of his companions in faith. To this day he is a pastor for many people. His "pious" books, as he liked to call them, have become quiet guides to vital Christian spirituality. This faith shows that it is, in the best sense of the word, fraternal, in that Rahner was ready to take up courageously all human questions and not to avoid any genuine need. Very early on, Rahner worked at clarifying the spirituality of the founder of his order and exploring, for example, the deeper meaning of the Ignatian "finding God in all things," and the experience of the "ever-greater God." Among his earliest works were treatises on the spiritual life according to the church fathers.

If one wishes to appreciate his interest in, and achievements for, practical theology and pastoral praxis, one has to understand that Rahner's theology is rooted in a deep spirituality, in a deeply personal experience of faith, and in pastoral activity. This practical dimension of his theological thought, then, is no subsequent application of a presupposed theology. Nor does it come primarily out of an "existentiell,"[59] personalistic or an habitual way of thinking of this theology. To be sure,

56. See "Jesus Christ," *Encyclopedia of Theology: The Concise Sacramentum Mundi* (New York: Seabury Press, 1975), 764–72.

57. See *The Church and the Sacraments*, trans. W. J. O'Hara (New York: Herder and Herder, 1963); "The Second Vatican Council's Challenge to Theology," *Theological Investigations IX*, 3–27.

58. *Theological Investigations IX*, 117–26; *Foundations of Christian Faith*, 448–59.

59. "Existentiell" refers to human existence in the concrete and to the ways in which the structures of human existence are given concrete content. "Existential," on the other hand, is a generic term applied to those characteristics or capacities of human existence (for example, self-transcendence, self-consciousness, and freedom) which make it specifically human and distinguish it from other modes of existence. Thus, for example, one's *existential* relationship to the Trinity and to Christ becomes *existentiell* through explicit, personal, formal prayer. "Existentiell," then, refers to one's subjective, personal appropriation. — Translation editor.

Rahner mastered numerous literary genres — from the stringent treatise to very personal prayer, for example, *Watch and Pray with Me*,[60]
which appeared under the name Anselm Trescher, which goes back
to his mother's family. He never denied that publications of this sort
were a special obligation for him. He often said that "several smaller
and larger 'pious' books are just as important to me as those which
claim to be theological works."[61]

The wooing mediation of the offer of revelation to human beings,
and from that the church's concern for their salvation, do not belong to
the "pastoral" consequences, but rather to the innermost driving force,
of his theology — a dynamic prior to all scholarly theology. It is only
logical, then, that Rahner was concerned, again and again, with the encounter of "theory" and "practice" in academic theology. The anthology
Sendung und Gnade (1959), subtitled "Essays in Pastoral Theology," is a
first impressive witness to the constant and numerous efforts he made
in this regard. Rahner's concern in presenting these essays was, above
all, to offer a service that arises primordially out of the very heart of
theology, and is directed at praxis and ultimately at its theory. The goal
of the essays flowed from the conviction "that the mission to the apostolate, and to pastoral care, is a saving event supported by God's grace.
For this reason pastoral theology is ultimately not psychology, peda-
gogy, sociology, and the like, but rather theology. Thus only that person
who trusts solely in God's grace will measure up to such a mission."[62]

What Rahner accomplished, actually and implicitly, in the different
essays in this volume was to develop, more and more in the follow-
ing years, into a scholarly concept of pastoral theology. *Sendung und
Gnade* contains a significant prolegomenon in the chapter entitled
"The Present Situation of Christians: A Theological Interpretation of the
Position of Christians in the Modern World."[63]

In this lecture delivered in Cologne in 1954, Rahner states that the actual situation of Christians in a present moment basically coconditions
their salvific activity. Eventually this notion then led to a new starting
point for practical theology as a scholarly discipline among the theological specialties. With the help of Heinz Schuster and the collaboration
of German-speaking pastoral theologians, Rahner drafted his *Plan und
Aufriß eines Handbuches der Pastoraltheologie* (Plan and Sketch for
a Handbook of Pastoral Theology).[64] The five-volume *Handbuch der*

---

60. Trans. William V. Dych (New York: Herder and Herder, 1966).
61. "Selbstporträt," *Forscher und Gelehrte*, ed. W. Ernst Böhm (Stuttgart: Battenberg,
1966), 21.
62. *Sendung und Gnade*, foreword to the third edition, 1961.
63. *The Christian Commitment*, 3–37.
64. Freiburg i. Br.: Herder, 1962. Not translated into English.

Pastoraltheologie (1964–72) tried to carry out this plan, insofar as it is even possible. The first three volumes, newly revised and updated, are also available in new editions. Translations into the major European languages have given this work an even wider circulation.

To be sure, not everything succeeded as originally planned. If Rahner himself had not personally taken a hand in the project, the first two volumes especially would hardly have been published. In retrospect it is clear that many areas were a little neglected or excluded from the start. For this reason the *Handbuch der Verkündigung* ("preaching") and the *Handbuch der Religionspädagogik* have only been published recently.

The basic overall concept is much more important than such concrete, individual sections, or thematic amplifications. Despite all the appreciation, however, it is precisely the methodological reflections that have scarcely found a real and lasting echo. For that reason, let me sketch the most important perspectives here:

1) In contrast to doctrinal, or essentialistic, ecclesiology, which tries primarily to describe the "enduring" nature of the church, in practical theology it is a matter of the church *inasmuch as* the church is a concrete historical reality, a reality which, with the help of a sociological-theological analysis, must come up with precepts for dealing with the daily accomplishment of its salvific concerns.

2) So understood, practical theology is not only intended for the "clergy" as the "subject" of the church's pastoral activities, it also turns its attention to the church as a whole, in the midst of the contemporary world. In so doing, it focuses upon all the official and nonofficial bearers of concrete responsibility for the faith, for example, the faithful and the pope.

3) The formal point of view of practical theology is that all ecclesial functioning is conditioned by the actual present moment. In addition, a thorough *theological* analysis of the present is necessary, an analysis which must find a nuanced viewpoint in all the statements of practical theology.

After years of not engaging in a scholarly, theoretical discussion such as one finds in the *Handbuch der Pastoraltheologie*, pastoral theology recently "joined the club" through the works of N. Mette and P. Neumann. Rahner's impulses, which, by the way, go beyond, and are not simply coextensive, with the *Handbuch*,[65] are, of course, not

---

65. See "Practical Theology within the Totality of Theological Disciplines," *Theological Investigations IX*, 101–14; "On the Problems Entailed in a 'Pastoral Constitution,'" and "Practical Theology and Social Work in the Church," *Theological Investigations X*, trans. David Bourke (New York: Herder and Herder, 1973), 293–317, 349–70; "The New Claims which Pastoral Theology Makes upon Theology as a Whole," *Theological Investigations XI*, 115–36; "Theology as Engaged in an Interdisciplinary Dialogue with the

just hidden in his expressly scholarly-theoretical treatises. Despite all subsequent nuances and corrections, Rahner's programmatical ideas still have a future because something like the initial impulse remains.

Karl Rahner was not a dreamy-eyed theologian, lost in the clouds of speculation, far from the reality of the church's present situation. He didn't play theoretical or historical mind-games for himself or for his own little clique. He always placed himself at his church's disposal. By name, or anonymously, he often handled many of her "hot potatoes." His collaboration at the council clearly showed that he could give up his own ideas and suggestions when the greater good and the common good were at stake. Often, during momentous theological consultations of the council, and in the following year, he put a stop to the endless, and often somewhat self-complacent debates, by stepping in suddenly, and saying with his own uniquely "grumpy charm" (Mario v. Galli): "Enough clever talk! We need a text!"

He saw his work for the church as an *offer* for better understanding the faith, about which one can decide in freedom, without using backroom politics and tricks to have "his" ideas prevail. Rahner knew that his dialogue with the real church could be fraught with conflict. He wrote the important essay *Free Speech in the Church*[66] in 1953, and he never tired of writing, or of taking a public position, if he thought that truth, love, freedom, or justice were being violated in the church. In this sense, he hardly ever espoused any splinter group within the currents in the church. He could only take the unpredictable position of one who wants to help in every way possible, and who speaks fearlessly for, or against, something, because he always remains concerned about the universal good of the church. It is for this reason that he always practiced a controversial and critical theology — without ever descending to the level of sheer grumbling, or vain knowing-better. If he criticized, then he only took a position if he had positive counter-suggestions to offer.[67]

In this effort, whether he had something to say or something contradictory to say, a charism — extremely rare among theologians — came to light. It is easy to have an abstractly loyal relationship to one's church. One can keep such a proper distance that basically one never comes into conflict with it. Many — be they conservative or progres-

---

Sciences," and "On the Contemporary Relationship between Theology and the Contemporary Sciences," *Theological Investigations XIII*, 80–93, 94–102; Perspectives for Pastoral Theology in the Future," *Theological Investigations XXII*, trans. Joseph Donceel (New York: Crossroad Publishing Company, 1991), 106–19.

66. New York: Sheed and Ward, 1959.

67. See *The Shape of the Church to Come;* "Opposition in the Church," *Theological Investigations XVII*, 127–38.

sive — demonstrate this by moving back and forth securely on the stilts of theological scholarship, above the immediate concerns of the real church.

Rahner took an active part in all the great questions without becoming a foot-dragging church officeholder, or a hawker of current interests that made headlines. What so seldom happens in the theological "business" is the passionate, pugnacious, ever-hopeful yes to the real church, despite every disappointment.[68]

At the same time Rahner knew that the contemporary church has a dangerous tendency toward an introverted narcissism, preoccupied with itself and with its "cares." Asked what he thought of the contemporary church on the occasion of his sixtieth birthday in 1964, he replied with a bit of a grumble: "The church, and all of us, ought to talk more about God and God's grace."

Rahner helped form the church and the theology of our time. For this he received many honors and great esteem. Times change. In 1968 he wrote: "Now I seem to be someone who must suddenly defend positions which are actually in the center of the church's tradition.... Indeed, a 'leftist' can become a 'rightist' because others have changed their positions, not because you have changed yours."[69] He often used the image of a war on two fronts, in which he had placed himself.

He remained faithful to his theological task in everything he did. In this sense there is nothing, or hardly anything, "private" that can be called "biographical," alongside his service. He stood totally in the service of the mission he undertook. This is the only way to grasp his unusual productivity. He used himself up for God and the people of the church.

And so, ultimately, he had an indifference toward, and distance from, theology as scholarship. He could say with clear irony: "I am no 'scholar.' In this work [of theology] I also want to be a man, a Christian, and, as much as possible, a priest of the church. Perhaps a theologian cannot desire anything else. In any case the science of theology, as such, was never important to me."[70] He valued precise scientific knowledge, but he feared the narrow-minded specialist.

As a great "generalist" or theological "universalist," he asked himself, seriously, how this immense task could be done responsibly in

68. See "Concerning our Assent to the Church as She Exists in the Concrete," *Theological Investigations XII*, trans. David Bourke (New York: Crossroad Publishing Company, 1974), 142–60.

69. *Die Antwort der Theologen* (Düsseldorf: Patmos, 1968), 13. See "The Church's Angry Old Men," *Karl Rahner in Dialogue*, ed. Paul Imhof and Hubert Biallowons, trans. ed. Harvey D. Egan (New York: Crossroad Publishing Company, 1986), 330–33.

70. "Selbstporträt," 21.

the face of the methods of theological specialization. "Forty years ago the ratio between that which I knew, and that which was available, with regard to the problematic, the knowledge, and the methods was perhaps 1:4; today it is probably 1:400."[71] He has shown how someone can do theology in such a situation. With a disarming openness, to the frustration of all scientific pretensions, he declared: "To a certain extent I want to be a deeply-thinking dilettante — and one who at the same time thinks deeply about his dilettantism and factors it into his thinking — but all with reference to theology's ultimately foundational questions."[72]

Rahner suffered from the excessive demands of thousands of questions, a long tradition, and life's complexities. He called the "method" of a fragmentary mastery "dilettantism." But who actually are the dilettantes in this case?

Rahner's work served the church and theology in a specific historical period. It is hard to say, today, how one can best describe this transitional period. Theologically, this step surely means — but not only! — the transition from a universally valid scholastic theology, in the broadest sense of the term, into a larger multiplicity of theological models that compete with each other, without detriment to a unity in the church's confession of faith. Since no one really knows where the journey is ultimately going, none of those people who believe that they have to go faster than Rahner should speak lightly about "overtaking" him. Those who entrust themselves to the power and the strength of Rahner's way of thinking come up with and raise questions, especially if they remain critical, which they cannot adequately answer so quickly.

Ultimately the individual assertions of this theology are not important, even though this theology need not shy away from them. What is important is the inner tension that survives lively oppositions and contradictory situations and makes them fruitful. Maintaining the unity-in-diversity of tradition and its interpretation, of past historical experiences and pressing contemporary concerns, of the inherited "substance" of the faith and critical reflection — this endures as his thought's excellent, and rare, basic characteristic.

And so this fundamental "transition" from one moment to the other is, ultimately, not a sign of a unique historical constellation, but rather an exemplary manifestation of Catholic theology in general. It is precisely in this regard that his theology can hardly ever be essentially "surpassed." Of course this example does not tolerate any imitation.

---

71. "Grace as the Heart of Human Existence," *Faith in a Wintry Season*, 19.
72. Ibid.

Rather it remains valid, as such, only if its one basic experience survives new challenges.

In this sense, Rahner is even now something like a classical theologian, full of the explosive power of his creative thinking, and of a unique spiritual presence which surprises us again and again. Rahner is like an Atlas, a giant who has taken upon himself the heavy burden of doing theology in our time, in a responsible and simultaneously creative way, and on behalf of all Christians, with the full effort of his whole self, to the very limits of his human capabilities.

IV. THE STRUCTURE AND USE OF THIS BOOK

At this point there are just a few things to say about the structure, selection, and arrangement of the texts — and, above all, their use.

1. Arrangement and Selection

The purpose of this anthology is to be neither a compendium of Rahner's theology, as Rahner himself has presented it in outline form in his *Foundations of Christian Faith*, nor a summary of the many statements in *Theological Investigations*. It is also not a "system" of Rahner's thought dreamt up by the editors. Despite all the correct conclusions coming from Rahner's reflections, most attempts at reducing his theology to a strict common denominator have forced it into a procrustean bed, and have robbed it of the freedom of its intellectual movement, as well as of its inexhaustible mystery.

This work is just an anthology, which takes selected material from Rahner's extensive writings in order to present to those who are interested a palette of the great themes, a series of impressive texts and important thoughts. One ought not to be deceived about the "systematic" which undergirds it. Of course it does take its cue from the structure of Rahner's theology, as seen in his *Foundations of Christian Faith*, his "short formulas of the faith," his numerous systematic treatises, and his various encyclopedia entries. However, it does not follow any of these models slavishly. Many texts could easily have been placed under another heading or in another place. For similar reasons, this anthology could not assemble all the themes of his theology. It would have been presumptuous to imagine that we could include everything. It is by all means conceivable that more specialized criteria for choosing will allow for other anthologies on Christian life, on pastoral care, and the like.

Nevertheless, we did try to present Rahner's thought whole and unabridged. We wanted to include all the essential perspectives and dimensions of his theological work — from the strict definition of concepts, his objections in the area of church politics, to the intimacy of prayer. A more systematically prepared American understanding strengthened us in our purpose.[73] Of course, readers must decide themselves whether the editors' good intention really succeeded.

2. The Editing of Texts

We did as little editing as possible. Reductions were unavoidable. What has been omitted in the text is not expressly noted. The text has been arranged uniformly with regard to format (abbreviations, quotations, and the like). For the sake of greater clarity, we made more use of paragraphing. Latin and Greek concepts, as well as technical terms, were both translated and explained. We did this, however, only the first time the word came up in a text. At times transitions in the text had to be recast. Only in one place (no. 22) did we make a change in paragraphs. Greek texts were immediately translated.

Quite a few places contained printing errors and oversights. Without damaging Rahner's unique and unmistakable style, several harsh expressions were carefully toned down. Footnotes were left out. The headings are mainly the work of the publishers, although often based on the formulation of the texts. For technical reasons (above all, because of the makeup of the pages) slight shortenings of the texts were necessary in several places, but none of them were significant. Those with scholarly interest should consult the original publications for comparison, as given in the footnote to each entry heading.

3. Reading Tips

The reader should enjoy as much freedom as possible in using this book. However, we recommend that the less-prepared reader not begin with the first section of this book. This first section presents a reflection on the whole of Christianity, and it is not easy to digest, for conceptual and linguistic reasons. Concrete anthropological phenomena (such as laughter, walking, aging, and the like), things about Christian life (such as Pentecost, the pilgrims' meal, judgment, and the like) are more easily accessible. Therefore we consciously recommend to the reader a choice of readings. This book wishes to invite the reader "to browse."

Of course, one can read it right through from beginning to end. Despite its marked limitation with regard to systematic composition, this book affords a certain overview of the breadth and dynamics of Rahner's thought. The bibliography at the end of this volume makes

---

73. Gerald McCool, ed., *A Rahner Reader* (New York: Seabury Press, 1975).

clear, of course, that this cannot be a smooth, royal road for making all of Rahner available in the easiest possible way.

The footnotes found with each entry heading, in addition to providing documentation, also serve to refer the reader to the complete texts. It may lead the person to reread, or to read for the first time, one book or another, be it *The Eternal Year* or *On Prayer.* Perhaps some readers will pick up the fundamental, early, philosophical works, *Spirit in the World* and *Hearers of the Word.*

All our efforts have only one goal: to guide people to Rahner's spirituality and thought, with as much authenticity and diversity as possible, and — what is more important to Rahner, as well — to prepare the reader who is open for an encounter with the living God: "All subtle theology, every dogma, all canon law, every adaptation, and all the church's nay-saying, all institutions, every office and all its power, every holy liturgy, and every brave mission has as its only goal: faith, hope, and love of God and human beings. All the church's other plans and actions would be absurd and perverse where she to abandon this commission and seek only herself."[74]

Translated by Robert J. Braunreuther, S.J.
Boston College

---

74. *The Church after the Council,* 31.

WHAT IS
CHRISTIANITY?

1 • A Short Formula
of the Christian Faith*

Christianity is the assent on the part of the whole community (church) formulated and held explicitly by that community to the absolute mystery which exercises an inescapable power in and over our existence, and which we call God. It is our assent to that mystery as pardoning us and admitting us to a share in its own divinity; it is that mystery as imparting itself to us in a history shaped by our own free decisions as an intelligent being; and this self-bestowal of God in Jesus Christ manifested itself as finally and irrevocably victorious in history.

I believe that what is definitive in the Christian faith is expressed here, and that too in a formula which, provided it is rightly understood and explicated, will also be found to cover the further contents of the Christian faith as well, as long as these are not taken to include those positive definitions freely enunciated by the church which belong to the dimension of historical and contingent fact as such, and which, moreover do not represent any particular problem on any reasonable approach to the question of intellectual honesty.

Let us examine the formula we have constructed, bearing in mind the provisos mentioned above. What it asserts first and foremost about Christianity and about belief in it is that God is the incomprehensible and impenetrable mystery, and that God must be recognized as mystery in this sense. Christianity is not a religion which, in its evaluation of human existence, postulates the idea of "God" as a recognized and acknowledged landmark, so to speak, one factor among the rest, which can be manipulated and combined with them so as to produce a satisfactory final estimate. On the contrary, Christianity is a religion that projects the person into the dimension of the incomprehensible surrounding and permeating his or her existence.

It prevents the person from falling on merely ideological grounds (for this is the ultimate significance of the Christian religion) into the mistake of supposing that there is a basic formula of existence which is comprehensible to us, which is available to us ourselves to manipulate, and on the basis of which we can construct existence.

---

* *Theological Investigations VII,* trans. David Bourke (New York: Herder and Herder, 1971), 60–64.

45

Christianity constitutes a radical denial of all such "idols." It aims at bringing a person into contact with God as the ineffable mystery without any diminution of his own human freedom, and without the hubris of attempting to control God. Christianity recognizes that a person knows God only when he is reduced to silence and adoration by the experience of this mystery. All religious utterances are true only insofar as they constitute the ultimate word introducing the silence with which he reacts to the presence of this mystery, in order that it may remain present to him in itself, and not be replaced by the mere idea of God.

But Christianity knows that this mystery permeates its own existence as the ultimate reality of all and as the truth of truths; that the Christian in his thoughts, in his freedom, in his actions, and in the conscious acceptance of his own death, always and unquestioning goes beyond that which can be defined, comprehended and conceptually manipulated in the dimension of the concrete and the particular which he encounters in the sphere of life and knowledge.

The Christian never simply "comes across" God (indeed in that case it would not be God at all) as one specific phenomenon among others within the sphere of human existence, one, therefore, which falls within the limits of his ideas and his actions. He is in contact with the living God as the all-encompassing and the unencompassed, as the ineffable upholder of being such that to call him in question is to call everything in question also, ourselves included; one who is not, so to say, conjured up by our questioning, but is already there in that he himself makes it possible for us to raise questions about him by providing beyond all question the basis from which such questions can be put, opening the door to them and raising us to the level at which we can ask them.

Rightly regarded, Christianity is not a fortress of truth with innumerable windows, which we must live in order to be "in the truth," but rather *one single* aperture which leads out of all the individual truths (and even errors) into *the* truth which is the unique incomprehensibility of God. But Christianity insists relentlessly, in season and out of season, that this overwhelming brightness that is darkness and silence to us, which encompasses our life and permeates everything, that is all other lights and the darknesses that correspond to them, shall not be lost sight of by us, that in our existence we shall not allow our attention to be drawn away from this strange and unearthly brightness, but rather face up to it, trembling indeed yet resolute (in our commitment to it), calling it by its nameless name, never endowing our own idols with that name.

But Christianity has something more to assert of this unearthly and ineffable mystery, and this is its real message. For the moment it makes no difference whether a person dares to learn of this real message of

Christianity from the innermost promptings of his own conscience as
moved by grace, or whether he has the impression that this message
constitutes the basic motive force, purged of all extraneous elements,
in the religious history of humankind (for in this too the mysterious
grace of God is at work), or even whether he simply receives this message from the witness of Christ and his apostles. In any case, the true
message of Christianity has this to say to us: God is the incomprehensible mystery of our existence which encompasses us and causes us
to realize, however painfully, the limitations of that existence, which
he himself transcends.

But he does not only present himself to us in this guise as the
ultimate horizon of the knowable, toward which the course of our existence as spiritual beings is oriented and by which it is corrected, even
while God himself remains remote and silent to us. He does indeed perform this function, setting us at a distance from himself so as to make it
possible for us to "return to ourselves" in knowledge and freedom and
thereby to give coherence and intelligibility to the environment of sensible experience in which we live, viewing it as a cosmic whole and as
our environment. And in the very fact of doing this he makes us experience for ourselves our own finite state. But there is more to it than this.
The mystery which we call God *gives himself* in his divine existence,
gives himself to us for our own in a genuine act of self-bestowal. He
himself is the grace of our existence.

We shall say, therefore, that what we mean by creation is that the
divine being freely "exteriorizes" his own activity so as to produce nondivine being, but does this solely in order to produce the necessary
prior conditions for his own divine self-bestowal in that free and unmerited love that is identical with himself. He does this in order to raise
up beings who can stand in a personal relationship to himself and so
receive his message, and on whom he can bestow not only finite and
created being distinct from himself, but himself as well. In this way he
himself becomes both giver and gift, and even more the actual source
of the human being's own capacity to receive him as gift.

Thus, the finite, of its very nature as finite, finds its ultimate fulfillment in God as the mysterious infinite. The "creator-creature"
relationship belongs necessarily and indispensably to the very mode of
reality as such, but does not constitute its actual content. God creates
because he himself wills to impart himself by "externalizing" and so
giving himself.

The distance between him and us is there in order that the unity
of love may be achieved. Creation, covenant, and law are there (as
providing a framework for the finite) in order that love may exist in
boundless measure. Obedience is imposed in order that we may re-

ceive God's freedom. We are set far from God in order that the miracle of his nearness to us to bless and even to forgive our sins may be made possible.

The purpose of all this is not that the mystery may be wholly penetrated and resolved by our minds, but rather that as mystery it may become the blessings of a person's spirit, which possesses this mystery directly and in a manner that draws it out of itself in order that in total self-forgetfulness it may love this mystery as its only true light and life.

This is the real content of Christianity: the ineffability of the absolute mystery that bestows itself in forgiveness and in drawing us into its own divine nature. Moreover, it bestows itself in such a way that we can sustain it, accept it, and once more really receive the capacity to accept it, from itself.

It can be seen, then, that this self-bestowal of God (upon the human being in the history that he shapes for himself as a free and intelligent being) has a threefold aspect. Now the three aspects involved, inasmuch as they mutually constitute the *self*-bestowal of God, are inherent in the divine nature as such. In this self-bestowal on God's part, therefore, what we Christians are accustomed to call God's triune nature is already present.

A further factor that belongs to the very essence of Christianity is the person from whom its name is derived, Jesus Christ. But the mystery that is Jesus Christ is bound up in the closest possible manner with the one mentioned above. The mystery of God's self-bestowal, in which God himself in his innermost glory becomes the absolute future of the person, has a history of its own because it proceeds from God himself as his free act, and because the person, as existing in the dimension of history, is involved in the historicity of humanity considered as a single whole. Also because he has to achieve the ultimate transcendentality of his nature, "divinized" as it is by God's self-bestowal, in the "space-time" dimension of history itself in and through a concrete encounter with the concrete world.

For it is in this that he exists, is aware of himself, and realizes himself. The self-bestowal of God, even though it constitutes the innermost and transcendental basis for the world's existence and its history, even though it represents the ultimate entelechy of the world, nevertheless has a history of its own, that is, an inner dynamism such that it manifests itself, unfolds itself, and achieves its fulfillment in space and time. We call this the history of salvation and revelation.

However, there is a point at which the manifestation of the divine self-bestowal as something offered on God's part, and as something freely accepted, even though accepted only with the help of God's grace, on the person's part, attains its acme and the stage at which it becomes absolute and irrevocable. It is the stage at which the dialogue between God and man who is *the* man, that becomes substantiated in him (so that it is not merely conducted by him as something distinct from his own essence) resolves itself in an absolute assent from either side, and manifests itself as such.

In other words, *the* man in whom this identity is achieved appears as God's absolute and irrevocable assent as uttered to and as accepted by humankind. And it is at this point precisely that we find what Christian faith means by the incarnation of the divine Logos. It is ipso facto present when the divine self-bestowal appears in history as absolutely and irrevocably uttered, and absolutely and irrevocably received. Admittedly there still remains the irreducible factuality of the history that has really been lived through, the fact that this takes place and is experienced precisely in Jesus of Nazareth.

What we mean when we speak of the "church" is the eschatological presence of God's truth and God's love in this entity by word and sacrament. And this means nothing else than that the historical facts are enduring and valid, that in Jesus of Nazareth the history of God's self-bestowal has manifested itself in an irrevocable form, and in this form remains present and remains the object of belief.

2 • The Sacramental Structure of the Christian Salvation-Reality*

Christianity is first and fundamentally Christ himself. It is therefore in the first place a *salvation-reality* which is given in the order of human history in the fact that the incarnate Son of the Father became, in virtue of his personal dignity and his membership of the race of Adam, the head and representative of the whole of humanity, and as such performed the act of worship of God and offered the absolute and final sacrifice that fundamentally redeemed humanity. The presence of this *fact of salvation* (as God's unique, free, historical act) in human history is the foundation of Christianity.

But this reality, in which Christianity first exists for us is: (a) posited by God himself. The crucial reality through which we reach God is therefore not *our* prayer and the offering made by *us* insofar as it is our own accomplishment, but an act of God himself, by means of which

---

* *Theological Investigations III*, trans. Karl-H. and Boniface Kruger (Baltimore: Helicon Press, 1967), 243–46.

the human being is capable of positing an act that pays homage to God and sanctifies himself; (b) It is "sacramental"; therefore, (c) the word is an essential constitutive part of it. These last two points we must here explain in greater detail in themselves and in their mutual connection.

Through the Logos's incarnation God's salvific will became a genuine reality in the order of human existence. That is why the human being does not find God in any process of rising beyond this world, whether this be conceived in an idealistic, gnostic, mystic, or any other fashion. He does not find God in the abandonment of the spheres of his "natural" existence (that is, of his existence as always given), but only in a turning to Jesus Christ, that is, to a reality within the sphere of his own existence and history, to Jesus in whom God himself came to us.

The salvific presence of God in the flesh, that is, *within* human history — the perennial stumbling block of all philosophy and autonomous mysticism — is nevertheless of such a kind that it is *not* immediately accessible to the grasp of human experience in its own inner *self*. This is excluded by the strictly supernatural character of the reality of this presence.

But if it is not only to exist "in itself" but also to be given "for us," to be "present" (and this is the only way for it to become a reality of *salvation*), then apart from the corresponding subjective a priori of which the human being has need in order to grasp it — the grace of faith, and so on — its proper, inner, total essence must contain an element that makes possible the presence of something transcending human experience without making it necessary for this reality to appear in its own proper self: the *sign* that makes present for us what exists in itself.

But for us, only the *word* can be considered as constituting such a sign. For all human reality — considered in isolation and apart from this supervening word that forms and interprets it — is out of the question as a sign indicative of the presence of a strictly supernatural reality, because such a nonhuman reality could function as a sign of this kind only in its *positive* being. But this would mean, in effect, that the natural being of a thing could have a univocal reference to a supernatural reality, and this is excluded from the beginning by the very supernatural character of that which is to be shown.

Such a reference can be effected therefore only by means of the word. For only in the word is there the possibility of *negation* pointing to another reality. Only the supervening of such a negation can transmute a positive mundane thing into the sign of a supernatural reality. We conclude, therefore, that among the intrinsic constitutive elements of the presence of a fact of salvation within *human* history — here in the first place the saving reality of Christ himself — must be numbered the *word* as sign.

This means in the first place that the Christian salvation-reality is essentially sacramental. For we may justly call sacramental all divine, supernatural salvation-reality that takes place in history and is therefore present to us only in *sign*. And this leads us to the conclusion that the word belongs to the fundamental constitutive elements of sacramental reality, and in such a way that the "sacramental" function is inherent in the word when it first makes its appearance in the essence of Christianity.

For if Christianity in its foundation and origin is not primarily the communication of truths (as true *propositions*) but the reality of the incarnate, crucified, and risen Son of God, and if *this* fundamental reality (as salvation-reality for us in the order of our existence) includes the *word* as an intrinsic element, then this can only mean that in its first *Christian* application the word is *sacramental:* a sign in which God's saving will is made present for us in our history.

The Christian word — or, to express it differently, the word insofar as it is Christian — is not primarily a discussion about something already given in other ways, not a means for reaching understanding between two persons about an object that each of them can attain in his own way, but a making present of the salvation-reality itself.

As applied to Christ this means that his revelation is not originally an imparting of true propositions, which perhaps no one would have thought of otherwise, but the self-revelation of his own being, a self-revelation by means of which he first becomes the Christ for us.

Christian preaching (that is, where it is not the "form of the sacrament" in the usual sense) is therefore nothing more than the further exposition of, or preparation for, the strictly sacramental word: it is always founded upon this, indeed it is in the broad sense itself "sacramental": the sign of the hidden and yet present salvation-reality of Christ, a sign which — in the case of the strictly sacramental word — itself brings about this presence.

3 • Christianity and World Religions*

The Catholic church is confronted by historical powers that she cannot neglect as wholly "secular," but which are important for her, even though they are opposed to her. It is her duty to establish a relationship

* *Grace in Freedom*, trans. and adapted by Hilda Graef (New York: Herder and Herder, 1969), 81–86.

with them and to understand their existence insofar as she cannot simply approve of them. But she must bear the scandal of their opposition and conquer it by herself becoming the higher unity that embraces it. This is what is meant by "open Catholicism."

One of the most difficult elements of this pluralism is the multiplicity of religions that exists even after two thousand years of Christianity and its missionary activities. For no other religion claims to be *the* religion and the absolutely unique and only valid revelation of the one living God. Moreover, today the existence of many religions threatens the individual Christian more than ever before. For in the past another religion was at the same time also the religion of a different civilization, with which there were only very peripheral contacts. It was the religion of foreigners. Thus it is not surprising that the existence of such a religion should not have affected oneself at all.

Today the situation is very different. Everyone is everyone else's neighbor and therefore, whether willingly or unwillingly, conditioned by a communications system embracing the whole planet. Every religion has become a question and a possibility for every person. Hence it challenges the absolute claim of one's own Christianity.

We would therefore explain the basic characteristics of a dogmatic Catholic interpretation of the non-Christian religions, and thus help to solve the problems of the Christian position with regard to contemporary religious pluralism. We call it a dogmatic interpretation, because we consider the question not from the empirical point of view of the history of religions, but from the dogmatic standpoint of Christianity's own conception of itself.

We begin with the statement that Christianity claims to be the absolute religion destined for all people, which cannot tolerate any other as having equal rights beside it. This thesis is the basis for the Christian theological understanding of other religions. Christ, the absolute Word of God, has come in the flesh and reconciled (united) the world to God through his death and resurrection, not only theoretically but in reality. Ever since, Christ and his permanent historical presence in the world that we call church are *the* religion which binds the person to God.

However, it should be noted that Christianity has a historical beginning in Christ. But this means only that this absolute religion, too, must come to all people historically confronting and claiming them as their legitimate religion.

Therefore, the question is: Is the moment in time at which this absolute historical religion makes existentially real demands on people the same for all, or has the beginning of this moment itself a history and thus is not the same in time for all people, all civilizations, and periods of history?

If we suppose that our second theory is correct, this means that we can understand our first thesis in a more differentiated way. For we shall state positively only that Christianity is meant to be the absolute and therefore unique religion of all people, but we leave open the question at which moment in time it is objectively binding for any person and any civilization. It should be noted that we are therefore concerned with the fact that a social entity is needed for salvation. Hence we may, indeed must, say without hesitation that this thesis implies that its social organization belongs to the very essence of religion.

Moreover, we may say that paganism continues to exist not because it has rejected Christianity, but because it has not yet met it in a sufficiently impressive encounter. If this is true, paganism will cease to exist in *this* sense, because the West has begun to enter the history of the whole planet. Or, to express it more cautiously, we enter an entirely new phase in world history, in which Christians and non-Christians, living in the same situation, confront each other dialogically.

Until the gospel actually enters the historical situation of a certain person, a non-Christian religion contains not only elements of a natural knowledge of God mixed with depravity caused by original sin and human elements, but also supernatural elements of grace. It can therefore be acknowledged to be a legitimate religion, even though in different graduations.

According to the first part of this thesis even non-Christian religions may be said a priori to contain supernatural elements of grace. This opinion is based on the theological principle that, as Christians, we must profess the dogma that God wills the salvation of all people even in the postparadisiacal period of original sin. On the other hand this salvation is specifically Christian, for there is no salvation apart from Christ, while, on the other, God truly and seriously wants all people to be saved. Both statements can be combined only by saying that every person is exposed to the influence of divine grace that offers communion with God, whether or not it is accepted.

The second part of our second thesis, however, goes further. It says that because of this pre-Christian religions, too, need not simply be regarded as illegitimate but that they, too, can very well have a positive meaning. This also applies to religions that, in their concrete forms, may contain many theoretical and practical errors.

This is shown, for example, by a theological analysis of the structure of the old covenant. For in the old covenant as it appeared in history there was much that was right and willed by God, but there were also a great many errors, wrong developments, and depraved ideas, while there was no permanent infallible authority to separate the two.

Hence we must give up the prejudiced idea that we may confront a non-Christian religion with the alternative of being either wholly of divine origin or a merely human thing. If in these religions, too, the person is under grace, the individual must have the possibility of a genuine saving relation with God.

The human person is a social being, and in earlier times he was even more radically involved in social ties. Hence it is unthinkable that he could have realized his relationship with God individually and interiorly, outside the actual religion which offered itself in the world around him. For, as has already been said, it belongs to the characteristics of a true, concrete religion that individual religious practice is embedded in a social religious order. Hence the salvation God wanted people to have reached them according to the divine will and permission in the concrete religion of the historical conditions and circumstances of their life, though this did not deprive them of the right and the limited opportunity to criticize and to pay attention to the reforming impulses that God's providence always inspired in such a religion.

If this second thesis is correct, Christianity confronts an adherent of a non-Christian religion not only as a mere non-Christian, but also as a person who may already be regarded in certain respects as an anonymous Christian.

It must be possible to be not only an anonymous theist but, as has been said, an anonymous Christian. There is a twofold reason for this. For the one who becomes the "object" of the church's missionary activities may have approached and even found salvation without having yet been reached by the church's preaching. Secondly, this salvation which the person has found must also be the salvation of Christ, because there is no other.

And so it is true that in the last analysis the preaching of the gospel does not make into a Christian a person absolutely forsaken by God and Christ, but that it transforms an anonymous Christian into a person who realizes his Christianity in the depth of his grace-endowed nature also objectively and in the church's communal confession.

This implies that this express self-realization of a formerly anonymous Christian is a higher phase of development of this Christianity, demanded by his nature. Hence we may on no account conclude that the preaching of Christianity is superfluous, because a person is an anonymous Christian without it.

Christianity is demanded, first, by the incarnational and social structure of grace and Christianity, and, secondly, by the fact that a clearer and more reflected comprehension of Christianity offers a greater chance of salvation to the individual than his status as an anonymous Christian.

True, we cannot hope that religious pluralism will disappear in the foreseeable future. Nevertheless, Christians themselves may well regard the non-Christian world as an anonymous Christendom. Therefore, it follows that today the church will not so much regard herself as the exclusive community of candidates for salvation, but rather as the avant-garde, expressing historically and socially the hidden reality which, Christians hope, exists also outside her visible structure.

The church is not the community of those who possess God's grace as opposed to those who lack it, but the community of those who can confess explicitly what they and the others hope to be. Of course, this explicit confession and the historical institution of this salvation of Christ which is offered to all is itself a grace and part of salvation. The non-Christian may think it supercilious that the Christian attributes all that is good and whole in every person to the fruit of Christ's grace and regards the non-Christian as a Christian who has not yet found himself.

But the Christian cannot do otherwise. Actually this seeming superiority is the way in which his greatest humility is expressed, both as regards himself and his church. For it lets God be greater than both the individual and the church. The church will confront the non-Christian with the attitude of Paul who said: "What therefore you worship as unknown, this I proclaim to you." Hence we may well be tolerant and humble toward all non-Christian religions.

4 • Christianity Is Not an Ideology*

It is really impossible to suspect Christianity of being an ideology by the mere fact that it makes absolute declarations with the claim to truth, in the perfectly simple and ordinary sense of this word, that is, because it makes declarations that can be called "metaphysical." On the one hand, they are declared with an absolute claim to truth and, on the other, they cannot be directly verified as valid on the empirical plane of natural science.

Of course, anyone who holds that every "metaphysics" is false or nondemonstrable cannot consider authentic Christianity, even as understood by itself, as anything but an ideology. That person may go on to reflect — in what would be an existentially irrational way — on why this Christianity can and should nevertheless have an essential significance for his life. He would then of course be overlooking the fact

* *Theological Investigations VI,* trans. Karl H. and Boniface Kruger (Baltimore: Helicon Press, 1969), 48–55.

that such a reflection on an irrational positing and ideologizing of life would itself imply a metaphysics, even though it be a bad one.

Of course, what has been said here is not meant to imply that the knowledge of faith and philosophical metaphysics are the same in their structure and merely differ with regard to their declared objects. It is true, all the same, that the Christian declaration of faith and metaphysics do coincide with regard to the just mentioned claim to truth, so that where the possibilities of a metaphysical declaration are denied in principle and from the outset, Christianity too can only be accorded the rank of a subjective ideology. For in this view, a subject before whom such an absolute claim to truth can be announced and to whom it can be imparted, just does not exist. In such a view only individual persons exist, individuals who try to make their existence a little more bearable and dignified by such mental fictions.

Hence, in defense against the reproach that Christianity is an ideology, it must in the first place be emphasized that metaphysics must not be suspected from the outset and in every case of being an ideology. This is shown by the very fact that the proposition stating that every metaphysics is in the last analysis a nonbinding ideology is itself a metaphysical proposition, whether it be expressed reflectively with theoretical universal binding force or is implied in the attempt to live life free from metaphysics (by an absolutely skeptical *epoché* regarding all matters beyond the immediate brute experience of life and natural scientific knowledge).

Relativism and skepticism, whether they be theoretically formulated or nontheoretically attempted in life, are metaphysical decisions. Metaphysics is inescapably given together with the human person's existence. He always interprets his existence within a horizon of a priori predecisions that have already preceded this experience and embrace it. True and genuine metaphysics goes further and, precisely speaking, only consists in reflection on those transcendental, inevitably given implications which actually bear their evidence and certainty already within themselves and are necessarily posited together with every intellectual and free exercise of human existence.

Metaphysics, as reflex knowledge, does not produce these implications but simply reflects on the implications there and so renders them systematic. It is therefore a systematizing of a transcendental experience that, as the unsystematic ground of every empirical experience and understanding of truth, essentially transcends the latter in insight and certitude.

This metaphysics can therefore unashamedly admit the unfinished nature of its reflection, the necessity of always beginning anew and its imperfection. And yet it can say quite confidently that its meaning, that is, transcendental experience itself, is still the common property of all persons open to the truth. It shows itself as such even in the plurality of metaphysical systems, even where these systems appear totally contradictory to the superficial regard of the ordinary person and even of the bad historian of philosophy, and thus gives the impression of being merely mental fictions and arbitrary subjective assumptions.

Only someone capable of utter silence and absence of any thought, that is, someone capable of living in a purely animal immediacy to his biological existence and who therefore would not even know anything about his metaphysical suspension of judgment (in other words, someone who would not exercise it at all), would be really free of metaphysics and could avoid the claim of being made for absolute truth.

However, if there can be a metaphysics, at least in principle, that cannot be simply disposed of as an ideology from the very start, then a fortiori Christianity cannot be rejected as being an ideology simply because the horizons of its declarations of faith do not coincide with the primitive, factual everyday experience and the experience of the empirical natural sciences.

The fact of a pluralism of world views cannot be a legitimate reason for dismissing every world view (insofar as one wants to subsume metaphysics and the Christian teaching of faith under this title) as a mere ideology. Precisely this attitude would itself go beyond the objects of empirical experience and their functional connections and would make experience as a whole — which as such is not an object of experience — the object of a declaration which by definition would then itself be an ideology.

The right relationship to the pluralism of world views and metaphysical systems cannot consist in a flat suspicion of every world view as mere mythology. It can only consist in an attitude that carefully and critically examines, holds itself open to further knowledge and modifications of previous knowledge, is modest, tries to discover the transcendental experience in all the "systems" put forward, and yet has also the courage to make decisions, to commit itself with the quiet assurance that absolute truth is already reached even in an historically conditioned, finite, incomplete, still open declaration — even though this absolute truth always ultimately remains that unspeakable, holy mystery that can no longer be confined in any system superior to it and manageable by us.

When and where metaphysics understands itself in the last analysis as that rational or, better, intellectual introduction to the attitude of openness toward the absolute mystery — an attitude that always holds sway in the ground of our intellectual and freely responsible existence but for this precise reason must not remain indifferent in itself for the person — then metaphysics loses its appearance of being merely an ideological fiction, even when confronted with the pluralism of world views of our existence.

This pluralism of world views destroys in reality only the rationalistic presumption of any false metaphysics which might maintain that in it the person can grasp the totality of reality right down to its last bases and so manage it in his own system, instead of — as in life — of being struck dumb in reflecting on the implications of the ground of total reality by which one is seized.

Proceeding from this, it can be seen under a still wider aspect that Christianity is not an ideology. We have already said that the basis of all metaphysically and valid knowledge of truth is transcendental experience (even before any objective and individual experience), an experience by which the person is always already referred to the unembraceable totality of reality and into its very ground, which is that always already present holy mystery that removes the person into the distance of his finiteness and guilt — and this we call God.

This transcendental experience possessed in knowledge and responsible freedom is again unsystematically also the basis, the necessary condition and horizon of everyday experience and as such is the first and proper "place" for the reality of Christianity, and this without prejudice to its historicity and history about which we will have to speak later.

Christianity cannot be an ideology because, on the one hand, this experience of transcendence, being the introduction to an absolute sacred mystery which is no longer grasped but which, on the contrary, lays hold of one, makes every ideology transcendent by its own transcendental necessity insofar as such an ideology turns a certain limited intramundane experience into an absolute one.

On the other hand then, insofar as Christianity is not abbreviated in any way and represents in its teaching the right interpretation of this transcendental experience as it really achieves itself in its own, unabridged being, Christianity signifies in its reality precisely this adequate transcendental experience. Thus Christianity cannot be an ideology.

This is not the place to ask in what sense such a starting point for the understanding of Christianity is to be found, and what effect it has, in Rudolf Bultmann and others. Can we not say that the reality of Christianity is what Christians are accustomed to call grace? Is grace not God's self-communication to the finite creature, the direct presence to God, the dynamism directed toward participation in the life of God who is above every finite and mortal creature?

Does not grace signify that the person, in spite of his finiteness and guilt, is superior to all worldly powers and forces, even when he suffers under them to the bitter end? Is not grace always offered to all persons on account of God's universal will and is it not effective in everything even when people close themselves to it in free guilt? Taking all this together, it means surely that the human person is someone who is borne by God himself and is driven toward direct presence to God in the very ground of his personal being. In other words, what we call grace is the real truth and the property, freely given by God, of the transcendental experience of the openness of the personal spirit to God.

If Christianity in its proper being signifies grace, and if grace is the innermost possibility and reality of the reception of God's self-communication in the very ground of human existence, then Christianity is none else but the deepest reality of the transcendental experience, the experience of the absolute and forgiving nearness of God himself who is distinct from and above all intramundane reality and yet is the one who in this very way (even in this absolute nearness) remains the holy mystery to be worshiped.

However, if this is the proper nature of Christianity, then every ideology has already been surpassed because every ideology is concerned with what is verifiable in intramundane experience, whether this refers to blood and soil, sociability, rational technologization and manipulation, the enjoyment of life or the experience of the person's own emptiness and absurdity, or whatever else, and it posits this as the basic condition of human existence.

Christianity declares these powers and forces, the masters of unredeemed existence, not merely theoretically but absolutely basically to be worthless idols that must never become our masters. It declares that the person has in the ground of his existence always already overcome these powers and forces in grace, and that the real question is whether he assents in his free actions to this his transcendental openness to God's immediacy through grace, which is eternal life — his free action itself originating once more from the power of this grace.

Therefore, since the basic fulfillment of Christianity finds its point of insertion in the very midst of the human person's transcendentality, a transcendentality that always arises above any intramundane ideology, even though merely or rather precisely because it is a transcendence toward the absolute mystery of God in his absolute and forgiving nearness), Christianity is from the outset no mere ideology. At least, it is not an ideology of immanence. However, the transcendence referred to here is not a superadded dimension to the realm of the human person's intramundane existence. Hence it cannot be regarded as a subsequent ideologization of human existence, as if it were superfluous for the fulfillment of human existence in the world.

Christianity, however, is also at the same time essentially a history, since it directs the human person's attention toward spatio-temporally fixed events of human history, understanding them as saving events that find their unsurpassing summit, center, and historical measure in the absolute saving event of Jesus Christ.

If this history itself is part of the nature of Christianity, and not just an accidental interchangeable stimulus of that transcendental, super-natural experience of the absolute and forgiving nearness of the holy mystery which overcomes all intramundane forces and powers, then Christianity appears clearly as the negation of every ideology of trans-manence and transcendence. (This must not be understood as the annihilation of transcendence, but must be seen as the negation of the ideologization of transcendence into a bare and empty formalization of genuine transcendence.)

Two things will have to be understood if we are to be able to think of this concept. First, it will be necessary to make clear the inner connec-tion between the genuine and unsurpassable historicity of Christianity in its turning to history regarded as a real event of salvation and the tran-scendental nature of Christianity understood as the openness by grace to the absolute God. In other words, it will have to be shown that gen-uine transcendentality and genuine historicity determine one another and that the human person by his very transcendentality is referred to real history, a real history he cannot "annul" by a priori reflection.

Second, it will have to be understood that by the genuine imposed nature of real history, the human person is empowered and indeed bound to take things really seriously even in his profane existence and to be really involved in the external historical reality, even where he recognizes and experiences by suffering the contingency and thus the relativity of this historical reality.

As regards the first question, it must be said straight away that the history of the human person, correctly understood, is not an element of mere chance imposed on the person in addition to his existence as a being of transcendence, but that it is precisely the history of his tran-scendental being as such. He does not live out his existence oriented to God in a pure or even mystical interiority, in some sort of submersion, running away from history, but lives it out precisely in the individual and collective history of his very being.

Hence Christianity can still be seen to consist absolutely in the grace-constituted transcendental being of the human person and yet in very truth be the actual history in which this being is achieved and which confronts the human person himself in spatio-temporal facticity. Truly there is then a history-of-salvation of the human word in which the divine word gives itself.

The church furthermore is truly the assembly of salvation and the sacrament, even though all these historical objectifications of the person's absolute depth-of-being open to God's grace only have and retain their own nature when all these historical manifestations appear as what they are, namely, as instruments of mediation and signs pointing to the incomprehensibility of a God who communicates himself in all truth and reality to persons through these signs so as to become directly present in an absolute and forgiving manner.

If and as long as these historical mediations are really mediations to the presence and acceptance of God's mystery, and while retaining their relative nature yet prove themselves even in this way as unavoidable for the human person's historical being in this aeon before the direct vision of God is reached, history and transcendence will never be subject in Christianity to an ideology of immanence, that is, to the idolization of intramundane powers, or to an ideology of transmanence and transcendence, that is, to the idolization in empty, formal abstractions of the person's transcendentality by grace.

Two further points must be noted in this connection. First, the human person's historicity, understood as mediation of his transcendental being elevated by grace, reaches its unsurpassable climax in Jesus Christ, the Godman. In him God's promise of himself to the world, its historical mediation and its acceptance by man have become absolutely one in a union that is not fusion and yet eliminates separation. Thus this represents God's historically unsurpassable eschatological communication to man himself through the history of grace in the world (without it being thereby possible simply to identify in some monophysite sense the historical mediation of God and God himself).

The human person can and must accept this mediation-by-immediacy to God as something quite irreplaceable, by humbly accepting it in his own transcendentality by grace as something that is historically ordained and freely contingent.

The person's reference to this historical mediation of his own grace inserted in the ground of his being does not take place merely or in the first place by a theoretical, historical knowledge about these historical events of salvation, a sort of knowledge that could be suspected as an ideology. It is given in an immediate, realistic manner which, through the living unity of the history of salvation, through the church (which is more than just the subsequent totality of the theoretical opinions of those who agree), through sacraments and worship, through what we call anamnesis, tradition, and the like, burst open any merely theoretical information.

Because the human person is mediated to the historical event of salvation and this mediation does not take place merely by way of theoretical information — since he experiences this mediation as the event of his own transcendental and supernaturally elevated being — he has always gone beyond the three above-mentioned basic forms of ideology.

Second, it must be stated that the necessary historical mediation of transcendentally established grace also draws the Christian's attention to the fact that he can and must also take his "profane" history absolutely seriously. He does this not by turning it into an ideology and by thus erecting it into an absolute, but by the fact of experiencing it as the concrete expression of the will of God who posits it in freedom: thereby he both removes it from himself as the conditioned and historically contingent and lends it the seriousness proper to the situation in which an eternal destiny is decided before God.

There is a final point to be stressed against the thesis that Christianity is an ideology. Ideologies mutually exclude one another in their doctrine and intention and are nothing more than the factor by which they negate and fight each other, since what is in fact common to them exists in a sense in spite of the ideological theory and not because of it.

Christianity, however, includes in its teaching what we will simply call "anonymous" Christianity. Christianity does not restrict that which constitutes its most proper reality, that is, forgiving and divinizing grace, to the circle of those who explicitly acknowledge the reflex and historical, instructive objectification of this ubiquitously active grace of God, in short, the explicit Christian doctrine and its bearer, the church.

Christianity, therefore, in view of God's universal salvific will and the possibility of justification even before reception of the sacraments, includes its doctrinal opponents in its own reality and hence cannot even regard them as opponents in the same sense ideologies do and must do.

Ideologies, if they are tolerant (which cannot be completely reconciled with the nature of an ideology) may indeed accept their opponents insofar as they are human beings or have some other neutral common basis. But no ideology can admit that what is really meant, what is specific in its own position, can be conceded to its opponents on the plane of theoretical reflection and social constitution. An ideology cannot admit a third possibility outside itself that could bring about this community of reality before and behind the differences of its reflex explicitness.

An ideology can never be greater than itself, whereas Christianity is more than itself precisely in the sense that it is the movement in which the human person surrenders himself to the unmasterable mystery and insofar as, fixing its regard of Jesus Christ, it knows that his movement actually finds the sheltering nearness of this mystery.

5 • Jesus Christ: The Synthesis*

The basic human hope and the experience of Jesus Christ sustain and justify each other in an ultimately indestructible bond that may be grasped by a person of integrity and reasonable conscience, as long as he assumes a stance of what Christians call humility in the face of the incomprehensible mystery.

The encounter with Christ is mediated both through the gospel of Christianity and of the church based on Jesus' message and also through the ultimate hope of God's grace.

What does a Christian see in Jesus? The answer may originate from various elements of experience and so the following considerations cannot represent the only possible description of the encounter with Jesus or own which is universally binding. On the other hand, the experience itself, for all its different aspects does possess a unity.

The history of Christianity, which has its own unique importance, envisions one man who loves and is faithful even unto death, whose whole human existence, embodied in word and action, lies open to the mystery which he himself calls, "Father," and to which he surrenders himself in trust even when his world is shattered. The dark chasm of his life is for Jesus the sheltering hands of his Father. He stands fast in his love for men and women. He is sure in hope, even when everything seems to collapse in the destruction of death. He was convinced that in him and his message the kingdom of God was at hand, that is, that God in direct love and forgiveness vigorously pledges himself to us, transcending all the good and evil forces that influence human existence.

For the person who listens to Jesus' message a new and decisive opportunity for the human being has come about, which is never to be surpassed. This experience also means that we are faced by a man who, in his life and death, does not fail to match up to the demands that are involved in being human. Thus Christianity is convinced that, despite every reason for skepticism in our experience of man, we may with innocent trust and total abandon surrender ourselves to the one man in absolute dependence.

---

* *Theological Investigations XVI*, trans. David Moreland, O.S.B. (New York: Seabury Press, 1979), 15–18.

Jesus' followers shared the experience of Good Friday without any illusions. And yet they then became aware, as a gift from Jesus himself, that his life is not in ruins, that his death is in fact a victory and that he is the one totally and finally accepted by God's mystery. In a word, they experienced the fact that he is risen.

Of course one should not conceive of this resurrection as a return to the limits of a life restricted by space and time and the facts of biology. One should rather think of it as the ultimate salvation of the one complete person, body and soul, in God.

The mystery is the "incomprehensible God" and so the manner of this acceptance cannot be given imaginative form. But whenever the absolute hope of the human person and the experience of Jesus' life and death meet, we can no longer reckon with Jesus' destruction without thereby denying this absolute hope and allowing the self-abandonment of the human person, whether willingly or not, to emptiness and futility.

If on the contrary we search for the historical personality who permits us to trust that in him our hope is fulfilled, then we cannot find any other name except the one presented by the witness of the apostles. The experience of Jesus gives us, insofar as we freely commit ourselves to our own hope, the strength and the heart to affirm from the center of our own experience and from the hope that lies within it, that he is risen.

The basic human hope and the historical experience of Jesus are bound together for a Christian as a unity. Jesus of Nazareth is accepted by God and in Jesus God has answered the question that the human person constitutes in his unlimited, incomprehensible nature. Human existence is here finally and gloriously blessed and the skeptical human question, fashioned in guilt and futility, is transcended. The courage to hope is sealed.

So Jesus is the ultimate answer that can never be surpassed, because every conceivable question is annihilated in death and he is the answer to the all-encompassing question of human existence in that he is the risen one. As Word of God he answers the question that we ourselves pose.

From this starting point there arise the statements about Jesus Christ contained in the traditional teaching and theology of the church, that is, orthodox christology. But the reverse is also true: whoever accepts Jesus as the unsurpassable Word of God, as the final seal of his own hope in history, is and remains a Christian, even if he cannot follow the traditional christological formulations or finds great difficulty in doing so, because they come from a framework of meaning not easily intelligible today.

Cross and resurrection belong together in the authentic witness to Jesus and in genuine and responsible faith in him. The *cross* means the stark demand for the human person to surrender self unconditionally before the mystery of his being that he can never bring under his control, since he is finite and burdened with guilt. The *resurrection* means the unconditional hope that in this surrender the blessing, forgiveness, and ultimate acceptance of the human person takes place through this mystery. It also implies that if the human person abandons himself to this movement, no further destruction lies in store.

Cross and resurrection clearly show how this self-abandonment is taken up by God in Jesus' fate, and how the possibility of self-surrender, the hardest task of our life, is irrevocably promised to us in Jesus Christ. For the Lord is an absolutely concrete fact. A person need only involve himself with this specific individual in unconditional love and he then possesses everything. Certainly one must die with him; no one can escape this fate. Why not, then, utter with him the words, "My God, my God, why have you forsaken me?" or "Into your hands I commend my spirit"?

In Jesus' destiny every human philosophy receives for the first time a truly specific and concrete form. What exactly this philosophy looks like or should look like is not exactly important. Once a person has reached Jesus, then it contains this simple message: just to be prepared to make the final act of hope and self-surrender to the incomprehensible mystery. Yet this covers everything because Jesus' fate, a death that is life, has brought this philosophy into being, not of course in mere talk about death but in the actual experience and suffering of death.

For us this moment still lies in the future. Our life is directed toward it without our knowing exactly when it will appear in our life. But only then has the essence of Christianity been grasped and conceived. A person can and should, however, prepare himself to be open to this event. The glory of our present existence is not thereby removed. Rather it gives everything its proper value and makes the burden light.

Christianity is thus simplicity itself because it embraces the totality of human existence and leaves all the details to the free responsibility of the human person, without providing an exact recipe for them. At the same time it is the hardest thing of all, a grace offered to all that can be and is received, even when unconditional hope has not yet discovered its seal in Jesus of Nazareth.

6 • Why Remain a Christian?*

Where are we to start when it is a question of stating and showing that one may have the courage of one's belief? If it is impossible to say everything, then we must choose and also determine our starting point somewhat arbitrarily.

I begin with the fact that I have — quite simply — always been a believer and that I have met with no reason which would force or cause me not to believe anymore. I was born a Catholic because I was born and baptized in a believing environment. I trust in God that this faith passed on by tradition has turned into my own decision — into a real belief — and that I am a Catholic Christian even in my innermost being. This, in the last analysis, remains God's secret and an unreflected reality deep down within me which I cannot express even to myself. I say that — in the first place — I, this believer, have not encountered any reason that could cause me to cease being what I am.

I understand that one would have to have reasons for changing in a way contrary to the pattern according to which one has set out. For anyone who would change without such reasons — who would not even be willing in the first place to remain true to the situation in life in which he has been placed and to the definite commitment of his spiritual personality — would be a person falling into emptiness, and no more interiorly than the shadow of a person.

If a person does not want to abandon his very self, then he must basically regard what is already there as something to be taken over and to be preserved until he has proof of the contrary. One can live and grow only out of those roots that already live, and precisely as they live — only out of that beginning in which one places one's original trust in life. What is transmitted to us may have provided us with lofty and sacred values. It may have opened up infinite vistas and taken hold of us by an absolute and eternal call. This alone, in the form of unreflected experience and simple practice without deceit or doubt, may not yet represent in the face of critical conscience and questioning reason any expressible and reflected proof of the simple truth of this tradition.

However, one thing has always remained clear to me — in spite of every temptation against the faith, which I believe I, too, have had to undergo — one thing has supported me as I kept fast to it: the conviction that we must not allow what has been inherited and transmitted to be consumed by the emptiness of the ordinary, of a spiritual indifference

---

* *Theological Investigations V,* trans. Karl-H. Kruger (Baltimore: Helicon Press, 1966), 4–9.

or apathetic and somber skepticism, but at the most only by something stronger, something that calls us to greater freedom and into a more inexorable light.

Certainly, inherited belief also has always been faith tempted and liable to temptation. But I have always experienced it as the faith that asked me: "Will you too go away?" and to which I could always merely reply, "Lord, to whom shall I go?" I have always experienced it as the faith, powerful and good, and the only possible reason permitting me to give it up would be the proof of the contrary. And nobody — not even my experience of life — has furnished me with this proof.

I realize that such a proof would have to go very deep and would have to be very comprehensive. There are, of course, many difficulties and many bitter experiences for the person in life. But it is quite clear that no difficulty could claim consideration as a reason against my faith unless it were equal to the dignity and deep-rootedness of what it is trying to threaten and change.

There may be many intellectual difficulties in the realm of the particular sciences — such as the history of religion, scriptural criticism, the early history of Christianity — for which I have no direct and, in every respect, satisfactory solution. But such difficulties are too particular and — compared to the reality of existence — too slight objectively speaking to be used as the basis for decisions about the ultimate questions of life. They are not weighty enough to be allowed to determine the whole, unspeakably profound depths of life.

My faith does not depend on whether exegetes or the church have or have not already found the correct interpretation of the first chapter of Genesis — on whether some decision of the Biblical Commission or of the Holy Office is the last word in wisdom. Such arguments, therefore, are beside the point from the very start.

Of course, there are other temptations which go deeper. But these are the very ones that bring out true Christianity, provided one faces them honestly and, at the same time, humbly. They reach the heart, the innermost center of life; they threaten and confront it with the human person's ultimate questionableness as such. But precisely in *this* way they can be for the person the labor pains of the true birth of Christian existence.

The argumentation of human existence itself makes the person feel lonely, as if placed into loneliness, as if involved in an infinite fall. It delivers him up, as it were, to his freedom — and yet he does not feel assured of this freedom. It makes him feel as if surrounded by an infinite ocean of darkness and an immense unexplored night — always managing to survive from one contingency to another. It leaves him fragile, poor, agitated by the pain of his contingent nature. Always it leaves him convinced once more of his dependence on the merely biological, on ridiculous social elements and on the traditional (even when one contradicts it). He feels how death is the final limit, beyond which he himself cannot pass. He feels the ideals of his life grow weak and lose their youthful luster. He experiences how one becomes weary of all the smart talk on the fairground of life and of science — even of science.

The real argument against Christianity is the experience of life, this experience of darkness. And I have always found that behind the technical arguments leveled by the learned against Christianity — as the ultimate force and a priori prejudgment supporting these scientific doubts — there are always these ultimate experiences of life causing the spirit and the heart to be somber, tired, and despairing. These experiences try to objectify themselves and to render themselves expressible in the doubts of scholars and of the sciences, no matter how weighty these doubts may be in themselves and however much they must be taken seriously.

For this very experience is also the argument of Christianity. For what does Christianity say? What does it proclaim? Despite the complicated appearance of its dogmatic and moral theology, it says something quite simple — something simple that all particular Christian dogmas articulate in some way (though perhaps it is seen to be simple only once these are given).

For what does Christianity really declare? Nothing else, after all, than that the great mystery remains eternally a mystery, but that this mystery wishes to communicate himself in absolute self-communication — as the infinite, incomprehensible and inexpressible being whose name is God, as self-giving nearness — to the human soul in the midst of its experience of its own finite emptiness. This nearness has become a reality not only in what we call "grace" but also in the tangible reality of the one whom we call the Godman. In these two ways of divine self-communication — both by their radical, absolute nature, and by reason of the identity of the "existence-of-itself" of God and his "existence-for-us" — there is also communicated, and thus revealed, to us the duality of an inner-divine relationship: in other words, what we profess as the trinity of persons in the one Godhead.

The human person, however, experiences these three absolute mysteries of the Christian faith (that is, the Trinity, the incarnation, and grace) by his inescapable experience of the fact that he is grounded in the abyss of the insoluble mystery, and by experiencing and accepting this mystery (this is what we call "faith"), as fulfilling nearness and not as a burning judgment, in the depth of his conscience and in the concreteness of his history (for both are constitutive elements of his existence).

That this radical mystery is nearness and not distance, self-surrendering love and not a judgment that casts out the human person into the hell of his own nothingness — this person finds difficult to accept and to believe. It may appear to us as a light almost darker than our own darkness. Indeed, it may take, and in some sense consume, the whole power of our soul and heart, of our freedom and our whole existence, to accept it.

And yet, is there not so much light, so much joy, love and glory, both internally and externally in the world and in the human being, to make it possible for us to say that all this can be explained only by an absolute light, joy, love, and glory — by an absolute being and not by an empty nothingness that cannot explain anything — even though we cannot understand how there can be this our deadly darkness and nothingness if there is the infinity of fullness, albeit as a mystery? May I not say that I am right to hold on to the light (even though it is faint) rather than the darkness — to the happiness rather than to the hellish torment of my existence?

If I were to accept the arguments against Christianity to which human existence gives rise, what would that offer me for my existence? The valor of the honesty and the glory of the resolution to face up to the absurdity of existence? But can one think of these as great, as obligatory and glorious, without implying once more (whether one really knows it or not, wants to or not), that there is something which is glorious and worthy of esteem? But how could this be, in the abyss of absolute emptiness and absurdity?

In any case, anyone who courageously accepts life — even a short-sighted, primitive positivist who apparently bears patiently with the poverty of the superficial — has really already accepted God. He has accepted God as he is in himself, as he wants to be in our regard in love and freedom — in other words, as the God of the eternal life of divine self-communication in which God himself is the human person's center and in which the person's form is that of the Godman himself.

For anyone who really accepts *himself,* accepts a mystery in the sense of the infinite emptiness which is the human being. He accepts himself in the immensity of his unpredictable destiny and — silently, and without premeditation — he accepts the one who has decided to fill this infinite emptiness (which is the mystery of the human person) with his own infinite fullness (which is the mystery called God).

And if Christianity is nothing other than the clear experience of what the human person experiences indistinctly in his actual being — which in the concrete is always more than just spiritual nature but is spirit, illuminated from within by the light of God's gratuitous grace — what reason could I have then not to be a Christian?

For when the person accepts himself in this way wholly and entirely, he accepts this light (that is, he believes) even though he does so unthinkingly and without expressing it. Thus, what reason should I have for not being a Christian, if Christianity means taking possession of the human person's mystery with absolute optimism?

I know of only one reason that weighs heavily on me — the despair, the lassitude, the sin I experience within me. This is the only reason that oppresses me — the crumbling away of human existence in the gray skepticism of our daily life, when we can no longer even raise a protest against mere existence, but just leave the tacit, infinite question that we ourselves are, well alone — a skepticism that cannot stand or accept this question but avoids it by losing itself in the wretchedness of everyday life.

This is not meant to deny that even everyday existence lived in the quiet honesty of patiently doing one's duty can also be a form of "anonymous" Christian living. Indeed, many a one (if he does not skeptically or stubbornly raise this way of living in its turn into an absolute system) may in actual fact grasp Christianity more genuinely than in its more explicit forms that can often be so very empty and be used as a means of escape before the mystery instead of openly facing up to it.

Nevertheless, the abyss opened up by the above reason could paralyze the infinite optimism that believes that the person is a finite nature endowed with God's infinity. If I were to give way to this argument, what could I put in place of Christianity? Only emptiness, despair, night, and death. And what reason do I have to consider this abyss as truer and more real than God's abyss? It is easier to let oneself fall into one's own emptiness than into the abyss of the blessed mystery. But it is not more courageous or truer.

This truth, of course, shines out only when it is also loved and accepted since it is the truth that makes us free and whose light consequently begins to shine only in the freedom that dares all to the very height. Yet this truth is there. I have called out to it and it has declared itself to me. This happiness gives me what I must give to it, that it may be and remain the happiness and strength of my human existence — it gives me the courage to believe in it and to call out to it when all the dark despairs and lifeless voids would swallow me up.

THE MYSTERY OF EXISTENCE

7 • The Mystery of the Human Person*

What do we mean by the human person? My reply, stripped to its essentials, is simple: The person is the question to which there is no answer. It is true that everyone goes through a large number of experiences in the course of his life. Drawing on those experiences, he gains knowledge about himself. It is also true that there are a large number of human sciences whose findings on the human person are continually growing. There is a metaphysical and even a theological science of the human person, and I am far from saying that it is all foolishness or uncertainty. On the contrary.

However, what is the situation with regard to our own experiences (including their extensions in reading poetry, looking at paintings and so on)? We go through them and then promptly forget about them. We have experiences and later we lose our understanding of the conditions which made them possible and we are unable to live them through again. Experiences should be lessons from the past for the future. However, the old situations in which they arose do not recur.

What do we really know about our earlier experiences? When we try to sort, evaluate, arrange, and reduce them to some sort of system, even in our own minds, we undergo a skeptical self-mistrust — one of the least trustworthy of feelings. We are afraid that this whole assessment of life's experiences is too much a prey to ill-thought-out prejudices — "prejudgments" — for us to have clear or certain knowledge about ourselves. When we hear others speak of *their* experiences (with all the selectiveness, arbitrariness and narrowness of which they are capable), we fear for our own experiences. We notice that each one of us has his "own" experiences, and only those. Yet we all want them to be in some way "objective."

And what do we really know about ourselves, once we have experienced how limited our own experiences are, how much "arranged" they are by our own freedom (which we can never knowingly grasp), and that they mean the renunciation of experiences which we could have had but did not have.

Who can say with certainty that he does not use his "experiences" (which are always at the mercy of a person's unconscious manipulation) to deceive himself about himself? We have all experienced the

---

* *Christian at the Crossroads,* trans. V. Green (New York: Seabury Press, 1975), 11–20.

fact that we are still a question to which we can give no answer on the basis of our own lives (as a collection of experiences). Experience gives answers, but no answer which would make what we are questioning — the human person as a unity and as a whole — intelligible. (It is not my purpose here to inquire into whether this one, all-embracing question is really directed at the intelligibility of the person, or whether this intention does not indicate the basic error as to the proper goal of this fundamental question, and therefore as to the person who is this question.)

And what about the conclusions of the natural sciences? Much of the answer to this question is expressed in our thoughts on "experience," because ultimately these sciences are no more than the systematically acquired results of human experience. Once it is established that these can give no answer to the question that is ourselves, the same may be said in advance of whatever is subsequently affirmed about them.

Do not misunderstand me: all praise to those sciences. If I am successfully operated on for appendicitis, if a sleeping pill induces peaceful sleep, if I need no longer live like Neanderthal man, if I can watch a football game in California by satellite; and if we can honestly say that we are not willing to forgo all this, despite our protests against consumer society, outrages, and injustice, if therefore we affirm it, then of course we are profiting by those sciences. We praise them with our lives; we should not revile them with our mouths.

Also the research they pursue can bring with it, in itself and not just because of the vital uses it discovers in things, a commendable euphoria of discovery and knowledge, even an aesthetic enjoyment. But do they give an answer to *the* question, or just an answer to questions? (Later on I shall reply to the objection that this distinction between question and questions is nonsense, that over and above the sum of questions there is no further question over which the individual need trouble either his heart or his head.)

The pluralism of these sciences is insuperable, and hence no answer can be extracted from their answers. By insuperable I mean that the findings of these sciences cannot be combined into a comprehensive "formula of the human" of which all particular findings would be merely applications and special cases, because the "psychic" (which is certainly a part of the person) cannot be reduced to the "physical," however much it may be the business of the human sciences to examine the unity (not identity) of spirit and matter and throw an increasingly penetrating and permanent light on it. This fundamental irreducibility exists because an identity of spirit and matter — if such there were — would still be an identity in thought of a subject; the thought of unity and the unity that is thought of would still be two different things, even if we could reduce everything to thinking and even if we could understand the content of thinking as a merely dependent function of thinking, which the "realists" of the modern natural sciences are least willing to do.

Further, because of the limitations of my IQ, the restricted time at my disposal for learning, and my freely chosen range of interests (as I emphasize this or that), the sum of all the human sciences cannot be accommodated in "my" (a single individual's) mind. A computer does not help, although it can be fed with vastly more knowledge than my brains. The computer is quite indifferent to the "knowledge" fed into it, and only a limited amount can be transferred to my brains even when the computer is fully programmed. Ultimately only the knowledge "stored up" by me from the computer is of significance to me. All I am left with is a very limited and ultimately a very arbitrary choice from everything that the human sciences might know "in themselves."

Presumably "other" knowledge — knowledge which is "out there" but not in my head — is used by others only so that they can control me without my noticing or being able to guard against it. And even supposing that the sum of all these sciences were in my head, they would still be only in *my* head as *my* thoughts, arranged by me and used by me as a free subject.

This subject of freedom — this free individual — would know of its own basic decisions (which can never be the adequate object of reflection, because reflection is always itself in the concrete, an act of freedom) nothing distinct and nothing exhaustive. The sum of scientific answers would, if they were the content of the free individual's thought processes, frame an unanswered question. And we can add, for the person who does not fully appreciate this, that in any case all these sciences are still "on the way."

They have more questions than answers. Even today the sum of the questions seems to grow faster than the sum of the answers. Therefore today's short-lived I — I who cannot wait for the infinitely extended future of the sciences (in which everything in any case would still be finitely clear), or console myself with this future in the obscurity of present-day science — am in actual fact and inescapably the subject who receives more questions than answers from the science which is really accessible to *me*.

What, finally, do we notice about metaphysics and the human person — about metaphysical anthropology? If it has a correct understanding of the human person, then it must grasp him as the essence of an unlimited transcendentality, as the subject who goes beyond (and in going beyond, creates himself as spirit) each individual (finite) object. It must grasp the person as the being who can nowhere come to a final standstill.

But this infinite extent of possible knowledge, insights, and experiences never reaches total fulfillment from within itself and with the means at its disposal. The space or "warehouse" in which experience, life, knowledge, happiness, pain, and so forth are stored is infinite, and so is always half empty (a generous estimate!).

Because we reach out beyond each finite object, but directly grasp only finite objects, we will never be content in this life, and so every ending is just a beginning. Hence the horrible tedium of it. We are constantly feeding new material into the warehouse of our consciousness. It constantly disappears into an infinite expanse which, not to put too fine a point on it, is just as empty as before. Our experience is like that of someone on a fixed bicycle: he pedals until he is ready to burst, but stays on the same spot.

It is easy to say that every moment of life offers something of beauty and that we should enjoy the present hour as it comes, without attempting to see beyond it. Anyone who takes this as a working principle has only to try it to find it does not work. At least once in his life that "beautiful" moment is filled with the emptiness of death. The anticipation of the person's transcendental nature beyond every individual thing (in which he has the impression of reaching forward into the void) is sometimes a part of that spiritual dying which in "biological" death is inevitable, even for the least sensitive. Why should we ever wish to hide it from ourselves?

At this point we are not looking at a "beyond" of which philosophy has nothing to say. In our lived existence, our acquired knowledge is a process extended in time. And our time is finite and ends with death, which is always close. In such finite time as this, the only product of a process of knowledge extended in time is a finite knowledge.

We see that quite clearly: the progress of knowledge means only that we experience all the more vividly the infinitude and permanent nonfulfillment of our questioning. The spirit's pride in never needing to come to a final standstill is also its ever sharper pain at never really getting there. We may, of course, dismiss this philosophy of transcendentality permanently unfulfilled in this life as mere fancy. Or we may assert that today it could hardly be called modern; or that such transcendentality is no more than the impulse behind the particular knowledge of the individual, in which function it has fulfilled its purpose without being able to lay any claims to significance in itself.

Nevertheless, this unfulfilled transcendentality remains, even though it may be pushed to one side. It is at work behind countless phenomena of individual and collective life: in boredom, the mists of which swallow up the variety of real life; in aggressive irritation at the present because it comes at us with such intolerable incompleteness that we are tempted to flee it into a kind of utopian dreamworld of the future; in psychological attempts to escape a world which seems (with every justification) too narrow and desolate; in the attempt to enhance or raise the finitely pleasant or finitely significant into pure enjoyment or an ideology; in the hope that the phenomenon of the finiteness of all these enhanced realities will cease to make its presence felt; in the attempt to overcome radical evil by acquiring an infinitude which will give us something more than the inevitably finite good; and so on.

I am not trying to maintain that it is impossible to drug oneself against the pain of transcendentality's nonfulfillment. Is any drug effective, however, in *all* the situations of life? And even if it should be, would its user not be freely opting for the human person's definitive unhappiness? Isn't damnation the freely chosen, definitive situation of the "bourgeois" who has no interest in the unattainable?

In the past, the evil which led to damnation could be lived only in actions which even in the realm of immediate experience were worked out as destruction and pain. Today, real evil can be lived out in "middle-class" normality insofar as that normality limits itself to the normal and attainable, rejects the sacred utopia of absolute hope as stupidity, and ultimately reaps its own punishment: condemnation to eternal narrowness.

The philosophy of unlimited transcendentality makes the person an unlimited question without its own answer. It reflects only what the experience of life and the human sciences already experience and suffer, and expresses the actuality of these experiences in their inner necessity.

What am I to say about faith and theology? Surely *they* promise a fulfillment of the individual's infinite capacity with the eternal "possession" of God who bestows himself, without any creaturely mediation, in his very own reality, just as he is, in and for himself? Yes, they do, and that is the individual's sacred hope. But this hope must *also* assert that even in eternal beatitude God remains the incomprehensible. How could it be otherwise? If God were comprehensible in his blessedness, he would be circumscribed, and the human person's transcendentality would reach out beyond God and triumph over God and turn itself into God. How, then, can God the incomprehensible be the person's goal and happiness? How (to turn the question round) is the person to be conceived if this incomprehensible God is his happiness?

There is no easy answer to this, because the conception of what is incomprehensible is a knowledge that cannot be calculated on other forms of knowledge and *their* comprehensibility. Understanding that one does not understand is a peculiar form of knowledge; it cannot be an isolated case on the margin of understanding to be totted up with other forms of understanding. Either an understanding of nonunderstanding does not exist because it is self-contradictory, or it must be the most fundamental form of understanding on which all other forms of conception depend.

The anticipation of transcendentality beyond the totally comprehensible (apparently into the void) must also be the supportive precondition of the understanding of God's incomprehensibility in the beatific vision. The vision must be the most radical and inevitable experience of God's incomprehensibility, and *therefore* the fulfillment of the human person's transcendentality toward the uncircumscribable. The incomprehensibility of God in the beatific vision must be understood not as the mere index of creaturely knowledge's finitude, as the buffer at which that knowledge is brought up short, but as the very "implosion" of its inner dynamism. If that is correct, the essence of knowledge itself is in fact changed: it takes on another essence for which incomprehensibility is no longer a limit that rebuffs but, precisely as incomprehensibility, the very object of its search.

The dry statement of God's incomprehensibility even in immediate vision is apt to puzzle most people and Christians. They think that the beatific vision will supply enough knowledge and perception to make them happy for eternity. They also say that once we see God, all the riddles and incomprehensible things in life will dissolve into radiant brightness and clarity, and that eternity is there for us to see that God has made everything good.

These Christians forget, however, that we cannot divide in God the incomprehensible from the perceptible, that what is seen is precisely what is incomprehensible, that this is true not only of God's "essence" but also of his free decisions disposing of our life and so of our eternity, that the sting of incomprehensibility (it could have been different; why was and is it just so and not otherwise for all eternity?) is not pricked out of our hearts, but will be experienced and felt with burning clarity in the vision of God as eternally valid, without there remaining the possibility of delusion or the faintest possibility that it will one day change. In Christian teaching, beatitude is the everlasting and irrevocable vision of God's incomprehensibility and therefore also (because it is grounded in the incomprehensibility of God's freedom) of our own incomprehensibility to ourselves.

Is it not true, then, that the human person is a question to which there is no answer. If the answer to this question is yes, then of course by the "answer" which is not, is meant an answer in which one fact is understandable as the compelling consequence of another, which itself (because there is no progression into infinity) is "comprehensible" simply in and by itself, which is to say…Yes, what exactly is it to say?

How far will individual realities "lead back"? And what is it to which, ex supposito, they do lead back? What does it mean to say that something must be understandable in itself and therefore necessary? We say this of God. But are we not really saying that this ultimate reality is incomprehensible? (Why do we not say "unfathomable?" Would it not be the same thing, and do we find it embarrassing to use the word "unfathomable" for fear that we shall notice the goal of our intellectual odyssey, namely, the incomprehensible?)

If, however, there is to be an "answer" to the unanswerable question which is the human person, then it can consist only in heightening, not in answering, this question; in conquering and piercing the dimension in which the question is posed in the way to which all questioning must conform; therefore, it must itself remain an unanswerable question.

To make a long story short (I could not in any case make it very long, because the real "answer," which does not and never can exist, cannot be derived from the question, and because therefore our only course, when we have come to an end of the hitherto existing dimension of the question into understanding, is a leap, into what is totally other), and in view of the incomprehensibility which makes an answer impossible: we must renounce any such answer, not experience this renunciation as in the least painful (otherwise where would our beatitude be?). We must let ourselves go into this incomprehensibility as into our true fulfillment and happiness, let ourselves be taken out of ourselves by this unanswered question. This incomprehensible venture, which sweeps all questions aside, is customarily referred to as the (devout) love of God. Only that turns darkness into light.

By "love" in this context, we are not to understand something the meaning of which we could grasp by comparison with other things. Instead we are to accept this description of letting ourselves go into the incomprehensible (whereby the letting go is at once destiny and act, and therefore free and willing) as the definition of love from which this word "love" takes its significance. (I am not inquiring here into how what we usually experience as and call "love" contains a part of what I understand by love here.)

"St. Teresa says of Satan that 'he does not love,' " writes Montherlant. That is correct, and it reveals the essence of damnation. The damned do not love and do not wish to love for eternity, and look for happiness in being dispensed from having to let themselves go into God's incomprehensibility. Satan believes he loses nothing by not seeing God, because in the logic of definitive guilt, guilt dispenses us from having to contemplate (= love) incomprehensibility, which we hate because by definition it does not surrender to us. Love, however, is the surrender by which we definitively relinquish control of ourselves and of everything else. For one who loves and knows what love is, the loveless person is damned.

If we wished to call the attempt to do without the incomprehensibility of love and the beloved "happiness" (one of many possible forms of happiness !), even Satan would be happy. He "comprehends" himself only as *he* wants to, relying on the alternative to selfless love, which is the effort toward self-assertion and autonomy. The one who loves has escaped this unhappiness, because in the loving leap into one alternative (the acceptance of God's incomprehensibility) the person has put the other alternative (isolated self-possession) behind.

The human person is the unanswerable question. His fulfillment and happiness are the loving and worshiping acceptance of his incomprehensibility, in the love of God's incomprehensibility with which we can learn to "cope" only by the practice of love and not by the theory of the desire to understand. (How could Aquinas say that the essence of happiness consists in an act of the intellect, when he knew that God is incomprehensible; when he prayed: "I worship you, O hidden Godhead," and knew that in the beatific vision God's incomprehensibility does not disappear? It comes to the light of eternity so radically and irrevocably that either we must travel to hell where, at least on the surface, one has no more to do with this incomprehensibility, or we must ourselves go with the happy despair of love into the incomprehensibility of God?)

Many people think they know where they stand: in themselves, in their society, in their life, or in their mission. Of course we know a lot about all these things. And why should not these insights be our food and escort on the road to the incomprehensibility of God and of ourselves? But we notice increasingly how all knowledge is really only the road to (known and accepted) incomprehensibility; that the proper essence of knowledge is love in which knowledge goes out of itself and the individual allows himself to go willingly into incomprehensibility.

We can cope with life's incomprehensibilities only if we do not try to master them with that philistine foolishness which often passes for brave lucid wisdom. In that way we can accept the fact that all the single insights of life (however modest, ambitious, loving, unsentimental, industrious, critical, "positive," intelligent, and so forth they may be) will never form a whole. We do not then imagine that there could be a well-tempered synthesis of all these disparate insights which could cater for them all.

All that I have said about the human person might strike the reader as being very abstract and pale. But the more exact and comprehensive physics becomes, the more obscure and abstract it is. And it is correct, even though only a minority understand it and yet conduct their lives by laws they do not understand.

The same may be said of a theory about the human person's true essence. It makes sense to think about it, and most people in day-to-day practice conform with this essence even though they do not understand it "theoretically." That does not matter, because this theoretical essence is not theory but love surrendering to the incomprehensible (which is the denial of theory).

Therefore, we may be human without "comprehending" it, because true knowledge even of one who knows can be gained only when he resigns his knowledge in favor of the blessed and eternal *docta ignorantia,* or the ignorance of the wise.

Yet how simple Christianity is. It is the determination to surrender to God's incomprehensibility in love. It is the fear that one does not do this, but instead draws a line at the comprehensible and so sins; the belief that Jesus managed to achieve this surrender and in doing so was definitively accepted by the one who enabled him to achieve it; the belief that in achieving this surrender in Jesus God has irrevocably promised himself to us as well.

A Christian is a true and most radical skeptic. If he really believes in God's incomprehensibility, he is convinced that no individual truth is really true except in the process (which necessarily belongs to its real essence) in which it becomes that question which remains unanswered because it asks about God and his incomprehensibility. The Christian is also the individual who can cope with this otherwise maddening experience in which (to formulate it with poor logic but accurate description) one can accept no opinion as wholly true or wholly false.

Anyone who in a hasty reading finds the above foolish and superficial should pause to consider that in any objection he might be tempted to offer, he is elaborating the only alternative with an empty no, and so lets it reach into this void. This reach is in fact the first act of openness to God's incomprehensibility, the invitation and grace to accept it and in his acceptance to find one's own incomprehensibility.

8 • Nature as Creation*

Christians know that in the light of revelation they have in principle the most comprehensive and, from a human point of view, the most authentic relation with nature. Their knowledge of nature, however, has a curious ambiguity about it, not because it is false or distorted, but because nature itself is ambiguous, and they have the courage to recognize its ambiguity and to accept it.

They see the vastness of nature, its splendor and power, its matter-of-factness, its beauty, its order and adaptability, its trustworthiness. They also know something of its unfathomable depths, its inexhaustibility. The psalms and the parables of Jesus give clear expression to this side of their relation with nature. Christians can even understand that humankind is tempted repeatedly by the glory of nature to worship it and to see it as God.

Christians also know a very different nature, a threatening, merciless, cruel, life-giving and life-destroying nature, a nature that humans experience as a multiplicity of impersonal and enslaving forces to which they seem to be helplessly delivered. They experience in themselves the power of death, the drive of instinct, the blind law of what is merely physical and chemical. Such things seem to pursue their own course without any concern for the claims of the spiritual person, for his or her freedom, dignity, and ethical responsibility. Nature thus appears to be simultaneously both ground and abyss, home and something foreign, bathed in splendor and sinister, heavenly and demonic, life and death, wise and blind.

They can only overlook one or other of its aspects when they deny a side of themselves, spirit or nature, the coming together of which constitutes the mystery of their being. They cannot deny themselves and become merely a part of nature, an animal with technical sophistication; nor can they so act as if the spiritual center of the person in its autonomy and freedom were somehow elevated above, and free from, nature.

How can a person be both? How can one endure the inescapable ambiguity of nature precisely as it applies to oneself? Here as elsewhere human beings must not abandon their role as the measure of all things. To measure nature in this way, however, is to recognize it and humankind as a part of it as an enigma.

To flee nature is to become rootless and artificial. To abandon oneself to it is to become inhuman, to become nothing more than the point

*Der christlicher Sonntag 13 (1961): 229–30. Trans. Daniel Donovan, University of St. Michael's College, Toronto.

at which nature's meaninglessness becomes cruelly self-conscious. In attempting to subdue nature one might win a thousand battles, but they will all end in final defeat, the defeat of death which either nature inflicts on us or which we bring upon ourselves through it.

There is no peace or meaning or final harmony in which only nature and the human person are involved. That final ground of meaning in which nature and humans are bound together in unity can be found neither in humankind nor in nature. If the problem is to be solved, it must be broadened to include another dimension. Some solution there has to be if we are not simply to fall into absolute nihilism before the question about the meaning of existence or, at least for a while, irresponsibly evade the question altogether.

"I believe in almighty God, the creator of heaven and earth, of all that is seen and unseen." In terms of our reflections, this means that behind humankind and nature lies a unity. Although *behind* them, it *truly* exists.

Spirit and nature, the spirit which we are and the nature in and out of which we live, are not the same. Every kind of monism, every attempt to reduce the breadth of our experience to a single element is an oversimplification that does violence to the pluralism of reality. And yet both, the human being as personal spirit in self-consciousness and freedom and nature as a less than spiritual reality, issue from the same creative ground. This ground which differs from humankind and the world and yet gives being and becoming to everything is what we call God. Thus nature and humanity are able to be both different and yet related to one another.

Neither idealism which tends to reduce everything to a manifestation of logical thought processes, nor materialism for which everything spiritual finally is nothing more than the universally present inner dimension of what is material, does justice to reality such as it presents itself to an impartial viewer. If there is to be unity and not oneness between the two aspects of our being, then there must be an original unity that lies behind the world and humankind, a unity from which they both come.

If that is the case, material nature is no longer radically foreign to spirit, no longer the dark and blind reality that can be nothing more than the uncomprehending opponent of humankind. What we think of as natural laws, finality, order, context, and the intelligibility of nature is a reflection, an image and likeness of the eternal creative Spirit from which in a free and spiritual act material reality comes. On the other hand, the spirit which we are, because it comes from the same creative act of God, encounters in nature something related to itself. It can calmly sink the roots of its life into this earthly world without worrying that by doing so it will be untrue either to its spiritual character or to its eternal task.

Humankind and nature are neither the same thing nor so radically opposed as to have to fight one another to the death. For both are made by the one creative love of an eternal ultimate reality that lies beyond all duality and which we name God. The *dark* side of our experience of nature reminds us of the unmistakable dignity of the human person as spirit, the light side of the same experience points to the fact that *nature comes from the same source as human spirit.* The true and originating unity of both realities, God, may well be to us darker and less comprehensible than that which it is intended to explain, the difference and unity of humankind and the world, but explain them it does. Real light is shed on both finite spirit and the world when they are seen in relation to the unspeakable mystery without which everything is flat and dull and tends to disintegrate. We can either lose ultimate meaning, which is always unity, or seek it there where alone it can be found, in the one creator of spirit and nature, in God.

With this, the question that we have been treating is not yet completely answered, the question how a human being, understood as a moral being, can exist in a nature which seems to be based on other laws than those which correspond to the dignity of a moral person. The ultimate presupposition for a positive solution to the question has already been given: *the origin and final goal of nature and humankind are one.* This and this alone undermines any final opposition between spirit and flesh, law of being and pure demand of value, facts and ethics, consciousness and object, logic and physics, an opposition that we are so often and to our despair tempted to see between humankind and nature. Only when theology is added to physics and ethics can one hope to resolve the tension between what is and what ought to be, between matter and humanity.

One thing should be added here and it follows from what has already been said. Where something springs forth from a source and is still underway, still in a process of becoming, its fulfillment, its perfect harmony, belongs to the future. The theology that traces the origin of humankind and nature back to God needs to be complemented by an eschatology of the eternal kingdom of God at the end of time. Situated between beginning and end, humans have the task, within nature and in fidelity to its laws, to fulfill their destiny as moral and spiritual beings.

9 • Life*

The contemporary world-picture is characterized by a predecision for unity and development. It sees matter, life, and spirit as held together in one single history of evolution. Such a concept is not necessarily false as long as it remains discreet and realistic and does not play down essential differences within this unity.

Actually, the idea of evolution does not exclude but includes an essential self-transcendence continually going on within it, since otherwise nothing would ever really become new. This self-transcendence has been conserved in some sense even within dialectical materialism under the idea of the "qualitative leap." The Christian philosopher and the Christian theologian will always conceive this self-transcendence, by which a being surpasses and "transcends" itself into something essentially higher, as happening under the dynamism of the divine being and under the continuous divine creative power.

Under this presupposition, however, evolution and essential self-transcendence (seen as the manner of the former) is an absolutely possible way of conceiving matter, life, and spirit as one connected reality and history and even to regard the divine self-communication to the rational creature by the grace of God's Spirit as the highest, freely given unsurpassable step and phase of this one evolution.

In such a predecided world-picture, *that* concept will be most easily suitable for understanding the content of the one evolving history which (a) expresses the reality in which it is given to us most immediately within this whole unity, and which (b) always makes what precedes and what follows this reality still comprehensible by means of this one history. Such a reality is "life," as we experience it in our own human life. Starting from this life, which is most close to us, is the most likely way of rendering matter and subhuman life intelligible, and this concept is also, as shown by the Bible, the creed, and dogmatic theology, suited for expressing the ultimate good of salvation, the perfection of the human person in God himself. It now becomes clear also that the concept of life actually enables us to have a continuous even though, of course, also gradual and analogous understanding of this one history of created reality.

We should look at life as a form first of all from the point of view of an inner unity and in a heterogeneous (i.e., physico-chemical and spatio-temporal) plurality which is not simply coordinated but hierarchically subordinated. Add to this the fact that this form has an "interiority" which governs and preserves, as from a central point, the

---

* *Theological Investigations VI*, 148–55.

self-construction, self-preservation, and relation to the environment, which at the same time separates and opens itself for the rest of the surroundings in a final and spontaneous relationship, and which conserves itself, incorporates, causes itself to appear in the whole and in all the parts, has the source and end of self-movement within itself and has a living-space and inner time-form all its own. Looking at life in this way, we will get a description of (to begin with, biological) life (without going into the distinction between animals and plants) which can be used as a model for understanding both higher and lower reality: that is, the one whole being and history of experienced reality.

To begin with then, we can understand inorganic matter as the first elementary step, as a collection of instruments, as a kind of vocabulary of biological life, as a boundary condition and value, and at the same time as a "deposit" for life. "Dead" matter is then the asymptotic zero-condition of life in which the interiority and openness-to-the-other of life approaches equally to the lower boundary-value. The individual material thing is apparently quite open to the totality of material reality, since it is a pure function of the whole and is completely tied up in the causal chains external to it.

Yet precisely in this way it has no true openness for the whole or reality; it exists merely as a moment of this reality itself, since it has not (yet) that interiority and that concentration in itself (at least as "form") vis-à-vis the whole (at least of an environment) which characterizes the living. It is lost in the other and hence in this absolute self-alienation it is also incapable of experiencing the other as such; it is not truly "open" since it is not interior to itself.

It has already, nevertheless, at least the passive possibility for such an interiority and openness, a possibility which grows in the same measure as it can be built up into heterogeneous systems which, if the "miracle" of self-transcendence toward self-possession and self-assertion should happen to them, signify precisely the interiorized form of the organic. Put in a different way, one could say and in this hit on the interconnection and distinction of the inorganic and the living in one blow: when the heterogeneous material system, built with a view to a unified, prescribed effort (at least of self-preservation) appropriates its orientation as such to itself, that is, interiorizes itself, then we have something living.

Starting from the concept of life, it is quite possible to understand the spirit and person as the radicalization and self-surpassing of life. The environment becomes simply the world, interiority becomes existence as a subject, assimilation of the environment by assimilation of nourishment becomes appropriation of culture and the machine, all through harmonization of the environment beyond the properly biological sphere; interiority of consciousness becomes self-consciousness; finite openness to the environment becomes infinite transcendence toward being as such.

It must be remembered in all this that we know of no personal subjectivity in our experience which is not in itself biologically alive and which does not presuppose itself as its own condition. It must be remembered that the fact of having to allow itself to be encountered which belongs to the "other" of the world, which is essential for commencing finite subjectivity, is precisely the nature of the biological, of the sensibility of the spirit, by definition. It must be noted that this is not contradicted by the Christian doctrine of the angels, since even they can be perfectly well conceived as mundane and cosmic beings, so that materiality and biosphere are merely different words for the sphere of the necessarily receptive spirituality and for intersubjectivity.

Seen in this light, the unity of nature of the finite spirit (even though transcendentally and infinitely open) and of matter is once more confirmed. Biological life and spiritual life have something in common in that they both constitute the unity of the one human life which is biological and sensible so as to be capable of being spiritual; even if the biological existed for itself alone, it would therefore remain valid that the openness toward the "other" grows in the same measure as, and not in inverse proportion to the degree of self-possession and self-direction arising out of an inner unity.

Where the openness of such life becomes unbounded and there thus appears the inner unity in the form of self-disposition, proper subjectivity and freedom, there is the real life of the spiritual person. Even this is always still "life" in the genuine "biological" sense, a life which the individual has not simply "in addition" side by side with his life as a spiritual person but rather as the inner, necessary moment of the life of the spiritual person itself.

Hence his spiritual life in his transcendence toward meaning in general, toward the world as such and its secret ground (God), is still always supported by corporeality, by *environment,* by spatio-temporal encounter, by sense experience, by witness, bodily intercommunication, and sociability. In short, it is true that the spirituality of the human person is and remains life in the very hard and sober everyday sense, and conversely, that his life is always and everywhere opened toward the breadth of the spirit.

In him it is impossible to live the biological life itself without the personal life, nature without culture, and natural history without the history of the spirit. Since, however, this inner unity of life is given in the form of *bios* and of spirit in that biological life constructs itself in a directly recognizable way into an ever greater and more complex interiority and into an ever wider environment (and both at once), it can be said without hesitation — presupposing any *essential* self-transcendence to take place under the divine dynamism — that life, transcending itself, unfolds itself in the history of nature into spiritual life itself.

According to Christian teaching, this one life finds its highest summit in God's self-communication. God is not only the ground and innermost dynamism of this one history of nature and the spirit. He is also its goal, not merely as the asymptotic final point toward which this whole movement is oriented but also in the sense that he gives himself in his most personal, absolute reality and infinite fullness of life, to the life of the human person as its innermost power (called grace) and as its innermost goal which communicates itself in its own proper reality. This is a sovereignly free, unowed self-communication but is as such the final fulfillment of life, because that toward which life is opened now becomes also its innermost ground and most interior possession, since the world of life becomes the life of life itself: eternal life.

Even here, this life of the human person does not leave behind or reject the corporeality of the one human being as if it were something nonessential. Whether one's biological side can still be called "biological" when the person is perfected in God is ultimately an indifferent question. The whole person (and hence also his spirit) will be changed. The whole person (and hence also his corporeality) will be saved. That we cannot imagine the preserved salvation of the bodily individual is not surprising: the whole glorified person is withdrawn from us in the absolute mystery of God.

God's self-communication, however, together with the divine Trinity given with it and with the historical appearance of this self-communication in Jesus Christ, constitutes the whole of what Christianity professes and hopes for, and that toward which the Christian lives. Because and insofar as the possession of this divine self-communication can be understood as the highest, most absolute stage of life, Christianity can be understood quite correctly as the teaching about life as such, as the profession of God, the *living* God, and of eternal life. For this reason, we always conclude the Credo with the words: "and the life of the world to come. Amen."

10 • The Human Person as God's Creature*

In the *Spiritual Exercises* of St. Ignatius of Loyola, the saint says: "The human person is created to praise, reverence, and serve God our Lord, and by that means to attain salvation. The other things on the face of the earth are created to help the person attain the end for which he is created" (no. 23).

If it is not to be misunderstood, the phrase "the human person is created" must be understood, not as referring to people in general, but as referring to me. Otherwise "the other things" are not clearly seen. What is meant here is "I" and no one else. It is true that there are others like me, but only in a certain sense. For each person must perceive the splendid and terrible reality, the fact that places him in isolation before God: that he is unique and exists once only.

He must do this: he cannot retreat into the mass; he cannot hide himself in that which holds always and for all. A human being: this is what I am, completely alone, however true it is that every other human being must also say the same of himself. In fact, what he says of himself is simply a generalization, but the "general" must here be heard, read, experienced, and accepted in the absolute solitude of the individual, in the existence that is on each occasion "mine."

What is said here then about "the human person" must be understood as referring to "me." When I say "I," everything else must fall back into that circle of the "other things" in regard to which I am the unique, incommensurable one, with a partner ultimately only in God, so that when I am afraid in this uniqueness, when I feel the dizziness and dread of this loneliness, I can take refuge only in God.

The phrase "the human person is created" must be read as a statement in the present tense. I have not been created once and for all in the past, but I am now the created one, my being created is something that is constantly taking place. Hence it must be said that I am the creature, now, uniquely. I am the one known to myself, that one who is directly the sole creature that has this characteristic of being immediately known, the characteristic which enables me to reach everything else. And at the same time I am the one unknown to myself.

I am being-present-to-myself, I am freedom. "I am" means: I am inescapably; I am the appointed beginning which cannot get back behind itself, and this beginning is "there." If I were to kill myself, if I were to protest against my existence, if — in Dostoievsky's words — I "wanted

---

* *The Priesthood*, trans. Edward Quinn (New York: Seabury Press, 1973), 19–22.

to return my entry card into this world," I would again be confirming my existence, I would again be placed before this absolute barrier that I am and that I am not nonexistent.

To say that I exist as a creature means further that I am finite and I know it. In me this finiteness becomes aware of itself and here alone becomes radically finite. I endure myself then; I know my limits, I over-step them and at the same time keep to them. Nevertheless I am: I am not merely appearance, not merely an illusion; not everything about me is unreality which could be overridden. I am as I am, inescapably as the known-unknown, as the being become present to itself and as that which is in control of itself, which — how incomprehensible it really is — is given into its own hands.

As such, however, I am always the one who is directed away from myself: I am present to myself and always look away from myself. This toward-which-I-am is God and we call him therefore the incomprehensible, absolute freedom, over which we have no control. When we say, "I am referred to God," we cannot simply add that all is then clear, but we are basically saying: "I am that one who, if he is really the one referred to God, can never 'become clear' to himself about himself." For if we are those who are referred to God, if we are *created,* then we understand ourselves adequately, we become transparent to ourselves, only when we understand God. And this is denied the creature for all eternity, even in the beatific vision. Or, better, it is not denied us, but the bliss of eternity lies in the fact that we are dealing with a God who himself is close to us as the incomprehensible mystery, and as infinite incomprehensibility lays hold on us down to the last fiber of our being.

11 • The Human Spirit*

Spirit is transcendence. Spirit grasps at the incomprehensible inasmuch as it presses on beyond the actual object of comprehension to an anticipatory grasp of the absolute. The "whither" of this anticipatory grasp — which in the act of grasping the individual and tangible attains the all-embracing incomprehensible — may be called obscure or lucid. Its reality, indescribable because nonobjectivated, may be experienced as a divine darkness, or greeted as the light which illuminates all else, since the individual object of knowledge is only present and definable in relation to it.

* *Theological Investigations IV,* trans. Kevin Smyth (Baltimore: Helicon Press, 1966), 42–43.

But in any case, this nameless region beyond all categories, on which the transcendence of the spirit lays hold without comprehending, is not an accessory or a preliminary sphere of darkness which is to be gradually lit up. It is the primordial and fundamental which is the ultimate transcendental condition of possibility of knowledge. It alone makes categorical clarity possible in the distinct knowledge of contours.

If then reason which gives shape and contour to the object lives by the indefinable; if the lucidity of the spirit comes from its being open to the divine and truly superluminous darkness — what are we to think of mystery? Can it be regarded as a defective type of another and better knowledge which is still to come? Is *ratio*, understood in the standard sense, just incidentally and secondarily the faculty of mystery, precisely because of its almost too taut tension? Or is it, in spite of the obscurity cast by the standard terminology, the very faculty which is originally and basically the faculty of mystery, and only derivatively *ratio* in the ordinary sense of the word, as supposed by Vatican I and the theology of the schools?

We are met by the same challenge when we consider the nature of spirit as being *one* in the *perichoresis* (circumincession) of knowledge and love. The positivism which places knowledge and love merely de facto beside one another in an unreconciled dualism must be excluded. For one thing — no one knows why — the same existent thing is both knowing and loving. Hence, in spite of a real multiplicity of faculties and acts, this one total relationship to itself and absolute being: a basic act, whose components are the interrelated and interdependent of knowing and willing, of insight and love, as we call them empirically.

But this must ultimately mean that while guarding the distinction between knowing and willing, we must understand the act of knowing in such a way that it will explain why knowledge can only exist in a being when and insofar as that one being realizes itself by an act of love. In other words, the self-transcendence of knowledge, the fact that it comes to be only *insofar* as it passes over into something else must be understood in this way: knowledge, though prior to love and freedom, can only be realized in its *true* sense when and insofar as the subject is more than knowledge, when in fact it is a freely given love.

This is only possible if knowledge is ultimately a faculty ordained to an object attainable only because the object is greater than the faculty. And what but the incomprehensibility of mystery can be such an object of knowledge, since it forces knowledge to surpass itself and both preserve and transform itself in a more comprehensive act, that of love?

12 • "You Are Dust!"*

The prayer that accompanies the distribution of ashes comes from Genesis (3:19), where the divine judgment is pronounced over all human beings, who had become sinners in their first parents. The divine judgment falls dark and hopeless over all: "For out of the earth you were taken; you are dust and to dust you shall return."

We dare not introduce into this text our platonic outlook on life, and think, "Oh, fine, the human body is clearly declared to be mortal. But what of it, for the soul is certainly immortal, and it can find no fault with this death, which in the long run isn't so bad." On the contrary, this text, this judgment is directed to the whole person: "You are dust."

Dust is an image of the whole human being. We may subsequently modify this image by distinguishing a twofold meaning: one meaning for the human body and one for the soul. Even in this distinction, however — which is certainly justified in itself — we stick to the one compact statement of scripture only when we do not forget that the assertion made in Genesis is concerned first of all with the whole person; and that this one assertion contains everything that pertains to the person, body and soul, even if it does so in different ways. *The human person,* therefore, and not just a part of his essence, is dust.

Understood in this way, dust is naturally an image, a graphic symbol. But it is an image that is fuller and deeper than our metaphysical ideas, which are often so remote and diluted. What, then, does this image tell us about the human person?

The symbol of dust was used as a declaration of the human person's essence not only in Genesis. "For he [God] knows our frame; he remembers that we are dust" (Ps 103:14). In Ecclesiastes 3:20 we read, "All are from the dust and all turn to dust again." Pessimistic? Yes, but this must be endured so that the joyous message of the new covenant can be grasped. Even pessimism can be inspired by God.

In the book of Job (4:19), the despondent Eliphaz complains in these words, "Even in his [God's] servants he puts no trust.... How much more those who dwell in houses of clay, whose foundation is in the dust, who are crushed before the moth." "I am merely dust and ashes," says Abraham to God, in order to move him to pity for a sinful race (Gn 18:27). And if a person's death is to be described, Qoheleth again has recourse to the image: "before the silver cord is snapped, or the pitcher is broken at the fountain, or the wheel broken at the cistern, and dust returns to the earth as it was.... Vanity of vanities, says the Preacher; all is vanity" (Eccl 12:6–8).

---

* *The Eternal Year,* trans. John Shea, S.S. (Baltimore: Helicon Press, 1964), 57–63.

Dust — truly a splendid symbol. Dust, this is the image of the commonplace. There is always more than enough of it. One fleck is as good as the next. Dust is the image of anonymity: one fleck is like the next, and all are nameless.

It is the symbol of indifference: What does it matter whether it is this dust or that dust? It is all the same. Dust is the symbol of nothingness: because it lies around so loosely, it is easily stirred up, it blows around blindly, is stepped upon and crushed — and nobody notices. It is a nothing that is just enough to be — a nothing. Dust is the symbol of coming to nothing: it has no content, no form, no shape; it blows away, the empty, indifferent, colorless, aimless, unstable booty of senseless change, to be found everywhere, and nowhere at home.

But God speaks to us: "You are dust." You — the whole of you — are dust. He does not say that human beings are only dust. It is an existential expression, not a complete formula of our essence. It can be spoken, though, even by itself, because the truth that it expresses must be experienced and endured to the full, so that whatever further is to be said about us (and there is a lot more, indeed everything, left to be said), this first assertion is not denied, watered down, nor essentially restricted.

For it lies in a completely different dimension. We are not a little dust and also at the same time and in the same dimension, still a lot more, so that to be a creature of dust would not be so bad. Rather, we are *all* dust, and are more than dust only when we really admit this dust-existence: I accept it, and "endure through it" with body and soul.

And because it is a question of an existential formula in this sense, then scripture can address this formula to human beings plainly, in all its harshness. Scripture need not add the comforting thought that we are more than dust, because this added notion, spoken in the wrong place, would be no comfort at all. Rather it would be the temptation not to take this dust-existence seriously, but to deceive ourselves about it.

Truly, then, scripture is right. We are dust. We are always in the process of dying. We are the beings who set our course for death, when we set out on life's journey, and steer for death, clearly and inexorably. We are the only beings who know about this tendency to death. We are dust!

To be sure, we are spirit, too. But left to its own resources, what is spiritual existence except the knowledge of things incomprehensible, the knowledge of guilt, and the knowledge that there is no way out of all this. We have enough spirit in us to know God. But what does this mean except that we know we stand before an unfathomable being whose ways are unsearchable and whose judgments are incomprehensible? What does this mean except that we stand before the holy one as lost sinners? What does this mean except that with our minds we grasp the meaning of what we are in reality: dust and ashes?

Perhaps this dust might want to boast that it is immortal spirit. If so, what would this boast mean except that this dust is, by its very nature, subject to the judgment, that as a sinner this dust has already been judged? What else would it proclaim by this boasting of its eternity except that it is dust, nothing but the commonplace, nothing but the abnormality of guilty indebtedness, nothing but anonymous insignificance, nothing but nothingness? Taken by itself, what is the spirit except the possibility of measuring the finite with an infinite norm, only to perceive with horror that the eternal cannot be reached.

And so through practical experience we come to realize that we are dust. Scripture tells us that we are like the grass of the field, an empty puff of air. We are creatures of pain and sin and of drifting perplexity, who are constantly and continually losing our way in blind alleys. We torture ourselves and others, because we do not know whether guilt comes from pain or pain from guilt. Despair is always threatening us, and all our optimism is only a means of numbing our hopeless, bleak anxiety. Dust, that is what we are.

It is not easy for the person to avoid hating himself (as Bernanos tells us). Actually, if dust really belongs to us, is really a part of us, then we shouldn't hate it. That is why oriental people, keenly aware of their origins, had such a remarkable relationship with dust, our proper image. He strews dust on his head, weeping and lamenting (Jos 7:6 ; 1 Sm 4:12; 2 Sm 1:2; Jb 2:12; Lam 2:10). In tears he throws himself down and sits in the dust for which he was made (Is 47:1).

The reason why we cast our enemies down into the dust, tread on them in the dust, and make them eat the dust, is because the proud hatred and triumph over an enemy really flares up in white heat at its own despair over itself (Is 25:12; 2:5; Jos 10:24; Ps 109:1; Mi 7:10; Ps 71:9; Is 49:23). What we hate in others is ourselves. We cannot stand someone else because we despair in our own selves as seen in others.

Dust doubtlessly has an inner relationship, if not an essential identity, with another concept of both Old and New Testaments: the concept of "flesh." "Flesh" certainly designates, in both testaments, the *whole* human being. It designates the whole person precisely in his basic otherness to God, in his frailty, in his intellectual and moral weakness, in his separation from God, which is manifested in sin and death. The two assertions, "we are dust" and "we are flesh," are, then, more or less essentially similar assertions.

From this conclusion, however, we must now go on to understand the change that the sentence "the human person is dust" undergoes in the Christian economy of salvation. The good news of salvation rings out: "The Word became flesh." St. Paul said that God sent his own Son in the likeness of human, sinful flesh (Rom 8:3). We can add to this and say that God himself has strewn his own head with the dust of the earth, that he fell on his face upon the earth, which with evil greed drank up his tears and his blood. Even more, we can say to him exactly what is said to us, yes, we can tell the eternal God: "Remember, man, that you are dust, and in death you shall return to dust." We can tell him what he told us in paradise, because he has become what we are after paradise. He has become flesh, flesh that suffers even unto death, transitory, fleeting, unstable dust.

But ever since then, as Tertullian says, this *caro* has become the *cardo salutis*. Flesh has become the hinge, the pivot of salvation. Since then, flesh designates not only the pivot and hinge of the movement into nothingness and death, but also the pivot and hinge of a movement that passes through dust's nothingness and forlornness into life, into eternity, into God.

Ever since that moment, the sentence of terrifying judgment, "dust you are," is changed for the person of faith and love. This is not the one who despairs at the downward movement of returning into the dust, and who "puts on the brakes" because he wants to stop this movement short of anxiety and terror. Rather, the individual of faith and love is the one who causes the movement to swing further, right into the midst of the dust and through it. This judgment still has a mysterious and shocking sense. The old sense is not abolished. The old sense must be endured and experienced in tears, in the experience of nothingness and of death, in evil and in dying, in the bitterness of internal and external limitations.

But even this existential sense of the pronouncement that we are dust contains another depth. The downward motion of the believer, the descent with Christ into the dust of the earth, has become an upward motion, an ascent above the highest heaven. Christianity does not set free from the flesh and dust, nor does it bypass flesh and dust; it goes right through flesh and dust. And that is why the expression "dust you are" is still applicable to us; rightly understood, it is a complete expression of our life.

When on Ash Wednesday we hear the words, "Remember, you are dust," we are also told then that we are brothers and sisters of the incarnate Lord. In these words we are told everything that we are: nothingness that is filled with eternity; death that teems with life; futility that redeems; dust that is God's life forever.

To say this is easy. To endure it is hard. But we have to endure it. In the boredom of everyday routine, in the disappointments that we experience in everything — in ourselves, in our neighbors, in the church — in the anxiety of time, in the futility of our labor, in the brutal harshness of universal history. Again and again we shall lie in the dust of our weakness, humiliated and weeping (grant, God, that this image shall never be realized in all its reality: in these days, a grave of atomic dust is all too possible). We shall experience again and again that we are dust. We shall not only be told this in a ceremony; but we shall experience it in life, and throughout life.

Just as the dying in baptism is only the beginning of a lifelong dying into the death of Christ, so too, the cross of ashes is only the renewed beginning of the return movement into the dust. Just as the sacrament of baptism is an image and symbol of the approaching humble reality of routine everyday life and of the splendor and glory hidden therein, so too, the sacramental ashes are an image and a symbol of the approaching humble reality of everyday life, and of the splendor and glory hidden therein.

13 • Freedom Received from and Directed toward God*

It would be a complete misconception of the nature of freedom to try to understand it as the mere capacity of choice between objects given a posteriori, among which, besides many others, there is also God; so that God would only play a special role in the choice made by this freedom of choice from among these many objects on account of his own objective characteristics but not on account of the nature of freedom itself.

Freedom only exists — as was seen explicitly already by St. Thomas — because there is spirit understood as transcendence. There is unlimited transcendence toward being as such and hence indifference with regard to any particular, finite object within the horizon of this absolute transcendence only insofar as this transcendence in every individual act concerned with a finite object is directed toward the original unity of being as such.

Moreover, this indifference exists only insofar as this act of transcendence (considered as the ground of every categorical personal relationship toward a finite subject and also toward the infinite represented in finite concepts) is supported by a conditional opening and

---

* *Theological Investigations VI*, 179–83.

extending of the horizon of this transcendence starting from itself, and of its goal, which we call God.

Freedom, therefore, has a theological character not only when and where God is represented explicitly and side by side with other objects in the objectivity of categories, but always and everywhere by the nature of freedom itself, since God is present unthematically in every act of freedom as its supporting ground and ultimate orientation. When St. Thomas says that God is recognized unthematically but really in every object, then this applies equally to freedom: in every act of freedom God is unthematically but really willed and, conversely, one experiences in this way alone what is really meant by God, namely, the incomprehensible "whither" of knowing and willing of the one original transcendence of the human being unfolding itself in knowledge and love.

The "whither" of transcendence cannot be mastered but consists in the infinite, silent mastery over us in that moment and indeed always when, by making a judgment on it, we begin to master something by making it subject to the laws of our a priori reason. It is not given merely as the whither of transcendence itself. This means that, since this goal is not experienced in itself but is only known unobjectively in the experience of subjective transcendence, every thesis of ontologism is already avoided from this point of view alone. Furthermore, its presence is the presence of such a transcendence that it is always given only as the condition of the possibility of categorical knowledge and not by itself alone. One can never go directly toward it. One can never reach out to it directly. It gives itself only insofar as it directs us silently to something else, to something finite as the object of direct vision.

It is decisive for the Christian understanding of freedom, however, that this freedom is not only made possible by God and is not only related to him as the supporting horizon of the freedom of choice in categories, but that it is freedom vis-à-vis God himself. This is the frightening mystery of freedom in its Christian understanding. Where God is understood in categories as merely one reality among others, as one of the many objects of freedom of choice — understood as a neutral capacity which is arbitrarily occupied with this and that — the statement that freedom of choice is choice even with regard to God would present no particular difficulty.

That freedom, however, is freedom vis-à-vis its all-supporting ground itself, that in other words it can culpably deny the very condition of its own possibility in an act which necessarily reaffirms this condition, is the extreme statement about the nature of created freedom which in its radicality leaves the usual neutrality of categories far behind. *It is decisive for the Christian doctrine of freedom that this free-*

dom implies the possibility of a yes or no toward its own horizon and indeed it is only really constituted by this.

This is true not merely and not even primarily when God is given and represented systematically in concepts and categories but also when he is given unsystematically but originally in our transcendental experience as the condition and moment of every activity directed toward the contemporary world in which we live. It is true in this sense that we meet God everywhere in a most radical way as the most basic question of our freedom, in all things of the world and (in the words of scripture) above all in our neighbor.

Why then, more precisely, is the transcendental horizon of freedom not merely the condition of its possibility but also its proper "object?" Why do we not act in freedom not merely toward ourselves, our surroundings, and the people around us either in conformity to reality or in a destructive way within that infinitely wide horizon of transcendence from which we freely confront ourselves and the world in which we live, and why is this horizon itself also the "object" of this freedom in our yes or no to it in itself?

This horizon is once more by definition the condition of the possibility of saying no to it. This means that in such a no it is unavoidably negated as the condition of the possibility of freedom and is also at the same time negated as an unthematic "object" or even (in explicit or practical "atheism") as a conceptually mediated object.

Thus, in the act of the negating freedom, there is present a real, absolute contradiction in the fact that God is affirmed and denied at the same time. In it this ultimate monstrosity is both withdrawn from itself and, by the fact that it is necessarily made objective and mediated in the finite material of our life in its temporal extension, made relative by being introduced into temporality.

The real possibility, however, of such an absolute contradiction in freedom cannot be denied, though it is indeed disputed and doubted. This happens in ordinary everyday theology whenever it is said that the only thinkable mode of freedom is that the infinite God in his reality can only assess a little "bending" of finite reality, the offence against a concrete and merely finite natural structure, for what it is, namely, something finite.

Therefore, God cannot reevaluate it as absolutely prohibited through his infinite sanction. He cannot designate it as something against his own will as such. The "will" against which such a sin really offends (such a theology would say) is, after all, the finite reality really willed by God, and to suppose an offence against God's will over and above this is falsely to turn God's will into a particular category of reality alongside the finite thing which is willed.

Yet there is the possibility of a free no toward God. Otherwise freedom would basically have no real orientation to the subject (of which we will have still to speak explicitly), that is, the fact that freedom is concerned with the subject itself and not just with this or that thing.

Let us grant that the act of freedom is really concerned with the subject itself, since this subject is transcendence. Let us grant furthermore that the individual intramundane beings encountered by us within the horizon of transcendence are not events within a space which remains untouched by what is in that space, but are the historical concreteness of the encounter and projection of this source and goal that support our transcendence. In this light freedom toward the encountered individual beings is always also a freedom toward the horizon, the ground and abyss, which allows them to present themselves to us and lets them become the inner moment of our receiving freedom.

Insofar as and because the horizon cannot be indifferent to the subject understood as a *knowing* subject but is systematically or unsystematically that with which this knowing transcendence is concerned, particularly if this "goal" is not its explicit object, to that same extent and for the same reason *freedom* — even though it is always exercised on the concrete individual things of experience and through this becomes what it is — is primarily and unavoidably concerned with God himself.

Freedom in its origin is freedom of saying yes or no to God and by this fact is freedom of the subject toward itself. Freedom is either indifferent to this or that, the infinite repetition of the same or of the contrary (which is merely a different kind of the same), a freedom of eternal recurrence, or the same "wandering Jew," or it is necessarily the freedom of the subject toward itself in its finality and thus is freedom toward God, however unconscious this ground and most proper and original "object" of freedom may be in the individual act of freedom.

We must add a second reflection to this, a reflection which alone brings to light the ultimate theological reason for freedom as freedom toward God, but one which can only be briefly indicated here. The supernatural and historical concreteness of our transcendence is never given as something merely natural but is always embraced and taken up by a *supernatural* dynamism of our spiritual being which tends toward God's absolute nearness.

In other words, God in the concrete is not present merely as the horizon of our transcendence, one which always withdraws itself and refuses to give itself; rather, understood as this horizon, he offers himself to be directly possessed in what we call divinizing grace. Given all this, the freedom in transcendence and in the yes and no toward the ground of this transcendence is given a directness toward God by which it becomes most radically capable of saying yes and no to God as such. This occurs, of course, in a way that is not contained in an abstract, formal concept of transcendental openness to a God who is merely the distant and uninviting horizon of all human existence and accomplishment.

14 • Freedom as the Total and Finalizing Self-Mastery of the Subject*

Freedom cannot be viewed in a Christian sense as an in-itself neutral capacity to do this or that in an arbitrary order and in a temporal series which would be broken off from outside even though, from the point of view of freedom, it could go on ad infinitum. Freedom is rather the capacity to make oneself once and for all, the capacity which of its nature is directed toward the freely willed finality of the subject as such. This is obviously what is meant by the Christian statement about the human person and his salvation and damnation when he, the free person, must answer for himself and the totality of his life before the judgment seat of God, and when the eternally valid sentence about his salvation or damnation in accordance with his works is passed by a judge who does not regard merely the appearance of his life, the "face," but the freely governed core of the person, the "heart."

It is true that human being's formal freedom of choice and decision is more presupposed in scripture than used as an actual theme. It is true also that the explicit theme in scripture, especially in the New Testament, is for the most part the paradox that human freedom, while remaining responsible and without being destroyed, is enslaved by the demonic powers of sin and death and to some extent even of the law, and must first of all be liberated to make way for an inner inclination toward the law (we will discuss this later). Yet it cannot be doubted that for scripture both the sinful and the justified are responsible for the actions of their life and to this extent are also free, and that freedom, therefore, is a permanent constitutive of human nature.

The proper nature of freedom, however, appears precisely insofar as freedom is the basis of absolute salvation and damnation in Christian revelation, and this finally and before God. For a merely profane everyday experience, freedom of choice may appear merely as the characteristic of the individual act of the human person, which can be

_____

* *Theological Investigations VI*, 183–86.

attributed to him insofar as it is actively posited by him, without this positing being already causally predetermined and in this sense forced by some inner human condition or some external situation.

Such a concept of freedom of choice atomizes freedom in its exercise and thus distributes it exclusively to the individual acts of the person, acts which are only held together by a neutral, substantial identity of the subject and of the capacities positing them all, as well as by the externals of spatio-temporal existence. Freedom in this sense is merely freedom of acts, imputability of the individual act to a person who remains neutral in himself and hence (as long as the external conditions are given for this) can always determine himself anew.

Once we see in a Christian sense, however, that by his freedom a human being can determine and dispose himself as a whole and finally, the idea of responsible freedom is changed and deepened immensely. This means that the individual does not merely perform actions which, though they must be qualified morally, also always pass away again (and which after that are imputed to him merely juridically or morally). The human person by his free decision really *is* so good or evil in the very ground of his being itself that his final salvation or damnation are really already given in this, even though perhaps in a still hidden manner.

Freedom is first of all "freedom of being." It is not merely the quality of an act and capacity exercised at some time, but a transcendental mark of human existence itself. If the human being is to be really and finally able to be master over himself, if this "eternity" is to be the act of his freedom itself, if this act is to be really able to make the individual good or bad in the very ground of his being, and if this goodness or badness is not to be merely an external, accidental event happening to the person (so that this act would merely, contrary to its goodness, draw something which remains good into damnation), then freedom must first of all be thought of as freedom of being.

This means that the human person is that being who is concerned in his very being about this being itself. He is always a being who already has a relationship toward himself, a subjectivity and never simply a nature. He is already a person — never just "something there" but always already "for himself" — "existing." Nothing happens to this being which does not affect its relationship to itself in some way. Or if it does, it becomes subjectively and salvifically significant only insofar as it is freely "understood" and subjectively taken over by the free subject as such in a quite definite way.

Its "ego" cannot possibly be passed over, it simply cannot be turned into an object and can never be replaced or explained by something else, not even by its own reflex representation of itself. It is genuinely original, never based on something else and hence cannot be derived from or proved by anything else. Its relationship to its divine origin must never be interpreted according to the notion of causal and formal relationships of dependence as operative in the categories of the realm of our experience in which the source keeps and binds and does not set free, and in which therefore independence and dependence grow in inverse and equal proportion.

The human person, by his freedom of being, is always the incomparable being who cannot be adequately classified into any system and cannot be adequately subsumed under any one concept. He is in an original sense the untouchable, but therefore also the lonely and insecure, a burden to himself, who cannot by any means "absolve" himself from this once-and-for-all lonely self-being and who can never "unload" himself on others.

Hence freedom is originally also not primarily concerned with this or that which one can do or not do. It is not originally the capacity of choosing any object whatsoever or the ability of adopting an individual attitude toward this or that. Freedom is rather the freedom of self-understanding, the possibility of saying yes or no to oneself, the possibility of deciding for or against oneself, which corresponds to the knowing self-possession, the understanding subject-nature of the human being.

Freedom never happens as a merely objective exercise, as a mere choice "between" individual objects, but is the self-exercise of the individual who chooses objectively. Only within this freedom in which the person is capable of achieving himself is the human being also free with regard to the material of his self-achievement. He can do or omit this or that in view of his own self-realization that is inescapably imposed on him. This self-realization is a task he cannot avoid and, in spite of all the differences within the concrete material of his self-achievement, it is always either a self-realization in the direction of God or a radical self-refusal toward God.

It must of course be realized that this basic nature of freedom is achieved over a whole period of time and that the total project of human existence, one's own total self-understanding or fundamental option, frequently remains empty and objectively unfulfilled. It must be borne in mind that not every individual act of freedom has the same actual depth and radical nature of self-disposal and that, although each individual act of freedom wants to venture total and final self-disposal, all such acts always enter into the totality of the one, total act of freedom of the one, whole temporally finite life, precisely because each one of these acts is exercised within, and receives its weight and proportion from, the horizon of the whole of human existence.

Correspondingly, the biblical and Augustine concept of the heart, the concept of subjectivity in Kierkegaard, the notion of *action* in Blondel, and the like, shows understanding for the fact that there is such a *basic act* of freedom which embraces and shapes the whole of human existence. This act is indeed realized and can be exercised only by means of those individual acts of the human person which can be localized in space and time and which can be objectified with regard to their motives.

Yet this basic act cannot be simply identified by an objective reflection with such an individual act; it does not represent either the merely moral sum-total of these individual acts nor can it be simply identified with the moral quality of the last of the free individual acts exercised (before death). The concrete freedom of the individual, by which he decides about himself as a whole by effecting his own finality before God, is the unity in difference of the formal fundamental option and the free individual acts of the person no longer attainable by reflection, a unity which is the concrete being of the subject of freedom having-achieved-itself.

In all this, to emphasize this once more and explicitly, freedom — precisely speaking — is not the possibility of always being able to do something else, the possibility of infinite revision, but the capacity to do something uniquely final, something which is finally valid precisely because it is done in freedom. Freedom is the capacity for the eternal. Natural processes can always be revised again and directed along a different path and are therefore for this very reason indifferent. *The result of freedom is the true necessity which remains.*

15 • Freedom and Ensnarement in Guilt*

If the Christian doctrine about the possibility of radical guilt in human existence is really to be understood, then we must also consider that the human being precisely as free subject, and not merely *in addition* to this, is a being in the world, in history, and in a world of persons. But this means that he always and inevitably exercises his personal, inalienable and unique acts of freedom in a situation which he finds prior to himself, which is imposed on him, and which is ultimately the

---

Foundations of Christian Faith, trans William V. Dych, S.J. (New York: Seabury Press, 1978), 106–10.

presupposition of his freedom. It means that he actualizes himself as a free subject in a situation which itself is always determined by history and by other persons.

This situation is not only an exterior situation which basically does not enter into the decision of freedom as such. It is not the external material in which an intention, an attitude or a decision is merely actualized in such a way that the material of this free decision then drops off this decision, as it were. Rather freedom inevitably appropriates the material in which it actualizes itself as an intrinsic and constitutive element which is originally codetermined by freedom itself, and incorporates it into the finality of the existence which possesses itself in its freedom.

The eternal validity of the free subject in and through his freedom is the final and definitive validity of his earthly history itself, and therefore it is also intrinsically codetermined by the elements imposed on it which have constituted the situation of the free subject in time. It is codetermined by the free history of all the others who constitute his own unique world of persons. However much it defends radically against making our own historical decision in freedom innocuous, the Christian interpretation of this situation of the free subject says that this situation, determined by his personal world, inevitably bears the stamp of the history of the freedom of all other human persons, and this precisely for the individual in his free subjectivity and in his most personal and individual history. Consequently, the guilt of others is a permanent factor in the situation and realm of the individual's freedom, for the latter are determined by his personal world.

The corporeality and objectification of each individual's original decision of freedom participates in the essence of this original free decision, and this is true whether the decision was good or bad. But they are not simply the original goodness or evil of this subjective, original free decision. They only participate in it, and therefore they are inevitably characterized by ambiguity. For while history is still going on, it always remains obscure whether they really are the historical, corporeal objectification of a definite good or evil free decision, or whether it only looks this way because this objectification has arisen only out of prepersonal necessities.

Moreover, this objectification of a free decision is always open to and capable of further determination. For the objectification of one person's free decision which has had an effect on the objectivity of a shared situation of freedom can become an intrinsic moment in the free decision of another. In this latter decision this objectification can acquire a completely different character without ceasing for this reason to be the result of the first free action.

According to Christian teaching objectifications of guilt are a part of these already existing elements in the situation of an individual's freedom. This seems to sound at first like something perfectly obvious. For every person has the impression that he has to decide about himself and to find himself and God in a world which is codetermined by guilt and by the guilty refusals of others. He knows from his own transcendental experience that there is freedom, and that this freedom objectifies itself in the world, in history, in time and space. He knows that such freedom includes the possibility of a radically evil decision, and he presumes that in this undoubtedly very inadequate and sorrowful world there are to be found objectifications of really subjectively evil decisions which have actually taken place.

This opinion is very natural. But if we think about it carefully and correctly, outside of the possibility of an absolute experience of one's own subjective evil objectifying itself in the world, it can really only claim to be probable at most. We could assume, first of all, that there has indeed always been the pressing and threatening possibility of really subjective evil in the world, but that this possibility has not become reality. We could assume that unfortunate situations which are detrimental to freedom and which always have to be worked through in the development of the human race never arise out of a really subjectively evil decision, but that they are the early stages of a development which begins from far below and moves upward, and is not yet finished. We could assume that perhaps there have necessarily been evil decisions of freedom objectifying themselves in the world, but that they are then improved and transformed by a subsequent change in this same subjective freedom, so that they no longer have any adverse significance for others which would constitute an essential obstacle to a good decision in freedom by these others.

All of these possibilities might appear very improbable. To a person who in a subjectively honest judgment faces himself not only as a possible sinner, but as a real sinner, it might appear absurd to assume that in the whole history of the human race he alone is such a sinner merely because he only has the possibility of judging about himself, while this possibility is not assured with regard to others, or at least not with the same clarity and certainty. It might strike such a person who has really experienced his own subjective guilt as absurd to believe that he and he alone has brought something evil into this world by his actions in freedom, something which he can no longer intercept completely and undo.

All of human experience points in the direction that there are in fact objectifications of personal guilt in the world which, as the material for the free decisions of other persons, threaten these decisions, have a seductive effect upon them, and make free decisions painful. And since the material of a free decision always becomes an intrinsic element of the free act itself, insofar as even a good free act which is finite does not succeed in transforming this material absolutely and changing it completely, this good act itself always remains ambiguous because of the codetermination of this situation by guilt. It always remains burdened with consequences which could not really be intended because they lead to tragic impasses, and which disguise the good that was intended by one's own freedom.

But this human experience, which is really quite obvious, is prevented from becoming innocuous by the message of Christianity and its assertion that this codetermination of the situation of every person by the guilt of others is something universal, permanent, and therefore also original. There are no islands for the individual person whose nature does not already bear the stamp of the guilt of others, directly or indirectly, from close or from afar. And although this is an asymptotic ideal, there is for the human race in its concrete history no real possibility of ever overcoming once and for all this determination of the situation of freedom by guilt. Throughout its history the human race can indeed, and always will strive anew to alter this situation of guilt, and even do this with very real successes and as an obligation, so that to neglect this obligation would itself be radical guilt before God. But according to the teaching of Christianity this striving will always remain codetermined by guilt, and even a person's most ideal, most moral act of freedom enters tragically into the concrete in an appearance which, because codetermined by guilt, is also the appearance of its opposite.

By rejecting an idealistic as well as a communistic optimism about the future, Christianity believes not only that it is giving witness to the truth, but also that it is performing the best service for a "better world" here and now. It believes that it has offered the world adequate moral imperatives and obligations extending all the way to responsibility before God and to the risk of *eternal* guilt. It believes that its historical pessimism is also the best service toward improving the world here and now, because the utopian idea that a world functioning in perfect harmony can be created by human beings themselves only leads inevitably to still greater violence and greater cruelty than those which persons want to eradicate from the world. Such a pessimism, of course, can become the excuse for not doing anything, for offering people the consolation of eternal life, and really for offering a religious attitude not only as the opiate of the people, but also as an opiate for the people. But this does not alter the fact that the radical realism which comes to expression in the pessimism of Christianity as we have formulated it with respect to the situation of our freedom is true, and that therefore it may not be disguised.

16 • Love: The Basic Human Act*

The spiritual life is not a mere series of actions endlessly succeeding each other toward the attainment of a spiritual goal: the past exists mysteriously in every moment. Thus, as a spiritual being, the human person acts, or at least, can act, in every moment with the resources of his entire past. His past is preserved in a concentrated form as the gathered experience of his life. The place from which a bullet was fired can be determined only by considering its whole path. Similarly a note sounded by a master violinist can be said to contain in essence that note as played by him up to the moment of its present perfection.

In a far greater measure the present action of a human being embodies his whole past: his knowledge obtained through effort or through suffering, the depth of his experience, the revolutions of his life, his joys and his sorrows. Memory may modify these to some extent, but they are none the less present. By all these influences, the present action is given its direction, its depth and resonance. The past is preserved and carried forward in the present action. At least, that is how it ought to be. Into the present free decision, a person is called upon to gather up all the past, thus bringing to it all that he is and was — in other words, the whole sum of his existence. The individual must seize the successive possibilities offered to him, and in doing so, he realizes what is eternal in him. Every moment is to be filled with his whole spiritual history which to him is the ever more enriched possibility of present freedom.

It is still more mysterious, yet true that in the grace of a present decision the human person can anticipate his future. This is not exclusive to such matters as resolution, planning, decision, premeditation, promise and vow, when the individual looks to the pattern of his future life. Besides, resolutions and similar spiritual and intellectual acts remain in the present tense, however important they may be for the future of the person: they become significant for his future only when actually

---

* *On Prayer,* trans. not given (New York: Paulist Press, 1968), 71–79.

carried out, and this carrying out is subject to a subsequent rather than to a present decision.

However, by saying that in a present action we can mysteriously anticipate the future, we mean something more than decisions which once taken cannot be altered and therefore exercise an ineluctable influence on later conduct. There are such facts, and they vary in significance. Marriage and holy orders — indeed, even living through a certain unrepeatable period of our lives — create facts which exercise an influence on future actions and decisions. Any future action must take these facts into consideration, and a person can no longer act as if they did not exist.

However, it is an equally important truth that an individual can take these facts into consideration in very different ways. He can change the face of his decisions, that is, he can either stand by his earlier decision to love a person, or he can betray this decision. His ordination to the priesthood can become more and more integrated into his life, or his life can be lived more and more outside his vocation. Indeed, he can become unfaithful to it.

Thus the fact created in the past is not actually evaded. Two opposite possibilities remaining after such facts have been created. For the future continues fundamentally undecided and undetermined. It is not this phenomenon to which we were referring when we said that the present moment can anticipate the future.

To explain what we mean, let us discuss an objection which might be put forward to disprove from the outset the possibility of such anticipation. Freedom seems to be incompatible with anticipation of the future. A person is always free, therefore also free in the future moments of his life. Hence it is impossible that the individual should anticipate his future to such an extent that he decides it in the present moment, filling as it were the present moment with the import of the future and anticipating what is still in the future. The future cannot be realized in the present moment. It seems that at this point the words of holy scripture (Mt 6:34) apply: "Sufficient for the day is the evil thereof."

One aspect of this objection is certainly to be maintained in our further considerations. Apart from exceptional cases to which we shall return later, the fact that in principle the entire life of a human being is free means that in no case can the free decision of the moment decide the future in such a way that a person knows for certain and in palpable manner that this decision has already shaped his future, and that thus the future has been decided here and now.

If this were not so, the future would be an almost mechanical unfolding of what has happened in such a moment. Life would no longer be shadowed by the incalculable future, and would be no longer subject to the law of responsible initiative. Theology teaches us, and the history of the saints bears out the truth, that there are cases in which an individual can know, through a free and complete conviction reached in the sight of God, that his life has reached a stage where his salvation is already assured. This is what theologians term "confirmation in grace." However, this is an exceptional case which can be left aside at this stage, because it occurs but rarely and need not be considered with reference to our own life. In such confirmation in grace, the person knows that, in a certain measure, his spiritual personality is already beyond the practical reach of sin.

As a general principle, such knowledge is not reconcilable with the freedom and uncertainty of our life on earth where decisions are made in ignorance and in blind trust, due to the uncertainty of our insecure position in the face of God. Our question, therefore, is still unanswered. Is it possible to try to anticipate the future even though the results of this venture may be uncertain?

One reason for answering this question in the affirmative is that freedom is not essentially — as a common misconception would have it — the capacity to accomplish, at least by desire, whatever we wish to do here and now. The correct definition of freedom is the individual's capacity to express his free personality completely, through decisions legitimately, freely, and finally made. Freedom therefore does not deny the possibility of creating internal (as distinct from merely external) facts which are definite and final. On the contrary, freedom has its ultimate meaning in this very possibility.

It is the very opposite of freedom to create conditions which are subject to alteration, change, reversion, or revision. Freedom achieves unique and permanent finality. The ultimate eternal destiny of the soul is not an accidental condition imposed on humankind as something which thwarts human freedom, as a foreign element which negates the very idea of that freedom. On the contrary, this destiny is the mature result of freedom itself.

Therefore, at any moment a free decision can anticipate a person's entire life, since it can be decisive of his lot in eternity. Every moment of free decision exerts a shaping influence on the entire growth of human personality, since it is the complete expression of what a human being really is within the depths of his own heart.

There are many of course who make narrow decisions dictated by the expediency of the moment rather than far-reaching decisions affecting their whole future and shaping their eternal destiny. Again success often depends on external conditions outside the control of free will. A person may fail a thousand times in his attempts so to gather up all the possibilities of his spiritual life into one moment of decision that all his future actions may receive a unifying significance from that decision. Yet the tendency to such decision is in us all, because it is part of the very essence of our freedom

A truly free decision always reaches forward to the whole of our life and is decisive of our eternal destiny. In most cases, it will ultimately fail to sustain its effect, either because this free decision was too weak and therefore incapable of reaching down into the very springs of our being, or because external circumstances beyond our control were too much for us.

It is scarcely possible to know with any degree of certainty whether our act of decision has completely succeeded in sustaining its effect. Nevertheless, in the moment of making such a decision human freedom really expresses itself as a desire to influence our whole future, to shape that future to the image of our decision, and thus to reach its effect even into eternity itself.

One such moment is inevitable. In death the thread of life is cut off, however much we might have liked to continue spinning the garment of our years. Although we never know how this can be done, and indeed although the appearances are inevitably against it, in death the human person completes his own pattern by dying his own death. In the moment of death he is what he has made of himself, freely and finally. The actual result of his life and what he wanted to be, freely and finally, become as one.

When exactly does death, in the sense of this action of freedom, occur; and when does an individual thus complete himself? What has been said of death is true inasmuch as, according to our faith, physical death is the free completion of the human being. However, we do not know whether this completion actually coincides in time with physical dissolution. What we know is that, apart from the exceptional cases to which we have referred, we can have no certainty that this moment of decision has been reached by us. Thus the moment of total decision lies always ahead of us, and we can only assume that it does not always coincide, and perhaps indeed very rarely coincides, with death in the physical sense.

The approach of physical death is generally accompanied by a reduction of consciousness, and it is unlikely that in this state the total decision can be taken. Since any free action can in itself become an act of total decision, it is at least probable that such a moment of total decision takes place at a time other than that of physical death. Since this total decision is the basic aim of freedom, we should indeed prepare for it at any moment.

What has so far been theoretically deduced from the nature of freedom is confirmed by experience. In the history of our own soul we remember moments which seemed indeed unforgettable. The experience, disposition, and intention felt by us at that moment seemed to be destined to remain deeply rooted within us. We realized that we could never go back on what we had freely chosen in that moment for the very reason that the choice was free. Advancing in age, we are sometimes overcome, gently and softly but with unspeakable rapture, by some awareness of God's grace taking possession of us. The divine huntsman will see to it that his game does not escape him. Our soul merely waits for the moment when his love will seize upon us finally. Let us not forget that such awareness of grace is an action involving our freedom, because it evokes a consent from the very depths of our being.

Even when such awareness proves to be an illusion, the very fact of this illusion seems to indicate our belief that there exists in reality what then appeared to us. When the mountaineer thinks he has reached the summit, a new stretch of the path opens up before his eyes, a stretch which was not yet visible when he estimated the distance he still had to cover. The illusion, in an individual case merely proves that our soul has been created for such moments when everything is finally completed. Suddenly, unexpectedly, and without any warning, there will come upon us what we had always hoped for, the fullness of life caught up in one moment of decision, the expression of freedom in its final perfection.

In freedom, we anticipate the whole unity of our life. Again and again, our anticipation will seize upon only a fraction of the whole, but we will not cease in our efforts to gather up past and future into that one decision of freedom from which our life will receive its final and definite truth and reality. Only God will hear when the hour of our glory strikes: unexpectedly and without knowing it ourselves, the fruits of our whole life will be in our hands. Whatever happens afterward in our life is but an exultant finale of a symphony, the final count in an election whose result is, beyond doubt, the ripening of a fruit after it has been gathered.

Let us call this great hour of our freedom, the unique and undisguised presence of the moment of eternity in time, the moment of "temporal eternity." The nature of this moment appears to us in a dark manner: indeed, being the fruit of freedom, the moment itself remains hidden. We know that it is of the nature of freedom to strive for this moment which is its fulfillment. Whether we are aware of it or not, we are always living in the attempt to reach this moment of fulfillment.

So far, we have endeavored to determine the moment of "temporal eternity" in its abstract form as the act by which a person disposes of himself and of all the possibilities of his life. The content of this act, however, is still undetermined. This act of freedom can be one thing or another, yes or no, ascent or descent, salvation or damnation, everlasting gain or eternal lose.

Let us therefore try to determine the full content of this moment, if it is indeed to be everlasting salvation, pure and final affirmation. It is through the love of God that the person succeeds in his attempt to secure his happiness in eternity. This definition is far from being self-evident. It is clear that not every act of the love of God is a moment of what we have called "temporal eternity." Every act of the love of God may be an attempt to achieve our unique moment of eternity in time; but only in very rare cases will we know with certainty whether we have succeeded in this attempt. In fact, except for one attempt, all these attempts are bound to fail. Needless to say, these failures are by no means insignificant in God's eyes or for ourselves. They are important and indeed indispensable exercises leading up to the supreme effort.

The identification of the act of love and the moment of eternity in time cannot take place unless we enter into it with our whole heart, our whole soul, our whole mind and strength, that is to say, unless we entirely spend ourselves in this act of loving freedom, making it final and irrevocable. Such an act of love can be attained but rarely, indeed only once, and this forever. When did we ever love God with our whole heart, our whole soul, our whole mind and all our strength (Mk 1:30)?

If we could fully understand the terrifying meaning of the words "whole" and "all, we would see that the commandment to love God with our entire being amounts to a commandment to direct our entire life toward the achievement of that moment of eternity in time. Our life would then be a continuous effort, until this grace is given to us. To strive for this success, in the moment of eternity in time, is the commandment of love. Every act of love tends toward that moment, in which it finds its fulfillment; but not every act of love is yet that unique moment.

In still another respect, it is not immediately evident that an act of love or indeed any human act can indeed be the true moment of eternity in time. We have said that in this moment an integration of our whole life takes place. It is by no means self-evident how love, and love only, is able to bring about this integration. Indeed, at this point we realize how little we really know about what we call love.

What is the fundamental act into which a human being can gather up his whole essence and his whole life? Which is the act that embraces everything, that comprehends everything and contains everything human: our laughter and tears, bliss and despair, mind and heart, everyday life and our moments of supreme happiness, compulsion and freedom, sin and redemption, past and future?

We hesitate to answer this question and yet the answer is clear. The love of God, and only the love of God, embraces everything. It brings a person face to face with God without whom he could experience nothing but a terrifying consciousness of emptiness and negation. The love of God alone unites all powers in a person — manifold, chaotic, and contradictory as they are — and directs them to God. The one and infinite God alone can create in the human being that unity which binds together what is manifold and contradictory without destroying it. Love alone makes the person forget himself, and it would indeed be hell if such self-oblivion could never be achieved.

Love alone can redeem even the darkest hours of the past, since love alone is brave enough to believe in the mercy of God. Love alone does not selfishly hold back: it is therefore able to dispose even of the future. Without love, the individual, anxiously guarding his finite ego, would husband his future and yield it but grudgingly. Love alone can, as it were, draw God on to this earth, thus integrating all earthly love in the moment of eternity.

To love alone, therefore, is given that persistency of courage which loves God who sees, through guilt, failure, and death, the bravery of his creature. The love of God is really the only total integration of human existence. Its sublime dignity and all-embracing greatness become clear to us when we understand this point. The full content of the moment of "temporal eternity" cannot be anything else, because without the love of God that moment would be nothing more than the secret judgment (Jn 3:18) and because, conversely, only in that moment can the love of God be what it desires to be and what it must be.

Much more could be said of this act of love in the moment of eternity in time. Above all, we must bear in mind that this act is grace, although it is the most sublime act of freedom. This moment is grace, because we can love God only through God's strength and power, because our love is only the response to his love, and because there is no love in us other than that which his Holy Spirit has poured out into our hearts. This moment is pure grace as such, because it transcends all the general grace of the love of God.

It is given only to the angels to be free at any moment to surrender entirely, to seize the very depth of all possibilities, and to smelt the core of life that it may be used without dross for the casting of a true image of God. Human beings are given this possibility only in those supreme moments of their lives granted to them by grace, when this possibility is given to them in such a way that they can really fulfill it. It is by grace that this moment is given to them, and it is by the superabundance of grace that this moment is given to them in such a way that they can fill it with the love of God. Thus the highest moment of freedom is essentially both grace and freedom. In that moment, freedom determines itself in the everlasting integration of an entire life.

17 • Propositional Knowledge and Primordial Consciousness*

It cannot be doubted that there exists in the natural order a kind of knowledge, which, while it is itself not articulated in "propositions," is the starting point of an intellectual process which develops into propositions.

Let us suppose that a young man has the genuine and vital experience of a great love, an experience which transforms his whole being. This love may have *presuppositions* (of a metaphysical, psychological, and physiological kind) which are simply unknown to him. His love *itself* is his "experience." He is conscious of it, lives through it with the entire fullness and depth of a real love. He "knows" much more about it than he can "state." The clumsy stammerings of his love letters are paltry and miserable compared to this knowledge. It may even be possible that the attempt to tell himself and others what he experiences and "knows" may lead to quite false statements.

If he were to come across a "metaphysics" of love, he might perhaps understand absolutely nothing of what was said there about love and even his love, although he might know much more about it than the dried-up metaphysician who has written the book. If he is intelligent, and has at his disposal an adequately differentiated stock of ideas, he could perhaps make the attempt, slowly and gropingly, approaching the subject in a thousand different ways, to state what he knows about his love, what he is already aware of in the consciousness of simply possessing the reality (more simply but more fully aware), so as finally to "know" (in reflective propositions).

In such a case it is not (merely) a matter of the logical development and inference of new propositions from earlier ones, but of the formulation for the first time of propositions about a knowledge already possessed, in an infinite search which only approaches its goal asymptotically. This process too is an explication. Here too there is a

---

* *Theological Investigations I,* trans. Cornelius Ernst, O.P. (Baltimore: Helicon Press, 1961), 63–65.

real connection between an earlier knowledge and later explicit propositions. But the starting point and the procedure are not those of the logical explication of propositions, which we first took as model for the development of dogma.

This case, which we are going to make use of in the field of dogma as a natural analogue for an explication other than that of the logical explication of propositions, must however be examined from a different angle. The lover knows of his love: this knowledge of himself forms an essential element in the very love itself. The knowledge is infinitely richer, simpler and denser than any body of propositions about the love could be. Yet this knowledge never lacks a certain measure of reflective articulateness: the lover confesses his love at least to himself, "states" at least to himself something about his love. And so it is not a matter of indifference to the love itself whether or not the lover continues to reflect upon it; this self-reflection is not the subsequent description of a reality which remains in no way altered by the description.

In this progressive self-achievement, in which love comprehends itself more and more, in which it goes on to state something "about" itself and comprehends its own nature more clearly, the love itself becomes ordered; it has an increasing understanding of what must properly be the foundation of its own activity, mirrors its own nature with increasing clarity, approaches as its goal, with an increasingly clear awareness, what it always has been.

Reflection upon oneself (when it is accurate) in propositions (that is, in *pensées* which the lover produces about his love) is thus a part of the progressive realization of love itself; it is not just a parallel phenomenon, without importance for the thing itself. The progress of love is a living growth out of the original (the originally conscious) love *and* out of just what that love has itself become through a reflective experience of itself.

It lives at every moment from its original source *and* from that reflective experience which has immediately preceded any given moment. Original, nonpropositional, unreflective yet conscious possession of a reality on the one hand, and reflective (propositional), articulated consciousness of this original consciousness on the other — these are not competing opposites but reciprocally interacting factors of a single experience necessarily unfolding in historical succession.

Root and shoot are not the same thing; but each lives by *the other*. Reflective consciousness always has its roots in a prior conscious entering into possession of the reality itself. But just this original consciousness possesses itself later in a new way, such that its life is now the accomplishment of that personal act of reflective apprehension by which it has enriched itself. Reflective consciousness would inevitably wither if its life were not rooted in the simpler basic consciousness, or if it were to reproduce this in every particular. The simple basic consciousness would become blind if, because it is richer and fuller, it refused to allow itself to grow out into a reflective consciousness involving *pensées* and "propositions."

18 • Intellectual Honesty and Human Decision*

It is not true to say that intellectual honesty is arrived at only when the subject is unencumbered (or, better, believes himself to be un-encumbered) by the burden of any radical human commitment. It is a great temptation to suppose that the intellectually honest person is the one who maintains a skeptical reserve; one who does not commit himself, and comes to no absolute decision; one who does indeed test all hypotheses but (the apostle's recommendation to the contrary notwithstanding) does not opt for any one of them; one who seeks to avoid error by refusing to commit himself definitively to anything; one who makes the radical mistake of taking the weakness of indecision (though it may be conceded that when this is only temporarily or partially present it may be a virtue) for the courage of the skeptic who is devoid of illusions.

No — intellectual honesty is not at all like this! Certainly there are cases in which human beings are so perplexed that they genuinely believe that they cannot truly proceed any further with a previously held position, as for instance in the case of an anguished atheist who in his despair can only see all existence as absurd, so that this absurdity hangs as a sort of Medusa's head before his eyes. Such a one must quietly reconcile himself to this position, and try to accept even this experience calmly. For even this, so the believer says, will be made by God to bring a blessing upon him. But he must not assert that this is the *only* proper attitude for the intellectually honest. How could he presume to know this ? How does he know that no one ever emerges from this purgatory or inferno? How does he know that no one ever has the strength to experience all this and still to believe?

In any case, whether we regard it as a curse or a blessing, freedom is inherent in our very nature (for our purposes it makes no difference how one interprets this freedom so long as one recognizes that it is

---

* *Theological Investigations VII*, 48–50.

inescapable). And this freedom of ours is such that it plays a vital part in even our most basic human decisions and attitudes. It is true of believers and unbelievers alike that there are no ultimate basic attitudes, no absolute standards of value or systems of coordinates for determining the meaning of existence such as might enable them to evade the struggles and hazards entailed in the responsible exercise of freedom.

This is not because it is sheer blind caprice that rules at this level, but because at this level it is no longer possible to separate one's basic views from the exercise of one's freedom. Hence it is that one who seeks to set himself free by being a skeptic, who refuses to commit himself or to make any position wholeheartedly his own on the grounds that he is anxious to avoid all danger of error — such a one does not remain free but has actually committed himself in the worst possible sense.

For he is living his life, living it once and for all, and thereby carving out a course that is irrevocable. In the very act of living his life he stands committed. If in spite of this he attempts to live without self-commitment, in a certain sense to remain in the dimension of "brute fact" and the biological, and if he attempts by these means to return the "entrance ticket" which admits him to the sphere of freedom and decision to remain "neutral," then this is itself in its turn a decision, and it is quite impossible to explain why there should be any better grounds for arriving at this particular decision than at any other.

Furthermore, there is no such thing as remaining poised in some dimension which is *prior* to decision. The attempt to remain neutral, therefore, is in practice only the refusal to bring one's powers of speculative thought to bear upon the decisions entailed willy-nilly in the fact of living one's life at all. For in this there is one decision at least which we must arrive at (even if our speculative thought upon the subject is only at the incipient stage): whether life is to be regarded as absurd or as filled with ineffable and mysterious meaning.

In short: intellectual honesty commands us to have the courage to make basic human decisions, however weighed down we may feel by uncertainty, darkness, and danger. For these obstacles are inevitably entailed by the fact that the minds with which we make our human decisions are finite and historically conditioned. And these minds of ours, while fully recognizing the disadvantages to which they are subject, still must decide.

Once this has been said, it must again be reiterated: we have to allow for the case of one who, in all responsibility and in accordance with the ultimate dictates of his conscience with regard to truth, finds himself so perplexed that he believes himself bound in duty to remain undecided upon many questions, and, indeed, as it seems to him, upon the most ultimate questions of all, in order to be true to that conscience; one who believes himself bound with all the resources of his spirit to keep an open mind and not to give any definitive answer in the sphere of speculative thought.

Such a one may, and indeed must, remain open to his conscience dictates. The enlightened believer will have only two points to make about this: first, that there is one thing that no one person can know about another. Suppose a person takes up such a stand at some point, whether proximate or remote, in the course of his existence. No one can know whether a decision made at that particular point does not ipso facto entail a definitive decision against the sacred as providing existence with its meaning. But neither does the individual have the right to bow down in worship before that particular meaning, when it is still remote from his own experience, merely on the grounds that the other feels himself compelled so to bow down, from a similar position of remoteness.

Second the believer, faced with someone who, in the name of responsibility to the truth and intellectual honesty, is maintaining with difficulty his openness to the question to which, as it seems to him, there is no answer, will draw his attention to the fact that even this decision, namely, that he can find no answer, does in fact constitute an assent to that which the believer himself calls the divine and blessed mystery of his existence; further, that the one who finds himself unable to find an answer has simply not yet been favored with the courage to define explicitly for himself that which he is already implicitly acknowledging in his life by the silent eloquence of his actions.

19 • The Divided and Enigmatic Nature of Humanity*

Recent decades in European cultural history have taken a strange turn for many people. They have experienced themselves as free and untrammeled, as answerable only to themselves and to the law of their own being, as autonomous persons. Wanting to be free, they fought against tutelage of every kind whether of church, state, society, convention, or custom. They fought for freedom, free science, free love, and

---

* *Von der Not und dem Segen des Gebetes* (Freiburg i. Br.: Herder, 1978), 28–31. Trans. Daniel Donovan, University of St. Michael's College, Toronto.

laissez-faire economics, for freedom of thought and of the press, freedom to organize and a thousand other freedoms. It was often a great and honorable struggle, but sometimes also a foolish rebelliousness and lack of restraint that confused freedom for self-destructiveness with true freedom.

While people were still raising the battle cry of freedom, they suddenly fell into in a strange kind of slavery, a slavery from *within*. In the heart of those who, because they had rejected every tie, every church and dogma, seemed so free, there unexpectedly arose a power that attacked and reduced them to slavery. To the extent that they rejected any external imposition of generally accepted norms and of binding principles of thought and action, they did not become free but fell under the sway of other powers that dominated them from within: instinct, ambition, lust for power, sexuality and pleasure. At the same time they experienced the inner powerlessness of crushing concern and insecurity, of loss of meaning, of anxiety and radical disappointment.

Another odd thing happened. Those who were thus engaged in struggling for their rights and their freedom inevitably had to take themselves very seriously. In their own eyes they became more and more precious and important. Their own inner life as the place where they could hope to affirm their distinctiveness became the object of an ever more radical self-affirmation, an ever more intense analysis, an ever more passionate love. The more they plumbed their own depths, the more they embarked on journeys of discovery into their inner life, the more ruthlessly they sought to ground the secrets of their hearts in science, art, and poetry, the more what they discovered became dubious. They wanted to discover themselves and in themselves the autonomous person in all his or her inviolable dignity.

After all the depth psychology, psychiatry, existential philosophy, and anthropology in which all the sciences come together in order to develop an understanding of human existence in all its depths including the unconscious, they discovered that at the deepest levels of their being they were not themselves but a vast and frightening chaos of anything and everything in which human beings are really only chance intersections of dark, impersonal forces, which arising out of blood and soil or genetic structure or a collective soul or nothingness — yes, why not even nothingness? — come together arbitrarily for a moment and flow uncontrollably through humans as through conduits, from one unknown to another. All that remained of the ego, the proud, glorious, individual ego was something like a cork bobbing on a vast sea driven to and fro by dark, ultimately nameless and blind forces. Do people today know any more of themselves than that they are a question within an unfathomable darkness, a question that only knows that the burden of its own questionableness is too bitter to be borne for any length of time?

As much as it may have turned out to be a journey into a limitless and pathless darkness, the preoccupation with the depths of human existence did produce *a* positive result: it revealed the breadth of human inwardness. What rational and enlightened people at the end of the nineteenth century knew about themselves in the light of their rather superficial education seemed so simple. They were constituted to some degree by the body but most of all by cleverness and reason. With science and technology on the rise and with metaphysics gradually disappearing like a morning mist before the brilliant sun, they were able to get to the bottom of everything. What counted for them were clear, scientific concepts, not mystery or mysticism or enthusiasm. The soul had no depths that even the shallowest person could not plumb. What in the landscape of the soul might appear as a swamp or a dangerous abyss could be handled with much enlightenment, a little morality, and good police.

Now, however, everything has become different. (This is true at least for some, because the word obviously has not gotten around to everyone.) People are beginning to notice again that on the foreground of the stage of human consciousness, that part exposed to the light of day, only a very small portion of what belongs to the soul is revealed. It has hidden depths to which, although they are a part of us, we have no easy access, depths in which demons may well lurk. It is full of mysterious psychic realities behind each of which stands something even more hidden and incomprehensible. It has depths in which in a concealed and almost unimaginable way there seems to be played out in advance by mysterious powers the life that we like to think of as exclusively the result of our own decisions. An ancient philosopher once said that the soul is in a certain sense all things. It is a truth that we have experienced and suffered in a new way. Those who attempted to ground themselves in themselves have fallen into an unfathomable abyss.

And so we have become indefinable and enigmatic to ourselves. There is within us a confusion of drives and possibilities, and we do not know which of them is the decisive one. How are we to understand ourselves?

20 • Individuality and Community*

Human existence, wherever we may meet it, is always found to be existence in the world, is always necessarily being with others, community. But each community will also be different according to the particular spheres into which human life unfolds. It may be an external joining of forces for the acquisition of an external necessity of life: a community of work. Here people are brought together by their common external activity, by a third thing which is as yet extrinsic to the human person.

The community of effort may consist in sharing in the creation of spiritual works of universal validity: science, art, law. These objective spiritual products are indeed, as such, independent of the arbitrary whim of the individual, and yet they do have a closer relationship to a person's being, insofar as they can come into real existence only as sustained by the spiritual experience of the individual: they strive for realization only in him.

And so from them, and from the work which they demand, arises the *community of spirit.* These spiritual products are communicated by means of speech. It is speech which first makes it possible to cooperate in the same spiritual work. Moreover, it brings the human being the possibility not only of pointing out such objective spiritual realities, such truths existing in themselves, but also of opening himself and revealing himself, of giving to the spiritual insight of others the possibility of penetrating with comprehension into one's own secluded, intimate interior. After all, only in speech (which does not necessarily mean sound) can the personal, spiritual countenance of a spiritual being be grasped, for this is always codetermined by liberty and therefore cannot be deduced from any other source. And so community of spirit can be extended by speech also into the community of those who reveal themselves by speaking.

Since such an unveiling of the inner secluded being of each person in himself avoids profaning the sacred character of the personal mystery only if it be offered and accepted in a love which makes of the two so much one that it is not an indifferent stranger who is allowed to enter into the sanctuary of one's being, the community of those who reveal themselves to one another by the spoken word refers us of itself to the community of love and must be conceived as its development. Thus we have the third kind of community we must distinguish, the *community of love.* It is founded upon a kind of mutual sharing of one's personal being, which is carried by love over into the other and inter-

* *Theological Investigations III*, 263–66.

mingles with his. Here the basis of community is no longer a third term in which people meet one another: in the love of person for person they meet one another in themselves.

But does this mean that in this highest form of human community the human person can carry his own being over into the inner sanctuary of the other to such an extent that he is able to surround with loving care everything there? Or are there spheres in the individual which are beyond the reach even of such love? Or, to ask the question this time from the viewpoint of the "beloved": Are there in him spheres whose essential meaning is such as to withdraw them from immediate, intimate sharing by another?

Yes: death — to begin with the clearest case — is a matter for each in himself alone with no reference to anything outside him. Everyone must die his own death for himself in supreme loneliness. But if it be true that all life points of itself constantly forward to death, that it is all the time a process of dying, then clearly death is merely a more obvious indication that there is present in the existence of everyone a deeper region in which the person is left to himself, a line of being pointing to himself alone.

In death it just becomes unavoidably evident in all its clearness that everyone has to make something of himself, to do and to suffer something by himself alone. What region of being is it, then, which reveals itself in death, which issues in it as its ultimate conclusion, which gives itself its final mark and seal in it?

It must be something in which the human being has to do simply with himself as such, something which is strictly his own task, which he alone can fulfill and in which no one else can substitute for him. But this is the case only where he himself is, in the strictest sense of the word, the task, where he is at once doer and deed, where doing and what is done are the same and both identical with himself. This is the case with human liberty, where with the whole force of the person's nature he gives its ultimate meaning and character to his whole being, where he forms his own existence into what he wants to be. Here he is essentially alone.

For the doing and what is done are inalienably his, they are as much his own as he is himself. For his action is the forming of his eternal physiognomy, it is himself in his eternal uniqueness. And hence only he himself can ever perform this act of eternal destiny. Everything that is done to a person, everything that happens to him, remains subject to the ultimate pronouncement of his liberty, in which he is still capable of understanding and accepting his lot (what is done to him, what is allotted to him); so everything that remains on this side of that ultimate personal verdict is not yet what finally counts in the human person.

Only to a being that is not free is its "lot" really its destiny. For the free being his destiny lies in himself. The choice which God has put into our hands we cannot confide to the care of any other.

But when the person with his whole being is called to a free decision about himself, he finds himself without intermediary before his God. For God is the beginning and end of this being, the norm of every decision, and also its ideal and exemplar, even when it is a case of that supremely personal actualization of the individual's being which is outside the uniformly regular and therefore not to be brought within the compass of any humanly accessible rule.

Consequently, in such a case God is still always there. He is not alongside one like a second being. He it is in whom we live and move and have our being. Indeed, in God alone do we possess in the first place that milieu and atmosphere which first renders possible and supports our innermost and most personal decision. This it is which is deepest and ultimate in us, and yet God is deeper than we are at our deepest level. He is beyond what is ultimate in us. And therefore God — and God alone — is not someone who has to wait in trembling expectation upon that word and decision of a person by which he strives to understand and form himself. God is before us, his willing and acting are therefore also before the person's inmost decision. God does not superimpose himself on an already constituted human being; God is already involved in his very constitution by his knowledge and action. He guides the hearts of kings (and in matters of the heart all are sovereigns); he has mercy on whom he wills in order that this person may have mercy on himself.

21 • The Child*

First and foremost the child is a *human person*. Probably there is no religion and no philosophic anthropology which insists so manifestly and so strongly upon this point as one of its basic presuppositions as does Christianity: the point, namely, that the child is already a human person, that right from the beginning he is already in possession of that value and those depths which are implied in the name of a human being. It is not simply that he gradually grows into a person. He *is* a person.

---

* *Theological Investigations VIII*, trans. David Bourke (New York: Herder and Herder, 1971), 37–43.

As his personal history unfolds, he merely realizes what he already *is.* He does not seek about in a void of indefinite possibilities ranging from all to nothing, to see what he can achieve by chance. He is equipped as a human being, given his allotted task and endowed with grace to perform it right from the very outset with all the inexpressible value and all the burden of responsibility which this entails. And this, because it comes from God and because his personal history, in spite of being inextricably bound up with the history of the cosmos and of the life principle as a whole, is related with absolute immediacy to God himself, to his original creative and inalienable design for him.

The child is the person whom God has called by a name of *his own,* who is fresh and unique in each individual instance, never merely a "case," a particular application in the concrete of a general idea, *always* having a personal value of his own and therefore worthy to endure forever. He is not an element in a process advancing and receding incalculably like the tides, but the unique explosion in which something final and definitive is constituted.

The child is the human being who is, right from the first, the partner of God; he who opens his eyes only to keep that vision before him in which an incomprehensible mystery is regarding him; he who cannot halt at any point in his course because infinity is calling him; who can love the smallest thing because for him it is always filled with the all; he who does not feel the ineffable as lethal to him, because he experiences the fact that when he entrusts himself to it without reserve he falls into the incomprehensible depths of love and blessedness.

The child is the person, therefore, who is familiar with death and loves life, does not comprehend himself but knows this, and precisely *in* this (provided only that he commits himself to the incomprehensible one in trust and love) has understood all, because thereby he has come into God's presence.

The child is a human being; the one, therefore, who always lives in a spirit of fraternity, leads a life of infinite complexity, knows no law other than that of endlessly journeying on and of great love and of that adventure which he can only recognize that he has come to the end of when he stands before God in his absolute infinitude. This is how Christianity views the human person and it sees all this already present in the child. And for this reason it protects the child while it is still in its mother's womb. It takes pains to ensure that the sources of life are not poured away upon the trifles of the lowlands of mere lust and desire. It has reverence for the child, for the child is a human being.

The child is a human being *right at the very outset.* Christianity is aware of the mystery of that beginning which already contains all present within itself, and yet still has to become all; the beginning which is the basis and foundation of all that is to come, its horizon and its law, and yet at the same time cannot even come to its own fullness except in what has still to come in the future.

Thus the state of childhood, too, is regarded as the beginning of the state of personhood. The child is already spirit and body united in a single entity. It is already nature and grace, nature and person, possessing itself yet exposed to the influence of the world and of history, and for all this it has still to become all things in the future. What is already present in the child has still to be realized, to become actual in experience.

And this unity which exists between the beginning and the stage of full development is itself in its turn a mystery which a human being lives and to which he is subject, but which he does not preside over or control by his own power. It is only when his final completion has been attained that this origin of his is revealed to him; the origin in which he was set on his course. For he began as a child and as a child of God. It is not until evening that the morning has completely passed away.

Childhood is a beginning in *two different senses.* The assertions of Christianity do not make reality in general, and above all the reality of the human person, any simpler than it in fact is. Thus Christianity has the courage to recognize the duality which the human being experiences in his existence even in the very beginnings of that existence.

Now the person's existence as an individual is historically conditioned, and viewed in this light he is not simply *pure* beginning, unaffected by anything that has gone before. In spite of the immediacy to God which is his right from his origins as that unique and particular creature, fresh from the hands of God, he is the beginning which springs up in the midst of a preexisting context, a history already wrought out by the human person before this particular individual arrived on the scene.

And this history is, right from the outset, also a history of guilt, of gracelessness, of a refusal to respond to the call of the living God. The history of the guilt of humankind taken as a unity right from the beginning of that history regarded as a single whole is also a factor in the history of the individual. The love which brings grace to the person, the love in which God himself with the fullness of his life gives himself to the individual is not simply, or in any obvious sense, an intrinsic element in a love which God might have born right from the beginning toward a humanity which did not fall into sin.

Rather, it is a love which endures despite the fact that sin rose to power in history right at the origins of the human race. In terms of the history of human existence this is the situation which the language of tradition calls original sin. It is a situation which radically and interiorly affects the individual, and in consequence of which the individual can count upon the grace which he needs, on the sheer proximity of God to shelter and sanctify him, not right from the beginning and in the very nature of humanity as such, but only in virtue of the redemption wrought by Christ.

And for this reason Christianity knows that the child and his origins are indeed encompassed by God's love through the pledge of that grace which, in God's will to save all humankind, comes in all cases and to everyone from God in Christ Jesus. Christianity cannot on this account regard the origins of childhood as a sort of innocent arcadia, as a pure source which only becomes muddied at a later stage and *within* the sphere of human cares in which the human being can control and guide his own course. It cannot view childhood as though prior to this stage it was simply the same as when it came from God as its eternal source, or as though for this reason, even in the context of the actual personal history of the individual and of humankind, childhood might once more be wholly purified of every kind of blemish.

No, Christianity views even childhood as already and inevitably the origin precisely of that person to whom guilt, death, suffering, and all the forces of bitterness in human life belong as conditions of his very existence. But since all this remains within the compass of God, of his greater grace and his greater compassion, therefore this realism with which Christianity reacts to the very origins of the human being in the child and its beginnings is far from being any kind of implicit cynicism.

Christianity's awareness of the guilt and tragedy which belong even to the beginning is, on the contrary, the necessary outcome of its awareness of the blessedness of grace and the redemption which overcomes this guilt and tragedy, and which comes both before and after it. For this is precisely the grace and redemption which the Christian experiences and to which he submits himself.

The child is a *child.* As soon as we look more closely into what is said about the child, especially in scripture, we notice that in reality it is almost always *presupposed* that we already know what a child is, so that no explicit information on this point is given to us. Thus the word of God itself indicates that we should rely upon the infinitely complex experiences of our own lives and our contacts with children in those lives as well as on the experience of our own childhood. It is the totality of this experience as summed up in the word "child" that holy scripture draws upon when it tells us that we must become as children, that we are "children" of God by grace, that even children can come to the messiah, and that they both need and are capable of attaining to the kingdom of heaven, that they can believe in Jesus, that to give scandal to them is a crime to be punished by a terrible death.

Thus scripture and tradition alike presuppose that we already know precisely *what* a child really is far more than they tell us this explicitly or treat of it as a distinct question. They leave it to our experience to determine what a child is, and what it means to be a child. But when we consider this experience of ours is it not dark, complex, and conflicting in character? Most certainly it is.

But even as such, it is sanctioned by scripture and tradition, and in this sense we are obliged to put up with the obscurity and complexity of our experience of childhood, not to try to iron out the complexities, but to endure them and still manage to be true to our own experience of children in arriving at an idea of what a child is. This is, in fact, only in conformity with the basic principles of which we have already spoken, namely, that the child is the human being himself in his incipient stages, and, what is more, the human person as divided within himself right at the beginning of his life and from the beginning onward.

In accordance with this, the genuinely Christian understanding and the Christian experience of the child is both idealistic *and* realistic at the same time. The New Testament, no less than antiquity, the Old Testament and Judaism, shows itself aware of the factors of immaturity and weakness in the child as can plainly be sensed not only in the writings of Paul (1 Cor 3:1; 13:11; 14:28; Gal 4:1–3; Eph 4:14; Heb 5:13), but also in the words of Jesus himself in the parable of the children in the marketplace who are sulky in their play (Mt 11:16ff.).

But this does not mean that the "little ones" are lightly estimated by Jesus in accordance with the attitude prevailing among his people and at his time. The children can serve him as examples of lack of false ambition, of not seeking for dignities or honors, of modesty and lack of artificiality in contrast to their elders, who are unwilling to learn anything from them (Mt 12:2ff.; 19:13 ff.). When Jesus holds up the child to us as the prototype of those for whom the kingdom of heaven is there, it cannot be said, even in a relative sense (much less in an absolute one), that what he is thinking of is its innocence. What is implied in this saying in which he holds up the child to us as an example is something far more important: that we can be like children in being receivers and, as such, carefree in relation to God, those who *know* that they have nothing of themselves on which to base any claim to his help, and yet who trust that his kindness and protection will be extended to them and so will bestow what they need upon them.

And thus without glorifying children or failing to recognize the radical insufficiency of their natures, Jesus does see in children those whom he can receive lovingly into his heart. This is what he means when he says "Of such is the kingdom of heaven" (Mt 19:14). They are those with whom he identifies himself. The woes he pronounces are designed to protect them against scandal, and, as he sees it, there is an angel who watches over their salvation and who continuously beholds the countenance of the Father in heaven.

For these reasons childhood is, in the last analysis, a *mystery*. It has the force of a beginning and a twofold beginning at that. It is a beginning in the sense of the absolute origin of the individual, and also the beginning which plunges its roots into a history over which the individual himself has no control. Childhood has the force of a beginning such that the future which corresponds to it is not simply the unfolding of some latent interior force, but something freely sent and something which actually comes to meet one. And it is not until this future is actually attained that the beginning itself is unveiled in its significance, that it is actually given and comes to its own realization, as a beginning which is open to the absolute beginning of God who is utter mystery, the ineffable and eternal, nameless and, precisely as such, accepted with love in his divine nature as he who presides over all things.

Such a beginning as this cannot be otherwise than mysterious. And because it is a mystery, and because as a beginning it bears all one's future life within itself, therefore life itself is mysterious, something which is already endowed with a certain autonomy, albeit in a hidden manner, and freed from external control. Hence, too, provided we reverently and lovingly preserve this state of being delivered over to the mystery, life becomes for us a state in which our original childhood is preserved forever; a state in which we are open to expect the unexpected, to commit ourselves to the incalculable, a state which endows us with the power still to be able to play, to recognize that the powers presiding over existence are greater than our own designs, and to submit to their control as our deepest good.

In this state we become guileless and serene — serene in a Mozartian sense even in those cases in which we weep and are overcome by dejection, because even these tears we accept as they are sent to us, recognizing that the sadness which they express is ultimately a redeemed sadness. And when our powers are at an end, we realize in a childlike spirit that our task too is at an end, since no one is tried beyond his own strength. When we take up this attitude, we make the mystery the protection and defense of our lives. We are content to commit them to the ineffable as sheltering and forgiving, to that which is unspeakably close to us with the closeness of love.

It is not as though the child as such has already achieved this in any fully developed sense. But this is how we see the person who, in spite of the perilous state in which he stands, is open to such self-commitment to the protection of the mystery of existence, recognizing that the duality of his nature is always more than compensated for by the deed of God wrought upon him.

And therefore the kingdom of heaven is for those who are children in this sense when, on the basis of this attitude of openness, and not without a certain *metanoia*, they become what they are — precisely children. Now this also implies, however paradoxical it may appear, that we do not really know what childhood means at the beginning of our lives until we know what that childhood means which comes at the end of them; that childhood, namely, in which, by God-given repentance and conversion, we receive the kingdom of God and so become children. It is in this sense that we only recognize the child at the beginning of life from the child of the future. And in the light of this, once more, we can understand that childhood invokes a mystery, the mystery of our whole existence, the ineffable element in which is God himself.

22 • The Challenge of Growing Old*

Old age is a special challenge in the Christian life. Human life, which is governed by what is human and therefore by what is Christian, is not a series of periods differing only in their biological and physiological characteristics. The biological difference, which is easy to see, permeates the human being in *all* his dimensions. In more profound philosophical and theological terms, this connection could also be seen the other way round: *because* the human being as a free temporal spirit has a history, he has a period of maturity and termination in a personal old age, and *therefore* a biological substratum which corresponds to that old age (which is primitively and positively intended) and makes it possible.

But we are not going to speak of this here. In earlier times, human societies (from primitive to highly developed cultures) awarded old age institutionally a particular role distinct from other people's. They acknowledged, at the social level, the human and Christian uniqueness of senescence.

For example, there was a council of wise elders, a minimum age for admission to high office, social customs which respected older people, a place of honor, a special dress, the council of elders as bearers of tradition, of law, of the administration of justice and of the control of "resources," and so on. Today experience and the passing on of experi-

---

* *The Religious Life Today*, trans. V. Green (New York: Seabury Press, 1976), 77–81.

ence are not so unequivocally tied to old people, and the latter often find themselves pushed rather to one side as inmates of old folks' homes. There is talk of the elderly as burdens on society. An age limit is set for certain social positions (even the cardinals' right to vote for a pope).

Yet, conversely, groups of old people can form something like "pressure groups" in politics, either through their own efforts or simply because of a top-heavy structure of the age pyramid, and we revolt against that. Ultimately it is simply that much has been changed in society and its relation to the elderly by the fact that proportionally there are many more old people in the population than before, their numbers have risen, their rarity value has dropped. Their function in society cannot be the same as in the past.

In any case old age has special characteristics (which are both privilege and burden) not given in any other period of life. The wisdom literature of the Bible pointed out a long time ago that a person can be mature and fulfilled many years before his time. But if one is to understand such an optimistic assertion (as a general observation) about a young person who is young psychologically and not only in years (in rapid inner age), such an assertion, strictly speaking, can only laud the fact that so fortunate a youth has filled and exhausted *his* period of life in an exemplary fashion. But it cannot seriously maintain that he has reaped in his early years, on the battlefield of his life, what one can actually sow and harvest only on the field of old age.

Old age is a grace — both mission, and risk — not given to everyone, just as, in the Christian understanding, there are other possibilities and situations reckoned as graces which are granted to some and withheld from others. That must be seen and accepted as part of "God's will." In this connection we should not take facile comfort in the ultimately erroneous thought that old age, like many other life situations, is a merely external situation which does not terminate in the definitive sequel of life but is merely like a costume in which a person plays a role in the theater of life which remains extraneous to himself, which he simply drops at death, which does not — even transformed — end in the personal definitiveness we call eternal life. Such an opinion (only superficially pious) does not take the human person's history really seriously. "Eternity" is the (transformed) definitiveness of history itself. Whether a person dies young or dies old, he takes this temporal destiny of his into his definitiveness as an inner moment of it.

Therefore growing old is a really serious matter. It is a grace, a mission, and the risk of radical failure. It is a part of human and Christian life which (like every other part of life) has its irreplaceable importance, one without substitutes. That is particularly true since old age must be understood not simply as life's running out but as life's "coming to definitiveness," even when that happens under the paralyzing influence of slow, biological death. More or less, the same thing may be said of old age as is said of death in its Christian understanding. We undergo death not in medical cessation but in the length and breadth of life, with all its different phases. But we cannot go into that here in any detail.

23 • The Pilgrimage of Life*

When we read of the Magi in the first twelve verses of the second chapter of St. Matthew, we are really reading our *own* history, the history of our own pilgrimage. Led by the star, three Magi from far off Persia struggled through deserts and successfully asked their way through indifference and politics until they found the child and could worship him as the savior-king.

It is our history that we read there. Or better: it *should* be our history. Do we not all have to admit that we are pilgrims on a journey, people who have no fixed abodes, even though we must never forget our native country? How time flies, how the days dwindle down, how we are eternally in change, how we move from place to place. Somewhere, and at some time or other, we come into existence, and already we have set out on the journey that goes on and on, and never again returns to the same place.

And the journey's path moves through childhood, through youthful strength and through the maturity of age, through a few festive days and many routine weekdays. It moves through heights and through misery, through purity and through sin, through love and through disillusion. On and on it goes, irresistibly on from the morning of life to the evening of death. So irresistibly, so inexorably does it move on that we often fail to notice that we fancy ourselves to be standing still, because we are always on the move and because everything else also seems to be going along with us, everything else that we have somehow managed to include in the course of our life.

But where does the journey lead? Did we find ourselves — when we awoke to our existence — placed in a procession that goes on and on without our knowing where it is leading, so that we have only to settle down and get accustomed to this motion, learn to tolerate it, and conduct ourselves in an orderly and peaceful fashion, and not dare to consult God's will to find out where this procession is really going?

---

* *The Eternal Year*, 42–48.

Or do we actually look to find a goal on this journey, because our secret heart knows that there is such a goal, however difficult and long the road might be? Is the human being merely a point in the world, in whom the world's nothingness is personified?

Does our spirit glow, only to realize painfully that it emerged from the darkness of nothingness to sink back into it again, just as a shooting star glows for a moment when it travels through our atmosphere on its dark journey to the empty universe? Do we run the course only to lose the way in the end? And does not the heart and the mind dare inquire beforehand about the law of the road, without growing stiff in terror over the speechless, helpless shaking of the head which is the only answer? Or cannot such a question be asked? But who could forbid the heart such a question?

No, we know very well that *God* is the goal of our pilgrimage. He dwells in the remote distance. The way to him seems to us all too far and all too hard. And what we ourselves mean when we say "God" is incomprehensible: ground of all reality; sea to which all the brooks of our yearning make their way; nameless "beyond" behind all that is familiar to us; infinite enigma that conceals all other enigmas in itself and forbids us to seek their definitive solution in what we know or in what can be experienced here on earth; boundless immensity in purest simplicity, in actuality, truth, light and life and love.

To him flows the huge stream of all creatures through all time, through every change and every succession. Does not our poor heart also have to set out to seek him? The free spirit finds only what it looks for. And God has promised in his word that he lets himself be found by those who seek him. In grace he wills to be not merely the one who is always a little farther beyond every place that the creature on pilgrimage has reached, but rather to be that one who really can be found, eye to eye, heart to heart, by that small creature with the eternal heart whom we call the human being.

Behold, the wise men have set out. For their heart was on pilgrimage toward *God* when their feet pointed toward Bethlehem. They sought him; but he was already leading them because they sought him. They are the type of those who yearn for salvation, yearn in hunger and thirst for righteousness. That is why they did not think that the human person could dare omit his one step just because God has to take a thousand in order for both to meet. They were looking for him, for salvation, in the heavens and in their heart. They sought him in seclusion and among people, even in the holy writings of the Jews. They see a strange star rise in the heavens. And God in his blessed kindness even allows their astrology, foolish though it may be, to succeed this once, because their pure hearts did not know any better.

Their hearts must have trembled a little when the theory drawn from their obscure knowledge of the Jewish expectation of salvation and from their astrology should now suddenly become applied in practice in a very concrete journey. Their bold hearts must have been a little frightened. They would almost have preferred that their hearts not take quite so seriously the noble principles of theoretical reason, principles so foreign to reality and so unpractical. But the heart is strong and courageous. They obeyed their hearts, and they set out.

And suddenly, just as they leave their native land behind them, at the moment when they dared to take the leap into a hazardous venture, their hearts become light, like the heart of one who has ventured all and is more courageous than is really possible — according to everyday proverbs. They travel over tortuous paths, but in God's eyes their path led straight to him because they sought him in sincerity. It frightened them to be so far from their familiar native country, but they knew that in journeying everything has to be transformed, and they marched on and on in order to find the native land that will be more than a tent by the wayside. They knew from their own deeds (life is more than the mind's theories) that to live means that we are always changing, and that perfection means passing through many levels of change.

So they journeyed. The way was long and their feet were often tired, their hearts often heavy and vexed. And it was a strange, painful feeling for their poor hearts to have to be so entirely different from the hearts of others, engrossed in their everyday affairs with such perfect stupidity, who looked with pity at these travelers walking past on a journey that was so uselessly squandering their hearts. But their hearts carry on to the end. They do not even know where the courage and strength keep coming from. It is not from themselves, and it just suffices; but it never fails as long as one does not ask and does not peer inquisitively into the empty reaches of the heart to see if something is inside, but bravely keeps on spending the mysterious contents of the heart. Their hearts cannot be intimidated. They do not look arrogantly upon those whom they pass. But they do move past them, and think, "He shall also call these people, when it pleases him to do so. But we dare not be disloyal to the light, just because it does not yet seem to shine for them."

From the scribes in Jerusalem they got sullen information; and a cunning commission from a king. But from these sources their ears heard only a heavenly message, because their hearts were good and were full of yearning. And when they came and knelt down, they only did what they had in reality always been doing, what they were already doing during their search and journey: they brought before the face of the invisible God now made visible the gold of their love, the incense of their reverence, and the myrrh of their suffering. Then their path led out from the land of salvation history. They disappear from our horizon as quietly as they came (like those who die). But whoever has once poured out his whole heart for the star, to the very last drop, has already encountered the adventure of his life in that single instant.

These men, who have disappeared from our horizon, had royal hearts. If their real journey continued on to the invisible, eternal light — indeed, if it really began only when they returned to their own country — then such royal hearts found their definitive home. And that is why we want to call them by that joyous name of days gone by: the holy kings from the East.

Let us also step forth on the adventurous journey of the heart to God! Let us run! Let us forget what lies behind us. The whole future lies open to us. Every possibility of life is still open, because we can still find God, still find more. Nothingness is over and done with for him who runs to meet God, the God whose smallest reality is greater than our boldest illusion, the God who is eternal youth and in whose country there dwells no resignation. We roam through the wilderness.

Heart, despair not over the sight of the pilgrimage of humankind, the pilgrimage of human beings who, stooped over with the burden of their suppressed terror, march on and on, everyone, so it seems, with the same aimlessness. Do not despair. The star is there and it shines. The holy books tell where the redeemer is to be found. Ardent restlessness urges us on. Speak to yourself! Does not the star stand still in the firmament of your heart? Is it small? Is it far away? But it is there! It is small only because you still have so far to go! It is far away only because your generosity is thought capable of an infinite journey. But the star is there! Even the *yearning* of the inner person for freedom, for goodness, for bliss, even the *regret* that we are weak, sinful people — these, too, are stars. Why do you yourself push clouds in front of the star — the clouds of bad temper, of disappointment, of bitterness, of refusal, clouds of sneering or of giving up — because your dreams and expectations have not been realized?

Throw down your defenses! The star is shining! Whether or not you make it the lodestar of your journey, it stands in your sky, and even your defiance and your weakness do not extinguish it. Why should we not, then, believe and go on the journey? Why should we not look to the star in the firmament of our hearts? Why not follow the light? Because there are people like the scribes in Jerusalem, who know the way to Bethlehem and do not go there? Because there are kings like Herod, for whom such news of the messiah only means inconvenience for their political plans, kings who even today make an attempt on the child's life? Because most people remain sitting at home with the sullen worldly wisdom of their narrow hearts, and consider such adventurous journeys of the heart as nonsense? Let us leave them and follow the star of the heart!

How shall I set out? The *heart* must bestir itself! The praying, yearning, shy but honest heart, the heart well versed in good works sets out, and journeys toward God. The heart that believes and does not become soured, the heart that considers the folly of goodness to be more sensible than the cunning of egoism, the heart that believes in God's goodness, the heart that will lovingly let its guilt be forgiven by God (this is harder to do than you may think), and that lets itself be convinced by God of its secret unbeliefs — that is not surprised at this, but gives glory to God and confesses — such a heart has set out toward God on the adventurous journey of a royal heart.

24 • Human Death*

The mystery of death is only distorted if it is viewed on the same level as the end of the animals and is conceived as a biological event which, in a certain way, has only adventitiously anything to do with the human being as such, owing to the fact that his biological end concerns something which is rather more than a purely material living being. The real nature of death as a total and totally human event is completely missed if one takes cognizance only of the traditional definition: a separation of body and soul.

For then death is seen only in one of its consequences, instead of in its essence, and we would have to force artificially and retrospectively into the expression "separation of body and soul" those elements which constitute the special character of human death, namely, the personal finality of the end, the fully human and indissoluble unity of act and suffering in death, the hidden outcome of a life which is reaching its full accomplishment, the birth of that eternity, which is not simply added as the continuation of earthly time, but is rather the fruit of a final, free, and absolute decision growing out of time itself, precisely inasmuch as it has been a human time.

From these and similar features of human death, which cannot be discussed here systematically in all their interconnections, let us select the one which has special bearing on the present topic: the voluntary character of death as such. Death is an act. Certainly it is the extreme case of something undergone, the event in which

---

*On the Theology of Death, trans. C. H. Henkey, revised by W. J. O'Hara , 2d edition (New York: Herder and Herder, 1965), 84–86.

what is obscure and beyond control disposes of the human being, ineluctably taking him from himself, in the ultimate depth of his existence.

Yet at the same time death is an act, and in fact the act of all acts, a free act. A person may be unconscious at the moment he is dying. Death may take him by surprise, if what we mean by death is the instant at the end, in which the death which we all die throughout our lives oriented toward this moment is manifested. But just because we die our death in this life, because we are permanently taking leave, permanently parting, looking toward the end, permanently disappointed, ceaselessly piercing through realities into their nothingness, continually narrowing the possibilities of free life through our actual decisions and actual life until we have exhausted life and driven it into the straits of death; because we are always experiencing what is unfathomable and are constantly reaching out beyond what can be stated, into what is incalculable and incomprehensible; and because it is only in this way that we exist in a truly human manner, we die throughout life therefore, and what we call death is really the end of death, the death of death.

Whether this death of death will be the second death or the killing of death and the victory of life depends completely on us. Hence, because death is permanently present in the whole of human life, biologically and in the actual concrete experience of the individual person, death is also the act of human freedom.

It must however be observed that the human person has to die his death in freedom. He cannot avoid this death imposed upon him as the work of his freedom. How he dies his death and how he understands it depend on the decision of his freedom. Here he does not carry something imposed on him, but what he chooses himself. That is to say that in the face of his immortality, the person must freely face death. He is asked how he wills to do this.

For when he opens the eyes of the mind at all, the individual inescapably sees the end, sees it all through life, perhaps dimly and not explicitly, perhaps deliberately avoids looking at it, "overlooks" it, but sees it all the same in doing so. And by freely accepting this human life oriented toward its end, the person freely accepts the movement toward the end.

But the question is, how does the human person understand this end toward which he freely moves, since he cannot do anything else than run the course of his life in freedom? Does he run protesting, or lovingly and trustingly? Does he view his end as extinction, or as fulfillment? People usually do not express their answer to this problem in abstract statements about death, but they live and tacitly carry out their free conviction through the actions of their life and the deeds of their daily existence, even when they do not know explicitly that by their life they are interpreting their death.

25 • On Work*

Work is, of course, the characteristic feature of what we call our working day or weekday. There are people who surround it with a halo and sing its praises as the expression of humanity's glorious creativity. Some misuse it also (and how often, too!) as a means of escape from themselves, from the secret and mystery of their own being, from that anguish which torments them in their striving after objective certainty.

But the true sense of work is to be found somewhere between these aberrations. It is neither the highest and noblest thing in life nor the drug prescribed to deaden the impact on the human person with respect to the mystery of his existence. It is just work, that's all, a tiresome thing but tolerable enough, nothing to make a fuss about, for it comes round regularly with the clock. It sustains life on the one hand and wears life out on the other. It is a thing that cannot be avoided, but when it does not deteriorate into unbearable drudgery, it can be reasonable and friendly.

Work never comes quite natural to us. Even when it starts out briskly as the setting in motion of our highest creative impulses, it has the habit of lapsing into the jog trot of dull, repetitive routine. It is perpetually plagued, too, with the need to make provision for the unexpected and for the drawback that what a person does not do from inner incentive but under compulsion from outside and at the behest of strangers, he merely puts up with; his heart is not in it.

Moreover, work requires the activity of the individual worker to be coordinated with the activities of the group and subjected to the regulation of a given rhythm; the work of each is a contribution to a common objective which, however, no individual worker has personally chosen. This calls for obedience and self-denial all round.

The first thing, then, that theology has to say about work is simply that it is, and will continue to be, work, tiresome and monotonous and involving the surrender of the worker's will to the demands of the daily round. As time goes on, work may become more and more productive as the result of new ideas and inventions, but, so far as the person is

*Belief Today, trans. M. H. Heelan, Ray and Rosaleen Ockenden, and William Whitman (New York: Sheed and Ward, 1967), 17–19.

concerned, its limits are fixed by biological factors which impel him steadily and inexorably toward the grave.

Work always has reciprocal relations with the world outside the workshop; they tend to be unstable, for the outside world can never be brought under complete control. And so work is likely to remain work, and to continue to be as scripture described it — a sign of the fallen state of humankind, a sign of the disharmony between what is within us and what outside, between freedom and necessity, flesh and spirit, the individual and society; and this disharmony can be overcome only by God's grace.

The phenomenon of sin, which is the result of this disharmony, gave rise in Christ (who was, of course, sinless) to the phenomenon of bodily redemption. Christ delivered us not only from death, the most radical effect of our fall, but from every other outward sign of our separation from God. In this way he has delivered us also from the tiresomeness, drabness, and (virtual) depersonalization of work. Through the grace of Jesus Christ, therefore, and not through any merit inherent in itself, work, when "done in the Lord," helps to form in us the attitude and disposition which God desires in those he invites to his eternal feast: that patience by which we can bear everyday witness to our faith, that faithfulness and detachment which spring from the Christian sense of responsibility, and that unselfishness which is the very food of love.

26 • Patience*

As soon as the subject of "patience" is introduced, one is immediately reminded of the opening words with which Cyprian of Carthage introduced his treatise on patience seventeen hundred years ago, to the effect that the listeners must already have what the speaker is trying to recommend to them, namely, patience, for without this he would not have any listeners at all. And in fact, if one were totally devoid of patience in any sense, then one would never be able to acquire it either, because the very act of acquiring it in itself entails the exercise of patience over a long period.

Some degree of patience, therefore, must be numbered among the basic attitudes of the human being, one that is deeply rooted in his nature. The reason for this is that it must, to a certain extent, support itself. It must already be there in order that it may be summoned up.

---

* *Theological Investigations VII*, 279–81.

It must be ready to hand in order that the higher degrees of it may be sought after.

Patience derives from something which is fundamental to the nature of the human being as such, namely, that he is both a person endowed with spirit and simultaneously a being subject to the limitations of time. Beings that are of their nature eternal have no need of patience. They have no further perfection to achieve beyond their present state. They do not look for anything further because the sheer eternity with which they are endowed means that their natures are already in the state of their due fullness and perfection.

Nonspiritual beings do not need patience because their consciousness is always limited to the present moment, and precisely in virtue of this fact they know nothing of continuous change as such, of the past and future as these affect them, even though they themselves are constantly undergoing a process of development and change.

But we are beings who are both endowed with knowledge and subject to time. We carry our past with us, and in our cognitive faculties we already reach out for that which has still to come in the future. We actually and consciously live through the process of change to which we ourselves are subject. The interplay of past and future acquires reality as our experience. Not only are we unable to hold back the process of transition and change, we cannot even conceal from ourselves our own inability to do this.

Our existence is governed by a single and uninterrupted process of change. We are empowered to see this existence of ours as a whole and to recognize as a law of its very nature that it must constantly press on to further developments. To recognize and accept this fact is what we might call "existential" patience, patience at the existential level. We patiently accept the fact that our existence is subject to change in this way, and yet that it retains its unity throughout the process of change.

But the very fact that we are this kind of being and cannot avoid being so, that we have this kind of nature and cannot escape from it — this in itself, once more, presents us with a task to accomplish, one in which it is possible for us to fail; something which we must do for ourselves, exercising courage and faithfulness, being consciously and deliberately true to our own nature in order to achieve it. For a person endowed with freedom and with spiritual faculties has in his makeup factors which are given, inevitable, and inescapable, and at the same time other factors which are mysterious and unpredictable. It is this that sets him the task of exercising his freedom responsibly.

The human person, therefore, must freely and consciously come to terms with this special quality in his own nature. He must recognize and accept himself as a being subject to constant and purposeful change, and at the same time endowed with cognition. He must not suppose that he is able to interrupt this change, must neither attempt to hold himself back at the stage which he has already achieved, nor attempt prematurely to achieve a stage which still awaits him in the future. In other words he must patiently accept the change to which his existence is subject for what it is, and recognize that it has a meaning and is directed toward a goal. Only then can he be said to be patient with this existential patience of which we have been speaking.

The point to be realized is this: What the individual has to recognize and accept with this elemental kind of patience is not simply those factors arising here and there in his life which are disagreeable, and which seem to him to be part of a meaningless lot imposed upon him from without. What he has to tolerate and endure with patience at its deepest and most elemental level is rather *himself* — himself considered as one who is on the way to some future goal, one who may neither stop and remain where he is, nor suppose that he is journeying into an empty and indeterminate void without any ultimate point of arrival. Our impatience with everyday vexations is simply a sign of the fact that at a deeper level of our life we have not succeeded in freely attaining to the virtue of this existential patience and making it our own.

There are those who seek to cling to the circumstances of the present moment with its pleasures, its successes, its seeming self-sufficiency even though all these are, of their nature, precisely transient and fleeting; those who cannot let go of what belongs to yesterday until what belongs to tomorrow has already been proved to be harmless and reassuring; those who cannot freely enter into new situations which seem to be more arduous or to hold out less promise, who cannot entrust themselves to the darkness or to that which is under the control of another; those who take fright at the silent power which presides over and controls our lives, and which is God, even though he alone knows and decides where this transitory existence of ours began and where it will end. Such as these are incapable of attaining for themselves this virtue of existential patience. They betray the fact that they do not possess this virtue by the impatience which they exhibit in their daily circumstances, and when they meet with the shortcomings, the pains and toils which belong to human life even at its most commonplace and everyday.

27 • On Illness*

Preaching God's word to the sick can be painfully embarrassing. The preacher himself is reasonably healthy, but has to speak to those who are not. He feels that they must be thinking: "It's easy for him to talk. He's in good health." Nor is it any help if he can say that he too has known serious illness. For he wasn't preaching when he was ill. And if he had been able to preach, he really doesn't know how he would have coped.

So all I can do at the beginning is to ask the sick to be ready to listen — even though they are not paid for it — almost in the same way as a traveler rightly looks at a signpost, notes its directions, and then leaves it behind him. The sick listener must also keep in mind the fact that illnesses are of so many kinds that it is almost misleading to speak of sickness in a general way. And yet, in speaking to the sick, it is impossible to address each one precisely with reference to his particular illness. For this reason too we are completely dependent on the benevolence and sympathetic understanding of the listener.

In the very last resort, the one whole life, in the midst and in spite of all the variety of things with which it is filled, is one single, great question, to be decided freely by each person: whether he will surrender himself trustfully and hopefully to the insoluble mystery we call God; whether he will entrust himself to it as to the holy, forgiving love which gives all things their ultimate meaning and gives itself to us.

Sickness is one of the events in which this one final question of life, which as such is always present, presses more clearly, is more rigorously stated, and demands our answer. For the sick person is, or at least can be, more lonely; he cannot so easily escape from the question which is really himself. His pain warns him of life's uncertainty; he is perhaps faced by the question which imminent death silently poses.

The sickness which a person experiences is not simply a fact, but also a task. We experience sickness itself as our own task, already fulfilled in one way or another, for good or ill, something which we do ourselves and do not merely endure. We should not merely react to sickness: this we have always done and the sickness which we experience in the concrete is always and already that sickness out of which our own reaction to it emerges and returns to us.

---

* *Opportunities for Faith*, trans. Edward Quinn (New York: Seabury Press, 1974), 135–37.

It is a reaction of confidence and resignation in one, or, also in one, a reaction of discouragement and distrustful obstinacy, an insistence that we must remain healthy in absolutely all circumstances. We should have confidence and resignation in one. Confidence: that is, the will and the joyous hope soon to be healthy again, because there are signs enough of this. But also resignation, accepting sickness because we can mature through it and because even death itself is not yet the end of hope and not the triumph of that absurdity which we experience at the surface of life, but blessing and grace. We should have both together: confidence and resignation.

If a sick person is close to death, he might ask how he can make his illness a task to be fulfilled with confidence and resignation, since his very situation means that he lacks the strength of mind to do this: to preach this sort of thing to him is pointless and to preach it to others, who do it without being told, is superfluous. It is true that, when our very last resources of mind and heart are really beyond our control, our task ceases and anything to be done about us and for us is left to the incomprehensible and gentle power of God, so Christians believe, and we have nothing more to do.

But we can never capitulate in advance and claim that we can do nothing more until we really have done everything and have made the effort without considering whether we can make it, but simply keep on with it. Fighting and not yielding, we should let God's providence overpower us. As long as we are alive, confidence and resignation in one should count as our task, to which we devote all our strength even to the very last.

A part of our task in sickness is to remain always open to others. Sickness can confront a person with himself in a fruitful way. But it can also have the bad effect of making us selfish, turning us back upon ourselves. It is a wonderful sign of the way in which an illness can lead the sick person to maturity if, as a result of it, he becomes kinder toward his own family, if he has a cheerful word of consolation and interest for them and does not merely expect others to speak to him in this way.

Even a sick person should make an effort not to take for granted the ministrations of those who are nursing him, as if it simply could not be otherwise. He should practice toward those on whose ministrations he depends those virtues which otherwise make relations between people human and Christian: gratitude, politeness, attentiveness to the human being in the other with his own troubles, the nobility of mind which can generously overlook the faults of others, even when they are burdensome to ourselves and are imposed on us by those from whom we think we have the right to demand everything because we are ill and in a public hospital.

Most of what I have said up to now is perhaps open to the objection that I've been moralizing, and this is the last thing to do when talking to the sick. This may be true. But I think it is both hard and at the same time liberating to regard the sick person as open to an appeal, as capable of action, and to tell him that he can still give his heart in confidence, resignation, in love for the other, even in the midst of his distress, and, if he does so in God's grace, it will liberate him and alone make his sickness what it really ought to be.

After all that has been said, it still remains true that sickness cannot be understood, that it is a part of a human being's incomprehensible lot which is not solved by any commendation of its blessing or by any complaint. There are questions which are answered only by leaving them unanswered and accepting them. If we attempt to answer them in any other way, we are deceiving ourselves and making use of mendacious ideologies to produce a pain-killing remedy which does not sustain us for long.

Among these questions, which must be accepted in silence, is also serious illness. Why this and not another, why me and not you, why just now and not at another time, why so hard to endure while also exhausting our strength, why so cruel also to those for whom the sick person is concerned, why leading so close to death, why death, why...?

Such questions cannot be avoided, and there are no answers which can solve them. If a person accepts the questions hopefully and without despair, without (at present) expecting an answer other than that which is already implied inwardly and mysteriously in the persistent question, he is professing his faith in God and his love, whether he knows this or not. And someone who accepts this question is already participating in the life, sickness, and redeeming death of him who in dying said two words which only together — but truly so — hold already the whole destiny of the person: the word acknowledging his being forsaken by God and the word that so gave his life into God's hands. The sick person who accepts the unanswered question lives by sharing in the life of Jesus, who cried on his deathbed, "My God, my God, why have you forsaken me?" who knew (as the Epistle to the Hebrews says) that it is a fearful thing to fall into the hands of the living God — whose awesomeness overwhelms us at these very hours — and who nevertheless said, "Father, into your hands I commit my spirit." Someone who lives with these two words of the Lord, who is sick and who, if God so decrees, dies, is in God's protection.

28 • Renunciation and Self-Realization*

Perhaps it is possible to say something of "psychological" importance even without psychology. Something said in a very abstract way can be concrete because it reveals more clearly what is universally valid but is easily obscured by things of secondary importance. Today one sometimes has the impression that people very often become unhappy because they want to be happy at any price. They are suffering from frustration anxiety: they think they might miss something, that something might escape them before they have to go; and at the same time they know that very soon they *must* go and that there is not much time left in which anything can happen to bring happiness. That is why they think that the most important thing is to take care not to let anything slip past them. But in reality this fear of not having consumed everything spread out on the table of life means that nothing is enjoyed: everything is merely "crammed" in, the digestion is spoilt. In the last analysis everything has escaped one after all, and nothing is really experienced because one wanted to experience *everything*.

It is easy to see that this is not the way. Everyone knows that really. For one only needs to bear this in mind — and here we use abstract terms, so that we can see better; the possibilities available to free action are always greater than what can be realized; one can never be everywhere at the same time; to embrace one possibility is always to renounce another, unless one had an unlimited lifespan. For a person always looks beyond what he has realized, and what he sees is not only the promise of new things to come, but also the renunciation of much, indeed, of everything except that minute portion which can be realized; there is much which will not come again, because it would only have been possible in the place now occupied by what has in fact been realized. Narrow reality is death to infinite possibility; the latter dies unborn in the womb of reality. All this, as we have said, is easy to see. The consequence is clear too, namely, that the ability calmly to let things go past is one of the great arts of life which are necessary to make our existence free and bearable.

But in reality this ancient wisdom of the necessity of "moderation" does not banish our frustration anxiety. For something in us asks, Why should we calmly let what is possible go by, and only hang on to so little? Perhaps we have got hold of the wrong thing and have let the right thing,

---

*Theological Investigations IX, trans. Graham Harrison (New York: Herder and Herder, 1972), 253–57.

the thing which can unbind us and hence redeem us, pass by. How is one to know? One cannot seriously test every possibility *as such;* one can only test the things one has *really* examined; consequently, one never knows, in being modest and restrained, whether one has put one's money on the wrong card or not.

So instead, "everything" — everything as far as possible, that is — must be tried, even if one knows that it is not really possible. Frustration anxiety continues to gnaw away; it knows it is senseless, but that does not kill it. The wisdom of moderation becomes just a mean-spirited means of frustration anxiety in an effort to extract as much as possible out of the empty fullness of what is possible. And so such wisdom is ultimately ineffective. All that remains is the desperate conviction that this does not work either. There is not only frustration anxiety. It also possesses a person. It does not energize life, but it steers it, and into the void.

Are we then left with only the alternative of renouncing the thirst for existence, renouncing the will, "seeing through" any initiation of action as the beginning of meaninglessness? But is it possible? Does it make sense? Is not this too another "art of living" in disguise, is it not again merely another form of the blind impulse of life, trying in this way to reach its goal, in this case at least the happiness of silencing its own wishes? And is it really possible on one's own, or is it the absurd attempt secretly to arrive back at a total yes by a total yes to a total no? For the activity of the will to live is itself still an act, and consequently it affirms what it wants to surrender. *Can* a person let go of himself totally, so that he can attain the calm ability to let go of individual possibilities, if he has not been taken out of himself? But by whom?

If death is life, that is, if to relinquish the particular is actually not to lose but to gain everything, frustration anxiety is defeated. Not as if the void were in itself actually the "fullness" — we do not really seriously believe that cheap dialectical trick of words. The "fullness" is not to be pieced together from the sum total of particular finite possibilities, but lies ahead of us as the one, whole, "absolute" future, which in Christian terms we are accustomed to call "God." He is ready to give himself to us if we succeed in "letting go."

It is true that we do not immediately come to possess this fullness as soon as the absolute future (which contains the as yet unappropriated fullness and desires to give itself to us) enables us to let go. Whenever this marvel really takes place, and we simply let go, calmly in harmony with it, frustration anxiety is conquered at its very roots. Petty reality is taken up as the promise of an infinite future, not as something which means the latter's death. We cannot "ascertain" that all this happens to us in actual fact; we can only do it as the final act, an act which does not take pleasure in itself nor affirm itself consciously, an act which is given to us as our own particular act.

"God," "grace," "justification," "freedom," "faith," "gift," "task," and all the other fundamental Christian concepts are realities in this event of calm renunciation, and they are secretly understood as such. Everything implied by these words — the abandoning of oneself in the hope of finding the incomprehensible fullness — takes place in the ultimately inaccessible depths of one's freedom when this freedom calmly "lets go," that is, lets the particular die, believing in hope that in this way (and ultimately *only* in this way) the whole, the fullness, "God" will be received. This is not done only *in order to* receive the whole, for the particular too may and must be willed in a spirit of calmness.

In Christian terms this kind of renunciation in letting things die in faith and hope is called taking up one's cross. As an act of *free* acceptance it takes a step in the direction of death's inevitability and is thus a preliminary exercise in the acceptance of that particular death which is our unavoidable lot. Scripture calls this "denying oneself and taking up one's cross."

Where human qualities are *fully* developed, even if this cannot be subjected adequately to concrete reflection, the acceptance (of the cross) does not only occur in freedom's uttermost depths (together with its permanently ambiguous objectifications in the history of the individual); it does not merely "occur," it also knows about itself, though in hope, not in the manner of reflection. Since a human person is an intercommunicative being and is only able to see himself clearly in another person, this acceptance knows about itself by perceiving another person — *the* other person — taking up his cross as the event of life. In him it can be seen that there is such an acceptance. As Christians we believe that we see Jesus of Nazareth as this other person taking up his cross. And in doing so we do not believe that he is only a sort of "productive example" for us which really might just as well not be there. We believe rather that God lays the cross upon us and, within it, his own fullness, because he wills Jesus of Nazareth and has accepted and worked in him as his own life in time and history.

The true "productive example" is the one which really empowers and enables us. For this reason Jesus of Nazareth is the "source of salvation," the redeemer. We Christians acknowledge him as the crucified; we confess him as the "risen" one, since, in the unity of the experience of the Spirit, who sets us free to take up the cross, and of the testimony of his disciples, we believe that in this death the arrival of God's life itself has taken place in the *whole* of human reality.

The person who, in a hope which no longer seeks to reassure itself, relinquishes himself in the depths of the mystery of existence, in which death and life can no longer be distinguished because they can only be grasped together, actually believes in the crucified and risen one, even if he is not aware of it (in conceptual terms). But to know of him explicitly is good and brings the promise of salvation. It is an assurance that one will be given one's own cross to take up as one's own, ultimate act of freedom.

Taking up one's cross has many forms. In what follows we shall dwell particularly on two of them. The first is to accept being disappointed — being "undeceived" — by life. At the very latest this happens in death, provided that one does not actually try to deceive oneself about it — which never quite comes off. In this connection it must not be forgotten that dying already takes place in life, for life is itself "death in abundance" (*prolixitas mortis*), as Gregory the Great says. The second form, perhaps the most radical case of disappointment — of being "undeceived" — occurs when one loves although this love does not, or no longer, "pays off," nor tries to take pleasure in itself as a heroic selflessness. The attempt to produce this kind of pleasure — which is at bottom impossible — is the aim of all those glorifications of life to be found in sentimental novels *à la Reader's Digest,* where everything ends happily without any genuine dying. Is it not true that many exponents of psychotherapy use this same treatment? Cannot one avoid facing the fact that life is a *dying* if one arranges things cleverly?

There are probably only two ways of living: being driven by frustration anxiety, and the acceptance of the cross, which, whether acknowledged as such openly or not, is the cross of Christ. Strangely enough, each of these ways of life can mimic the other. Probably it must be so; otherwise we could "judge" ourselves. What the psychologist gets direct hold of is never one or other of these ways of living in itself, but at best its objectification, which is always equivocal. What seems to be a neurotic, even culpably incurred frustration anxiety, can be that very dying by which, in a hidden acceptance, the cross of life is taken up in suffering. What presents a "healthy" and "balanced" appearance can be the result of a frustration anxiety which is driving the person to avoid taking up his cross.

Basically one need not be afraid that the acceptance of one's cross necessarily leads to passivity and resignation in the face of the concrete tasks of life. The individual who does not fear death, or rather, who accepts the abiding fear of death, can enjoy the particular good things of life which come to him because they are a genuine promise of the absolute future. He is able to risk his whole self. He is free to love without sparing himself. He does not need to overtax this life's happiness and thus spoil it.

29 • Laughter*

By "laughter" we do not mean the sublime heavenly joy that is the fruit of the Holy Spirit, nor the joy that "spiritual persons" like to talk about in soft, gentle terms (a joy that can easily produce a somewhat insipid and sour effect, like the euphoria of a harmless, balanced, but essentially stunted person). No, we mean real laughter, resounding laughter, the kind that makes a person double over and slap his thigh, the kind that brings tears to the eyes; the laughter that accompanies spicy jokes, the laughter that reflects the fact that a human being is no doubt somewhat childlike and childish. We mean the laughter that is not very pensive, the laughter that ceremonious people (passionately keen on their dignity) righteously take amiss in themselves and in others. This is the laughter we mean. Is it possible for us to reflect on this laughter? Yes, indeed, very much so. Even laughable matters are very serious. Their seriousness, however, dawns only on the one who takes them for what they are: laughable.

Is laughter such as we mean proper even to a spiritual person? Naturally, if it doesn't suit us, we should not toil over it. Such laughter must come from the heart — yes, from that heart that not even the saint is complete master of. In order to be a spiritual person, then, one does not need to force this laughter when it doesn't come of itself. We do not doubt the spiritual worth of someone who doesn't laugh in this way. By no means. The question is only this: whether or not the spiritual person must rightly call this laughter into question, whether or not he has to attack it as incompatible with the dignity of a spiritual person. No! Not at all! Let us explain and justify this laughter. When we do so, laughter shall smilingly tell us very serious things.

In the most pessimistic book of the Bible we read: "There is a time to weep and a time to laugh; a time to mourn and a time to dance" (Eccl 3:4). This is what laughter tells us first of all: there is a time for everything. The human being has no fixed dwelling place on this earth, not even in the inner life of the heart and mind. Life means change. Laughter tells us that if as people of the earth we wanted to be always in the same fixed state of mind and heart, if we wanted always to brew a uniform mixture out of every virtue and disposition of the soul (a mixture that would always and everywhere be just right), laughter tells us that fundamentally this would be a denial of the fact that we are created beings. To want to escape from the atmospheric conditions of the soul — the human soul that can soar as high as the heavens in joy and be depressed down to death in grief — to want to escape by running

---

* *The Eternal Year,* 49–55.

under the never-changing sky of imperturbability and insensitivity: this would be inhuman. It would be stoical, but it would not be Christian. This is what laughter tells us first of all.

It speaks to us and says, "You are a human being, you change, and you are changed, changed without being consulted and at a moment's notice. Your status is the inconstancy of transformation. Your lot is to stop and rest at no one status. You are that manifold, incalculable being that never factors out without a remainder. The being that can be broken down into no common denominator other than that which is called God — which you are not, and never will be. Woe to you if, while immersed in time, you should want to be the never-changing, the eternal; you would be nothing but death, a dried up, withered person.

"Laugh with me," says laughter. "But not all the time! Always and everywhere I want to be quite little, like God's great and noble creatures. Only the laughter of hellish despair should be continual on this earth. Only the devils should laugh like this, not you. But laugh sometimes, and laugh with ease. Do not be afraid of laughing a little stupidly and a little superficially. In the right spot this superficiality is deeper than your toiling thoughtfulness, which was suggested only by a spiritual pride, a pride that does not want to endure being a mere human being. There really is a time for laughter; there has to be, because this time, too, is created by God. I, laughter, this little childish simpleton who turns somersaults and laughs tears, I am created by God.

"You cannot encircle and capture me. You cannot put me down on your spiritual budget in so many precisely figured columns, like nickels, dimes, and pennies. It is hard to prove that, according to God's will and according to the principles of ascetical and mystical theology, I am supposed to crop up, to turn my somersaults just where I please. But for all that, I am one of God's creatures. Let me into your life, then. Don't worry, you won't lose anything by letting me in. The fact that you shall still weep and be sad takes good care of that worry."

Laugh. For this laughter is an acknowledgment that you are a human being, an acknowledgment that is itself the beginning of an acknowledgment of God. For how else is a person to acknowledge God except through admitting in his life and by means of his life that he himself is not God but a creature that has his times — a time to weep and a time to laugh, and the one is not the other. A praising of God is what laughter is, because it lets a human being be human.

But it is more, this harmless laughter. True, there is a laughter of fools and of sinners, as the wise Sirach instructs us (21:20; 27:13), a laughter which the Lord cursed in his woes (Lk 6:25). Naturally, we do not mean this laughter: the evil, unhappy, desolate laughter which seeks to help us escape the incomprehensibility of history by trying to comprehend this drama of history as a cruel, silly trick, instead of revering it as a divine comedy, serene and confident that its meaning will one day be clear to us.

We are thinking here of that redeeming laughter that springs from a childlike and serene heart. It can exist only in one who is not a "heathen," but who like Christ (Heb 4:15; cf. 1 Pt 3:8) has thorough love for all and each, the free, detached "sympathy" that can accept and see everything as it is: the great greatly, the small smally, the serious seriously, the laughable with a laugh. Because all these exist, because there are great and small, high and low, sublime and ridiculous, serious and comical, because God wills these to exist — that is why this should be recognized, that is why everything should not be taken as being the same, that is why the comical and the ridiculous should be laughed at. But the only one who can do this is the person who does not adapt everything to himself, the one who is free from self, and who like Christ can "sympathize" with everything; the one who possesses that mysterious sympathy with each and every thing, and before whom each can get a chance to have its say.

But only the person who loves has this sympathy. And so, laughter is a sign of love. Unsympathetic people (people who cannot actively "sympathize" and who thus become passively unsympathetic as well) cannot really laugh. They cannot admit that not everything is momentous and significant. They always like to be important and they occupy themselves only with what is momentous. They are anxious about their dignity, they worry about it; they do not love, and that is why they do not even laugh. But we want to laugh and we are not ashamed to laugh. For it is a manifestation of the love of all things in God. Laughter is a praise of God, because it lets a human being be a loving person.

But it is more, this harmless, innocent laughter of the children of God. All that is fleeting is an image, even the pleasant and rather casual laughter of everyday life. And in this case we do not even need to discover the likeness. The word of God itself has declared the real analogies. Scripture accepts this laughter that almost always borders on the trivial. Laughter, not merely a smile. Laughter, not merely joy and confidence. And scripture makes this small creature (which, of course, will have to grow dumb and dissolve into nothingness when it treads the halls of eternity) into a picture and likeness of God's own sentiments. So much so that we would almost be afraid to attribute to God the harsh, bitter, scornful laughter of pride. The thrones in heaven laugh (Ps 2:4). The Almighty laughs at the wicked man, for he sees his day already approaching (Ps 37:13). Wisdom, speaking of the ungodly, tells us that the Lord shall laugh them to scorn (Wis 4:18).

God laughs. He laughs the laughter of the carefree, the confident, the unthreatened. He laughs the laughter of divine superiority over all the horrible confusion of universal history that is full of blood and torture and insanity and baseness. God laughs. *Our* God laughs; he laughs deliberately; one might almost say that he laughs gloatingly over misfortunes and is aloof from it all. He laughs sympathetically and knowingly, almost as if he was enjoying the tearful drama of this earth (he can do this, for he himself wept with the earth, and he, crushed even to death and abandoned by God, felt the shock of terror). He laughs, says scripture, and thus it tells us that an image and a reflection of the triumphant, glorious God of history and of eternity still shines in the final laugh that somewhere springs out from a good heart, bright as silver and pure, over some stupidity of this world. Laughter is praise of God because it is a gentle echo of God's laughter, of the laughter that pronounces judgment on all history.

But it is still more, this harmless laughter of the loving heart. In the beatitudes according to Luke (6:21), this is what we find: "Blessed are you who weep now, you shall laugh!" Of course this laughter is promised to those who weep, who carry the cross, those who are hated and persecuted for the sake of the Son of Man. But it is *laughter* that is promised to them as a blessed reward, and we now have to direct our attention to that point.

Laughter is promised, not merely a gentle blessedness; an exultation or a joy that wrings from the heart tears of a surprising happiness. All this, too. But also laughter. Not only will our tears be dried up; not only will the great joy of our poor heart, which can hardly believe in eternal joy, overflow even to intoxication; no, not only this — we shall laugh! Laugh almost like the thrones; laugh, as was predicted of the righteous (Ps 51:8).

It is a most awful mystery, this laughter of finality, this laughter which will accompany the saved as they depart this drama of universal history, this laughter that on high will be the ultimate (as incessant weeping in the depths), when stage and auditorium of universal history have become empty forever.

But you shall laugh. Thus it is written. And because God's Word also had recourse to human words in order to express what shall one day be when all shall have been — that is why a mystery of eternity also lies deeply hidden, but real, in everyday life; that is why the laughter of daily life announces and shows that one is on good terms with reality, even in advance of that all-powerful and eternal consent in which the saved will one day say their "Amen" to everything that he has done and allowed to happen. Laughter is praise of God because it foretells the eternal praise of God at the end of time, when those who must weep here on earth shall laugh.

The seventeenth, eighteenth, and twenty-first chapters of Genesis tell a strange story, the story of Abraham and his wife: how he became the father of all believers in receiving the promise of a son, because he believed, against all hope, in God who makes the dead live and calls into being that which does not exist (Rom 4). In the telling of this promise and its fulfillment, it is also said that the father of all believers and his wife — she who in her hopeless old age bore him his son, from whom Christ is descended — laughed (Gn 17:17; 18:12–15; 21:6). Abraham threw himself on his face and laughed. Sarah laughed to herself. "God has made me a laughing stock," she says, when she had borne the son of promise. The laughter of unbelief, of despair, and of scorn, and the laughter of believing happiness are here uncannily juxtaposed, so that before the fulfillment of the promise, one hardly knows whether belief or unbelief is laughing.

Fools laugh, and so do the wise; despairing nonbelievers laugh, and so do believers. But we want to laugh in these days. And *our* laughter should praise God. It should praise him because it acknowledges that we are human. It should praise him because it acknowledges that we are people who love. It should praise him because it is a reflection and image of the laughter of God himself. It should praise him because it is the promise of laughter that is promised to us as victory in the judgment. God gave us laughter; we should admit this and — laugh.

30 • On Getting About*

Getting about is one of our most common everyday activities, so common that we never give it a thought until something turns up which restricts or prohibits the use of our legs. Then the ability to get about suddenly becomes a wonderful boon, a heaven-sent blessing. Human beings, unlike plants, are not tied to a circumscribed environment. They can seek out an environment for themselves, decide to change it, choose another and — off they go. The feeling of freedom that this ability to get about gives us is evident even as we go on our daily round, despite the fact that the direction of our steps is dictated by the demands of the job. All this going about breeds in us the spirit of the roamer, the seeker, who does not know where he is going, much less when he will get there. A time comes, however, when we feel we want to make for a definite goal and not just wander about aimlessly.

---

* *Belief Today*, 20–22.

We sometimes speak of a "walk" or "way" of life. Now we find in scripture that Christians were at first known as those "belonging to the Way" (Acts 9:2). When the Bible wishes to impress on us that we should not only listen to the word of God but practice it, it tells us that we must not only live in the Spirit, but "walk" in the Spirit. Again, one of the most time-honored elements in public celebrations, secular as well as religious, is a procession. Human life, too, is often described as a pilgrimage, and a pilgrimage certainly connotes an uncommon amount of getting about.

These are a few indications (there are many more) that our lives have long been likened to the primitive, natural, everyday phenomenon of getting about. And this purely physical activity of continually moving from one place to another warns us that we have here no sure abode. We are still wayfarers heading for a destination but uncertain of the way, pilgrims, wanderers between two worlds, beings in transition, borne along by some external power, but retaining the ability to guide and direct our course. We do not always succeed, however, in reaching the destinations we plan for ourselves.

We see, therefore, that the progress of a free and responsible human being as he goes on his everyday round typifies the person's whole existence. His faith reveals to the Christian the goal of his existence and assures him he will reach it. He is borne along incessantly by some power conscious of itself and of not having fulfilled its purpose, a power ever seeking, ever believing it will find its goal in the end, because (and how could it be otherwise?) that goal is God himself toward whose second coming, in the person of Christ, our own future moves inexorably.

So we have to keep on getting about, to keep on seeking our goal. The holy one, for his part, will come and look for us if we only go toward him, walk in his way. When we have found him — or rather when he has found us — we shall learn that our meeting had already been determined by the power that bore us on toward God, and that the stirring of that power within us was the sign that God had come to meet us. And that power is what we call God's grace.

31 • Seeing and Hearing*

Seeing and hearing are clearly the fundamental modes of human experience. To be able to say this we do not need to raise the old question of how many senses a human being actually possesses. Touch can perhaps be understood as a rudimentary form of seeing and it is clearly only in the domain of seeing and hearing that it becomes human experience, that is, that it presents another person or another thing as objectively perceived.

And what eater and smoker has not noticed that taste in the darkness is not fully itself? But even those who doubt this may take what we are going to say as meaning that hearing and seeing can be regarded as the particularly clear and exemplary kinds of spontaneous human experience generally. They need not therefore reject what follows as mistaken from the start.

Now a banal common-sense "philosophy" will regard hearing and seeing simply as two gates through which our human world and our environment enter into the domain of our subjectivity, as two bridges by which we cross the gap between "subject" and "object." Such everyday philosophy (that of Greco-Roman and Western provenance, at any rate) will simply accept those two gates and bridges as factual data, with the subconscious feeling that "in themselves" they could be quite different from what they are and would then convey quite different experiences. It will point out that other biological organisms clearly have quite a different sensory world, that because of our particular senses very much escapes us which in itself is just as directly present around us, that the actual senses we possess are a very arbitrary a priori filter (though biologically useful) which selects a priori, shuts out much, opens no access to many things.

We do not see infrared, we do not hear the acoustic waves which a bat uses with its "radar," we have no direct receptive organ for radio waves, and the like. Consequently, we only approach a wider range of material reality with the help of interposed apparatus. In short, we regard our powers of hearing and seeing more or less as an old wireless set which is unfortunately incapable of receiving short waves. Then at most we console ourselves for this primitive quality of our receptive mechanisms by saying that they are sufficient after all for the immediate indispensable purposes of life and in *that* respect are not badly constructed.

Clearly, however, this "common-sense philosophy" of seeing and hearing is too primitive. In the first place a genuine metaphysics of the

---

* *Everyday Faith,* trans. W. J. O'Hara (New York: Herder and Herder, 1968), 196–204.

human person cannot (though we cannot indicate the reasons for this here) regard our sense organs on the model of a microscope which is added to our will to see and which allows as much to be seen as its structure permits, this structure being independent of the person seeing. We do not merely *have* sense organs, we *are* sensibility. Our corporeality and therefore our sensibility is built from within, from the personal-intellectual subject himself.

It is the permanent mode in which spirit (i.e., the free subject open from the start to the totality of all possible reality) has of itself entered into the world. It cannot therefore be the case at all (if this view, which can only be indicated here, is correct) that the apparatus for hearing and seeing represented by our sense organs was fitted on to us from outside and could just as well be different. Their biological adaptation to their purpose is only intelligible as an expression of the fact that they are appropriate to us precisely as intellectual, personal beings who stand in real relation to the world generally, not just to our particular environment. (The dog as a nasal animal is, of course, from the biological point of view just as adapted by his sensibility to his life. So the question could be raised, for what purpose we have furnished ourselves with our apparatus precisely in this way.)

We must therefore say, however bold the thesis may be, that if a receptive spiritual nature as such (not ours, which is already retro-determined by its sensibility) "proceeds" and constitutes its "receptive apparatus" on the basis of its own purposefulness, it will hear and see just as we do.

Seeing and hearing are precisely the ways in which the spirit opening itself to the whole of reality as such admits this reality in direct encounter. (And this meeting which one goes out to and admits — by hearing and seeing — is ultimately meant as loving communication of corporeal spiritual persons in such a way that in it the promise of the absolute mystery of God is found. Seeing and hearing on the one hand and intercommunication on the other imply in their unity and difference the problem of the relation between the aesthetic and the moral and religious, which cannot of course be gone into here.)

Naturally it is impossible here to give grounds for this thesis of the origin of sensibility in spirit itself, which thereby shows itself to be sensitive by its very nature. This may be considered laughable, and as a warning it may be pointed out that someday on a distant star intelligent corporeal beings may be discovered who communicate with their environment by senses quite different from sight and hearing. It may be objected, too, that the present state of our scientific knowledge of the world proves that on the one hand the human spirit aims at the whole of the world's reality but that hearing and seeing directly offer only a tiny section of that reality. On this basis the spirit has to find its way indirectly into the totality.

Consequently, as a corporeal spirit it could certainly be conceived as having wider gates to the world from the start. Nevertheless, let this thesis stand, and the question raised what it involves if it is properly understood. In the first place it is not ultimately the case that hearing and seeing only furnish slight initial material which is elaborated by the scientific mind until this achieves its own self-constructed world of knowledge. On this view only the latter is the spirit's own, and at the same time nearest to the real world "in itself," as a conscious image of the objective world. And so the sensory material would only be a strange and ultimately amorphous intermediary between the objective world and the world of the spirit.

Because the spirit makes the sensibility proceed from itself as its own faculty (as Aquinas says) and retains it within itself ("the soul is the form of the body" [*anima est forma corporis*]), the spirit itself is perfectly in act when, in accordance with its nature as spirit (that is, on its own basis with its limitless horizon and with all that it is), it actually hears and sees, accomplishes that "turning" (one might almost use the term "conversion") to the image, without which there is no true knowledge, as Thomas knew, in his doctrine of the *conversio ad phantasma*, and Kant also, for whom a concept without a perception remains empty. The concrete form in its "light," given to it through the medium of colors, the articulate word with the intelligible perspective it implies, both with the infinity in which they stand, bring fully into act the spirit itself.

What is also given by or in addition to this visible and audible form is of two kinds, which must not be confused. An amalgam of the two must not falsely take on the appearance of being what the spirit in truth is seeking. First, there is the clear horizon of the spirit's limitless range; only in this is the concrete form what it is, standing out in relief but causing that horizon to be experienced when the form is seen or heard: the infinity of the enveloping mystery of holy silence. When we have forms heard or seen whose source is there, which lose themselves in that, cause that invisible and unutterable to be experienced, we have "primordial forms" (of nature or art) as, for example, the Apollo which Rilke contemplates in his poem, or "primordial words."

"Behind" these primordial forms there is nothing, for with them everything is present, the infinite mystery which in them is *there*. "How did St. Benedict see the world in a coal? — In all things everything is hidden and concealed," we read in Angelus Silesius (*The Cherubinic Wanderer*, IV, 159). Only if we see or hear in this way can we really see and hear. That we for the most part do not see and hear like that, but in a technical and utilitarian way see things as possible objects of active manipulation in the service of our biological self-affirmation, whether everyday or scientific, is no argument against it, but only against us in our inauthenticity and mediocre anonymity.

We have laboriously to relearn such hearing and seeing today. What is called "composition of place" in religious meditation has its basis here. Similarly the doctrine of the "spiritual senses" in a long Christian tradition and the practice of the "application of the senses" in mystical contemplation in Ignatius Loyola. And a Christian would have to reflect here on what the First Letter of John says, "What we have heard, what we have seen with our eyes, what we have looked upon and touched with our hands, concerning the word of life...." He would have to realize that the meaning of the incarnation of God's Logos and the fundamental experience evoked here by John would be destroyed if we were to suppose that seeing and hearing are merely the spring-board which we leave behind in order to attain true knowledge of an abstract, nonsensory and wordless kind.

Second there is abstract, conceptual science. No one must despise it. It belongs to human beings, they must dare to undertake it, not only for his biological self-affirmation but because the human person is "spirit-in-world." It also belongs to the practical activity by which, not content with a purely contemplative relation to the world, he must fulfill himself.

But where philological and historical learning, all that belongs to the moral sciences of humanity, does not return to sight and hearing of concrete forms, they become empty talk. Where philosophy and theology are no longer in possession of fundamental words, they cease to be true philosophy and theology, language which subjects us to mystery.

And the natural sciences? They have certainly enormously extended knowledge and power over things. But if their mathematically formulated statements about functional relationships in the physical world are not to become pure mathematics and webs of formal logic, they cannot lose the connection of reference to what is directly given in sense experience. What they mean physically and not merely mathematically can always ultimately only be made intelligible on the model of objects of direct sight and hearing. They imply an intention to exercise power, directed ultimately at what we corporeally experience.

This widening of the biological vital space and theoretical knowledge of a scientific kind ultimately stands at the service of that spirit which becomes open to absolute mystery in simple spontaneous sight and hearing of the world around it or in loving interpersonal relationships. And so all sciences lead back to that fundamental seeing and hearing of the primordial forms through which the holy and enveloping mystery becomes known to a human being especially when the primordial form is the human person himself, the human face, the ever unique word of his love.

Is there not a conflict between seeing and hearing? Almost the whole Greek and Western tradition of philosophy has surely regarded the human person as contemplating the "phenomenon" of being, whereas Christian tradition from the Old Testament down to Luther's assertion that the ears alone are the organ of the Christian, has surely understood the word addressed to us with power, which brings what it utters, "passive" hearing as opposed to "active" gazing, to be the fundamental mode of authentic human existence?

Isn't the complaint made that people nowadays will not read (that is, hear) anymore, but only want to look at pictures? It would be a foolish undertaking to attempt to settle the dispute between eyes and ears and decide which of them derives more directly and more radically from the one source of authentic human life. Those who read in the Bible the saying of Jesus that the ears and eyes of his disciples were blessed (Mt 13:16) will perhaps not seek to settle the dispute at all because it is not a genuine one. For both are ways of possessing the world and both are modes of personal relationship and derive from the same ground. Together they form a single contact with the world and the one domain of the presence of the sacred mystery. We might simply say with Angelus Silesius (*The Cherubinic Wanderer* V, 351): "The senses are in the spirit all one sense and act; he who sees God tastes, feels, smells and hears him too."

But is it true that people today are changing from a humanity of the ear and the word into one of eye and sight? Of course it is quite conceivable for there to be epoch-making changes in the way the ultimate confronts a person (as, for example, people of the Old Testament had a book of God but were not allowed to make any image of God). But the change in question which is so much lamented at the present time might be explained much more simply, to the extent that it really exists.

One might say that through modern sciences in their almost limitless differentiation, through the enormous number of books, through the unimaginable character of the statements of modern natural sciences, through the "demythologizing" of theology (which always also involves the removal of pictures and images from it, however fatefully necessary this process may be), the amount of talk (and vocabulary) in contrast to earlier times, has increased so monstrously in comparison with what is visible, that the appetite for the pictorial is now at bottom merely a legitimate attempt to preserve a balance between seeing and hearing.

That empty talk is, as a consequence, paralleled by an equally futile and insatiable appetite for things to look at, is deplorable and threatening but not surprising. But a human being is "born to see and appointed to gaze." He can and must always relearn how to see. With the concentrated gaze which makes forms blossom out before him, in their purity and as they emerge from their roots in mystery. They may be forms in perfect simplicity and beauty, or forms which (like the crucified) inescapably represent what is incomprehensible from the dark depth of our destiny, forms which God has shaped or which we have composed for him. And because seeing is really the person's act (more than the passivity of hearing), the human being himself is manifested in seeing, steps before us, reveals himself in the way he sees and what he makes to be the object of his gaze.

According to scripture, in the individual's eyes we read his fear, his nostalgia, his pride, compassion, kindness, wickedness, ill-will, scorn, envy, and falsity. We make ourselves by seeing and form ourselves by gazing. But we have to learn how to see. It is not only the "effort of understanding" (Hegel) that is demanded of the person, but also the effort of "contemplation," because he has been given the grace of sight.

The sublimest of discourse is the last moment before silence falls, the silence which expresses the ultimate. The human being perhaps most easily learns to be silent when he is gazing. We Christians long for the "vision of God," and confess Christ to be the image of God (2 Cor 4:4) as well as his Word; it is therefore an important task and a holy, human, and Christian art to learn to see. We only think we have always been able to, and that nothing is easier. May we say, adapting a saying of scripture, He who has eyes to see, let him see? May we say that only those who have learned to see (with the eyes of love) will be blessed? Those who have learnt to see with an eye which is "sound" (Mt 6:22) have the true "view of the world."

32 • Primordial Words*

There are words which divide and words which unite; words which can be artificially manufactured and arbitrarily determined, and words which have always existed or are newly born as by a miracle; words which unravel the whole in order to explain the part, and words which by a kind of enchantment produce in the person who listens to them what they are expressing; words which illuminate something small,

---

* *Theological Investigations III*, 295–301.

picking out with their light only a part of reality, and words which make us wise by allowing the manifold to harmonize in unity.

There are words which delimit and isolate, but there are also words which render a single thing translucent to the infinity of all reality. They are like seashells, in which can be heard the sound of the ocean of infinity, no matter how small they are in themselves. They bring light to *us,* not we to them. They have power over us, because they are gifts of God, not human creations, even though perhaps they came to us through human beings.

Some words are clear because they are shallow and without mystery; they suffice for the mind; by means of them one acquires mastery over things. Other words are perhaps obscure because they evoke the blinding mystery of things. They pour out of the heart and sound forth in hymns. They open the doors to great works and they decide over eternities. Such words, which spring up out of the heart, which hold us in their power, which enchant us, the glorifying, heaven-sent words, I should like to call primordial words (*Urworte*). The remainder could be named fabricated, technical, utility words.

It is true of course that we cannot divide words once and for all into these two categories. This division refers much more to the destiny of words, which elevates them and dashes them to the ground, which ennobles them and degrades them, which blesses them and damns them — just as in the case of human beings.

We are not speaking here of worn-out words which are preserved, impaled like dead butterflies, in the showcases of dictionaries. We mean living words in their living being and movement, just as we utter them in propositions, speeches, and songs. Words have their history too. And as in the case of the history of the human person himself, there is only one true master of this history: God. In fact, God himself became the subject of this history when he spoke such words in the flesh of this earth and when he had them written as his own words.

Innumerable words, according to the use we make of them, are raised up to the ranks of the one type, primordial words, or — which is unfortunately mostly the case — slide down to the level of the other type, utility words. When the poet or the poor man of Assisi exclaims "water," what is meant is greater, wider and deeper than when the chemist, debasing the word, says "water" for his H_2O.

According to Goethe, water is like the human soul — you cannot substitute H_2O for that. The water which is seen by humans, which is praised by the poet, and which is used by the Christian in baptism — this water is not a poetic glorification of the chemist's water, as if he were the true realist. On the contrary, the "water" of the chemist is much rather a narrowed down, technical derivation of a secondary kind from the water of a human being. In the word as used by the chemist, a primordial word has been fated to sink down to the level of a technical word of utility, and in its fall it has forfeited more than half its being. In its fate is reflected the lot of humanity through thousands of years.

Let no one think with foolish superficiality that it does not matter whether a word has more or less content; that as long as one clearly knows what content a word and the concept it expresses have, everything is in order and one word is as good as another.

No, primordial words are precisely the words which cannot be defined. They can only be taken apart by being killed. Or does someone think that everything can be defined? It cannot. All definitions have constant recourse to new words, and this process must come to a stop with the ultimate words, whether these are absolutely the last possible words or merely those which constitute in fact the final point of the human person's reflective self-interpretation. And yet these ultimate words possess only that "simplicity" which conceals within itself all mysteries. These are the primordial words which form the basis of a human being's spiritual existence! They are given him. He does not arbitrarily construct them, nor can he cut them up into convenient pieces, which is what is meant by "defining."

This is all very obscure, someone will say. Granted, thinking which divides and recomposes the pieces like a mosaic is clearer and more easily grasped. But is it more true, more faithful to reality? Is "being" clear? But of course, says the shallow mind, that is being which is not nothing. But what is "is" and what is "nothing"? Whole books have been written, and from this ocean of words there has been obtained only a little jug of stagnant water.

Primordial words always remain like the brightly lit house which one must leave behind, "even when it is night." They are always as though filled with the soft music of infinity. No matter what it is they speak of, they always whisper something about everything. If one tries to pace out their boundary, one always becomes lost in the infinite. They are the children of God, who possess something of the luminous darkness of their Father.

There is a knowledge which stands before the mystery of unity in multiplicity, of essence in appearance, of the whole in the part and the part in the whole. This knowledge makes use of primordial words, which evoke the mystery. It is always indistinct and obscure, like the reality itself which by means of such words of knowledge obtains possession of us and draws us into its unsounded depths. In primordial words, spirit and flesh, the signified and its symbol, concept and word, things and image are still freshly and originally one — which does not mean, simply the same. "O star and flower, spirit and garment, love, sorrow and time and eternity!" exclaims Brentano, the Catholic poet.

What does this mean? Can one say what it means? Or is it not precisely an uttering of primordial words, which one must understand without having to explain them by means of "clearer" and cheaper words? And even if one had explained them with the most scholarly profundity, would one not have to return to these words of the poet, to these primordial words, in order to understand, in order intimately and truly to grasp, what it was that the long commentary "really" wanted to say? Blossom, night, star and day, root and source, wind and laughter, rose, blood and earth, boy, smoke, word, kiss, lightning, breath, stillness: these and thousands of other words of genuine thinkers and poets are primordial words. They are deeper and truer than the worn-down verbal coins of daily intellectual intercourse, which one often likes to call "clear ideas" because habit dispenses one from thinking anything at all in their use.

In every primordial word there is signified a piece of reality in which a door is mysteriously opened for us into the unfathomable depths of true reality in general. The transition from the individual to the infinite in infinite movement, which is called by thinkers the transcendence of the spirit, itself belongs to the content of the primordial word. That is why it is more than a mere word: it is the soft music of the infinite movement of the spirit and of love for God, which begins with some small thing of this earth, which is seemingly the only thing meant by this word. Primordial words (as one might explain it to the theologian) have always a literal meaning and an intellectual-spiritual meaning, and without the latter the verbal sense itself is no longer what is really meant. They are words of an endless crossing of borders, therefore words on which in some way our very salvation depends.

Are we perhaps here, in order to say, house, bridge, fountain, gate, urn, fruit tree, window,
At the most: pillar, tower... but to *say,* please understand, Oh to say, what the things themselves never intimately thought to be.... (Rilke, *Ninth Elegy*)

Only someone who understands these lines of the poet has grasped what we mean by primordial words and why they have every right to be, indeed must be, obscure. This does not of course mean that one may drape one's own confused superficiality with primordial words of this kind to pass them off as profound, or that one should speak in an obscure way where one could speak clearly. It means only that the primordial words reflect the human person in his indissoluble unity of spirit and flesh, transcendence and perception, metaphysics and history. It means that there are primordial words, because all things are interwoven with all reality and therefore every genuine and living word has roots which penetrate endlessly into the depths.

There is one aspect of these primordial words which we must consider more explicitly than we have done so far: the primordial word is in the proper sense the presentation of the thing itself. It is not merely the sign of something whose relationship to the hearer is in no way altered by it; it does not speak merely "about" a relationship of the object in question to the hearer: it brings the reality it signifies to us, makes it "present," realizes it and places it before us. Naturally the manner of this presentation will be of the most diverse kinds, depending upon the kind of reality evoked and the power of the evoking word. But whenever a primordial word of this kind is pronounced, something happens: the advent of the thing itself to the listener.

Something happens not merely for the reason that the human being, as a spiritual person, obtains possession of reality only by knowing it. It is not only the knower who obtains possession of the reality known by means of the word. The reality known itself takes possession of the knower — and lover — through the word. Through the word the object known is transferred into the person's sphere of existence, and its entry is a fulfillment of the reality of the object known itself.

Many a person will be tempted to think that being known is for the object a matter of indifference, which is attributed to it only externally. He will take this opinion to be a corollary of his unequivocal objectivism. To be sure, he will grant that the world is real *because* it is known by *God* and his love: in this one case reality is constituted by the very fact of standing within the sphere of God's light.

Leaving aside the fact that even this truth can be considered too superficially, our "objectivist" will deny that the case of the knowledge of reality by *other* knowers is in any way similar. It is of course true that the realities of this earth do not cease to exist, if no one apart from God knows them and recognizes them in his knowledge. And yet they are more fully themselves and arrive at the complete fulfillment of their being only when we know and speak them. They themselves acquire, to use the expression of Rilke, an intimacy of being when they are known. Why?

Let us reflect upon this: Does not everything have its being in the whole? Does not even Sirius in the gloom of the subspiritual already faintly tremble whenever a child throws its doll out of the cradle? Is not each person completely himself, entirely brought to that fulfillment which he should have and which God has eternally planned for him, only when *all* persons are made perfect in the kingdom of God? Must not all individuals wait for their ultimate fulfillment upon the complete fulfillment of all things?

Now, in the realm of the spirit is not the completion of the individual precisely the completion of his knowledge and his love? Therefore, it is through them that the other is completed. The fact that I am known, recognized, and loved, that is *my* completion. And this completion in knowledge and in love, in being known and being loved, is not merely a completion on the "plane" of the "intentional," but a fulfillment of the reality, of the being itself.

For reality itself is, in the measure of its being, knowing and being known in unity. All realities sigh for their own unveiling. They want themselves to enter, if not as knowers at least as objects of knowledge, into the light of knowledge and of love. They all have a dynamic drive to fulfill themselves by being known. They, too, want to "put in their word." The word is their own fulfillment, in which they arrive at the point where all reality, because it draws its origin from eternal spirit, finds its ultimate home: in light. If these realities are persons, then this fulfillment will be realized in the exchange of the word of love which is mutually bestowed. If they are subspiritual realities, then they attain their salvation in the fact that they are lovingly spoken by all beings who are capable of knowing and loving — not by God alone.

Everything is redeemed by the word. It is the perfection of things. The word is their spiritual body in which they themselves first reach their own fulfillment. Hungering for knowledge and love, things pluck in their spiritual word-body at the hearts of those who can know and love them. Invariably the word is the sacrament by means of which realities communicate themselves to human beings, in order to achieve their own destiny.

What we have said about the redeeming mission of the word is true in some way of every word. But it is especially true of primordial words. We do not mean by this, of course, only single words, but all that is said by a person to bring things in a powerful and compact way out of that darkness where they cannot remain, into the light of the human person.

33 • Hearer of the Word*

The first requisite for the human being's hearing the word of the gospel without misunderstanding is that his ears should be open for *the* word through which the silent mystery is present. More indeed is

---

* *Theological Investigations IV*, 358–62.

expressed in the word of the gospel than we grasp wordlessly, than we can also master without words. For in this word comes what is incomprehensible, the nameless, silent power that rules all but is itself unruled, the immense, the abyss in which we are rooted, the overbright darkness, by which all the brightness of each day is encompassed — in a word, the abiding mystery which we call God, the beginning who is still there when we end.

Now, strictly speaking, every word that is really a word, and strictly speaking, only the *word* has the power of naming the nameless. No doubt, the word expresses, designates and distinguishes, demarcates, defines, compares, determines and arranges. But as it does this, he who has ears, he who can see (here all the senses of the spirit are at one) experiences something totally different: the silent, mystic presence of the nameless. For that which is named is conjured up by the word.

And so it advances from the encompassing, quiet and silent source from which it arises and where it remains secure; that which is described and distinguished by the word, by the distinctive name, combines with the other as it is distinguished from it, in the unity which comprises the comparable and akin, and so points silently back to the one origin, loftier than both, which can indeed preserve both unity and distinction in one.

The word puts individual things in order, and so always points to a fundamental background order which cannot itself be ordered but remains the perpetual a priori antecedent to all order. One can miss all this when one hears words. One can be deaf to the fact that the clear spiritual sound can only be heard when one has first listened to the silence beyond each distinct sound, the silence in which all possible sounds are still gathered up and at one with each other.

One can disregard one's own comprehensive hearing, by allowing oneself to be enslaved by the individual things one hears. One can forget that the small, limited region of the determinative word lies within the vast, silent desert of the Godhead. But it is this nameless being that words try to name when they speak of things that have a name; they try to conjure up the mystery when they indicate the intelligible; they try to summon up infinity when they describe and circumscribe the finite; they try to force the human person to allow himself to be gripped, as they grip and grasp. But a person can be deaf to this eternal meaning of temporal words, and still grow proud of his stupid, unreceptive hardness of heart.

Hence words must be spoken to him, which are such that he recognizes that they are uttered by those whom he must take seriously, and that he sees that these words call upon him to decide whether to dismiss them as meaningless or to strive to listen to them long enough in truth and love until he understands that their whole meaning is to utter the unutterable to make the nameless mystery touch his heart gently, to make the unfathomable abyss the foundation of all that the foreground supports.

Christianity needs such words; it needs practice in learning to hear such words. For all its words would be misunderstood, if they were not heard as words of the mystery, as the coming of the blessed, gripping, incomprehensibility of the holy. For they speak of God. And if God's incomprehensibility does not grip us in a word, if it does not draw us on into his superluminous darkness, if it does not call us out of the little house of our homely, close-hugged truths into the strangeness of the night that is our real home, we have misunderstood or failed to understand the words of Christianity. For they all speak of the unknown God, who only reveals himself to give himself as the abiding mystery, and to gather home to himself all that is outside himself and clear — home to him who is the incomprehensibility of silent love. Yes, he who would hear the message of Christianity must have ears for the word where the silent mystery makes itself unmistakably heard as the foundation of existence.

The second requisite for the hearing of the Christian message is the power to hear words which reach the *heart,* the center of the human being. If God as the mystery wishes to enunciate himself in the words of Christian revelation, the word will aim at the *whole* person, because this God wishes to be the salvation of the whole human being. The word seeks him out at his original unity, out of which the multiplicity of his existence grows and in which it remains comprised: the word seeks the *human* heart.

And hence the words of the gospel message are necessarily words of the heart: not sentimental, because that would not be heart to heart; not purely rational words of the intellect, since this can be understood merely as the faculty which grasps and masters the comprehensible, and not as the primordial faculty which allows itself to be gripped and overwhelmed by the incomprehensible mystery and is therefore called the heart for preference, if one is thinking of this primordial faculty of the inmost human spirit.

Thus, to be a Christian, one must be capable of hearing and understanding the primary words of the heart. And these are not merely concerned with the human person's scientific rationality and his dispassionate pseudo-objectivity. They are not just signposts for the biological will to live and the direction of the herd instinct. They are, so to speak, sacral, even sacramental: they help to effect what they signify and penetrate creatively into the person's primordial center.

This capacity and readiness must be developed by practice, so that the primary words do not glance off the shell of preoccupations, are not choked in the indifference and cynical nihilism of the human being, are not drowned in chatter, but like a lance piercing mortally a crucified man and opening up the sources of the spirit, may strike the inmost depths of a person, killing and bringing to life, transforming, judging, and graciously favoring.

We must learn how to listen under the severe discipline of the spirit and with a reverent heart which longs for the "striking" word, the word that really strikes us and pierces the heart, so that mortally stricken and blissfully surprised, the heart may pour the libation of the muted mystery which it concealed into the abyss of God's eternal mystery and so, being freed, find blessedness.

The third requisite for the proper hearing of the message of the gospel, which we choose to mention here out of many others, is the power of hearing the word which *unites*. Words distinguish. But the ultimate words which call to the all-pervading mystery and reach the heart are words that unite. They call to the origin and gather all into the unifying center of the heart. Hence they reconcile; they free the individual from the isolation of his loneliness; they make the whole present in each one; they speak of one death and we taste the death of all; they voice one joy and joy itself penetrates our heart; they tell of one man and we have learned to know all persons. Even when they speak of the dire loneliness of an individual uniquely isolated, they notify the hearer of his own isolating loneliness and point to the one sorrow of all and their one task, which is that they still have to seek the true unity of many divided hearts.

Thus the authentic words unite. But one must be able to hear them, otherwise one cannot understand the message of Christianity either. For it speaks only of one thing, the mystery of love, which wishes to strike home to the human heart as judgment and salvation: a love which is not a feeling but the true substance of all reality as it strives to manifest itself in all things. Only when one can hear the secret sound of unifying love in sundering words, has one ears to perceive truly the message of Christianity. Otherwise, Christianity too is only a distraction beating on the ear with a thousand words that tire and stupefy the spirit, because it is asked to accept too much that fits in nowhere, which means death to the heart, because it ultimately loves only one thing, it can hear only one thing, the word of union which is God himself, who unites without dissociating.

The fourth and last requisite for the hearing of the message of the gospel which we shall mention here, is the capacity of recognizing the inexpressible mystery *in* the word which speaks of its bodily form, inseparable from the word but not confused with it: the power of becoming aware of the incarnational and incarnate incomprehensibility, of hearing the Word become flesh.

And in fact, if we are Christians, and not just metaphysicians delving into the obscure grounds of being, we must remember that the eternal Word, where the obscure but personal unoriginated origin indicated by us as "Father" in the Godhead expresses himself absolutely and knows himself eternally, has become flesh and dwelt among us. The *Word*, where the unoriginated mystery is in possession of itself, the infinite Word which has none other beside it because it alone of itself says all things that can be said: this has become flesh, and without ceasing to be all has become this particular thing, without ceasing to be always and everywhere expresses itself "here and now."

Therefore, since then, in this Word made flesh the human word has become full of grace and truth. It is not just a sort of silently signaling finger, pointing away from what it delimits and illuminates into the infinite distance, where the incomprehensible dwells, silent and unapproachable: the incomprehensible itself, as grace and mercy, has entered the human word. In the region encompassed by the human word, infinity has built itself a tent, infinity itself is there in the finite. The word names and truly contains what it apparently only hints at by a silent signal; it brings on what it proclaims; it is the word which really only attains the full realization of its being in the sacramental word, where it really becomes what God's grace made it as he uttered his eternal Word itself in the flesh of the Lord.

And therefore, the Christian must be open to the grace bestowed on the word in the Logos who became man. He must be schooled in the mystery of the Word which through the Word made flesh is the embodiment of the infinite mystery and no longer just a pointer pointing away from itself to the mystery. Deep down within the narrow earthly well of the human word the spring that flows forever gushes forth, the flames of eternal love leap out of the burning bush of the human word.

This propriety of the word, in its true and full reality, is already grace in the word, and the power of hearing such a word in its true sense is already grace of faith. But ever since the human word has existed as the embodiment of the Word of God which abides forever, and ever since *this* Word has been heard in its permanent embodiment, there is a brightness and a secret promise in every word.

In every word, the gracious incarnation of God's own abiding Word and so of God himself can take place, and all true hearers of the word are really listening to the inmost depths of every word, to know if it becomes suddenly the word of eternal love by the very fact that it expresses the human being and his world.

If one is to grow ever more profoundly Christian, one must never cease to practice listening for this incarnational possibility in the human word. One must have the readiness and the capacity to find *permanently* the whole in the individual; one must have courage for what is clear and definite, in order to become aware of the inexpressible; one must bear and love the candor of what is close at hand, to be able to reach the distant One, who is not, however, silent indifference.

34 • The Contemporary Inner Threat to Truth*

The contemporary human being suffers to no small extent from an incapacity to realize the meaning and value of truth in itself. At any rate he finds it extremely difficult to do so. It should be noted that what we are immediately concerned with here is not truthfulness but truth. For we shall only acquire a real and effective understanding of what truthfulness means when we have renewed our understanding of the meaning and value of truth itself.

However, today this understanding is threatened. It is not possible here to point out the historical causes and origins of this state of affairs, in which our understanding of truth is imperiled. This would take us too far back in history. The religious dissensions and conflicts; the breaking up of society into many self-contained units; the antimetaphysical positions which are characteristic of modernity; the purely descriptive positivism of modern natural science; the recognition that the knowledge of the individual is conditioned by far-reaching sociological factors; the deliberate manipulation on the part of political forces of the conclusions of the sciences and of public opinion; the fact that today the individual has a direct and vivid realization of how manifold opinions, religious and moral outlooks are in the world; the experience of sudden and worldwide revolutions in thought taking place almost overnight — these and similar manifestations are in part causes and in part symptoms of what we are speaking of here. The contemporary human being labors under the false impression that only in those cases in which empirical reality is quite directly subject to diagnosis and control on part of the human person is there much chance of gaining any accurate knowledge of such reality.

The contemporary human being regards his own thoughts as unverifiable, as mere opinion, as a view which can neither command reality

---

* *Theological Investigations VII,* 229–34.

in all its aspects nor offer any very strong grounds for confidence in the reliability of his own cognitive processes. This attitude of relativism and skepticism on the part of the contemporary person with regard to his own cognitive processes leads to a further phenomenon, still more important than the first.

The contemporary person (and this extends very largely into the sphere of faith itself) is really very far from feeling that truth is important in itself; that it has a value either in itself or even, considered as knowledge, that it has any significance in itself for salvation. In other words, the contemporary person is by no means convinced that a deficiency in truth, quite regardless of whether it is culpable or not, could imperil his own life either in the temporal or the eternal dimension.

We have only to apply the experiment to ourselves to realize the truth of this. Let us ask ourselves, then, whether we are really convinced of the fact that knowledge of divine truth as such constitutes a factor which is essential to salvation itself, such that without it, regardless of the reasons why one may have failed to discover this truth, it is simply impossible to attain to salvation at all.

Or again we may ask ourselves whether our position may not fairly be summed up somewhat as follows: We hold that if one does know the truth, it is certainly excellent and good, because then one can and must act in conformity with the real facts that one has thereby grasped. But for all that, in the last analysis we do draw a distinction between the sphere of the technical and the practical on the one hand, and the higher spiritual sphere of dispensations and principles on the other.

In the former sphere if one fails, no matter how inculpably, to realize and apply the rules, then something unpleasant and injurious may ensue. In the latter sphere, however, if indeed it exists at all, any mistakes we may make cannot possibly result in the same injurious effects. For here one can only be held responsible for *those* mistakes which consist in morally culpable acts (and these only to the extent that they are morally culpable).

I believe that it is only by submitting our ideas to this kind of experiment that it is brought home to us how great a danger we all stand in of denying the value of truth *as* truth; how much we all hold, without realizing it, that truth is only valuable as providing the prior condition for coping rightly with reality.

For we can only adopt a right practical attitude toward reality when we know what properties it has in itself, and what reactions this or that mode of behavior may be calculated to produce in it. Perhaps this may serve to bring home to us how far we have moved in our inmost convictions from the position that knowledge as such (though admittedly this comes to its full fruition in love) constitutes in itself *the most radical mode of communication with reality.* May we not actually have reached the position of thinking of knowledge as providing merely a *starting point and prior condition* for such communication with reality, and, indeed, not always even an essential prior condition for it at that?

The successes achieved in the whole interrelated complex of the natural sciences, the developments in technology and other revolutionary changes within the social scene, have all unintentionally contributed to the fact that human beings have come to prize truth merely as a means of gaining control and mastery over the environment in which they exist (and from this point they have then gone on actually to define the nature of truth in terms corresponding to this essentially functional view).

This control over the environmental factors in human life does not consist in knowledge as such; other means are used in the pursuit of it, namely, technology, medicine, practical genetics, and the like, and so a basic attitude to life is arrived at in which something is regarded as true only when it can be put to some "practical use," and all other kinds of knowledge, which cannot be shown to have this particular kind of contribution to make, are regarded as mere opinions, mere speculative positions which are adopted, secondary side effects to be ascribed to hereditary or racial factors, social conditions, and so on. In short, the concept of truth here is that of a skeptical pragmatism, which each one may seek to justify for himself whether on biological or sociological grounds according as he wishes.

In the light of this it is easy to understand why to one who allows these ideas to influence his own thought to any significant extent it really does seem quite right that that ideology is true which is de facto effective and powerful. It is true insofar as it claims to shape the future in conformity with the only sort of reality which it will recognize as reality at all: reality on the material and sociological plane with an ideology to correspond to this.

Knowledge is reduced to a mere tool, enabling the individual so to cope with his material and sociological reality that he can gain control over it. This in turn leads to the further conclusion that he is truthful and honorable who assimilates himself to the sociological ideology which has power to shape the future. For it is this, in fact, which constitutes the real and the effective. Anyone, therefore, who succeeded in reawakening his contemporaries to a sense of what the nature of truth really is in itself would be performing a vital task indeed.

Such a one would also have to enable his contemporaries to achieve a renewed grasp of truthfulness as the initial capacity, prior to all presuppositions, to achieve truth in itself, truth in its own unique essence. In saying this we must of course recognize that the person is free to use this initial capacity of his or not as he chooses, and he may culpably misuse it and so fall into error.

But if we are to attain to the unique essence of truthfulness as defined here, the concept of truth on which we must fix our gaze is not one which can be defined in purely neutral and general terms. Certainly it is possible to conceive of truth in a wholly general sense as equivalent to "correctness or accuracy," the idea that a proposition must correspond to reality quite regardless of what this proposition refers to.

To define truth thus would be to do exactly the same in the dimension of knowledge (something which is, in principle, perfectly possible) as one does in the dimension of being when one understands "being" as signifying the being of a "something or other" completely undefined and in the void, the being of a "not-not-being." When we understand being in this way as merely the unique self-identity of the "something-or-other being," we have obtained no true view of being. We have further to understand that there is *being* as such, being in the absolute.

This constitutes the absolutely primary basis (the very root foundation for all truth and all being) for all human knowledge of being, such that even though it is not explicitly adverted to, without it no such knowledge would be possible at all. It is only on the basis of this primary and implicit awareness of being as such, then, that we can really apprehend what is meant by the being of any given existing thing in its reality.

What this *properly* means must be based on the ultimate priority of being in the absolute. In the same way, too, truth in its original and ultimate sense is not the correctness of a proposition which is equally valid in all its possible applications, but truth in the absolute, which the person encounters as the horizon, omnipresent and all-encompassing, to every "concept" in which the individual and the particular are grasped.

The human being is conscious of this all-encompassing horizon to his ideas not as an explicit object for investigation in itself, but rather as that which constantly impinges upon his awareness. And this truth supports all other particular truths and is not itself supported by any. It is that which is uniquely self-authenticating (in itself) and, precisely in virtue of this fact, that which is to us the incomprehensible mystery.

It is only on the basis of these factors, which we have only been able to indicate in what has been said above, that the ultimate nature of truthfulness as such can be discovered: it is the basic sense of truth as the initial and absolutely primary communication with reality at its most absolute, and at the same time at its most all-embracing. It is that sense considered as basic receptivity, submissiveness, readiness not to refuse or to resist that which impinges upon it. It is the openness of the human person as spirit to being in the absolute (that which provides the basis for the being of all that is).

It is that sense, that initial perception, in which we accept with our minds the mystery of which we are conscious as the foundation and support of all reality, and which we call God, the unique truth of truths which bears its own meaning within itself. It is the basic acceptance of this mystery even though it has no use for us, even though it cannot be exploited by technology and cannot be made to contribute to our biological self-assertion, our physical well-being, our diversion or our enjoyment.

It is that sense of truth which is strict and exacting in its claims upon us, and only bestowed upon us as such; that initial perception which demands a response not merely from the human rational faculty as refined and developed by technological training, but rather, demands from our spirit, from our whole person, the ultimate decision which is ours to make as free. It is at this level that it demands our response, and at the same time makes this response possible.

It must be reiterated that those who define truth as "the adequation of statement to the objective state of affairs" are viewing it only as it appears to be, and only in a quite superficial connection, and so as a property which applies with equal validity to every correct proposition. In fact truth, like being, is first and last a property inherent in reality itself (considered as the "able-to-be-made-manifest" as actually revealed), and simultaneously inherent in knowledge too (considered as openness to the self-manifestation of being).

As such, it is an analogous entity, and an analogous concept. For this reason it is precisely not applicable in any primary or basic sense in contexts dealing with the practical usefulness of a formula for the technical manipulation of material objects or for predicting the outcome of processes in the natural order.

It is not in such contexts of practical living that truth achieves its true applicability, but rather in another context, one in which the human person as spiritual being realizes and possesses his own subjectivity, himself as a whole (a process which ultimately includes the love and freedom pertaining to truth); in which he experiences his own finitude, which he likewise comprehends, accepts, and endures as a whole; in which, faced with the question of being as such, being in its totality, he holds firm to the ineffable mystery; in which he does not shrink from the questionableness, the radically contingent nature of all individual entities, all of which point him on to the nameless infinite; in which he does not seek to grasp reality by taking possession of it for himself, but rather suffers himself to be grasped by it in its unfathomable depths; in which he does not speak but rather falls dumb with adoration. It is in this context that truth in its proper and ultimate sense comes into its own, and it is here that it enters our lives. And it is the acceptance of this ultimate essence of truth, the truth that so constantly goes unrecognized, that constitutes truthfulness in its primary and most basic form; it is this that is presupposed in other contexts in which truthfulness signifies the assent of the free individual to truth.

35 • "Freedom": A Contemporary Slogan*

Every age has its own great and dominant ideals, its slogans (using this term in a wholly positive, or at least a neutral sense) in which it sums up its hopes and its desires. A dominant idea of the kind we have in mind, in which everything is drawn into a synthesis, may on this account be very imprecise, if only because — to put it briefly — a human being cannot arrive at a definition of the whole when he does not himself stand outside it, or assign what is an ultimate practical goal to a place in a system of coordinates which is different from, and higher than, itself.

Such slogans, key concepts, and all-epitomizing ideals belonging to a particular age may undergo changes. For an individual whose awareness is safeguarded against falling into a mere pluralism of totally disparate realities, they are both necessary and justified. Slogans of this kind should not be blamed on the grounds that they are not susceptible of any full analysis or exact definition, even though of course this fact again should not wrongly be exploited as a blank check to justify us in producing mere phrases where exact answers and precise reflective thought are possible.

The human person is in fact a being such that his reflections upon himself and his understanding of his own existence are invariably only approximate, if only because the reflective thought itself as it develops is subject to intellectual perspectives and motivations which are incapable of being in their turn objectified, reflected upon, or subjected to critical analysis.

In this situation slogans play their part. They are intended to sum up the awareness and the aims of a given epoch, without thereby standing for a process of reflection which is total and all-embracing, or capable

---

* *Theological Investigations XIII*, trans. David Bourke (New York: Seabury Press, 1975), 108–11.

of being analyzed down to the last detail. A given epoch — it may be precisely the present one — can have several such slogans and dominant ideas. In the present age the term "freedom" certainly constitutes one such. It is true that for at least two hundred years it has been included among the ideals of all movements in social politics, but even so it has still not lost its power of attraction. It has become a watchword throughout the world, and peoples of very widely differing stages of economic and cultural development have fastened upon it.

Precisely on this account it is, of course, almost inevitable that the word "freedom" has come to stand for an entity which is almost indescribable, and in fact is unknown. The social scientist, with his rational and empiricist approach, would therefore be justified in saying that freedom has become, to such an extent, an indeterminate entity, something which bears a different meaning for every individual, every nation, and every social group, that any social politics capable of giving an account of itself in rational terms will find this concept totally intractable.

But even the practitioner of this science of social politics should at any rate concede that such a slogan *exists,* that it makes its impact in the minds and hearts of individuals, and that therefore, whether it is welcome or not, it does on any showing make itself felt as a force in the field of social politics. We can also understand that the reason why this term should already have made so strong an impact for so long, and should still be making it today, is that freedom has still not become something that can be taken for granted, something no longer capable of stimulating any movement.

Presumably it would indeed be perfectly possible for us in all sincerity to uphold the position that, at least in the Western industrial countries, the degree of social freedom already achieved is greater in relation to the broad mass of peoples than has been achieved in any previous age. But even though this fact can presumably be adduced, it still does not make freedom something that can be taken for granted, something which, since it already exists for many individuals and in a notable degree, is no longer of concern and no longer capable of serving as a slogan to express the expectations and demands for social change in the future.

For in the sphere of society, freedom is always a relative concept, related to the sum total of what human beings value as capable of achievement within a foreseeable space of time. For people of a particular age, or at least according to their opinion, whether true or false, the sum total of these physical, medical, economic, and social changes which they demand may be very great. And in these circumstances, when these physical, medical, and the like, factors in practice remain stable, they feel that their freedom is needlessly restricted by this lack of change, when in principle change is possible. And they feel this even though, materially speaking, the freedom they enjoy is far greater than that of peoples of some former age, who must have regarded the restrictions upon their freedom as in practice more or less unalterable.

Now the situation today is that the sum total of economic, social, and other changes which (at least in the opinion of individuals) might be introduced is immense — regardless of whether this opinion is altogether correct, or whether further distinctions would have to be drawn in order to make it so. And for this reason contemporary human beings are far from feeling that they enjoy a particular freedom, especially in the case of those who no longer recognize their existing situation as the outcome of free and creative activity on the part of those who overcame conditions of economic and cultural chaos so as to bring it about, and hence regarded it as manifestly praiseworthy. Today many, especially younger persons, are reacting against the contemporary social situation by aggressively demanding more freedom. But I believe that we should view this in the way that we have indicated above.

Presumably it would not be very meaningful if we sought to explain this aggressive demand simply by saying that in a technological and industrial age and, in conditions in which the population has increased enormously by comparison with earlier ages, the economic, social, political, and legal conditions in which people have to live have become so complex and so difficult to change that even when they are regarded as inevitable, they are still felt to restrict the freedom of the individual in the highest degree. In a certain sense this may be justified. But as an explanation of the aggressive demand for more freedom it is straightway open to the objection that in former ages the person, living as he did in simpler situations of life and social conditions, did not in any sense enjoy any more freedom, either for the shaping of his own life, for going where he liked, for choosing his own philosophy of life, forming the sort of social groups he wanted, choosing the goods he thought best, and so on.

The sole difference between this and former ages is simply this: the compulsions of former ages, which allowed the human being less freedom, were felt to be more or less unalterable, and therefore the demand for more freedom could not be regarded as capable of fulfillment in any effective sense.

But this brings us back once more to the explanation we have adumbrated at an earlier stage as to why there is so aggressive a demand for greater freedom today, even though, objectively speaking, there has never been more freedom than there is today. Now this enables us to give a certain description of what is meant by freedom as such at the level of social living. On this showing, freedom would be a condition in which it is possible to get rid of a situation which is regarded as undesirable and capable of being abolished. In arriving at the judgment that a given social situation is undesirable, it is possible that another situation, the one that replaces the previous one, is regarded as desirable. And this view in turn may be justified or unjustified, or may be arrived at with or without the agreement of the majority of one's contemporaries, with or without appealing to this.

But it may also be the case that in struggling against the existing situation we do not make any attempt to consider in detail the future situation which is intended to replace it. In other words it is a matter of indifference to those advocating the change whether they fall out of the frying pan into the fire. The characterization of freedom in the social sense which we have given is, of course, at a very formal level. But surely the reason for this is to be found in the fact that it actually *does* take very different forms at the material level as well, this freedom which individuals and groups desire when they put forward their demands for more freedom.

We could of course draw a distinction between genuine and merely supposed freedom, and say that a greater freedom is to be found in those cases in which an individual, without being hindered by external factors, can direct his own human and individual nature in general, and the value attached to it, and in which he has greater scope for this in terms of the possibilities and the means at his command.

But while in itself such a definition of the nature of social freedom would be justified so far as metaphysical anthropology is concerned, it too would fail to bring us any closer to the answer we are seeking because precisely on this point, of how we should rightly understand the nature of the human person and his dignity, very different ideas are put forward, and any description of freedom, if it is to be effective at the level of social politics, must take into account the pluralism of anthropologies which exist today and come to terms with it.

36 • Christian Faith and Secularization*

We ought to be very careful in our judgment about the "secularization" of contemporary life. The plough and the sickle of former times were also secular objects. Today they have been replaced by

---

* *Grace in Freedom*, 78–79.

tractors and threshing machines; thus there is not only a change in image and proportions, but there are also more objects in this world which can obstruct the religious view because they are so fascinating and so large. But they are there by rights, and as Christians we must simply accept the fact that there will be ever more man-made reality which is neither "numinous" nature nor profane in the bad sense.

To say it quite simply: the loaf of bread has become much bigger, thank God, but a person can still realize that one does not live by bread alone, for he has always been tempted, not only now, to think the opposite. We make secularization only more dangerous if we dramatize it. And, let us be frank: Is it really so certain that formerly, when religion and the church played a greater part in public life, people really had more true faith, hope, and charity, which, after all, are more important than anything else? God alone knows. The faith that is attacked by our secular world and is left to the free decision of the individual may well be more genuine.

Further: Is the seemingly secularized ethos of our time which speaks (and, let us hope, not only chatters) of the freedom and dignity of the human being, of responsibility and the love of one's neighbor, is this ethos a result of Christianity or not? It is its legitimate son, even though it is often a prodigal son who squanders his property far from his father's house.

How could this ethos remain alive unless people still believed, even without admitting it, that they are children of God destined for eternal life? Is not this belief genuinely Christian, and could it remain alive at all apart from Christianity? And would this ethos still be so alive, indeed propagating itself, unless it were still living by the side of explicit Christianity? Surely the secularized ethos of our society receives its power from Christianity. Perhaps this, too, may be a case of living off the money of one's parents, but not wanting to admit that one did not earn it oneself.

By the way, the United States is often regarded as a prime example of a secularized country. But on closer inspection we shall find that many heterogeneous elements do, indeed, exist there side by side, but that the churches are nevertheless extraordinarily "present" in public life. Apart from the social services run by the state in which, after all, Christians have as much a share as everyone else, it must be said that the participation of "humanists" in private charitable enterprises for the poor, the sick, neurotics, lepers, and so on, is relatively modest. All honor to Albert Schweitzer, for example. But most private works of mercy, it seems to me, are done by practicing Christians. Humanists attach too much importance to their own emancipation from Christianity and its "social power," and this prevents them from actual positive engagement.

And finally, if we do not want the world to be submerged by a pagan secularism without God and without hope, we ought not to compile statistics and make forecasts, but should bear our Christian witness in the marketplace by word and deed. Everything else we can and must leave to God.

37 • When Are We Peace-Loving?*

When are we peace-loving? A lover of peace, I think, is someone who can change his view, since it is only in this way that there can be any hope of agreement between "opponents" who have hitherto held different opinions. That person alone is a lover of peace who is even prepared to accept defeat in a division of opinion, who is prepared in principle to admit his "opponent" to be in the right, who is willing to end the discussion with a different attitude from that with which he started it. That person alone is a lover of peace who can bring himself to commend the very person whose opinions and decisions he thought he had to oppose and resist. That person alone is a lover of peace who shows politeness and patience even to someone who gets on his nerves.

We are peace-loving only if we classify the attitudes and endeavors of others as little as possible under simple, general concepts which can easily be rejected, if we are constantly overcoming also our thinking in clichés, constantly making the effort to see behind the words the reality itself, on which perhaps there is no real disagreement. We are peace-loving only if we measure *ourselves* by the ideal but *others* by what is really possible, if we do not defend our social prestige, if we fight honestly and fairly even though this fairness diminishes our chances of victory. We serve peace only if we really understand that it is possible to incur responsibility even by hesitation and silence, if we respect politicians only when they prove themselves otherwise to be human beings and not merely the representatives of our own selfishness, if we distrust politicians particularly when they are much too ready to admit that we are in the right and to confirm our own opinions.

The gospel blessing on peacemakers comes upon us only if we defend not only our own but also others' freedom, if we slowly learn to be

---

Opportunities for Faith, 103–5.

really sensitive not only to the wrong done to ourselves but likewise to wrong done to others. The peace-lover also possesses small, ordinary virtues: he is polite to those over whom he himself has power and does not cringe before those who are more powerful than he is; he draws the attention of a person in the wrong to his mistakes and keeps silent about them before others; he does not insist on his own importance and does not consider himself irreplaceable; he knows that for all of us self-criticism burns itself out more quickly than self-defense, that we should be able to give up responsibility and should not think that we ourselves can do all for the best; he knows that it may occasionally be better for the other to do something *well* than for ourselves to have done it *better*, since the other's freedom — which is the really better — can nourish only when he is allowed to do well what he can do.

The peace-lover does not allow any brutal alternatives to be forced upon him; he tries to formulate the arguments of his opponent better and more convincingly than the latter can do himself, since the peace-lover does not want to gain a cheap victory by making a fool of his opponent. The peace-lover will not be one-sided when he sees that this is the result of jumping to conclusions, because he knows that we are still one-sided when we think that we can see all sides.

The peace-lover is polite when politeness is likely to be to his own detriment and perhaps considers bluntness appropriate when politeness could only be to his advantage. The peace-lover respects the "signs of the times," but he does not worship them. He does not think that God is always on the side of the big battalions. He plays his part, calmly and boldly, knowing that others have a different part and that the symphony of the world sounds quite convincing, not where we, the individual players, stand and play, but where the sound is heard of one only, of God.

38 • Creative Hope for Peace*

Someone who wants to fulfill his mandate for peace must be hopeful and begin his action for peace at the point where he is at the time. The peace which is not yet, but for which we have a mandate, that peace, that is, which is still to come, can come to be only as a result of historical acts freely undertaken. This peace is not only the spontaneously emerging product of a necessary evolution in the economic,

---

Opportunities for Faith, 105–7.

social, and political dimensions. This peace is really future, it has to be achieved; it is not simply there already, concealed in the present. But future can be made only by those who hope. Future is first of all always utopia, which only the hopeful person can plan and seize for himself in advance. Future is that which is recklessly willed in complete freedom, without reassurances, and in this sense it is what is hoped for as distinct from what is merely planned and calculated.

Without this creative hope the peace of the future cannot come: without the hope which is action and not mere cosy expectation.

This future peace cannot be achieved by creative hope as an isolated, individual work which might be completed within the sphere of our own existence without affecting or changing other things within that sphere. The peace of the future is rather the result of much more far-reaching and radical changes which transform our whole existence. To say that peace is the work of justice is to see it as derived from the whole of human existence. Only when a higher justice permeates all dimensions of existence, when far-reaching changes of awareness and very substantial changes in all social institutionalism are successful, can the peace of the future come.

The mandate of creative hope for peace is therefore by its very nature extended to the creative action of hope for a very radical change of the human being, his society, and his environment. Hope for peace becomes hope for the one future in its wholeness which is entrusted to the human person as his deed. This whole future is certainly in the first place an intramundane future. But this latter is in fact also the necessary mediation of that eschatological hope which means God himself and gains from this standpoint its final worth and the radical seriousness with which it lays claim to us as its hopeful agents.

Peace is only another name for the whole future successfully achieved; but at present that future is shrouded in darkness. It cannot be calculated merely in the planning offices of the futurologists, since these in the last resort can know the future only as implied in the present, not the really new future of creative hope, however much that which can be calculated and planned may enter into this new future and the planning itself be a factor of the creative hope. If the mandate of peace is extended and elevated in this way to the greater mandate of the new future and to a creative hope, it must not be understood as ideologically innocuous, as if hoping were mere expectation and the new future as a whole only that which makes demands on *nobody* precisely because it is the mission of *all*. Although it is an act of freedom, creative utopia of the new future in hope is certainly also the incalculable gift of history and its Lord. So too is the peace of this new future.

We should, however, be liars if we were to say that we are the ones who hope for this future and its peace, unless at the point where we stand here and now we are doing what serves the cause of peace. But we are doing this only if each of us in his own place, in his own particular situation, in regard to the people he is constantly meeting, succeeds in thought, word, and deed in overcoming his selfishness. This does not mean restricting our peace mandate merely to ethics and to a field that is prior to the social and political sphere, for this very act of gaining a real victory over our selfishness simply cannot take place merely within the field of interpersonal relationships. This act itself has always a social dimension, social consequences which, however slowly, change the institutionalisms of society.

Opinions may well be and remain very divided on how radical such changes will have to be in order to produce the peace of the new future, whether they can be effected in many small steps or only by great revolutionary moves; but the recognition of this fact and the obligation of tolerance involved in it must not be made an excuse for those who really want no change and therefore no true peace. But in any case, in such a situation someone who is thinking more in evolutionary terms, who advocates many small steps toward a true peace, must ask himself whether this is what he is really doing or whether his program merely conceals the fact that he wants to stay where he is.

And anyone who thinks that only large steps, only radical changes in society, can serve true peace in a new future, anyone who fights for this view, must likewise see that he is bound nevertheless to gain small victories over his own egoism until greater moves and revolutionary changes are actually possible. For, without such modest victories over the egoism concealed almost to the point of identity in all of us, even the most far-reaching social revolutions would mean no more than the replacement of one tyranny by another, a new form of war and not true peace. The small steps are for all part of the mandate of peace, for, if they are really taken, there is already concealed in them secretly and almost invisibly the miracle of creative hope, the quiet dawn of a new future.

39 • The World and the Angels I*

In our reflections we are starting out from the assumption that if there are angels, they are to be understood, not a priori as Leibnizian monads, but as cosmic powers and authorities for which, with all their

---

* *Theological Investigations XIX*, trans. Edward Quinn (New York: Crossroad Publishing Company, 1983), 260–66.

subjectivity and personality a cosmic function (that is, one related to the world) is an essential constituent. If we could not make this assumption, then obviously there could be no talk of a primarily natural knowledge of the existence of angels.

It may certainly be claimed, particularly at the present time, that a theology of the cosmos is very undeveloped. Of course, elements of such a theology of the cosmos are to be found scattered in a traditional textbook theology. The createdness and temporal nature of the world as a whole are mentioned there; an angelology of the traditional kind can scarcely fail to include some cosmic aspects; a defense of the unity of the human race must include some consideration of the biosphere, particularly if there is no longer any attempt to defend traditional monogenism; in anthropology a substantial unity of spirit and matter is maintained with reference to the human being, even though the older metaphysics of "prime matter" (*materia prima*) scarcely appears in textbook theology and consequently little can be seen of the unity of spirit and matter as a cosmic unity; in eschatology there is usually a brief mention of the new heaven and the new earth, but it really does not become very clear whether, why, and how the definitive consummation of created spirit-persons and of their history carries with it also the consummation of the material cosmos or has little to do with this material cosmos.

Perhaps all the questions that ought to be raised in a theology of the cosmos are so obscure in themselves that it is easy to understand the ineffectiveness of such a theology. The fact remains that in theology human beings and their relationship to God are at the center of attention and it is in this light that all theological statements must be understood in their meaning and validity. This corresponds to the nature of revelation and theology, and to an absolutely fundamentally legitimate development of the philosophical understanding of the human person, in which the latter gradually came to be seen, not so much as part of a cosmos, but as a transcendental subject with a world of his own which he projects in thought and action.

But this development of the history of ideas in modern times was also coexistent with a contrary tendency: the earth moved away from the center of the cosmos and became an insignificant particle in an immense cosmos which continually became, and is still becoming, greater for human knowledge; but the human being himself became increasingly clearly perceptible as the product (intentionally or accidentally) of a history of nature of the material cosmos. From this standpoint, too, a theology of the cosmos is required, particularly since the doctrine of the substantial unity of spirit and matter in the human person (with all its consequences: salvific importance of history as such, incarnation of the Logos, resurrection of the body, etc.) simply forbids us to pursue an absolutely acosmic theology and anthropology.

Such a theology of the cosmos would have to work out the theological significance of the interpretation of the cosmos as a world continually coming to be. The older premodern world on the whole understood world and earth as static factors created by God once and for all, offering for all time a fixed stage on which the human person and the person alone could carry on his history. Today we rightly speak of a history of nature; we are aware of a world that is always and everywhere coming to be and we understand the history of humanity also as a part of this history or at least as conditioned by it, even though a serious and cautious metaphysics of grades and orders of being (taking really seriously the differentiatedness of the world) recognizes essential differences between entities in the cosmos and is consequently aware of qualitative leaps, of real self-transcendence of one grade of being into a higher grade, which is possible only as a result of God's creative dynamism in the world. The recognition of essentially different grades of being (from real subjectivity, personality, and transcendentality to being as a whole) does not, however, imply a denial of the one material cosmos and its evolution taking place in a continually new self-transcendence of an inferior grade.

In the light of such a basic conception of the world (in which the human being is no longer seen without more ado as the center of a world constructed statically around him, as the one who is absolutely and in every respect underivable, but in which he represents a peak and an effect of a world evolution), the question can no longer be avoided as to whether that subjectivity rooted in materiality which we know as the human person is the only one toward which this world evolution of the material cosmos has developed in continually new self-transcendence. This question must be raised in view of the vast immensity of the material cosmos as a world coming to be.

If we imagine the cosmos as a world coming to be, and as oriented in its becoming to subjectivity, then it is really not to be taken for granted that this aim has been successful only at the tiny point we know as our earth. At this stage in our reflections, admittedly we should not forget what has been learned from this history of human subjectivity. A personal and free subjectivity oriented in unlimited transcendentality to being purely and simply (and, consequently, to the ground of being which is God) is the center of the cosmos, even though this human subjectivity rests on a materiality which as such cannot be regarded as the center of all that is material, even if it made sense at all to speak of a material center of this material cosmos.

But even if we do not forget this human subjectivity, through which *everything* is the world of the human being, the world he has, however great it may be and however great it may still come to be, the question in fact remains open as to whether the immense growth of the material cosmos has served only for the emergence in particular of human subjectivity.

Traditional theology especially, with its conviction of the existence of angels (of angels who have a common salvation history together with human beings), cannot start out from the axiom that in regard to God there can really only be human subjectivities. The question, then, can seriously be raised even if we have not or would not have any opportunity of answering it unequivocally.

If this question is raised, it does not mean (although this perhaps is possible and justifiable) that we are asking here about beings existing on other "stars" as subjects with more or less the same biological corporeality as that which we know as our own. It is true that the latter question could also be raised, because it cannot be regarded simply and absolutely as improbable that somewhere else in such an immeasurable cosmos there are the same chemical and physical preconditions as with us for the "chance" of the emergence of life and that this life then develops according to the strict laws of evolution (with and in qualitative leaps) toward something essentially like ourselves.

This question about "human beings on other planets" is one that has recently been raised afresh and more urgently because it inevitably also brings up theological problems. But it is a question that will not be pursued further here, since at the present time it is not only unanswerable, but refers to living beings which at least up to now have not been incorporated in our own existential and theological sphere of life and thus existentially and theologically have no more relevance for us than any sort of "dead" star anywhere in the universe.

The question will, however, be raised here as to whether this general starting point of a world coming to be, oriented to subjectivity, might not lead to some conclusions about the conceivability and probability of angels. If we speak of "angels," it is assumed from the outset that (1) they have an essential connection with the world and (2) they have for us an existential relevance that we denied to possible "human beings on other planets," since the existential sphere of life of the latter (at least up to now) does not overlap with ours.

If there are such "angels" who fulfill this second precondition, their relationship to matter, essential as it must be, is to be understood as different from ours and from that of the hypothetically assumed "human beings on other planets." Such an essential relationship of subjectivity and matter must by its very notion be understood always as a limited regionality of matter, which is interiorized and (if desired) organized and subjectivized by this finite subjectivity. But this limited regionality of a subjectivity need not be understood as like that of a human corporeality. This material regionality can be understood as much more plural and more differentiated, more complex, and as embracing more material individual realities than is the case with human corporeality, *and* this greater and more comprehensive, subjectively interiorized regionality ought also to be able to incorporate into itself as partial elements those individual realities that we know as human beings. It would be wrong to regard such an idea a priori as too abstruse. A free subjectivity of the human being, open to the whole of reality, which at the same time is the ultimate organizing principle of a peristalsis of the digestive organs, is not a priori more probable than the idea envisaged here.

As already pointed out, such a higher principle of unity and order of a material regionality, greater and more differentiated than the human body, does not mean that the individual realities incorporated into this more comprehensive system are in any sense suppressed by this principle and no longer realizable in accordance with their proper nature. A higher principle of order respects the essential nature of the individual realities it organizes and gives them a further determination only in the directions in which they are ambivalent and open. Nor is it inconceivable from this standpoint that such a higher principle of unity and order of a material regionality should incorporate into this unity and order also realities which are themselves already subjectively polarized and interiorized.

In other words, even a human reality which itself represents a corporeally limited system of matter and subjectivity can be conceived as integrated into such a higher system, if and insofar as this corporeality itself has a potentiality for a higher and more comprehensive order. If two subjectivities are thus understood as graded principles of unity and order, with one above the other, then, of course, such a gradation, and sub- and superordination, is originally present in connection with this organizing function in regard to matter as such only insofar as these two principles extend to a smaller ("body") or greater material area ("angelic region"), but not (as is obvious) insofar as both principles as intellectual subjects of freedom have an infinite openness to being as a whole and to God: that is, they are distinguished in the light of the range of their starting point within materiality and not in the light of their goal (God).

It can readily be admitted that we seem at first sight to have become involved in our reflections in a consideration of the nature of the "angels" and have apparently moved away from the question of their existence, returning to points already touched on. But in the last resort this apparent deviation is justified. For the question can now be more clearly stated: If angels are understood in this way, can they be thought of as existing in the light of the conception of an essentially material world, moving progressively toward increasingly higher subjectivity and a genuine unity of plural material realities?

We might think in the first place that a continually advancing subjectivizing and interiorizing of the material cosmos is also the task of the human person, going beyond the area of his biological corporeality in his knowledge and activity into the world as such (and not merely set in his environment as fixed by his corporeality), thus subjectivizing and interiorizing the cosmos in possibilities and ways which he is only now beginning slowly to discover (astronautics, for example). The question, of course, might also be asked whether the time of the world must now be regarded as having lasted so long and being so far advanced that those more comprehensive subjectivities to which the evolution of the world is tending must already exist, or whether they belong to a future still to come. (By analogy with some other theological problems it might then be said that the angels are perhaps not protological but eschatological beings.) But the human being's destiny of activating in deed and thought a greater subjectivizing and interiorizing of the cosmos does not exclude the possibility that this goal of the cosmos can and should be attained in other and higher ways, particularly since the person's somatic starting point imposes on the fulfillment of this task limits which (as can easily be understood) cannot in fact be surmounted, although they are prior to the absolute fulfillment of this task.

The question of time seems more difficult to us. It might be asked whether the evolution of the world has "already" arrived at "angels." Our conception of angels seems to see them mainly as the end product of an evolution of the world, while traditional theology regards them as (also cosmic) principles at the beginning of the world. Here there are certainly difficulties and obscurities which are not to be denied or minimized, but it can admittedly be asked whether that finite physical time which begins according to currently accepted ideas of modern physics with the "big bang" (which can certainly not itself be simply identified with the beginning of the world in a theological sense) is the very time in which the material cosmos evolves under the necessary and already present principles of order which we call "angels."

Whatever we think exactly of the way in which such angels come to be, they have in any case an essential relationship to matter, and, consequently, the history of the latter is also their own history, so that they do not become acosmic if we place them as principles of unity and order at the beginning of the history of the material cosmos, the history that we know as that of our material cosmos. In this history, then, angels, too, would reach the fulfillment of their nature as organizing and unifying regional principles of the material cosmos. It might then be asked if they could not (without any inconsistency) be both at the beginning and at the end of a material history, in a way similar to that in which the human intellectual subject is at the beginning and end of a history of the body, without implying that the "soul" (which must be seen as present at the beginning of this corporeal history) had no history itself. Over and above all this, in principle, the possibility cannot be a priori excluded that the history of nature in regard to matter may develop toward such more widely ranging regional and interiorizing principles more rapidly than it did toward the emergence of the human being.

It could certainly be assumed that subjectivity on the narrow basis of our biological corporeality is attainable only with greater difficulty and more slowly (and also more "casually") than on the basis of a more comprehensive materiality, that nature's feat of subjectivity within a small corporeality (known as the human being) needed a longer start (called the biosphere) than would be required for cosmic subjectivity as a whole. It cannot then simply be claimed that "angels" in this sense must be no more than goals still to be reached in a cosmic evolution. It is by all means conceivable that world evolution (with qualitative leaps), in the light of its nature and existence, has already reached those subjectivities with a greater material regionality which we can call angels.

40 • The World and the Angels II*

All our reflections hitherto seem to have made the existence and nature of "angels" conceivable, but no more than that. Are there in fact in the world of our experience any indications that this thing, whose nature and existence can be conceived and expected, actually exists and makes itself known? With our conception of these "angels" in particular we certainly do not expect the existence of such "angels" to be made known by their effects, suddenly and unexpectedly interposed in isolation at certain individual points in the natural and normal course of material events. A priori we do not count on this sort of miraculous intervention of angels at purely individual points in space and time to make known their existence.

---

* *Theological Investigations XIX*, 266–71.

But, we might ask, can the existence of such principles of the cosmos become known only in this way or is there a possibility of such an experience which does not necessitate the interruption of the material course of things and which is described and investigated by physics and chemistry? A possibility of this kind seems conceivable if the negative criterion just mentioned is kept in mind and in the light of the nature of angels as understood here.

If the human person becomes aware of unities and orders of a greater, but particular, kind, which, on the one hand, are conceivable in the light of the individual elements of such a unity and order and are sustained by these elements without detriment to their own immanent laws, and which, on the other hand, exist without being required or necessitated by these structural elements themselves, so that in order to "explain" them we would need to have recourse to mere "chance" or even directly (which is unlikely) to a creative institution by God alone, then an individual has the right to think of organizing and unifying principles of these unities and orders, whose existence is not adequately explained by that of their elements.

Human beings seem to have always had and to be able to have today such experiences of unities and orders in the world of nature and the history of humanity, to be interpreted and explained in this way; in fact, it seems that in the course of the history of humanity such experiences have been the real although less obvious reason for belief in angels, and not only those dubious "spiritualistic" experiences with which supporters and opponents of the existence of angels are usually occupied. Both in nature and also in human history, and, moreover, in the interconnection and unity of nature and history there are experiences of unity and order, experiences which seem to be adequately interpreted only if such principles of unity and order are presupposed and if it is understood that the materialities out of which these unities and orders are constructed do not themselves provide an explanation of these orders. "Plurality of itself does not become unity" (*Non enim plura secundum se uniuntur*), as Aquinas rightly says.

At this stage of course, even before we catch sight concretely of these particular orders and unities, the old problems emerge from the debate between hylomorphism, holism, reduction of the biological to cybernetically interpreted chemical systems. For all these and similar theories are meant to provide the right answer to the question of exactly how complex unities are to be understood, when they seek to prevail against their "environment" and thus to make their unity clear. But, although it might seem appropriate, we cannot, of course, go into all these difficult problems here.

The problems are particularly difficult in the field of theology, since theology *of itself* cannot defend the principle of a fundamental essential difference between the purely material and the biological, but must remain neutral on this point and leave it entirely to the free discussion of the philosophy of nature. For theology as such, this kind of essential difference (despite all the unity of evolution and self-transcendence) is certainly present only when it is a question of the human person's spiritual subjectivity in unlimited transcendentality toward being as a whole and so toward God.

Which of these systems of the philosophy of nature (apart from anthropology) is right is a question on which theology cannot have an independent opinion in the light of its own principles. But since the interpretation of those greater unities and orders (which are more comprehensive than any of the particular, material, living, individual human realities taken in isolation) is supposed to be a matter of natural knowledge, this incompetence of theology in regard to the theories mentioned is not simply irrelevant for our question.

It can, however, be said that if and insofar as a theological anthropology accepts as a fact the existence of material systems (at least in the human being) whose unity and order is at least partially determined by a unifying substantial principle, it cannot appeal to interpretations available in the philosophy of nature of the order and unity of individual biological realities, excluding holistically or cybernetically any higher principle for this order and unity, and then assert a priori that there cannot be higher and more complex unities within the material cosmos established by higher substantial principles. This should be obvious particularly because we must certainly distinguish in principle between the structure of a complex entity on the one hand and the unifying ground of this structure on the other, and cannot assume a priori that the elements of such a structure alone in their diversity themselves contain the ground of the unity of this structure.

Of course it is impossible, particularly here, to deal terminologically and objectively with the complex of questions coming ontologically under the heading of substance and structure. These two terms may offer an immense field for debate; but if the term "structure" is understood in its traditional sense (that is, as the result of a unification, and not as the principle of this unification and unity), if, moreover, we at least leave open the question of whether a synthesizing "from below" is not for us a concretely tangible process of a self-transcendence (in the sense indicated, of creating something qualitatively new), then we cannot regard structure at any rate as an unequivocal alternative to substance, substantial form, and so on, and claim the right to go back from the structure to the real principle of this structure.

Where then, we ask finally, is it possible to discover concretely such unities and orders of a particular but greater kind, for which a proper principle of unity, order, and structure can be postulated: a principle which, since the unity and order it establishes are more comprehensive than those of the human body, possesses at least that subjectivity and transcendentality which is proper to the human spiritual principle?

It is, of course, possible here to do no more than hint at an answer to this question, since more concrete and better substantiated answers would lead us into the whole length and breadth of the particular sciences, and since, in view of the technically rationalistic mentality of the contemporary human being and the mathematically-quantitatively operating sciences involved in this, a mystagogy would be required for the genuine experience of such orders and unities — a mystagogy correcting the modern mentality and thus making effective the experience of these unities and orders.

Nevertheless, both within the history of nature as such and also in the history of humankind, as well as in the interconnection of the history of nature and human history, embracing a variety of material realities in space and time, there are unities distinguishable from one another and containing in themselves a unity and order which at least gives the impression that it is not explicable purely and simply by the casual assemblage of its formative elements and preconditions, although, of course, quite definite circumstances and conditions must be present in these elements for such an ordered unity to be able to emerge in a particular form within the cosmos as a whole.

The necessity of such conditions "from below" may not, of course, be disputed or obscured. But it would not really contradict the explanation of this ordered unity envisaged here if it were clearly proved that such an ordered unity always and necessarily emerges if these conditions are fulfilled from below. (The theologian, for instance, will not deny that, if the biological preconditions and factualities are present for human procreation, a human being will necessarily emerge, although the "human soul" thus emerging qualitatively transcends the event of such a biological procreation as much as the intellectual subjectivity of the human person always surpasses his biological reality as such, although the latter is incorporated into the former as an intrinsic constituent.)

In the history of the evolution of life, it seems that there are such ordered unities, complexes of plural meanings, which go beyond the biological individual realities. At the particular stages of evolution of flora and fauna, together with their mutual interdependence, unities delimitable from one another can be distinguished; a particular period of evolution is characterized by a uniform style which is common also to those individualities in such a period which are not directly derived from one another; by and large in an individual period everything is coherent, although this common physiognomy of an epoch cannot be interpreted merely as our own subjective impression.

Many causes can be suggested, of course, for the rise and decline of such an epoch in the history of the evolution of life, just as the most diverse individual causes can be assigned for the death of a human being; but the impression is given (despite all these possible external causes) that in the last resort such a period dies from within itself, outgrows itself and *wants* to die, just as with the individual human being (despite his external breakdown) death is his own death coming from within, and what we call "chance" is the executor of an internal necessity.

If someone considers such a period in the history of nature with its unity, its common style, and its one destiny and does not think that he has understood the one totality as such when he has grasped its elements and their "accidental" coordination, despite all the positivism of the sciences at the present time, he can have the courage to perceive a unifying principle in such a unity.

The same can certainly be said (and more emphatically) in regard to the periods of the history of humankind and in regard to the histories of individual nations and other historical unities that can be observed. Here, too, things do not go in utter shapelessness; here in particular there are unities clearly distinguishable from one another, each with a particular style of its own; here, too, each period of universal history, of the history of a nation, or of a particular civilization has its internal drama and dialectic, its beginning and its end, has a common physiognomy, although this entire unity and peculiarity cannot be made intelligible solely by human beings, who directly carry on this history and realize throughout time unities of meaning that they themselves had by no means foreseen. These historical structures of meaning, extending in time over several generations, have, of course, their preconditions from below in all the individual empirical causes (geographical, biological, meteorological, sociological, etc.). But the very fact that these causes from below are really plural in character and mutually independent may lead us to wonder whether their blind, casual concurrence alone can explain the historical structures of meaning emerging from that concurrence.

If the Christian in face of such a question is inclined to find an answer promptly and directly in an appeal to God's providence ruling over and in history, this answer is not wrong but raises the further question of *how* this providence of God is to be understood as concretely *carried out,* whether it does not itself come to prevail through real principles, created by God, establishing order and unity, principles described in the book of Daniel as angels of the nations. When we observe that such unities of meaning of a greater even though particular spatio-temporality emerge in history, when we learn that they are not wholly and ultimately due solely to shortsighted historical planning by human beings or still less have their ground in "chance," in the unplanned coincidence of subhuman causes, but when at the same time in seeking for the sufficient reason of such unities today particularly it is impossible to appeal to a "direct" intervention of God's providence, the presumption at least of such "angels of the nations" is justified.

41 • The World and History as the Event of God's Self-Communication*

For how do we Christians picture the world — what we are and experience, with all that thus belongs to us? As one, vast, all-embracing, all-distinguishing event: the self-communication of God. God whom none can call by name, none comprehend, so that all we say of him must fall short of that incomprehensibility, that unspeakable abyss which sweeps everything away into its blinding darkness. But this God is our concern. It is he who penetrates the labyrinth of our minds, encompasses the realm of our experience with his mystery of morning and evening, is already existent before our own beginnings and yet remains eternally remote even when we have reached the end of all our ways in pursuit of him; and sink exhausted to the earth. We must always reckon with him; we must call on him though we can give him no name; and when we present our final reckoning, he must be there to ensure that there is a remainder, that we do not end in nothing.

We say of this God that the world is the event of his self-communication, the ecstasy of his love that would lavish itself outwardly on that which he is not. The tremendous outburst of his love, already sufficient to itself, creates from nothingness a world on which it can freely lavish itself. God's love, which in its eternal glory needs nothing, creates not so as to guide the world as an external force by remote control in the elliptical orbits of finitude, but in order to entrust himself to *his* world, thus letting it become the fate of divine love.

This love beggars comprehension. Judging by the forms in which it manifests itself, one might think it a monstrous blind force. It calls

---

* *Servants of the Lord,* trans. Richard Strachan (New York: Herder and Herder, 1968), 16–20.

forth aeons and worlds apparently only to let them subside again into the void; it allows the absurdity of culpable denial of itself to enter its creation; it quickens and kills, seems indifferent to individual beings, acts often as naked force, is deaf to the despairing cry of the oppressed and the ghastly rattle of the dying, is blind to the innocent helplessness of children that moves even our hardened hearts. But this love, that like the tidal wave of an infinite ocean roars through all space and time, uprooting everything, sweeping everything away, creates the material world and its tremendous evolution so as to make spirit, and the history of spirit, in it and of it. For after all, because of its essential orientation to spirit the material world is sustained from the outset by the creative dynamism which has as its goal the history of personal freedom, of which the material world is one element, intrinsic or extrinsic.

If this spirit is created and thrust into an immeasurable, free, open history, it is so that God can communicate his very self, so that in contact with the world he who always is may become what he always is: the ecstasy of love, which though it overburdens us, has made us such that only under this burden, which *is* love, can we be happy, though we can also forfeit this love by renouncing it in deadly sin. This totally incomprehensible God is the future, literally open to infinity itself, in the form of unfettered and immeasurable love, that knows no other law but itself. It does all things, suffers all things, permits all things, so that it may embrace all things in itself, descend into every abyss, break above every mountaintop, and triumph in all things and over all things, by lavishing itself on us and causing us to accept it as God's one mystery.

This love has a temporal history and is the driving force behind the history of this world; but it is not merely the hidden spring in the world's remotest depths; it also wishes to be manifested in the world's events and in people, in human love, in free acts, in sacrifice unto death, in faith, hope, charity, whatever forms these may assume in the space and time that is our history. And the nearer this one history, sustained by God's self-communicating love, draws to the ultimate goal where this love will be "all in all," victoriously consuming all things — provided a person has not rejected it outright — the more unmistakable its manifestation in history will be. Love has already found the predestined shape of its victory; even now the world's history unfolds not only by virtue of self-communicating love but also within the time of victory made manifest, the time of Jesus Christ, who unites within himself the radical, historical manifestation of God's definitive gift of himself to the world, and the world's acceptance of that gift.

Human history flows on in the time of Christ that will never pass; but even in its historical manifestation it is encompassed by God's victorious self-gift. Indeed, this manifestation has become history even more radically, history even within the world of steadily widening prospects; it is the human history of people active in a hominization of the world and a human self-manipulation on a scale yet undreamed of. And it is still a history that seems to human beings a growing chaos — an impenetrable mix of sin and holiness, light and darkness; a history of simultaneous ascents and downfalls, of blood and tears, of noble achievements and rash presumption; a history that is appalling and magnificent, an ooze of endless trivia and yet a high drama; a history in which the individual is freed from the degradation of self-alienation and is reduced to the status of total insignificance among the billions of his brothers and sisters; a history of arrogant might and the inexorable demands of "planning," yet increasingly unpredictable, with a growing pluralism of cultures, economic systems, political systems; an ever more variegated human consciousness, and trend toward a society of the masses; so that this pluralism, with all the schizophrenia it begets in the consciousness of the individual, is compressed into a highly inflammable density by a human history ever more closely knit, ever more one.

In the midst of all this history, at a thousand different times and places, in a thousand forms, the one thing occurs which produces and sustains it all: the silent coming of God. This *can* happen. But whether it really does, and where, is the unfathomable secret of God, and of the person's fundamental freedom. But it can occur anywhere, in forms ever new, and does in fact occur, though we can never point with certitude to any particular evidence.

The event exists, though always shrouded in the incurable ambivalence of all that is human. It may occur anywhere: in a comfortable bourgeois sickroom, where the sick man, still hoping against hope, in a final act of surrender allows death to take possession of him in the last dread solitude; in the mudholes of Vietnam; in the ultimate honesty — and it does exist — of a person who thinks himself an atheist and yet keeps doggedly on along the road to the unknown, nameless God, praising him; in the stern practicality with which, full of silent unselfishness, an individual tries to serve his brothers and sisters in a research laboratory; where a child opens his heart to God; where a person is smitten with compunction for a guilt that seems fathomless to his fellows; in the bliss of love and in the horror of despair, incomprehensibly accepted, in life and in death, in glory and banality, in things sacred and things profane.

This mystery may occur anywhere, because everything originates in this self-communicating love of God, because it embraces even guilt, and because already it has, in Jesus Christ, brought forth the event of its triumphant historical manifestation. It is the indissoluble beginning of both God's victory and ours, the triumph that manifests itself in such ordinary, humble garb that anyone can find the improbable courage to believe and hope that God's tremendous love occurs even in one's own appalling humdrum life, where nothing seems to happen but birth and death, and in between, amid emptiness, and the guilt no one is spared, a little longing and a little faithfulness

42 • Evil and the Devil*

Even if the existence of demons is assumed and upheld as a fact, the concrete ideas of them in popular theology and more especially in the ordinary piety of Catholics need a decisive demythologization. This is something that must be considered for a while here. As such, this demythologizing has no need of any particularly modern insights. It is sufficient to apply to the ideas of the demons those fundamental and universal insights on evil which were long ago developed by a Christian metaphysics of finite freedom, of the nature of the good and of culpable evil.

There is no absolute evil. All evil is finite; it is not a positive reality in itself but a want of good in an entity that remains good in its substance as coming from God and indestructible. In its origin, in its possibility of becoming definitive, in its coexistence with an absolute God and his unrestricted good, freedom, and power, freely posed wickedness is certainly a mystery which resists a rationalistic solution and cannot simply be understood as merely the unavoidable reverse side of the good, as an irritating phenomenon in the coming to be of the good.

But this need not prevent us from seeing the wickedness of the wicked, the guilt of the guilty, even in its possible finality, as deficiency (although freely posited) of the good in a good entity, as something that would not and never could be evil if it were not and did not still remain good in very many respects and dimensions of reality. We can be evil and do evil only if we remain good and behave well (even though in a defective way).

Even in an evil action of freedom of the most radical kind, the good is affirmed as condition of the possibility of freedom and goodness, and realized in a positive sense, although not to the extent and in the radicalism possible and required in the particular concrete situation. If we do not want to be Manichees and if we do not want to see evil

* *Theological Investigations XIX*, 255–59.

and good as consisting in an absolute dualism of two equal powers, we must always and everywhere keep in mind the fact that even evil lives by the good and always continues to realize the good, that evil as absolute and forthright corruption would utterly destroy as an entity this entity that had become evil.

All this, however, is true of the devils and demons, if they exist. They have a nature that is good and created by God that is not removed, but, again, posited, even by their free and definitive decision against God. Not that the finalized decision by these demons against God can be seen as a superficial patina clinging only externally to a reality created by God, so that the question might be asked why this patina is not swept away and the reality created good by God preserved. Wickedness freely chosen is certainly a determination reaching to the very heart of the personal reality created by God. But it is a determination of this reality created by God and therefore good and remaining good in its substance and self-realization.

A popular idea of devils, however, is that they are beings consisting of nothing but opposition to God, of hatred and negation. This popular idea confuses evil with what has become evil, "wickedness" (*malitia*) as such with actual "evil" (*malum*); it identifies evil beings with the pure essence of evil, with what is nothing but wickedness. But there are not and cannot be any such evil beings.

If the demons reject God, their rejection is a defective mode of their always positive nature and its realization, which always has a positive meaning and positively contributes only to the goodness of the world. Even more mythological would be an idea of demons as impish, malignant spirits whose action and behavior really contain in their substance nothing but a destruction of positive realities, although that action can be understood only as a realization of what is positively good.

It is a mythological idea to suppose that in order to realize their nature in the world, with the good necessarily involved in it and with the negative present in and about this good through their decision, these evil spirits need a "permission," understood up to a point juridically and legally, from God who permits them in one place and forbids them in another to inflict damage, without this having anything really to do with the nature and the cosmic function they possess, whether good or bad.

If and insofar as events in the cosmos and its history are also conditioned by the existence and self-realization of such powers and authorities, these events are not properly to be understood as effects of new initiatives on the part of these demons, oriented only to evil as such, but as consequences of their nature and their cosmic function, which are always the expression of an essentially good nature *and* determined also by the evil decision.

When the effects produced by these demonic cosmic powers are regarded merely as purely destructive, we are involved in principle (whether we notice it or not) in a kind of Manichaeism, or we adopt a childish attitude and ascribe to the demons behavior like that of small boys throwing stones at the windows of their school. Mythological, too, is the idea of a conflict and opposition between God and the demons, with God and the devil struggling against each other as more or less equally matched partners, engaged in an absolute antagonism.

The demons (if they exist) are radically dependent on God, sustained entirely in their activity by a positive collaboration of God, planned from the outset in their activity together with the evil involved in it by God's providence totally independently of any other influence; in a properly metaphysical sense there cannot be a struggle between God and the devil, since the latter from the very outset, always and at every moment, in all his powers and in all his activity, is completely dependent on God.

The difference between the demons and God and their dependence on him are, in any case, as great as the difference and dependence on our part: that is, infinite. Compared with one another, they and we may display considerable differences in knowledge and power. But the difference does not place the demons in the role of an anti-God. And if, in particular with traditional textbook theology, we ascribe to them a superhuman measure of intelligence and power, we should certainly not regard them as present in almost childishly trivial manifestations which are of little importance either to world history or to salvation history.

And if with traditional textbook theology we take seriously into account the intelligence and power of these agencies, we shall not suspect that they are involved when a saint falls down the stairs or some poor girl shows symptoms of schizophrenia or epilepsy which in other cases are certainly due to natural causes and are not interpreted there in terms of demonology.

If we recognize the existence of such nonhuman spirit-persons, particularly if we regard them as belonging to a higher order despite their relationship to the world, we simply cannot conceive their activity as a sporadic interference intended *only* to do harm in the chain of causes and effects otherwise perceptible to us, but must see it as the effect of this higher order as such, which does not cancel the essential achievement and connection of the lesser orders, but takes up the latter intact into the higher order.

We no longer assume today that the biosphere can establish its power and its own internal laws only by partially abolishing and disturbing the normal course of the sphere of the physical and chemical. Higher systems do not remove the lower ones, but incorporate the latter while preserving them in their own existence. If there are superhuman created-and-personal realities, they form within the unity of the one cosmos a higher order in the world as a whole.

Nor is this structural system, produced from the unity of all created realities in the one cosmos, removed by the sin of personal realities within this system of the one cosmos as a whole; for even "evil spirits" by their decision can give a false direction to other individual realities (or, if the latter are personal in character, at least can attempt to do this), and they can realize these evil intentions of theirs only in a positive affirmation of their nature and function.

If we wanted to continue with such speculations within the scope of a traditional Catholic angelology and demonology, we could point to the vast intelligence and great freedom of these beings which mean that their radical and definitive culpability makes sense only as a result of wanting to be like God in the sense of rejecting such a deification through *grace*. But if this is assumed, it becomes even more clear that the natural cosmic function of the demons (like that of the other angels) must not be seen as canceled, but only as determined also by their refusal of God's offer of himself out of free, gracious love. Then the really demonic element in the world would be that fainthearted despondency in which the creature fears for itself and will not venture freely to entrust itself to the absoluteness of the love in which God seeks to bestow, not something befitting the creature, but himself.

In brief: if we want to pursue angelology and demonology at all, we must remain on the level of the first initiative for such a theory and not degrade these cosmic powers and authorities to goblinlike, ghostly, malicious spirits who are more stupid and more wretched than feeble human beings.

43 • The Need of Redemption*

The need of redemption signifies *first of all* the condition in which the human being inescapably finds himself in his own experience, and which he feels to be incomplete, ambiguous, and full of suffering. And he feels this to be so in all the dimensions of his reality so that the

---

* *Encyclopedia of Theology* (New York: Seabury Press, 1975), 1519–20.

experience of this state, as both individual and collective, is practically identical with his existence itself.

For the Christian interpretation of the human person, however, this condition does not consist solely in the unavoidable frictions of material, biological, social, and personal development. It does not consist solely of social grievances or the finite character of human existence (biological or spiritual). This condition must not, however, be falsely exaggerated to the point of denying the very *capacity* for salvation, as in the pessimistic existentialism which holds that existence is absolutely and irremediably absurd and that frank recognition of this fact is the human being's authentic truth. But this attitude can in fact be regarded as recognition that the human person cannot save himself. Then the contrary opinion (the Marxist view, whether applied collectively or regarded individualistically) would be the modern form of "superstition" (M. Blondel).

Christianity acknowledges the person to be capable of salvation, ultimately because even his freedom is finite and remains comprised within God's creative love. But the human being is also in need of deliverance, primarily and ultimately from his *guilt*.

Certainly a finite guiltless being which had to grow and develop would have felt the pain of incompleteness as a deficiency, in the process of becoming. But the Christian view of the human being knows that, concretely and radically, suffering is more than merely "growing pains," and in fact is the manifestation of guilt. And only where guilt is abolished can there be any question of redemption.

This guilt however, both as the state of original sin and as the action of individual freedom, cannot be removed by the person himself. For it is not merely a transgression of certain objective norms belonging to this world. If it were, and if we leave out of account a deeper analysis of freedom as mutual communication between human persons, in which the phenomenon of a guilt impossible to annul by the human being himself can be experienced, then it would be conceivable that person might be able himself to undo the consequences of his transgression, remove his guilt and so finally come to an arrangement with God as the guardian of these regulations concerning creatures.

Guilt in the concrete order as "sin" is the free no to God's direct, intimate love in the offer of his self-communication by uncreated divinizing grace, and therefore essentially an act which has dialogic character. And because free, it aims at finality, definiteness. Such an act, however, is directed to the absolutely sovereign, free God and is essentially an answer, dependent on God's call and offer. Through a no to divine love of that kind, the human person of himself can no longer reckon on the continuance of that love, especially as it is the love of the absolutely holy and just God who is the absolute contradiction of such a refusal. Only if that love freely endures even in the face of such a refusal and, as divine and of infinite power to set free, goes beyond that guilt, is forgiveness possible, that is, is there any possibility of the human person freely loving, responding in a genuine dialogue, made possible by God.

Hence only on the basis of forgiveness of sin is definitive salvation conceivable as personal fulfillment and deliverance from the trials of suffering. For while suffering and death are manifestations of guilt in the depths of existence, complete "beatitude" in all dimensions can only come as God's eschatological gift. It is not a goal that can be achieved by the person himself.

The experience of humanly ineradicable guilt as the ground of the person's need of redemption is felt in very different degrees. That is understandable in view of the existence of the human being and his situation in the history of salvation. It does not rule out the fundamental assertion of the need for redemption as the condition of understanding Christian soteriology. A merely rudimentary sense of guilt or an apparently total lack of it may itself be culpable repression, "suppression" of the true situation of the human person (Rom 1:18).

It may simply be due to a very primitive stage of development in the individual, in which a true sense of guilt is not possible. It may be a sign that the powerful (though inarticulate) grace-given sense of living within the domain of divine (forgiving) love to some extent outweighs and overlays the sense of guilt (although in principle both grow in direct proportion). It may be that in some individual the possibility of radical guilt has remained a mere possibility through God's preserving grace, and that this possibility as such is less easily recognized in act than guilt itself (though that is not necessarily so, as we see from the saints' consciousness of sin).

Finally, the profound individual experience always requires an effective example and "catalyst" in the experience of humanity and its history of calamity (especially as interpreted by the revealed history of perdition and salvation). And an individual, culpably or not, may not be sufficiently confronted with this experience in its entirety.

All these factors may be combined in very different ways in the individual and cannot be adequately distinguished by conscious introspection. (For example, concupiscence antecedent to freedom but still inculpable, as opposed to concupiscence which is culpably ratified by freedom, cannot entirely be distinguished by reflection.) Hence there are difficulties regarding the individual sense of guilt, all the more so as many acts are objectively but not subjectively guilty and can be analyzed even by the person concerned in terms of his own oppressive past, social factors, and the like, and so "cleared up." Methodical guidance is needed to initiate human beings into the recognition of their guilty situation.

Here, however, it is ultimately decisive to understand that this admission of guilt (the manifestation of the "wrath of God"; cf. Rom 1:18) will *in fact* be really radically ventured and achieved only by those who encounter and accept God's forgiveness. The need for redemption is concretely grasped in the act of accepting redemption. Otherwise the human person does not gauge the radical truth of his guilt; he will deny it or interpret it in some other way. Consequently, initiation into the need for redemption is encouragement to believe in the love of God and accept it as unmerited and unconditional (and so therefore not ended by guilt), in the knowledge that even to accept this love is the work of this love.

ON THE
LIVING GOD

44 • The Word "God"*

It is natural to begin with a brief reflection on the word "God." This is so not merely because, in contrast to a thousand other experiences which can get a hearing even without words, it could be that in this case the *word* alone is capable of giving us access to what it means. But for a much more simple reason we can and perhaps must begin a reflection on God himself with the word "God." For we do not have an experience of God as we have of a tree, another person and other external realities which, although they are perhaps never there before us absolutely nameless, yet they evoke their name by themselves because they simply appear within the realm of our experience at a definite point in time and space, and so by themselves they press immediately for a name. We can say, therefore, that what is most simple and most inescapable for us with regard to the question of God is the fact that the word "God" exists in his intellectual and spiritual existence.

We cannot evade this simple, although ambiguous fact by looking to a possible future and asking if a human race could ever exist in which the word "God" would absolutely disappear. In this case, either the question whether this word has a meaning and refers to a reality outside of itself would not arise anymore, or it would arise at a completely new point where what had earlier been the origin of this word would have to achieve presence in a new way and with a new word. In any case, the word exists among us.

Its existence is prolonged even by an atheist when he says that there is no God, and that something like God has no specifiable meaning; when he founds a museum without God, raises atheism to the level of a party dogma, and devises other similar things. In this way even the atheist is helping the word "God" to survive longer. If he wanted to avoid that, he would not only have to hope that this word would simply disappear in human existence and in the language of society. He would also have to contribute to this disappearance by keeping dead silence about it himself and not declaring himself an atheist. But how is he to do that if others, with whom he must speak and from whose language sphere he cannot completely withdraw, talk about God and are concerned about this word?

The mere fact that this word exists is worth thinking about. When we

---

* *Foundations of Christian Faith,* 44–51.

speak about the word "God" this way, we do not only mean of course the German word. Whether we say *Gott* or "God" or the Latin *deus* or the Semitic *el* or the old Mexican *teotl,* that makes no difference here. It would, however, be an extremely obscure and difficult question to ask how we could know that the same thing or the same person is meant by these different words, because in each of these cases we cannot simply point to a common experience of what is meant independently of the word itself. But for the time being we shall pass over this problem whether the many words for "God" are synonymous.

There are also, of course, names of God or of gods in places where a pantheon of gods is worshiped polytheistically, or where, as in ancient Israel, the one, all-powerful God has a proper name, Yahweh, because they were convinced that they had quite definite and specific experiences with him in their own history. Without prejudice to his incomprehensibility and hence his namelessness, these experiences characterize him and thus bestow upon him a proper name. But we shall not discuss here these names of God in the plural.

The word "God" exists. This by itself is worth thinking about. However, at least the German word says nothing or nothing more than that *about* God. Whether this was always the case in the earliest history of the word is another question. In any case the word "God" functions today like a proper name. One has to know from other sources what or who it means. Usually we do not notice this, but it is true. If we were to call God "Father," for example, or "Lord," or the "heavenly being," or something similar, as happens all the time in the history of religion, then the word by itself would say something about what it means because of its origins in other experiences we have and in its secular usage. But here it looks in the first instance as though the word confronts us like a blank face. It says nothing about what it means, nor can it simply function like an index finger which points to something encountered immediately outside of the word. Then it would not have to say anything about what it means, as is the case when we say "tree" or "table" or "sun."

Nevertheless, because this word is so very much without contour (and it is because of this that the first question has to be: What is this word really supposed to say?), it is obviously quite appropriate for what it refers to, regardless of whether the word may have originally been so "faceless" or not. We can prescind, then, from the question whether the history of the word began with another form of the word. In any case, the present form of the word reflects what the word refers to: the "ineffable one," the "nameless one" who does not enter into the world we can name as a part of it. It means the "silent one" who is always there, and yet can always be overlooked, unheard, and, because it expresses the whole in its unity and totality, can be passed over as meaningless. It means that which really is wordless, because every word receives its limits, its own sound and hence its intelligible sense only within a field of words. Hence what has become faceless, that is, the word "God" which no longer refers by itself to a definite, individual experience, has assumed the right form to be able to speak to us of God. For it is the final word before we become silent, the word which allows all the individual things we can name to disappear into the background, the word in which we are dealing with the totality which grounds them all.

The word "God" exists. We return to the starting point of our reflection, to the plain fact that in the world of words, by which we form our world and without which even so-called facts do not exist for us, the word "God" also appears. Even for the atheist, even for those who declare that God is dead, even for them, as we saw, God exists at least as that which they must declare dead, whose ghost they must banish, and whose return they fear. One could not be at peace about him until the word itself no longer existed, that is, until even the question about him would not have to be asked anymore. But it is still there, this word, it is present. Does it also have a future? Marx thought that atheism too would disappear, hence that the very word "God," used in affirmation or in denial, would disappear.

Is a future for the word "God" conceivable? Perhaps this question is meaningless because a genuine future is something radically new which cannot be calculated in advance. Or perhaps this question is merely theoretical and in reality it becomes a challenge to our freedom, whether we shall go on saying "God" tomorrow as believers or as unbelievers, challenging each other by affirming, denying, or doubting. However the question about the future of the word "God" might be settled, the believer simply sees only two possibilities and no other alternative: either the word will disappear without a trace and leave no residue, or it will survive, one way or another a question for everybody.

Consider for a moment these two possibilities. The word "God" will have disappeared without a trace and without an echo, without leaving any visible gap behind, without being replaced by another word which challenges us in the same way, without at least only a question, or better, *the* question even being raised by this word because people do not want to say or hear this word as an answer. What would it be like if this hypothesis about the future is taken seriously?

Then the human being would no longer be brought face to face with the single whole of reality, nor with the single whole of his own existence. For this is exactly what the word "God" does and it alone, however it might be defined phonetically or in its genesis. If the word "God" really did not exist, then neither would these two things exist anymore for the human person, the single whole of reality as such and the single whole of human existence in the mutual interpenetration of both aspects.

The human being would forget all about himself in his preoccupation with all the individual details of his world and his existence. On this supposition, he would never face the totality of the world and of himself helplessly, silently, and anxiously. He would not notice anymore that he was only an individual existent, and not being as such. He would not notice that he only considered questions, and not the question about questioning itself. He would not notice anymore that he was only manipulating in different ways different aspects of his existence, and never faced his existence in its unity and totality. He would remain mired *in* the world and *in* himself, and no longer go through that mysterious process which he *is*. It is a process in which, as it were, the whole of the "system" which he is along with his world reflects deeply about itself in its unity and totality, freely takes responsibility for itself, and thus transcends and reaches beyond itself to that silent mystery which seems like nothingness, and out of which he now comes to himself and his world, affirming both and taking responsibility for both.

The human being would have forgotten the totality and its ground, and at the same time, if we can put it this way, would have forgotten that he had forgotten. What would it be like? We can only say: he would have ceased being human. He would have regressed to the level of a clever animal. We can no longer say so readily today that a human person exists when an earthly being walks upright, makes fire, and fashions stone into tools. We can only say that the human person exists when this living being in reflection, in words and in freedom places the totality of the world and of existence before himself in question, even if he might become helplessly silent before *this* one and total question. Perhaps it would even be conceivable, and who can know for sure, that the human race, although it would survive biologically and technologically, would die a collective death and regress back into a colony of unusually resourceful animals. Whether this is a real possibility or not, the believer who uses the word "God" would not have to dread this would-be "utopia" as a disavowal of his faith.

For he is familiar with a merely biological consciousness and, if we want to call it such, an animal intelligence in which the question about the totality has not arisen and for which the word "God" has not become part of its destiny. Nor would he be all that confident about saying what such a biological intelligence can accomplish without entering into that destiny which is characterized by the word "God." But the human being really exists as a human being only when he uses the word "God" at least as a question, at least as a negating and negated question. The absolute death of the word "God," including even the eradication of its past, would be the signal, no longer heard by anyone, that the human person himself had died.

As we said, perhaps such a collective death is conceivable. This would not have to be any more extraordinary than the death of an individual person and of a sinner. When the question would no longer exist, when the question would simply have died and disappeared, then naturally one would no longer have to give an answer, but neither could he give a negative answer. Nor could this lacuna, if one conceived of it as a possibility, be made an argument that what is meant by "God" does not exist, because if it were, one would have to give an answer, although only a negative answer, to this question. Hence the fact that the question about the death of the word "God" can be raised shows again that the word "God" still survives even in and through the protest against it.

The second possibility to be considered is: the word "God" will survive. Every individual in his intellectual and spiritual existence lives by the language of all. He has his ever so individual and unique experience of existence only in and with the language in which he lives, from which he does not escape, and whose verbal associations, perspectives and selective a prioris he appropriates, even when he protests against them and when he is himself involved in the ever-ongoing history of language. One has to allow language to have its say because one has to use it to speak and use it to protest against it. A final and basic trust cannot reasonably be denied it if one does not want to be absolutely silent or contradict himself. Now the word "God" exists in the language in which and from which we live and accept responsibility for our existence.

But it is not just some accidental word which appeared suddenly in language at some arbitrary moment and at another disappeared again without a trace, like "phlogiston" and other words. For the word "God" places in question the whole world of language in which reality is present for us. For it asks about reality as a whole and in its original ground. Moreover, the question about the totality of the world of language exists in that peculiar paradox which is proper precisely to language because language itself is a part of the world, and at the same time it is the whole of it as known. When language speaks of anything it also expresses itself, itself as a whole and in relation to its ground, which is distant but present in its distance. It is precisely this that is pointed to when we say "God," although we do not mean thereby identically the same thing as language itself as a whole, but rather its empowering ground. But for this very reason the word "God" is not just any word, but is the word in which language, that is, the self-expression of the self-presence of world and human existence together, grasps itself in its ground. This word *exists,* it belongs in a special and unique way to our world of language and thus to our world. It is itself a reality, and indeed one that we cannot avoid. This reality might be present speaking clearly or obscurely, softly or loudly. But it is there at least as a question.

At this point and in this context we are not yet concerned with how we respond to this word and this event, whether we accept it as pointing to God himself, or whether in despairing rage we refuse to allow this word to make demands upon us, because, as part of the world of language, it would force us, who are also a part of the world, to face the totality of the world and of ourselves without being able to be the whole or to master it. And at this point we are also leaving entirely open the question how this original totality is defined and related to the world of plurality and to the multiplicity of words in the world of language.

At this point we can only call attention to one thing somewhat more clearly than before, since it touches upon the topic of the word "God" directly. If we understand correctly what has been said about the word "God" up to now, then it is not the case that each of us as an individual thinks "God" in an active process and that in this way the word "God" enters into the realm of our existence for the first time. Rather, we *hear and receive the word "God."* It comes to us in the history of language in which we are caught whether we want to be or not, which poses questions to us as individuals without itself being at our disposal. The history of language which is given to us, and in which the word "God" occurs as a question to us, is in this way an image and likeness of what it announces. We should not think that, because the phonetic sound of the word "God" is always dependent on us, therefore the word "God" is also our creation. Rather it creates us because it makes us human beings.

The real word "God" is not simply identical with the word "God" which appears in a dictionary lost among thousands and thousands of other words. For this dictionary word "God" only represents the real word which becomes present for us from out of the wordless texture of all words through their context and through their unity and totality, which itself exists and is present for us. This real word confronts us with ourselves and with reality as a whole, at least as a question. This word exists. It is in our history and makes our history. It is a word. For this reason one can fail to hear it, with ears, as scripture says, which hear and do not understand. But it does not cease to exist because of that. In antiquity Tertullian's insight about "the soul being naturally Christian" (*anima naturaliter Christiana*), that is, the soul that is Christian from its origins, is derived from the inexorability of the word "God."

It exists. It comes from those origins from which the human person himself comes. Its demise can be thought of only along with the death of the human being himself. It can still have a history whose changing forms we cannot imagine in advance precisely because it is what keeps an uncontrollable and unplanned future open. It is our opening to the incomprehensible mystery. It makes demands on us, and it might irritate us because it disturbs the peace of an existence which wants to have the peace of what is clear and distinct and planned.

It is always open to Wittgenstein's protest, which bids us to be silent about things which we cannot speak about clearly. Notice, however, that he violates this rule in formulating it. The word itself agrees with this maxim if correctly understood. For it is itself the final word before wordless and worshipful silence in the face of the ineffable mystery. It is the word which must be spoken at the conclusion of all speaking if, instead of silence in worship, there is not to follow that death in which the human person becomes a resourceful animal or a sinner lost forever.

It is an almost ridiculously exhausting and demanding word. If we were not hearing it *this way,* then we would be hearing it as a word about something obvious and comprehensible in everyday life, as a word alongside other words. Then we would have heard something which has nothing in common with the true word "God" but its phonetic sound. We are familiar with the Latin expression *amor fati,* the love of one's destiny. This resolve in the face of one's destiny means literally "love for the word that has been uttered," that is, for that *fatum* which is our destiny. Only this love for what is necessary liberates our freedom. This *fatum* is ultimately the word "God."

45 • Images of God*

Think of the false images of God that are found everywhere and therefore also in us. It is all very odd. We human beings recognize the faults of others, their stupidity, their obtuseness, their cowardliness, their narrow-mindedness, their sentimentality, their traumata, their twisted feelings, their inferiority complexes. But how difficult it is to admit the same things in ourselves, to say: What I see in others is presumably in me too; presumably I am as little inclined as these others are — with their irritability, their complexes, their finiteness, which I

---

* *The Priesthood,* 10–12.

know — to recognize myself as I really am and face the cracks in my own nature.

This observation holds too in regard to the narrow, constricted, untrue and ready-made images of God which human beings always set up to a certain extent as idols and thus shut out the nameless God who simply cannot be pinned down in shape and form, in an image. God transfixed in a concept, the God of the clerics is a God who doesn't exist. But don't we too often have an idol and don't we worship it when we turn religion, faith, the church, the message of Jesus Christ, from what it ought to be into a profession? This amounts to identifying with God ourselves and the world which we ourselves want to uphold and defend. Then God is really never more than a high-sounding word behind which we ourselves are masquerading, God transfixed in a concept as compared with the God who is constantly and increasingly experienced as a living, infinite, incomprehensible, ineffable reality and person: this God is one of those idols which presumably we may also constantly discover in ourselves.

The child's sweet, kind God is another idol. The narrow-minded God of the pharisee obedient only to the law is yet another. The God we think we know by contrast with the God of incomprehensible love, love that is harsh and able to kill; the God taken for granted by so-called "good Christians," who behave as if they could not understand the atheist's anxiety and uncertainty and as if the latter were merely stupid or malicious: this self-evident God of the good Christians is also an idol of which we must beware. God — least of all the true God — is not a collective title for religion. In the religion of the Vedas we can see most clearly how all priestly activity, religion with all its machinery, can become so inflated, so autonomous, that religion ends by giving its stamp to God instead of God defining religion.

Something like this really can happen to us. Let us ask where the idols, the false concepts of God, are in our own personal piety. If we think that everything ought to make sense, to be palpable; if we think that things ought to go well for us, that everything in our life should always be crystal clear; if we think, with the aid of a manual of moral theology or with any other concepts, norms, principles — no matter how true, how correct — we could so shape our life that it would run absolutely smoothly; if we think that God must be at our disposal as long as and because we serve him; if we think it isn't right that things should go badly; if this is how we think, then behind these cherished illusions there is a false image of God and this is what we serve. If these images are shattered by God himself and his life, by his guidance and providence, then one thing should be clear from the beginning: what is disappearing is not God, but an idol.

46 • Troubled Atheism?*

There was to be found toward the end of the eighteenth and beginning of the nineteenth centuries a theoretical and practical atheism which really was so unpardonably naive and so culpably superficial as to assert that it knew that there is no God. It did not produce any great intellects, and it belongs essentially to the past, even though it has only today become a mass psychosis and the dogma of a militant political *Weltanschauung.*

The case is quite different with "troubled atheism" if we may so call the phenomenon which we are contemplating. Alarm at the absence of God from the world, the feeling of no longer being able to realize the divine, consternation at the silence of God, at God's shutting himself up in his own inaccessibility, at the senseless secularization of the world, at the sightless and faceless materiality of the laws of the world up to the point where it is no longer merely a question of nature but of the human being — this experience, which imagines that it must interpret itself theoretically as atheism, is a genuine experience of deepest existence (even though a false interpretation is partially bound up with it) which the common thinking and speaking of Christianity is far from having learnt to take into account.

Fundamentally, however, it is only the realization that God does not belong within the world view, that the real God is not a demiurge, that he is not the spring in the clockwork of the world, that wherever anything happens in the world which forms part of the "normal" makeup of the world it is always possible to discover for it a cause which is not God himself. This realization, which corresponds only to a hypothetical atheism postulated for the purpose of the world view, and which Thomas Aquinas has already materially established when he says that in the natural order of things God acts through causes distinct from himself, this realization of troubled atheism is fundamentally only the growth of God in the spirit of humankind.

We now experience in a novel way and at a radical level with precedence what we always knew notionally with the First Vatican Council but always soft-pedaled, that God is inexpressibly elevated above everything that is or can be thought outside himself. If this is true — and it forms part of the foundations of the Christian faith — then God is elevated above every expressible statement of the world; he does not belong within such a statement; he can be spoken of only in a qualitatively different kind of statement.

That this is so is realized by humankind today, since it has come

---

* *Theological Investigations III,* 390–93.

gradually into possession of a scientific picture of the world which is as profane as the world which is not God, since he is inexpressibly elevated above it, so that there obtains no analogy between it and him which would not immediately reveal itself as surrounded by a still greater unlikeness. The truth of God and the view of the world are two things. We are just discovering today that one cannot picture God to oneself in an image that has been carved out of the wood of the world.

The contemporary intellectual has the duty which is at once pain and grace of accepting this realization, of not suppressing it in a hasty and cheap apologetic for an anthropomorphic "belief in God,'" of interpreting it rightly, that is, of understanding that it has in truth nothing to do with atheism in the proper sense. Let us freely admit to ourselves the crisis of faith. It will do no harm. We cannot discover God ruling in this world of ours quite so naively as was done in former times. We cannot do this, not because God is dead, but because he is greater, more nameless, more in the background, more incomprehensible. God *is:* that is not a proposition which one can range alongside the other propositions which constitute science.

God is: this proposition is more original than any meeting with the world because — whether we have heard it or missed hearing it — it is already stated when we begin in wonderment to ask in the sciences how we can intellectually organize the world in which we find ourselves in order to dominate it and snatch away from it a part of its dominion over us. But because the proposition "God is" is of such an utterly different kind, because though it can be heard as prestated in all other propositions its sound can also by that very fact always be drowned by all these other propositions, since in our scientific-worldly-experimental knowledge its object makes itself known through that of other propositions, and never as such for itself and alongside of other objects, for that reason God is so far away. We are far away from him, because he is the unconditioned and unlimitable, whereas we are conditioned and it is the lot of our knowledge to grasp by delimiting.

The world view and the truth which is proper to it, specific, creaturely, finite, are the sum of what can be expressed, delimited, calculated; but the absolute truth that God is, is the affirmation that he is the incomprehensible whose extension does not fit into the system of coordinates and areas which we set up to express a tangible reality by catching it up in this net of limitation.

Such knowledge cannot have the definition, the exactness, which is appropriate to that knowledge which builds up the world picture of today. Not because the former is less certain and more vague than the latter, but because it is the knowledge which intends what cannot be defined, whose content masters us and not we it; in which we do not take hold but are taken hold of; in which is stated the only self-evident reality which is by that fact incomprehensible to us.

If great spiritual processes have their meaning and their promise in spite of the fault and the foolishness of human beings, out of which they grow with one — but only one — of their roots, then the crisis of faith, the existential anguish of our time in case God should be lost to it, an anguish and a feeling which does not grow only out of the malice and superficiality, the pride and moral fault of human persons also has its meaning. God becomes greater. He recedes into a distance which first makes it possible to glimpse his boundlessness.

We Christians can be bound by a feeling of brotherhood and sisterhood, not to the militant atheists, but quite certainly to those who are agonized by the question of God, those who are silent, reserved, averse to noisy conviction: all of us have called upon the silent incomprehensibility of God with or without the name, both in us and in them the question of the most exact picture of the universe as a whole is not one that answers itself; they and we have experienced something of what we read in the scriptures: "My God, why have you forsaken me?" We hold the opinion concerning them, since we have no right to judge them, that they only think that they do not believe; we know of ourselves that we rightly express what is present in them too in the center of their spirit and the depths of their conscience without their being able themselves to articulate it conceptually, namely, that everything is encompassed, sustained, known by the knowing and loving, ineffable mystery which we call God.

This is the truth of truths, the truth which makes us free; the truth which opens. Without it everything limited, every individual truth within the picture of the world becomes the prison in which the person dies the death of an animal — although a clever one. This one truth leads indeed into the incomprehensible, the immense, into a dimension in which we are disposed and do not dispose, the adorers and not the rulers; we are taken into a vastness in which we cannot by ourselves find our way; we are caught in the grip of a destiny which is not guided by us. But the courage or, better, the believing and trusting love which entrusts itself to such incomprehensibility is the act in which the human person assents to his own most intimate being without tremblingly failing in his speech before it, in which he assents to the endless possibility of endless reality.

47 • God Is Far from Us*

We suffer not only from lacking the contentment and the carefree security of life, not only from sitting in darkness and in the shadow of death, but above all — dare we be bold to say how it really is? — we suffer because *God* seems to be far from us.

God is far from us. This is not a statement that applies to everyone. It is not a statement that should alarm the God-filled heart. But it is also not a statement in which the person to whom it applies dare take pride, thinking that at least the bitterness of his heart is infinite. This is not a statement that trumpets forth a characteristic that the person should ignore, a characteristic that would seem to prohibit God from bestowing his nearness and the certainty of his blessed love, as if despair makes a person's heart greater than good fortune does. To make the distance of God into the proud nobility of the human being (as do many forms of that interpretation of life called existential philosophy) is sin, at once stupid and perverse. In many people, God's distance is simply a fact that is there and that demands an explanation. It is a pain, the deepest pain of the fasting season of life, the season that lasts as long as we travel as pilgrims, far from the Lord.

God's "distance" here does not mean that a person denies the existence of God or that he ignores God's existence in his own life. This may often — but by no means always — be a false reaction to the situation that we mean. Here God's distance means something that can be found just as well — indeed, even above all — in believers, in human beings who yearn for God, in persons who gaze out toward his light and the gladness that his nearness brings. Even these persons (yes, especially these) can and must often experience what we mean: to them God seems most unreal — he is mute and silent in refusal, as if he embraces our existence only as an empty, distant horizon would embrace it; our thoughts and the demands of our heart go astray in this pathless infinity and wander around, never to find their way out.

God's distance means that our spirit has become humble in the face of an insoluble puzzle. It means that our heart is despondent over unanswered prayers, and is tempted to look on "God" only as one of those grand and ultimately unbelieved-in words under cover of which people hide their despair, because this despair no longer has the power to accept even itself as real. God seems to us to be only that unreal, inaccessible infinity which, to our torment, makes our tiny bit of reality seem still more finite and questionable. This infinity makes us seem homeless even in *our* world, because it leads us to the extravagance

---

* *The Eternal Year,* 66–72.

of a yearning that we can never fulfill, and that even he does not seem to fulfill.

Yes, it appears that contemporary Western humankind, more than the people of earlier times, must mature expiatingly in the purgatory of this distance from God. If in the destiny of individuals it happens that besides the blessed day of the near God, there is the night of the senses and of the spirit, in which the infinity of the living God comes nearer to human beings by seeming to be more distant and not at all near, why should such times not also be experienced in the destiny of nations and continents? Why shouldn't this, in some way and in some measure, be the holy lot of all? (That the blame for such a condition belongs, perhaps, to one particular era, is no proof against the fact that this condition can be a "blessed fall" [*felix culpa*].)

Seen from this point of view, the declared atheism of many people, theoretical as well as practical, would then be only the false reaction to such an event — false, because impatient and mistaken. It would be reactionary in the proper sense: it clung to the childish experience of the near God as claim and condition of worshiping acknowledgment. When that childish experience is gone, then a person can no longer start with God, and there is nothing for him. The atheism of our day, then, would be the stubborn blocking off of the self against calling out in the dark purgatory of a choked-up heart for the God who is always greater than the God thought of and loved the day before.

Enough. There is a distance of God that permeates the pious and the impious, that perplexes the mind and unspeakably terrifies the heart. The pious do not like to admit it, because they suppose that such a thing should not happen to them (although their Lord himself cried out, "My God, my God, why have you forsaken me"); and the others, the impious, draw false consequences from the admitted facts.

If this God-distance of choked-up hearts is the ultimate bitterness of the fasting season of our *life*, then it is fitting to ask how we are to deal with it, and (for us it is the very same question) how we can today celebrate the fasting season of the *church*. For when the bitter God-distance becomes a divine service, the fasting season of the world changes into the fasting season of the church.

The first thing we have to do is this: stand up and face this God-distance of a choked-up heart. We have to resist the desire to run away from it either in pious or in worldly business. We have to endure it without the narcotic of the world, without the narcotic of sin or of obstinate despair. What God is really far away from you in this emptiness of the heart? Not the true and living God; for he is precisely the intangible God, the nameless God; and that is why he can really be the God of your measureless heart. Distant from you is only a God who does not exist: a tangible God, a God of a human being's small thoughts and his cheap, timid feelings, a God of earthly security, a God whose concern is that the children don't cry and that philanthropy doesn't fall into disillusion, a very venerable — idol! That is what has become distant.

Should one not endure such a God-distance as this? Indeed, we can truly say: in this experience of the heart, let yourself seemingly accept with calm every despair. Let despair fill your heart so that there no longer seems to remain an exit to life, to fulfillment, to space and to God. In despair, despair not. Let yourself accept everything; in reality it is only an acceptance of the finite and the futile. And no matter how wonderful and great it may have been, let it be really you: your own self, you with your ideals, you with the preliminary estimate of your life (which was sketched out and planned with such shrewd precision), you with your image of God, that satisfies you instead of the incomprehensible one himself.

Make *yourself* block up every exit; only the exits to the finite, the paths that lead to what is really trackless, will be dammed up. Do not be frightened over the loneliness and abandonment of your interior dungeon, which seems to be so dead — like a grave. For if you stand firm, if you do not run from despair, if in despair over the idols which up to now you called God you do not despair in the true God, if you thus stand firm — this is already a wonder of grace — then you will suddenly perceive that your grave-dungeon only blocks the futile finiteness; you will become aware that your deadly void is only the breadth of God's intimacy, that the silence is filled up by a word without words, by the one who is above all name and is all in all. That silence is God's silence. It tells you that he is there.

That is the *second* thing you should do in your despair: notice that God is there. Know with faith that he is with you. Perceive that for a long time now he has been waiting for you in the deepest dungeon of your blocked-up heart, and that for a long time he has been quietly listening to you, even though you, after all the busy noise that we call our life, do not even let him get a word in edgewise, and his words to the person-you-were-until-now seem only deadly silence. You shall see that you by no means make a mistake if you give up your anxiety over yourself and your life, that you by no means make a mistake if you relax your hold on self, that you are by no means crushed with despair if once and for all you despair of yourself, of your wisdom and strength, and of the false image of God that is snatched away from you.

As if by a miracle, which must be renewed everyday, you will perceive that you are with him. You will suddenly experience that your God-distance is in truth only the disappearance of the world before the dawning of God in your soul, and that the darkness is nothing but

God's brightness, that throws no shadow, and your *lack of outlets* is only God's incomprehensibility, to whom no road is needed, because he is already there. You shall see that you should not try to run away from your empty heart, because he is already there, and so there can be no reason for you to flee from this blessed despair into consolation that would be no consolation, into a consolation that does not exist. He is there. Do not seek to hold him fast. He does not run away. Do not seek to make sure of yourself and to touch him with the hands of your greedy heart. You would only be clutching at a straw, not because he is distant and unreal, but because he is the infinite who cannot be touched. He is there, right in the midst of your choked-up heart, he alone. But he is all, and so it appears as if he were nothing.

If we do this, then peace comes all by itself. Peace is the most genuine activity: the silence that is filled with God's word, the trust that is no longer afraid, the sureness that no longer needs to be assured, and the strength that is powerful in weakness — it is, then, the life that rises through death. There is nothing more in us then but God; God and the almost imperceptible and yet all-filling faith that he is there, and that we are.

But one thing more must still be said: this God-distance would not be the rising of God in mortal, choked-up hearts if the Son of Man, who is the Son of the Father, had not suffered and done just this with us and for us and on our behalf in his own heart. But he has suffered and done all this. It happened in the garden, from whose fruit human beings wanted to press out the oil of joy, the garden that was in truth the garden of the lost paradise. He lay on his face; death crept into his living heart, into the heart of the world. Heaven was locked up and the world was like a monstrous grave; and he alone in that grave, choked up by the guilt and helplessness of the world.

As refreshment, the angel who looked like death passed him the cup of bitterness, that he might sink into agony. The earth wickedly and greedily gulped down the drops of blood of his mortal terror. God blanketed everything as with a night that no longer promised day. One can no longer separate him from death. In this vast death-silence — men slept, dulled by grief — in this death-silence the small voice of the Son floated somewhere, the only sign from God that was still left. Each moment it seemed to be stifled. But a great miracle took place: the voice remained. The Son spoke to the awful God with this tiny voice that was like a dead man's, "Father" — he spoke to his own abandon-ment — "Your will be done." And in ineffable courage he commended his abandoned soul into the hands of this Father.

Ever since that moment, our poor soul, too, is laid in the hands of this God, this Father, whose former decree of death has now become love. Ever since that time, our despair is redeemed, the emptiness of our heart has become fulfillment, and God-distance has become our homeland. *If* we pray with the Son, and, in the weary darkness of our heart, repeat his prayer in the garden. In pure faith. No storm of rapture will spring up, when his words mysteriously rise up somewhere in the depths of our hearts as our own words. But their strength will suffice. For each day it will be just enough. So long as it pleases God. And this is enough. He knows when and where our heart will be sufficiently purified — only here on earth can it be purified — to endure also the dazzling dawn of his blessedness. Our poor heart, that now in faith in Jesus Christ shares with him the night, which to the believer is nothing other than the darkness of God's boundless light, the darkness that dazzles our eyes, the heavenly night, when God really is born in our hearts.

48 • Natural Knowledge of God?*

We know from the teaching of the church that the one God as principle and goal of the world can be known with intrinsic certainty "by the light of natural reason" from the objective world. All that is immediately given in this declaration is that such knowledge is possible for human nature. We say "for human nature," that is, concretely, this possibility of knowing God (concerning the content and extent of which more will be said in a moment) is something which belongs to the constitution of the human being even in independence of revelation and the vocation which raises him by grace to a participation in the life of God in trinity.

It is a possibility, then, which the human person still has even when he has as a sinner lost the possibility of participating in God's personal life; one which consequently is still operative where and insofar as human philosophy and religion lie under the law of sin; and so one which must in some form or other necessarily be met with in the non-Christian world of human religion and philosophy, simply because he is a human being.

The phrase "rational knowledge from the world" demarcates this way of reaching God, first, from a personal divine revelation to the human person (both as inner illumination by grace and as exterior historical revelation). Further, this knowledge is distinguished from an

* *Theological Investigations I*, 82–83.

immediate experience of God (whether present in fact or not), as this is understood in every form of ontologism, no matter whether it is mystical or rational in tendency. Third, the phrase guards against a conception of experience of God which would make it something purely irrational, emotive, not available to critical examination and incapable of mediation by rational concepts and statements.

Moreover, only a *possibility* of this kind of knowledge of God is in question. A whole series of problems arises here. Does this possibility ever become a reality, and if so to what extent? How does this realization come about ? Is it due in fact to human nature alone, or are there in fact causes at work such as primitive revelation and the supernatural grace which falls to every person's share? How far does this realization depend not merely on rational and logical factors but also on a moral decision, on which again both the inherited and the personal sins of the human being have their influence as well as healing supernatural grace? For the concrete acquisition of this knowledge of God in an actual individual, how far is growth in awareness of values always a presupposition, how far are sociological preconditions required like language, education, and training of the religious sense?

All these are questions on which no decision is made in the Vatican Council's definition. Taken by itself, all that is said in this definition about the content of the rational knowledge of God is that God can be known as cause and end of the world. Nothing is finally decided about the question as to whether God can be known as creator of the world, in the strict theological sense of the word "creation."

What in concrete terms forms the content of this possible natural knowledge of God, appears perhaps most simply when we try to determine the *theological sense* of this pronouncement about a possibility of human nature; for it becomes immediately apparent that revelation could have absolutely no interest in determining a possibility of human nature, since it always has to deal with the concrete person, the individual, then, who is always within the supernatural order.

The theological sense of this decision (which in the last resort must always be related to a theological situation and not a purely natural one, in which, just in itself as a fact purely of this world, revelation would have no interest) is clearly this: that in this conception of human nature alone is it possible for a human being to be a potentially receptive subject of theology and of revelation.

It is only if the human being stands before God always and of necessity and on every presupposition, even, then, as sinner, as turned away from God and deprived of the free gift of divine life — "by nature," then — that he is that being who has to come to terms with revelation, who has the power to perceive revelation, for whom the failure to perceive revelation involves not merely deficiency but guilt.

Precisely in order to be able to experience God's self-disclosure as *grace*, that is, to be able to apprehend it as neither obvious nor immanent (just a part of the divine constitution), the human being must be a subject who in the very nature of things has to come to terms with God's disclosure or withholding of himself. Only if it is in the nature of things that he has something to do with God can he freely and spontaneously experience God's self-disclosure as it is actually promulgated in revelation: in other words, precisely so that revelation might be grace, it is necessary at least in principle that the human person should have something to do with God from a locus which is not already grace.

49 • Experience of Self and Experience of God*

If we are to speak of the experience of self *and* the experience of God, then the first point to be established is that they constitute a unity. Obviously what we mean by unity here is not simply an absolute identity. For when, in experiencing ourselves as subject, we see ourselves as "transcendental," even then this "transcendental" subject is absolutely different from that which we mean when we speak of "God." Even the most radical truth of self-experience recognizes that this subject which we are is finite, even though, precisely as such, and in its sheer transcendentality, it contains an absolute orientation toward the infinite and the incomprehensible through which it is this without being identified with it. In other words, therefore, its nature is constituted by something, and experiences itself as so constituted, which it must perforce refuse to identify itself with.

While, therefore, experience of God and experience of self are not simply identical, still both of them exist within a unity of such a kind that apart from this unity it is quite impossible for there to be any such experiences at all. Both would be lost constantly, each in its own way. This unity implies, of course, not only that every experience of God (like every other knowledge of God) as it exists in the subject is a process in which this subject is at the same time made present to itself and experiences itself. Taken by itself, such a unity would in fact still not

---

* *Theological Investigations XIII*, 124–29.

constitute any *characterization* of the experience of God as such, for in every spiritual act of knowledge or freedom, whatever it is concerned with, the subject is made present to itself.

Or, to put it in Thomas Aquinas's terms, a "complete return of the subject to itself" (*reditio completa subjecti in seipsum*) takes place. The unity between the experience of God and the experience of self is too ultimate and too all-embracing for it to consist solely in the simple fact that, as in every other "subject" of human knowledge, so too in the knowledge of God, the subject experiences himself at the same time. This unity consists far more in the fact that the original and ultimate experience of *God* constitutes the enabling condition of, and an intrinsic element in, the experience of self in such a way that without this experience of God no experience of self is possible. In other words, the personal history of the experience of God signifies, over and above itself, the personal history of the experience of the self.

Of course the point could equally well be formulated the other way round. The experience of self is the condition which makes it possible to experience God. The reason is that an orientation to absolute being, and so to God, can be present only when the subject (precisely in the act of reaching out toward absolute being) is made present to himself as something distinct from his own act and as the subject of that act. In accordance with this we can then likewise go on to assert: the personal history of experience of the self is the personal history of the experience of God.

All this is certainly something which cannot be said of every "subject" of experience. It is true that there is no experience of the self without the passive experience of subjects of some kind of an a posteriori character in the personal life of the individual concerned, subjects which are offered to the individual in the course of his life by his environment and his social milieu. To that extent the "return" to the self necessarily also involves in all cases a "projection" into the world outside. So much is this the case that true observation of the self at the level of explicit reflection upon oneself (whether scientific or nonscientific) constitutes only a very secondary and supplementary process in the totality of the human experience of the self.

Nevertheless, the knowledge of a particular individual subject within the world does not constitute the necessary condition enabling the human being to experience himself or the subject of that projection in which this experience is achieved. Yet without any experience of God, however nonthematic and nonreflective in character, experience of the self is absolutely impossible. And hence it is, as we have said, that the personal development of experience of the self constitutes the personal development of the experience of God and vice versa.

The unity which exists between experience of God and experience of the self as here understood could of course be made clear
in a process of transcendental reflection. Inevitably some of the factors involved in this have already been indicated in what we have said
so far. The transcendentality of the human person in knowledge and
freedom, as it reaches up to absolute being, the absolute future, the
incomprehensible mystery, the ultimate basis enabling absolute love
and responsibility to exist, and so genuine fellowship (or whatever
other presentation we may like to make in fuller detail of this human
transcendentality) is at the same time the condition which makes it
possible for the subject strictly *as* such to experience himself and to
have achieved an "objectification" of himself in *this* sense all along. But
this philosophical argument for the unity between experience of self
and experience of God will not be pursued any further in the present
context.

In place of this, attention may be drawn to a theological consideration which shows that such apparently remote and abstract lines
of thought have, after all, a concrete bearing upon life. The unity between the experience of God and the experience of self is the condition
which makes it possible to achieve that unity which theological tradition recognizes as existing between love of God and love of neighbor,
and which is of fundamental importance for any right understanding
of Christianity.

In order to achieve a clearer view of this, a preliminary consideration
must be included at this point. The only way in which a human being
achieves self-realization is through encounters with another person, a
person who is rendered present to his experience in knowledge and
love in the course of his personal life, one, therefore, who is not a thing
or a matter, but a person.

Of course an individual experience of self on the part of the subject,
taken in isolation and abstracted from the totality of the course of a
human life, is conceivable in connection with an individual piece of
material "subject-matter." In that case "I come to know something"
would be the formal structure of an experience of self of this kind
in connection with a piece of "subject-matter" which, following the
custom of the philosophers of old, we conceive of, not without reason,
as a material object.

In reality, however, the situation is different. Another person is not
any "piece of subject-matter," one of many in which the experience of
self can be achieved. The true, living, and concrete experience of life
which is identical with the experience of self in the concrete has, in
relation to its "pieces of subject-matter," a structure in which not every
item has an equal value.

Despite the ascendancy nowadays enjoyed by the sciences oriented toward material realities, and which also include the human being as one such material reality within their area of subject-matter, the experience of life is an experience of other persons, one in which material objects are encountered as elements connected with, and surrounding concrete persons and not otherwise.

Life in its full sense is in the concrete achieved in knowledge and freedom in which the "I" is always related to a "Thou," arising at the same moment in the "Thou" as in the "I," experiencing itself in all cases only in its encounter with the other person by recognizing itself to be different from that other person, and at the same time by identifying itself with that other person. The original objectivity of the experience of self necessarily takes place in the subjectivity of its encounters with other persons in dialogue, in trustful and loving encounter.

A human being experiences himself by experiencing the other *person* and not the other thing. The human person could not achieve a self-withdrawal from a world consisting exclusively of material objects any more than he could from his own body, the concrete experience of which as it de facto exists also in fact presupposes an encounter with the physicality of other persons. Self-experience is achieved in the unity between it and the experience of other persons. When the latter is harmoniously achieved, the former succeeds as well. He who fails to discover his neighbor has not truly achieved realization of himself either. He is not in any true sense a concrete subject capable of identifying himself with himself, but at most an abstract philosophical subject, and a person who has lost himself.

The subject's experience of himself and of the Thou who encounters him is one and the same experience under two different aspects, and that too not merely in its abstract formal nature, but in its concrete reality as well, in the degree of success or failure with which it is achieved, in its moral quality as an encounter with the real self and with another person in love or hatred. Thus the concrete relationship of the subject to himself is inextricably dependent upon the factor of how a subject encounters other human beings.

Now assuming all this (though this statement of ours constitutes only a cursory adumbration of it), we can inquire into a further implication of it, one contained in the doctrine of the Bible and the church, namely, that love of God and love of neighbor constitute a unity. In other words, it follows from this Christian doctrine that in view of the fact that on the one hand the experience of God and the experience of self are one, and on the other that the experience of self and the encounter with our neighbor are one, that all these three experiences ultimately constitute a single reality with three aspects mutually conditioning one another.

Now this also implies the converse, namely, that the unity between love of God and love of neighbor is conceivable only on the assumption that the experience of God and the experience of self are one. The unity which exists between experience of self and experience of God, which at first seemed to be formulated and pointed to in purely philosophical terms, is also an implication of that principle, basic to Christianity, that love of God and love of neighbor are one.

We must think of these three relationships of the subject to himself, to God, and to his neighbor, not simply as separate from, and existing side by side with one another like the relationships which a single subject bears to another contingent being which he chances to encounter, or to the subject-matter of a posteriori experience. These relationships, on the contrary, are present, as a matter of necessity, all at once, and as mutually conditioning one another, in every act of the subject endowed with intellect and freedom, whatever form this act may assume. Only if we recognize this can we say that the love of neighbor is the fullness of the law, and that in it the destiny of the human being as a whole is decided.

Only then can we say that person discovers himself or loses himself in his neighbor; that the human being has already discovered God, even though he may not have any explicit knowledge of it, if only he has truly reached out to his neighbor in an act of unconditional love, and in that neighbor reached out also to his own self.

In brief, among many other reasons which might be adduced for the unity of this experience, but which cannot be developed here, there is a theological one too, namely, the unity between love of God and love of neighbor. This statement can be maintained in its real and radical significance only if the relationship inherent in every act posited by the subject is extended to God and also the neighbor with the same transcendental necessity as it is to the subject himself, if God and other human beings (human beings in principle and in general, even though this is then concentrated in the concrete other subject whom he encounters as a matter of irreducible contingency in the course of his personal life) constitute not particular factors confined to one area within the total scope of the experience, but are realities present as a matter of transcendental necessity opening up and sustaining the experience in its totality.

50 • God Is No Scientific Formula*

It may be said that God is not present in the realm of science and in the world organized by it, that the scientific method is therefore a priori a-theistic, since it is concerned only with the functional relationships of the individual phenomena. The believer will not contradict this. For God may not be used as a stop-gap. For what happens in this sphere, that is, what can be proved experimentally, can certainly not be what we mean by God in the proper sense of the word.

God is not "something" beside other things that can be integrated into a common homogeneous system. If we say "God" we mean the whole, not indeed a sum of phenomena to be examined, but the whole in its incomprehensible and ineffable origin and ground which transcends that whole to which we and our experimental knowledge belong. This ground is meant by the word "God," the ground which is not the sum of individual realities but which confronts them freely and creatively without forming a "higher whole" with them. God is the silent mystery, absolute, unconditioned and incomprehensible. God is the infinitely distant horizon to which the understanding of individual realities, their interrelations and their manipulation must always point. This horizon continues to exist just as distantly even when all the understanding and action relating to it have come to a standstill. God is the unconditioned but conditioning ground, the sacred mystery because of this everlasting incomprehensibility.

If we say "God" we must not imagine that everyone understands this word and that the only question is whether what all mean by it really exists. Very often the person in the street believes it to mean something which he rightly denies, because what he imagines it to mean really does not exist. He thinks it is a hypothesis for explaining phenomena until science can give the true explanation, or someone to frighten children until they realize that nothing extraordinary happens if they are naughty. The true God is the absolute, sacred mystery to which one can only point in silent adoration. For he is the silent abyss and thus the ground of the world and of our knowledge of it. He is incomprehensible in principle, for even if we were to discover a "world formula," it would not even explain ourselves, and this formula, precisely because it was understood, would again be enveloped in the infinite mystery.

For the mystery is the only thing that is certain and that goes without saying. It calls forth the movement which examines whatever can be explained, but it is not gradually exhausted by this movement which we call science; on the contrary, it grows with the growth of our knowledge.

---

* *Grace in Freedom*, 191–95.

Hence we cannot imprison God in an exact formula, we cannot assign a place to him in a system of coordinates. We can only stammer of him and speak of him vaguely and indirectly. But we ought not to be silent about him only because we cannot speak of him properly. For he is present in our existence. True, we may always miss him, because there is no definite point which we might indicate and say: There he is. Hence we may be told to be silent about what cannot be expressed distinctly. But the believer will, because of his own experience, understand a "troubled" atheist who is silent before the dark secret of existence. Simone Weil's words, namely, that the person who denies God may be nearer to him than one who only speaks of him in clichés, may well be applied also to many who call themselves Christians. Such a person may be nearer to God because of his unfulfilled metaphysical longing, that is, if he does not selfishly enjoy, but truly suffers it. For in this case he knows more of God than the so-called believer who regards God as a question which he has long settled to his own satisfaction.

Nevertheless, God is there, not here or elsewhere, but everywhere in secret: where the ground of all silently confronts us, where we encounter the inescapable situation of responsibility, where we faithfully do our duty without reward, where we realize the blissful meaning of love, where death is accepted in the midst of life, where joy no longer has a name. In all such modes of his existence the human being is involved in something other than the strictly definable. Hence he must become more conscious of transcending what is individually determined; he must accept this transcendence — perhaps against much resistance — and finally courageously defend it. This speaking of God may ultimately only point to the question which is the human person himself and thus hint at God's mystery in silence; the result may be less adequate than any statement on another subject; the answer, aimed at God's bright "heaven," may ever again fall back into the dark sphere of the person or may consist in inexorably upholding the question that transcends any definition, formula, or phenomenon. At least in such efforts, whether successful or not, a human being continues to question; he does not despair and he will receive an answer because just this question is blessed with the experience of the incomprehensibility which we call God.

If a person who has experienced this trusts that this incomprehensibility, ineffably close, communicates itself protectingly and forgivingly, he can hardly be called a mere "theist" anymore. For such a person has already experienced the "personal" God, if he understands his "formula" correctly and does not imagine that God again becomes merely a "good" man. For what this truly and blessedly means is that God cannot be less than a human being, endowed with personality, freedom, and love, and that the mystery itself is free protective love, not an "objective order" which one can, after all, possess (at least in principle), and against which one could ensure oneself. Such a person has already understood and actually accepted what Christians call divine grace. The primeval event of Christianity has already taken place in the center of existence, namely, the direct presence of God in the human being in the "Holy Spirit."

However, much must happen before this person will become a Christian in the full, authentic sense of the word, namely, the encounter of this primeval Christian event with its own historical appearance in Jesus Christ, in whom the ineffable God is present to us also in history, in word, in sacrament, and in the confessing community which we call the church. But this necessary and holy institutional Christianity only has a meaning and is not ultimately a sublime idolatry if it really introduces the human being to the trusting, loving surrender to the holy and nameless mystery. This surrender is accomplished by freedom, which receives itself from this silent mystery, and thus our answer comes from the "Word of God" itself.

Of course the person of our scientific age, brought up, as he thinks, to sober exactness, will call such talk emotional, mere poetry and cheap comfort. For it is no formula according to which we ourselves experiment in order to arrive at a palpable result. This talk babbles of the one experiment of life which the mystery accomplishes in us.

And in every life, even in that of the scientist and technocrat, there are moments which will draw him into the center of existence when infinity looks at and calls him, who is now one with the responsibility of existence itself. Will he then shrug his shoulders and look the other way? Will he only wait until he is "normal" again, that is, absorbed by his interest in research and his daily life?

Perhaps one may often react in this way, making the commonplace person who forgets himself in material things the measure of all things, even when he investigates the universe — but will such an escape always be successful? Will he then be quite honest with himself? Surely this flight may not really be caused by sober objectivity, and a human being may even pretend to venerate the incomprehensible silence while his whole attitude actually remains an escape and he only wants a superficial and guilt-ridden well-being in order to escape from the claim of the incomprehensible. Could this escape succeed even when life no longer permits a person to pass on to research and the daily round? Perhaps he may even violate the ultimate dignity of both daily life and research because he refuses to let them reach into the sacred sphere of mystery which surrounds them. One can master life with scientific formula insofar as one has to make one's way among various events, and this may be frequently successful. But the human being himself is grounded in an abyss which no formula can measure. We must have sufficient courage to experience this abyss as the holy mystery of love — then it may be called God.

51 • The True God*

Let us ask ourselves what we know of this true God. In this respect, I must again recall what I said at first, when we were talking about the correct concept of God, of the God we do not grasp but who grasps us, whom we do not sustain but who sustains us. For our primal experience is not in fact of thinking of God, of knowing him, but of being grasped by him and known by him. My knowing, my loving, my longing, my fear, are already sustained from the very beginning by an incomprehensibility which in fact is called God; and indeed it is only when this primitive experience of God is somehow present in a more vital way through talking about God that this very talk of God makes sense, only then does reflection on God also acquire a deeper meaning. This is what we mean when we speak of the true God.

We mean by God, as Vatican I puts it, he who is ineffably exalted above all that is or can be thought of outside himself. We mean the God beyond our mind; we mean the God who is also "greater than our heart" (1 Jn 3:20) in such a way that this power overwhelming our heart is also the source of both our deepest grief and our greatest bliss. We mean — if we may speak in this way at all — the God who is infinite in all his attributes.

Think of his knowledge and wisdom, his power, his truth, his truthfulness, his fidelity, his goodness, his beauty, his eternity, his immensity, his ubiquity. Think of his freedom, his justice, his mercy; remember that "God" means just what the human person cannot say, that blazing reality which is and remains for us the absolute mystery, mystery most of all when we see him face to face for all eternity. Remember that it is God who once again sustains our knowledge when we know him; remember that God is the very word for that which marks our freedom in its ultimate, autonomous independence and yet does not belong to us. That God is the very name for the fact that something can surpass itself and that this power of self-transcendence, by being effective in us and

* The Priesthood, 12–15.

becoming — so to speak — our own innermost strength, is precisely the power that must be acknowledged as what we are not.

Remember that God is simply the incomprehensible. That is how he is the eternal, personal, knowing, self-possessing primal cause of our existence. He is the personal God who is absolutely identical with his freedom, so that we cannot — so to speak — get behind this freedom of God and cannot seriously attempt to get the measure of his freedom by making a concrete comparison with some being that can be distinguished from him.

Think what it means when we say that God lives, God sees me, continually and forever. Think what it means when we say that God is active, he sustains me, he knows beginning and end, he brings about my destiny, he takes me seriously, he continually establishes me in my proper reality; he sends me away from him and by that very fact holds me to him; he makes me a free being, even in regard to himself, and by that very fact is my lord; he is closer to me than I am to myself and by that very fact he is infinitely distant from me.

Think what it means that God loves me. Don't think that this proposition, as it is understood here by Christian faith, is a philosophical statement. It is the innermost experience of our existence, but — precisely because it is the innermost experience of our life — it is already sustained by his infinite grace. God loves me. What a tremendous thing this is when I know what is finite and infinite, what is limited and unlimitable; when I know that the absolute loves me, that is, even in his own being and freedom and through these, he is such that he grasps me, has made my nothingness a factor in his own life, has given himself to me in the innermost, free unrelatedness and inwardness of his person, in what we call grace. All this is true even if I don't know it, even if I don't think of it, even though the narrow space of my being is felt in some way to be empty, narrow and small at the very point where it is inundated by God's infinity. All this is said when we say that God loves us.

We have said nothing. And if you or I, if we, imagine that something has been said, we are deceiving ourselves. For, as the Fourth Lateran Council says, no sort of similarity can be perceived in him which is not intersected by a deadly — and for that very reason lifegiving — still greater dissimilarity. But this is just how God is to be named, just how these things are to be understood: "hidden Divinity" (*latens Deitas*), which in this incomprehensibility of its eternal mystery has given itself into our heart. "Reverently I adore you, hidden Divinity" (*Adoro te devote, latens Deitas*).

52 • God in the Old Testament*

The religion of the Old Testament is commonly spoken of as *mono-theism*. This basic characterization is quite just, provided that we understand what we mean by "monotheism" when we apply the term to Old Testament religion. Monotheism must not be understood here as a metaphysical denomination of a static kind, to be applied with equal justice to Deism. In the last resort, the monotheism of the Old Testament is not based on the rational considerations of a human being who is seeking for the ultimate unity of the world and can only find it in a transcendent source of all things; rather, it is based on the experience of Yahweh's saving deeds in the midst of this world and in the history of his people.

The heart of Old Testament monotheism is the fact that Yahweh, that is, the definite person with a proper name who actually intervenes in the history of a people and of all human persons by his own free will, has seized hold of this definite people, without regard to their natural qualities, has chosen it and made it his own people by entering into a covenant with it; and as the jealous God, has forbidden it to venerate all other numinous powers so that he might establish his uniqueness as the only God with whom his people can be concerned.

Old Testament monotheism involves a conscious recognition of this fact: it knows that this person Yahweh, freely active in history, can alone legitimately claim the title El-Elohim; that all other Elohim are not such in reality, are nothings; that this Yahweh is the absolute sovereign Lord of the world and of nature (so that every kind of worship of Baal, as a cult of the powers of nature and fertility, is a service of idols and nonsensical); that this Yahweh is wholly spirit and person, on whose free "creation" absolutely everything depends.

The further working out of this conscious recognition could safely be left to the historic development of this basic idea of Old Testament monotheism; it forms in fact the greater part of what is revealed in Old Testament history. This history does not of course advance by a merely human reflection upon the basic datum we have described, but rather through an experience of the unceasing novelty of Yahweh's personal action (so that really it is not a history of theology, but a history of revelation and salvation, of God's own speech and action in the world).

A cosmological metaphysics ascends to a first cause in the world, to an intellectual first cause, and thence to a first cause transcending the world, and thus (in principle, at least) proceeds until it has in fact achieved some understanding of God as person (in purely formal

---

* *Theological Investigations I*, 92–94.

terms, of course); in this way it terminates in the ultimate question as to whether and how this personal God might not only continue to cause the world but also — appearing alongside the world, as it were — might wish to deal with it.

The development of the Old Testament conception of God proceeds in exactly the reverse order: first comes the experience of God as a free person active in the world, a person generous and abundant, who reveals himself in his proper name, who calls and chooses; and it is only from this historical experience of who Yahweh is that it becomes progressively clearer *what* he is — not just *a* god, not just *a* powerful lord in the history of perhaps this people alone, but *the* Lord of the history of all peoples and so Lord of nature too: the transcendent, spiritual cause and source of all reality, lifted up above every earthly limitation.

This Lord (because of the original starting point of his people's knowledge of him) is not dissolved in the empty indistinctness of an impalpable metaphysical concept, but remains in his absolute transcendence of all earthly things concretely and unambiguously *he*, just as he wished in his sovereign freedom to show himself, in the course of the unique history of his covenant with this people. A brief formulation of what we have learnt would run as follows: the basic form of Old Testament monotheism is not, "One God exists" (there is a single primary cause of the world), but "Yahweh is the unique God."

53 • God in the New Testament*

The first thing that strikes us when we try to find out how the people of the New Testament thought about God is the unquestioning assurance which characterized their consciousness of him. It never occurred to these people to raise the question of his existence as such. The New Testament knew nothing of all those characteristic features of our consciousness of God today: an anxious sense that questioning must come first, a sense that it is first necessary slowly and reflectively to lay a firm foundation before any sort of intimation, developed feeling, or recognition of God can be admitted; a feeling that God never fails to withdraw himself from the grip of the human being's questions; a fear that after all God may be nothing but a monstrous projection of our subjective needs and yearnings; a suffering in religious doubt.

For the New Testament God is in the first place simply there. He

---

* *Theological Investigations I*, 94–96, 98–100.

is there: in spite of all his incomprehensibility and sublimity, all the fear and trembling, and the overwhelming joy which this divine reality may have in store for human beings, nevertheless, as simply the most evident fact of all, the fact in no need of proof or explanation, he is really there. For the people of the New Testament the question is not whether the reality of the world which they can see and touch might perhaps point beyond itself to the infinite darkness of a wholly other; all they are concerned with is how this God, who has always been given and self-evident, actually behaves, so that the human being might for the first time learn how things really stand with himself and the world.

It is not the immediate reality of the world and its visible magnitude which serve as a kind of permanent base from which, subsequently as it were, God is going to come within reach, but just the reverse: it is only under God that human beings find their own reality and the reality of the world really clear and comprehensible. This unquestioning assurance of God's existence does not arise from any properly metaphysical considerations, nor is it troubled or put off balance by the awareness that this kind of genuine knowledge of God is absent in the rest of the New Testament world.

First, then, this unquestioning assurance does *not* really arise from *metaphysical* reflection. Proofs for the existence of God are never produced. There is never any guidance on how the individual might by himself develop a consciousness of God, nowhere an appeal to a need for God with the intention of eliciting a conscious conviction of his existence.

The New Testament is indeed aware of a self-consistent possibility of knowing God from the world. The one and only true God, his "power" and "divinity" (this abstract metaphysical term occurs only twice in the New Testament), his "wisdom" and the "kingdom of God," God's sanction of the natural moral law as a divine ordination (1 Cor 1:21; Rom 1:32; 2:14), can be known through what is made (Rom 1:20) always and everywhere, hence in independence of God's historical action in the world (Rom 1:21); and they can be known with such certainty that the refusal to acknowledge God by revering him or giving thanks (Rom 1:21) involves moral guilt, which provokes the wrath of God (Rom 1:18).

For St. Paul, something knowable exists in God, which while remaining objective, presents itself openly for the human being's recognition (Rom 1: 19). According to St. Paul again, the character of the world as created must always have been apparent to human beings (Rom 1:20). There is always the possibility for the world of a "wisdom" that can come to know God from the wisdom of God objectivized in the world (1 Cor 1:21). In spite of its certainty this possible knowledge of God, which is moreover always somehow present in actual fact (Rom

1:19–21), always essentially involves the human being's moral and religious decision. Although God is never far from human beings (Acts 17:27), their situation is such that they must seek him; so that in consequence of this character of the knowledge of God as *decision,* it is uncertain whether they will in fact touch him and find him (Acts 17:27).

But for the actual consciousness of the people of the New Testament this metaphysical possibility is *not* the *existential* support and cause of their consciousness of God. The metaphysical knowledge of God is never discussed at length. It is never invoked by the people of the New Testament as far as their own experience of God is concerned; reference is only made to it so as to show how ignorance of God is comprehensible as moral depravity, to convict someone who does not know God of sin.

Even where this metaphysical possibility is briefly touched on in the context of an apologetic for monotheism (Acts 17:22ff.), the final motive of conversion to the living God is not the metaphysical argument but the historical activity of God himself revealing himself in the foolishness of the cross (1 Cor 1:18ff.) and the resurrection (Acts 17:31). These are facts which are brought home to people not in the form of a truth in itself basically reasonable and available at all times for inspection, by helpful guidance and instruction, but by preaching and proclamation, by an announcement which exacts not intelligent comprehension but obedient acknowledgment.

The *inner reason* for the unquestioning assurance of God's reality, the basic reason for this unquestioning assurance which characterizes the human person's consciousness of God in the New Testament is the simple and massive fact that God had *revealed himself,* that by his action he himself had intervened in the history of this people and so had given testimony to his own actuality.

Above all else the people of the New Testament are convinced that God had revealed himself in the Old Testament history of the people of the covenant. "In many and various ways God spoke of old to our fathers by the prophets" (Heb 1:1). Their God is the God of the fathers (Acts 3:13), the God of Abraham, Isaac, and Jacob (Mt 22:32), who showed himself to Abraham (Acts 7:2), who by the covenant had made the people his people (Mt 2:6) and himself Israel's God (Lk 1:68).

The people of the New Testament see this God at work throughout the history of this, their people (Stephen's speech, Acts 7:2–53; St. Paul's preaching at Antioch, Acts 13:16–41). They know God by seeing his action in the saving history peculiar to Israel. So too the prophetic monotheism of the Old Testament is for them the foundation of their knowledge of God.

But their knowledge of God is not derived just from his self-disclosure in the past history of their people; they experience the living reality of God in his new activity in their own history. God reveals himself anew to them too. God has spoken to them in his own Son *now* (Heb 1:2), now made known his saving grace (Ti 2:11; 3:4; 2 Tm 1:10) through the Son of God, through whom they have come to faith in God (1 Pt 1:21). The Son has declared God to them, whom no one has seen (Jn 1:18); they have seen the Son of God with their own eyes, have heard him and touched him with their hands (1 Jn 1:1). God's glory shines for them in the face of Christ (2 Cor 4:6; Jn 12:45).

For the people of the New Testament and just *their* situation in the plan of salvation, an indissoluble bond connects their experience in faith of the reality of Christ and their knowledge in faith of God. Hence the large number of expressions in which Christ and God are associated: eternal life is the knowledge of the only true God and of him whom he has sent (Jn 17:3); the turning away from idols to the service of the true and living God and the waiting for his Son are, as it were, the basic formula of Christianity (1 Thes 1:9–10).

What St. John preaches is "fellowship" with the Father and his Son (1 Jn 1:3). Salvation is fulfilled in "the knowledge of God and of Jesus our Lord" (2 Pt 1:2). And these two realities do not stand unrelatedly side by side, nor are they connected merely objectively; they are now so inseparably connected even in the experience of the believer that whoever abandons one does away with the other too: "No one who denies the Son has the Father" (1 Jn 2:23).

The New Testament does indeed allow for a true and enduring knowledge of God even without the possession in faith of his Son. But in that crisis in which the person whom Christ has encountered has to make a decision, this kind of true knowledge of God, such as the Jews perhaps have (cf. Rom 2:17ff.), ceases to be the only knowledge which matters to the New Testament: that knowledge which brings a person into real relationship with the living God as savior. And in this sense those who do not have the Son do not in fact "know" God at all, not as though it were only as Father of the Son precisely that they do not know him.

So the Lord can say: "If I glorify myself, my glory is nothing; it is my Father who glorifies me, of whom you say that he is your God. But you have not known him; I know him" (Jn 8:54–55). Because they do not acknowledge and love the Son come from the Father and sent by him (Jn 8:42), they no longer acknowledge the God whose sons they are convinced they are in virtue of the old covenant.

But the people of the New Testament, the witnesses of the whole reality of Christ (Acts 2:22,32; 3:15; 10:39; 13:31), have had the living, tangible experience of Christ, his reality, his miracles and his resurrection. They have encountered God there. They know him from his living, powerful action among them in Christ. The primary thing is not a carefully constructed philosophical conception of God, but God's own concrete self-disclosure to them in Christ.

54 • The Uniqueness of God in the New Testament*

When Jesus was asked which was the first of all commandments and answered that it was the commandment of love — and this is the heart of the Pauline and Johannine message too — he himself in this critical context (Mk 12:29ff.) cited the Shema: "Hear, O Israel: the Lord our God, the Lord is one." The scribe can only confirm Jesus' profession of the faith of his people, once more in the words of the Old Testament (Dt 6:4; 4:35): "He is one, and there is no other but he" (Mk 12:32).

This confession of the *one* God runs through the entire New Testament. In Jesus' own words, eternal life is that they should know the only true God (Jn 17:3) and be mindful of the glory which is from this *one* God alone (Jn 5:44). Thus testimony to the uniqueness of the sole God is consistently recurring throughout the New Testament.

Now this monotheism is not just a fragment of tradition taken over from the Old Testament, although it is in fact usually expressed in the old traditional formulas. It is bound up with the basic Christian confession; and when Christ wanted to state as briefly as possible what that eternal life was which he offered us, he spoke of the knowledge of the one true God (Jn 17:3). When St. Paul, in the earliest portion of the New Testament, sums up what has come about in the Thessalonians who have become Christians, once again the first item to be mentioned is conversion to the living and true God in opposition to the many false gods (1 Thes 1:9). And from God's uniqueness St. Paul derives support for two of his central themes: the calling of the Gentiles to the same rights in the New Israel (Rom 3:28–30; 10:12; 1 Tm 2:4–5) and the unity of the multiple workings of the Spirit among Christians in the one body of Christ (1 Cor 12:6; Eph 4:6). Again the notion "the gospel of God" seems in many places (Rom 15:16; 1 Thes 2:2,8,9), in view of the context, to have the sense, "gospel of the one true God." Confession of faith in the one true God is one of the essential elements in the gospel of Christ.

* *Theological Investigations I*, 100–104.

The central significance of New Testament monotheism becomes still clearer when we try to discover what is meant by this teaching. This confession is not concerned with a mere metaphysical matter of course, merely the primary cause of every sort of reality, necessarily conceived as of an ultimate unity. This one God is indeed spoken of as the primary cause of all things, "from whom are all things" (1 Cor 8:6). He is the "Father of us all, who is above all and through all in all" (Eph 4:6), "the same God who inspires all in everyone" (1 Cor 12:6). He gives to all life and breath and all things (Acts 17:25); "in him we live and move and have our being" (Acts 17:28), so that "he is not far from each one of us" (Acts 17:27); and because of this ontological relationship to the world, it is possible in principle, according to St. Paul, for God to be known from the world in his "deity" (Rom 1:20). We have already noted that this metaphysical knowledge of God is a buried knowledge, only brought to some understanding of itself by actual contact with God's revelation in action; but even apart from this fact the confession of the "one God" of its very nature goes beyond knowledge of a unified first cause and end of the world. Here too we have an instance of what has been called "prophetic" monotheism.

In the first place, it is not simply a matter of establishing the uniqueness of this one God in a neutral way; rather, he is confessed in faith: "for us there is one God" (1 Cor 8:6), although (and because) there are "many 'gods' and many 'lords' " in the world (1 Cor 8:5), although (and because) behind the polytheism in the face of which monotheistic confession is made, there stand real demonic powers and not just error and misconception.

As in the Old Testament, the one God of whom confession is made is not primarily the end term of autonomous knowledge, but the living, acting God who makes himself known by his own action. And so the formula for the New Testament does not run, "There exists one God," somewhat in the sense of the Enlightenment, "We all believe in one God"; but on the contrary, he who has actively manifested himself in Christ and in the pneumatic reality of salvation which has come into being with Christ, that is the unique God.

And here too it is distinguished from Old Testament monotheism: the *Father* of our Lord *Jesus* Christ is the unique God, and just this is the denial of Judaism. Because the one God whom the people of the New Testament confess is the living God who was at work in the saving history of the Old Testament and definitively revealed himself in his Son, the people of the New Testament like to go on using the old expressions "God of the fathers," "God of Israel," "God of Abraham, Isaac, and Jacob," and speak in the manner of the Old Testament about "our" God, or quite personally "my" God.

On the other hand they speak also of the God and Father of our Lord Jesus Christ, or again more briefly of the God of our Lord Jesus Christ (Eph 1:17). This concrete God is the unique God intended when monotheism is professed. Anyone who confesses the one God, and does not thereby intend to confess in this God the God of the fathers and of our Lord Jesus Christ, certainly does not mean the God of whom the primitive church made confession: "For us there is one God" (1 Cor 8:6).

The uniqueness of the divine nature in the world and in history is *not* supposed to be something established in a merely *static* way. God's uniqueness has first to become operative in the world and in history. God must first *become* for humans the unique God. For human beings to confess the unique God does not imply merely the confession of a fact but the acceptance of a task; for this God who acts in history intends precisely by this means to extend his "Lordship," the acknowledgment of his unique divinity, so it is truly only by a slow process that he becomes the unique God (2 Cor 6:16), until at the end of time he will really be "God, all in all" (1 Cor 15:28).

In consequence, it is precisely in the commandment of all-embracing and exclusive love for this one God that monotheism finds its achievement. For in this alone can it become apparent whether the one God is really God, and indeed the unique God, for those who confess him. They must have no idols beside God, neither Mammon (Mt 6:24) nor the belly (Phil 3:19), neither statues (1 Cor 10:21; 12:2; 2 Cor 6:16) nor forces of the cosmos (Gal 4:8ff.), neither local rulers (Acts 4:19; 5:29) nor the emperor in Rome (Mk 12:17), nor again the angels (Col 2:18).

What matter is to serve God and give him what is his, to listen to him and rely on him alone; what matters is to remain faithful to God in the face of the gravest threats, to the point of death by martyrdom: a continually new "turning to God from idols, to serve a living and true God" (1 Thes 1:9) — in this Jesus and primitive Christianity see the real meaning of "one God." As a profession of faith monotheism may have been a matter of course to the people of the New Testament; in the actual conduct of their lives it was always a new task.

From what has been said it becomes a little clearer perhaps — this is an old problem of the schools — how there can be a "belief that God is one" (cf. Jas 2:19). The question which concerns us here is whether, on the basis of what has been said about the content of New Testament monotheism, it is possible to explain at least in part how the first article of the creed as such can be an object of faith — which St. Thomas Aquinas, for instance, denied (I, q.2, art. 2, ad 1; II–II, q.1, art. 5). There is nothing wrong in saying that anyone who has recognized that an ultimate cause of the world exists cannot at the same time believe this in faith. In this sense St. Thomas is perfectly correct when he says: "it is impossible for one and the same thing to be known and believed by the same person. Hence it is equally impossible that one and the same thing be an object of science and of belief for the same person."

But this sort of faith is not in question at all in monotheistic faith, as we have seen. We do not believe by faith in a unified, ultimate cause of the world, which as such is known and not believed in; but we believe by faith in a person living and active in history, of whose existence we can become aware because of his activity, before it is known as the absolute being which is the foundation of everything: we believe what this person says, namely, that he and he alone is the absolute God. It is *possible* to believe that Yahweh, that the Father of our Lord Jesus Christ (both understood as proper names in the strict sense), is the unique God, because logically it is not yet necessary nor is it possible that, before the content of this self-disclosure is known, the person who reveals these things should be known in that respect precisely in which he reveals himself by actually speaking.

55 • God as Person in the New Testament*

For the people of the New Testament God's personal being is a living reality. Their knowledge of God is not the result of their own theoretical study of the world but of their experience of God's living activity among them. The countless examples of living prayer in the New Testament are so many testimonies to the personal God in whom primitive Christianity believed; and they indicate at the same time in what sense the concept of God's personality must be understood here: the God of the New Testament is a God whom human beings may address as *Thou*, in a way in which only a personal being can be addressed as *Thou*.

We shall see in more detail what was involved in thinking of God as a person by attempting to set out the individual elements in this conception of a personal God.

God is he who acts; he who is free; he who acts in a historical dialogue with human persons; and he who in the true sense tells us about his "attributes" — which would otherwise remain hidden — only through this activity.

---

* *Theological Investigations I*, 104–12.

God is the one who *acts*. In metaphysical knowledge of God from the world, where God is apprehended in the sense of the Vatican definition as the "ground and goal" of all reality, God is also in a certain sense one who acts, he who sets up all reality. We may leave out of account here the fact that because of original sin the unity of the one transcendent God is concealed by the human person's subjection to a plurality of cosmic powers which he makes into idols.

But even setting this aside, God's activity is in a certain sense concealed in "natural" theology by the mere fact that for the metaphysician absolutely *everything* is an objectification of God's activity. In this way God's activity remains absolutely transcendent: it has no "here and now" within the world such that in this "here and now" it might be grasped and experienced in distinction from all that it is not. Because *everything* is God's action, this action fades, as it were, into the anonymity of the "always and everywhere," as far as human knowledge is concerned, for human knowledge remains essentially dependent on recognizing something by bringing it into relief against other things of a different kind.

Now what characterizes the experience of God in the New Testament (as of course it did in the Old Testament too) is that it knows of a definite and distinct activity of God *within* the world: it knows of God's saving activity in history, an activity which, as God's new, free initiative, neither instituted jointly with the world nor already contained in it, possesses a quite definite "here and now" in the world and in human history, distinct from all other being and becoming.

The New Testament does indeed also know with complete assurance that *everything* is, moves, and lives in him (Acts 17:27), God as "the God." It sees the "Father of all" (Eph 4:6) at work everywhere, in nature too; it sees how he makes the sun rise and the rain fall, clothes the lilies of the field and feeds the birds of the air, as the God of the fruitful seasons, sating the human heart with food and gladness (Acts 14:17). It sees him at work, too, in the history of humanity as a whole, the spreading abroad of the various races as the historical epochs succeed each other, the coming and going of peoples (Acts 17:26).

But close observation shows that the New Testament completely lacks any expression of numinous feeling for the cosmos, excited by the world, its greatness, and glory. And this is quite apart from the fact that the New Testament, when it speaks of the glory of the lilies, also remembers that they wither and are cast into the oven, and is generally aware that the whole of creation has been caught up in the sinfulness of human beings and is thus remote from God, groaning for the revelation of its own glory (Rom 8:22).

Thus on the one hand the New Testament is capable of seeing God powerfully at work in the whole of reality and history, and on the other God never becomes for it the mysterious glimmer of an absolute immanent in the world; the world is never deified but remains always the creature of the Lord beyond all world who shapes it freely by his word.

And this is because the New Testament has experienced God's activity *within* the world, and for that reason there can never be any uncertainty about that activity of his either, from which the total reality of the cosmos derives. For the New Testament, God's self-revelation in the world is never a quality which adheres uniformly to every reality in the world. In his sovereign freedom he has chosen a people for himself to the exclusion of all others and made it his people (Acts 13:17ff.); this people alone possessed the covenant and the giving of the law and the promise (Rom 9:4;Jn 4:22); he has sent his Son (Rom 8:3; Gal 4:4), so that upon this unique historical event depend the human being's entire salvation and the transfiguration of the whole world (Acts 4:12; Eph 2:18).

The New Testament is strongly conscious of a sharply defined saving activity of God within the whole of human history, which as a whole possesses no immediate relation to God's salvation at the start. So strong is this consciousness, that the calling of nations to reconciliation and community with God is not inferred from some metaphysical knowledge of God's necessary goodness but is the great mystery of God's free election, hidden from all humanity, yet disclosed contrary to all expectations, God, as it were, suddenly calling all nations to salvation in spite of the elective, discriminatory freedom of his love (Acts 11:17–18; Eph 2:11ff.). It is from this experience of God's free personal activity within history that the confession of God as *creator of the world,* simply speaking, also acquires its specific validity and clarity.

First, we may say that in the New Testament (as in the Old Testament) it is never claimed that natural knowledge from the world includes as one of its objects a free creation of a temporal world "out of nothing." We leave undecided the question whether and how far the character of the world as *created* in the strict sense is available to natural theology. The New Testament (like the Old) accepts its knowledge of the world's createdness in the strict sense from the God who speaks and reveals himself. Further, the human person only really learns what *creating* is from God's powerful activity in history, unconstrained by any prior obligation. It is here that the human person experiences concretely the truth that God "calls into existence the things that do not exist" (Rom 4:17), a formula which is on the one hand related to God's free activity in the history of Abraham, and on the other is used by the New Testament as a clear expression for creation "out of nothing."

Thus knowledge of God's historical activity within the world and knowledge of his creative omnipotence through his mere word over against everything which is not he, complete and support each other reciprocally. Because he is Lord of heaven and earth, he can maintain his sway in sovereign power and freedom over the destinies of the world and of human beings (Mt 11:25; Acts 4:24ff.; Eph 1:11). And in this sway over history the human person has a deep impression of God's free and unconstrained sovereignty in action, his creativeness — "the immeasurable greatness of his power" (Eph 1:19) which shows itself with power in the resurrection, gives us "faith in the working of God" (Col 2:12), and so allows us to experience concretely and vividly the fact that God is "he who accomplishes all things according to the counsel of his will" (Eph 1:11).

This God who acts in nature and in human history is one who acts *freely.* God manifests himself as person in his activity precisely by the fact that this activity is voluntary and free. Precisely because the activity even in his world arises from God's spontaneous resolution, which is not something given along with other ingredients in the original constitution of the world, its tendencies and finalities, it becomes clear that this active God is the God transcending natural and human worlds, that God's activity is not just another word for the world-process, that his will is not just another word for "fate." It is on the basis of a concrete experience of free irruptions into the historical course of the world, novel and unexpected and extrinsic to the world's immanent dynamism, that the people of the New Testament recognize God as a free, transcendent person.

They do indeed know of the *eternity* of God's definitive decree, the purpose of his will to lead all history and the whole world to their definitive goal (Rom 16:25; 1 Cor 2:7; Eph 1:4; 3:9; Col 1:26; 2 Tm 1:9), and go on at once to reflect on it; and what is true of this divine purpose is obviously true of God's historical activity in the world in general. And this is to say that God's freedom has determined from the very beginning a goal for the world and for human beings which is in fact infallibly pursued and attained in the history of the world.

But it is certainly not to say that this final unified and definitive plan of salvation had always been so deeply imprinted upon the world from the very beginning and objectified there that, from the very beginning, everything was going to run its course according to a natural law, in such a way that, as in Deism, God would throughout the whole of time merely be the spectator of the immanent unfolding of that reality which he had created in the beginning.

God's plan of salvation has rather been an absolute secret of his, concealed from all earlier ages and generations, and which only now, in the last times, becomes objectively real and thereby makes itself known. The reality of salvation in Christ has now emerged in the world for the first time (Ti 2:11; 3:4) and *in consequence* become manifest (2 Tm 1:10); so that revelation is not just instruction about something which has always been the case, but the unveiling of the new unfoldings of God's free activity.

That this activity of God in Christ takes place precisely now and not at some other time (Heb 1:2; Col 1:26; Rom 16:25), that it emerges over against the human being lost through sin; that contrary to every human standard it is aimed at the poor, the weak, the foolish among people (Mt 11:25; Lk 1:51ff.; 1 Cor 1:25ff.), to human beings who can lay absolutely no claim to it in justice; that it is thus pure grace — from all this the individual person learns that this activity is God's really new, original initiative, his free doing.

Disciplined by this experience of God's incalculable freedom as shown in the basic facts of our salvation, a person of the New Testament is now capable of seeing God's free activity at work *elsewhere* throughout nature and grace. What is distinctive in individual natural bodies is just as much the work of his freedom as the overwhelming and incomprehensible differentiation in his mercy and his reprobation, as the vocation to offices and gifts, as the appointing of a time for the end.

The eternity and immutability of God's free decree on the one hand, and its incalculability in terms of the previous situation of the world on the other, belong together and together form the presupposition for any proper human attitude to God. On the one hand, one can rely in faith on the fact that God is faithful and true, that his decrees are unchangeable and without repentance.

On the other hand, what is still to come about by God's act, in its existential concreteness, continues to remain within God's sovereign power of disposal, and remains for us a mystery only fully to be unveiled at the end of all the ages; and for that reason this free God is never at the power of human calculations: God remains free Lord.

Because the God who acts is set over against human beings, and because he has mercy on whom he will and hardens whom he will (Rom 9:15–18), his free and sovereign dispensation is first and last for our "existence" (in the modern sense of the word). St. Paul does not even begin to try to formulate a theodicy in respect of God's free choice in grace: "But who are you, a man, to answer back to God?" (Rom 9:20) The rightness and holiness of God's decision rests in itself alone, precisely because it is free; it is not to be traced back to some necessitating source which has the lucidity of its necessity.

In the third place God shows himself as person in that he deals with the human person in a historical *dialogue,* that he allows the human being, his creature, really to be a person too. Some brief explanation is needed of what we mean by this.

Every purely metaphysical knowledge of God which starts from immediately perceptible reality and penetrates to its ultimate cause — and calls it God — always at least runs the risk of conceiving the world as a pure function of God, in such a way that the world becomes a pure expression and objectification of this cause, merely a derived function of God (as opposed to the risk of making God into merely the inner meaning of the world). Thus it is almost impossible for metaphysics to avoid the danger of forgetting the two-sided personal relationship between God and the created spirit, the danger of not understanding that the personal God so transcends the world that he can allow this world, which is totally dependent on him, a genuine activity, even with regard to himself; that what is totally dependent on him acquires through his own agency a genuine independence with regard to him; that God can set human beings free with regard to God himself.

Further, this relationship between God and human beings, which is so obscure for metaphysics, is seen at its clearest precisely in the *saving* history of God's dealings with human persons. The human being takes part in a real *dialogue* with God. He gives God's word to him the answer which he, the person, wants to give. And his may turn out contrary to God's will. The individual can harden his heart (Rom 2:5; Heb 3:13); he can resist the Spirit of God; he can obey or not obey God's will; he can contradict God; he can shut the doors of his heart to God when he knocks; he can set his will in opposition to God's plan of salvation.

The existence of powers in the world which are hostile to God and which are yet creatures of the one God, cannot be separated from this reality of a personal independence of the created spirit; the reality of sin, its inexcusability before God, God's wrath over sin, his summons to reconciliation, prayer, the existential genuineness of which depends on the human being's having a genuine initiative with regard to God — all these realities witnessed to in the New Testament presuppose the same bi-personal relationship between God and human beings.

God's activity in the course of saving history is not a kind of monologue which God conducts by himself; it is a long dramatic dialogue between God and his creature, in which God confers on human beings the power to make a genuine answer to his word, and so makes his own further word dependent upon the way in which human persons do in fact freely answer. God's free action never ceases to take new fire in human activity.

History is not just a play in which God puts himself on the stage and creatures are merely what is performed; the creature is a real coperformer in this human-divine drama of history. And so history has a real and absolute seriousness, an absolute decision, which is not to be relativized as far as the creature is concerned with the remark — at once true and false — that everything rises from God's will and nothing can resist it.

The scriptural basis for what has just been said lies in the simple and yet incomprehensible fact that in the Bible the almighty, absolute, the "ruler of all" (Rv 1:8), through his own personally expressed word, calls upon his creature, the work of his hands, to do his will; and that accordingly this word which calls upon someone else cannot be meaningless, although it proceeds from him who has the power to do all things.

Although the creature is given free play in this way, the power to make a real answer to God, God retains the last word: not only in the sense that as the stronger physically, so to speak, he finally acts in such a way that no reaction of the creature can follow his action, having no further power to withstand it; but also in the sense that even the creature's sinful act, while it does indeed involve total disaster for the creature itself, is nevertheless incapable of leaving the field of God's ultimate will — the will by which God wills his glory.

For God's power is revealed even in those vessels of his wrath which have fallen into destruction (Rom 9:22, 23). So far as we have any knowledge of it from God, the history of the world, from the point of view of the world and in isolation, closes with a shrill disharmony never to be resolved. What is exterior to God is never in itself resolved into an ultimate, all-embracing harmony; and yet, and precisely in this way, the world proclaims the glory of the God whose ways are unfathomable and whose decisions are inscrutable.

A creature can be reconciled with this end of all the world only if it unreservedly gives glory to God, and loves him and adores him precisely in the unfathomable, inappelable freedom of his will; loves him, then, more than itself, so that solidarity with God's will is more important to it than solidarity with anything else, like itself created.

It is only after reaching some understanding of the living and free personal being of the transcendent God who is able to enter into an active dialogue with the world, that we can begin to examine the teaching of the New Testament about God's "attributes." For we have to know God as person before we can understand that the decisive question for human beings is not, strictly speaking, *what* God is, but as *whom* he wishes freely to show himself with regard to the world.

A person does not strictly speaking have *attributes* with respect to another person: he has freely and personally adopted attitudes. And this is above all true of God's absolute, sovereign being as person with regard to his world. Certainly these free attitudes which God has adopted with regard to the world, have, so to speak, a metaphysical structure, arising from God's necessary nature; but the attitude actually adopted is not unambiguously laid down in consequence of this structure.

He can have mercy and he can harden the human heart; he can enlighten them and he can send "upon them a strong delusion" (2 Thes 2:11) or a "spirit of stupor" (Rom 11:8), without thereby ceasing to be the holy one (Heb 12:10; 1 Pt 1:15) and his judgments ceasing to be true and just (Rv 19:2). With respect to this God of the New Testament, then, everything depends for the human being on how God in fact behaves with regard to the person, not just on how he necessarily is in himself.

The experiences by which a person learns about God in saving history are not just exemplifications, instances to show the attributes of God as a metaphysical entity which the individual knows in its necessary character; they are experiences containing a teaching of which the human being can only become aware through the experience. This experience therefore always remains new and unexpected; what is learnt from it is not identified with something always and already there, but itself occurs for the first time. The kernel of what the New Testament declares about God's "attributes," then, is not a doctrine about God as an abstract metaphysical entity, but an announcement about the concrete, personal countenance which God shows to the world.

56 • On the Personal Being of God*

The statement that God is a person, that he is a personal God, is one of the fundamental Christian assertions about God. But it creates special difficulties for people today, and rightly so. When we say that God is a person, and this in a sense which as yet has nothing to do with the question about the so-called three persons in God, then the question about the personal character of God becomes a twofold question: we can ask whether God in his own self must be called a person; and we can ask whether he is person only in relation to us, and whether in his own self he is hidden from us in his absolute and transcendent distance.

Then we would have to say that he is a person, but that he does not by any means for this reason enter into that personal relationship to us which we presuppose in our religious activity, in prayer, and in our turning to God in faith, hope, and love. We shall not have touched the

---

* *Foundations of Christian Faith*, 73–75.

real difficulties which such an assertion about God as person creates for people today until we have discussed explicitly the relationship between God and the human person, the self-communication of God to the human being in grace as the transcendental constitution of the person.

If we prescind from these difficulties for the time being, then the assertion that God is a person, is the absolute person who stands in absolute freedom vis-à-vis everything which he establishes as different from himself, this assertion is really self-evident, just as much as when we say that God is the absolute being, the absolute ground, the absolute mystery, the absolute good, the absolute and ultimate horizon within which human existence is lived out in freedom, knowledge, and action.

It is self-evident first of all that the ground of a reality which exists must possess in itself beforehand and in absolute fullness and purity this reality which is grounded by it, because otherwise this ground could not be the ground of what is grounded, and because otherwise the ground would ultimately be empty nothingness which, if the term is really taken seriously, would say nothing and could ground nothing.

Of course the subjectivity and personhood which we experience as our own, the individual and limited uniqueness through which we are distinguished from others, the freedom which has to be exercised only under a thousand conditions and necessities, all of this signifies a finite subjectivity with limitations which we cannot assert with these limitations of its ground, namely, God.

And it is self-evident that such an individual personhood cannot belong to God, who is the absolute ground of everything in radical originality. If, then, we wanted to say that in this sense God is not an individual person because he cannot experience himself as defined in relation to another or limited by another, because he does not experience any difference from himself, but rather he himself establishes the difference, and hence ultimately he himself is the difference vis-à-vis others, then we are correct in saying that personhood in this sense cannot be asserted of God.

But if we proceed this way, then we could do the same with regard to every transcendental concept which is applied to God. When I say that God is the original meaning, the ground, the absolute light, the absolute being, and so on, then I have to know what ground, meaning, and so on, are supposed to mean, and I can make all of these assertions only in an analogous sense. This means that I can make them only within that movement in which the comprehending subject allows his comprehension, as it were, to flow into the holy, ineffable, and incomprehensible mystery.

If anything at all can be predicated of God, then the concept of "personhood" has to be predicated of him. Obviously the statement that "God is a person" can be asserted of God and is true of God only if, in asserting and understanding this statement, we open it to the ineffable darkness of the holy mystery. Obviously, precisely as philosophers, we know what this statement means more concretely and more exactly only if, following an ultimate maxim of genuine philosophizing, we do not fill the philosophical a priori in its empty formality and formal emptiness arbitrarily, or arbitrarily leave it empty, but rather allow this formal assertion to receive its content from our historical experience. In this way we allow God to be person in the way in which he in fact wants to encounter us and has encountered us in our individual histories, in the depths of our conscience, and in the whole history of the human race.

Hence we must not make the formal emptiness and empty formality of the transcendental concept of person, which is asserted of God, into a false god, and refuse from the outset to allow him to fill it through personal experience in prayer, in one's personal and individual history where God draws close to us, and in the history of Christian revelation. From this perspective a certain religious naiveté, which understands the personhood of God almost in a categorical sense, has its justification.

The ground of our spiritual personhood, which in the transcendental structure of our spiritual self always discloses itself as the ground of our person and at the same time remains concealed, has thereby revealed itself as person. The notion that the absolute ground of all reality is something like an unconscious and impersonal cosmic law, an unconscious and impersonal structure of things, a source which empties itself out without possessing itself, which gives rise to spirit and freedom without itself being spirit and freedom, the notion of a blind, primordial ground of the world which cannot look at us even if it wants to, all of this is a notion whose model is taken from the context of the impersonal world of things.

It does not come from that source in which a basic and original transcendental experience is really rooted: namely, from a finite spirit's subjective and free experience of itself. In its very constitution a finite spirit always experiences itself as having its origins in another and as being given to itself from another — from another, therefore, which it cannot misinterpret as an impersonal principle.

57 • God Is Love*

Of all that human beings have learnt by experience about God in saving history the decisive thing is that out of his grace God the Father has called us in his Son to the most intimate community with him: it is summed up in the proposition: "God is love" (1 Jn 4:16). But to see what this proposition means we must undertake a somewhat more extensive inquiry. With regard to God's personal activity, the New Testament understands that the free, living God can act differently at different times, can enter into different relationships with human beings. The decisive feature of this understanding is that it involves a knowledge of the fact which is precisely *not* a matter of course for the New Testament understanding of God, that the free, incalculable God has spoken his last, *definitive* word in the dramatic dialogue between God and humanity.

God is the free and the transcendent, whose potentialities could never be exhausted in a finite world, and who in consequence is never really bound by what he has done. But he *has* bound himself: he has taken up a position with regard to humanity and the finite which he himself freely declares to be definitive, and of which he himself says that he will never go beyond it again and never withdraw from it.

And because the only time which really signifies before God does not follow the periodicity of stars and clocks but rather that of God's ever new, free acts in his world, time really stands still when God has spoken his last word. And as this has in fact happened, the "fullness of time" (*kairos*) is in fact accomplished (Mk 1:15), the end of time has come upon us (1 Cor 10:11; 1 Pt 4:7).

The inner temporal form of the world, derived from God, is at its end, even if this last *kairos* may last for thousands of years by astronomical measures. We must realize what it means for the infinite one to say that this deed, which he has now done and which inevitably carries within itself the contingency of a free act in the sphere of the finite, is his *last* deed; that of all the innumerable possibilities which remain open to him, none will be realized after this deed; that the mode of his action at precisely this moment shall abide for all eternity.

If we are now to characterize this unique situation, one which can never be surpassed and which has never existed before, we must in the first place distinguish it against God's previous modes of behavior, and second we must determine what is peculiar to it with regard to time and intrinsic content. It was said earlier that in the last analysis the New Testament does not offer a doctrine of God's attributes, but

---

* *Theological Investigations I*, 117–25.

an account of those ever new attitudes of God of which the human person had experience in the course of history. And we have just seen that the "fullness of time" of the New Testament is characterized by the fact that God's attitude as it is experienced there is the definitive one.

Our problem then may be formulated in terms of two questions: First, how is this attitude distinguished from God's previous attitudes, those of the Old Testament and in the time before Christ? And second, what in fact is this attitude or disposition considered precisely in the terminal situation of the New Testament?

According to the Epistle to the Hebrews, God expressed himself in the world by his speech and activity in manifold ways. But his last and definitive word, his last and definitive act, which has come to pass in the "proper time" (1 Tm 2:6; 6:15; Ti 1:3) of the new and eternal covenant and is now present, is not just the latest in a series, but the "fullness" of all earlier times (Mk 1:15; Gal 4:4), and yet precisely something new with regard to what had gone before.

If this is the case, then this final disposition must be distinguished from anything *earlier,* which with regard to it is drawn into a unified order; and at the same time this disposition must be understood as the goal of all that has gone before, which finds its fulfillment in this disposition.

In other words, this "end-time," which is the goal and "fullness" of everything before it, puts all God's previous saving speech and activity — however manifold and various this may be — over a common denominator, and thus stands in essential distinction from the whole of what had gone before; and yet the whole must be resolved into this teleological fulfillment.

We must bear this relationship in mind when we ask by what distinguishing features we are to know the God of the New Testament from the God of the Old. After all we have said, it should be clear that we are not just asking the harmless question as to what human beings understood about God in Old Testament and New Testament times. We are not concerned with the subjective conceptions of the peoples of the two covenants, with the growing knowledge of something in itself unchanging, but with a difference in God's own "attitude."

It is of course impossible to set out here the whole doctrine of the New Testament concerning the difference between the old and new covenants, between the time before Christ and the time in Christ, although this would be the only really concrete way of showing how the God of the fathers differs from the God of our Lord Jesus Christ.

Here we must follow a simpler way. We shall simply start from the usual (and, it would seem, justified) view of this difference, that in the New Testament, and in the strictest sense there alone, God revealed himself as God of *love,* as love *itself.* In concrete terms, then, our first question becomes how and why God's love, become manifest in Christ, is distinguished from God's behavior in the Old Testament and is at the same time its fulfillment.

At first sight the anticipated conclusion does not seem very probable: God seems to have shown himself as one who loves even in the time of salvation *before* Christ. In what follows, only the barest outline of Old Testament teaching can of course be offered, and that with the utmost reserve.

First, then, we find references there to what might be called a metaphysical love of God. When we hear that God loves everything that is (Wis 11:24), that Yahweh gives everything its nature and that his mercy embraces all that he has made (Ps 145:9), when the Psalmist celebrates the whole of creation as a work of God's graciousness and goodness (Ps 136:1–9), what we have is the reflections of a natural theology: the goodness (the value) of reality is traced back to its source in the source of all being, which in consequence is also conceived of as good.

What was said earlier about natural theology in general holds good for this metaphysical goodness of God; it is knowable and in a way familiar; it is hidden because of original sin and is only clearly disclosed when human beings come to know God in the supernatural history of salvation. But a "love" like this does not really set up a personal I-Thou relationship between God and the human person. The person is aware of being borne by a will in some way directed to value and the good, but this is not enough to let him turn round, as it were, so as to enter into a personal relationship of community and reciprocal love with this source of his own ontological value.

Again, we often hear in the Old Testament of God's goodness and mercy, as they are shown in his personal, historical activity. God has chosen his people; he has in a special way shown his goodness, his mercy, and his love in a special personal guidance, in election and covenant. For the Old Testament, and especially for the prophets, the very fact that he has entered into relationship with human beings in so personal a way is itself an expression of his inconceivable mercy and grace, a revelation of his love. And the climax of his love in the Old Testament is that he does not allow himself to be turned away by the unfaithfulness of his people, Israel's repeated falling away from its God; that he does not give up his desire for a personal relationship because of the adultery of his people. We could put this more sharply and say that for the Old Testament God's love is shown by the fact that he enters into a personal relationship with his people and that he does not abandon it in spite of their rejection of him. But that is all this love seems yet to mean.

Certainly there is a constant celebration of Yahweh's mercy and graciousness, his compassion and his readiness to forgive, with regard to all creatures in general and the people of the covenant in particular. But if we are justified in identifying God's goodness with a genuinely personal love, it follows that we cannot really draw any conclusions from language like this as to whether God already loves human beings there in the sense that as someone wholly personal in his very essence he wants to give himself to them. Goodness, forbearance, mercy, solicitude are still attributes which can characterize the conduct of a master to his servant. Consequently, a relationship of this kind still does not mean that this solicitous and just and lenient ruler wishes to have anything to do with the servant in his own personal life. He can continue to be distant and inaccessible. Surely it was the beginning of something new and personal for God to have freely exercised his dominion over all that he has made in such a way as to enter actively into the world and intervene in it by his own personal initiative, as it were, surrendering his sovereign upliftedness above everything finite by becoming a fellow-actor with his world.

This is a new beginning which, looking back from the New Testament, we can only understand as a moment in God's movement toward the creature, a movement in which he wished to entrust himself to us in his transcendent identity, in the inner mystery of his own personal life. But this could not yet be seen in the Old Testament. The fact that God in his personal activity takes human beings into his service, makes them, by a divine historical act, what he already is by nature, the fact that God accepts them as his servants and personally communicates his will to them and has personal dealings with them — all this was already so inconceivable a marvel that it could only be described by *using* the image of paternal or marital love.

But that it was already in fact a love which drew the human person up to God only became evident in the new covenant. It has further to be remembered that God's loving treatment of human beings in the Old Testament is intrinsically oriented toward something to come, to a new covenant. Now this great promised thing remains curiously obscure and ambiguous in the Old Testament. Is this new greater thing only the establishment of God's rule in the world, which is still going to leave the person merely God's servant, or is it going to be something more? Is God's law going to be completely established at some time in the future, and is this rule going to be one in which God precisely wills to be more than just the Lord who establishes himself in the world by the jealous affirmation of his own being? Is God going to be beloved Lord or lordly Beloved?

All these promises were existential utterances of God, not just predictions; and of their very nature (until God should have bound himself by speaking his last, definitive word), they were held in abeyance so long as it was not known what answer God's free collocutor, the human being, would give to these promises in the dialogue which forms the history of salvation.

In the Old Testament, then, God's love for the human being (so long as it does not mean just God's metaphysical relationship to his creature, something quite general and unexistential and implying no personal communion at all) consists in the very fact that he desires and makes possible a personal encounter with the person, that he seeks this relationship urgently and maintains it in being, and that (provisionally, at least) this relationship was not abandoned in consequence of a turning away from God on the part of the human being.

But it was concealed in the mystery of God's eternal decree that this relationship would go beyond that between a master and his servant and that it would be irrevocable. For God had still not done anything in human history which would unambiguously and irrevocably open a way for human beings to the depths of God's own personal life. And in consequence, that love for God to which the person was summoned, was still provisional, until it should be known how God himself wanted to love him. The human being was commanded to love God with the whole force of his being; but it was still hidden in which of two ways this should be.

This unconditional assent by the human person to God in his freedom, would it be the humble love of a servant for his master, who, precisely because by his love he affirms God to be as God wishes to be, remains far from his sovereign majesty and unapproachable light, not presuming to an intimate relationship with God such as would involve really unrestricted personal communion with him? Or does this loving affirmation, which the person utters blindly and unconditionally, draw him into the depths of God's inner life?

When in the Old Testament the human person uttered this affirmation of his loving trust in God, he was inevitably swept up into the universal teleology of God's entire redemptive action, even when the goal of this activity was still hidden from him. Ready to be just a servant, he was already son; but just this was hidden from him until *the* Son of the Father came, and it thus became manifest in human history what the secret of God's purpose had always been.

When we say that God is love, and that this is what finally characterizes God's free, historical behavior in the fullness of time, in the "fullness of time" of the New Testament, we mean to say two things. First, this is in fact a free *act* of God in Christ, an event, not an attribute: the coming to pass of the New Testament in Christ. Second, it is the event in which God's inmost life is communicated to human beings, in his love for them, fully and without restraint.

A genuinely personal love always has these two marks. Love is not the emanation of a nature but the free bestowal of a person, who possesses himself, who can therefore refuse himself, whose surrender therefore is always a wonder and a grace. And love in the fully personal sense is not just any relationship between two persons who meet in some third thing, whether this "third thing" is a task, a truth, or anything else: it is the ceding and the unfolding of one's inmost self to and for the other in love. The discussion which follows will be divided in accordance with this twofold distinction; not that the whole saving reality of the New Testament is to be depicted in this way, but rather that it will be considered only with regard to these two points.

a) That God is love, that he has received human beings to the most intimate communion with himself in love — this has become manifest in the sending and incarnation, in the cross and glorification, of his only begotten *Son*. It has become manifest not merely in the sense that the Christ-reality may be taken as a particular instance, from which may be read off what attitude God has necessarily adopted with regard to humanity; but it has become manifest in the sense that all God's free activity in the whole history of salvation has been directed to this event from the very beginning and thus rests on this single decision; and that this free purpose of entering into unrestricted personal communion with human beings first became finally irrevocable and unconditional through God's act in Christ.

Christ is the "end of the law" (Rom 10:4), the fulfillment of the times (Mk 1:15), what became manifest in him is the "love of God" (Rom 5:8). God so loved the world that he gave his only begotten Son (Jn 3:16). It is not for nothing that the great argumentative movement of the Epistle to the Romans on the theme of the new epoch which has just opened, reaches its climax in a hymn which, beginning with a celebration of the love of the elect for God, goes on to the love of Christ and comes to rest in the certainty of "the love of God in Jesus Christ, our Lord" (Rom 8:28ff.).

It is in the Christ-reality that God's love is really and truly present for the first time; it is there that it has first really appeared, there for the first time really objectified itself (Rom 5:8); and through this real being-present in the world it has become manifest. And it is by this means that a definitive and unsurpassable *fact* has been brought into being; for Christ abides eternally: he has brought eternal redemption into being; he has entered into the eternal tabernacle and sits on the right hand of God. It is by this means that the promises have first emerged from their existential abeyance and ambiguity, and have been really established (Rom 15:8); so that no future epoch and no conceivable stage of development (Rom 8:38) is ever going to annul this definitive event of God's love for us.

b) Moreover, God has bestowed his very self upon us in Christ: "our fellowship is with the Father and with his Son Jesus Christ" (1 Jn 1:3; "fellowship" was frequently used in koine Greek for conjugal association); and our fellowship is with the Holy Spirit (2 Cor 13:13). This fellowship of love is produced by the Pneuma of God, through whom God pours forth upon us his love for us (Rom 5:5; Gal 4:6; 1 Jn 3:24; 4:13); and in this Spirit God's most intimate personal life is unfolded to us. For he is the Spirit who searches the "depths of God," which none knows and searches but the same Spirit of God (1 Cor 2:10) and so leads us into the deepest intimacies of God's knowledge (Jn 15:26; 16:13; 1 Cor 2:12; 1 Jn 2:20, 27).

So this Spirit of God, who is the realization in us of God's personal love and in whom God has unfolded to us his ultimate depths, is the Spirit of adoption (Gal 4:4–6), who gives us testimony of our adoption (Rom 8:15). Through him we are children of God (1 Jn 3:1, 2), called to know him as we are known, to see him face to face (1 Cor 13:12). In this way we are taken up into the most intimate community of life with the God of whom it is said that no one has seen him or can see him (Jn 1:18; 1 Tim 6:16), whom only the Son knows (Mt 11:27; Jn 3:11, 32; 7:29), and in consequence only he to whom the Son reveals it (Mt 11:27) by giving him a share in the nature and rights of his sonship (Rom 8:17, 29; Heb 2:11, 12).

It is not our concern here to inquire further into the nature of this grace and sonship. Even so it is clear enough that this relationship is inseparably dependent upon the reality of Christ, and owes its existence as a reality precisely to God's free self-disclosure once and for all in Christ.

"God is love" is not primarily, then, a statement, illuminating in itself, about the nature of God, but the expression of the once-for-all, undeniable and unsurpassable experience in which mere human beings have come to know God in Christ: an expression of the experienced fact that God has bestowed his own entire self on us. Certainly, insofar as God's free disposition in the "fullness of time" of Christ is the unsurpassable communication of all that God is and can be by essence and freedom, it is also a communication of the divine nature. But this depends inseparably on the fact that God, as person, freely wished to love us; and in the knowledge of this truth the entire reality of Christianity is contained.

58 • God, Our Father*

The God of the philosophers is no "Father," but the incomprehensible ground of all reality which escapes every comprehensive notion because he is a radical mystery. This is always only the beyond, the inaccessibly distant horizon bounding the small sphere we are able to measure. He certainly exists for us also in this way, as the unanswered question that makes possible any answerable one, as the distance which makes room for our never-ending journey in thought and deed. But does this ineffable being which we call God exist only in this way? That is the question.

True, the distance which philosophical theology establishes between God and ourselves is still necessary to prevent us from confusing God with our own idols, and thus it is perhaps more than philosophy, it is a hidden grace. But the question whether God is only unapproachable ineffability must be answered in the negative. He is more, and we realize this in the ultimate experience of our existence, when we accept it without rejecting or denying it under pretext of its being too good to be true. For there is the experience that the abyss protects, that pure silence is tender, that the distance is home and that the ultimate question brings its own answer, that the very mystery communicates itself as pure blessedness. And then we call the mystery, whose customary cipher is "God," Father. For what else are we to call it?

Much paternalism in our world has certainly tried to invest custom and inherited power with a glory designed to prevent us from bearing freedom and responsibility ourselves, as well as the loneliness resulting from both. We experience the technical achievements of this world not exactly as an expression of tender, fatherly feelings but rather as hard and inhuman. The pressure of life often prevents us from realizing what we mean by calling God Father, a concept distilled from our notions of human fatherhood.

Nevertheless, if we are resolved to let God be God, if we adore him as an ineffable mystery, not to be inserted as a definable factor into the sum of our life, we may suddenly experience him as communicating himself, as merciful and forgiving, indeed, as grace, and thus call him Father; though mother, love, or home would express this just as well, because they also describe a primeval experience, preserving the bliss of the secret hour.

"Father," however, is also a good word and suited to the world which is given to us and through which we must express him. For there will always be fathers in this world, and even today we experience them

---

* *Grace in Freedom,* 196–99.

not only as exercising an irksome authority, but also as the power that supports us by sending us forth into our own life and liberty.

Applied to God, the word "Father" signifies the origin that is without origin, the ground that remains incomprehensible, because it can be comprehended only through his grace that keeps us while we emerge from it. "Father" means the serenely loving seriousness, the beginning that is our future, the creative power that accomplishes its work patiently and without haste, which does not fear our desperate complaints and premature accusations. He sends us his mystery, himself, not anything else as partial answers; he sends himself to us as love and thus answers the question which we ourselves are, and thus reveals himself as "person," disposing of himself in full knowledge.

Such experience exists, and not only momentarily, but always. It opens itself to us always new, in serene detachment. Nevertheless, it is difficult to encounter this experience; for its opposite is quicker and imposes itself more brutally. But we need not have this experience by ourselves, for in this respect, too, no person lives to himself alone. Even our most intimate, unique experiences happen in our life because they encounter similar ones in others, and thus meet themselves. The history in which we live our common life together is the place where everyone finds himself.

Now there we may find a man who called himself simply the Son and who said "Father" when he expressed the mystery of his life. He spoke of the Father when he saw the lilies of the held in their beauty, or when his heart overflowed in prayer, when he thought of the hunger and need of human beings and longed for the consummation that ends all the transitoriness of this seemingly empty and guilty existence. With touching tenderness he called this dark, abysmal mystery, which he knew to be such, *Abba* (which we ought almost to translate as "daddy").

And he called it thus not only when beauty and hope helped him to overcome the incomprehensibility of existence in this world, but also when he met the darkness of death and the cup in which was distilled all the guilt, vanity, and emptiness of this world was placed at his lips and he could only repeat the desperate words of the Psalmist: "My God, my God, why have you forsaken me?" But even then that other, all-embracing word was present to him, which sheltered even this forsakenness: "Father, into your hands I commend my life."

Thus he has encouraged us to believe in him as the Son, to call the abyss of mystery Father, to realize both our origin and our future in this word alone, and thus to measure the dimensions of our dignity, of our task, of the danger and experience of our life. True, only the crucified is *the* Son. But he is also the sign that we all are truly children of God and dare and must call Father this true God himself, and not only the finite idols we ourselves imagine and create. Because he is the Son, we are empowered to set aside the daily experience of the absurdity and torment of this life, to realize the true ground of this experience and to change it into an incomprehensible but blissful mystery by calling it Father.

Can we say anything more improbable? But how else can we break through the mere semblance of truth, which we shortsighted "realists" regard as truth itself, and come to the authentic truth that makes us blessed? For may truth not redeem and save? That is the question which decides our life. Whoever opts for the blessed truth calls it "Father." And we may be allowed to hope, if someone thinks that, in order to remain true, he must opt for a deadly truth, he has nevertheless loved in his heart the blessedly protecting truth of the Father, because he has been faithful to the truth he thought bitter.

59 • Non-Christian and Christian Conceptions of God*

In a certain way all the influences actually at work in the human being's religious life will play a part in the non-Christian conception of God: the human person's natural knowledge of God ascending from below through the world, the deterioration due to original sin, grace and primitive revelation.

Consequently, all three factors will be seen most clearly at work at that point in the conception of God which is formally decisive for the Christian conception, namely, in God's free, personal existence transcending the world as *Lord* of nature and history. Granted that even in the person's fallen state his nature and divine grace are still continually active, it will never be possible that the consciousness of a God, unique, transcendent, free and freely treating with the human being in history, should disappear.

But if the human person lives in a fallen state, and if in the last resort sin is the will not to allow God to be God and the attempt to shut the world in upon itself, then every non-Christian religion, insofar as it is and must be qualified theologically as sin, is bound to give God's infinity the meaning of all infinity of powers and forces active in the world, will be in fact a polytheism.

---

* *Theological Investigations I*, 84–86.

Each one of these religions, in a metaphysical and religious pursuit of unity which is quite justified in itself, will try to comprehend the multiplicity of deified powers and forces of the world in a unity; and so inevitably each will turn into a form of pantheism. Each will be guilty of forgetting God as person and as free to enter into historical communication with the world by his revealing word; and in the last resort each will become devotion to the world instead of obedience to the unique and living God. All these elements (in varying measure, of course) will be met with in every non-Christian religion.

It becomes basically impossible, then, to interpret any one of them in terms of an absolutely clear-cut formula, by means of which it should be distinguished merely negatively from the Christian conception of God. Which of the elements present in it actually decides the issue before God for the *individual* person and his concrete, existential achievements is in the last resort not for us to judge.

Inversely, we may note three corresponding features of the *Christian* conception of God. In the first place, it will confirm that knowledge of the unique, transcendent, personal God which is always stirring into life, whether naturally or supernaturally, even outside the history of revelation; and, precisely from the viewpoint of revelation, it will free what is naturally true in non-Christian religion and philosophy from the encumbrance of sin, allowing what is supernatural in these truths to appear *as* such, and restraining the attempt to claim it as part of the person's innate, inadmissible nobility.

Second, the Christian conception will always express God's passionate protest against every kind of polytheistic or pantheistic deification of the world caused by original sin and everywhere at work, even today. Third, it will alone be able to say unambiguously and definitively just how the personal, transcendent God desires in *actual fact* to stand to the world in his sovereign freedom: namely, as the God who actually discloses his inmost self to human beings out of grace, so compelling them in a unique, climactic situation to an absolute gravity, either bliss or damnation; as the God who gives his definitive sanction to the world in the incarnation of his Son and so precisely summons it to share in his triune life.

60 • God and Creatures*

Our existential insensitivity and the weakness of our power of realization regarding nondivine realities which fall, or ought to fall, into
the sphere of religious acts is at least partially due to a false, basically
unchristian, pantheistic, or theophanistic conception of God. The true
God is not the one who kills so that he himself can live. He is not "the
truly real" which like a vampire draws to himself and, so to speak, sucks
out the proper reality of things different from himself; he is not the *esse
omnium* ("the being of everything)."

The nearer one comes to him, the more real one becomes; the
more he grows in and before one, the more independent one becomes
oneself. Things created by him are not maya, the veil, which dissolves
like mist before the sun the more one recognizes the absolute, that
is, the more religious one becomes. We do indeed feel this way, and
it would be important to answer the question as to why we feel like
this. But this basic existential condition, no matter how deep and even
humble it may seem to be, is itself again a pride due to original sin and
something profoundly unchristian.

One loves "the absolute," but not God who is the creator of heaven
and earth. Basically one hates created reality, since it is not the absolute in itself; one calls it the relative, the contingent, that which —
in relation to God — is determinable in a merely negative sense, the
mere limitation of being which in itself is infinite, which alone matters:
and one forgets that precisely this conditioned reality is what is loved
unconditionally by the unconditioned, that it therefore has a validity
which makes it more than something merely provisional — something
which dissolves in the face of God — and that this created unconditioned reality forbids us (in spite of all philosophy which, even in our
case, is not yet sufficiently baptized) to evaluate it in a purely negative
sense even in relation to God.

No one can say that these are themselves merely ontological expressions which are of no importance for the religious act. No, precisely
when we come face to face with the absolute by a religious act in the
course of our existential realization — and if we do this in a *Christian*
and not in a platonic sense (and in this context, even every form of Aris-
totelianism and every Western philosophy right up to German idealism
is still far too platonic) — *then* (and hence in the very heart of the religious act) we come face to face with that absolutely serious love of
what has been created by that love: the valid, eternal, living reality, that

---

* *Theological Investigations III*, 40–43.

which truly is, precisely because — and not even though — it exists through this love.

We arrive at that which has a significance of its own, that which cannot be passed over, which is not simply already to be found "supereminently" in God (for otherwise he would not have loved it effectively and in a truly, creatively free way). When we come thus in a religious way to this God of the truly serious and unconditional love of created reality, however, then we must love him as he is, then we must not maliciously try to turn him in our religious act into someone he precisely is *not*, namely, into a God without a world. Instead, we must love everything loved by him with his love, and so must love it in that precise way — not as something provisional, as the cloud which, breaking up its contours, dissolves in the presence of the infinity opening up before us — but precisely as something valid in the sight of God, as something eternally justified and hence as something divinely and religiously significant before God.

A pluralistic world of the numinous finds its meaning and its justification in the sight of the God of Christianity. The effort of holding on to this truth is the effort of overcoming our unchristian outlook and of solving the *sinful* dilemma into which original sin throws us: God *or* the world. A polytheistic, or polytheistically tinged, enslaving veneration of the powers and forces of this world is merely the other side of the same guilty dilemma: the numinous nature of the world without the one, living God. But the opposite springs from the same cleavage: the God-lessness of the world. We today are in danger of honoring God (or at least of trying to honor him) and of letting the world itself be God-less.

The Christian attitude, however, would be to honor the world as something willed and loved by God, and to do this in a properly balanced way, since this love given to the world is itself of varying degrees; hence it would be Christian to pay a truly religious veneration where the world has already found the finality of its eternal validity before God in the morning and evening summits of its spiritual history, that is, in the angels and the saints.

It should, therefore, be a task of theology to think much more deeply, and in a much more vital manner than it has done up until now, about why, how, and in what dependence of the basic religious acts on God, what it calls *dulia* (veneration), in contrast to *latria* (adoration), is in truth a genuinely religious act, and how, as such an act, it can and must be exercised more independently and not merely as an act which simply resolves itself into the act of *latria*.

Signs of the great difficulty of such a Christianization of the basic religious act directed toward God are to be seen even within the theory of Christian mysticism. This theory has always been tempted (even in

St. John of the Cross) to let everything in the mystic act disappear in the face of God, so that over and over again subsequent corrections of such a start on a pantheistic basis were found to be necessary to enable the mystic to hold on to the fact that he may and can still occupy himself with the humanity of Christ.

It can be seen, at any rate, that the question of whether one can still take other realities beside the reality of God seriously and realize them in a religious act is a question of the first order and importance in Christian thought. That it does not take on this importance in ordinary piety is no argument against this statement. Ordinary piety, for which God is after all *from the very start* one reality *beside* many others, naturally does not experience any difficulty in regarding St. Anthony as a most noteworthy, important, and effective figure, side by side with the Holy Spirit.

But then, in this case, this does detract from God and from our true relationship to him who does not tolerate any strange gods before him (not even those in whose case one carefully avoids using the name of God). But when God becomes more and more truly God for us — the consuming fire, the simply incomparable, the one who in his grace has become near after being most radically distant — then only a mature Christian relationship to God would be still capable of recognizing and realizing in this burning flame and blinding light that this makes the rest of reality loved by him even more real, even more true and valid, and that in this boundless sea of fire of infinite degree everything is not destroyed but finds its real life, not only in itself but also for us. Yet because such maturity is also a beatifying task of our religious development in God's true grace, which always works differently from what we ourselves might imagine, it is our duty to make an effort to attain it.

Leaving creatures is the first and, for us sinners, always new phase of finding God. Yet it is merely the first stage. Service toward creatures, the mission away from God back into the world, may be the second phase. Yet there is still a third: to find the very creature itself, in its dependence and autonomy, *in* God, in the midst of the jealously burning inexorableness of his being all-in-all; to find the creature even in the very midst of this — the small in the great, the circumscribed in the boundless, the creature (the very creature itself) in the creator — this is only the third and highest phase of our relationship to God. For there we who have gone out from the world to God return with him in his entrance into the world, and are nearest to him there where he is furthest away from himself in his true love of the world; there and in this we are nearest to him because, if God is love, one comes closest to it where, having given itself as love to the world, it is furthest away from itself.

61 • God's Self-Disclosure and the Human Word*

God's self-disclosure in the human word of revelation would nullify itself if it were not bound up with the inner light of grace and strictly supernatural faith. If God were to speak of himself insofar as he is not revealed through his creation, which is distinct from himself, and use human words without the supernatural elevation of the hearer, his utterance would come only under the subjective a priori of the finite spirit as such. And his utterance, if not simply nullified, would be necessarily degraded to an element of the self-understanding and the possibility of self-understanding of the mere creature. It would no longer be a real self-disclosure of God.

For here too it is true that whatever is received is received according to the manner and nature of the recipient. It is also true here that knowledge is essentially a process of coming to awareness of self in him who knows. It is enlightened self-possession, so that everything that is received is grasped as an element of this self-accomplishment. Though the human being is undoubtedly, even as spirit in the natural order, absolute openness to being in general, and hence to God who is cause and principle of this spirit, still, if God's communication about himself were received without grace, it would only be grasped as a moment of this self-accomplishment of the human person within the world (even if it came as something infinitely open).

Only where the act of hearing in what we call grace is really the coaccomplishment of an act of God in a strictly supernatural participation of God himself, and not merely of a quality *created* by him, can the divine utterance be strictly supernatural, that is, qualitatively supernatural in itself and not merely distinguished as regards the mode of communication from any communication made through merely created things. A divine utterance which is divine by reason of its own nature has no meaning unless it is directed toward a divine hearing.

Part therefore of the expression of divine revelation is the Holy Spirit, as the strictly supernatural self-communication of God. He does not enter in merely as the guarantee of its correctness or as the originator of a process of efficient causality on the part of God which takes place per se in the region of the finite. He is there as the thing uttered itself and only with this can the human utterance be God's self-utterance. Here we have at once that infinite openness in the closed revelation,

---

* *Theological Investigations IV*, 11–14.

and the dynamism of self-development, whose only limits are in the beatific vision itself.

It is also true (and this is part of the fundamental dogma of a Christianity of the incarnation) that this self-communication of God really takes place in the human word, and not merely on the occasion of it. Human words are not merely the external occasion for a pneumatic or mystic experience of transcendence directed toward the God who is nameless. Spirit and word can only be possessed in their indissoluble unity, undivided and unconfused.

Hence the human word is open from the start to the infinitude of God. (This it is, insofar as it is natural, by virtue of its *potentia obedientialis,* and so far as it is supernatural, by virtue of its being uttered by the Spirit and by virtue of its elevation by the Spirit.) And the divine Spirit is given in and through this word, assumed by himself, in his own infinity and concrete reality.

Here we have a very special and unique conjuncture which is usually overlooked in theology. There are two modes of knowledge in the region of natural knowledge. In the first, we have an actual experience of the reality in question, in itself or in its effects, and on this basis and in view of this we form our concepts and judgments in its regard. We then constantly start out from these concepts and judgments, to return constantly to the experience of the thing itself, whence we are enabled to form anew our concepts and judgments and subject the previous ones to a critical investigation, because we can have the thing itself without any assertion about it. In the second, there exists a type of knowledge which does not possess the thing itself but relies on the assertion of another and so is unable to make direct experimental contact with the thing itself and make itself independent of the judgments communicated to it. The second is what happens in all that is called *testimonium.*

Now, the Catholic, antignostic and antimystical view of the reality and truth of divine revelation makes the first mode impossible. That is, we cannot make ourselves independent, in our pilgrim state, of the assertions made in the testimony to revelation. Further, we cannot — like the modernists — set up a wordless state of experience with regard to what is meant in faith, to derive thence new and original statements of revelation in the form of intellectual assertions.

From all this the average theology of the schools concludes (without really thinking much about it) that revelation is to be conceived of in accordance with the second of the two modes of human knowledge mentioned above and will be mere verbal testimony, which only indicates something not truly possessed and does not impart the thing itself. That is precisely what is incorrect.

In the word of revelation which comes through grace we have something intermediate and higher, between the two modes of knowledge named above: in the word the thing itself is given. Behind the verbal testimony of God in human concepts we cannot go, to reach a wordless possession and experience of the divine reality itself. That will only happen when the Word utters itself in the immediacy of the final fulfillment. All the same, we now have not only the utterance, but also the thing itself: God's self-communication to the spirit in his own proper reality — which is already the homogeneous beginning of the vision itself.

This of course can only be said if the Spirit who activates the supernatural hearing of the word of God is not merely a heavenly element of consciousness in the act of faith but really enters in as the light of faith. This does not necessarily mean that this light of faith must be present to the believing mind as a conscious datum and object, distinguishable from the other objects of consciousness. But there must be a genuine presence of the light of faith to consciousness, even though as a datum it is not in the state of an object or the object of reflection.

62 • A Prayer: God of My Life*

I should like to speak with you, my God, and yet what else can I speak of but you? Indeed, could anything at all exist which had not been present with you from all eternity, which didn't have its true home and most intimate explanation in your mind and heart? Isn't everything I ever say really a statement about you?

On the other hand, if I try, shyly and hesitantly, to speak to you about yourself, you will still be hearing about *me*. For what could I say about you except that you are my God, the God of my beginning and end, God of my joy and my need, God of my life?

Of course you are endlessly more than merely the God of my life — if that's all you were, you wouldn't really be God at all. But even when I think of your towering majesty, even when I acknowledge you as someone who has no need of me, who is infinitely far exalted above the lowly valleys through which I drag out the paths of my life — even then I have called you once again by the same name, God of my life.

And when I give praise to you as Father, Son, and Holy Spirit, when I confess the thrice holy mystery of your life, so eternally hidden in the

---

Encounters with Silence, trans. James M. Demske, S.J. (Westminster, Md.: Newman Press, 1966), 3–10.

abysses of your infinity that it leaves behind in creation no sign that we could make out by ourselves, am I not still praising you as the God of my life? Even granting that you had revealed to me this secret of your own inner life, would I be able to accept and realize this mystery if your life had not become *my* life through grace? Would I be able to acknowledge and love you, Father, and you, eternal Word of the Father's heart, and you, Spirit of the Father and the Son, if you had not deigned to become through grace the triune God of my life?

But what am I really saying, when I call you *my* God, the God of my life? That you are the meaning of my life? the goal of my wanderings? the consecration of my actions? the judgment of my sins? the bitterness of my bitter hours and my most secret joy? my strength, which turns *my own* strength into weakness? creator, sustainer, pardoner, the one both far and near? incomprehensible? God of my brethren? God of my fathers?

Are there any titles which I needn't give you? And when I have listed them all, what have I said? If I should take my stand on the shore of your endlessness and shout into the trackless reaches of your being all the words I have ever learned in the poor prison of my little existence, what should I have said? I should never have spoken the last word about you.

Then why do I even begin to speak of you? Why do you torment me with your infinity, if I can never really measure it? Why do you constrain me to walk along your paths, if they lead only to the awful darkness of your night, where only you can see? For us, only the finite and tangible is real and near enough to touch: Can you be real and near to me, when I must confess you as infinite?

Why have you burnt your mark in my soul in baptism? Why have you kindled in me the flame of faith, this dark light which lures us out of the bright security of our little huts into your night? And why have you made me your priest, one whose vocation it is to be with you on behalf of men and women, when my finiteness makes me gasp for breath in your presence?

Look at the vast majority of people, Lord — excuse me if I presume to pass judgment on them — but do they often think of you? Are you the first beginning and last end for them, the one without whom their minds and hearts can find no rest? Don't they manage to get along perfectly well without you? Don't they feel quite at home in this world which they know so well, where they can be sure of just what they have to reckon with? Are you anything more for them than the one who sees to it that the world stays on its hinges, so that they won't have to call on you ? Tell me, are you the God of *their* life?

I don't really know, Lord, if my complaint is just or not — who knows the heart of another person? you alone are the reader of hearts, O God, and how can I expect to understand the heart of another when I don't even understand my own? It's just that I can't help thinking of those others, because — as you well know, since you see into the depths of my heart, O hidden God from whom nothing is hidden — often enough I feel in myself a secret longing to be like them or, at least, to be as they seem to be.

Lord, how helpless I am when I try to talk to you about yourself! How can I call you anything but the God of my life? And what have I said with that title, when no name is really adequate? I'm constantly tempted to creep away from you in utter discouragement, back to the things that are more comprehensible, to things with which my heart feels so much more at home than it does with your mysteriousness.

And yet, where shall I go? If the narrow hut of this earthly life with its dear, familiar trivialities, its joys and sorrows both great and small — if this were my real home, wouldn't it still be surrounded by your distant endlessness? Could the earth be my home without your far-away heaven above it?

Suppose I tried to be satisfied with what so many today profess to be the purpose of their lives. Suppose I defiantly determined to admit my finiteness, and glory in it alone. I could only begin to recognize this finiteness and accept it as my sole destiny, because I had previously so often stared out into the vast reaches of limitless space, to those hazy horizons where your endless life is just beginning.

Without you, I should founder helplessly in my own dull and groping narrowness. I could never feel the pain of longing, not even deliberately resign myself to being content with this world, had not my mind again and again soared out over its own limitations into the hushed reaches which are filled by you alone, the silent infinite. Where should I flee before you, when all my yearning for the unbounded, even my bold trust in my littleness, is really a confession of you?

What else is there that I can tell you about yourself, except that you are the one without whom I cannot exist, the eternal God from whom alone I, a creature of time, can draw the strength to live, the infinity who gives meaning to my finiteness? And when I tell you all this, then I have given myself my true name, the name I ever repeat when I pray in David's Psalter, *Tuus sum ego.* I am the one who belongs not to himself, but to you. I know no more than this about myself, nor about you, O God of my life, infinity of my finiteness.

What a poor creature you have made me, O God! All I know about you and about myself is that you are the eternal mystery of my life. Lord, what a frightful puzzle a human being is! He belongs to you, and you are the incomprehensible — incomprehensible in your being, and even more so in your ways and judgments. For if all your dealings with me are acts of your freedom, quite unmerited gifts of your grace which knows no "why," if my creation and my whole life hang absolutely on your free decision, if all my paths are, after all, your paths and, therefore, unsearchable, then, Lord, no amount of questioning will ever fathom your depths — you will still be the incomprehensible, even when I see you face to face.

But if you were not incomprehensible, you would be inferior to me, for my mind could grasp and assimilate you. You would belong to me, instead of I to you. And that would truly be hell, if I should belong only to myself! It would be the fate of the damned, to be doomed to pace up and down for all eternity in the cramped and confining prison of my own finiteness.

But can it be that you are my true home? Are you the one who will release me from my narrow little dungeon? Or are you merely adding another torment to my life, when you throw open the gates leading out upon your broad and endless plain? Are you anything more than my own great insufficiency, if all my knowledge leads only to your incomprehensibility? Are you merely eternal unrest for the restless soul? Must every question fall dumb before you, unanswered? Is your only response the mute "I will have it so," that so coldly smothers my burning desire to understand?

But I am rambling on like a fool — excuse me, O God. You have told me through your Son that you are the God of my love, and you have commanded me to love you. Your commands are often hard because they enjoin the opposite of what my own inclinations would lead me to do, but when you bid me love you, you are ordering something that my own inclinations would never even dare to suggest: to love *you*, to come intimately close to you, to love your very life. You ask me to lose myself in you, knowing that you will take me to your heart, where I may speak on loving, familiar terms with you, the incomprehensible mystery of my life. And all this because you are love itself.

Only in love can I find you, my God. In love the gates of my soul spring open, allowing me to breathe a new air of freedom and forget my own petty self. In love my whole being streams forth out of the rigid confines of narrowness and anxious self-assertion, which make me a prisoner of my own poverty and emptiness. In love all the powers of my soul flow out toward you, wanting never more to return, but to lose themselves completely in you, since by your love you are the inmost center of my heart, closer to me than I am to myself.

But when I love you, when I manage to break out the narrow circle of self and leave behind the restless agony of unanswered questions, when my blinded eyes no longer look merely from afar and from the outside at your unapproachable brightness, and much more when you yourself, O incomprehensible one, have become through love the inmost center of my life, then I can bury myself entirely in you, O mysterious God, and with myself all my questions.

Love such as this wills to possess you as you are — how could it desire otherwise? It wants you yourself, not your reflection in the mirror of its own spirit. It wants to be united with you alone, so that in the very instant which it gives up possession of itself, it will have not just your image, but your very Self.

Love wants you as you are, and just as love knows that it itself is right and good and needs no further justification, so you are right and good for it, and it embraces you without asking for any explanation of why you are as you are. Your "I will have it so" is love's greatest bliss. In this state of joy my mind no longer tries to bring you forcibly down to its level, in order to wrest from you your eternal secret, but rather love seizes me and carries me up to your level, into you.

When I abandon myself in love, then you are my very life, and your incomprehensibility is swallowed up in love's unity. When I am allowed to love you, the grasp of your very mystery becomes a positive source of bliss. Then the farther your infinity is removed from my nothingness, the greater is the challenge to my love. The more complete the dependence of my fragile existence upon your unsearchable counsels, the more unconditional must be the surrender of my whole being to you, beloved God. The more annihilating the incomprehensibility of your ways and judgments, the greater must be the holy defiance of my love. And my love is all the greater and more blessed, the less my poor spirit understands of you.

God of my life, incomprehensible, be my life. God of my faith, who lead me into your darkness — God of my love, who turn your darkness into the sweet light of my life, be now the God of my hope, so that you will one day be the God of my life, the life of eternal love.

JESUS CHRIST

63 • Jesus of Nazareth between Jews and Christians*

Believing Jews will confess and in doing so will be in agreement with us Christians that to be believing Jews they have to hold to the special covenant of the living God with Israel. What an extraordinary claim is already implied in this. It affirms the infinite, transcendent, supramundane God who created the world, its people and history out of nothing. Rejecting any glib divinization of the world through pantheism, it confesses a single God who in the infinite transcendence of his incomprehensible being is radically distinct from the world and who yet embraces it in the freedom of his creative word. Near to everything through the total dependence of all created reality on him, he is distinct in his infinite superiority to every creature. Of *this* infinitely distant and incomprehensible God, Israel confesses, in a remarkable paradox, that he has sealed with it, with precisely this people, a unique covenant. This is true even if the covenant is not a source of national pride but is a blessing for *all* people and even if the grace of the living God in a mysterious and historically indiscernible way rules the history of all other peoples as well.

Israel confesses that this absolute and incommensurable God appears in the *midst* of its history, here and now, with his word, chooses and makes distinctions, is near or far as he wills. He does not indifferently, as it were, carry the whole sweep of history as its distant ground, both near to and far from everything in the same way. Israel confesses that the one, infinite God acts not just everywhere but with historical determination, here and now, in and on itself. If it were not to believe this, it would have to deny that it was chosen for a unique covenant; it would have to reduce the covenant to a mere instance of God's universal and fundamentally equal activity. God would remain purely transcendent and would no longer be a partner *in* history but rather the metaphysical ground of all history.

If Israel has experienced and confessed *this* God of concrete history, then we Christians believe that we are more true to the fundamental law of their experience when we believe and confess that the free and

---

* "Bekenntnis zu Christus," in *Juden, Christen, Deutsche,* ed. H. J. Schultz (Stuttgart: Kreuz Verlag, 1961), 152–56, 158. Trans. Daniel Donovan, University of Saint Michael's College, Toronto.

273

personal involvement of God in history, the near approach of God to creation, the manifestation of the divine and incomprehensible mystery, has a history and is moving toward its final and unsurpassable highpoint, not as consuming judgment but as the nearness of love. God was really there in silence, in the burning bush, in the word of the prophet, that is, always in a specific here and now, in one place and not in another, now and not then, present in a chosen earthly reality and not simply there as a mystical atmosphere permeating everything. If this is true, how can the definitive, unsurpassable presence of God, the presence that means the final and irrevocable redemptive acceptance of humanity in spite of finitude and guilt, be other than through God's making his own human existence with its life, word, silence, and death? The very nature of a human being, after all, is radical openness to God. That is what we Christians confess when we believe in Jesus Christ as the Son of God.

Rejection of this faith is secretly carried by a mythological, docetic or monophysite misunderstanding of it. God does not transform himself into something earthly. Jesus is not simply the appearance of a human being, the livery of a disguised God. Jesus is truly human; he worships, is obedient, experiences his own mortal finitude, falls mute before the incomprehensible mystery we call God. This human reality, God has truly made his own. It is a reality that he could not deny because he created it. We confess that the God who turns to humankind in a personal way is so uniquely present in his Word in Jesus that without identifying God and a creature, that presence can only be expressed by saying that Jesus *is* the Word of God. The man Jesus achieves in a unique and radical way the possibility of a dialogical and free relationship to God precisely because his reality has been embraced by God in an unsurpassable fashion. Nearness to God and the self-actualization of the creature grow not in inverse but in direct proportion.

What happened in Jesus in a pure and unique way is a promise for the rest of us. It reveals that we can only understand and grasp our own being and the being of God when we see ourselves as pure orientation to God, and God as that blessed infinity which in freedom is no longer distant but near and which offers itself to us. To understand what we confess of Christ is to recognize that it cannot be affirmed of everybody. And yet his uniqueness gives us the courage to believe that we are and can be true sons and daughters of God, born from God, participants in divine nature.

People, whether they know it or not, already believe in Christ, if with mind and heart they let themselves fall into the inscrutable mystery of God. In doing so they dare, in spite of their incomprehensible, guilty and death-oriented nothingness, to feel and to understand themselves as true children of God. If we think that as human beings we have to go through life on the watch for the place where the infinite question that we are and the answer that God alone is might have come together, where else would we find the courage to say, "It has happened and we have found it?" than in Jesus of Nazareth?

It is said that he has not redeemed us because the guilt and misery of history are still with us. Must one not ask in return: Do you seriously expect the definitive kingdom of God *within* history? For whom would this kingdom be there? Not for those who are already dead and not for us who are on the way to death. But our heart too longs for the coming of God. Can it be other than that God has already entered into the heart of this finite world and of our cruelly sinful history and taken on and suffered its finitude, tragedy, and guilt, and by so doing brings the kingdom of glory as the end of world history.

Is it not so that those who truly believe in eternal life, a life that brings history to a conclusion and is not itself of "this world," have the best chance to create in this world a bearable life? Neither despair is able to do it nor the hubris which thinks itself capable of transforming history into the definitive kingdom of God. Those who before the end of history struggle in radical hope and total commitment for the betterment of this world confess, whether they know and consent to it or not, that the root of all history has already been healed. For those who are neither naively optimistic nor rationalistic, such a confession cannot be understood as knowledge of something self-evident and necessary. It can only be understood as faith in what is not self-evident, faith that this root was made whole by a particular act or event.

We Christians believe that this event is named Jesus Christ. Because we believe in *this* kind of redemption from the depths, we are always able to begin again and to do what can be done so that at the end we will be blessed. If through grace we find the courage to love unconditionally the God who alone finally is responsible for the world, then there exists even in this world peace, the kingdom, and salvation. We must ourselves do God's will. It is not done for us. Redemption through Christ does not imply a denial by God of our duty but rather the gift that enables us to fulfill it. When we have failed and are guilty, it comes as the incomprehensible gift of forgiveness, a gift that in our interpretation of life we must not take for granted but rather receive from God's grace. Even this can only take place in the gift of penitential and loving acceptance of God's grace by *ourselves,* in the gift of our conversion to God which is always the beginning of our own free action. Can one think of an authentic relation to God (if one understands what this word means) other than in the confession that the highest form of our own activity is again grace. Redemption through the Son and our own responsible action do not thus contradict one another.

If the messiah were *only* human, how could he be the final moment in the history of salvation, how could he be more than one in the incomplete series of God's messengers, of whom none can be the last one, how could he be more than the prophet of what is provisional? Certainly Jesus did not understand himself in this way as even a critical search for the historical Jesus would have to admit. He thought that with him the very kingdom of God had decisively dawned and that in relation to him the fate of the world was being determined. A messiah or prophet could not be thought of in this way if he were only one of God's messengers, someone who spoke *a* word of God, but never the final word. Even if, in the world of Jesus, the messiah tended to be thought of as a kind of prophet, divine fulfillment always goes well beyond human expectations. How could it be otherwise?

When we Christians dare to express our faith in Jesus Christ in this way before Jews, then it seems to me that always and especially today another thing has to be said. The one in whom we believe and whom we confess and love as the Son of God and as our salvation and hope is from their race. Precisely because in him flesh and not theology became the pivot of salvation, as Tertullian said, what stands in our scriptures as a word of Jesus remains eternally true: "Salvation is from the Jews" (Jn 4:22). For ourselves who have been grafted onto the true olive tree of history and of the promise, the olive tree that is Israel, it is important to say: Jesus loved his people, he prayed for them as he was dying, he forgave them and redeemed them. They are guilty in regard to him precisely as we are, not more and not less. Thus this people *is* redeemed. Nor does God repent of his promises. If the saving will of God in Christ Jesus, as we confess it, so embraces Israel that we are seen by God in Israel rather than Israel in us, can we then imagine as Christians that this will of God is powerless? Can we, as at first glance Paul seems to have done, simply look to the distant future for the fulfillment of our hopes for Israel's recognition of Jesus Christ? Christianity may and indeed today must reflect more explicitly than at its beginnings on individuals and their salvation. It cannot any longer think only of a reconciliation between the Lord and a future Israel, for the Israel of yesterday and today is the chosen, called, and redeemed people. And so we Christians dare to hope that the apparent no of Israel to Jesus comes out of a deeper and more enigmatic yes of faith.

Paul says that the temporary no of Israel has been used by God to further our blessing, the blessing of the Gentiles. Why this is so is difficult to understand. The Gentile Christian, however, accepts it on the basis of the New Testament and hopes that the no of Israel which redounds to our benefit, as threatening to salvation as it appears and can be, is finally a no behind which is hidden the true and saving yes to Jesus Christ. It is perhaps hidden because the grace of giving the incarnate Word of God to the world would have been for Israel unbearable.

64 • Seeking Jesus Christ*

Freely tending toward finality, the human person has to be concerned with himself as one and whole. Admittedly, he can permit himself to be driven through the diversity of his life, occupied now with one, now with another, detail of his life and its possibilities. But he is expected to have in mind and to be responsible in freedom for the oneness and wholeness of his existence; he has to be concerned with *himself,* with his "salvation."

If he does this, he will find himself in a peculiarly and fundamentally embarrassing situation. Since it is a question of the totality of his existence, it seems that here this very totality alone as one and whole can be important for salvation; it seems that no particularity of his life, of his individual and collective history, can from the outset, from the nature of the case, be crucial for this one and whole. It seems therefore that, however much in other respects he remains unquestionably a historical being, in the question of his salvation the human being must become unhistorical.

He may attempt in a variety of ways to place the one totality of his existence before himself, regardless of history: becoming aware of himself in a mystical experience in the depths of his being, seeking salvation in the contemplation of this totality; trying to grasp in a metaphysical upswing the eternal truth that hovers constantly over history and assures him of his everlasting nature beyond the many-colored variety of his history; seeking his real truth, while exposing in a spirit of skeptical resignation all truths as historically and sociologically conditioned. But all this is irrelevant in the last resort since in all these and other conceivable ways the person thinks he can find himself as one and whole only outside his authentic historical existence: history as such seems to be beyond salvation merely the outward show that disguises the person's true nature in a thousand empty appearances.

If however a person is sure that he can also achieve and experience his salvation only in his history (since he becomes aware of himself

* *Theological Investigations XVIII*, trans. Edward Quinn (New York: Crossroad Publishing Company, 1983), 145–48.

and realizes his freedom in contact with his contemporaries and his environment, that is, in history, and cannot even in metaphysics or mysticism really step out of his history), he looks for another human being in whom, by God's free power of course, such salvation has really been achieved and as achieved becomes perceptible to him, in whom then because of his solidarity with him, for himself too not only the abstract possibility of salvation, but salvation also as promise for his hope becomes concretely apparent.

The person who really seeks his salvation and knows that he is responsible for it in his freedom looks in the history of the one humanity to which he belongs for a human being in whom this salvation has not only occurred as promise to himself, but also becomes *tangible* as victoriously achieved by God's power and permits him to hope for it, concretely as more than a merely abstract possibility for himself. Whether such an achieved and thus also experienced salvation event is merely *sought* in history or is already actually found there, is not a question that need be considered at this stage in our reflections.

The person at least sought in this way we may call the absolute salvation bringer (although our reflections on this point must be somewhat hasty and spasmodic), since, as we said, it is a question, not merely of the fate of an existing individual solely for his own sake, but of one that promises salvation as a firm hope for *us* and assures us effectively by God's grace of our salvation. This of course assumes that the person who is sought and who has reached salvation exists in an absolute solidarity with us and that we can offer and do actually offer to him the same solidarity.

In our human situation as it is in fact, this salvation achieved in the persons sought cannot be understood as occurring otherwise than by death, since it is only there that history is completed, freedom becomes definitive, the human being surrenders himself freely and finally to the mystery of God, and thus the person's transcendence into God's incomprehensibility and his history reach their definitive unity. But since it is meant to be the effective promise of salvation for us, God's gift of himself to us and not merely the individually isolated fate of this person, this death rescuing the person for salvation, as achieved and saved for us into God, even though in an absolutely once-and-for-all experience, must also become tangible: that is, the death of this person must be capable of being understood as passing into what we describe in traditional Christian terminology as the resurrection of this person. This also implies of course that this person (still being sought) in his life and his self-understanding was such and is historically grasped by us as such that we can believe seriously in this life as redeemed, in his "resurrection." But, on these assumptions, such a person, hitherto to some extent projected a priori by our question about salvation, can certainly be understood and described as absolute salvation bringer.

Seen merely as such a person, he is not himself salvation, for, in view of the human being's boundless transcendentality beyond any particular good and in view of this transcendence as radicalized by what we describe as grace, this salvation can only be God himself and can be given immediacy and finality only by the self-communication of this God. But this person who is sought is the absolute salvation bringer insofar as his consummation occurring through death and resurrection in the power of God in solidarity with us is for us the irrevocable sign that God has promised himself as the consummation of our salvation.

As we said at the very beginning, we cannot attempt also here to prove expressly and in detail that what is meant, at least implicitly, by the absolute salvation bringer thus depicted and sought is the same as what the classical christology of the church means and teaches in talking about incarnation, hypostatic union, God's eternal Word becoming man in the unity of one person and in the unconfused duality of a human and divine reality.

But we think that this proof is possible in principle and we presuppose it here as possible and practicable. When, *in* the redeemed destiny of one human being, in that destiny experienced as redeemed, a person grasps God's promise of salvation to himself, he is practicing christology explicitly or implicitly; if in his history he seeks such a human being, he is practicing "seeking" christology explicitly or implicitly. And, since a person can really only culpably suppress the question of his own salvation, such an explicitly or implicitly realized seeking christology involves in every human being today also the presence in transcendence and grace of the prerequisite that he is seeking and will eventually find his own private christology.

65 • Approaches to Jesus Christ*

The first approach consists in *love of neighbor.* Jesus himself shows us what this means in Matthew 25, where he asserts an identity between himself and our neighbor. Every love for one's fellow human being has, at least in its nature, the character of an absolute commitment of one's personal existence to that person. Hence where there is real love, it is achieved whether consciously or unconsciously, in the

---

* *Theological Investigations XIII,* 197–200.

hope that, despite all the questionableness and fragility by reason of which that person cannot in any sense supply a complete justification of the absolute character of the love that is borne to him, such a commitment is reasonable, and need not necessarily meet with ultimate disappointment.

Now in Jesus and through him this hope has been confirmed. In his person a man appears in palpable and historical guise for whom and in whom it is manifest (to those who believe) that that love in which a person lovingly commits himself to him can, in its absolute character, no longer meet with disappointment. This person, therefore, can enable us to commit ourselves in love to our fellow human beings too, justifying us in this and enabling us to hope in the total and unreserved character of this commitment.

But let us imagine an individual who, in virtue of his very existence, his human lot, and the final and definitive outcome of this, provides an absolute justification for a total and unreserved love for himself and his brethren, and overcomes all ultimate reserves on his part as the subject of this love with regard to the ultimate questionability of the beloved. Such a person as this is (though this is a point which we cannot develop further here) precisely he whom the Christian faith in its traditional formulation acknowledges as the Godman, as that man who is one with God to such an extent that if we commit ourselves to him unconditionally in the sureness of faith and hope, then the goal of this love of ours, which embraces both the beloved and ourselves, becomes God himself, and no longer solely an individual man in all his radical questionability.

But for the same reason the converse is also true: he who loves Jesus as one who lives, with a love that is justified and sure of itself, and in an attitude of absolute trust that recognizes its absolute basis in Jesus himself, such a one has already accepted Jesus as him whom the Christian faith proclaims, whether he does or does not understand the classic and abidingly valid formulas of christology.

A second approach, leading to an understanding of what Jesus is and is for us, can be discovered in the *experience of death*. This approach is primarily connected with what has been said with regard to love of neighbor as leading to an understanding of Jesus. The absolute character of such love seems in fact to be threatened in the most radical sense by the very fact of experiencing the death of the beloved.

And even if we say that such love is asserting that the beloved survives as a final and definitive force, still this would in its turn lead to the further question of what grounds there can be for so boldly hoping that the beloved does remain as a final and definitive force in this sense, and where *that* man is whose fate, regarded as brought about by God, enables the victory which such a final and definitive state represents to be manifested to our eyes in historical terms.

But even apart from this, the experience of death constitutes an approach enabling us to understand the reality of Jesus and his significance for us. However much each individual may die his own death, it still remains true in the deepest sense that death is the common fate of all human beings, and that in it they are united among themselves by having to endure that which is most extreme and most ultimate. And no one is justified in adopting an attitude of indifference to his fellow.

But at what point in our personal history do we achieve the concrete hope what is most ultimate and extreme in our existence, in which we are absolutely torn apart from ourselves, is not the victory of the sheer empty nothingness of the human being, but on the contrary opens onto the absolute blessedness of the love of God and his eternity?

In the end it is only in a man whose "resurrection" is experienced in faith and hope as the crown and fulfillment of our common death. But if in such a resurrection the final and definitive assent of God to us is recognized as the true reality of the death of Jesus and of our own death, then the risen Lord is believed in, as the unsurpassable word of salvation uttered by God to us, and as the bringer of eschatological salvation. And again we can assert this: he who is thus believed in, in the power of a hope that overcomes death and as the basis of this hope, is precisely he who is acknowledged in the Christian faith as the incarnate Word in whom God has definitively and victoriously uttered himself to us.

On this basis it becomes, properly speaking, ipso facto intelligible why and how we can designate the factor of *hope in the absolute future* as an approach enabling us to understand what Jesus is and what he means for us. We are speaking of a hope which hopes on behalf of all, and, moreover, hopes for a final and definitive victory as the outcome of the history of humankind, even though it cannot point to any definable goal already filled out with a content which we can recognize (for to do this would be to turn from the incomprehensible and mysterious God of the future to make an idol of the future itself fashioned by our own hands).

Such a hope as this must necessarily search history to discover how far it has already advanced in its course toward the future. This is not in order to anticipate the absolute future by already formulating it in ideological terms, or in order falsely to transform it into a goal to be constituted as such by human beings themselves. Rather, it is because this hope must render an account of itself in the concrete.

It should not be prohibited from inquiring into the "signs of the times," seeing that it is genuinely hoping for its own fulfillment, and that this, after all, is destined to be achieved in and through history. Nor should it restrain itself, from motives of false diffidence, from noticing in history that history itself has already entered upon a phase in which the possibility of an ultimate collapse of history into the void of God as its absolute future is already past.

Once we have, in a spirit of faith, seized upon the "resurrection" of Jesus, then we have grasped the fact that the one and single history of the world as a whole can no longer fail, even though the question of how the personal history of the individual will turn out remains open, and belongs to the absolute future of God which brings blessing indeed, but still at the same time remains at the level of incomprehensible and indefinable mystery. But once the word of God's self utterance, in the case of a concrete individual in history, is present never again to be withdrawn, and accepted in faith as the absolute future of history, then that unity between God and human beings is present and believed in too, which Christian faith acknowledges in the "hypostatic union."

The questions must be asked how we can love our neighbor unreservedly, committing our own lives in a radical sense on his behalf, how such a love is not rendered invalid even by death, and whether we can hope in death to discover not the end but the consummation in that absolute future which is called God. And anyone who does ask these questions is seeking thereby, whether he recognizes it or not, for Jesus. He who really keeps alive this threefold question and does not suppress it will not find it in itself so difficult to discover the answer to these questions in history in the person of Jesus, provided Jesus is preached to him aright.

And provided he opens himself to the answer to this threefold question constituted by Jesus and his life in death and resurrection, then he gains too an approach which will enable him to understand the traditional christology, which at first sight seems so difficult to understand, but, ultimately speaking, conveys no other message than that in Jesus God has uttered himself to us victoriously and unsurpassably as the blessed response to that threefold question which is not merely something human beings ask themselves, but which they really are.

66 • "I Believe in Jesus Christ"*

Today one cannot say anything of religious and theological significance about Jesus Christ himself without also describing the essence of *faith* itself as an act whereby Jesus is seen as the Christ. In referring to this faith first of all as an occurrence — and as having a "content" only within the particular context of that occurrence — it must be clear at the outset that this faith is to be understood as more than the merely private subjectivity of which we today are justly suspicious, by being faith within *the* church and under obedience to what the church's authoritative faith says. Hence we can immediately see the point of a mandatory confession of faith today too. The man Jesus commits himself to human beings in the faith of the church and with the church. To wish to find this faith by relying solely on oneself would be a fatal individualism.

This faith occurs as a result of an absolute trust, by which one commits *oneself* to the other person and thereby embraces the rights and privileges of such a total self-abandonment with a hope without reservations. This extends to all areas of existence which, on account of the absolute quality of this self-abandonment, do not need to be seen totally nor to be specified in advance. The person to whom one thus commits oneself can be addressed in the most varied ways depending on the dimensions of one's own self and the nature of one's absolute commitment: simply "Lord," "Son of God," "forgiver," "savior," and a thousand other names which have become his since the New Testament.

Hence an important but secondary question is which of the many aspects of this total claim is most suitable for any particular person's encounter with him: whether the apparently completely private aspect, for instance, whereby one confidently lays hold on his forgiveness of one's own guilt, or within the cosmic perspective of universal history, whereby one accepts him in trust as the omega of the development of the universe, the meaningful conclusion of history. The most diverse approaches to him are all intended to be gateways to the one radical self-commitment of the whole human being to Jesus Christ, and it is only in this sense that they have any meaning at all.

Similarly we are not concerned here with the question of what is required for a person so to find the concrete man Jesus that this act of total self-surrender to him successfully takes place. Although it is no less decisive for the understanding of christology and the subject under discussion, we cannot here enter into detail as to why what we mean when we say "God" is the same as what is known and accepted as

---

* *Theological Investigations IX,* 165–69.

the ultimate ground of this free act of confident, hopeful, and loving self-surrender to the other person.

Once we have assumed this, we can say the following: where someone is *justified* in trusting himself to another person *absolutely,* and where this other person on his own account is able to accept this absolute trust and give it a basis, authorized by God and by no one else, then this other person is in such a unique and radical union with God that the relationship can be rightly and radically interpreted for all time in the way orthodox Christian faith affirms — irrespective of how such a committed person himself understands and interprets the experience.

If we are honest, we contemporary human beings will admit that the doctrine of God's incarnation seems at first sight like pure mythology which can no longer be "realized." But if we listen closely to what *real* Christian doctrine says about the Godman, we notice that there is nothing to be "demythologized" in this fundamental dogma, but that it only needs to be understood correctly to be *completely orthodox and at the same time worthy of belief.* If we say "God is made man" in the ready-made patterns of our everyday speech, we either think automatically of God being changed into a man or else we understand the content of the word "man" in this context as an outer garment, a body in its constituent parts or something similar, by means of which God himself renders himself visible on the stage of his world's history. But both interpretations of this statement are nonsensical and contrary to what Christian dogma really intends to say. For God remains God and does not change, and Jesus is a real, genuine, and finite man with his own experiences, in adoration before the incomprehensibility of God, a free and obedient man, like us in all things.

Then what does this fundamental affirmation of the Christian faith mean? It is unexceptionable and legitimate from the point of view of dogma if we consider on the one hand that, in the sense we have outlined, a man who is able to receive an act of unconditional trust in God authoritatively and on his own account, must be in a quite unique union with God; and it is conversely also legitimate to try to formulate the fact of this union, the abiding mystery of the divine sonship of Jesus and of the incarnation, in primarily existential categories, that is, in terms which express the human person's total spiritual and cognitive nature.

The human being exists all the time as one who comes from somewhere and as one who is spoken to; as one who answers yes and no and who comes from and returns to the mystery we call God. This fact of issuing from an origin and proceeding to an end is the essence of the spiritual creature. The more radically this fact is realized in actuality, the more independent, that is, the freer the person is.

Therefore, the realization of thus originating in a source and being bound for an end is to an increasing extent the gift of God *and* the human person's act. If a person receives this human essence from God in such absolute purity and integrity and so actualizes this relationship with God that he becomes God's self-expression and his once-for-all pledge of himself to the world he calls into existence, we have what we call "incarnation" in a dogmatically orthodox sense.

Similarly in the doctrine of the unity of the one divine person and the two — divine and human — natures, the mystery described in ontic and substantial categories is the same as that which can also be expressed in existential terms. The only necessary condition for interchanging the types of statement is the awareness that every existential statement automatically includes an ontological one and vice versa.

It is essential, however, that we understand that this act on the part of such a person is already the act of God in creating and sustaining him as he is. It is also absolutely necessary not to misunderstand the relation between God and the human person as a merely peripheral and supplementary "state of mind," leaving the human person's actual existence basically untouched, and unable to influence it radically. To understand this correctly, one only needs to grasp the fact that God has not merely "uttered" the human being as the open question which we are in respect to him, but that he has uttered this question in such a way as to provide it with the possibility and potential of accepting itself as such unconditionally and totally — thereby accepting God himself.

The message of the faith concerning Jesus Christ is neither myth nor fairy tale, but it tells of the unique occasion which saw the radical achievement of the *ultimate* possibility of human existence. Faith has the courage to accept Jesus of Nazareth as the one who, from the depths of his being, grounded in God, has surrendered himself in obedience to this God and has been accepted as such by him — this is made plain by the resurrection. He was *able* to do this because he was and is the one who *had always* been accepted by God. What he is in reality occurred and appeared in history in his life, namely, in God's pledging of himself to the world, made irreversible in and through the radical, divinely initiated acceptance of this pledge in the true man Jesus.

Looking now from the other angle, whoever experiences in faith that he trusts Jesus of Nazareth absolutely, that in him God gives his pledge unconditionally and irreversibly, that in respect of Jesus his own concrete encounter with another person in trust and love becomes absolute and he thus experiences what is meant by "God" — such a person may interpret this experience how he will, well or ill, adequately or unsatisfactorily; in reality he believes what we orthodox Christians call "incarnation": the unconfused and inseparable unity of God and man, in which God remains totally God, the human is radically human, and both are one, uncompounded and inseparable, in this Jesus who is the Christ of faith.

If we entrust ourselves to him in a radical way, and exist in attendance on him alone, we experience directly *who* he is, and this trust of ours is *founded* on who he is. This circle cannot be broken. Whether one knows it explicitly or not, one is always seeing God and man in one. The Christian believes that in Jesus of Nazareth he finds both as one. Love for all other people finds its justification here and discovers its ultimate ground, and all such love leads to the one man in whom this union of God and man, intended for everyone, appears in its historical uniqueness and utter finality — Jesus Christ.

The church is right to value highly its ancient christological formulas, the product of a long and troubled history of the faith. Every other formula — and there may be others — must be tested to see whether it clearly maintains that faith in Jesus does not acknowledge merely a religious genius or the prophet of a passing phase in the history of religions, but the absolute mediator of salvation now and always. But wherever and in whatever way a person accepts this in faith and trust, he enacts in such faith what Christianity confesses concerning Jesus of Nazareth, crucified and risen.

67 • The Birth of the Lord*

Look at the Lord and see how he subjects himself to time! What a venture — to risk entering a certain family at a certain time with the divine life! The appearance of God in the flesh!

Often we suffer in the circumstances we find ourselves in — circumstances that are the result of former history and the factors that were at work in it. Often we are the plaything of politics and suffer greatly because of it. We look apprehensively into the future. We ask how, under such conditions, the life that we have planned for ourselves can even be possible. Afraid of life and mistrustful of its unfolding, we constantly ask ourselves if the real order is going to give us the material necessary to shape our lives.

The Word of God risked entering into this dull reality to become a troublesome outcast, the member of a dispossessed family, and a citizen of an enslaved land. He is born in poverty, in a stable, because

---

* *Spiritual Exercises,* trans. Kenneth Baker, S.J. (New York: Herder and Herder, 1965), 146–50.

Mary and Joseph were not admitted to the inn. Thus St. Paul was able to say of him: "He became poor for your sake, even though he was rich" (2 Cor 8:9). But even this poverty was not exceptional — no one noticed it. What Mary and Joseph were forced to experience in Bethlehem was probably not a great shock to them. Rather, they accepted it as the normal treatment of poor people.

Nevertheless, a birth in such lowly and ordinary circumstances, at least according to our way of thinking, hardly seems suitable for the beginning of a magnificent life. All the circumstances of Jesus' birth indicate a birth that is poor, very ordinary, and terribly common; it is neither extremely poor nor of such a nature that one could predict a noble life from it. His birth is also unrecognized by others: it takes place somewhere in the outskirts, and the people of the time were busy with other things. A few wretched shepherds find it a heavenly event; world history pays absolutely no attention to it.

The very fact of being born, however, is something distressing. "To be born" means to come into existence without being asked. Contingency and being called unasked into existence are factors that belong to the reality of the finite spirit. The starting point of our life that determines it for all eternity in such a way that we can never escape it, is in the hands of another. The acceptance of this unchangeable situation is something that belongs to the fundamental facts of human and especially of Christian existence. The human reality of the Word could not have a fate different from that of creation, at least from the moment that it was provided for by the creative power of God. Even the Lord had to begin!

We can imagine the most wonderful things about the glory of this child who was given to us, but his birth, in any event, is a descent into privation. Through his birth, he truly put on *our* history. How we can and must reconcile this fact with the prerogatives that theology rightly ascribes to him, is another question. We should notice here that he came into the world the same way we did in order to come to terms with the pregiven facts of human existence, and to begin to die. In number 116 of his *Spiritual Exercises,* St. Ignatius wants the exercitant "to see and consider what they [Mary, Joseph, and the others] are doing, for example, making the journey and laboring that our Lord might be born in extreme poverty, and that after many labors, after hunger, thirst, heat, and cold, after insults and outrages, he might die on the cross, and all this for me." According to St. Ignatius, we are supposed to look at the life of the Lord without whitewashing it, without romantic phrases, and without a debilitating humanism. In the meditation on his birth, we should be able to see this point clearly: At his birth, the incarnate Word begins his death march and everything that is mentioned in the history of his birth is an early announcement of his end in utter poverty, weakness, and death.

With this perspective of the history of the birth of Christ we still should not forget that a new and eternal reality appeared in this birth. This reality is not only an eternity such as the connatural immortality of a spiritual subject, but also the eternity of a personal subject that has value in the eyes of God: life in the "glory of God." The child who then began his life's journey from his mother's womb remains forever as a divine reality. When we look at God now, we always see the man whose history began with this blessed birth. Through this birth, God's kindness and his love for us, his "philanthropia," appeared (Ti 3:4–7). On the other hand, human beings really only become lovable when the happy ending of their life is guaranteed, when God establishes the beginning of this end by inserting his own blessedness into human life to carry it along. Only in this way is human living made really bearable. Otherwise, it is only a question to itself and to others — a question to which there is no answer, because there is just too much involved in it: Transcendence toward the infinite, finiteness, spirit and body, an eternal destiny and the passing fate of time, plenitude and want.

For the fundamental questions relative to our human existence, we have no other truly concrete answer but that there is a man who was born as a member of our race and who was like us in all things. His human reality — and therefore ours too! — has meaning and direction, yes, and even an intelligibility surpassing our powers of comprehension, because here the eternal Word of God, the blessed self-expression of the originless mystery, was born, and because God, since he wanted to manifest *himself*, revealed himself as man. This is the beginning of "the end of the ages" that, according to St. Paul, has come upon us (1 Cor 10:11).

Before this event, the dialogue between God and humanity was an open thing — no one knew which way it would go or how it would be terminated. God kept the details of its further development to himself (Eph 3:9). No one could tell from the history of the world before the coming of Christ how it would end. But with the birth of our Lord, God's final Word is spoken into the world: He establishes his Logos as the Word of the world, so that now, as it were, the Word and the call of God plus the answer of the world coincide in one Godman and for all eternity have become hypostatically one. It is for this reason that world history, that is really engaged in a dialogue with God, is closed right here. And nothing unexpected can ever really happen again. Therefore, the rejoicing of the angels and the mysterious announcement of the "glory" of God on earth accompany this birth. Up to this moment, God had refused to make this announcement and in fact could not make it, because the world lacked the peace and the inner unity that proceed from the "good pleasure" of God.

Now the only open question is the one that is directed to us: How will we respond to the final Word of God directed to the world — a word of mercy, of God's coming to it, and a word that signifies its total acceptance by God? The world-horizon of our human existence is now necessarily this Word of God who has come into the world. We cannot remain neutral to a world-horizon of this kind. It must be the source both of our disturbing restlessness and of our heartfelt joy. Now we should consider these events in our hearts as Mary did (Lk 2:19).

68 • The Everydayness of Jesus' Life*

That which is amazing and even confusing in the life of Jesus (and the reason why we do not notice it anymore is that we are accustomed to ignore it) is that it remains completely within the framework of every-day living; we could even say that in him concrete human existence is found in its most basic and radical form.

The first thing that we should learn from Jesus is to be fully human! The courage to do this — to live from day to day under the threat of sickness and death, to be exposed to one's own superficiality and to the superficiality of others, to be a member of the masses, and so forth — is not at all easy. (Humanism and the Renaissance are fundamentally only an escape into a utopia that is just apparently heroic!) But if the Word of God assumed a concrete human existence in Jesus, then this must clearly be so great, meaningful, important for the future, and so full of possibilities, that God did not become anything else but a man just like this when he wanted to go outside of himself.

Moreover, in his life Jesus is a man of scandal. This is something that we are always tempted to protest against! If we look at his life through the eyes of an unbelieving historian, then we meet a man who was born in a miserable corner of the earth, who begins his life unnoticed by others (even his parents did not understand him!), who is pushed around by the politics of the time, and who, after a short public life that is hardly very important, dies in agony on a cross.

There is nothing magnificent in this life! In a certain sense, Jesus did not even live at all, at least not in the way we would expect a spiritually rich human life to be lived. He passes up everything that we

---

* *Spiritual Exercises,* 121–25.

consider necessary to make our lives abundant and full. To be sure, he remarked that the lilies of the field are clothed with more beauty than Solomon in all his glory, but at the same time he said that they were only grass that would wither on the next day. He passes up marriage, art, and even friendship, for the men he gathers around him do not really understand him, so that he really remained very much alone. He does not pursue politics or science. He did not solve any of the social problems of the time. He showed no resentment toward these things. He did not despise them. He just did not busy himself with them. The only thing we can really say about Jesus is that he was a very pious man.

Most likely, we would have imagined the human life of God in quite different terms. Naturally, the incarnate Son of God should have been pious. He should have shown us how to pray to the living God correctly. But in addition to that, he should have had time and care for many other things. We should have expected that he would compose a magnificent literary work; we should have especially expected that he would reform the world politically and socially, that he would establish in some visible way the kingdom of God.

We would like to find some traits in Jesus' life that would make him a bit more congenial. But we find none of this! What Paul said of Jesus is very true. "He humbled himself." The Word of God truly hid his glory in his humanity. Obviously he was not concerned about manifesting his divine majesty in his humanity. But if the Word as the first and last spiritual principle of all creation reveals himself in Jesus, is present in him, then does not the metaphysician have the right to expect that all of creation would, as it were, be gathered together in him so that he might really be the quintessence of the world, the concentration of everything that is good and beautiful?

Jesus, however, passes up everything. At the most, he allows himself a simple pleasure occasionally: a banquet, deep friendship with John, a look at the temple — but even in this case, it is his disciples who call his attention to the beautiful building. He is silent and passes by like one for whom everything in a certain sense is already dead, or at least very provisional. All of those things are the "other" for him; they are not the kingdom of God, and therefore he does not consider them essential.

It is difficult for us to accept the fact that Jesus really cannot do anything else but save souls. We really would not have anything against that, even if he did this very intensively. But we would like to see this zeal combined with some other things that are very dear to our hearts.

Certainly, we should follow the Lord, that man of scandal, with discretion. In a certain sense, we need the world. There are many things that we can and should incorporate into our lives, and there are many things that we should enjoy with gratitude to God — to borrow a phrase from St. Paul. (In fact, it is our duty to continue the life of Jesus in many areas of human endeavor where he was not "allowed" to go in accordance with the will of his Father.)

We should not be filled with resentment. We should not conduct ourselves like those "ascetics" who make their renunciation of the goods of this world easier for themselves by converting the objects of their renunciation into something bad. We should not be fanatics. We should follow Christ in joy and happiness. In order to be able to do that properly, we should have many different experiences of this world — sin only excepted. The dialectic human situation of using and leaving the things of this world applies also to the following of Christ. And yet, as Christians, we must take the scandal in Jesus' life very seriously. This is and remains the basic form of his history that irresistibly forces us to make a decision.

What we said earlier about standing apart from this world, what Paul means when he says, "You have not received the spirit of the world," what St. John means when he demands, "do not love the world and what is in it!" and especially what Jesus demands when he warns us not to receive our glory from ourselves — all of that is presented to us in the figure of Jesus of Nazareth in a most concrete form, and forces us to come to a decision. We should always keep this clearly before our eyes: Jesus demands a renunciation, even in Christian world-affirmation, that is composed of a truly interior poverty animated by faith. This attitude produces a fullness of life that only Jesus can.

69 • Jesus' Self-Consciousness*

If we look at Jesus' life historically, though on a modest scale, we can affirm that Jesus had a human self-consciousness though one which may not be identical in monophysite style with the consciousness of the divine *Logos,* as though it and the entire reality of Jesus were ultimately passively controlled, put on therefore like a uniform, by the sole active divine subject. Jesus' human self-consciousness was at that distance from the God whom he called his Father that is proper to a created being: he was free, and yet obedient; he worshiped and yielded to God's incomprehensibility like any other human consciousness.

Quite apart from an essential sense of self, maintained throughout a lifetime, the sense of self, that is, of a profound nonreflective con-

---

Mediations on Hope and Love, trans. V. Green (New York: Seabury Press, 1977), 42–44.

sciousness of being radically and uniquely close to God (as is apparent from the special nature of his behavior toward the "Father"), the self-objectifying and verbalizing (self-)consciousness of Jesus also has a history. It works up to the horizon of understanding and shares in the ideas of Jesus' environment, not "condescendingly," for others, but so that he himself becomes part of that environment. Jesus' consciousness learns and has new, surprising experiences; it is threatened by the ultimate crises of self-identification, even if those crises, no less acute because of it, are subject to an awareness that they too remain hidden in the will of the "Father."

His relationship to the Father, which is given (and only thus given) in that consciousness, is something that Jesus objectifies and verbalizes for himself and for his audience by means of what is often known as "imminent expectation" — the news of a new and ultimate imminence of the kingdom of God. It is customary, of course, to see that as meaning a short chronological interval before the coming of the kingdom of God, and to make that short interval the decisive point of that expectation. Jesus, however, rejects that viewpoint and yet announces an imminent expectation of the kingdom of God.

If we play down the question that Jesus finally left open: namely, that of the ultimate meaning of the "nearness" of the coming day of Yahweh, because this "nearness" of his proclamation on the one hand and the knowledge of the obscurity of the day on the other hand, as they existed in Jesus' consciousness, cannot be synthesized into a higher unity, it is permissible to speak of an "error" in Jesus' imminent expectation. In such an "error" he merely shared our lot, because to err in that way is better for the human being in history (and therefore for Jesus too) than to know everything already, and thereby to forgo the darkness and anguish of a situation of trial and decision undertaken in the spirit of hope.

But if we should presuppose a notion of "error" which is more appropriate to the nature of human existence, there is no reason to speak of Jesus' making a mistake in his imminent expectation. A genuine human consciousness *must* have an unknown future in front of it.

The imminent expectation that Jesus verbalized in chronological terms was the right way for him. It was the way offered him by his situation to understand the closeness of God calling him to make an unconditional decision. Only an enthusiast for a false and unhistorical kind of existentialism or idealism, who thinks that he is able to decide for or against God (in some situation beyond history), is really surprised at this objective translation of the facts governing a decision about salvation into the form of "imminent expectation." That is the case, even if other people (for instance, we of the twentieth century) have to (and ought to) translate this poignant new situation of the choice about salvation into different objective terms.

70 • The Core of Jesus' Proclamation*

Jesus' proclamation of an imminent expectation of the kingdom of God has, therefore, to be interpreted correctly. In it he proclaims the closeness of the kingdom as the situation of absolute decision for absolute salvation or its opposite as given "now" and only now. But in Jesus' proclamation this situation is so constituted that God offers salvation and nothing else to all human beings as sinners; God, therefore, does not merely set up a situation which is permanently ambivalent as far as human freedom is concerned, but decides this through his own action in favor of human salvation without thus dispensing the person from his own free responsibility for his salvation.

Jesus does not unite the proclamation of the triumphant existence of the kingdom of forgiveness for sinners by God himself with a call to free conversion in human beings, in a "system" comprehensible to the person outside his attitude of acceptance in hope. That may be justifiably described as the historically perceived core of Jesus' message. The rest of his message can be understood only from that basis: his struggle against the dominance of a law that sets itself in God's place; against all legalism and the absolute elevation of religious or secular powers in the world; against any merely pious morality, such as a justification by works which tries to set itself up against God.

If (and insofar as) the proclamation of the absolute nearness of the kingdom of God in the foregoing sense constitutes the core of Jesus' message, it is true to say that Jesus proclaims the kingdom of God and not himself.

This man Jesus is (authentically) man (pure and simple), because he forgets himself for the sake of God and human beings who are in need of salvation, and exists only in that particular state of self-oblivion. A pronouncement about himself by Jesus (which of course exists) is therefore only conceivable when and because it occurs as an inevitable aspect of *the* closeness of God proclaimed by Jesus in his own self-occurrence. Jesus' "function" reveals his "nature."

This nearness of God is the closeness of the salvation which God

---

* *Meditations on Hope and Love*, 44–51.

himself ordains in the continuing freedom of the human person. It is not to be conceived as existing in Jesus' consciousness as a given and uniform situation; it is not an already universally given human existential which can at most be forgotten and suppressed, and for that reason only has to be preached anew. For Jesus that nearness of God is with him and his preaching in a new, unique, and henceforth unsurpassable way.

Why that is the case for Jesus, and (according to the preaching of the pre-Easter Jesus) independently of his death and his resurrection (which of course considerably enlighten and resolve this question in another way), is not easy to say. Is Jesus in that preaching expressing no more than his unique relation to God, which he does not find in others, but wants to mediate to them, as far as they are capable of receiving it? Would the kingdom come "quickly," and in its full glory, if Jesus' message were not rejected? Did Jesus "have to" preach on that hypothesis? In the end we have to say of this whole problem that Jesus' rejection, death, and resurrection help us to place it appropriately. Ultimately, we cannot and must not ignore Jesus' end and fulfillment; we cannot expect a straightforward resolution of the problem.

Conversely, however, Jesus' preaching of the nearness of the kingdom of God (given only with him) is our own decision-situation (now). It is also true for us in spite of our — still uncertain — dependence on a still extensive human history. Through that preaching, at least insofar as it is confirmed by Jesus' death and resurrection, we have an absolute decision-situation, for we enjoy an offer of salvation from God, which did not exist before Jesus. In any case, an individual can never put himself in the situation of humankind as a whole.

I have spoken of an indissoluble connection between the imminence of the kingdom of God proclaimed as something new by Jesus *and* his "person." More exactly: the pre-Easter Jesus holds that new nearness of the kingdom will occur *through* his proclamation of that very nearness.

It is now easier to understand how Jesus could identify the kingdom of God with himself in that way, before his death and his resurrection were allotted a place in (his) theology. It is also easier to understand why the significant core of his preaching was this kingdom of God and not, directly, himself.

Of course the new imminence of the kingdom of God preached by Jesus as something new and not yet given, is not merely a relatively greater degree of imminence than hitherto, which itself could be exceeded and therefore dissolved by an even greater nearness and urgency of God's call. Such an idea of Jesus' function, corresponding to that of any prophet who always knows that he will be replaced by others, who will preach another, new word of God, is rendered impossible by Jesus' imminent expectation. He is the last call of God after which no other is to come or can come on account of the definitive nature of the self-communication of God (who represents himself in no other way) in the declaration that the power of divine mercy essentially constitutes this self-communication of God in the freedom of human beings.

But this thesis isn't exactly easy to understand. It does not degrade Jesus to the status of any prophet or religious ranter. Why is the givenness of that which is proclaimed (the nearness of the kingdom of God) dependent on Jesus' preaching? Perhaps it is because otherwise we would know nothing of what is proclaimed and then it would not be so effective, since what isn't known can't be accepted in human freedom? But if that were the answer, we would have to explain how and why, without this proclamation by this particular Jesus, we would know nothing about what is proclaimed: namely, the nearness of the kingdom of God.

What is more, in *what* would the new, insurpassable immanence of the kingdom of God consist, if it were there, not explicitly without Jesus' proclamation, but of itself, independent of Jesus' proclamation? How could we explain, in terms of Jesus' religious experience, that is, the fact that he knows about an imminence of God's coming as something radically new, if he tells the ignorant only what did not indeed exist before this proclamation, but would have happened quite independently of it? When, where — in other words — can Jesus have learned what he knew?

If we consider carefully the notion of a purely gnoseological necessity of Jesus' preaching of the kingdom, we must confess that he did not preach anything really new, but only, even though in a prophetically definitive style, proclaimed the old news in a new way. In fact his originality is often questioned. That is justifiable if we overlook the fact that his preaching proclaims a hitherto nonexistent and therefore radically new nearness of God which is present only through his, Jesus', preaching. Looked at soberly, there is no more to say than that: Jesus experienced a relationship to God which on the one hand (in comparison to others) he experienced uniquely and in a new way, and which on the other hand he looked on as exemplary for other persons in their relationship to God. He experienced his unique and new "filial relationship" to the "Father" as meaningful for all human beings, inasmuch as in it, as far as all were concerned, God's movement toward them occurred in a new and irrevocable way.

In this unique and, as far as we are concerned, exemplary relationship to God, the pre-Easter Jesus is able to experience the imminence of the kingdom of God in his person. Thus he knows that the coming of the kingdom is indissolubly bound up with *his* preaching and is, in fact, his very preaching.

Through his death and resurrection, of course, all the foregoing is ultimately (and only then ultimately) rendered definitive in itself and for us. But we now understand how Jesus was able, even before Easter, to recognize and experience himself as the absolute bringer of salvation, even if that self-interpretation obtains its ultimate credibility (as far as we are concerned) from Easter, and only then is revealed in its ultimate profundity. In himself Jesus experiences that absolute, triumphant turning of God to himself which had not existed previously in that way among "sinners," and perceives it to be meaningful, valid, and irreversible for all persons. The pre-Easter Jesus, too, in terms proper to his own self-understanding, was already proclaiming the kingdom of God, as it had not existed historically before, and as it was there *through* and *in* him.

If what has been said about the self-understanding of the pre-Easter Jesus is correct, then Jesus is, in a unique and unsurpassable way, the Son of the eternal God. He is not to be reduced to the level of a prophetic figure, a mere religious genius, or a secular messiah. In his life and his proclamation, Jesus is in person the ultimate and unsurpassable Word of God to the world. We might object that one word does not mean much, because it "only" includes the God-given triumphant mercy of God, which encompasses history as a whole with all its guilt and stumbling, and expresses God himself as the absolute human future.

But if this all-encompassing Word has also to be filled with all God's words and the answers of human beings that occur in the whole of human history, then this open and (in the above-mentioned respect) eternal Word is definitive, because it communicates to history as a whole its coming in God's incomprehensible glory. Hence it cannot be surpassed. All history to come, and all its unforeseeable individual futures, are at work in this Word, yet cannot lead beyond it. It is the Word of the absolute, all-reconciling future-containing God himself, and not something merely preliminary to God.

If Jesus in his person, in the unity with God from which he speaks, and in his word is that Word, and if that Word is pronounced by God (because it can be said only by God), then Jesus one and entire is pronounced from eternity as the intentionally triumphant self-communication of God to God's world. From the beginning of existence he is intended by God as that Word, even when that Word, in order to be and to be heard by us, had to unfold and expound in a human history. Christians are right to say that this Word of God, in which God communicated himself in his ultimate definitive nature and in a historically perceptible manner, was born at Christmas.

71 • The Will for the Cross*

Let us, however, take a closer look at the sacrificial disposition of Jesus himself. It is the will for the cross, the obedience unto death, the voluntary sacrifice of his life by the one who has power to give his life or to keep it, by the one who gave it because this was his Father's will. It was therefore a will for sorrow, for the chalice of bitterness, for destruction, because God was to be glorified precisely by such a voluntary acceptance of suffering.

We can just get an inkling as to why precisely such suffering and dying was the form of glorifying God surpassing all other possibilities and the one by which the only begotten Son of God revealed his Father. Suffering and dying are the destruction of what is human; they are a task of one's own fulfillment, one's own pleasure and honor. But from the human point of view, such a task of self-affirmation shows — more than anything else — that all salvation comes from God. It is not by elevating his own self and by perfecting his own being that a human being can find the God who, without the person's merit, forgives the sinner and calls him out of the sphere of his natural desire of perfecting self to the infinity of his own divine life. The new life itself is God's grace, is his gift.

No amount of suffering, death, dark night, and denial of the unruly will to live could have forced God to come down to man. But such active renunciation of one's own happiness as is contained in surrender to pain and sorrow is still the clearest practical confession of the fact that the person, conscious of his own powerlessness in the face of the God of forgiveness and elevating grace, expects his salvation from above and not from himself, and hence can and will sacrifice his ego and its values, those values which are powerless to procure his salvation.

Such a will to sacrifice animated Jesus as he offered himself to God in order to win for us forgiveness and grace, and this one and the same will to sacrifice also makes Christ a victim pleasing to God when he

---

* *Theological Investigations III*, 162–63.

offers himself ritually to God on our altars as the eternal high priest: the will to die so that the Father may be honored, and so that it may be made known that he is all in all, and the human person is nothing before him.

72 • "Behold the Man"*

The human person is a complex and changeable being. It is no blame to him not always to be the same, nor is it demanded of him that he shall be so. For this reason it is difficult to define who and what he really is. There is much that he himself cannot speak of with any willingness. He flees from himself. He is able to do this because it is only possible to reflect upon and speak of one's self when one has time and leisure to do so. But among the factors which are intrinsic to his makeup there is one, in particular, that he finds it impossible to speak of, one that reduces him to dumbness. How might a portrayal of the human being be expected to appear if it were designed to throw precisely this element into relief? The element that makes him what he is, yet what he is unwilling to admit that he is, and is not prepared to be.

It would have to be the picture of someone dying, for though we are indeed unwilling to die, we are nevertheless given over to death to such an extent that death pervades all things for us even in this present life as a sinister power. The dying person would have to be suspended between heaven and earth, for we are not fully at home either here or there. Heaven is too remote from us, and earth too is far from being a dwelling place in which we can feel ourselves really secure. The individual in our picture would have to be alone. For when we arrive at our final hour, the impression is that our fellow human beings feel shy and embarrassed (because they, in fact, are not yet ready for that stage in their lives), and that they leave us alone.

The person in the picture would have to be depicted as though two intersecting lines, one horizontal and one vertical, were passing through his body. For the human heart is, so to say, bisected by, and becomes the point of intersection for two such lines. The horizontal one extends out on either side of it as though striving to include the whole world within its ambience. The vertical one points sheer and undeviatingly upward as though in an effort to concentrate the whole person exclusively upon him who is uniquely one.

The one in the picture would have to be nailed fast to these. For

---

* *Theological Investigations VII*, 136–39.

our freedom upon this earth extends only to a certain point, the point at which it becomes limited and circumscribed by the inescapable necessities of life. The person in the picture would have to be represented with his heart pierced through, for at the end everything has been transformed into a lance which spills our heart's blood to the last drop. He would have to wear a crown of thorns, for the deepest pains come not from the body but from the spirit. And finally, since all human beings are in the same condition as this one man, this solitary figure would, in spite of his solitariness, have to be flanked on either side by other figures, the exact replicas of himself.

We might go on from this to represent one of these figures as despairing and the other as hoping. For we never know altogether for sure whether there is more hope or more despair in our hearts as we draw nearer to death. This would more or less complete the picture. It would not represent all that is in the human being, but it would show what must be shown of us precisely because we are unwilling to accept this particular aspect of ourselves as true (to entertain doubts on this point is simply another way of shrinking from the recognition of this truth). All the other truths which also apply to us do not need to be represented in the picture, because we are ready and eager to recognize them as it is. Our consideration of what such a picture would reveal to us about ourselves poses a question for us which we must answer. And yet this is a question which we are unable to answer by ourselves.

This picture of ourselves which we view so reluctantly is the picture which God has set before our eyes in the death of his Son on Good Friday. And when this picture of man was to be set up before us, one of those taking part in this drama said: "Behold the man!" (Jn 19:5) Again, in his writings Paul says of the Christians that they are those before whose eyes Jesus Christ was portrayed as crucified (Gal 3:1). To some it is a stumbling-block, to others folly, but to those who have been called it is the power of God and the wisdom of God (1 Cor 1:23f.).

Now if God thus sets before our eyes the picture from which we have been copied, then as we view this picture, we are not looking merely at the radical instability of our own existence. Then, in the very act of forcibly confronting *us* with the question that *we* are, God also gives us his own answer to this question. It is only because he knows the answer that the drama conjured up by his unfathomable love has brought home to us the question that we ourselves are. And since his eternal Word has itself become man and, in the fullness of his human nature, has died upon the cross of our existence, he has spoken his answer to us, and thereby given us the initial spark of courage which we need in order to look upon this picture of ourselves, which was concealed from us, to hang it in our private rooms, to set it up by our waysides, and to plant it over our graves.

To what extent, then, is this the answer of God to the question that we ourselves are?

The answer to this question might be stated in a single sentence which the fathers of the church have repeated again and again: "All that was received and accepted is redeemed." All that he accepted is redeemed because thereby it has itself become the love of God and the fate of God. He has accepted death. Therefore, this must be more than merely a descent into empty meaninglessness. He has accepted the state of being forsaken. Therefore, the overpowering sense of loneliness must still contain hidden within itself the promise of God's blessed nearness. He has accepted total failure. Therefore, defeat can be a victory. He has accepted abandonment by God. Therefore, God is near even when we believe ourselves to have been abandoned by him. He has accepted all things. Therefore, all things are redeemed.

Does this pass unnoticed by us? Do we feel ourselves imprisoned in the stifling incomprehensibility of our existence, brought up against a blank wall, and unable to find any escape? Do we find ourselves quite unable to feel that everything is redeemed? Do we imagine that the darkness of Good Friday has in reality lasted continuously ever since the first Good Friday of all? Do we believe that we could accept him, the crucified one, as the image of our existence, were it not for the fact that we do not know how this man, so surrounded by pain and the darkness of death, can also be the salvation and the light of God for us in the extended death that is our life? How is the miracle of Good Friday faith brought about? It is the miracle of grace. No proof can be advanced to justify it.

But let us kneel beneath the cross, and there pray: "Lord I do believe, help thou my unbelief!" At least for the space of one moment let us command all else to silence, the anguish of our own heart and the poignant question of our spirit. Let us be silent in order that we can *listen,* and so, hear just this one word issuing from the lethal darkness of this man in the moment of his death: "Father into your hands I commend my spirit." And then — O miracle of grace! — we are able to believe that everything has been accepted by God and redeemed. For let us look more closely into this death of his, and hearken more attentively!

There is one here who is in mortal straits. He has been spared nothing. He has no illusions. This is death. He has no intention whatever of playing the hero in it. There is nothing of the poseur in him. He is not the sort of person who still acts a part even in the moment of death. He has known what is in the human heart. Those about him, therefore, have not made his death any easier, neither those whom we call his enemies, and who feel themselves to be so, yet for whom he prays, nor those few others who, since he has managed, even in this moment of his death to think lovingly of them, have made the act of dying even harder for him. He has drained the cup of life, almost to the last dregs. All is darkness without and within. He is alone with the suffocating malice of the entire world, which is stupid and at the same time diabolically malignant. He knows that the guilt of the world which clutches ravenously for his heart and life, is not the sort of misunderstanding that turns out on closer examination to be a harmless mistake.

It is the incomprehensible guilt which leads to condemnation. He is alone with this. The light of his Father's nearness is transformed, so to say, into the dark fire of judgment. There is only abandonment and powerlessness left, burning and yet unutterably dead. Death in its stark reality has penetrated to his heart and pierced its way into the innermost depths of his human life — death as absolute. "My God, my God, why have you forsaken me?"

And when abandonment and death have pervaded his whole life in this sense, then listen to what he says: "Father into thy hands I commend my spirit." It is a fearful thing to fall into the hands of the living God, when in an act of inconceivable love, one has identified one's self in spirit with the sins of the world. And yet when he did thus fall into the hands of the living God, what he said was: "Father, into thy hands I commend my spirit."

If there is one word in all this which is immediately and in itself worthy of our belief, it is this one. This word, uttered by him in this moment, *must* be accepted. There is God the Father. One can commit all things to his hands — all things. In such a way that all things are accepted by him.

One is not forced to believe this word, uttered from the cross to us and extending beyond us into the unfathomable depths of the mystery of existence. But one can believe it. One has only to hearken to him and to keep one's eyes fixed upon him. Then the crucified one, who is the image of our existence, also tells us the answer which God has given in him, the divine Word incarnate, to the question that we ourselves are.

73 • The High Point of Jesus' Mission*

On the cross, the Son of Man attains the high point of his mission. For the sake of this "hour," he came into the world. The glorification which he asks of the Father in his priestly prayer — "Father, the hour has come; glorify your Son that the Son may glorify you" (Jn 17:1–2) — is nothing else but God's will that the incarnate Word descend into death's incomprehensibility with all the love of his heart. His glorification begins when he is nailed to the cross and hung between the highest and the lowest, abandoned and rejected by heaven and earth alike. Now he is the lamb of God who takes the sins of the world upon himself, the perfectly obedient one who came into the world to serve so that he might hand over his life as a ransom for many.

On the cross, the saying of his that he "must" suffer is realized (Lk 24:26). This is the remarkable and incomprehensible *dei* of the original Greek text of scripture by means of which the seemingly insoluble connection between God's sovereign direction and human freedom, between God's love and human guilt, is proclaimed to all. In its own way, it also announces that contingent world history has taken on a certain aspect of absoluteness. That Jesus died on the cross "had to be," and everything else, his life and work, all of his words — and even the totality of world history — can only be properly interpreted from that starting point.

Of course this high point of Jesus' mission is also the supreme catastrophe of his life. This is so true that even his mission seems to disappear into deathly silence! The crucified Lord is betrayed and abandoned by his friends, rejected by his people, repudiated by the church of the Old Testament. When he dies a painful death, he is even abandoned by God himself. He who did not know sin has become sin in this abandonment (2 Cor 5:21), so that his life is given over completely to death.

The catastrophe of Jesus' life, however, is also the deepest and most personal act of his life: For, by his obedience, he is able to absorb that which is absolutely foreign to him and that which is threatening to destroy him, so much so that, being changed into him, it becomes something absolutely near and something breaking forth in power. Obedience has many different functions in our lives. For example, it is necessary for the existence and growth of any kind of common life; it is necessary for learning, since only the person who believes another actually and not just theoretically — and directs his life accordingly — is able to transcend himself to such an extent that he is not locked within himself, and thus deprived of any real knowledge of himself.

* *Spiritual Exercises*, 236–40.

Jesus' obedience, his own desire to be "obedient" (Phil 2:8), his submission to the will of the Father, cannot be described even approximately with worldly categories. There is a certain mystical sense about them that is proper to Jesus. This certain something is present in our obedience when we follow Christ. When Jesus could have destroyed his vulgar, ignorant enemies, and when he could have had ten legions of angels at his disposal — if God's will had not been otherwise — then we encounter in his obedience the silent, incomprehensible yes to his end, to an excruciating death in abandonment. We encounter in his death a yes to all that everyone really despises, a yes to that which no one can take from another, one's death, a death through which one already attains the Father.

If we can enter into this attitude even partially, we will begin to understand that the saints, who could obey without getting angry or bitter and were dumb enough to obey when commanded, could tumble into the most holy life of God with their silent obedience — an obedience brought into the world by the incarnate Son of God.

Jesus' greatest act on the cross is not only his yes to abandonment and suffering, but also his yes to God's incomprehensibility. Jesus' death is his own free act of falling into the consuming judgment of God. But Jesus can only accomplish this as a perfect act of his unconditioned love of God. For the ordination of the sovereign freedom of God, when it is seen to proceed from his absolute holiness, justice, and goodness, can only be accepted and born by another lover who lets himself go in love. In this way, he accomplishes the incomprehensible — something that must be present in every love if it is really going to be love. Since love is the only act rooted in the human person's essence by which he can let go of himself in order to get away from himself and so really find himself for the first time, love alone is somehow a "given" that is itself inexplicable and incomprehensible. Only love can adequately express what is really characteristic of the human being. Thus he can only attain his own true reality by giving himself in love.

Of course a person should protect himself. He should take care of himself and worry about the salvation of his soul. There is and must be a legitimate self-love! But in the last analysis, we can only love ourselves by loving God and not ourselves, by loving his ways and not our ways, by loving the one who is not a metaphysical abstraction of infinite perfections, but the living God who ordains the cross and death and all those things that "ought not" to be.

For the person who does not love but just wants to know, who therefore necessarily only agrees with the god of his own making — for this person, a God who is the sum total of everything incomprehensible must be a frightful scandal. The endurance of God's incomprehensibility reached its peak for Jesus on the cross. It becomes so much a part of him that his very life is poured out in the death-dealing cry, "My God, My God, why have you abandoned me?" (Mt 27:46).

Jesus experiences death not as a biological fact, but as the absolute darkness of hell. We could almost say that he himself becomes this darkness, which, of course, does not justify the contention that Jesus underwent the pains of hell. For this darkness of his debilitated life is not the ultimate fact of his existence. The ultimate fact is the great love which prompted him, in the midst of his own darkness, to say to another who was crucified with him: "this day you will be with me in paradise!" (Lk 23:43), and to utter with confidence: "Father, into your hands I commend my spirit!" (Lk 23:46)

These words do away with hell! In fact, we could say that the only reason Jesus is not in hell is because he brought the incomprehensible, absolute power of his love into hell with him. It is a terrible thing to fall into the hands of the living God. On the cross, Jesus handed himself over to this God in perfect obedience and love — and there was no endless terror. There was only the blessedness of entering into the still greater love of the God of grace.

Jesus' sacrifice on the cross is not an unsurpassable moral event because — in the sense of a superficial "satisfaction theory" — it can be attributed to the Word and so achieve a certain infinite "value" or "worth." Rather, this sacrifice is the personal act of the Word himself! And this does not make it less creaturely and free, but it makes it even more genuinely so. For the closer a creature comes to God, the more autonomous it is, the more free it is, the more it "is" simply.

Therefore, the incarnate Word is really able to experience all the dimensions of human existence as his very own: the dignity of a mission, the abyss of ruin, the consummation of obedience, and the deep love of the heart — a heart that can say "Father" to this God who still stands before him as the consuming fire of judgment, a heart that can surrender its poor life into his hands.

74 • The Cross as the Revelation of God's Love*

The cross of the Lord is the revelation of what sin really is. The true world is the one that appears right here: the world in which the cross of the incarnate God is raised on high. The cross of Christ mer-

---

* *Spiritual Exercises*, 240–42.

cilessly reveals what the world hides from itself: that it, as it were, devours the Son of God in the insane blindness of its sin — a sin whose Godless hate is truly set on fire upon contact with the love of God.

How could it have even a ray of hope when it kills this man, when it destroys him and blots him out right at the point where he came into his own? Even though it is true that a person cannot sin without knowing what he is doing, and without being guilty for his sin in the eyes of the God of love and merciful understanding, still it is no less true no matter how paradoxical it may seem — that sin and the malice of sin appear to be harmless, that sin tries to manufacture a good conscience; it is no less true that sin can act as if everything is not really so bad after all, so that finally its presence in the world is hardly noticed.

Although most of us are rather dull, ordinary clods rendered harmless by our tepidity, it still remains true that the sins we commit really and truly "crucify the Son of God on our own account"(Heb 6:6). We are deceived if we think that we could not actually do that, or that, at most, it could only "happen" to us in such a way that we would not be responsible for it. What our own experience leads us to feel about ourselves is basically the consequence of many sins — of our first parents, of the whole world, or our own.

The truth about ourselves is what the cross of Christ says to us about our baseness and its hellish possibilities. Therefore, we should turn our gaze to the crucified Jesus and tell ourselves in the midst of our sinfulness: he loved me and offered himself up for me. "In this the love of God was made manifest among us, that God sent his only Son into the world, so that we might live through him. In this is love, not that we loved God but that he loved us and sent his Son to be the expiation for our sins" (1 Jn 4:9–10). We should meditate on that; we should also consider these words of St. Paul: "But God shows his love for us in that while we were yet sinners Christ died for us" (Rom 5:8).

Also, from a theological point of view, it is not easy to understand why we are loved by God precisely through Christ's death, why he transformed this death into the revelation, yes, into the only revelation of his love, with the final result that we only receive his love through his death. All we can do in our meditation is simply to accept this fact with love. "He loved them to the end!" says St. John (Jn 13:1).

That goes for us, too! The Word loved us to the end! With his own life, he shared our end and our death. Because he was a lover and remains a lover for all eternity, the world is saved. The salvation of the world grows out of the strangely incomprehensible, even paradoxical, unity between the death-dealing revelation of sin which inflicts a terrible paroxysm on God himself who came into the world in order to destroy death by his own death, and between the ineffable outpouring of his love which did not hesitate to sustain sin and death. Out of death and love! "Where sin increased, grace abounded all the more!" (Rom 5:20), and, "God has consigned all men to disobedience, that he may have mercy upon all!" (Rom 11:32)

All of us try to block God's door to the world in such a way that it can never be opened again, and we try to lock ourselves in the prison of our own finiteness so that we can never get out again — even if we wanted to. But if we turn around in our prison so that we can see what a pitiable state we are in, then we encounter Christ who has entered into our loneliness and embraces us there with the outstretched arms of the crucified. Because he is present where we have incarcerated ourselves, we are no longer able to close the prison of our finiteness. We can still be lost, but then we lose our life in the midst of salvation. And so long as we are walking in this "present time," in the "now," we really do not have to do anything but allow ourselves to be embraced by the crucified. We could almost say that it is much more difficult to be lost than to be saved, for the one who wants to save us is God himself, who showed his supreme love for us by dying on the cross. It can be important for us to tell ourselves this frequently, for we are always tempted to stay in sin because we do not dare to believe in the magnificent love of God, and because we do not want to believe that God will forgive us our sins.

When we consider the crucified in this way, we should also look at his pierced heart — that heart which is open "so that there might be a refuge of salvation for all penitents!" If properly understood, the devotion to the Sacred Heart of Jesus belongs to the very essence of Christianity. Therefore, it is always present wherever true Christianity is present, even if it might not be recognized explicitly as such. The only reason we are saved is because the heart of the incarnate Word was pierced through and streams of living water flowed from it. The pierced heart of Jesus Christ is the center of the world in which all the powers and currents of world history are, as it were, bound together into one. The ultimate meaning of the frightful multiplicity of all the things God has created and his most comprehensive statement about them is: the heart, in which his love was pierced through.

75 • Gratitude for the Cross*

In commemorating the death of Jesus as the ground of our salvation and of our final hope for life, we should not at the outset overlook the fact that it is in the ordinariness of life that we hope that we are saved and redeemed and set free. Here already is a reason for gratitude for the cross. The ordinariness of Jesus' destiny, which we believe to be our redemption, became in fact saving because it was accepted by God. It did not fall through death into the void but was caught up and given definitive meaning in the loving and blessed incomprehensibility of God. And thus an ordinary life, so like the life that we ourselves experience, witnessed in a conclusive way to the self-giving love of the mystery we call God.

In and through his death, Jesus' life was marked by an unimaginable dreadfulness that he alone as someone who gave himself in trust and love to God could experience. All the terrible things that led to his death, the injustice done him, the execution by the political and religious powers of the time, the brutality he suffered, were finally only preliminaries to a death that we all die and which everywhere in its incomprehensibility and in the final loneliness and impotency into which it leads is equally terrifying.

Although there can be enormous differences in our experience before death, the terror of death itself is the same for everyone. If by God's grace this terror did not bear within itself the hope of an incomprehensible life, and if this inner mystery of death had not become believable for us through the death of Jesus understood as the coming of the definitive love of God and as a passage into that fulfillment, which we call the resurrection, then we might well despair. Through the death of Jesus, ordinary death, which is common to us all and which we share with him, has become full of blessed hope. That death which is the fate of everyone, which reveals everything as provisional and passing, and which seems to involve all things in one and the same process of destruction, has itself become a sign of limitless hope and gives to all the rest its final dignity and meaning.

Everything that in its meaning, glory, and blessedness seemed to reach only to the fast-approaching border of death has now an infinite glory and promise which no death can any longer limit. If all our days are ordinary because they lead inevitably to that great equalizer that is death, they have also become, for those who in faith rightly understand the death of Jesus, feast days in which the event of an eternal life

---

* *Herausforderung des Christen: Meditationen und Reflexionen* (Freiburg i. Br.: Herder, 1975), 42–46. Trans. Daniel Donovan, University of Saint Michael's College, Toronto.

is celebrated and the banality of this life receives an eternal dignity. Everyday life can thus become gratitude for the cross.

Although there are many grounds that might be mentioned for gratitude for the cross, our reflection about it is rooted in the experience that in Jesus God appeared and that through God's act the redeemer and the redeemed are one and the same. To carry this reflection a step further, this unity of redeemer and redeemed is intended, through the grace of God which comes to us from the cross of Jesus and which leads on to the universal triumph of his resurrection, to become a reality in us. What is characteristic of our gratitude for the cross consists precisely in our identity with the crucified one.

What constitutes the saving act of Jesus on the cross? To this question a thousand right answers might be given because what is being asked here sums up in itself all the incomprehensibility of God and of humankind, an incomprehensibility that no single formulation can exhaust. The scriptures offer the most varied answers to our question. It is not my intention to list them here. In dying, Jesus stood as a human being before that abyss of death that puts everything into question and renders it impotent. He let himself fall into it, accepting it in faith and hope. Through the true mystery of death, which we call God, that last cry of despair which alone we humans of ourselves can bring to death, was transformed into a final and free abandonment of self in faith, hope, and love. In this abandonment the incomprehensibility of the God of the abyss dawned as pure blessedness.

Naturally Jesus' death has a meaning and a dignity that we cannot attribute to our own. It was the once and for all, irrevocable and unrepeatable word of God's power to us, the act of *the* Word of God. As fundamental as this is for Christians, it remains true that his abandonment of self in faith and hope into the incomprehensibility of death in which God dwells is also demanded of us in our death. In us, too, the redeemed and the redeemer must become one; salvation by another and salvation by oneself, when seen in their ultimate significance, do not represent contradictions for a Christian. Self-abandonment in death will only escape being an act of despair if we do it in the power of God's act in us, in the power of the "Spirit" which made possible and perfected Jesus' own self-abandonment. His death becomes for us the promise that the same Spirit will effect in our death this marvel of transformation of doubt into an acceptance of the incomprehensibility we call God. We cannot simply *know* that this marvel of hopeful self-abandonment is taking place in us, but we can firmly hope that it is.

It remains true that the saving self-abandonment of Jesus reaches out, if we allow it, to embrace us. We die in him and with him. This self-abandonment, of course, has to be exercised in ordinary, everyday life, in the unavoidable and yet calm acceptance of the renunciations that it entails, with its banality and barrenness, its hidden and thankless moments of bitterness. If in this way we learn how to die with Jesus and thus go to meet the hoped-for miracle that in our death through the Spirit of God who bestows God's acceptance we will willingly abandon ourselves, then our life will become in its sober ordinariness an act of gratitude for the cross.

Many will give thanks through the calm sobriety with which they embrace life and death as these come to them without explicitly knowing that their very calmness is the result of God's grace or that they are reenacting the redemptive pattern of the life and death of Jesus. Those who in explicit faith have encountered the crucified Christ, the one who has gone through death into the life of God, know that they can expect something more and something different from their death than a despairing muteness, the beginning of a definitive and silent emptiness. For Christians the blessed hope of infinite openness that is present in both life and death becomes a duty, which finally God is and the fulfillment of which he gives us.

Christian spiritual literature often affirms that the pious must and indeed *can* accept with gratitude and even joy the bitterness of their life, its disappointment, pain, and hopelessness, the slow and yet inexorable approach of death, as their "cross." This affirmation and demand are incomprehensible. Gratitude for the cross is certainly anything but a self-evident possibility. That we accept bravely and without self-pity the harshness that is a part of life together with its vitality, strength, and glory, is a demanding aspect of life that is by no means easy. But where what might be called the "cross" really enters into our life and begins to dominate it, where pain no longer affirms strength, where effort is no longer the price that we willingly pay for achievement and success, where trials and disappointments are the precursors of death which itself can promise nothing more than a fall into emptiness, there gratitude for the cross becomes incomprehensible. Gratitude seems to take its possibility and its strength from life, whereas what is now being asked is that we give thanks for life's destruction.

It would appear that in life we can only give thanks through life for life and not for death, but that in fact is what both the cross of Jesus and our cross primarily are. In this rather hopeless situation we might at least take consolation in the thought that when nothing further can be done, we are free from all obligation. This, obviously, would include gratitude for the cross. To Christians, however, and to those who in the depth of their being are anonymously but truly Christians, a great and finally incomprehensible promise has been made. In death they will not only be saved, as it were, from without by God's power, but this saving act of God will enable them to save themselves. Through an act that is both theirs and God's, they will be able in death to abandon themselves and thus experience gratitude for the cross. Such gratitude consists ultimately in the acceptance, through God's gift, of Christ's cross and of our own. The Christian hope is that God himself with his power will be with us in the abyss of our powerlessness at the moment of death so that not only will life follow death but death itself through God's power becomes our own act by which life is created. Willing self-abandonment is a deed that creates eternity.

Because God and human beings are not in competition with one another, dividing up, as it were, our reality between them, this pure act of God on our behalf is at the same time our own highest act. The acceptance of death which brings salvation and in which God gives himself to us is thus itself the perfect form of gratitude for the cross. Death which is our own cross and our sharing in the cross of Christ is not just an event at the end of life but is something that takes place throughout the whole of life. Every awareness of limitation, all bitterness and disappointment, every decline in our powers, experience of failure, emptiness and barrenness, pain, misery and need, oppression and injustice, all such things are precursors and even parts of that one death that we die throughout life.

The willing and hopeful acceptance of the many experiences of death in life are a part of that one experience of gratitude for the cross which we both suffer and do by dying in self-abandonment. Gratitude for the cross thus becomes a blessed part of everyday life. It does not consist in profound theories, eloquent words or elevated feelings. Nor does it forbid us to struggle courageously for life, freedom, and joy wherever we can. True gratitude for the cross is the calm and honest acceptance of that slow process of dying that takes place throughout life. Such gratitude is basically simple. Because everyone, even if only anonymously, encounters the cross of Christ, all are asked whether they are willing to express their gratitude for the cross.

76 • Jesus' Resurrection*

If we are to speak of the resurrection of Jesus and the credibility attached to it, then properly speaking we should explicitly state and

---

* *Theological Investigations XI*, trans. David Bourke (New York: Seabury Press, 1974), 206–14.

make clear certain principles at the level of existential ontology and anthropology upon which we shall be basing our arguments.

We are accustomed to think of the human being to some extent in a dualistic sense, and because of this we find it difficult to grasp the fact that what is meant by the definitive state of the human person, his state of being redeemed and having attained to salvation, is basically speaking the same as that which we call the resurrection of Jesus and of the human person in general. For basically speaking, it is inconceivable either in terms of modern anthropology or biblical anthropology that there should be any absolute division between a fate which we attribute to the physical side of the human being and the fate which he undergoes at the spiritual level and in his personhood.

Now if we evaluate and understand this point correctly, then the following two statements have exactly the same meaning: first, "This crucified one is he who has been received by God in such a way that he, together with his fate and the decision which that fate involves, has been ratified by God as having an eternal validity"; and second, "He has risen."

It is necessary for us to recognize the fact that for ourselves, too, we can hope for no other definitive form of deliverance than that which, on any correct understanding of Christian terminology, we call resurrection. And if we did perceive this more clearly, then we would see that right from the outset the individual may justifiably and confidently ask this question of history itself: Is there any point within this history at which I find an event which makes it possible for me confidently to assert, "So-and-so is the one who has been accepted and saved by God; in other words, the one who has risen from the dead"?

We should begin by reminding ourselves of all these general perspectives and prior assumptions for our understanding, if we intend seriously to inquire into what is truly meant by the resurrection of Jesus, and why it is worthy of belief. Even here it is not a question of a miracle of God being inserted into a spiritual situation in which nothing of the kind could possibly be expected at all. It can perfectly well be the case that it is only through the a posteriori experience that an a priori perspective of hope already transcendentally present within us is brought to the stage of conscious and explicit realization. But when it is brought to this stage we recognize it as something which has been present all along, although, it may be, in a very unexplicated way. This is the one principle which should be borne in mind from the outset and all along in seeking what the resurrection of Jesus means.

Second, we should achieve for ourselves a clear understanding of what really can be meant in *theological* terms by resurrection. The moment we picture to ourselves a dead man returning once more into our temporal dimension, with the biological conditions belonging to it, we have conceived of something which has nothing whatever to do with the resurrection of Jesus, and which cannot have any kind of significance for our salvation either. In fact, to say that any individual has risen from the dead must precisely be tantamount to saying: "This man in this fate of his which seems so absolutely negative, has in a true sense, as himself, and together with his history, really attained to God."

What it does not say, however, is this: He has once more extricated himself from the process of death, and is once more there on the same plane as ourselves. This is in fact precisely not any sort of concession to the modern spirit of the time, after the manner of the demythologizers, but belongs so obviously to the very content of dogmatic teaching that this dogmatic teaching itself would otherwise have no Christian meaning whatever. Once we recognize this, then, precisely on *this* basis, and not merely on the basis of contemporary exegetical criticism, it becomes evident that the question of whether we could touch the risen individual, whether he could eat, and so on, is absolutely secondary, not merely because it suits us today to take this line, but because it is positively demanded by any true understanding of the ancient dogmatic teaching of the church.

One who has achieved the definitive finality of his own existence cannot be subject to the material changes we undergo. He cannot exist in a temporal dimension such as belongs to us. He cannot remain dependent upon other physical entities such as temperature, tactibility, and the like. In other words, even if we were to take all these stories in an extremely literal sense, we would still even then have to interpret them as meaning that in terms of the range of experience and understanding open to us the individual risen from the dead had undergone "in himself" a process of *transposition.*

It should be clear that this "transposition" sets the risen individual "in himself" on a different plane just as much as it attests the fact that he has been eternally and definitively saved by God. To questions such as whether, if we were already even now in a glorified state, we could see the marks of the wounds of the risen Lord, whether then we would still have a head and hands in the same way that we do now, and so on, we should in principle reply: This is something which we do not know and the reason that we do not know it is not that we adopt an attitude of critical skepticism and are no longer willing to accept very much by faith, but rather that the intrinsic meaning of the dogmatic teaching itself does not admit of answers being found to questions of this kind. Whether Christendom has or has not always recognized this fact so clearly as is entailed by the radical nature of resurrection — this too in its turn is a secondary question.

As Catholics we believe in a development of dogma, that as the awareness of our faith becomes more and more developed, we achieve a deeper understanding of the dogma itself. And under certain circumstances certain conceptual models, or perhaps even errors which have crept into our understanding at an earlier stage, are gradually eliminated in this process. The ultimate goal of the process itself is not that in this way we shall gradually argue away the very substance of the dogma itself, so as to leave no room for it in our world, but rather that from its own true and innermost center an ever better understanding may be achieved of what it truly signifies. Even Paul recognized that all realities, and so too the conceptual models we use to understand them, undergo a radical transformation that extends right to the ultimate roots of their nature.

Hence we cannot, on the basis of the models we currently use to understand existence, vividly portray to ourselves what eternity is like. On any radical view this is just as impossible in the case of the soul or spirit of the human being as it is in the case of the physical side of his nature. Yet because we are inclined to accord a certain priority of value to the spiritual side, we find it easy to suppose that at the spiritual level we can live on throughout all eternity in the same mode as that in which we are living in the present.

Yet this is quite untrue. We know nothing of the "last things" (*eschata*) beyond the fact that we are and that we receive the history of our own reality and free decision and our relationship to God as something that is permanently definitive. We have no conceptual models to explain to ourselves precisely how this comes to be. All we know is that we cannot conceive of the human being as a sort of space rocket with two stages, in which the lower stage, that which is called the "physical side," will one day fall away so that then a "spirit," with the special dimension of reality belonging to it, will continue on alone to enter definitively into the glory of God.

We know that the human person is one and cannot be separated into two compartments. If we believe in a consummation then we believe in *our* consummation. The fact that in accordance with the intrinsic complexity and historical development of human nature this consummation must appear different in respect of each particular element in the person — this too is, admittedly, a point that is clear. But as for any positive conceptual model showing us *how* we should represent this to ourselves — this is something which we do not and should not have, for if we did have it, then quite certainly we should be misinterpreting the meaning of "eternity."

All this is very obvious to the individual when he is thinking of *his own* resurrection according to the affirmation which we make in the creed. But obviously it also applies to the case of the risen Lord. For in fact he is risen in that which we call his human nature, his human reality. If he then manifests himself to the disciples in a quite specific mode, then inevitably this has the force of a "transposition" of that which he himself is into our conceptual world.

Yet it is clear from the outset that we can never adequately separate this "for us" aspect of the risen Lord from the "in himself" aspect of him. I cannot work out for myself whether or not the glorified wounds of the physical side of Jesus actually exist in the "in himself" dimension which belongs to him as risen. I do not even know whether one who has been glorified has a head. I have no positive grounds for denying it, but, ultimately speaking, I do not know it, and, moreover, it is a matter of indifference. All this still does not in the least alter the fact that I believe that I am not simply some transitory element in this world, but rather, that as this particular individual, the physical side of whose nature I must include in my concept of myself, I have a kind of existence which is destined to endure, for which I am answerable to God, and which will have an eternal validity in his life.

If we have ever devoted any intelligent consideration to these matters, then, while of course not all those particular questions are immediately clear which we can raise with regard to the resurrection and appearances passages, still many of these questions will cease to appear to us of such acute and radical importance. Of course this in itself is still not enough to provide an answer to the question of precisely *how* the disciples really did experience, at the ultimate heart and center of this Easter experience, the existence of Jesus as delivered from death, and so in some sense having an abiding and eternal validity in God.

This too is a point on which not much can be said. Why is this? It is because we ourselves have precisely not undergone this experience. But even *in* an experience of this kind, of one who, having been delivered, definitively possesses his own history, the true heart and center of this experience is of course, in the very nature of the case, not something which can initially be verified by touching him with our hands, and so on, or laying them upon a wound in his side. It is obvious from the outset that we cannot weigh and measure the risen Lord, cannot photograph him with our cameras, that even a team of television reporters could not make a documentary about him. He does not belong to the world of our experience. For this reason it is extremely difficult now to express in more precise terms exactly *how* the apostles experienced this.

Nevertheless, we can from the outset say this much: If they had been able to touch him in the same way that we touch things at the everyday level, this would in fact not have constituted the true experience of the definitive state which this man Jesus had attained to at all. For in that case the more solid the disciples would have felt such experiences to be at that time, and within the dimension of this world, the less they would have experienced that in which the essence of resurrection in fact consists: the fact that this man is he who has been definitively delivered.

We must simply say: These disciples did maintain that they had undergone this experience, and these individuals actually described this experience. But in these descriptions of theirs it is clearly apparent that they were very conscious of one fact, and actually point to it with what is relatively speaking considerable exactitude, the fact, namely, that their experience was no mere subjective impression of some abiding validity in Jesus, such that it still maintains a permanent force for us; the fact that the point of departure in this experience was him and not their own subjectivity; that it constitutes something quite different from visionary experiences in other contexts with which these men were perfectly familiar. In the case of Paul, too, we find him on the one hand uncompromisingly presenting himself as a mystic gifted with visions and similar phenomena; yet at the same time, on the other, being plainly conscious of, and emphasizing (even to the point of using a different terminology), the fact that the experience of the risen Lord is something quite different.

The question still remains: Is the experience which these disciples attest for us susceptible of abstract investigation and explanation in rational terms, or is any such rationalizing abstraction contrary to the experience asserted by them to have taken place, on the grounds that if we do subject it to this rationalizing process, even that which they do record of it in all honesty thereby ceases to have any further validity?

At this point the Christian says: "Well, I accept this experience from themselves as being unique, but at the same time as something which has really been attested. I believe with them." If we say, with the exegetes of our own time, that the resurrection is not an event that took place in historical fact, but that the historical fact consists rather simply in the faith and the conviction of the apostles and disciples about the resurrection, then this again is not a statement which the dogmatic theologian, on any right understanding of this statement, concedes to the exegete and the historian only reluctantly and with a "gnashing of teeth."

The situation is, rather, that here too we have something which is at basis obvious from the very nature of the case, and, moreover, from the very nature of the case as the dogmatic theologian views it from his *own* standpoint. For one to rise from the dead in such a way as to rise into the incomprehensibility of God obviously, in the very nature of what is signified by this, is not something which is intrinsically included, or should be included, in the dimension of historical experience as found in other contexts. This, however, is in no sense to exclude the fact that this experience involves *some reality* which is not identical with itself as such.

The disciples do not create the resurrection of Jesus *by* their experience. Rather, they experience (this is a witness that we must accept from them if we are willing to believe at all) the resurrection of Jesus. The Catholic interpreter of the apostles' experience of the resurrection says, "What I accept from them is that they had experience of one who had risen." He does not say, "I postulate the experience of Jesus in virtue of the fact that I postulate an experience of faith."

And it is in this sense, too, that Paul understands the resurrection. If we wish to deny this experience to the apostles and Paul, then that is a matter for our own free decision. But what we cannot say on any showing is what Bultmann and others have said in their interpretation of the resurrection, namely, that the apostles themselves would also have understood it in this sense. What the witnesses of the resurrection intended to convey was that in the risen Lord they experienced a reality which is immediate, radical, and inseparable from the saving significance which this event bears for us.

On the other hand, however, God would have had no reason to cause an individual to rise from the dead unless that individual had some significance for us. Thus we can uncompromisingly state that Jesus properly and radically became he who had risen from the dead only when he had attained precisely to *that* point toward which everything tends as its goal, and at which he is present in my faith too as he who has risen from the dead. The very fact that reality quite in general is a single reality which is intended to be made present in the subject endowed with spiritual faculties — this fact in itself is enough to justify us in making the assertion we have just made. Whether we refuse to accept the apostles' witness to this experience of theirs or not — that is a matter for ourselves.

But in any case if we are honest, we must not assert, as the skeptics so often do, that it is possible in the twinkling of an eye to provide a serious explanation of this experience of the apostles (which, after all, is on any showing a piece of historical data) even without according to the experience as its subject matter that reality which it is intended to have in their eyes. If anyone says they were precisely people who were religiously inclined, who could not bear to be parted from their master, and so precisely ended by conjuring up the idea that he had risen from the dead — if anything of this kind is intended to be taken as a serious explanation of the apostles' experience, then this again belongs to the realm of uncritical rationalism. And even though nowadays this "explanation" is usually formulated in somewhat loftier and more polite terms, it still belongs to this realm of uncritical rationalism.

If anyone understands the resurrection aright, if at the center of his own existence he yearns for his own "resurrection" since, on any true anthropology, he can only understand himself as a person who hopes for that which is described in terms of resurrection, then, in my belief, he has also achieved an a priori perspective such that, while it certainly does not excuse him from the *free decision* of faith in the resurrection of Jesus, still at the same time it does justify him in believing in such a thing as the resurrection of Jesus, that is, in accepting the Easter experience of the disciples as a matter of his own intellectual honesty.

Incidentally, it may be said that the disciples were not stupid or primitive men. We have only to represent their concrete situation to ourselves. There is someone who was a very nice man, put forward very remarkable ideas, and who was yet condemned and killed by the legitimate political authorities and also by the religious authorities accepted by the disciples themselves. How on this showing are the disciples, without something more than this happening to them, to arrive at the idea that it is all quite otherwise than it seems, that the reality has, after all, turned out gloriously? The Easter experience of the disciples really cannot be explained away as simply as the skeptics suppose.

But let us put the question to ourselves once more: If we are skeptics and doubters, have we any positive meaningfulness to offer for our lives and the lives of others? Anything which makes life itself more meaningful? And if in reply to this we sought to say, "Oh yes, all that about the resurrection of Jesus would certainly be very beautiful, but it is too beautiful to be true," then the reply to this would be to ask, "Why should not a person prefer the darkness of his existence to consist in faith in an absolute light than to commit himself to this darkness as one who has been banished from the light?"

This is all the more true in view of the fact that the human being as he is does not, after all, basically speaking, or in his life as he lives it in the concrete, allow himself to fall into the void of the absurd. For, in spite of everything, he is, in his existence, one who is decent, loving, faithful. In the very act of achieving the fullness of his existence he still says again and again, "There is a light."

And basically speaking is not the attitude of Christians precisely tantamount to saying, "Despite all that is unintelligible, dark, cruel and brutish, there is a hope justified even prior to any theoretical process of reasoning, that existence has a meaning"? Now if this meaning is such that it affects the whole person, and not merely a spiritual element within him, then it thereby asserts that the human being will be the risen one. But once he achieves this plane of thought, then once more it does not involve any *hara kiri* of the intelligence when he believes that message of the apostles, on which they have staked their lives, that they have had the experience of *the* risen one as the instance of resurrection that is radically first and provides the foundation for all the rest. And it is he who justifies us in hoping for our resurrection.

77 • The Easter Message*

It is difficult in well-worn human words to do justice to the joy of Easter. Not simply because all the mysteries of the gospel have difficulty in penetrating the narrow limits of our being and because it is even more difficult for our language to contain them. The message of Easter is the most human news brought by Christianity. That is why we have most difficulty in understanding it. It is most difficult to be, do, and believe what is truest, closest, and easiest. For we people of today live by the tacitly assumed and therefore to us all the more self-evident prejudice that what is religious is purely a matter of the innermost heart and the highest point of the mind, something which we have to do for ourselves alone and which therefore has the difficulty and unreality of the thoughts and moods of the heart.

But Easter says that God has done something. God himself. And his action has not merely lightly touched the heart of some human being here and there, so that it trembles at the inexpressible and nameless. God has raised his Son from the dead. God has called the flesh to life. He has conquered death. He has done something and triumphed where it is not at all a question merely of interior sensibility but where, despite all our praise of the spirit, we are most really ourselves, in the reality of the earth, far from all that is purely thought and feeling, where we learn what we are — mortal children of the earth.

We are children of this earth. Birth and death, body and earth, bread and wine — such is our life. The earth is our home. Certainly, for all this to be so and to be splendid, spirit has to be mingled with it like a secret essence, the delicate, sensitive, perceptive spirit which gazes into the infinite, and the soul which makes everything living and light. But spirit and soul have to be *there*, where we are, on the earth and in the body. They have to be there as the eternal radiance of earthly things, not like

---

* *Everyday Faith*, 76–83.

a pilgrim who, not understood and himself an alien, wanders once like a ghost across the world's stage in a brief episode. We are too much the children of this earth to want to emigrate from it forever one day. And even if heaven has to bestow itself for earth to be endurable, it has itself to come down and stand over this abiding earth as a light of blessedness and itself break forth as radiance from the dark bosom of the earth.

We belong here. We cannot become unfaithful to the earth, not out of autocratic self-will, which would not suit the sons and daughters of serious, humble mother earth, but because we must be what we are. But we suffer from a secret and mortal sorrow which lodges in the very center of our earthly nature. The earth, our great mother, is itself in distress. It groans under its transitoriness. Its most joyful festivities suddenly resemble the beginning of funeral rites, and when we hear its laughter, we tremble in case in a moment tears will be mingled with it. The earth bears children who die, who are too weak to live forever and who have too much spirit to be able entirely to renounce eternal joy. Unlike the beasts of the earth, they see the end before it is there and they are not compassionately spared conscious experience of that end.

The earth bears children whose hearts know no limits, and what the earth gives them is too beautiful for them to despise and too poor to enrich them, the insatiable. And because the earth is the scene of this unhappy discord between the great promise which haunts them and the meager gift which does not satisfy them, the earth becomes a fertile source of its children's guilt, for they try to tear more from the earth than it can rightly give. It can complain that it itself became so discordant through the primordial sin of the first man and woman on earth, whom we call Adam and Eve.

But that does not alter the fact that the earth is now an unhappy mother, too living and too beautiful to be able to send her children away even to conquer a new home of eternal life in another world, and too poor to give them as fulfillment what she has contributed to give them as longing. And because the earth is always both life and death, it mostly brings neither, and the sad mixture of life and death, exultation and lament, creative action and monotonous servitude is what we call our everyday life. And so we are here on the earth, our home, and yet it is not enough. The adventure of emigrating from what is earthly won't do, not out of cowardice but out of a fidelity imposed on us by our own nature.

What are we to do? Listen to the message of the resurrection of the Lord. Has Christ the Lord risen from the dead or not? We believe in his resurrection and so we confess: he died, descended into the realm of the dead and rose again the third day. But what does that mean, and why is it a blessing for the children of the earth?

The Son of the Father has died, he who is the Son of Man. He who is at once the eternal plenitude of the Godhead, self-sufficient, limitless and blessed as Word of the Father before all ages *and* the child of this earth as son of his blessed mother. He who is both the Son of God's plenitude and the child of earth's need, has died. But the fact that he died does not mean (as in a really unchristian way we "spirituals" shortsightedly think) that his spirit and soul, the vessel of his eternal Godhead, have freed themselves from the world and the earth, and, as it were, fled into the immensity of God's glory beyond the world because the body which bound them to the earth was shattered in death and because the murderous earth showed that the child of eternal light could find no home in its darkness. We say "died" and immediately add "descended into the realm of the dead and rose again." And this gives the "died" quite a different sense from the world-forsaking sense which we are tempted to attribute to death.

Jesus himself said that he would descend into the heart of the earth (Mt 12:40), that is, into the heart of all earthly things where everything is linked into one and where in the midst of that unity death and futility sit. In death he descended there. By a holy ruse of eternal life he allowed himself to be overcome by death, allowed death to swallow him into the innermost center of the world so that, having descended to the primordial forces and the radical unity of the world, he might establish his divine life in it forever.

Because he died, he belongs in very truth to this earth. For although the human person — the soul, as we say — enters in death into direct relation to God, it is only when the human body is laid in the earth that he enters into definitive unity with that mysterious single basis in which all spatio-temporal things are linked and in which they have, as it were, the root of their life.

The Lord descended into death into this lowest and deepest of all the visible creation. He is there now, and not futility and death. In death he became the heart of the earthly world, divine heart in the very heart and center of the world where this, prior even to its unfolding in space and time, sinks its roots into God's omnipotence. It was from this one heart of all earthly things in which fulfilled unity and nothingness could no longer be distinguished and from which their whole destiny derived, that he rose.

And he did not rise in order finally to depart from here, not so that the travail of death which gave birth to him anew might transfer him to the life and light of God and he would leave behind him the dark bosom of the earth empty and without hope. For he rose again in his *body*. That means he has already begun to transform this world into himself. He has accepted the world forever. He has been born again as a child of the earth, but of the transfigured, liberated earth, the earth which in him is eternally confirmed and eternally redeemed from death and futility.

He rose, not to show that he was leaving the tomb of the earth once and for all, but in order to demonstrate that precisely that tomb of the dead — the body and the earth — has finally changed into the glorious, immeasurable house of the living God and of the God-filled soul of the Son. He did not go forth from the dwelling place of earth by rising from the dead. For he still possesses, of course, definitively and transfigured, his body, which is a piece of the earth, a piece which still belongs to it as a part of its reality and its destiny. He rose again to reveal that through his death the life of freedom and beatitude remains established forever within the narrow limits and sorrow of the earth, in the depth of its heart.

What we call his resurrection and unthinkingly regard as his own personal destiny, is simply, on the surface of reality as a whole, the first symptom in experience of the fact that behind so-called experience (which we take so seriously) everything has already become different in the true and decisive depth of all things. His resurrection is like the first eruption of a volcano which shows that in the interior of the world God's fire is already burning, and this will bring everything to blessed ardor in his light. He has risen to show that that has already begun. Already from the heart of the world into which he descended in death, the new forces of a transfigured earth are at work. Already in the innermost center of all reality, futility, sin, and death are vanquished and all that is needed is the short space of time which we call history after the birth of Christ, until everywhere and not only in the body of Jesus what has really already begun will be manifest.

Because he did not begin to save and transfigure the world with the superficial symptoms but started with its innermost root, we creatures of the surface think that nothing has happened. Because the waters of suffering and guilt are still flowing where we are standing, we think the deep sources from which they spring have not yet dried up. Because wickedness is still inscribing its runes on the face of the earth, we conclude that in the deepest heart of reality love is extinct. But all that is merely appearance, the appearance which we take to be the reality of life.

He has risen because in death he conquered and redeemed forever the innermost center of all earthly reality. And having risen, he has held fast to it. And so he has remained. When we confess him as having ascended to God's heaven, that is only another expression for the fact that he withdraws from us for a while the tangible manifestation of his glorified humanity and, above all, that there is no longer any abyss between God and the world.

Christ is already in the midst of all the poor things of this earth, which we cannot leave because it is our mother. He is in the wordless expectation of all creatures which, without knowing it, wait to share in the glorification of his body. He is in the history of the earth, the blind course of which in all victories and all breakdowns is moving with uncanny precision toward his day, the day on which his glory, transforming all things, will break forth from its own depths. He is in all tears and in all death as hidden rejoicing and as the life which triumphs by appearing to die. He is in the beggar to whom we give, as the secret wealth which accrues to the donor. He is in the pitiful defeats of his servants, as the victory which is God's alone. He is in our powerlessness as the power which can allow itself to seem weak, because it is unconquerable. He is even in the midst of sin as the mercy of eternal love, patient and willing to the end. He is there as the most secret law and the innermost essence of all things which still triumphs and prevails even when all order and structure seems to be disintegrating.

He is with us like the light of day and the air which we do not notice, like the hidden law of a movement which we do not grasp, because the part which we ourselves experience is too short for us to discern the formula of the movement. But he is there, the heart of this earthly world and the secret seal of its eternal validity.

Consequently, we children of this earth may love it, must love it. Even where it is fearful and afflicts us with its distress and mortal destiny. For since he has entered into it forever by his death and resurrection, its misery is merely temporary and simply a test of our faith in its innermost mystery, which is the risen Christ. That this is the secret meaning of its distress is not our experience. Indeed it is not. It is our faith. The blessed faith which defies all experience. The faith which can love the earth because it is the "body" of the risen Christ or is becoming it.

We therefore do not need to leave it. For God's life dwells in it. If we seek the God of infinity (and how could we fail to?) *and* the familiar earth as it is and as it is to become, in order to be our eternal home in freedom, then one way leads to both. For in the Lord's resurrection God has shown that he has taken the earth to himself forever.

Caro cardo salutis, said one of the ancient fathers of the church with an untranslatable play on words: the flesh is the hinge of salvation. The reality beyond all the distress of sin and death is not up yonder; it has come down and dwells in the innermost reality of our flesh. The sublimest religious sentiment of flight from the world would not bring the God of our life and of the salvation of this earth down from the remoteness of his eternity and would not reach him in that other world of his.

But he has come to us himself. He has transformed what we are and what despite everything we still tend to regard as the gloomy earthly residue of our spiritual nature: the flesh. Since then mother earth has only borne children who are transformed. For his resurrection is the beginning of the resurrection of all flesh.

One thing is needed, it is true, for his action, which we can never undo, to become the benediction of our human reality. He must break open the tomb of our hearts. He must rise from the center of our being also, where he is present as power and as promise. There he is still in movement. There it is still Holy Saturday until the last day which will be the universal Easter of the cosmos. And that resurrection takes place under the freedom of our faith. Even so, it is *his* deed. But an action of his which takes place as our own, as an action of loving belief which takes us up into the tremendous movement of all earthly reality toward its own glory, which has begun in Christ's resurrection.

78 • The Glorified Lord*

Christ is also the Lord who ascended into heaven! His resurrection and ascension are the fruits of salvation — a salvation bringing the destiny of the world to its appointed end. In this regard St. Paul says that "the end of the ages" has come upon us (1 Cor 10:11). If God accepts the world, if he carries out his descent into it in such a way that he experiences the abandonment of death as the appearance of sin and Godlessness in order to include it in his glorification, if he takes a piece of this world, which always remains just that, into his glory with him, then the world is indeed irrevocably accepted, and no one can ever wrench it from the hand of the resurrected and ascended Lord. Then the world has ascended to heaven in his person

In this way, the world entered into its final phase. We might even say that thus the heart of this despairing world has been changed into something good. Ultimately, the world has already been set right, for he, the living center of history and even of nature, became flesh and is even now glorified. Thus everything that happens in the world now is either an effect of his victory or a last-ditch battle of those worldly powers that were conquered by his cross.

---

* *Spiritual Exercises,* 246–50.

It will always be difficult for us to look at the world and the world's history in this way. But this only means that we have not yet come to the inner realization that the final victory is really already present in our hearts — hearts into which Christ has poured his spirit of victory over the world.

The resurrected, ascended Lord is the end of the ages! He is the heart of the world! He is standing before the throne of the Father as the Son of Man. The words of Psalm 110 apply to him: "Sit at my right hand!" Here he is the high priest celebrating the eternal liturgy of creation (Heb 8–10), for he has truly ascended to heaven, taking with himself what is ours. In such wise is he standing before the Father! As one belonging to us, he has thus actually become our blessedness, a piece of God's inner life. Naturally, this "piece" remains a creature, but for all that it still belongs irrevocably to God.

If our knowledge of metaphysics helps us to see how God is absolute in the full sense of the word, outside of time and history, beyond becoming and progress (to borrow an expression from the mysticism of the Middle Ages), then this does not mean that he interferes with his creation from time to time. Rather, its true significance is that he holds eternally within himself the results of creation's history as his own reality, and lets it participate in his own life for all eternity. This is nothing else but the glorification of the world and of human beings, which can only happen through grace. Of course this glorification can only be believed in grace, for only under the influence of grace can a person muster up the boundless optimism to be convinced that God has already begun to be "all in all" (1 Cor 15:28).

That is what must be continued in our own "private" saving history. We are the ones who "live together with Christ," who makes us "sit with him in the heavenly places" (Eph 2:6), because we "were buried together with him...and in him also rose again" (Col 2:12). In other words, just as his cross and the totality of his life have become a part of our life, so also is his resurrection a factor in our present existence.

We would have a mistaken notion of our imitation of Christ if we thought it would bring us into one stage of his life after another. We have already risen with Christ! Because he has risen and because we possess his Spirit, we already have the "pledge" of our future glory (Eph 1:14) in that Spirit about whom St. Paul writes to the Philippians that he will make our body like to the body of his glory (Phil 3:10). Basically, this resemblance is already present in us, but it still must be made manifest!

The resurrection of Christ is not only a saving event that tells us now what we will one day become, but is not actually ours at this moment. Rather, it is *the* reality that determines, right now, all history and therefore the personal situation of each one of us — both externally and internally. Externally, because we live in the aeon of Christ and are thus at the end of the ages! Internally, because we already possess his glorifying Spirit! This must be the source of Christians' confidence in ultimate victory!

And such confidence cannot be based on the cleverness of church politics. It is also very far removed from the expectation that we will always be successful in this world. There is no this-worldly advantage for the church's persecuted and for her martyrs to tell them in the midst of their sufferings that the church will be even more glorious after they are gone. This is not the kind of victory-confidence that has been given to us!

We can only understand it as an inner conviction proceeding from these words of Christ: Have confidence, I have overcome the world! What we consider to be our field of existence, what we feel to be the "powers" influencing our destiny — these things are more appearance than anything else. Actually, our whole situation is much different from that. Of course Jesus also says: You will be afflicted in the world. We would surely be surprised if it were not so. But then he immediately added that he has already overcome the world, and that therefore we should have trust. If the world in which we live has already been overcome by Christ, then we are not justified in saying: "Sure, he has done all right, but we are still in the same old predicament."

That is not so! Of course we are with him in the new order only because we believe. Naturally, the situation is not such that we first have the experience: Aha, everything is going just fine! — so that we are then led to believe. Instead, somehow or other this faith and this experience mutually determine each other. Only the believer can have this experience — and because he has it, he believes.

We read in Hebrews (3:6) that Christ stands as the Son over his own house: "And we are his [God's] house if we hold fast our confidence and pride in our hope." Now we can really approach the throne of grace with confidence. In the power of Jesus' blood, we also have access to the Most Holy. We should not throw this confidence away. We should tell ourselves again and again: The love and mercy of God are final. The love of the Lord will never again be overcome!

In the eighth chapter of his Letter to the Romans, St. Paul lists the worldly powers he had experienced: life and death, the world, angels and principalities, good and evil, things present and things to come, height and depth, all creation — and then he says that nothing can separate us from the love of God that has appeared in Christ Jesus our Lord. We should gradually come to a realization of the superiority of those who have risen with Christ to life.

Not in the sense that we become bold in a worldly sense; nor in the sense that we would imagine ourselves to be freed from all further sadness and affliction. But in the sense that, in spite of everything, we are somehow mysteriously surrounded by something greater, by the victory of Christ — and from that we get our courage. Truly, through Christ we are already beyond time and the power of time, beyond past history, beyond sin and the weight of the flesh, beyond death.

Of course this victory-confidence of ours is almost identical with the weakness of the cross, because the victory was obtained on the cross. Therefore, we are still walking in fear and trembling. But still in a fear that is self-composed. We must consider the cross the test of our faith, and at the same time realize that God is stronger in us than is our own fear of the cross. We should have this viewpoint in mind when we consider the future of the church and out own future: Nothing can separate us from the love of God in Christ Jesus our Lord! In accordance with the mind of St. Paul we should add to that, the resurrected and glorified Lord! This view is also a grace — one that must be prayed for and one that makes us blessed. But it also demands the complete gift of our hearts: We must, as it were, break away from ourselves with a realization supported by faith that everything that happens in this world, no matter how painful and cross-filled, is really already penetrated with the victory of Christ — the same Christ who rose from the dead and ascended into heaven.

79 • Christ's Ascension into Heaven*

We are celebrating the festival of Christ's ascension. We know that, properly speaking, we are thereby celebrating the conclusion of the festival of Easter, Easter once again, because by his resurrection the Lord has already entered into his full and final consummation. Thus what Christendom is celebrating in this festival, and what it is thereby making explicit, is something which, even though it was already implicitly contained in our Easter faith, is nevertheless new, something which goes beyond what we celebrated at Easter. This is the recognition of the fact that in the fullness of glory upon which he has entered the Lord has been withdrawn from his followers; that the full unveiling of the Easter glory which is to embrace all things is something for which we are still waiting; that the "little while" is still continuing, in which the fullness of our life in Christ is still withheld from us and from the world itself.

---

* *Theological Investigations VII*, 181–85.

Thus the festival of the ascension is, in a very true and proper sense, the festival of faith as such; the festival, therefore, not so much of the real facts in which we believe, but of faith itself. For faith does in fact imply holding fast to that which we have not experienced for ourselves. It implies a building on invisible foundations, a committing of one's self to that which only seems to be there because of the actual act of trust and self-commitment in itself.

But when we let the Lord go, and do not cling to him, so that he is hidden until the end and is only present among his own in a mysterious manner in his Spirit, then we are saying that we are ready to perform precisely that act which we call faith. This is an eschatological entity. It cannot be reduced to the formal acceptance of any kind of truth such as is always possible and viewed wholly in abstraction from the content of belief. To believe is to live by the future, to exist in the power of that which, even though it is the center of our own existence, nevertheless, has been withdrawn into the future that awaits us. It is a living by anticipation, a being true to a reality that lies in the future. In a single word, it is eschatological existence. Ascension is the festival of faith as such.

In this sense the ascension becomes the festival of holy pain. He has departed from us. It is frightening that we feel so little pain about this. He himself thought that he had to console us. But our hearts, so withered and shallow as they are, respond to his consolation merely with amazement. We have to spend a long time in recollecting ourselves before we can realize — perhaps — even to some little extent, the fact that we should be inconsolable at the fact of his remoteness from us.

For this, we would have really to be holding fast to him. We would have to be overwhelmed with terror and anxiety at the void which his departure leaves for us. Now, at last, someone was there who is not superfluous; someone who does not become a burden but bears burdens because he is good — good in so unobtrusive a manner that we were already at the stage almost of taking his goodness for granted; someone who called the impenetrable riddle that lies behind all apprehensible things his Father, and in doing so gave the impression of being neither incredibly naive nor tastelessly presumptuous, one indeed who almost led the world into the temptation of taking it for granted when he allowed us, too, to utter the words "Our Father" into this divine darkness. It was the compassion of God and his wisdom that were with us in him. At last we were able to think of God in a manner somewhat different from the abstractions of the philosophers.

At last one was there who really knew something, and yet did not have to be abstruse in speaking of it; one whom one only had to make contact with, whom one dared to kiss, whom one struck on the shoulder in friendliness; someone who sought nothing for himself — and in these trivialities we had everything, *everything* made physically present to us: God, his pity, his grace, his nearness.

Now he has gone. He wanted to console us by saying that precisely by so doing his Spirit, and in this living Spirit of his, himself would come to us. That is a consolation. Oh yes. For if he were only physically present to us, without his Spirit taking possession of us, his presence to us would be of as little avail as to a Judas who sits at his side or kisses him. But when his Spirit is in us, then we are his, the Lord's, and he is ours. But the fact that we have him only in order to seek him, to be able to seek him and to have to seek him, that he should be among us only in order that it may still be revealed to us what we are in virtue of this fact — this makes the joy and blessedness of possessing him in his Spirit a pain as well.

It is the pain of waiting, the pain of the birth-pangs of eternal life, the pain of hope, the pain of pilgrimage. Yet if only we could feel this blessed pain, this grace of the festival of the ascension, more ardently and more keenly! But we are content with this life. Today we are often proud that our loyalties are to the earth (though naturally this can have a good sense). We do not look above or into the future like the men of Galilee. We keep our gaze fixed on the foreground of our lives and on the present. We are not those who wait, those who look, those who are unsatisfied; not those who hunger and thirst for that justice which is to be found only in the future, that future which will bring us the return of the Lord if we keep watch for it. May God give us the grace to celebrate this festival as a festival of blessed pain!

The ascension is a festival of the future of the world. The flesh is redeemed and glorified, for the Lord has risen forever. We Christians are therefore the most sublime of materialists. We neither can nor should conceive of any ultimate fullness of the spirit and of reality without thinking too of matter enduring as well in a state of final perfection. It is true that we cannot picture to ourselves in the concrete how matter would have to appear in this state of final endurance and glorification for all eternity. But we have so to love our own physicality and the worldly environment appropriate to it that we cannot reconcile ourselves to conceiving of ourselves as existing to all eternity otherwise than with the material side of our natures enduring too in a state of final perfection.

And — one shudders at the "blasphemy" which such an idea must represent for the Greek mentality — we could not conceive of the divine Logos either in the eternal perfection which belongs to it forever otherwise than as existing forever in the state of material incarnation which it has assumed. As materialists we are more crassly materialist than those who call themselves so. For among these it would still be possible to imagine that matter as a whole and in its entirety could, so to say, be raised at one blow onto a new plane and undergo a radical qualitative change such that, for purposes of definition, it could no longer be called matter, because this future state would be so utterly different from the former one in which it originated. We can entertain no such theory. We recognize and believe that this matter will last forever, and be glorified forever. It must be glorified. It must undergo a transformation the depths of which we can only sense with fear and trembling in that process which we experience as our death. But it remains. It continues to perform its function forever.

It celebrates a festival that lasts forever. Already, even now, it is such that its ultimate nature can survive permanently; and such too that God has assumed it as his own body. "You did not spurn the virgin's womb nor the blessed eternity of matter" (*Non horruisti virginis uterum. Non horruisti materiae beatam aeternitatem*). And already for this world as a whole the process of fermentation has commenced which will bring it to this momentous conclusion.

It is already filled with the forces of this indescribable transformation. And this inner dynamism in it is called, as Paul boldly confirms for us in speaking of the resurrection of the flesh, the holy Pneuma of God. It is a free grace. It is not the sort of entity which the world could lay claim to as something proper to itself, something belonging to it autonomously and as of right. But it is the true, the ultimate perfection of the world in all its power, which brooded and hovered over the primordial chaos, and which will preserve all things and perfect all things which were and are. And this power of all powers, this meaning which is the ultimate meaning of all meanings, is now present at the very heart and center of all reality including material reality, and has already, in the glorified flesh of the Son, brought the beginning of the world triumphantly to its final goal of perfection.

The ascension is the festival of the true future of the world. The festival we are celebrating is an eschatological one. In this celebration we anticipate the festival of the universal and glorious transfiguration of the world which has already commenced, and which, since the ascension, has been ripening and developing toward the point where it will become manifest.

And there is a truth which we must repeat yet again, even though it is one which we have already seen from the obverse side of the same single reality, and have already stated. Considered as an event the ascension does not only have the connotation of departure and distance. On the contrary, it is a festival of the nearness of God. The Lord had to die in order really to come close to us. For the physical nearness of those who are still imprisoned in the flesh, and who have not yet passed through death, is precisely remoteness; though it is a nearness, the sweetness of it is, nevertheless, only the pledge of the true nearness that can only be achieved in the future.

And if the death, resurrection, and ascension of the Lord constitute one single event, the particular aspects and phases of which cannot be separated one from another, then the separation implicit in this festival is simply another way of expressing the nearness of the Lord in his Spirit, which has been imparted to us through his death and resurrection. Thus he is closer to us than he ever was; closer than he was during the time when he was still in the flesh, closer so long as his Spirit is in us, so long as his life and his death have taken possession of us, so long as his Spirit in faith, hope, and love has loosened the fetters of our finite state and turned it into the infinitude of his Father, so long as we have abandoned the merely finite and, by his Spirit, become strong enough boldly and lovingly to sustain the most intimate and, at the same time, the most "other-worldly" reality of the incomprehensible mystery of God.

In his death the Lord has broken the old vessel of the Spirit and has left it unrepaired. Properly speaking, the infinitude with which the world has been endowed is the one new vessel into which his Spirit is poured out, for his body, even though it is truly glorified, no longer separates him from us. Rather, it has itself become a sheer openness to the world. The ascension is the festival of the true nearness of the Lord in his holy Spirit.

And it is in this sense that the ascension is the festival which celebrates our preparation for Pentecost. This festival is simply a transition from the Easter of Christ to the beginning of our Easter, which we call Pentecost. For our sharing in the Easter of Christ is achieved through the Spirit of Christ bestowed at Pentecost. And thus we celebrate the ascension of Christ by watching and praying for his Spirit: Come and be near to us as Spirit, since you have withdrawn from us your nearness in the flesh.

In all these great festivals of Christian living let us beware of intoxicating ourselves with great words. It is not the majesty of the words of theological speculation that constitute the realities in the communication of which the true celebration of such festivals consists. Rather, it is the reality of the Spirit of grace himself which both celebrates and is celebrated in us. But this reality, as the living and life-giving, the victorious and the transforming, can also be experienced in microcosm; best of all, perhaps, in keeping faith with him in a spirit of joy and thanksgiving to God for the life of spring, in the courage and joyfulness which we show in our everyday life, in the calmness, tolerance, and love which we show to our neighbor, and many other small miracles of grace of this kind in the ordinary course of life.

And all liturgical celebration achieves its meaning only if it finds a true and sustained projection of itself in the ordinary course of life in this way. For where the Spirit performs the miracle of faithfulness and courage in our poor lives from day to day, there is the Spirit of Christ. And where the Spirit of Christ is present, the true festival of the ascension of the Lord is celebrated.

80 • The Eternal Significance of Jesus' Humanity*

That God himself is man is both the unique summit and the ultimate basis of God's relationship to his creation in which he and his creation grow in direct (and not in inverse) proportion. This positive creation, not merely measured in relation to nothingness but also in relation to God, reaches its qualitatively unique climax, therefore, in Christ.

For, according to the testimony of the faith, this created human nature is the indispensable and permanent gateway through which everything created must pass if it is to find the perfection of its eternal validity before God. He is the gate and the door, the alpha and omega, the all-embracing in whom, as the one who has become man, creation finds its stability. He who sees him, sees the Father, and whoever does not see him — God become man — also does not see God.

We may speak about the *impersonal* absolute without the non-absolute flesh of the Son, but the *personal* absolute can be truly *found* only in him, in whom dwells the fullness of the Godhead in the earthly vessel of his humanity. Without him every absolute of which we speak or which we imagine we attain by mystical flight is in the last analysis merely the never attained, objective correlative of that empty and hollow, dark and despairingly self-consuming infinity which we are ourselves: the infinity of dissatisfied finiteness but not the blessed infinity of truly limitless fullness. This, however, can be found only where Jesus of Nazareth is, this finite concrete being, this contingent being, who remains in all eternity.

The decisive factor for the basic question of our whole reflection is, however, the following: Jesus, the man, not merely *was* at one time of decisive importance for our salvation, that is, for the real finding

---

* *Theological Investigations III*, 43–45.

332 • THE CONTENT OF FAITH

of the absolute God, by his historical and now past acts of the cross, and the like, but — as the one who became man and has remained a creature — he is *now* and for all eternity the *permanent openness* of our finite being to the living God of infinite, eternal life; he is, therefore, even in his humanity the created reality for us which stands in the act of our religion in such a way that, without this act toward his humanity and through it (implicitly or explicitly), the basic religious act toward God could never reach its goal.

One always sees the Father only through Jesus. Just as *im*-mediately as this, for the directness of the vision of God is not a denial of the mediatorship of Christ as man. One will have to say that, on the one hand, this truth of the objective and subjective mediatorship of Christ as man is hardly likely to be ever in danger of being theoretically denied by anyone who is a Christian but that, on the other hand, it has not yet by a long way been thought through and conceptually worked out as much as it ought to be.

We reflect in most cases merely on the historical and moral mediatorship of the Son of Man during his life on earth. Consequently, the humanity of Christ becomes unimportant in our average religious consciousness of faith. We still know somewhere or other in our conceptual knowledge of faith that there is this humanity and that it is blessed and glorified and in possession of the beatific vision. One will perhaps give a pious thought to the consideration (not, of course, in dogmatic theology) that "besides" the beatific vision (in which every other knowledge and beatitude is given supereminently, so that one does not really see what else could still be of interest) one might still be able to derive an "accidental" joy from the humanity of Christ in heaven.

Yet where is the clear knowledge, expressed in ontological terms, of the fact that it remains eternally true to say that no one knows the Father except the Son and those to whom he wishes to reveal it: he who sees him, sees the Father? Where is the clear consciousness that, here and now and always, my salvation, my grace, my knowledge of God, rests on the Word in our flesh?

The fact that it is very difficult to formulate, prove, and explain all this exactly and sufficiently clearly in metaphysical terms is no reason for quietly passing over these things. It is easier to show with some semblance of truth that this is impossible. Yet, after all, this is the same for all truths of faith. Theologians are not immune from the danger of denying or silently suppressing truths of faith by means of rationalistic philosophical stratagems, even when these truths are completely obvious in the church's unreflected consciousness of faith without being already explicitly stated in "Denzinger."

Attempts to bring this truth into a clear light have already been made and should be further extended and deepened. The doctrine of the eternal liturgy and intercession of Christ in heaven is part of this. One should ask oneself whether, looked at from this "existential point of view," the doctrine of the physical, instrumental causality exercised by the humanity of Christ for all grace, does not recognize a truth — although perhaps in a questionable way and one which has not yet attained its own particular presuppositions — a truth which must absolutely be preserved.

Every theologian should allow himself to be asked: Have you a theology in which the Word — by the fact that he is man and insofar as he is this — is the necessary and permanent mediator of all salvation, not merely at some time in the past but now and for all eternity? Does your theology really see him in this way, so that by being this Godman he also is so bound up by his humanity with the religious act that this act goes (consciously or unconsciously) through this humanity to God, and so that this humanity is essentially and always the mediating object of the one act of worship (*latria*) which has God for its goal?

It should be pointed out that this Christ-question concerning our basic religious acts does not signify merely that one can "also" adore the one who has become man, and this "even" in his human nature. Happily, this truth is to be found in every dogmatic theology. Yet unfortunately it does not say in every dogmatic theology that if the religious act really wants to reach God, it *always* and in every case has and must have exactly this "incarnational" structure, which must also have its subjective parallel to the basic objective condition, namely, that in the incarnate Word, God has communicated himself to the world, so that this Word remains eternally the Christ. This incarnational structure of the religious act in general does not mean, of course, that this must always be something explicitly conscious or that, given the confined area of our earthly consciousness, it would be possible, beneficial, and necessary to strive for such an explicit consciousness of passing through the incarnate Word always and in every act.

81 • The Christological Dogma*

If Jesus is the historical, unique, and irrevocable communication of God in his human reality, with history, body and soul, and a personal human freedom in his life and death, and if this self-communication of

---

Meditations on Hope and Love, 57–61.

God means God himself and not merely a gift which is distinct from him (in being created and finite), and if we do not conceive such finite gifts of God as having a saving effect for us; if there is no doubt whatsoever that this self-communication of God is a matter of God himself as he is in and for himself; and if he gives himself to us thus and in Jesus, then a unique and definitive union exists in Jesus between him and God: a unity given from the beginning (even though it must of course unfold in such a way that we have to say, straightforwardly and resolutely: In Jesus, for him, and through him for us, there is God whole and irrevocable: God as himself — though of course as the incomprehensible and nameless).

God himself is represented in no other way. That of course appears in the traditional doctrinal formulas of the councils of Ephesus and Chalcedon in the fifth century, which taught that the eternal Logos of the Father took up the entire, undiminished and free human reality of Jesus as his own and united it with himself, so that this reality, without any reduction of autonomy and freedom, even in regard to God, became the reality and manifestation of God as he is in himself.

In this sense, Christian dogma states boldly that Jesus "is" "God" and the "eternal Son of the Father"; that his human reality in birth, life, death, and ultimate fullness can and must be asserted of God himself; and that the characteristics of God can and must be asserted of Jesus.

Of course, in such statements of fact and in such divine and human predications of the one Godman Jesus, and in accordance with official church teaching, we have to add that this "factuality" has a significance that makes it essentially different from similar factual statements in and about our everyday world.

In normal circumstances (for instance, Peter is a man), it is a question of plain identity between subject and predicate. In the christological statements, however, we are faced with a mysterious unity of God and Jesus in which all the divine and the human reality may no longer be conceived as identically the same, because they are not so, but remain "unmixed" — as the Council of Chalcedon stresses.

That must always be taken into consideration in the attribution of divine predicates to Jesus; when, for instance, we say: God was born, God died, or Mary is the mother of God. If we forget that absolute difference in this mysterious unity of God and man in Jesus, we are not more faithful or pious, but heretical; we are in fact monophysites.

We must think of the way in which the divine sovereign freedom of God ordains the man Jesus and his freedom as set over against us. If we wanted to think of this "influence" of God on Jesus in freedom in some other way (in the way, for instance, in which a higher principle of control in us permeates the lower levels and dimensions of our reality), then we would (in the formulation of traditional christology) turn from the divine and the human reality to a (complex) single "nature." We should then be monophysites and monothelites. We should be heretics.

If, in contradistinction to traditional christological terminology, we think of an active center of freedom with a free finite personality of the kind appropriate to a human being, set at an infinite distance from God, and use the term "person" in a human sense, then of course Jesus has a created human personality; in that sense he is a human "person."

To assert the opposite would be erroneous; in fact that belief is rejected by the church as monophysitism, a rejection emphasized in the condemnation of monothelitism — of the belief, in other words, that only a single active center of freedom exists as the mysterious unity of God and man in the one Jesus whole and entire.

In traditional church terminology when we speak and must speak of the one, single divine "person" in Jesus, then we refer to God, insofar as he accepts and encompasses the wholly "personal" reality of the authentic man Jesus, without canceling it, so that it really becomes God's being among us, the irrevocable Word of God's acceptance in himself for us.

We need not deny that the traditional christological statements of the church's magisterium can also be misunderstood and are in fact (though without any guilt) wrongly understood by Christians; by which I mean that they are understood in a monophysite sense. Christians and non-Christians rightly find these monophysite formulations mythological.

Since we certainly cannot further explain the "how" of the hypostatic union (and don't in fact have to), these official church formulas ultimately say no more to us than that God in himself has communicated himself to us as our absolute future, reconciliation, and forgiveness, and that he has done so in the one whole reality and history of Jesus, from the beginning to the end of his own eternal definitiveness. If we understand and believe that, then we are Christians.

But the traditional doctrinal formulations of the church on christology do prevent us from reducing Jesus to the level of a religious genius, of a religious prophet (even one still without an equal) after whom fundamentally new and similar types can come. Perhaps we are slow today to offer structures of thought and terms and concepts which might enable us in the future to express and preserve the mystery of Jesus in other than the traditional terms, in formulas more directly accessible to us today. Perhaps we need formulas which help us more to avoid the danger of a monophysite identification of God and man in Jesus, without that leading to another heresy — a new version of an old nestorianism (as it was understood by the church in the fifth century), which sees Jesus, ultimately, as no more than an ordinary even if divinely gifted man. But even if other kinds of christological expression become conceivable in the future, and are composed and perhaps even accepted by the official teaching church, now as in the future the traditional christological formulations retain their significance.

82 • The Credibility of the Dogma on the Incarnation*

First with regard to the "idea" of the Godman, the essential content of the teaching that the Logos became incarnate in our human mode of existence. To a conscience which is intellectually honest and truthful, this "idea" is worthy of belief. The only factors which it presupposes are these: first, that human person understands himself as the being which constantly transcends its own nature and reaches out to the mystery of God even as this mystery bestows itself upon the human being. It must further be understood (and this has already been indicated at least in brief) that the idea of the Godman is already implied as the eschatological climax to that process of historical mediation and revelation in which the transcendental self-bestowal of God is realized. At any rate, it is implied as a conceivable goal which this process is open to attain.

It is vital, therefore, to rid this idea of all mythological misconceptions. The human side of the Godman is no passive puppet, no mask through which God makes himself known. It constitutes no fresh attempt on God's part in which he strives once more to achieve as redeemer in the world what he failed to achieve as creator of it. The Godman is truly man in that he is set apart from God as his worshiper, in that he is free and obedient, in that his human nature is subject to historical circumstances, progresses, and develops (this applies to his religious experience as well, because nearness to God, personality, and genuine creaturehood grow in the same, and not in inverse proportions).

And the Godman does not represent a second intervention on the part of God as creator, this time taking place in the already established order of the world, but rather the climax to a history of the world that is also the history of the spirit and the history of salvation. It is to this climactic point that God has ordered the whole of history from its very

* *Theological Investigations VII*, 67–70.

inception. He has done this through his own self-bestowal, which exercises a decisive influence upon all the constitutive factors in history, for this self-bestowal of God in history constitutes an "existential," a fundamental orientation of history, which transcends all its particular modalities.

Thus the incarnation, considered as the climactic and focal point of history in this sense, had already, by its redemptive power, more than overcome the guilt arising from the misuse of freedom even before it was incurred. The incarnation remains a mystery of the divine self-bestowal. If it is viewed in this context, it is impossible to dismiss it as being a mere mythologem, even though, admittedly, it does not compel acceptance by the intellectually honest mind either. In spite of this it is credible, worthy of belief.

Believers, therefore, and those endowed with a reasonable sense of history, are not disappointed to find that the incarnation, both in the manner in which it takes place in history and in the manner in which it is recorded in the New Testament (on a true reading of this), is just as hidden and unremarkable, considered as an event, as the deed of grace in general by which the human being is made a sharer in the divine. This is what one would have expected a priori. Both the incarnation and the deed of grace in history as a whole are accomplished in acts of practical and "down-to-earth" compassion performed in the context of everyday human life. And yet even in this context this deed of divine grace bears a wonderful witness to itself if we can only view this plane of human existence with minds that are willing to believe.

A further point that is essential is that this "idea" of the Godman has been realized in concrete objective fact precisely in Jesus of Nazareth. It is essential that we should accept it as concrete fact at this particular point in space and time. Admittedly this means relying on the information that a particular fact has taken place in history, and for the person's pride in his own capacity to transcend particular historical facts this is always a scandal.

The human being is tempted to hold a priori that there can be no question of a truth that is merely "historical" providing the explanation of his own existence. But it is precisely the intellectually honest who can be self-critical enough to understand that real history cannot be dismissed in favor of theories concerning historicity.

History in the concrete, the deeper meaning of which is never sufficiently realized, is necessary as the medium in which human nature as free and intellectual being can operate on the spiritual and transcendent plane. And again, it is precisely the intellectually honest individual who can understand that the human being must commit himself to the finite dimension of space and time in order to render the eternal present to himself not merely as an abstract concept but as a reality actually present within him.

It must be admitted that the courage to commit one's self to the concrete in this way is indispensable for faith. It must be unreservedly conceded that even to prove in terms of scientific exegesis that Jesus himself understood himself to be the Son of God in the metaphysical sense of the Christian dogma is far from easy. But one who can read, interpret, and translate will not expect Jesus himself to express himself in the formulas of theological metaphysics, and will not feel this to be necessary in order to say what such formulas mean. And given the recognition of this, it is not in principle impossible to supply such a proof.

While this remains a difficult task for the individual in the concrete, with all the possible or impossible conditions to which he is at present subject, it is not the sole means to which the intellectually honest can have recourse in order to establish how Jesus thought of himself, and to justify his interpretation on this point.

If the idea of the Godman is worthy of belief; if in fact in the history of human thought intellectuals have had the courage to believe in the concrete embodiment of this "idea," yet solely and exclusively as realized in Jesus; if we have not, so to say, artificially constructed the circumstances of his life in the laboratory of our own minds, but rather found ourselves faced with them as preexisting facts; if we commit ourselves enough to give these facts a chance to prove themselves sound and valid; if finally we find ourselves already belonging to the community of those who believe and if we find God in that community — what reasons could validly be advanced for holding that we were unjustified in doing all this?

83 • The Two Basic Types of Christology*

We must now proceed to delineate the first type, the "saving history" christology. In it the eye of the believer in his experience of saving history alights first on the man Jesus of Nazareth, and on him in his fully human reality, in his death, in the absolute powerless and in the abidingly definitive state which his reality and his fate have been brought

---

* Theological Investigations XIII, 215–21.

to by God, something which we call his resurrection, his glorification, his sitting at the right hand of the Father.

The eye of faith rests upon this man Jesus. He is, in the concrete sense described, the content of the specifically Christian experience, and the experience of saving history. Through him, as faith sees it, God's ultimate and irrevocable utterance of salvation to human beings is made. The fact that God is gracious to the human person despite his attitude of culpable protest, and the fact that this grace imposes itself victoriously — this is something which becomes definitively and unsurpassably clear to the experience of faith in this man Jesus.

Jesus of Nazareth is not merely an utterance of God to us which, viewed in the light of the development of the history of salvation and revelation, always remains at the level of the provisional and conditional turning of God to human beings, but rather the definitive, unsurpassable, and victorious — in other words, eschatological — utterance of God to humanity. And because of this, and to the extent that it is true, Jesus cannot be subsumed into the category of prophet and religious reformer.

On the contrary, it could be demonstrated, even if we must forego this here for want of time, that from this starting point of christology which we have just defined, the classic statements of Chalcedonian christology can be arrived at provided that we interpret these in themselves aright. And for this precisely, the starting point mentioned above has, conversely, an indispensable and crucial importance.

The point of departure for this christology, therefore, is the simple experience of the man Jesus, and of the resurrection in which his fate was brought to its conclusion. It is he whom the person encounters in his existential need, in his quest for salvation. And in Jesus he experiences the fact that the mystery of the human being, which it is not for the person himself to control, and which is bound up with the absurdity of guilt and death, is, nevertheless, hidden in the love of God.

Where Jesus is present in this sense, there is in fact present too an orthodox — a Chalcedonian, if we like to express it so — christology, even if, through our own limitations, or because of the liability to misunderstanding inherent in the Chalcedonian formula, the explication in terms of faith of this basic experience of Jesus and in Jesus in faith is actually not attained to.

We have already said that a basic experience of this kind of the fate of Jesus can be described as the deed of God wrought upon him and upon us, and so too the Chalcedonian interpretation of that fate can be expressed as a descending christology, though this does not mean that this *precise* descending christology, in contrast to the second basic type of christology, need necessarily be saying more than what was already clearly present at the starting point: Jesus in his human lot is *the* (not a!) address of God to humanity and, as such, eschatologically unsurpassable.

In this basic type of christology, in which Jesus is from the outset seen within the context of the individual person's quest for salvation in the concrete human conditions of his life, the cosmos as such does not enter into the question. As the creation of God and as the world which is in a fallen state, this is simply there beforehand as the stage on which the event of Jesus in saving history takes place. And properly speaking, it makes no difference to this to say that this world has, in the providence of God, been conceived of all along in such a way that its true function is to be the stage for this saving event.

This appears above all from the fact that the possibility and actuality of sin, to which this saving event represents the answer, does not itself in turn appear as conditioned, permitted, and mediated by this saving event. Any transition of this christology into the second basic type could at most be arrived at on the basis of the conviction that the promise of the Spirit given through Jesus signifies not merely the salvation of the human person, which is measured by his own personal need, but rather the self-communication of the absolute God as he is in himself to human beings.

For our present purposes we shall not attempt to show how the various exceptional varieties of this basic type, whether orthodox or heterodox in character, can be derived from it, and also how they make their appearance in history. And a further task which must likewise be foregone is that of devoting a fuller consideration to the question of what may be concluded from this basic starting point of christology with reference to an orthodox, sober, and prudent theology of the Trinity, and also with regard to the question of the preexistence of the divine Logos.

The second basic type of christology has, with all the necessary provisos, been called the metaphysical type, a descending christology. In this formulation the term "metaphysical" is taken in its broadest sense — in other words, not merely as having that meaning which is familiar to us from the classic Western philosophy of being.

If and to the extent that a christology clearly goes beyond the original experience of Jesus by the believer (whether justifiably or unjustifiably, this is not the question for the present), then it is metaphysical. This also applies, for instance, to a christology which originally, and not merely in a derived sense, speaks of a communication of *idiomata* from the *kenosis* and the death of God, and intends such paradoxical statements in their full seriousness. It would in fact be possible to speak in these terms in a derived sense of the conclusions following from the first basic type of christology.

In any case the metaphysical christology as intended here clearly finds its point of departure and the possibility of verifying it in the first basic type of christology. But this does not alter the fact that what we are dealing with here is a basic type which is different in its entire conception. It can, of course, be present in various ways more intensively and more clearly. If we want to designate it in its fully characteristic form, we can surely isolate two special characteristics in it.

First, the approach here consists in a markedly "descending" christology, which, at least formally speaking, constitutes something more than a mere inversion of the ascending christology found in the first basic type. The preexistence of the Logos, his divinity, his distinction from the Father, the predicate "Son of God" ascribed to the divine Logos as him who preexists in this christology, are regarded as manifestly belonging to him from the first, and assumed more or less to be statements based upon the verbal assertions and convictions of Jesus himself.

This preexistent Logos who is the Son of God descends from heaven, becomes man, that is, assumes a human reality as his own, in such a way that this preexistent Logos also achieves a visibly historical dimension and appears in the very history which as preexistent he has already shaped and molded. In this statement of a "descending" christology we are not at present concerned with the question of whether and how it is covered as implicitly included also in the ascending christology of the first basic type.

If we have rightly understood it, this is certainly the case. But the decisive factor in this descending christology is, after all, precisely that it proceeds, as something that is self-evident and does not need any further recourse to the experience of Jesus in saving history, from a doctrine of the Trinity, the Logos, and a preexisting Son of God. And these assumptions are properly speaking based not upon the experience in saving history of the crucified and risen Jesus, but are made known through verbal teaching by this same Jesus, a teaching which is placed upon his lips and regarded as his "very words themselves" (*ipsissima verba*).

And in this approach we are abstracting from the question of whether this is, historically speaking, justified or not. God has become man. For this second type of christology this is, from the point of view of religion and theology, not a justifiable interpretation of a more original experience of saving history, but the supreme and primary axiom of this christology, though of course we are also aware that there is a history behind the revelation of this axiom itself.

Hence the statement of faith that Jesus Christ is God does not need any further explanation so far as this line of thought is concerned, whereas in the first basic type of christology the same statement has an interpretative force — though of course a justified one — and comes as the conclusion of an elaborate argument, since our critical understanding of it has to be acquired from the more original experience of saving history.

Second, this descending christology, as found in the second basic type, implies a doctrine concerning the cosmic and, if the term may be permitted, transcendental significance of the incarnation. It is the Logos that created the world that becomes man. But from this there follows the further implication that this process of becoming man constitutes something more than a mere isolated event marking a particular point in space and time, and belonging to a particular category, in a world which for the rest is comprehensible even on other grounds, but is rather the supreme point in the relationship of the divine Logos to his world in general.

Creation is then regarded as the enabling condition for an element in the self-emptying, self-uttering, and self-communicating of God. Because, and to the extent that, God will not empty himself and bestow himself in an act of love into a void of nothingness, the world becomes that which opens itself to receive its own glory, which is sufficient for it.

The human person, on this basic conception, is not that which is "self-evident" in itself, or the empty question waiting to be answered by God, but precisely that which comes to be if, and to the extent that, God himself utters himself; that which is precisely contained within a question, and also an answer of God in which God himself expresses himself. World is not simply accepted as that which is already given, but comes to be in that God himself utters himself, and in this self-utterance of his in the Word become flesh, imposes the finality and unsurpassability of this self-utterance.

The incarnation is not so much an event in space and time, simply to be accepted in its factualness, but is rather the historical supreme point of a transcendental, albeit free, relationship of God to that which is not divine, in which God, himself positing this nondivine, enters into it in order himself to have his own personal history of love within it. Saving history, as the history of the forgiveness and reconciliation of the human being in his guilt, is embraced and integrated within a relationship of God to the world which is established prior to guilt with a view to the history of God's own incarnation within his world, and admits of the presence of guilt in the world only as a possibility of radicalizing this relationship of God to the world, sustaining it always and throughout from the first, the relationship of love in which God lavishes himself upon the world.

For this basic type it is, ultimately speaking, not a decisive factor whether it is developed more in terms of existential ontology or of cosmology — whether, in other words, the human being is conceived of as belonging to a world or whether the world, together with the human person, is conceived of as God's self-utterance — provided only that this self-utterance of God is thought of as achieving its point of eschatological irreversibility in Jesus.

The fact that these two types are not merely basic types but *the two* basic types of christology should surely be conceded. If we take sufficiently into account the formal character of the characterization of these two basic types, the two types concerned could, of course, materially speaking, be made to undergo extraordinary variations. And hence the impression may emerge that there are very many other types of christology which can likewise be claimed to be basic types.

But let us take the transcendentality and the historicity of the human person as constituting the two poles of our basic understanding of humanity. Then, for our understanding of what is meant by Jesus Christ, there can be only one conception, in which the person remains freely within his history, from which in fact he can never be separated so as to achieve a state of total transcendentality, and in which he finds his salvation. This means there is one conception according to which the individual radically brings to bear his metaphysical powers in order to proceed from the question of what he is as subject and what the whole of reality is in one, and attempts once more to understand what he has initially freely experienced in history as his salvation.

This in itself already provides a starting point for a more precise definition of the relationship which the two basic types bear to one another. It is clear that the second basic type constantly presupposes that experience of sacred history which is experienced in the first basic type, as its abiding basis and as the necessary criterion for rightly understanding the assertions it contains. Precisely today it is necessary, for an understanding of faith which is appropriate to the modern situation, to make clear whence this second basic type derives.

This is not to maintain, even implicitly, that the second basic type is really superfluous, and, especially today, simply makes it more difficult to believe in Jesus as the eschatological bringer of salvation. Even in the New Testament as a whole the frontiers are, after all, crossed, from a statement belonging to the sphere of the first basic type to statements belonging to the second. And in principle this procedure is justifiable even if the titles of dignity attributed to Jesus in the New Testament point to him as man in his function as bringer of salvation without directly or ipso facto consciously reflecting upon his preexistence as a God who is, on the one hand, "in himself" the incomprehensible origin and, on the other, he who can utter himself in historical terms and so justifies what is really meant in statements about the Trinity.

The human being as a whole, and in the spiritual development of humanity as such, is always too he who asks questions at a metaphysical and transcendental level. He is always he who cannot have any eschatological hope as a person of this earth unless he affirms that a continuity exists through all the discontinuity between the history of the natural order and the history of the human spirit.

Jesus constitutes the eschatological response of God primarily not in words but in the deliverance of concrete reality. And precisely if this is true, then this response of God is ipso facto an event of this material world, albeit one which brings about eschatological transformations in it. If we also conceive of God's totally free act as one — an act through which the world's one reality and all worldly events are both intrinsically united and reciprocally distinguished — then we should inquire into the intrinsic unity which exists between the creation of the world and that unique event within this world which we recognize in faith in Jesus of Nazareth.

All descending christology of the second basic type may have a secondary and interpretative character. It may again and again, in order to achieve intelligibility and to justify its own propositions, be forced to return to the quite simple experience of Jesus of Nazareth. Nevertheless, it is legitimate, inevitable, and sanctioned by the fact that the church, right from the earliest times down to the present day, has discovered Jesus of Nazareth precisely in these statements of Chalcedonian christology which seem so abstractly metaphysical, almost irreligious, and strangely inquisitive in character. It has discovered him there afresh again and again.

84 • The Christian Doctrine of Redemption*

The really fundamental problem of soteriology is probably that the crucifixion certainly cannot be regarded as an attestation (directed to us) of God's forgiving love, which moves *us* to believe in this love. It has to be acknowledged as the *cause* of our salvation. On the other hand, if we are not to fall into primitive anthropomorphism, the truth must not be obscured that God is not moved and his mind is not changed by history.

Encyclopedia of Theology, 1525–27.

What happened on the cross proceeded from God's forgiving will as its effect, and did not determine that will. Since that is so, the real problem, at least for understanding Christian soteriology in our situation at the present day, is why this original forgiving will of God does not simply effect forgiveness "vertically from on high" in the same way and directly at all points of space and time, but comes to humankind from a definitive historical event, which itself is the "cause" of forgiveness.

Systematic soteriology must begin with the relation between two elements. One is the salvific will which determines the human being always and everywhere in the supernatural existential, and offers of God's divinizing and forgiving self-communication to the free personal existence of the person. The other is the *history* of salvation and revelation. This "transcendental" saving will of God is not produced by history, but causes history, yet in such a way that this history is the history precisely of the transcendental saving will of God (at least as regards the term on which it bears). This corresponds proportionately to the general relation between human transcendence and human history.

The saving will of God is realized, and finds effect among us, by taking historically concrete form, so that in this sense its historical manifestation is its effect and its ground. Saving will and its historical manifestation are not opposed to one another like cause and effect extrinsically related to one another, but are like inner constituents of one whole, which mutually condition and form the basis of one another.

This history of salvation as the concrete accomplishment of God's transcendental saving will, which by the term on which it bears is itself historical, forms a unity. Moreover, it is constituted in its unity by all the dimensions of the human being (unity of matter as the spatio-temporal "field" of personal history; unity of origin [God]; unity in necessary personal intercourse in community and society; unity of goal of this history [perfect kingdom of God] as genuine final cause).

In this unity of history as that of the transcendental self-communication of God who creates and constitutes history in order to give himself (unity of nature and grace), each factor of history (and so also of the history of every single person) is dependent on every other; the totality of this history (which is united by a real principle, not by an "idea" or "plan" of God) is the situation of the salvation history (of the "subjective" redemption) of the individual free creature.

The history of salvation understood in this way as a unity does not consist merely of a series of homogeneous single events of equal importance. It tends toward a victorious culmination which gives a direction to this history which is irreversible. It therefore tends toward an "eschatological" culmination.

This culminating point which as goal, as *causa finalis,* supports the whole history of divine self-communication, and in its victorious power brings it to definitive manifestation, is realized when God himself makes this history his own in the Godman (as absolute bringer of salvation), although it is also a history of sin and its historical manifestations (results of sin: domination of death and of the law), and when this acceptance of the sinful world on the part of God is also answered by acceptance on the part of the world, an acceptance which was predestined in the former.

Consequently, objectively (in exemplar) and so subjectively, the *irreversible* acceptance is given and historically manifested as a unity of God and world (in all its dimensions). The radical acceptance of divinizing self-communication on the part of the creature occurs, however, by death. For death, as action, is the definitive acceptance of self by the free being, and, as undergone, it is the acceptance and endurance of the situation of guilt which is that of the free being.

Both acceptances occur and are manifest definitively through the resurrection as the saving fulfillment of death. Since the being and destiny of the Godman as the eschatological culmination of the history of the transcendental saving will of God is an element in the one single salvation history of all, history as victorious redemptive *situation* enters for *all* into its eschatological stage and its eschatological manifestation. (This is the case however the individual in his freedom responds to this situation. As long as history continues, the possibility of salvation remains immediately offered and inescapably present, and this is something that is not at all a matter of course or necessary.)

On this basis it is also understandable in how radical a sense the Godman's being and destiny is a glorification of God, which means the salvation of the world. The glory of God in the world is not *only* a formal abstract quality of any moral action whatsoever conformable to the will of God. It is the historically irreversible manifestation of God communicating himself as merciful love, which imposes itself victoriously and concretely manifests itself when it transforms the manifestation of refusal of such love, death, into an expression of love in the obedience unto death of the Godman.

Inasmuch as the history of God's transcendent self-communication in the above-mentioned sense is the ground of this saving will itself (because an intrinsic element of this saving will) and this history is based in all its phases on its irreversible goal and culminating point (as final cause) and unfolds by moving toward this *eschaton,* Christ and his destiny (the *complete* accomplishment of which appears in the resurrection) are the cause of salvation as historically constituting the historically irreversible saving situation for all.

And yet saving history *as a whole* (in dependence on its intrinsic final cause) goes to constitute the salutary situation of the individual. This becomes clear, for example, in the teaching about the church as mystical body of Christ and sacrament of universal salvation (Vatican II: *Lumen Gentium,* art. 48), the treasury of the church, and the like.

The attempt might be made to comprise this saving causality of the cross of Christ even more clearly in ontologically differentiated terms. Here, however, we can only point to the analogous problem of the causality of the sacraments, which are historical manifestations of grace and, precisely by being so, are also causes of grace. If in the theology of the sacraments the strict concept of the causality of sacramental signs is formed, and we see that sign (real symbol) and cause are not two simply coupled properties of the sacrament, but form a radical unity (sign *as* cause — cause *as* sign), then this concept of cause might also be applied to the saving event of Christ as the primordial sacrament of redemption.

85 • Incarnation and Imitation*

The human person's opportunity and obligation to imitate Christ, established by the incarnation, is not primarily and essentially an imitation of the particular moral virtues and acts of the Godman, but first and last an imitation in the acceptance of human existence.

The human being as person is precisely the one who has to deal with his own nature, who in his being present to himself, his "complete return to himself" (*reditio completa ad seipsum*) (Aquinas), and in his freedom actively disposes not of just anything, but of himself: in both, the human being is that one who is placed before himself and asked how he will come to terms with himself.

In the light of this transcendence and this freedom and this dependence on the absolute God, it is by no means obvious that this person is in harmony with himself. He can protest, so to speak, against this preexistent reality; he can feel that he is "condemned to freedom"; he can rebel against this constriction which is imposed on him, which befalls him and which he experiences, which he knows but can never overcome. In other words: he really has a free relationship to his own life which bears the character of a decision.

All sanctity, all sin can be regarded in the last resort as a person's

---

* *The Priesthood,* 78–81.

acceptance or rejection of this, his own human existence. Every sin is really a no to this human nature and to the control it possesses in advance over human freedom, human life, and human nature, always understood, of course, as the actual nature, nature with its supernatural vocation through participation in the life of God.

In the light of this, imitation of Christ then means first and last the acceptance of our own human existence with its goal: the achievement in our turn of that assumption of human nature which the eternal Logos himself achieved.

To be in harmony with what now in fact belongs to this nature, with its corporeality, its sexuality, its constriction, its death-trend, with its pain, its shared existence with others, its earthly origin, with its in-corporation into the history of nature and the rest of humankind, its association too with the principalities and authorities which we call angels: all this is properly speaking the task that life puts before us.

All that we call moral, ethical, is nothing other than the ought-character of this objective confrontedness with oneself and one's existence. When this existence is accepted, the ought-character of this existence is then ipso facto fulfilled and all this holds (whether we know it or not) in the concrete, thoroughly christocentric order of reality; all this is an achievement of the assumption of humanity, of human existence, by the eternal Logos who himself accepts his image in it or — better — projects himself as the image of the Father into the nondivine, thereby expressing the human reality, so that in the assumption of human existence by Christ and the Father we are ourselves assumed.

This cannot be understood of course as an assumption of any kind of abstract human nature, of something that could be reduced to a purely formal structure — as, for instance, "rational animal." What is always meant is actual human existence: that which is projected by the Father in the Logos, which is expressed by the Logos himself in his incarnation, which is conceived and willed from the first as sharing the world of the incarnate Logos.

This human nature we always accept, not as something we have understood, but as something imposed on us as the enigma of our own existence. Hence no one succeeds in getting away from this christocen-trism of human life. Every human being must thus confirm his freedom in the acceptance or rejection of this human existence of his and — up to a point — is inescapably really bound to do this.

Through Christian revelation we know more of this ontological depth of human life, but every person has to deal with this life as it is, known reflectively or as something not understood, with which he is necessarily faced. Whether he knows it or not, everyone accepts

Christ with the free acceptance of his existence or rejects in protest the Christ imposed on him.

In regard to this imitation of Christ, it must be remembered that this humanity as it exists in Christ, in the actual shape of that life's destiny, is also the existential of our own life. We are not simply projected and sustained by the Logos who has assumed an abstract human nature, but by the Logos who willed and accomplished this human life in fact as his revelation and self-utterance in the finite world. That is why everything concrete about this human life tells us what is really intended with us.

The Christ-conformation of existence is not merely the result of the abstract assumption of human nature by the Logos, but comes about through the actual shape of existence. That is why we meditate on the life of Christ, why we say we will imitate our Lord in his poverty, why we say that our life is a participation in the death and in the cross of Christ.

All these things have a certain contingency in the life of Jesus; they did not need to be so, they are again concrete expressions of a free attitude of the Logos, who wanted to reveal himself just in this way. But it is just this actual shape of the life of Jesus which then becomes the law of our life, whether we can draw this conclusion in a theoretical, abstract moral philosophy or moral theology, or not. In regard to this life we cannot ask Jesus why he did this or that; at any rate, we cannot ask about everything, down to the last detail.

The life of Jesus as form of our life cannot be regarded merely as an alternative: either to reject it, to consider it as invalid for us, or to prove it to be appropriate in actuality by the standards of an abstract, fundamentally essentialist philosophy of the human person and what he ought to do. The Lord is the ultimate standard; there is none higher than he, since the ultimate standard of necessity is revealed to us just in this actual person.

For it is just here that the Logos became man and not simply any man, but this man, so that we cannot really accept a division in the life of Jesus between what is important for us and what can be left aside, however true it may be that the structure of this life bears within itself and thus also creates for us variations of significance and of necessity. All this remains a factor of this unique historical norm, and the imitation of Christ can be measured by no other standard than Jesus himself and his life.

86 • A Prayer to Jesus Christ*

Lord Jesus Christ, you yourself have shown me a way to a faith that is real and determines my life. It is the way of the ordinary and actively generous love of neighbor. I meet you on this road, as unknown and known. Guide me on this path, Light of Life. Let me walk it in patience, always further, always new. Grant me the incomprehensible strength to venture toward people and to give myself in the gift. Then you, yourself, in an unexplicable union with those who receive my love, step forward to meet me in my neighbor: You are the one who can take on the whole life of humankind, and you remain at the same time the one in whom this life, handed over to God, does not cease to be love for humankind.

My faith in you is "on the way" and I say with the man in the gospel: "I believe; Lord, help my unbelief." Guide me along your path, you who are the Way to my neighbor, my unknown, looked-for brother or sister, and therein are God, now and forever.

Amen.

Jesus, you asked that boundless, totally revealing and probing question of human existence which I myself am. But this happens not only through words, but through your entire earthly life, not half-way and with hesitation, as in my case. I, on the other hand, cling to the particular which is safe and prefer a death which I am solely made to endure by death itself as absolute ambiguity, but do not actively participate in. You, of course, died freely, and in you God asked this boundless question as his own, embraced it himself, and raised it up into that answer which is his own blessed incomprehensibility.

What the church, whose baptized member I am, tells me about you often sounds incomprehensible to me. Teach me through my life what is meant by it. I want to be patient and be able to wait. I will try to translate it for myself over and over again into that which I experience in you. But I shall also broaden and incorporate what I experience into that which your church believes and proclaims about you.

You *are* yesterday, today, and in eternity, because your life cannot have been lost before God. You are the infinite question in which I and my dying life participate, namely, human being. You are the Word of God, because in you God promised himself to me and spoke himself as answer. You are God's answer because the question which you are, as the dying crucified one, has been definitely answered with God, in

---

* *Prayers for a Lifetime*, ed. Albert Raffelt (New York: Crossroad Publishing Company, 1984), 80–82.

your resurrection. You are Godman, both uncommingled and forever undivided. Let me be yours in life and death.

Amen.

Jesus, all the church teaches about you is good and I gladly say over and over again before it: "I believe; Lord, help my unbelief." But the church's teaching about you is good only because it intends to illuminate my own particular inner perception of you, no, *you yourself,* as you speak yourself through your Spirit into my heart, and as you silently meet me in the events of my life, as the experience of your indwelling grace.

You meet me, Jesus, in my neighbor toward whom I have to venture without guarantee in that fidelity to conscience which does no longer pay; in all love and joy which is still only promise and asks me for the courage to believe in *eternal* love and joy; in the slow rising of the dark waters of death in the pit of my heart, in the darkness of that death which is a lifelong dying in the ordinary way of difficult service in everyday trials; everywhere you meet me, you are in everything, unnamed or called by name. For I search for God in all things in an effort to flee from deadening nothingness, and in all things I cannot abandon the person I am and love. Therefore everything proclaims you, the Godman. Everything calls out to you in whom as man one already possesses God without once more having to let go of humanity, and in whom as God one can find humanity without having to fear meeting nothing but the absurd.

I cry out to you. The last strength of my heart reaches out for you. Let me find you, let me meet you in the whole of my life so that slowly I also come to understand what the church tells me about you. There are only two final words: God and human, one *single* secret to which I totally surrender in hope and love. It is in being twofold that this mystery is truly one, one in you, Jesus Christ. As I put my hand into your wound, I say to you with the doubting and questioning Thomas: "My Lord and my God."

Amen.

THE HOLY SPIRIT

87 • The Holy Spirit as the Fruit of Redemption*

As the Lord who rose from the dead and ascended on high, Christ can send out the Spirit. The fact that he has done just that and is still doing it is a sign that he has truly entered into the most holy sanctuary of God. If we want to get some idea from the life of Jesus just how our lives are going to turn out, then we cannot ignore the impact of Pentecost and the outpouring of the Spirit as the fruit of the redemption.

We should try first of all to consider the Holy Spirit as the third person of the one Godhead. And we should not forget that we have real relations to each of the three divine persons. Our knowledge of them is not something that is unimportant to us. The God who gives himself to us in grace, in whose life we participate by grace, and whom we will one day see face to face, is a trinitarian God whose nature subsists in three persons.

Of course the "how" of this subsisting is absolutely incomprehensible for us. If our theology is cold and abstract, then it can easily happen that the possession of this absolute mystery seems unfruitful in our lives. But the fact still remains that God is triune in his inner life, and that we are involved through grace in his interiority. If we accept the words of scripture as we find them, then we do not get involved in "appropriations" in the sense that statements applicable to God in general are distributed haphazardly to the three persons.

No. The relations of the Father, the Son, and the Spirit to us — relations which are expressed in scripture — are fundamentally the immanent Trinity itself. Therefore, we do not have to occupy ourselves so much with psychological speculation on the Trinity (in the vein of St. Augustine), which, though it may be very sublime, leads to a dead end. Such speculation may be very profound and beautiful and magnificent; it even deserves our respect, since it is the result of a thousand years of theologizing about the Trinity.

But the first thing we must do is listen simply to what scripture tells us about the Spirit. *That* accepted, believed, lived, embraced, and loved in the depths of one's being — that is the Holy Spirit! There he encounters us as he is and not as a mere abstract appropriation. In

---

* *Spiritual Exercises*, 251–56.

any event, our true, supernatural life consists in the communication of the divine Spirit, and everything a person can say about the essence, glory, and end of the Christian can be summed up by saying that he has received the Spirit of the Father and in this way has been filled with the divine life. That explains everything else!

A further consideration would be that the glorified Lord is the source or fountainhead of this Spirit. We can add to that: "The Lord with his pierced heart." St. John says: "for as yet the Spirit had not been given, because Jesus was not yet glorified" (7:39). But Jesus was glorified because as the corporeal love of God he was raised on the cross and pierced through by the guilt of the world. He became the source of the Spirit for us because he sacrificed himself and poured out his blood for us. According to 1 John 5:6ff., there is no Spirit except in the blood of the redeemer. The living water that flows out of the heart of the messiah (Jn 7:38) comes from the pierced side of Christ immersed in futility and weakness.

If we have the feeling sometimes that God has left us without buoyancy and enthusiasm, without an interior glow, and even without the Spirit, then we should ask ourselves whether or not we are refusing to accept the cross, penance, failure, weakness, and the emptying out of our own hearts. Could it not be that this is the reason why we have so little experience of the powerful movements of the Spirit in our own lives and in the life of the church? "Give your blood and you will possess the Spirit!" is an adage of the early monks.

That is still true today. Without being touched in the heart, there is no Spirit, for the source of this Spirit is the glorified Lord who gained his triumph on the cross in the midst of weakness and Godforsakenness. The fountains of everlasting life, according to St. John, spring forth from the depths of the earth. Because he came in water and blood, we are saved! For those of us who are close to him, blood and the water of the living Spirit are very closely related.

We should try to get inside of the reality of the "graced" human being — a reality which is given through the communication of the Spirit from the Father and the Son — by quietly going over what scripture has to say about the Spirit of God and of Jesus Christ.

In this connection, we should think of the names given to the Spirit in the New Testament. He is the "Holy Spirit," the "Spirit of the thrice-holy God," the "Spirit of the Father and of the Son," the "Spirit who was poured into us," the "Paraclete," the "Comforter" and "Advocate," the "Spirit of freedom," the "seal of our redemption" by which we are truly stamped as those accepted by God and belonging to him, the "first fruit of the redemption," the "pledge" in which the beginning of eternal glory is already given to us, as it were, by prepayment, the "strengthening and comforting anointing." He "enlightens" and "inspires."

He it is "who lives in our bodies as in a temple," "sanctifies us into a dwelling place of God," "makes of us the sanctuary of his church." He is the "Spirit of the new creation through whom the Lord makes all things new," "out of whom a person must be born again" in order to really be the person he is supposed to be for all eternity. his goal is life and freedom. He is the divine opposite of what the New Testament calls *sarx*, that is, the flesh which is weak and perishable, attached to sin, sullenly closed to God, and a stranger to the Spirit. That flesh is marked out for death, but nevertheless it fancies itself to be life. In contrast, the Spirit is the arouser of the glorified body, the "Spirit of adoption giving us testimony that we are the children of God." St. Paul says of this Spirit (1 Cor 2:10ff.) that "he searches the depths of God," and as such imparts to us the true basis of our knowledge of God.

We should never forget that our theology is not just the product of human cleverness striving for its own deification with the use of certain metaphysical and historical data. Its real source is Christ's gift to us of everything he received from the Father. Ultimately we can theologize because the Spirit is given to us as the searcher of the depths of God, and as the living anointing of wisdom. The theological system we have so carefully worked out is a faint shadow touching only the surface of that luminous nature of ours which struggles along in concepts. It is only a reflection of what is present in the center of our human existence — much more clearly and really, in actual self-reflection, yes, and in a true possession of the known. Even when we are speaking about the mystery of the life of the triune God, we are not speaking in mere concepts, but from experience, because, prior to all theology, the Spirit, who searches the deep things of God, has already become our Spirit.

The Spirit of God breathes where he will; he does not ask our permission; he meets us on his own terms and distributes his charisms as he pleases. Therefore, we must always be awake and ready; we must be pliable so that he can use us in new enterprises. We cannot lay down the law to the Spirit of God! He is only present with his gifts where he knows that they are joined with the multiplicity of charisms in the one church. All the gifts of this church stem from one source — God.

What Paul says in the twelfth chapter of his First Epistle to the Corinthians is still true today! This should give us the strength to overcome every form of clerical jealousy, mutual suspicion, power-grabbing, and the refusal to let others — who have their own gifts of the Spirit — go their own way. That is what the Spirit wants from us!

He is not as narrow-minded as we sometimes are with our recipes! He can lead to himself in different ways, and he wants to direct the church through a multiplicity of functions, offices, and gifts. The church is not supposed to be a military academy in which everything is uniform, but she is supposed to be the body of Christ in which he, the one Spirit, exerts his power in all the members. Each one of these members proves that he really is a member of this body by letting the other members be.

If we read the seventh chapter of the First Epistle to the Corinthians carefully, we will note that the Spirit is also the Spirit of virginity. After St. Paul has defended his teaching in this matter, he closes with the words: "And I think that I have the Spirit of God" — even in this regard! This connection also shows up in other passages where St. Paul characterizes the Spirit as a spirit of prayer; and again where he relates the Spirit to the practice of continence in marriage.

In the New Testament, the Holy Spirit is also called the principle of the Christian community — the principle of *koinonia.* In 2 Corinthians (13:13), he is spoken of as the giver of this community in which the redeemed are open to the Father and the Son. God's intercourse with the creature and the creature's with God, and even the intercourse of creatures between themselves — which is only possible and truly free under the influence of charity, where everything belongs to one and still every other can truly be himself, without being reduced to nothing because he has been deprived by the others and without himself being compelled to deprive others in order to assert himself — this intercourse really *is* the Holy Spirit.

According to Jesus' words contained in John 20:23, the Spirit is the principle of the forgiveness of sins: The Lord equipped his disciples with the Spirit so that they could forgive sins. Moreover, the Spirit is introduced as the principle of prayer: he it is who groans in us with ineffable sighs, because we have been sanctified by him. He prays in us so that our prayer acquires an almost infinite range and a divine depth. The New Testament keeps telling us again and again to pray in the Holy Spirit. We should remind ourselves occasionally of the dignity and depth of our prayer.

According to 2 Timothy (1:7) the Holy Spirit is communicated to priests through the laying on of the hands of the apostles as the Spirit of power, love, and self-control. The Spirit is also characterized in the writings of the New Testament according to his fruits. In this connection, we should read the fifth chapter of the Letter to the Galatians. In sharp contrast to human self-seeking, St. Paul enumerates as the fruits of the Spirit: love, joy, peace, patience, kindness, goodness, faithfulness, gentleness, continence.

88 • Pentecost*

If we wish to understand what Pentecost really is, we must first recognize one point: Christmas, Good Friday, Easter, and Pentecost (in other words, all those "once and for all" events which we celebrate in the great festivals of Christendom) are so closely interconnected that they merely represent the temporal development of one and the same salvific event, the time structure of a single deed of God performed in history and upon humanity.

This deed of God, one and indivisible, yet taking place in a historical process that is phased, is the definitive and irrevocable acceptance of humanity in the incarnation of the Logos. In that the Logos assumed a human "nature," he necessarily assumed also a human historicity, so that this assumption of the reality of human nature was only complete when he had brought the history of this reality to its consummation by his death.

What is unique, new and "once and for all" in this single historical event of assuming human nature and human history is its definitive finality. Always and everywhere where human history has been wrought out, the dialogue between God and the human person, issuing in salvation or perdition, has taken place. Always and everywhere, therefore, the Spirit has been present to judge and to endow with grace.

But this single dialogue, which runs continuously through the whole history of humanity, was open. Before the incarnation of the Logos no word of God had entered into world history as an event, no word which God imposed finally and definitively, no word in which God addressed himself definitively and irrevocably to the world, no word which expressed him definitively and exhaustively, no word which disclosed the ultimate and all-comprehending plan of God, no word which brought out the meaning of the real climax in the drama of world history, no word which drew this drama to its ultimate issue and brought out its ultimate meaning.

And still less was it revealed before Christ what the import of this ultimate and all-embracing word would be, whether it would import judgment or grace, remoteness or nearness, Lordship or Fatherhood, the relationship of servant or of child, law or grace, the order of created nature or the freedom of the Spirit of God imparting itself and thereby bestowing the infinitude of God upon humanity.

The dialogue lasted throughout the whole history of humankind from the beginning up to Christ. But the last word was not yet spoken. The whole of it still remained open. History was able to develop in

---

* *Theological Investigations VII*, 195–97.

either an upward or a downward direction. All was still ultimately in the balance. Every commitment was provisional and subject to revision. Every dispensation was subject to change and decay. One age might be followed by another which abolished the provisions of the first, and did not really so much as allow what was unique and proper to it to be brought to its fullness.

But since the Word has taken flesh and submitted to death and to the other conditions of our history, and has subjected itself to these conditions in a final and irrevocable manner because it assumed our human nature as a factor most intimately inherent in itself, now everything is different, everything has become final.

However much the individual has to experience his own private destiny as still open and undecided, since the incarnation, death and resurrection of Christ human history as a whole has already arrived at its goal. It has been assumed by God forever. It has been endowed with grace to all eternity. It can never more be abandoned. The factor of sinfulness in it has already been included in this gesture of acceptance on God's part, and has been outweighed by the power of the grace which has conquered it. The world is predestined to salvation and not to perdition, to life and not to death. God no longer waits for the decision of the world as though it had to say the last word.

On the contrary, he has spoken the ultimate word as his own Word, and *at the same time* as that of the world itself. And this word is reconciliation, life, light, victory, and the glory of God himself, which he himself has implanted in the innermost depths of the world itself to become its glory. And all this is now no longer hidden in the eternal decrees of God (though it has, of course, been present in these right from the beginning, albeit in a manner which was not available to creatures to recognize and to examine), but has rather become manifest, has been brought into being and given objective reality in the world itself, rooted in the very heart of the world to become the active principle that directs it to its goal. The result is that this active force inherent in the world already bears within itself all the fullness of perfection, and has already imparted this fullness to the world.

When, therefore, we say that at Pentecost the Spirit has descended upon all flesh, then we no longer say this only of that Spirit which has always presided in the world, for we are speaking of the eschatological Spirit, the Spirit as the irrevocable gift. This is the Spirit of the eternal predestination of the world as a whole to life and to victory, the invincible Spirit which has been implanted in the world and in its history, and indissolubly wedded to it.

This Spirit was not there before Christ, and since Pentecost it has been revealed that *this* Spirit is the Spirit of Christ, that in its outpouring and its work in the world it shares in the finality of Christ himself; that it is the Spirit of the crucified and risen Christ, and therefore the Spirit who will no longer disappear from the world and from the community of Christ. It has been revealed that the Spirit is the Spirit of the risen Christ, and that it has been promised as such irrevocably and invincibly to the world — it is this that was revealed at Pentecost and was accepted in an attitude of faith by those upon whom the Spirit descended.

89 • The Holy Spirit and the Church*

Easter and Pentecost are the two festivals in our ecclesiastical year which go back to apostolic times. This is because they were already included in the synagogal calendar, in which they fall at the same time of year, although admittedly their content there is different.

In the time of the early church Easter and Pentecost were not, properly speaking, two distinct festivals, or even two distinct "festal cycles" existing independently side by side. Rather, Pentecost is the culmination of Easter. Easter is the "glorification" (*doxa*) of the redeemer Christ, a glorification which includes his exaltation upon the cross and his exaltation at the right hand of the Father in a single festival.

Pentecost is the manifestation of that phenomenon which the Lord speaks of in John, "If anyone thirst, let him come to me and drink. He who believes in me," as the scripture has said, "out of his (the messiah's) heart shall flow rivers of living water." And John adds to this: "As yet the Spirit had not been given because Jesus was not yet glorified," and further, "It is to your advantage that I go away, for if I do not go away the Counselor will not come to you."

Out of the death and resurrection by which the Lord is taken away from the world, therefore, springs up the Spirit. If Jesus is not glorified, it is not given. It will only be poured out if Jesus, by his death, has overcome the world and its prince. On the cross water and blood flow down from his pierced side as a sign of the fact that the living water of the Spirit, which springs up to eternal life, and which is to flow as a stream from the heart of the messiah, can only come from the Lord "glorified" in his crucifixion. The Spirit only comes in water and blood. *Because* Easter, that is death and resurrection, has come, *therefore* Pentecost has come. And Pentecost is only the event to which all the

* *Theological Investigations VII*, 186–92.

events of Easter are oriented with an intrinsic teleology of their own in order to find their fulfillment in Pentecost.

But we must ask ourselves what Pentecost really is. It is the festival of the descent of the Holy Spirit, the festival in the baptism of the Spirit, the festival of the "pouring out of the Spirit of God upon all flesh," the beginning of that dwelling of the Spirit permanently and enduringly "in the vessel of the flesh and in the church," to quote Irenaeus.

Truly Pentecost is not a mere transitory visitation by the Spirit, a mystical ecstasy lasting for a moment. It is not even, in the first instance, a charismatic gift bestowed personally upon the apostles, as it were, as private mystics or charismatics. Rather, Pentecost, in all its external expressions which seem so strange, is at basis only the outward manifestation of the much more vital fact that henceforward the Spirit will never more be wholly withdrawn from the world until the end of time.

For this permanent dwelling of the Spirit in the world is only the outcome of that overshadowing of the Spirit which took place in the incarnation of the Son of the Father. And because the church is nothing else than the visible manifestation of the Spirit in the world, therefore the church, which was born of the water and blood flowing from the dead body of Jesus, from the "second Adam" asleep on the cross, only becomes visible and manifest for the first time at Pentecost.

Let us develop these ideas a little further. "The Spirit was not yet given," John declares, referring to the time when Jesus was not yet glorified. And yet we pray: "You who spoke through the prophets." Even in this short declaration of faith, therefore, we acknowledge that the Spirit was at work in the world even before Christ, because we know that many times over and in many ways God spoke of old to our fathers. There was no Spirit and yet there was a Spirit.

How can these two statements be reconciled? Is it merely that before the redeemer came the Spirit was present in a lesser degree, so that now he is poured out in abundant measure upon us? No, though certainly this is also true. But taken in isolation, this answer would not suffice, and would not meet the crucial difficulty. Formerly the Spirit was never in the world in the way that it is in it now, now that the fullness and the end of the ages have arrived. The Spirit of whom we speak is the Lord, for the Lord is Spirit, God is Spirit.

But how is God in the world? Can he manifest himself within the confines of this finite state? He himself as he is, can he impart himself — not his gifts, his finite works, but *himself* — to human beings? It might be said that he reveals himself in creation. Well, but this is only the hem of his garment, the curtain that veils him. For creation, nature as the theologians call it, tells us of God only as one who is remote, since the process of nature is cyclic, and it turns back upon itself. Of itself nature does not open up any way to man which can lead him into the inaccessible light of the depths of the Godhead, into the inner life of God himself, into his presence and before his countenance.

God himself, therefore, had to come in order to lift us out of the cycle of birth and death, and in order to build a way for us by which we could be led out of the bondage of our humanity, confined as it is to the finitude of its own nature and of the world, into the life of God himself. And *this* God who comes into *this* world for *this* purpose we call the Holy Spirit. The Spirit of God in the Christian sense, the holy Pneuma, is present where the deliverance of the person from the world and from sin and from finitude is achieved, and where the way is opened for him to enter into the presence of God himself.

But how is the Spirit to come upon us? How can we possess him, or — to put it better — how can we allow ourselves to be possessed by him? At what point in this finite state of ours does he decide that we shall be allowed to break into the life of the infinite? Does he not move where he wills? Is his work not so mysterious and incalculable that the human being never knows whence he comes or whither he is going, or where he will allow himself to be found? Are not the ways by which the Lord, the Spirit, comes not untraceable, so that we only know where he is to be found when he has already taken possession of us? Is there anything visible, apprehensible, to which we can point and say: "Behold, here and now lay hold of this. Then you can be sure that the Spirit who moves where he will has taken possession of you?"

Yes, there is such a thing, because we believe in the incarnation of the eternal Logos, because God himself has entered into the dimension of history, into the confines of space and time; because of his free grace he has assumed forever a part of this finitude of ours which belongs to space and time: that part which we call the humanity of Jesus. He has assumed this and made it his own life in such a way as to keep it evermore as belonging to his own being. Therefore, there is a "here and now" in the world into which God has come in order to deliver us and to lead us into his own life, in which there is no "here and now."

In Jesus of Nazareth we have the living God of the living Spirit and of grace. The church is nothing else than the further projection of the historicity and of the visibility of Jesus through space and time, and every word of its message, every one of its sacramental signs, is, once more, nothing else than a part of the world in its earthiness, with which the Spirit has united itself indissolubly since the day on which the Logos became flesh.

At Pentecost this Spirit has become manifest. Not merely the Spirit who moves intermittently and mysteriously here and there, who takes a prophet and uses him as his "instrument" so long as he wills to do so, but who never remains lastingly among us, and who provides no lasting sign of his presence and power, but the Spirit of the Son who has become man. That is why — something which seems so contradictory — Peter's sermon, delivered on the very day on which the Spirit descends straight from above into the hearts of the apostles, does not invite the penitents to look upward too, to see whether the Spirit coming from the realm which is beyond time and beyond history is not descending upon them as well.

No, he has only one message for them: Be baptized! It is in the "here and now" of the sacramental sign that the Spirit of Pentecost is present. And he is in this sign evermore and always. It is at that point, therefore, at which the visible sign is effected by the visible messenger, that Pentecost takes place. It is at that point that the Holy Spirit becomes present.

Prior to the death and glorification of Jesus this was not the case, and it is for this reason that at that time the Holy Spirit had not yet been given. Previously there was indeed a Spirit of God, but not a Spirit of God made man. Before the incarnation of the Logos the invisible was not present in a mode that was visible and *lasting*. There was a juridical order which God had instituted for the people of Israel. But this juridical order did not constitute a church. It was binding upon the people of that time, but it did not bring about any grace, any Holy Spirit. There was a Spirit, but it merely hovered and did not actually descend at any point. It never became "visible."

Now, on the other hand, in the fullness of time, a visible mode of this kind has actually been achieved, in the incarnate Logos and in his body, the church. *Ubi est ecclesia ibi et Spiritus Dei; et ubi Spiritus Dei illic et ecclesia et omnis gratia.* These are the words of Irenaeus: "Where the church is, there is the Spirit of God; and where the Spirit of God is, there is the church and every grace." *In ecclesia posuit Deus . . . universam operationem Spiritus.* "God ordained that the entire work of the Spirit should take place in the church." And where the Spirit is active, there, at any rate remotely, a stage is achieved in the construction of the visible body of the church.

Thus for Catholics the life of the Spirit, wherever it occurs, is always included within the fold of the church. And everything else is not the life of the Holy Spirit but rather mere religious excitement. There is no Holy Spirit apart from the holy body that is the church. For this reason we are only "spiritualized," that is, taken possession of and permeated by the Holy Spirit, we only act in and by the Holy Spirit if we are incorporated in the body of the church.

For Pentecost is the festival of that Spirit *cujus non sunt participes omnes qui non currunt ad ecclesiam,* "in whom only those who hasten to the church have a share." Once more we are quoting the words of Irenaeus. And when Paul tells us that the Spirit quickens while the letter kills, the letter here refers to the old covenant. But the Spirit which quickens is that which rested upon Jesus of Nazareth and which lives on in the visible historical church. We must not let the church begin only at that point at which it no longer gives us unease.

Because the church is there, therefore there is also a continual Pentecost. Therefore the outpouring of the Spirit upon all flesh is still continually taking place. Therefore we ourselves can still pray continually: *Veni Sancte Spiritus,* "Come, Holy Spirit." And because we say this prayer in the church, therefore we know that we are heard. For the Spirit of the Lord is not far from us.

But for all this may we not sometimes ask: Where, then, is the Spirit in us? Where are his mighty works, his fire and his rushing wind? Do we not all too often seek in vain for the Spirit in the visible church? Are not many indeed true to the letter without possessing the Spirit, orthodox without being moved by the Spirit of God? And does it not sometimes seem as though there were, after all, more of the Holy Spirit in many movements of religious enthusiasm than there, where the Holy Spirit has built his temple forever?

Certainly the Holy Spirit remains always in his church. This church will always be the place in which he dwells in order to descend upon all who await him there with hearts ready to receive him. But for us as individuals all this is far from being a comfortable guarantee that he is able to work in us as he would wish to, and as the times demand that he should be at work. We cannot have a comfortable guarantee of this merely on the grounds that we go in and out of the house of the Lord. He is not to be found apart from the letter of the new covenant, but not everyone who recognizes this letter as sacred and says "Lord, Lord" is ipso facto a Christian filled with the Spirit, spiritual in the sense that God, our own responsibility, and our own age demand that we should be spiritual.

Only he who is a member of the church *and* independent, humble *and* daring, obedient *and* conscious of his own personal responsibility, a pray-er *and* a doer, adhering to the church in her past *and* in her future — only such a one as this makes room for the Spirit of God at Pentecost, who appears in the form of a mighty rushing wind, the Spirit who is always ancient and always young — for this Spirit to do its work in him, to renew the face of his own soul, to use those who are his own in order to transform the earth as well.

And yet — is this the ultimate answer, the solution to every riddle? Where is the Spirit in us, even though we offer him a willing heart in spite of all denials, though we wait for him, though we do not say that we are children of Abraham, knowing very well that God is able to raise up such children even from stones, and to fit them as living stones into the temple of the Spirit? The Spirit comes in tongues of fire and signs and wonders when it pleases *him* to do so.

But for ourselves, he has commanded *us* to believe in him, in his power and in his presence, even when we do not feel them. The Lord has commanded us not to think out beforehand how we should bear witness to him, because in the moment when we do have to bear such witness — not necessarily before that moment — the Spirit will come to our aid. But in doing this he has also warned us against obstinately seeking to have a tangible and perceptible assurance of his advent to us. Our task is to regard our feebleness as a sign of his complete power; to live in hope against all hope. He who gives the honor to God in this way, and does not seek to possess it for himself, he who commits himself to God in faith without vision, in him the Spirit lives and works.

Insofar as externals are concerned in such a case, everything seems drab and everyday, a mere fulfillment of one's duty, patient expectation, wearisome struggles against manifold temptations. But viewed from within, Christian life consists of a *sobria ebrietas spiritus,* a clear-sighted and sober intoxication by the Spirit. The Spirit lives within us. There his light shines quietly and, as it were, with an inner life of its own. There his power is growing, though still hidden, as seed grows even though the husbandman sleeps.

But when the hour of testing arrives, then — perhaps when we least expect it — the Spirit of wisdom and power will be with us. In this time, then, we will pray for the Holy Spirit, for the good Spirit whom the Father gives to all his children who ask him for it. We will seek him in his church. With Mary, who was overshadowed by the Spirit, and with Peter, as once in the room of the Last Supper, we will "be of one mind, constant in prayer." We will ask God for a humble, and at the same time a bold heart, one which is ready to receive the Spirit of freedom and love, for a believing heart that does not demand signs and wonders, rather for faith to believe that it is not in the context of pageantry, but a spirit of quiet and recollection that the living God fills the hearts of believers with the Holy Spirit who is eternal life.

90 • The Holy Spirit and the Mysticism of Everyday Life*

Why is it that we do not dare to call ourselves mystics, and perhaps for very different reasons cannot take any personal part in these charismatic movements and practices? Do we have any experience of the Spirit? Do we merely nod respectfully in the direction of other people's experiences which we ourselves find rather elitist? Do such people merely offer reports of a country that we have never seen and whose existence we are content to accept much as we might credit that of Australia if we have never been there?

We accept, and even confess as Christians supported by the testimony of scripture, that we can have such an experience of the Spirit, and *must* have it as something offered to us in our essential freedom. That experience is given to us, even though we usually overlook it in the pursuit of our everyday lives, and perhaps repress it and do not take it seriously enough.

If I try to bring the reader's attention to such experiences, it seems inevitable that a few theoretical remarks on the innermost nature of human knowledge and freedom should precede more practical statements about personal experience. The reader will have to excuse the summary and rather abstract nature of what I have to say in a somewhat restricted space. Only by talking about knowledge and freedom can I show and analyze the structure and specific nature of our spiritual experiences, and indicate why in our reflective, verbalizing objective minds we can easily overlook those experiences, and imagine that they do not exist at all. Therefore, I request special patience and attention in considering my initial theological remarks.

We should consider human knowledge and freedom together, because in spite of the great differences between them, ultimately they have a common structure. In knowledge and freedom the human being becomes the very essence of transcendence. That may sound rather pretentious but it is unavoidable, and what I refer to in these terms is, in the end, the ultimate ineradicable essential structure of the human person, irrespective of whether the everyday person and the empirical scientist care to notice it or not.

In knowledge and freedom the human being is always simultaneously concerned with the individually characterized and specifically definable individual object of his everyday experience and his individ-

---

* *The Spirit in the Church*, trans. John Griffiths (New York: Seabury Press, 1979), 11–15, 17–24.

ual sciences, and at the same time with something beyond all that — even when he takes no notice and does not name or refer to this "something else" always present outside and beyond the ordinary. The movement of the mind or spirit toward the individual object with which he is concerned always aims at the particular object *by* passing beyond it. The individually and specifically and objectively known thing is always grasped in a broader, unnamed, implicitly present horizon of possible knowledge and possible freedom, even if the reflective mind, only with difficulty and only subsequently, succeeds in making this implicitly present fragment or aspect of consciousness a really specific object of consciousness, and thus objectively verbalizes it.

The movement of the spirit and of freedom, and the horizon of this movement, are boundless. Every object of our conscious mind which we encounter in our social world and environment, as it announces itself, as it were, of itself, is merely a stage, a constantly new starting point in this movement which continues into the everlasting and unnamed "before-us."

Whatever is given in our everyday and scientific consciousness is only a minute isle (though it may be big in one sense and may be magnified by our objectifying knowledge and action, and continuously and increasingly so) in a boundless ocean of nameless mystery, that grows and becomes all the clearer the more, and the more precisely, we express our knowing and wanting in the individual and specific instance. If we tried to set a boundary to this empty-seeming horizon of our consciousness, we would find that we had already passed through and beyond that very barrier that we sought to establish.

In the midst of our everyday awareness we are blessed or damned (have it how we will) in regard to that nameless, illimitable eternity. The concepts and words which we use subsequently to talk of this eternity, to which and into which we are constantly referred, are not the original actual mode of being of that experience of nameless mystery that surrounds the island of our everyday awareness; but they are merely the tiny signs and idols which we erect and have to erect so that they constantly remind us of the original, unthematic, silently offered and proffered, and graciously silent experience of the strangeness of the mystery in which, in spite of all the light offered by the everyday awareness of things, we reside, as if in a dark night and a pathless wilderness. (There we are in darkness and a desert place — but one that reminds us of the abyss in whose depths we are grounded but can never plumb.)

Anyone who wants to can, of course, irritably and as if tried too far, let the matter drop and continually repress it. He can try to ignore the night that alone makes our tiny lights visible and enables them to shine forth. But then an individual acts against his own ultimate being, because this experience of his orientation to boundless mystery, if seen for what it really is, is not some extraneous spiritual luxury but *the* condition for the very possibility of everyday knowing and wanting (even though he usually overlooks this and fails to consider it in the to-and-fro of everyday life and the pursuit of knowledge).

If we were to use the term "mysticism" to describe this experience of transcendence in which we always, even in the midst of everyday life, extend beyond ourselves and the specific thing with which we are concerned, we might say that mysticism occurs in the midst of everyday life, but is hidden and undeclared, and that this is the condition of the very possibility of even the most ordinary, sober and secular everyday experience.

In this unnamed and unsignposted expanse of our consciousness there dwells that which we call God. The mystery pure and simple that we call God is not a special, particularly unusual piece of objective reality, something to be added to and included in the other realities of our naming and classifying experience. He is the comprehensive though never comprehended ground and presupposition of our experience and of the objects of that experience. He is experienced in this strange experience of transcendence, even though it may not be possible to arrive at a more exact metaphysical characterization of the unity and variety between the transcendental experience of the spiritual subject in knowledge and freedom, on the one hand, and the experience of God himself which is given in the transcendental experience, on the other hand. This kind of definition is too difficult a philosophical undertaking and unnecessary in the present context.

Nevertheless, the unlimited extent of our spirit in knowledge and freedom, which is ineluctably and unthematically given in every ordinary experience, allows us to experience what is meant by God as the revealing and fulfilling ground of that expanse of the spirit and its unlimited movement. Transcendental experience, even when and where it is mediated through an actual categorial object, is always divine experience in the midst of everyday life.

But even if we ignore the question whether such transcendental experience of God in the Holy Spirit could properly occur in instances of undirected absorption, in a state of consciousness void of objects of any specific kind, and in mystical experience for its own sake, there are in any case actual experiences in our existential history in which this intrinsically given transcendental experience of the Spirit occurs more obviously in our conscious minds: experiences in which (to put it the other way round) the individual objects of knowledge and of freedom with which we are concerned in everyday life, by their very specificity, more clearly and insistently reveal the accompanying transcendental spiritual experience, in which by themselves and implicitly they indicate that incomprehensible mystery of our existence that always surrounds us and also supports our everyday awareness, and they indicate it more clearly than is otherwise usual in our ordinary and banal everyday life. Then everyday reality of itself refers to this transcendental experience of the Spirit which is implicitly and apparently featurelessly there and always there.

This indication, which is always associated with our everyday reality conceived in knowledge and freedom, and more insistently brought to our attention in certain situations, can also be intrinsically given by reason of the positive nature of that categorical reality in which the magnitude and glory, goodness, beauty and illumination of our individual experiential reality promise and point to eternal light and everlasting life. But it is already understandable that such a form of reference is most clearly experienced where the graspable contours of our everyday realities break and dissolve; where failures of such realities are experienced; when lights which illuminate the tiny islands of our everyday life go out, and the question becomes inescapable whether the night surrounding us is the absurd void of death engulfing us, or the blessed holy night which is already illumined from within and gives promise of everlasting day.

When therefore I refer in the following primarily to those experiences which in this second way allow transcendental experience of God in the Holy Spirit to go forward, that does not mean that people and Christians are forbidden to let this experience of God occur in the first way, and thus to receive it. Ultimately the *via eminentiae* and the *via negationis* are not two ways or two stations, one behind the other on a way, but two aspects of one and the same experience (though, as I have remarked, for the sake of clarity it is quite justifiable to lay special stress on the *via negationis*).

I can now refer to the actual life-experiences which, whether we come to know them reflectively or not, are experiences of the Spirit. It is important that we experience them in the right way. In the case of these indications of the actual experience of the Spirit in the midst of banal everyday life, it can no longer be a question of analyzing them individually right down to their ultimate depth — which is the Spirit. And no attempt can be made to make a systematic tabular summary of such experiences. Only arbitrarily and unsystematically selected examples are possible.

Let us take, for instance, someone who is dissatisfied with his life, who cannot make the goodwill, errors, guilt, and fatalities of his life fit together, even when, as often seems impossible, he adds remorse to this accounting. He cannot see how he is to include God as an entry in the accounting, as one that makes the debit and credit, the notional and actual values, come out right. This human being surrenders himself to God or — both more imprecisely and more precisely — to the hope of an incalculable ultimate reconciliation of his existence in which he whom we call God dwells; he releases his unresolved and uncalculated existence, he lets go in trust and hope and does not know how this miracle occurs that he cannot himself enjoy and possess as his own self-actuated possession.

There is an individual who discovers that he can forgive though he receives no reward for it, and silent forgiveness from the other side is taken as self-evident.

There is one who tries to love God although no response of love seems to come from God's silent incomprehensibility, although no wave of emotive wonder any longer supports him, although he can no longer confuse himself and his life-force with God, although he thinks he will die from such a love, because it seems like death and absolute denial, because with such a love one appears to call into the void and the completely unheard of, because this love seems like a ghastly leap into groundless space, because everything seems untenable and apparently meaningless.

There is the person who does his duty where it can apparently only be done, with the terrible feeling that he is denying himself and doing something ludicrous for which no one will thank him.

There is a person who is really good to another person from whom no echo of understanding and thankfulness is heard in return, whose goodness is not even repaid by the feeling of having been "selfless," noble, and so on.

There is one who is silent although he could defend himself, although he is unjustly treated, who keeps silence without feeling that his silence is his sovereign unimpeachability.

There is someone who obeys not because he must and would otherwise find it inconvenient to disobey, but purely on account of that mysterious, silent, and incomprehensible thing that we call God and the will of God.

There is an individual who renounces something without thanks or recognition, and even without a feeling of inner satisfaction.

There is a person who is absolutely lonely, who finds all the bright elements of life pale shadows, for whom all trustworthy handholds take him into the infinite distance, and who does not run away from this loneliness but treats it with ultimate hope.

There is someone who discovers that his most acute concepts and most intellectually refined operations of the mind do not fit; that the unity of consciousness and that of which one is conscious in the destruction of all systems is now to be found only in pain; that he cannot resolve the immeasurable multitude of questions, and yet cannot keep to the clearly known content of individual experience and to the sciences.

There is one who suddenly notices how the tiny trickle of his life wanders through the wilderness of the banality of existence, apparently without aim and with the heartfelt fear of complete exhaustion. And yet he hopes, he knows not how, that this trickle will find the infinite expanse of the ocean, even though it may still be covered by the grey sands which seem to extend forever before him.

One could go on like this forever, perhaps even then without coming to that experience which for this or that individual is the experience of the Spirit, freedom, and grace in his life.

For everyone makes that experience in accordance with the particular historical and individual situation of his specific life. Everyone! But he has, so to speak, to dig it out from under the rubbish of everyday experience, and must not run away from it where it begins to become legible, as though it were only an undermining and disturbance of the self-evidence of his everyday life and his scientific assurance.

Let me repeat, though I must say it in almost the same words: where the one and entire hope is given beyond all individual hopes, which comprehends all impulses in silent promise,

- where a responsibility in freedom is still accepted and borne where it has no apparent offer of success and advantage,

- where someone experiences and accepts his ultimate freedom which no earthly compulsions can take away from him,

- where the leap into the darkness of death is accepted as the beginning of everlasting promise,

- where the sum of all accounts of life, which no one can calculate alone, is understood by an incomprehensible other as good, though it still cannot be "proven,"

- where the fragmentary experience of love, beauty, and joy is experienced and accepted purely and simply as the promise of love, beauty, and joy, without their being understood in ultimate cynical skepticism as a cheap form of consolation for some final deception,

- where the bitter, deceptive and vanishing everyday world is withstood until the accepted end, and accepted out of a force whose ultimate source is still unknown to us but can be tapped by us,

- where one dares to pray into a silent darkness and knows that one is heard, although no answer seems to come back about which one might argue and rationalize,

- where one lets oneself go unconditionally and experiences this capitulation as true victory,

- where falling becomes true uprightness,

- where desperation is accepted and is still secretly accepted as trustworthy without cheap trust,

- where a person entrusts all his knowledge and all his questions to the silent and all-inclusive mystery which is loved more than all our individual knowledge which makes us such small people,

- where we rehearse our own deaths in everyday life, and try to live in such a way as we would like to die, peaceful and composed,

- where — (as I have said, we could go on and on):

- there is God and his liberating grace. There we find what we Christians call the Holy Spirit of God. Then we experience something which is inescapable (even when suppressed) in life, and which is offered to our freedom with the question whether we want to accept it or whether we want to shut ourselves up in a hell of freedom by trying to barricade ourselves against it. There is the mysticism of everyday life, the discovery of God in all things; there is the sober intoxication of the Spirit, of which the fathers and the liturgy speak which we cannot reject or despise, because it is real.

Let us look for that experience in our own lives. Let us seek the specific experiences in which something like that happens to us. If we find them, we have experienced the Spirit which we are talking about. The experience of eternity, the experience that the Spirit is more than a piece of this temporal world, the experience that the meaning of the human being is not contained purely in the meaning and happiness of this world, the experience of the wager and of the trust which no longer possess any obvious ground taken from the success of this world.

From there, we can understand what kind of secret passion is alive in persons of the Spirit and in the saints. They want to have this experience. They want repeatedly (out of a secret fear that they are caught up in the world) to ensure that they are beginning to live in the Spirit. They have tasted the Spirit.

Whereas ordinary people treat such experience only as an unpleasant though not wholly avoidable disruption of normal life, in which the

Spirit is only the seasoning and garnishing of another life but not of one's own, people of the Spirit and the saints have tasted pure Spirit. The Spirit is something they drink straight, as it were, no longer as a mere seasoning of earthly existence. Hence their remarkable life, their poverty, their longing for humility, their passionate wish for death, their readiness to suffer, their secret longing for martyrdom. It is not as if they were not also weak. It is not as if they did not also have continually to return to the ordinary atmosphere of everyday life. It is not as if they did not know that grace can also bless everyday life and rational action, and make them steps toward God. It is not as if they did not know that we are no angels in this life and are not expected to be. But they know that as a spirit the human being (in real existence and not merely in speculation) must really live on the borderline between God and the world, time and eternity, and they try continually to make sure that they are also really doing that, and that the Spirit in them is not only the means of a human way of life.

Now, if we experience the Spirit, then we (at least as Christians living in faith) have already experienced the supernatural — perhaps very anonymously and implicitly. This is probably so that we cannot and should not turn our daily lives inside out and upside down in order to see the supernatural. But we know if we release ourselves to this experience of the Spirit, if the tangible, speakable, and enjoyable founders, if everything sounds deathly silent, if everything has the taste of death and of downfall, or if everything disappears into an incomprehensible, so to speak, white, colorless and intangible blessedness, then not only the spirit but the Holy Spirit is actually at work in us. Then the hour of his grace has come. That is the time of the apparently strange groundlessness of our existence which we experience: the groundlessness of God who communicates himself to us, the beginning of the coming of his infinity, which no longer has any paths, which is enjoyed like nothingness because it is infinity. When we have cast off and no longer belong to ourselves, when we have denied ourselves and we have moved an infinite distance from ourselves, then we begin to live in the world of God himself, of the God of grace and eternal life.

That may seem unusual to us at first, and we are constantly tempted to take fright and return to the trustworthy and close at hand; indeed, we often have to do so and should do so. Yet we should try to grow used to the taste of the pure wine of the spirit, filled by the Holy Spirit. At least we should do so to an extent that enables us not to reject the chalice when it is proffered to us.

91 • The Triune God I*

Christians, for all their orthodox profession of faith in the Trinity, are almost just "monotheists" in their actual religious existence. One might almost dare to affirm that if the doctrine of the Trinity were to be erased as false, most religious literature could be preserved almost unchanged throughout the process.

It cannot be denied that the *incarnation* is so theologically and *religiously* central in Christian life that on that account the Trinity is always and everywhere irremovably present. Yet when the incarnation of God is spoken of, theological and religious intention is today concentrated on the fact that "God" has become man, that "a" person of the Trinity has assumed flesh — but not on the fact that this person is precisely that of the Word, the Logos.

And this state of affairs is not surprising. For since St. Augustine, contrary to the tradition preceding him, it has been more or less agreed that each of the divine persons could become man. From which it follows that the incarnation of the second person in particular throws no light on the special character of *this* person within the divine nature.

No Christian can seriously deny that there is an understanding of the doctrine of the Trinity in terms of the economy of salvation, that there is an experience of the history of salvation and revelation of a threefold kind. The history of revelation and salvation brings us up against the ineffable mystery of the incomprehensible, unoriginated God who is called Father, who does not live and remain in a metaphysical remoteness, but who seeks in all his incomprehensibility and sovereignty and freedom to impart himself to the creature as its eternal life in truth and love. This one and incomprehensible God is unsurpassably close to human beings historically in Jesus Christ, who is not simply one prophet in a still continuing series of prophets but the final and unsurpassable self-promise of this one God in history. And this one and the same God imparts himself to us in the innermost center of human existence as Holy Spirit for salvation and for the consummation which is God himself.

For Christian faith then there are two utterly radical and definitive and unsurpassable factualities, modes of existence, of the one God in the world, factualities which are the final salvation freely granted by God to the world, in history and transcendence. As permanent, these two factualities are always to be distinguished, even though (and this is not to be specially explained here) they are mutually dependent. It

---

* *Theological Investigations IV*, 79–80; *Theological Investigations XVIII*, 114–16.

is of course not clearly obvious from the outset that there are only *two* such factualities of God himself *in* himself *for* his creation.

If we could presuppose the doctrine of the immanent Trinity on the two internal divine processions as *only* two, it would be easy to answer the question of the exclusiveness of the two divine modes of factuality for the world. But, since we must first of all here understand the economic Trinity as immanent, the question is not so easy to answer at this point. But (and this may suffice here) we could say that the diversity, unity, and mutual dependence of the human being's historicity and transcendentality provide an adequate aid to understanding for the distinction, unity, and exclusiveness of the two factualities of God, assuming, however, that we regard the human person from the outset as the image of God and do not forget that this image "human being" must from the outset be such that he can be the recipient of God's self-communication: that is, what is to be communicated must necessarily correspond to the nature of the recipient of the communication, and vice versa.

If, with all the unity and mutual interdependence, there is really a permanent duality of the divine modes of factuality in God's self-communication to the world, this means at least that there is what we describe as the economic Trinity. The unoriginated God, who imparts himself in two different modes of factuality and because of the unity and diversity of these two modes and because of the incomprehensible sovereignty which he retains even in his self-communication, may not be understood simply in a lifeless identity with these two factualities. In this salvific economic Trinity the unoriginated and permanently sovereign God is called Father; in his self-communication to history, Logos; in his self-communication to the individual's transcendentality, Holy Spirit. (We prefer to use here the term "Logos," which is also authorized by the New Testament, since at this point we want to avoid the question of whether the "Son" of the Father, who is Jesus according to the New Testament, designates even in the earliest New Testament statements, as distinct from later statements of the New Testament or of the magisterium, an exclusive salvific economic mode of factuality of God and thus an immanent mode of subsistence of God, or more fundamentally the unique unity of the man Jesus with God-Father as such.) For the Christian, then, there is undoubtedly a salvific economic Trinity.

In regard to this statement, however, it is essential to see and acknowledge that the duality of God's factualities for us does not get in the way of the factuality of God in himself or that the latter is not mediated by something that is not God. Logos and Holy Spirit are not to be regarded as mediating modalities which are different from the one God. For since Christianity rejects any neoplatonic, Plotinian, gnostic, or similar idea of a descending self-emptying God, they would then have to be regarded as created realities, which, like all other created realities, would by their nature point to the God who always remains remote, but would not mediate God as such in his innermost reality.

In God's *self*-communication to the creature, radically understood, the mediation itself must be God and cannot amount to a creaturely mediation. These reflections, however, would seem largely irrelevant even to a religious person who is a theist, if he wants to remain obediently and humbly alone, looking to the incomprehensible God from an infinite distance, not venturing at all to realize that this infinite and incomprehensible God might also be the God who is utterly close and immediate and not only the infinitely remote creator-God. But if and when the thirst for God in himself imparted to the human being by God himself is admitted, if and when the ultimate unsurpassable statement of revelation that God himself as such wills to give himself to us is heard and accepted, in the sense in which this statement emerges clearly in the New Testament in the experience of Jesus and his Spirit, then it is impossible to avoid the admission that there is a twofold self-communication of God in diversity and unity, the modalities of which in their unity and distinction are again God himself strictly as such.

92 • The Triune God II*

We suppose that, when God steps outside of himself in *self*-communication (not merely through creation, positing other realities which are not himself), it is and must be the Son who appears historically in the flesh as man. And it must be the Spirit who brings about the acceptance of the world (as creation) in faith, hope, and love of this self-communication. Insofar as this one self-communication of God, which occurs necessarily in these two complementary aspects, is *free,* the incarnation and the descent of God's Spirit are free, even though the connection between the two moments is necessary.

The fact that it is precisely the Logos who became man and the Spirit who "sanctifies" is a free event, if and because God's self-communication is free. Hence the question can only be how the incarnation and the descent of the Spirit can, in the properties we know about them through revelation, be so "conceptualized" or understood that they look like moments of the *one* self-communication of God,

---

* *The Trinity,* trans. Joseph Donceel (New York: Herder and Herder, 1970), 86–87, 106–15; *Encyclopedia of Theology,* 1461–62.

hence as *one* economic Trinity, and not merely as two "functions" of two divine hypostases, which might be exchanged at will.

God is revealed as communicating himself in absolute and merciful presence as God, that is, as the absolute mystery. The historical mediation of this transcendental experience is also revealed as valid, as bringing about and authenticating the absolute experience of God. The unique and final culmination of this history of revelation has already occurred and has revealed the absolute and irrevocable unity of God's transcendental self-communication to humankind and of its historical mediation in the one Godman Jesus Christ, who is at once God himself as communicated, the human acceptance of this communication, and the final historical manifestation of this offer and acceptance.

And in this unity of God's transcendental self-communication and its definitive historical mediation and manifestation, the fundamental mystery of the triune God is also revealed, since what is involved is the communication of God in himself. For this mystery is merely the ground of God's action on us — the *in se* of the *quoad nos* of God — in history and transcendence, God in his incomprehensible primordiality, God in his real capacity to enter the human being's transcendence and history: Father, Son, and Holy Spirit.

Inasmuch as history mediates transcendence, the Son sends the Spirit; inasmuch as transcendence makes history, the Spirit effects the incarnation of the Logos; inasmuch as the appearance in history implies the manifestation of reality, the incarnate Logos is revealed as the self-utterance of the Father in truth; inasmuch as God's coming among us in the center of our life signifies his love and ours, the Pneuma is revealed in his intrinsic reality as love.

If through the intermediary of history we come to know the transcendental absolute presence of God in his self-communication, and accept it by means of itself, we know by the act of faith itself what we mean when we speak of the Trinity and thereby sum up the whole form and content of our Christian faith and its revelation and the history of revelation, and are baptized in those three names.

When *today we* speak of person in the plural, we think almost necessarily, because of the modern meaning of the word, of several spiritual centers of activity, of several subjectivities and liberties. But there are not three of these in God — not only because in God there is only *one* essence, hence *one* absolute self-presence, but also because there is only *one* self-utterance of the Father, the Logos. The Logos is not the one who utters, but the one who is uttered. And there is properly no *mutual* love between the Father and Son, for this would presuppose two acts. But there is loving self-acceptance of the Father, and this self-acceptance gives rise to the distinction.

Of course, that which we call "three persons" in God exists in God with self-awareness. There is in God a knowledge of these three persons (hence in each person about himself and about the two other persons), a knowledge about the Trinity both *as consciousness* and as *"object"* of knowledge (as known). But there are not three consciousnesses; rather, the one consciousness subsists in a threefold way. There is only one real consciousness in God, which is shared by Father, Son, and Spirit, by each in his own proper way.

Hence the threefold subsistence is not qualified by three consciousnesses. The "subsistence" itself is as such not "personal," if we understand this word in the modern sense. The "distinctness" of the persons is not constituted by a distinctness of conscious subjectivities, nor does it include the latter. This distinctness is conscious. However, it is not conscious for three subjectivities, but it is the awareness of this distinctness in one only real consciousness.

While formerly "person" meant directly (*in recto*) only the distinct subsistence, and cosignified the rational nature only indirectly (*in obliquo*) — according to the thinglike way of thinking of the Greeks — the "anthropocentric turn" of modern times requires that the spiritual-subjective element in the concept of person be first understood.

Hence the church faces a situation that did not always exist. On the other hand, it is evident that the regulation of language, which is necessary in a church as a community of a shared social worship and confession, cannot be undertaken by the single theologian at will. The only thing he can do at present is *also* to use the concept of person in the doctrine of the Trinity, and to defend it, to the extent of his power, from misunderstandings that it is threatened by. The magisterium forbids him to suppress such concepts on his own authority, but also obliges him to work at their fuller explanation.

What would such an explanatory concept be that would explain and correctly interpret the concept of "person"? Does it correctly and completely correspond to the concept that is to be explained?

In order to answer this question, and to summarize our previous considerations, we must (once more) start from our basic axiom. The one self-communication of the one God occurs in three different manners of given-ness, in which the one God is given concretely for us in himself, and not vicariously by other realities through their transcendental relation to God. God is the concrete God in each of these manners of given-ness — which, of course, refer to each other relatively, without modalistically coinciding.

If we translate this in terms of "immanent" Trinity, we may say: the one God subsists in three distinct manners of subsisting. "Distinct manner of subsisting" would then be the explanatory concept, not for person, which refers to that which subsists as distinct, but for the "personality" which makes God's concrete reality, as it meets us in different ways, into precisely this one who meets us *thus*. This meeting-us-thus must always be conceived as belonging to God in and for himself. The single "person" in God would then be: God as existing and meeting us in this determined distinct manner of subsisting.

The expression "distinct manner of subsisting" needs more explanation. We consider it better, simpler, and more in harmony with the traditional language of theology and the church than the phrase suggested by Karl Barth: "manner of being." First, if we prescind for a while from the word "manner," it says simply the same as the definition of "person" in Thomas: "that which subsists distinctly (in a rational nature)," and the same as the corresponding Greek word.

What is meant by subsisting can become clear only in our own existence, where we encounter the concrete, irreducible, incommutable, and irreplaceable priority and finality of this experience. This-there is what subsists. Thus our basic axiom is once more confirmed. Without our experience of Father, Son, and Spirit in salvation history, we would ultimately be totally unable to conceive at all of their subsisting distinctly as the one God.

There are advantages in speaking of the "distinct manner of subsisting" or of God in three distinct manners of subsisting, rather than of person. "Three persons" says nothing about the unity of these three persons, so that this unity must be brought from outside to the word by which we designate the three persons. Of itself, "manner" at least suggests the possibility that the same God, as distinct in a threefold manner, is concretely "three-personal," or, the other way around, that the "three-personality" cosignifies the unity of the same God.

We must keep in mind, however, that regarding the Trinity, "distinct *manner* of subsisting" should not be understood in such a way as if this "manner" were something subsequent, a "modality" without which the substantially real might also exist. The concrete Godhead is necessarily in these manners of subsisting. It is impossible, except through a merely conceptual abstraction, to conceive of a Godhead that would, as real, be previous to these manners. That is why the one God is Father, Son, and Holy Spirit.

Let us further test the usefulness of the expression "distinct manners of subsisting" (while here and now methodically avoiding the word "person") by formulating a few basic statements about the Trinity with the help of this concept. We may say, then, that:

- the one God subsists in three distinct manners of subsisting,

- the manners of subsisting of Father, Son, and Holy Spirit are distinct as relations of opposition; hence these "three" are not the same one;

- the Father, Son, and Spirit are the one God each in a different manner of subsisting and in this sense we may count "three" in God;

- God is "threefold" through his three manners of subsisting;

- God as subsisting in a determined manner of subsisting (such as the Father) is "somebody else" [ein andere] than God subsisting in another manner of subsisting, but he is not "something else" [etwas anderes];

- the manner of subsisting is distinct through its relative opposition to another one; it is real through its identity with the divine essence;

- the one and same divine essence subsists in each of the three distinct manners of subsisting;

- hence "he who" subsists in one of such manners of subsisting is truly God.

If we consider these and similar formulations, which may be made with the help of the concept "distinct manners of subsisting," we may safely state that they say exactly as much as the formulation which uses the word "person." We have already said and must not repeat the advantages of the use of the concept "distinct manners of subsisting" as compared with the concept of "person" and what difficulties it entails. This concept, which intends to be nothing more than an explanation of the concept of person as meant in the doctrine of the Trinity — an explanation which is legitimated by the truly Thomistic definition of the "person" — should not, as we said above, induce us to give up the use of the concept of person. But using it together with the concept of person may serve the purpose of overcoming the false opinion that what is meant by "person," especially within the doctrine of the Trinity, is clearly evident. He who starts with this false opinion may verbally protest to the contrary, may emphasize the mysterious character of the Trinity, may know of the logical difficulties in reconciling the three "persons" with God's unity. Despite all this he will have great trouble avoiding a *hidden* prereflective tritheism.

93 • The Triune God and Monotheism*

The statement that the "Logos and the Holy Spirit are God himself" is not an attenuation or the obscuring of monotheism rightly understood, but its radicalization. Monotheism as a religious and theological statement is not an abstract metaphysical theory about a remote absolute, but a statement about the sole absolute, about the God with whom we have to deal concretely in salvation history.

If this God of concrete salvation history realizes there his absolute and unconditional self-communication in history and transcendence, then on the one hand the diversity of these modes of factuality cannot be denied, but on the other this mode of factuality cannot be thrust between the one God and the creature graced by God as something merely created, which would then establish God's remoteness and not his closeness.

If and insofar as (and this of course cannot be questioned) creaturely mediations between God and human beings can be conceived and do in fact exist, and when these occur in the field of the human person's religious relationship to God and thus have a numinous quality, there is really always a danger of an explicit or disguised polytheism. The human being seizes on such a mediation, grasps it absolutely firmly, affirms it at least implicitly in this firm grasp as God himself, and yet in truth it is no more than a finite creature that cannot by any means convey God in himself.

For the Christian, then, the religious monotheist is inescapably confronted by certain alternatives. He may demythologize in a theoretical monotheism all (even permanent and unavoidable) mediations of his relationship to God (whether these are understood as word, scripture, sacrament, or institution, etc.) as purely created, in the last resort thrusting the absolute God into an infinite remoteness; thus he becomes a merely theoretical monotheist, for whom God is as distant as the supreme divinity among ancient and primitive religious figures, because in the concrete he has to cling to these particular and finite mediations of explicitly or surreptitiously polytheistic character. *In practice,* then, religion becomes again devotion belonging to the present world and is simply a numinous transfiguration of that world.

Or the person takes radical monotheism seriously, but at the same time for his own part refuses to see the mode of factuality of the monotheistic God as itself divine, and then he must see God's mode of

---

* *Theological Investigations XVIII*, 116–18.

factuality as radically creaturely and finite and lying on this side of the abyss between God and creature; thus he ends up again with a merely theoretical and abstract monotheism, which places God at an infinite distance, and in the actual practice of religion necessarily clings to these created mediations as all that he can regard concretely as properly religious, whether they are called commandment, scripture, covenant of God, or anything else.

In either case he will hesitate uncertainly between an abstract monotheism, which simply cannot take entirely seriously what is proper to religious monotheism, and a concealed polytheism, which in practice makes absolute those created realities which are supposed to convey God to him, although they are finite. (It seems to me that we might follow this hesitation between an abstract monotheism and an unadmitted polytheism up to the modern Western history of ideas in Hölderlin, Rilke, Kerenyi, Heidegger, and others.) There is a continual attempt to distinguish between the divine and the gods.

Or, finally, the religious monotheist, sustained by God's grace itself, has absolute confidence that the absolute God as such has come absolutely close to him. But then he must consider the mediating modes of factuality as themselves divine in the strict sense of the term. He must say both these things, even though he cannot offer for this dual statement any higher synthesis, surpassing it, making intelligible from a more fundamental standpoint the statement that the one sole God as himself is close to us in two modes of factuality and that these two modes of factuality are themselves God.

This absolutely comprehensive dual statement is therefore the radicalization of that monotheism which comes within a religious dimension. For the monotheistic God is the God who is close to us in concrete salvation history. It is only when created modes of mediation (although these *also* exist) in the ultimate sense are denied to him that he is really the sole God, close to us who is present as himself in salvation history.

The proposition of the identity of God's modes of factuality with God himself is only the converse of the proposition that any purely created mediation between God and the human person removes this God into an absolute remoteness, turns a concrete into an abstract monotheism, and permits us to be implicitly polytheistic in the concreteness of our religious life. God must mediate to himself through himself; otherwise he remains remote in the last resort and in this remoteness is present only by the divisive multiplicity of created realities which point to God's remoteness. This is the meaning of the proposition on the divinity of the two fundamental modes of God's factuality in the world and it thus also means that concrete monotheism is taken completely seriously.

94 • A Prayer at Pentecost*

Lord, today is Pentecost, the day we celebrate when you, raised above the highest heavens, sitting at the right hand of the Father, poured out on us the Spirit of the promise, so that you in your Spirit might remain with us all days until the end, and through him continue in us your life and death to the glory of the Father and to our salvation.

Lord, consider the spirits which oppress us and give us the spiritual gift of discernment. What gift would be more appropriate to Pentecost?

Give us the knowledge, enduring in everyday life, that if we seek and long for you, the spirit of serenity, peace and confidence, freedom and simple clarity is *your* Spirit, and every spirit of unrest and fear, of narrowness and of leaden depression is at most our spirit or is that of the dark abyss.

Give us your spirit of consolation. We know, Lord, that we should, must, and can be true to you even in desolation, dryness, weakness of soul. Nevertheless, we may also ask you for the spirit of consolation and strength, joy and confidence, of growth in faith, hope and love, of vigorous service and praise of your Father, for the spirit of calm and peace. Banish from our hearts spiritual desolation, darkness, confusion, inclination for base and earthly things, hopelessness and mistrust, tepidity, sadness and the feeling of abandonment, discord and the choking feeling of being far from you.

But if it pleases you to lead us by such ways, then leave us at least, we beseech you, in such hours and days, the holy spirit of fidelity, constancy and perseverance, so that we may go on our way in blind trust, maintain direction and remain true to the resolutions which we made when your light was shining on us and your joy filled our hearts. Yes, and give us rather, in the midst of such desolation, the spirit of courageous enterprise, of defiant "Now's the time!" in prayer, self-control and penance.

Give us then absolute confidence that we are not abandoned by your grace even in those times of abandonment, the confidence that you are more than ever with us when unfelt, as the power which wills to be victorious in our weakness. Give us the spirit of true remembrance of the kindness of your loving visitations in the past and of vigilant watch for the tangible evidences of your love, in the future. At such times of desolation cause us to confess our sinfulness and wretchedness, humbly experience our weakness and acknowledge that you alone are the true source of all good and of all heavenly consolation.

When your consolation comes to us, let it be accompanied by

---

* *Everyday Faith,* 96–98.

the spirit of humility and of readiness to serve you even without consolation.

Give us always the spirit of courage and sturdy determination to recognize temptation and occasion of sin, not to argue with them to make no compromise with them, but plainly to say no, because that is the simplest tactics in the fight. Give us the humility to ask for advice in puzzling situations, without insincere loquacity and self-complacency but also without the stupid pride which suggests we ought always to try to manage by ourselves. Give us the spirit of heavenly wisdom, so that we may recognize the real danger points of our character and life, and watch and fight most faithfully where we are most vulnerable.

Give us, that is, *your* Pentecost Spirit, the fruits of the Spirit, which your apostle tells us are love, joy, peace, patience, kindness, goodness, faithfulness, gentleness, self-control. If we have this Spirit and its fruits, we are no longer slaves of the law but free children of God. Then the Spirit will call in us: Abba, Father. Then he will intercede for us with sighs too deep for words. Then he will be the anointing oil, seal and pledge of eternal life, the spring of living water which wells up in the heart and flows to eternal life, and whispers, Come home to the Father.

Jesus, send us the Spirit. Give your Pentecost gift more and more. Make the eye of our spirit clear and our spiritual powers sensitive, so that we can distinguish your Spirit from all others. Give us your Spirit, so that it may be true of us that "If the Spirit of him who raised Jesus from the dead dwells in you, he will give life to your mortal bodies also through his Spirit who dwells in you." It is Pentecost, Lord. Your servants and handmaids ask with the boldness you commanded them to have. Let it be Pentecost in us also. Now and forever. Amen.

THE PEOPLE
OF GOD
IN HISTORY

95 • Witness to the World's Salvation*

In this world of God, of Jesus Christ, and of incomprehensibility there is to be a community to bear witness to Jesus; to attest God's vouchsafing of himself to the world, and its inevitable victory. This community does not coincide with the community of God's children, for by the infinite power of God's historical gift of himself those children are found everywhere, in all ages, in a countless multitude of forms, in all colors. And conversely: in inextricable confusion on the threshing floor of this community of witnesses the wheat and chaff of world history still lie unwinnowed. But what really happens in the depths of world history must be explicitly attested, and its historical manifestation must be proclaimed and occur anew by that very proclamation.

This must be, because the ultimate truth and reality of this tremendous history not only exists in Christ but has also become manifest in him, has been definitively fixed in that manifestation. So this community of witnesses comes from Jesus for the salvation of *the world* (not merely for their own salvation), attests him, points back in faith to him, his death, and his resurrection, and forward in hope to the revealing of his victory.

This community must be the community that dares to declare aloud, in, and despite, all the wretched bourgeois narrow-mindedness that is part of its lot, that the dreary plain of our existence also has peaks soaring up into the eternal light of the infinite God, peaks we can all scale, and that the awful bottomless abysses still hide God-filled depths we have not sounded, even when we think we have experienced everything and found it all absurd. Unequivocally and audibly the witness of this community, with its incomprehensible courage which dares contradict all of the human person's miserable experience, should shout out its invincible faith: God exists; God is love; love's victory is already won; all the streams of bitter tears that still flow through our land have dried up at the source; all darkness is but the darkest part of the night that heralds the dawn; life is worthwhile.

This testimony is the raison d'être of the community called the church, insofar as it is more than a mere part of the totality of humanity which God will never allow to escape from his love. Its true, ultimate nature, the real work that it is set, is not how to teach human

---

* *Servants of the Lord*, 21–23.

beings a little respect for God, not how to wring a little decency and kindness from their brutal selfishness, is not the law, but the gospel that God triumphs by his own doing and victoriously lavishes himself on this humanity and its world — is witness to that most improbable of facts which is the only ultimate truth.

Now since this community always gives the same witness, she must herself be *one,* and she requires cohesion and order; since she points back to Jesus Christ and ahead to him, this unity, this cohesion, and this order must come from Jesus Christ; since she is the community of witness to God's eschatologically victorious bestowal of himself to the world, since the historical manifestation of this bestowal happened in Christ as a permanent promise and this age in which we live is the last aeon of history, the community herself cannot perish; her witness, even her unity and order, are subject to the victorious mercy in which God gives himself to the world.

She is there, the community of this witness; she does her work and justifies her existence whether she be great or small, for she does not witness for herself but for the salvation of the world, which takes place both inside and outside her own circle; but neither can she exempt anyone from the call to share in witnessing to God, his Christ, and the approaching kingdom of God; she must summon all to effect and experience in themselves this salvation of the world by witnessing to it before the world. And she knows that should an individual turn a deaf ear to this summons, he would also lose that to which he is meant to bear witness. She also knows she is the community which proclaims God's salvation for others, for everybody: the salvation which is there for all and takes place in glory for all who do not culpably reject it. She knows she is the community that proclaims an absolute hope from which she may exclude no one. This community is called the church.

96 • The Church: The Basic Sacrament of the World's Salvation*

If we take in all due seriousness the statement that the church is the basic sacrament of salvation for the world, we shall realize that what it is intended to say is this: the church is the concrete historical

---

* *Theological Investigations X,* trans. David Bourke (New York: Herder and Herder, 1973), 14–24.

manifestation, in the dimension of a history that has acquired an es-chatological significance, and in the social dimension, of precisely *that* salvation which is achieved through the grace of God throughout the entire length and breadth of humanity.

The relationship between the church and this salvation of the world is the same as the relationship between the sacramental word and grace in the process of salvation which takes place in the life of the individual. In this process of salvation in the life of the individual these two entities are intrinsically connected but not identical with one an-other. Inasmuch as this process is subject to the conditions of time, either of the two entities involved can precede the other. Grace can already be present when the sacrament has not yet been conferred. A sacrament, even when validly conferred, can still have to wait for its fulfillment through the grace which is signified by it.

In the same way the church is the authentic manifestation of grace in history, a manifestation which offers itself as salvation *universally* and to *all,* a manifestation which is indeed intended to be presented and borne witness to as a visible historical entity with a sacramental significance, and as something that can be described and pointed to in the explicit preaching of the gospel.

But at the same time the reality of the church is not *only* present where it has already fully achieved this status of being explicitly and visibly a social entity, the nature of which can be reflected upon and described, in other words, where it is fully ecclesiastical in character and so itself as a part of the church achieving its own unique impact as a concrete historical phenomenon. But for this very reason the converse is also true. The manifestation of grace which achieves this objective reality in the church is a *manifestation* and a *sign* of that grace wherever it may take effect. In other words, the church as manifestation of grace is a sacramental sign of the grace that is offered to the world and history as a whole.

From the Christian point of view the world, humankind and human history can certainly not be understood merely as the sum total of all those individuals who are each working out their own personal salva-tions, or of the private lives of such individuals insofar as salvation is being worked out in them. If this were the case, then there would have been no need for the incarnation of the Logos in the unity of the human race. All that would have been necessary would have been a purely spiritual message of God directed to the depths of the individual's own private conscience, in other words, the kind of salvation history that is susceptible of a purely existentialist interpretation.

But against this the message of salvation addressed by God to humankind considered as a unity in this sense has the character of a primordial or basic sacrament. It embraces the individual and his personal history but is in itself Christ or the abiding continuity of his existence in history which is the church. This message of grace to the world, which has this quality of being a "basic sacrament" does indeed take effect in the lives of individuals.

Indeed it is intended to be brought to reality at the individual and sacramental level in the explicit word of preaching and in the form of the concrete sacrament. In the same way, in fact, this message of grace to the world, with its fundamentally sacramental character, is constituted by the common life of those who have received baptism and celebrate the Christian eucharist.

But this message does not achieve its effective force only in those contexts in which it is given concrete realization in the explicit word of preaching and in the sacraments, insofar as these are addressed to or conferred upon the individual. Grace can always take effect in the world even apart from the individual instances of the preaching of the word and the conferring of the sacraments, but wherever it does take effect this grace is already visibly being signified as an element in saving history as realized in this world in virtue of the fact that the church itself has this force of being a basic sacrament.

So far we have only been able to indicate our basic position. But taking this as our standpoint, we can achieve an understanding of a new "experience" of the church, precisely the experience that the church is still the basic sacrament of salvation for the world in just those contexts in which the world is not the church. The Christian of today and tomorrow will experience his Christianity *as ecclesiastical* by thinking of it not primarily and essentially as one of many interpretations of the significance of the world which compete with one another in the world's marketplace, not as a sum total of theories which are put forward at the same level as statements about the realities of this present world, so that the attitude underlying the Christian theories appears to represent a negation of these other speculations about the meaning of human existence.

The Catholic must think of and experience the church as the "vanguard," the sacramental sign, the manifestation in history of a grace of salvation which takes effect far beyond the confines of the "visible" church as sociologically definable. The sacramental sign of a Christianity that is anonymous, that is "outside" the church in the sense that it has not yet realized its true nature, but at the same time "within" the church even though it has not achieved its "ultimate self-realization."

This is not because otherwise there would simply be no Christianity at all outside the visible church, but because the Christianity that does exist there has not come to its full maturity as an objective entity, and therefore has not yet realized its own nature in the explicit awareness and reflective objectivity of the creed as actually formulated, of the sacraments as supplying objective reality, and of the visible church itself as providing an organized structure definable in sociological terms, all of which is, in fact, achieved in the church itself.

The Christian will regard non-Christians (in order to simplify the problem we shall set aside the question of non-Catholic Christians) not as having no part in Christianity or as standing altogether outside salvation because they are not Christians, but rather as anonymous Christians who do not realize what they truly are in virtue of grace in the depths of their own consciences; what they are, namely, in virtue of something that they achieve at a level which is perhaps wholly un-adduced, but is none the less real; something which the Christian too achieves in that *he* goes beyond this and recognizes what he is doing as a matter of objective reality in the reflective processes of his own conscious thought.

All this must be so if it is not the case that God, with a view to bestowing eternal salvation on human beings, suddenly permits their goodwill to count in place of the reality itself. For basically speaking, this view would render invalid the doctrine of the necessity of the church and grace as mediating salvation and not merely as something which people are commanded by God to embrace. Here, there can be no doubt.

The awareness of the *professed* Christian, his faith as able to be formulated in propositions, as "in conformity with the creed," is some-thing that empowers him and actually obliges him as a matter of duty to incorporate himself as a member in the visible society of the church. And this faith of his is a part of Christianity in its fullness, and is a grace which once more facilitates and renders more secure precisely that which is already present in the depths of human existence and human awareness, so that it is this that he is actually acknowledging by his faith.

There can be no doubt that the Catholic rightly feels and values his explicit membership in the church as an unmerited grace, as a blessing, as a promise of salvation. But it must be admitted that in doing this he is also aware of a fear that plumbs the very depths of his being. For the greater the grace the greater the danger, and more will be demanded of him who has received more. Again, he never knows whether he is in fact measuring up to what is demanded of *him* in particular, as distinct from others. He knows — this too can be accorded its due importance — the words of Christ which tell us that many will come from the east and from the west, but the children of the kingdom shall be cast into the exterior darkness (Mt 8:11ff.).

Again, the constitution *Lumen Gentium* invokes a saying of Augustine (no. 14) to draw a distinction between "heartfelt" (*corde*) and merely "corporal" (*corpore*) membership of the church. The Catholic Christian knows that he belongs to the church *corpore*. But *what he does not know for certain* is that he is actually *living* in it by faith and love. This is something which he can only *hope* for and which he must hope for. But because the Christian hopes for the salvation of others also, because he is sufficiently aware of modern theological developments to recognize that he can hope for this (even if he cannot know it for certain), because it is easier for him today than it was formerly to conceive in theological terms how it is possible to be a "Christian" (here this is intended to signify someone living in the grace of God and of Christ even when he does not know the name of Christ or feels compelled to reject him) — because of all this, *therefore* he can only regard himself and professed Christians, the church, as the vanguard of those who are journeying toward the salvation of God and his eternity through the roads of history.

For him the church is, in a certain sense, the uniformed section of the army of God. It represents that point at which the intrinsic nature of the life of God made man as projected into the world is also made manifest at the historical and social level (or better, is made manifest most clearly, since to the eye enlightened by faith the grace of God is not totally devoid of all embodiment even outside the church). The Christian knows that the light of morning on the mountains is the beginning of the day that lights up the valleys. It is not a day that is confined to the higher levels, and so condemns the darkness below.

We may recall the Christian teaching that there is no absolute principle of evil, that evil is that which is not, that the one unique God is good, and that he wills what is good for the church as well, that that which is real is also the good, so that it follows that a true realist must think well of reality. The Christian knows that it would be blasphemous to suppose that in the last analysis it is easier to do evil than good, or that on a "sober" and realistic view of reality it is the evil that is in possession there and not the good, or that, ultimately speaking, evil will survive when good has disappeared.

The Christian knows that it is not the humility of the creature but rather its pride that prompts such ideas, or that makes it suppose that it is able, at least by embracing the evil, to emancipate itself from God, for this is simply a stupid lie. The Christian knows that in fact it is precisely the achievement of his own existence that is demanded of him, to believe in the light when he is in the darkness, to believe in blessedness when he is in pain, to believe in God as the absolute in the midst of the relativity to which he is subject. He knows that revelation in its progressive unfolding lays bare our sins to us only in order that we may believe in the forgiveness of God. (Guilt *alone* and taken by itself is something that we could already have experienced in our pain, our death, and our powerlessness to escape.)

When Paul regards the unbelief of the Jews as only temporary (Rom 9–11), we may ask how this is to be interpreted at least in a theology which, while it wants to do Paul full justice, can no longer think simply in "collectivist" terms. This statement should not lead us to credit Paul with the opinion that it was only later generations of Jews who would be believers, while the earlier ones remained *totally without faith in any sense.* Only one who is "collectivist" to the point of being unchristian can suggest this kind of uncompromising solution to the question.

In Paul's own thought an idea which he held firm to, and which constituted the inner kernel of his own personal conviction, was that the grace of God would emerge victorious over "unbelief." He himself may or may not have regarded the process by which this was to be accomplished as already having explicitly and definitively attained its full development. But in any case it makes no difference to the point at issue how far he did actually hold this view.

The faith of the people of Israel, which became manifest as a phenomenon only in their later history (admittedly even this is still not apprehensible to us in any assured sense as a predestination of the individual to salvation), must be a sign of the fact that in earlier ages too God had already had compassion on this people in a manner which we can neither discern nor comprehend (once more nothing definite is implied in this with regard to the salvation of the individual as such). For why otherwise should we take as the defining characteristic of Israel as a whole the faith of her later stages of development and not the unbelief of her earlier period? How otherwise could it be preferable to say: "Israel as such will be overtaken by God's grace" rather than: "This people has rejected God?"

In the light of this the Christian is fearless and untroubled in the view he takes of the world — that world which is filled with a thousand opinions and philosophies of life. He does not need anxiously to scrutinize the statistical data to see whether, not only in theory but in actual fact as well, the church is the greatest organization based on a philosophy of life or whether her rate of growth is in proportion to that of the world population. Certainly he will regard the world with missionary zeal.

And this is a point which is also included in the Constitution on the Church and the Decree on the Missions. These are especially concerned to ensure that the quite astonishingly optimistic note they strike with regard to the salvation of the world shall not obscure the need for the church's missionary activities or weaken the missionary zeal of Christians.

In this connection one question may be left open and not treated here: namely, whether we have already arrived at the clearest possible "synthesis" between this optimism with regard to salvation and the inalienable duty of Christians to be missionaries of the gospel. In any case the Christian will bear witness to the name of Christ. He will be resolved to impart his grace to others, for he possesses a grace of which those others are deprived — are *still* deprived, precisely the grace of belonging to the church *corpore* and not merely *corde*. Only when they have this grace will they actually be contributing to that basic sacramental sign that is the church.

Moreover, it is this grace that summons the entire world to make space in human living, in its dimensions of freedom and of physical concretion too, for that divine life which has all along been at work at the very roots of human nature as the offering of God to communicate himself to us, regardless of whether this offering is accepted or refused. It is this grace too which not only impels history forward to that blessedness in which its ultimate consummation is to consist, but is also intended to be incarnate in history itself in full measure and in manifest form.

But the Christian is aware of a further point. His zeal has the greatest chance of success when his enthusiasm for his missionary vocation is tempered by calmness and patience. He knows that he must imitate the patience of God (which, according to Paul, is positively salvific rather than condemning in its meaning). He knows that God has willed this world to be as it is because otherwise it would not be at all, and that even that which is "merely" *permitted* is simply permitted precisely as an element in something that is willed (and not merely permitted) by God. He knows further that this which is willed by God can and must be hoped for not merely as the revelation of God's justice but also as the revelation of his infinite kindness to humankind.

The Christian knows that God does not begin the work of his grace only at that stage at which someone takes it up in the name of God. For this reason, when he is faced with one who, so far as his "philosophy of life" is concerned, has no intention of being a brother, the Christian nevertheless goes to meet him boldly and hopefully as a brother. He sees in him one who does not know what he truly is, one to whom it has not yet been made plain what he nevertheless may be presumed already to be achieving in the depths of his own human living. (So true is this that we have an absolute duty to assume this in hope, and it would be a failure in charity to hold anything less about the non-Christian, for should I as a Christian simply and absolutely take it for granted that the non-Christian with whom I am in contact is devoid of God's grace?) In this other person the Christian sees Christianity in its "anonymous" or unacknowledged form at work in a thousand ways.

He knows that a human being is always more and always achieves more in his human living than he himself can express. Ultimately speaking, the reality of our existence as humans always goes beyond the interpretations we ourselves place upon it in theory. Now if the Christian recognizes all this, then he cannot consider it rash or out of place to assume that even though the non-Christian interprets himself quite otherwise, still by God's grace some kind of "unacknowledged Christianity" is already present in him or even is actually, though all unconsciously, being put into practice.

If the Christian interprets his own *self* (rightly understood) as at the same time justified and sinner (*simul justus et peccator*) or as, arising from this, at the same time a believer and an unbeliever (*simul fidelis et infidelis*),even though he intends to be a believer and only this, then it is no impertinence either if he interprets the non-Christian as one who is perhaps "at the same time a believer" even though he intends to be only an unbeliever.

If the Christian sees that the non-Christian is kind, charitable, and true to his own conscience, he will no longer be able to say nowadays "All those are 'natural' virtues," for in fact, ultimately speaking, these only exist in the abstract. He will no longer say: This is certainly just the "outward brilliance which the vices of the pagans display," as Augustine does. On the contrary he will think, "There the grace of Christ is at work even in one who has not yet explicitly called upon it but who, at the same time, has already hungered after it in the unexpressed and unacknowledged longings of his heart. There is one in whom the unspeakable groanings of the Spirit have already called in supplication upon the silent but all-pervasive mystery of existence which we Christians know as the Father of our Lord Jesus Christ!"

Supposing that the Christian sees the "pagan" dying willingly. Supposing that he notices how the other willingly submits, as though no other course were open to him (Oh yes, another course is open to him, for he can summon up the ultimate resources of his entire existence and use them to assume a last and absolute attitude of protest and absolute cynicism and doubt) to a death in which he falls into the bottomless abyss which has never been plumbed to the full (because in order to include God it must be infinite). Supposing that the Christian himself recognizes in this basic willingness of the non-Christian, which is no longer an articulate attitude at all, that this abyss into which the non-Christian is falling is the abyss of a meaningful mystery and not of a despairing void.

If the Christian sees all this, then he sees also in one who is dying in this way him who is nailed to the saving cross of human existence *at the right hand of Christ.* And he sees that precisely *this* real situation in the concrete, in which this dying man finds himself, wordlessly utters the plea "Lord remember me when you come into your kingdom."

Why should it not be so? The sheer transcendence of human nature need not always be used as a mere means with a view to asserting one's right to earthly existence. It can be accepted and endured, and then it can also be elevated by grace in such a way that, liberated from its downward tendency toward the finite, it becomes the dynamic impulse that urges us upward toward the God of eternal life, inasmuch as he, in the ultimate reality of his own nature, considered as that which has been communicated and is to be communicated further, is the ultimate goal and destiny toward which the human being is supernaturally directed.

This orientation toward God implanted in the spiritual transcendence of the human person by grace goes beyond his nature and liberates him from his earthly bent. Moreover, it is sound Thomistic doctrine that it also alters the final goal, the "formal object" of what the spirit can achieve. And because of this, even though it may not actually set any new object before the individual's vision, it is *in actual reality* a "revelation," and that too not a "natural" revelation but one that is grace-given. Moreover in the sense that as revelation it is "uttered" by God to human beings on the level of his freedom and personhood, it can already be considered "verbal" and, insofar as it is accepted at this level, as faith.

We are dealing, therefore, with the submission of someone in obedience and love to the infinitude of his own transcendence as to something which is beyond his control. The person submits himself to this transcendent dimension in his own being not in the measure that it can be grasped by us, but rather in the measure that we are grasped and contained by it as something beyond our control. Now if this is so, why should not this attitude of obedient and loving submission on the part of the individual be so transformed, even in the present by the ordinations of God's will to bestow supernatural salvation on human beings, as to become something more than merely the spiritual transcendence which is in this sense natural to them?

Why should not God bring it about by his own act that this spiritual transcendence really becomes in us that interior tendency which draws us into the life of God? And supposing the individual accepts this tendency implanted in him in the sense that he willingly submits to the control of that which he cannot comprehend in its incomprehensibility, why should not this be enough? (Is it really necessary to insist that of course all the demands of natural and supernatural ethics are to be thought of as implicitly contained in this, though admittedly only in such a way that their authentic orientation to God can be achieved, "subjectively" speaking, in the concrete life of the individual even in those cases in which the most far-reaching errors at the material level with regard to particular moral norms are to be found? This is something which is shown in the experience of Christians as well as that of pagans.)

Now on this showing, when the Christian preaches Christianity to the "non-Christian," he will take as his starting point not so much the basic attitude of wanting to make the other something which he simply has not been hitherto. Rather, he will attempt to bring him to himself. Of course this cannot mean that Christianity is, as the modernists hold, simply the explication of the religious needs of human nature. Rather, it is because God in his grace, and because of his will to save all human beings universally, has already long before *offered* the reality of Christianity in its truest and deepest essence to the individual, and because it is perfectly possible, and even probable, that the individual has already freely accepted this reality without consciously adverting to it.

These, then, are the factors which will influence the Christian of today and tomorrow in his view and experience of the church. He will think of it not as making itself felt only infrequently and with difficulty, not as one of the numerous "sects" into which humankind is divided, not as one of many elements in the pluralism of society or the pluralism in the intellectual life of humankind. Instead of this, the Christian will think of the church rather as the visible and apprehensible form of that which already has a unifying force at the interior level, as the historical expression of that which is universal to all people and, in a true sense, evident to all (for all that it has been freely instituted by God, for it is precisely God and not any particular finite being which has instituted it!).

The church appears to the Christian as the sheer rendering present in visible form of the nature of the human person as subject to God's designs (for example, human nature as it exists in "historical fact" and to which a supernatural calling has been granted). In short, the church appears to the Christian as the fundamental sacrament of a grace which, precisely because it is offered to all, presses forward to express its sacramental significance in history even where the individual sacrament (of baptism) has not yet been conferred.

But precisely on this view of the church this grace is never simply *identical* with that which constitutes its effective sign. Rather, in virtue of the particular concrete sign which it institutes in the present, and through which it is itself made present (both aspects must be expressed), it assures us that its power extends *everywhere.* We can say in all calmness: through the sign of the particular sacrament as it is conferred the grace of God assures us that its power extends everywhere, even to those areas where the specific sacramental sign has not yet been applied as such in the concrete to those specific individuals in whom we hope that the grace of God will powerfully take effect.

For these individual sacramental signs taken together (and in unison with other factors contributing to the church's makeup) precisely constitute the church, since she is, in fact, the community of those who have been baptized and who celebrate the eucharist. But in virtue of the fact that she is the sacrament of salvation for the world, she is also the promise of grace to it.

It must be remembered that the history of humankind is *one and single,* so that there is an intrinsic unity between everything that it contains from Abel to the last living human being, and each individual has a connection with all the rest, not merely those living at the same time or in the same place as himself, but with all human beings right through the ages.

Now if this is accorded its due significance, then the church is to be thought of as the leaven working through the lump of dough that is the whole of humanity. And its influence is not confined to that particular part of the "dough" where it can actually be seen taking effect and so which has itself been turned into an active element in the process of fermentation. On the contrary, the leaven that is the church is at work everywhere and for all. Its influence is extended to every age and is present precisely in those parts of the flour which, so far as we can see, have not yet been turned into leavened dough.

To the kind of Christian whom we have in mind, therefore, and who belongs to the new image of the church, the church herself will appear as a promise extended to the world outside the church. And this is true not only on the condition that, or to the extent that, this world has already itself come to belong to the church. The promise is not only an assurance that this world will increasingly come to belong to the church, but is the real hope that it will be possible for the world to be redeemed through the church, even in those areas of it where its inclusion in the church has not acquired the status of a palpable fact of history.

97 • The Closure of Revelation*

It is a doctrine of the church, though not in the strict sense a defined one, that revelation "was closed with the death of the (last) apostle(s)" (Denzinger, nos. 2020ff.). What does this proposition mean? It would be false to interpret it as meaning more or less that when the last apostle died there was left a fixed summary of strictly drafted propositions like a legal code with its clearly defined paragraphs, a sort of definitive catechism, which, while itself remaining fixed, was going to be forever expounded, explained, and commented upon. An idea like this would do justice neither to the mode of being proper to intellectual knowledge nor to the fullness of life of divine faith and its content.

When we try to discover the profound reasons for the completeness of revelation, we begin to see how we should approach the interpretation of this proposition. To start with, revelation is not the communication of a definite number of propositions, a numerical sum, to which additions may conceivably be made at will or which can suddenly and arbitrarily be limited, but a historical dialogue between God and human beings in which something *happens,* and in which the communication is related to the continuous "happening" and enterprise of God. This dialogue moves to a quite definite term, in which first the *happening* and *consequently* the communication comes to its never to be surpassed climax and so to its conclusion.

Revelation is a saving happening, and only then and in relation to this a communication of "truths." This continuous happening of saving history has now reached its never to be surpassed climax in Jesus Christ: God himself has definitively given himself to the world. Christianity is not a phase or epoch of a history of world civilizations which could be displaced by another phase, another secular "aeon."

If formerly, before Christ, something took place in history, it was and is invariably conditioned, provisional, something with its own limited range and endurance and thus leading to death and emptiness: one aeon after another. The present always dies in the future. Each age goes by in successive rise and fall, infinitely far from the true eternity which abides beyond; each carries its own death within it from the moment of its birth: civilizations, nations, states, or intellectual, political, economic systems.

Before Christ, even God's enterprise in revealing himself to the world was "open": times and orders of salvation were created and displaced each other, and it was still not apparent how God was going at last to respond to the human answer, usually negative, to his own ini-

---

* *Theological Investigations I,* 48–49.

tiating act, whether the ultimate utterance of his creative Word would be the word of wrath or of love. But "now" the definitive reality is established, one which can no longer become obsolete or be displaced: the indissoluble, irrevocable presence of God in the world as salvation, love, and forgiveness, as communication to the world of the most intimate depths of the divine reality itself and of its trinitarian life: Christ.

Now there is nothing more to come: no new age, no other aeon, no fresh plan of salvation, but only the unveiling of what is already "'here" as God's presence at the end of a human time stretched out to breaking point — the last and eternally the latest, newest day. It is because the definitive reality which resolves history proper is already here that revelation is "closed."

Closed, because open to the concealed presence of divine plenitude in Christ. Nothing new remains to be said, not as though there were not still much to say, but because everything has been said, everything given in the Son of love, in whom God and the world have become one, forever without confusion, but forever undivided. That revelation has been closed is a positive and not a negative statement, a pure amen, a conclusion which includes everything and excludes nothing of the divine plenitude, conclusion as fulfilled presence of an all-embracing plenitude.

98 • Scripture as the Book of the Church*

We regard scripture as the church's book, the book in which the church of the beginning always remains tangible as a norm for us in the concrete. Indeed it is norm which is already distinguished from those things which are found in the original church but which cannot have a normative character for our faith and for the life of the later church. If the church in every age remains bound to its origins in its faith and in its life; if the church as the community of faith in the crucified and risen Jesus is itself to be in its faith and in its life the eschatological and irreversible sign of God's definitive turning to the world in Jesus Christ, a sign without which Jesus Christ himself would not signify God's irreversible coming into the world and would not be the absolute savior; and if this church of the beginning objectifies itself in scriptural documents at least in fact, and also does so necessarily given the historical

---

Foundations of Christian Faith, 371–75.

and cultural presuppositions in which the church came to be, then in all of this together we have a point of departure for understanding the essence of scripture.

It is also a point of departure from whose perspective we can arrive at an adequate and at the same time a critical understanding of what is really meant by the inspiration of scripture and by a binding canon of scripture. Since scripture is something derivative, it must be understood from the essential nature of the church, which is the eschatological and irreversible permanence of Jesus Christ in history. It is to be understood from this perspective as something normative in the church. (From this perspective the Old Testament can be understood not merely as a collection of documents about the history of Israel which are of interest for the history of religion, but rather can be understood as a part of what is normative for Christian faith.)

Scripture, we are saying, is the objectification of the church of the apostolic age which is normative for us. We have already said in another context that for a variety of reasons we may not understand the duration of this apostolic age in too limited a way. Hence we may not consider it in too primitive a fashion as ending with the death of the "twelve" as the "apostles" and with the death of Paul without getting into superfluous theological difficulties. We cannot of course simply deduce the exact temporal duration of the apostolic age from theological principles. But there are no special objective difficulties in saying that, according to the self-understanding of the ancient church, the age ended with the writing of the final books of the New Testament, and hence around the first decades of the second century.

This obviously involves a bit of a circle: the apostolic church is supposed to be normative, and hence the apostolic age is the criterion for what can be valid as scripture. And, conversely, we are defining what can be valid as the apostolic age from the duration of the history of the canon. But by the very nature of the case this circle belongs to the essence of a historical reality which itself determines the scope of its "beginning" to some extent. Consequently, from the mass of things which are found in this initial period it knows essentially what should have a normative character for it in the future, but it does not know this with a clarity which can any longer be made completely rational.

Given these presuppositions which we have done no more than indicate, we can say then: the church of the apostolic age objectifies itself in scripture. Therefore, this scripture has the character and the characteristics which belong to this church in its relationship to future ages of the church. What this means more precisely will follow as we now try in the coming sections to say something about the canon and the formation of the canon, and about the inspiration and the inerrancy of scripture. We shall do this more from the perspective of the traditional data of the church's official doctrine and the theology of the schools.

It is not possible here to trace the history of our knowledge of the scope of the canon. That is a task for the introductory course in the biblical sciences which we cannot assume here. The difficulty in this undertaking for the dogmatic and systematic theologian was just indicated: the canonicity and the inspiration of the individual parts of what is in fact the New and the Old Testament should not be constituted by being recognized by the church, a notion which the First Vatican Council rejected (cf. Denzinger, no. 3006); but the scope of the canon, and hence the inspired character of the individual books in the strict and theological sense, is only known to us in fact through the teaching of the church.

But as we can see from the history of the canon, this teaching of the church cannot be grounded by saying that by means of an oral tradition which goes back to the explicit testimony of the first recipients of revelation (for example, the apostles until the death of the last apostle) the church has acquired through explicit testimony a knowledge of what is inspired and what is not inspired in the scriptural deposit of the apostolic age, and consequently has acquired a knowledge of what belongs in the canon of holy scripture. We shall indeed have to agree with the First Vatican Council that inspiration and canonicity cannot be constituted by means of a recognition of definite books on the part of the later church, by means of a recognition which comes to these books from outside, as it were, and which dictates to them from outside a higher value than they have by themselves.

But if we understand the origin of these writings themselves as a moment within the formation of the original church as something which is normative for future ages, as a moment in the process in which the essence of the church in the theological sense comes to be, as a moment in the constitution of this essence which can certainly have a *temporal* duration, then to derive the essence of scripture from the essence of the church does not fall under the censure of the First Vatican Council. During the apostolic age the real theological essence of the church is constituted in a historical process in which the church comes to the fullness of this essence and to the possession of this essence in faith. This self-constitution of the essence of the church until it reaches its full historical existence (and it is not until then that it can fully be the norm for the future church) implies written objectifications.

Therefore this process is *also,* but not exclusively, the process of the formation of the canon: the church objectifies its faith and its life in written documents, and it recognizes these objectifications as so pure and so successful that they are able to hand on the apostolic church as a norm for future ages. From this perspective there is no insuperable difficulty with the fact that the formation of these writings and the knowledge that they are representative as objectifications of the apostolic church do not simply coincide in time, and that the formation of the canon was not finished until the postapostolic age. In this understanding the canonicity of scripture is established by God insofar as he constitutes the church through the cross and the resurrection as an irreversible event of salvation, and the pure objectifications of its beginning are constitutive for this church.

From this perspective, or so it seems to us, we can also clarify what is called "inspiration" in the church's doctrine on scripture. In the documents of the church it is said again and again that God is the *auctor* (author) of the Old and New Testaments as scripture. The school theology which is at work in the encyclicals of Leo XIII and up to those of Pius XII tried time and again to clarify by means of psychological theories how God himself is the *literary* author or the writer of holy scripture. And it tried to formulate and to clarify the doctrine of inspiration in such a way that it becomes clear that God is the literary author of scripture.

This, however, did not deny (and the Second Vatican Council affirmed it explicitly) that this understanding of God's authorship and of inspiration may not reduce the human authors of these writings merely to God's secretaries, but rather it grants them the character of a genuine literary authorship of their own.

This interpretation of the inspired nature of scripture which we have done no more than sketch can of course be understood in such a way that even today one does not necessarily have to accuse it of being mythological. In any case it cannot be denied in the Catholic church that God is the author of the Old and New Testaments. But he does not therefore have to be understood as the literary author of these writings. He can be understood in a variety of other ways as the author of scripture, and indeed in such a way that in union with grace and the light of faith scripture can truly be called the word of God. This is true especially because, even if a word *about* God is caused by God, it would not by this very fact be a *word of God* in which God offers himself. It would not be such a *word of God* if this word did not take place as an objectification of God's self-expression which is effected by God and is borne by grace, and which comes to us without being reduced to our level because the process of hearing it is borne by God's Spirit.

If the church was founded by God himself through his Spirit and in Jesus Christ, if the *original* church as the norm for the future church is the object of God's activity in a qualitatively unique way which is different from his preservation of the church in the course of history, and if scripture is a constitutive element of this original church as the

406 THE CONTENT OF FAITH

norm for future ages, then this already means quite adequately, and in both a positive and an exclusive sense, that God is the author of scripture and that he inspired it.

Nor at *this* point can some special psychological theory of inspiration be appealed to for help. Rather, we can simply take cognizance of the actual origins of scripture which follow for the impartial observer from the very different characteristics of the individual books of scripture. The human authors of holy scripture work exactly like other human authors nor do they have to know anything about their being inspired in reflective knowledge. If God wills the original church as an indefectible sign of salvation for all ages and wills it with an absolute formally predefining and eschatological will within salvation history, and hence if he wills with this quite definite will everything which is constitutive for this church and this includes in certain circumstances scripture in a preeminent way, then he is the inspirer and the author of scripture, although the inspiration of scripture is "only" a moment within God's primordial authorship of the church.

99 • Truth and the Development of Dogma*

In the first place it is obvious that a revealed truth remains what it is, remains precisely "true," that is, it corresponds to reality and is always binding. What the church has once taken possession of as a portion of the revelation which has fallen to her share, as the object of her unconditional faith, is from then on her permanently valid possession.

No doctrinal development could be merely the reflection of a general history of humanity, a history of civilizations containing nothing but the objectification of the everchanging sentiments, opinions, and attitudes of a continual succession of historical epochs. Such a historical relativism is simply false, metaphysically and still more theologically.

Yet all human statements, even those in which faith expresses God's saving truths, are finite. By this we mean that they never declare the *whole* of a reality. In the last resort every reality, even the most limited, is connected with and related to every other reality. The most wretched little physical process isolated in a carefully contrived experiment can only be described adequately if the investigator possesses the one comprehensive and exhaustive formula for the whole cosmos. But he does

---

* *Theological Investigations I*, 43–45.

not possess such a formula; he could have it if and only if he could place himself in his own physical reality at a point which lay absolutely outside the cosmos — which is impossible.

This is even more true of spiritual and divine realities. The statements which we make about them, relying on the Word of God which itself became "flesh" in human words, can never express them once and for all in an entirely adequate form. But they are not for this reason false. They are "adequately true" insofar as they state absolutely nothing which is false. Anyone who wants to call them "half false," because they do not state everything about the whole truth of the matter in question, would eventually abolish the distinction between truth and falsehood.

On the other hand, anyone who proposes to regard these propositions of faith, because they are wholly true, as in themselves *adequate* to the matter in question, that is, as exhaustive statements, would be falsely elevating human truth to God's simple and exhaustive knowledge of himself and of all that takes its origin from him. Just because they are true, an infinite qualitative difference separates them, in spite of their finitude, from false propositions, however hard it may (even often) be in individual cases accurately to determine in the concrete where the boundary lies between an inadequate and a false statement.

But because our statements about the infinite divine realities are finite and hence in this sense inadequate — that is, while actually corresponding to reality, yet not simply congruent with it — so every formula in which the faith is expressed can in principle be surpassed while still retaining its truth. That is to say, in principle at least it can be replaced by another which states the same thing and, what is more, states it not only without excluding more extensive, more delicately nuanced prospects but positively opening them up: prospects on to facts, realities, truths, which had not been seen explicitly in the earlier formulation and which make it possible to see the same reality from a new point of view, in a fresh perspective.

Now this evolution within the same truth is not, at any rate not necessarily, the play of empty curiosity; it can have an essential significance for the human being and his salvation. The human mind is not like a photographic plate, which without preference or alteration simply registers anything which falls upon it at a particular isolated moment. Rather, in order simply to understand what he sees or hears, a human being must react, take up a stand, bring the new experience into connection with what he already knows or has been affected by or dealt with, the whole historical sum of his experience. He must find a place for his own reality, his own life and conduct in the order of divine truth, and direct his life accordingly. And this is a matter of faith and love and observance, in worship, in the ordinances and the activity of the church, and in his day-to-day life in the world.

And so he can never abstract from what he is, from his ever new, changing historical reality. For it is not just his unchangeable metaphysical "entity" which he has to insert into the economy of God's message, but his concrete, historical "contingent" reality, his "existence" with all it includes: his talents, his particular, limited and evolving endowments; the spirit of his time, the possibilities of his epoch; his concepts, which, granting all the fixity of metaphysical truth, are none the less historically conditioned; the particular task, always changing and always sharply defined, which is set him by his inescapable situation in the world — and this situation again must never be thought of as just the result of a secular historical development, but is itself the result of Christ's government of his church, as he gradually leads her, sometimes by new ways, through a changing reality to his own single truth.

If a human being does all this — and he must do it, because he always has his eye (metaphysically and theologically) on the absolute, though always from a finite historical viewpoint — no change takes place in the divine reality, nor do the true propositions concerning this reality become false. But there is a change in the perspective in which he sees the reality through these propositions: he expresses this reality differently, he can state something new about it which he had not explicitly noticed before.

The decisive feature of such a change is not "progress" in the sense of acquiring a sort of plus-quantity of knowledge (as though the church were somehow to become "more clever"), but (in principle, at least) the change, the new look, of the same reality and truth, appropriate to just this age of the church: it is change in, not of, identity. By this again is not meant that the change is necessarily an entire abandonment of the earlier view or perspective; this would be a conception of change as we see it in the material and not in the spiritual realm.

The mind of humanity, and even more the church, has a "memory." They change while they preserve, they become new without losing anything of the old. We today have our own philosophy, while we still philosophize with Plato and his abiding truth. And still more we have our theology, which bears the undeniable stamp of our time, while we continue to learn anew from scripture, the fathers, the scholastics. If we fail either to preserve or to change, we should betray the truth, either by falling into error or by failing to make the truth our own in a really existential way.

100 • What Is "Demythologizing?"*

All human knowledge is always bipolar: conceptual and intuitional at the same time. Even the most abstract and most precise metaphysical notions still include their particular intuitional element. Under certain circumstances an intuitional *happening* may belong and be suited to this necessary intuitional element just as much as the static image. The boundary between the image and what is meant by it is not to be found at exactly the same point in all "meant" realities, if only for the simple reason that even something directly representable can be "meant" (for example, the cessation of new births, and the like).

The "proto-historical" (Gn 1–3) and the "eschatological" must of their very nature show the greatest distance for us between their representation or image on the one hand and the intended or meant object on the other hand. Although something can be meant only together with and under cover of a representation (an image, a representable happening), it is possible to mean realities and happenings which cannot be represented (for example, the "depth" of the soul, the *"sub"*-conscious, the "pure" spirit).

The human person can recognize the inadequacy of such notions, in which the representing element is taken "as a makeshift" from some other reality than the one meant by the notion itself, and hence he can criticize and change this element. He does this, not by doing away with this element and obtaining a "pure" concept of the object itself and in itself alone — which is beyond what can be represented — but by modifying his representation and looking at the reality anew. This can be done since the reality though not representable in itself can still be conceived from different points of "view," and thus the person gains a clear understanding of the various points where the individual image and representation is merely an image and representation without applying simply as such to the referred-to object in itself.

When someone undertakes in this sense a critique of the representation-schemata of the religious concepts which are used for a dogma, and does so cautiously and slowly, in the constant endeavor (under the control of the magisterium of the church) of not losing anything of the content of faith in the process, then he does not "demythologize," but does something which theology has always done and must always do. And conversely, if he does *this,* he can easily see that *he* has no cause to demythologize and that such a demythologizing is ultimately nothing else but his own, in itself perfectly justified method

---

* *Theological Investigations II,* trans. Karl-H. Kruger (Baltimore: Helicon Press, 1963), 208–9.

(if properly applied), which has been badly applied in this particular case, because one has — rightly — emptied out the bath water and — unjustifiably — the child with it.

This critique of the schemata of representation always remains unfinished; for we can always conceive something only with the help of *other* "representations." The "critique" is, therefore, of necessity, just as inadequate in relation to the object in itself as the "criticized" proposition. In many cases in theology it will not be possible at all to say where *precisely* the meant object stops and the "mere" image begins.

In such cases the believing Christian and theologian will abide by the usage of the scriptures and tradition in theology and even more so in the proclamation of the faith, because he knows, after all, that he has there an image which has been sanctioned and which allows the matter itself to be seen correctly, even though it is impossible in this case to achieve an adequate reflective separation of the two elements.

There are of course notions whose representative element is of such a basically human and at the same time objectively unavoidable kind, that these notions, once they have been found, cannot really be replaced by any better ones. But in every concept there takes place a "conversion to the phantasm" (*conversio ad phantasmata*), as St. Thomas says. All knowledge about any reality, no matter how supramundane the object and strict and abstract the notion, is knowledge in "likenesses and parables."

101 • The Holy Church*

Because the church must praise *God's grace,* she must also profess herself to be the holy church. She must sing: "You have loved us, O Lord, and redeemed us by your blood; you have made us to be a kingdom and made us priests to God your father" (Rv 1:5–6).

This hymn of praise to the grace of God in the profession made by the holy church, a profession belonging to the innermost core of the Christian credo, must now be clarified in its theological traits, and this from several points of view. This profession made by the holy church is a profession of the *visible* church. It is, of course, a profession of *faith.* Certainly, what is professed is *actually* seen, and acknowledged as seen, by the grace of God and in the light of faith (without thereby

---

* *Theological Investigations III*, 94–97.

questioning the apologetic, faith-testifying function of the holiness of the church as a mark of the true church of Christ).

But this holiness of the church is not by this fact something which is present merely as something absolutely beyond experience, as something merely believed to be present in a completely hidden way in the church and contrary to all history and experience, merely believed to lie under the sole outward impression of the church's hopelessly sinful state and failure, and yet believed by a despairingly paradoxical "nevertheless." This holiness makes the church "a sign lifted up for all peoples" (*signum elevatum in nationes,* Denzinger, no. 1794). One meets her if one looks for her and wants to see her with a humble and open mind; she shines out, she proclaims herself in a real way, one can meet her. God's deed in giving his grace to us is witnessed in her works which are such that we can praise the Father on account of them (Mt 5:16); it is witnessed in its fruits which are love, joy, peace, patience, tenderness, goodness, faith, modesty, continence (Gal 5:22ff.).

This manifested, "proclaimed" holiness of the church is not merely a pure "facticity" which can be observed subsequently here and there and contrary to all expectations. It can be seen to be rather something which is ordained by God in his decrees. It is indeed always an act of the human being's free love and of the free obedience of his faith.

But precisely this act is determined and given gratuitously by God; precisely this act is borne and guaranteed by the greater power of the grace of God, God who of himself no more allows the church as a whole to break out of his love than out of his truth. And this is not because human beings could not do so but because God grants the grace to the church really to do freely what he wants of her; not merely her word and her objective preparations for salvation (preaching and the sacraments), but also her "existential" being is intended to proclaim the final victory of grace, since in Christ on the cross God has the last word in the dialogue between himself and the human race, and this word is the effective word of mercy.

Hence the church *must* in *all* ages proclaim — even though in a sense ashamedly, yet quite clearly — that she is the holy church. She knows what she thus affirms of herself, not merely by her past experience of herself by God's mighty deed which has been promised to her by God's word before she had any — otherwise very problematical — experience, and which goes beyond and anticipates this experience. The proclamation of her own holiness is an eschatological statement of faith and not merely a kind of judgment of history which condescends not to overlook the good which "after all also exists" over and above everything ugly.

Yet precisely in this way, this statement must be a concrete one. If the church were simply to say that she is the holy one and mean by this simply that this has to be said in general — as it were, at random and without indicating anything absolutely definite, but simply because it is not very likely that God's word and grace should nowhere gain a real and final victory — then she would really have proclaimed grace and its holy law merely as a possibility and as a challenge, but not grace as the victorious power and the law as fulfilled by grace.

In this case, she would, after all, be preaching a merely abstract "idealism"; she herself would be an ideal and a postulate but not the God-given fulfillment which has already surpassed everything merely morally demanded, everything which merely ought to be. She would, after all, be merely the law and not the Spirit which is poured out. She herself would be on the side of the law which is the goad of sin; she would be merely on the side of those to be redeemed and not the tangible expression of the grace of redemption.

If this were so, then the more the church would speak about holiness — the clearer and more forcibly she would proclaim the mere demand for holiness — the more she would be the Old Testament synagogue of the law. Yet she is, after all, distinguished from the latter precisely by the fact that she does not proclaim the law as a demand (although she must do this also, since we, her listeners, are always in transition from the servitude of the flesh to the freedom of the Holy Spirit); rather, she proclaims the fulfillment of the law which has been accomplished in us by the grace of God.

Hence she must be able to state her holiness in the concrete. She must have a "cloud of witnesses" whom she can indicate by name. She cannot merely maintain that there is a history of salvation (without it being known exactly where it takes place with real, final success), but she must *really relate* that very eschatological history of salvation which she is herself. The prize of her actual saints belongs to her innermost being and is not merely something which she "also" achieves "on the side," something which has been inspired by a purely human need for hero worship.

The mission to praise the grace of God as something which has come and conquered contains the obligation of the church to call herself the one who is holy throughout the ages, and to make this statement about herself in a concrete way as seen in the prize of the saints given by name. The church must, therefore, begin with Mary, the protomartyr, and the apostles; but she cannot stop there. She must retain the power which was active in the primitive church when she "canonized" our Lady, the protomartyr, and the apostles, otherwise she would simply have been the holy church at one time without being it *still:* she could no longer actually praise the grace of God, which has really been granted to her as something which saves and sanctifies.

102 • The Sinful Church*

There is, however, a further hindrance and danger to faith besides the deep bitterness of human existence and the great variety of philosophies of life in the world. I am referring to the assembly of believers itself — the church. She is indeed the holy church, even in the view of any unprejudiced student of history. She is the sign which, lifted up above all nations, bears her own testimony to her divine origin and life by her inexhaustible fruitfulness for all holiness.

But she is also the sinful church, because we her members are sinners. And this sinfulness of the church does not merely mean the sum total of the, as it were, private faults and failures of her members, including even those who bear her highest and most sacred offices. The sinfulness and inadequacy of the members of the church have their effects also in the actions and conduct which, insofar as they take place within the sphere of human experience, must be designated as the actions and conduct of the church herself. Sinful human nature, insufficiency, finiteness, shortsightedness, a falling short of the demands of the times, lack of understanding for the needs of the times, for her duties and for the trends of the future — all these most human characteristics also belong both to the officeholders and to all the members of the church, and they also take effect by God's permissive will in what the church is and does.

It would be silly self-deceit and clerical pride, group egoism and cult of personality as found in totalitarian systems — which does not become the church as the congregation of Jesus, the meek and humble of heart — if she were to deny all this, or tried to hush it up or to minimize it, or made out that this burden was merely the burden of the church of previous ages which has now been taken from her.

No, the church is the church of poor sinners; she is the church which does not have the courage to regard the future as belonging to God in the same way as she has experienced the past as belonging to God. She is often in the position of one who glorifies her past and

---

* *Theological Investigations V,* 15–18.

looks askance at the present, insofar as she has not created it herself, finding it all too easy to condemn it. She is often the one who, in questions of science, does not only proceed slowly and carefully — intent on preserving the purity of the faith — but also often waits too long and who, in the nineteenth and twentieth century has sometimes been too quick to say no when she could have pronounced a yes earlier than she did — with, of course, the necessary nuances and distinctions.

She has quite often in the past sided more with the powerful and made herself too little the advocate of the poor. Often she has not proclaimed her criticisms of the powerful of this world loudly enough, so that it looked as if she were trying to procure an alibi for herself without really coming into conflict with the great ones of this world. She often places more value on the bureaucratic apparatus of the church than in the enthusiasm of her Spirit; she often loves the calm more than the storm, the old (which has proved itself) more than the new (which is bold and daring).

Often in the past, she has in her officeholders wronged saints, thinkers, those who were painfully looking for an answer, and theologians — all of whom wanted merely to give her their selfless service. Often before, she has warded off public opinion in the church, although according to Pius XII such public opinion is essential to the well-being of the church. Not infrequently she has mistaken the barren mediocrity of an average theology and philosophy for the clarity of a good scholastic tradition. She has often shown herself more in the role of an anathematizing judge to those outside her fold, to the Orthodox and Protestants, than in the form of a loving mother who meets her child halfway — as far as she can possibly go — in all humility and without being controversial. She has frequently failed to recognize the Spirit which is really her own when, as is its way, it has breathed where it would through the alleys of the history of the world and not merely through the sacred halls of the church herself.

Often before, she has let herself be pulled down by heresies and other movements — contrary to her proper nature and the fullness of her truth (although without ever denying that truth) — to the level of the one-sidedness of her opponents. And often in such cases she has represented her teaching, not as the more comprehensive yes to what was the "proper" and latent meaning of the heresy, but rather as what appeared to be a purely dialectic no given to such a heresy.

According to every human estimation she has missed many a golden opportunity in the achievement of her task, or has wanted to seize it when the *kairos* for it was already past. Not infrequently, while being under the impression that she was championing the lofty inexorability of the divine law (which is certainly her sacred duty), she was really acting like a common, nagging governess, trying narrow-mindedly and with too average an understanding of human existence to regulate life by the typical "examination of conscience" still found in [outdated and bourgeois] devotional books.

She has too often asked merely for well-ordered good breeding which never puts a foot wrong, instead of asking for a mind with high ideals, a loving heart and courageous life. To many minds she has not been able to give an authentic enough account of herself for people to see guilt and dark fate existing only outside her. All this is true. All this represents a temptation to faith, a burden which may impose itself on the individual and almost stifle him.

But first of all, are we ourselves not part of this burden which weighs on us and threatens our faith? Are we not ourselves sinners too? Do we not also belong to the tired grey company of those in the church who obscure the light of the gospel by their mediocrity, their cowardice and their egoism? Do we really have the right to cast the first stone at the sinful woman who stands accused before the Lord and is called the church — or are we not ourselves accused in her and with her, and delivered up to mercy for good or ill?

And furthermore, we surely know that reality and truth can be achieved only on earth, in history and in the flesh and not in an empty idealism. Surely we know today more than ever before that the person finds himself only in a hard and clearly demanding community and that any kind of solipsism — every attempt at self-preservation by the precious, self-cultivating individual — is an ideal of the past which in any case was always wrong. Knowing all this, only one way is left open to the contemporary human being: he must bear the burden of the community, seeing it in the true way, the real freedom of the person and of truth. Regarded in this light, the church of sinners may indeed remain a heavy burden to us, but she will no longer be a scandal to us which destroys our courage of belief.

Finally, we seek God in the very flesh and bones of our existence. We must receive the body of the Lord. We want to be baptized into his death and be included in the history of the saints and great souls who loved the church and remained loyal to her. One can achieve all this only if one lives in the church and consequently helps to carry her burden — the burden which is our own. As long as the sacrament of the Spirit and the body of the Lord is celebrated in her, all human insufficiencies are after all passing shadows which may frighten us but cannot kill.

Our love, our obedience, our silence, and our courage, where necessary, profess our belief in the true church and her spirit of love and freedom to the official representatives of the church, as did Paul to Peter. And these are much holier and hence always much more powerful realities in the church than all mediocrity and all the traditionalism which will not believe that our God is the eternal God of all future ages. Our faith can be tempted by the concrete form of the church; it can mature by it and does not need to be killed by it, unless we have already let it die beforehand in our own heart.

103 • The Church and Freedom*

One should go on to prove more exactly why, and above all how, the church is the quasi-sacramental tangible element, and the historically visible factor of the redemptive liberation of human freedom. Insofar as she is, or rather has, God's Spirit, she is or has freedom, and to her alone can we strictly apply the text: Where the Lord's Spirit is, there is freedom. She is the "where" of spiritual freedom. Insofar as she is different from the Spirit living and ruling within her, the church is the historical quasi-sacramental sign of this Spirit, and hence also of freedom, by which the "pneumatic" freedom is signified and made present.

One should now go on to inquire into the way in which the church is the effective sign of this spiritual freedom in her being, her word, her sacramental action, and in her history. First of all, she *proclaims* this freedom in her *word* which is the message of Christ. She does not do this by teaching subsequently *about* freedom which would exist even without this teaching; but, on the contrary, she renders freedom present *by* proclaiming it.

She gives human beings this freedom by effectively obtaining the divine Spirit or freedom for them in the sacraments. Her *life* is a *sign* of this freedom, insofar as she lives the love of God and neighbor in her sanctified members. And love, precisely to the extent in which it forgets itself, relinquishes self-assertion and serves others — for the sake of others it even lets itself be bounded by many an earthly and legal limitation. Love frees the human person from himself. It makes him free for the boundlessness of God and of his eternal life. But even this can unfortunately only be briefly outlined here.

One thing, at any rate, must be firmly borne in mind from what

* *Theological Investigations II*, 97–98.

has been said: the reality and the notion of freedom are not merely something which belongs to the human person's natural being, which the church, as the guardian even of the natural order, would then in addition defend and regulate in its ordered exercise and in the different fields in which such freedom is lawful. Freedom is rather a proper theological notion which expresses a reality belonging strictly to the order of grace, and much more than this psychological freedom of choice and freedom as a right of the person. Freedom is a theological notion expressing a reality which in the strictest sense of identity is itself the gift of salvation, rather than being merely a presupposition for salvation. For the real, true, and ultimate freedom, which must be gifted to our freedom to free it from guilt, law, and death, is the sacred Spirit of God itself and of his Christ. Hence the church is the indispensable, existential place of this freedom, insofar as and because this Spirit can be had only in the church, since it is her inner reality and she its external sign.

104 • The Priest*

The priest is the proclaimer of the word of God, officially commissioned and appointed as such by the church as a whole in such a way that this word is entrusted to him in the supreme degree of sacramental intensity inherent in it. His work as proclaimer of the word in this sense is essentially directed toward the community (which is at least potentially in existence).

To express the matter quite simply, he is the one sent by the church to proclaim the gospel in her name. He is this in the supreme mode in which this word can be realized, namely, that of the anamnesis of the death and resurrection of Christ which is achieved in the celebration of the eucharist.

In defining the concept of the priesthood in these terms we are not seeking to set it apart from the episcopal office. The very fact that medieval theology denied that episcopal consecration had a distinct sacramental character in itself shows that it is not altogether easy to separate the two entities from each other, even though since the Second Vatican Council the position of the medieval theologians can no longer be maintained.

---

* *Theological Investigations XII*, trans. David Bourke (New York: Seabury Press, 1974), 36–38.

On the basis of this definition of the concept it becomes clear that the priest is not simply a "cult official," and that this task of bearing witness to the word of God as exhibitive and effective of salvation is one that lays claims upon his whole existence (viewing this from the theological standpoint), regardless of the extent to which it may also determine his calling in secular society or how far it may or may not supply his economic needs. Since the essence of his priesthood consists in proclaiming the word of God, this imparts to it from the outset a *missionary* character. It orients him from the outset toward a community, regardless of whether he can assume this as already in some sense in existence, or whether he has to create it from the beginning, and regardless too of what the precise sociological constitution of this community may be.

What we have said does not rule out either the possibility or the fact of there being quite different ways in which the "ministry of the word" may be realized, these too being "official" ways and capable of being sacramentally imparted to an individual as a commission from the church.

In this connection the *concrete form* which a priestly commission of this kind may assume in the social structure of the church and in secular society may *vary very greatly,* and many of the functions which are actually exercised by priests can in practice also be conceived of as special and nonpriestly official functions in the church without the theological essence of the priesthood itself being affected by this.

The way in which the word is proclaimed, the concrete form of the community to which the priest is attached, the precise manner in which the various official functions, whether actual or possible, are coordinated in the church, and the status of the priest in secular society — all these are factors which can very greatly. But we should not identify all these from the outset with that which constitutes the real theological essence of the priesthood. Not only are all these factors subject to change as a matter of empirical fact, but the church herself ought actively to take the initiative in imparting ever new forms to them.

Up to the present there has been a failure to realize sufficiently the extent to which official functions in the church in general and the priesthood in particular are capable of being changed in this way, both interiorly and exteriorly. Often the indelible character of the priesthood has been appealed to by those opposed to ideas of change of this sort. Contemporary exegesis, the history of dogma and of the church, the sociology of the church, and the needs of the church in the present day all compel us to a radical reappraisal of the mutable and immutable factors in the Catholic priesthood.

If this reappraisal is carried through boldly enough, two points will become clear: first, there is indeed an abiding element in priestly office such as justifies an individual in the concrete circumstances of his life, as a man of today, in entering upon it boldly and confidently; second, from the standpoint of dogmatic theology almost unlimited scope is available to the church in subdividing and giving concrete form to her official institutions in those ways which most effectively correspond to her own mission and the contemporary situation.

105 • Ministry of the Word*

What is a priest? The names applied to the priesthood by the New Testament are concerned mainly with its external structure. The "apostle" is the envoy, "bishop" means supervisor, "presbyter" elder. It is remarkable that scripture characterizes the content of the priestly office only in this one respect: as ministry of the word (Acts 6:4). Even where the administration of baptism is particularly named as the commission given to the apostles, it appears as the means to becoming "disciples" of the new teaching of Christ (Mt 28:19). And St. Paul puts his mission of proclaiming the good news before the command to baptize (1 Cor 1:17). Moreover, baptism itself takes place "in the word of truth" (Eph 5:26), in calling upon the "name" of Christ (Acts 2:38ff.), in the "name" of the blessed Trinity (Mt 28:19). May we not then describe the priest as the man to whom the word has been entrusted? Is he not quite simply the minister of the word? But of course we must state more clearly what word is here in question.

The word which is entrusted to the priest as gift and mission is the *efficacious* word of *God* himself.

It is the word of *God*. The priest is not speaking of himself. His way does not lead human beings, their world and the experience of this world in which the person encounters himself, into the light of the person's consciousness of himself. His word does not redeem, in the sense indicated above, the things of the *world* from their gloomy and blind darkness by orienting them toward human beings. The word of the priest is the word of God. It is spoken by God in the infinite condescension of his self-revelation, and brings the inner and most intimate light of God into the person's darkness. It enlightens the one who comes into the world and admits God himself into the individual through the faith which it awakens.

---

* *Theological Investigations III*, 302–7.

The word of God is the eternal Logos of God who was made flesh, and therefore could also and in fact did become the word of man. All the words of God previously spoken are only the advance echoes of this word of God in the world. So much therefore is the word possessed of divine nobility, that we can call the Son, the eternal self-comprehension of the Father, nothing else but the *Word.* It was precisely this person who is the *Word,* not another person of the most holy Trinity, who became in the flesh the word of God directed to us.

If God wills to make himself known to the world in that which he is in his most proper, most free self, beyond the realm of his creative power, he can do this in only two ways: either he seizes us and the world immediately into the dazzling brilliance of his divine light, by bestowing upon his creatures the direct vision of God, or he comes in word. He cannot come to us in any way other than in the word, without already taking us away from the world to himself. For he wants to give himself to us precisely as that which simply as the creator of realities outside himself he cannot reveal.

That is possible only because there is present something in the world, one thing alone, which belongs to God's own reality: the word, which sets the creature free from its muteness by pointing beyond the whole created order. In it alone lives in a conscious way that transcendence which both negates and liberates. It alone is capable of making God present as the God of mysteries to the person who does not yet see him, in such a way that this presence not only *is* in us by grace, but is *there* for us to perceive. Thus the word, as the primordial sacrament of transcendence, is capable of becoming the primordial sacrament of the conscious presence in the world of the God who is superior to the world.

This word has been spoken by God. He has come in grace and in the word. Both belong together: without grace, without the communication of God himself to the creature, the word would be empty: without the word, grace would not be *present* to us as spiritual and free persons in a conscious way. The word is the bodiliness of his grace. This does not apply only, and in the perspective of our present life not primarily, to the sacramental word in the strictest theological sense. It already applies to the word of faith in general. This word is one of the constitutive elements of the presence of God in the world, which is not yet transfigured, and therefore dwells as yet in faith and not in vision. This word is necessary, if God is to mean more to us than the ultimate ground of extradivine reality, if God is to be for us the God of grace who communicates to us his own intradivine glory.

This word, which makes God present in the world as God, and not merely as ultimate cause of the world, is a free word. It is a free act of love. Therefore it cannot be discovered at all times and in all places in the world. It cannot be gained from the world. It is an event. It must be spoken: through Christ and through those whom he sends.

For the presence-to-us of the reality of the divine self-revelation as expressed in this word always remains dependent upon this word being spoken and repeated. If it cannot be spoken by Christ himself until the end of time, then it must be carried on by others. The others cannot take hold of this word by their own power, in the way in which one "takes up" a theory which one has once heard and propagates on one's own account and at one's own risk.

If it were so, how could they know that it has remained the word of God and not been transformed into a human theory, which suffocates the original divine word under a chaotic mass of human interpretation? How could one prevent the message, which is an event in history, from becoming mere theology about it? The word of God must "run on," but it must be borne by those who are sent. We call the messenger and the herald of the word of God the priest.

Therefore, what he says is a proclamation, a *kerygma,* not primarily nor ultimately a doctrine. He is handing on a message. His word, insofar as it is his word, is a signpost pointing to the word spoken by another. He must be submerged and unseen behind the message he delivers. As priest he is not primarily a theologian, but a preacher. And because there is preaching, there is theology, not vice versa. For the same reason it is the preaching church with her demand for faith which is the norm of theology. It is not the "science" of theology which is the norm of a "popularizing" (*haute vulgarisation*) which could be called preaching.

The word whose proclamation Christ has entrusted to the priest is an *efficacious* word. It produces an effect. This is not primarily because it influences the salvation of him who hears and believes it. That comes in the second place. No, this word is efficacious because it is not merely discourse about something that would remain equally real and effective if it were not talked about. It can be said of the weather and of the moon that they would exist in any case even if poets did not speak of them and meteorologists did not publish weather reports (although even this is not entirely true). Here the case is quite different.

For the salvation of God is love. But all love achieves its own fulfillment only if it is accepted and answered. It can be answered only in freedom. And freedom exists only where there is consciousness of spirit and wakefulness of heart. Because this is so, God's grace itself only reaches its own fulfillment when it is spoken. Then it is really *present.* It is present in virtue of being proclaimed. The word first translates the love of God into the human sphere of existence *as* love, to which human beings can respond. The word is consequently the efficacy of love. It is an efficacious word.

The efficacy of the word of God can naturally have very different grades and degrees. This depends on what kind of word of God is in question, how and by whom it is spoken. But wherever it is really a case of the word of God *itself* as a delivered message, there we are in the presence of the efficacious word: wherever, that is to say, it is not merely theology in an exclusively human sense which is practiced, as a merely human reflection *about* the word of God. (We leave out of account for the moment the question whether theology does not cease to be theology, if it no longer speaks the word of God itself, aided by supernatural powers of grace and of the light of faith.)

But the effective power of the divine word itself, which allowed God in expressing himself to "pitch his tent" among us (Jn 1:14), is different. *He* has "told us all" that he has received from the Father, namely, himself with Godhead and manhood, flesh and blood, with his life and death, with his short span of time on earth and the eternity which he acquired. But *we* have to speak him in many different ways. We cannot with all our words say him completely, although *he* has confided to us a multitude of words. Of his one glory we can say sometimes more, sometimes less. We have to speak him into the undelimited dimensions of human existence, into all the heights and depths of our life. The one white light from him must be refracted in all the prisms of the world.

There are many efficacious words spoken at the command of Christ. These words are of varying efficacy in themselves and in the persons who hear them. When is the most concentrated, the most effective word spoken? When is everything said at once, so that nothing more has to be said because with this word everything is really *there?* Which is *the* word of the priest, of which all others are mere explanations and variations?

It is the word which the priest speaks when, quietly, completely absorbed into the person of the incarnate Word of the Father, he says: "This is my body...this is the chalice of my blood...." Here only the word of God is spoken. Here is pronounced the *efficacious* word. Words can be spoken about higher realities, about the eternal mystery of the most blessed Trinity. But these words themselves are only there "for us," meaningful and of existential import, because the Son of the Father knows no other divine glory than that into which he has brought his and our human existence; because he has become man; because he has a body which was delivered up; and because he has taken on our blood which he shed for us. The greatest mysteries thus only exist for us because the mystery of the humanity and death of the Lord exists.

The most effective way of speaking about these mysteries, too, is by speaking effectively about the body and blood of the Lord. But it is the word of consecration that speaks of this. It speaks in such a way, that what was spoken of is now present. Everything is then present: heaven and earth, Godhead and humanity, body and blood, soul and spirit, life and death, church and individual, past and eternal future; everything is gathered together into this word. And everything that is evoked in this word really takes place: "mystery of faith," "sacred banquet," "communion" (*mysterium fidei, sacrum convivium, communio*). In it God already becomes in reality, even if only under the veil of faith, all in all. Here there is not a discourse "about" death and life. Death and life are proclaimed until he comes, and in coming bring us what is already here and already celebrated in mystery: the handing over of the Son and with him of the world to the Father.

This efficacious word has been entrusted to the priest. To him has been given *the* word of God. That makes him a priest. For that reason it can be said that the priest is he to whom has been entrusted the word. Every other word that he speaks, that he reflects upon, that he theologizes over, that he proclaims, for which he demands faith, for which he is prepared to pour out his blood — every other word is only explanation and echo of this one word.

In it the priest, his person wholly absorbed into Christ, says only that which Christ has said. And in it Christ has said only one thing: himself as our gift. Though the priest may make known mysteries as distant as the stars, in the depths of the divine being — he can do this because he can show under the forms of this earth him who came to us from those eternal distances as the Son of the Father and brought with him everything that the Father gives him from all eternity and ever continues to give; and he is present under the forms of this earth because over these humble signs there remains constantly poised the word: "This is my body...."

If the priest preaches Jesus, his life and death, then what he says is not mere talk, because by his word he is present among us who lived this life and died this death for our salvation. If he preaches sin, judgment and damnation, he can only do this because he lifts the chalice of the blood which was shed for our sins, and because he preaches the death which was the judgment on our sins and our salvation. If he speaks of the earth, then he cannot forget that he lifts up the fruit of our poor fields and vineyards as a sacrament into the eternity of heaven. If he speaks of the human person, of his dignity and his depth, he alone can tell the real truth about him — *Ecce homo!* — and truly show the flesh of sin, which is laid on the altars of God in sacrifice.

It is with true consolation that we are able to maintain: the priest is he to whom the efficacious word of God has been entrusted. One might also say: the priest is he to whom the primordial word of God in the world is entrusted, in such a way that he can speak this word in its absolute concentrated power.

106 • Women and the Priesthood*

On 15 October 1976 the Sacred Congregation for the Doctrine of the Faith published with the approval of Pope Paul VI a "Declaration on the Question of the Admission of Women to the Ministerial Priesthood." In what follows we shall put forward some theological reflections on this declaration. These — if only because of the limits of space on the one hand and the vast range of the theme on the other — will be restricted to the properly theological aspect of the question involved and in fact to the theological aspect of *this* declaration, not to all the theological problems raised by the question of the possibility or nonpossibility of the ordination of women as such. Thus we limit our reflections to the strictly theological aspect — that is, to the question as to whether it is certain that Christian revelation in its unchangeable substance excludes women from the priestly ministry in the Catholic church.

If a theologian seeking a strictly theological statement of the question does not approach the basic content of the declaration from the outset with an unambiguously preconceived opinion or with strong but understandable feeling, if he is ready to respect in principle the teaching authority of the Congregation for the Doctrine of the Faith, he will first of all raise the question of the theological qualification of the declaration.

The answer must be given straightforwardly and without prejudice that it is an authentic declaration of the Roman authorities on faith. Such a declaration obviously carries a certain weight merely in virtue of the formal authority of the Roman magisterium, independently of the arguments put forward by that authority; it cannot be judged by a theologian simply as a statement by some other theologian, the importance of which would be no more than the importance of the arguments put forward. Nevertheless, despite papal approval, the declaration is not a definitive decision; it is in principle reformable and it can (that is not to say a priori that it must) be erroneous.

If the declaration appeals to an uninterrupted tradition, this appeal is not necessarily and justifiably an appeal to an absolutely and definitively binding tradition, an appeal to a tradition which simply presents

---

* *Concern for the Church: Theological Investigations XX*, trans. Edward Quinn (New York: Crossroad Publishing Company, 1981), 35–47.

and transmits a "divine" revelation in the strict sense, since there is obviously a purely human tradition in the church which offers no guarantee of truth even if it has long been undisputed and taken for granted.

With this declaration, which has an authentic but not defining character, the fundamental question is whether the appeal is to a "divine" or a merely human tradition. The decision itself of course seems to imply the former, but does not make this absolutely clear, particularly since it is admitted that hitherto the undisputed practice did not call for any more precise and closer reflection: that is, there has been scarcely any reflection on the precise nature of this tradition in actual practice.

We are, then, dealing here with an authentic but in principle reformable declaration from which error is not certainly a priori excluded and not with a simple reference to an absolutely certain doctrine of faith which is clearly and irreformably binding for other reasons. What should be the attitude of the theologian and believer to such an authentic but in principle reformable declaration of the Roman magisterium is perhaps expressed most clearly in the letter of the German bishops on 22 September 1967 to all those charged by the church with the proclamation of the faith, which need not be quoted at length here. This instruction speaks unashamedly of the fact that "errors can occur and have occurred in the exercise of the church's teaching authority," that the church has always been aware of this possibility, says so in its theology, and has worked out rules for dealing with the situation.

The situation of the theologian with regard to the theological qualification of the Roman declaration in question is not a simple one. He must bring to such a decree the respect it deserves; nevertheless, he has not only the right but also the duty of examining it critically and, under certain circumstances, of contradicting it. The theologian respects this decree by attempting to appreciate as impartially as possible the reasons it puts forward, by respecting as a matter of course the consequent practice of the church as binding for him (at least for the present), by seeing as reinforced by the decree the conclusion that the general awareness of the church in regard to the legitimate opportunities of women in the church as a whole has not yet reached the point at which we could speak of a general change of awareness.

The theologian, however, has also the right and duty of critically examining this Roman declaration, even to the point of regarding it as objectively erroneous in its basic thesis. In the nineteenth and twentieth centuries (to say nothing at all about earlier times) there is a whole series of declarations of the Roman authorities on faith which have meanwhile been shown to be erroneous or at least largely obsolete. Such progress in knowledge is absolutely necessary for the effectiveness of the church's proclamation and simply cannot be conceived in practice without this sort of critical cooperation on the part of the theologians. It might indeed be said that such processes of revision have frequently taken too slow a course during the past hundred and fifty years, to the detriment of the church, because theologians exercised their indispensable function too nervously and under the threat of the church's disciplinary measures. With the increasingly rapid development and change of awareness in secular society today, these processes of revision can sometimes become more urgent and require more than formerly the honest and sincere work of theologians, even if this is wearisome and can at first expect little gratitude or recognition on the part of the Roman magisterium.

The essential argument of the declaration takes the line that the practice of Jesus and the apostles, which makes no suggestion of the ordination of women to the priesthood, cannot be explained in the light of the sociological and cultural situation at the time and therefore assumes an intention on the part of Jesus which is not historically and sociologically conditioned: that is, it holds for all times and must be respected faithfully by the church at all times. This argument is clarified by a reference to the fact that Jesus (and, up to a point, also Paul) in his sociological and religious appraisal of women took up a position completely opposed to the depreciation of women at the time and thus could have spoken out against the exclusion of women from positions of leadership in a secular or religious community, if he too had regarded this exclusion as caused merely by the sociological situation at the time. What must be said about these arguments?

Before reaching the crucial point of our own opinion after a proper critique of this argumentation, here are some brief preliminary observations. In the entire course of the argumentation it is never made sufficiently clear on whom the burden of proof really lies in the whole controversy. If the declaration says, for example, that the opposite thesis is not and cannot be proved, it shifts the real burden of proof to its opponents. But is this really justified as long as the basic thesis of the declaration has not been established as certain or (in other words) when at least the possibility must be envisaged of explaining the practice of Jesus and the apostles simply by the sociological and cultural conditions of their time, particularly since the declaration admits that some of Paul's ordinances on the behavior of women are influenced by "the customs of the period" and therefore "no longer have a normative value"?

The argumentation of the declaration is defective also in other ways. Thus the transition from the concept of the apostle and the twelve to the concept of the priest (and bishop) in the declaration is too simple to fit in with our present-day knowledge of the origins, structure, and organization of the primitive church. If we appreciate the difficulties created by these discoveries, which cannot be ignored, we may wonder whether it is possible to deduce from Jesus' choice of men for the college of the twelve any definite and unambiguous conclusions with regard to the question of an ordinary, simple leader of the community and presider of the eucharistic celebration in a particular congregation of a later period. The declaration leaves out all the difficult questions about the concrete emergence of the church and its origin from Jesus, although they are of the greatest importance for its theme.

It might also be asked whether, in view of the cultural and sociological situation at the time on the one hand and the "immediate expectation" (generally admitted today as a fact) on the other, it is possible to look at all to Jesus and the apostles for a plan in regard to the structure of the communities which (over and above what might be deduced for the church from the event of salvation in Jesus' death and resurrection) could really be related to later times unambiguously and forever.

Nor does the declaration make use of a clear and comprehensive concept of the priestly ministry. In the fifth and sixth sections especially the proper function of the priest seems to be restricted more or less to the sacramental power of consecration, so that we almost get the impression that the declaration would be prepared to concede to women practically all ecclesiastical functions except this one (and "the official and public proclamation of the message," which hardly seems consistent with Jesus' commission to the women — mentioned in the second section — "to take the first paschal message to the apostles themselves"). But there can be no doubt that such a narrowing down of the concept of "priest" must rouse very serious dogmatic and particularly pastoral misgivings.

We come finally to the crucial point in the argumentation of the Roman declaration. Once more a preliminary observation must be made. A practical rule of action can be culturally and sociologically conditioned and be open to change, and actually change, as a result of a changed cultural and sociological situation, and yet at an earlier stage may not only have existed and been sociologically recognized, but may even have been morally binding. Such a situation and the rules derived from it may have been "objectively" opposed to more general and more fundamental moral principles also recognized and affirmed at the time, but not then seen or only slowly seen clearly as opposed in the consciousness of a society. As a result the more general principle only slowly changed the situation in that society and made it aware of a new and more concrete rule of action, although previously a contrary concrete rule not only existed in fact but was at the time morally permitted or even binding, since it was impossible or only possible by immoral violence to change the sociological situation from which it had emerged.

This fundamental consideration certainly does not need to be supported by examples or substantiated in principle. If someone wants examples, he has only to recall the institution of slavery during the first Christian centuries, polygamy in the Old Testament, the laws of war in the Old Testament, or the church's prohibition of usury until well into the eighteenth century. In all these cases it is decisively important to observe that a concrete rule of action coexisted with more general moral principles, while being really "in the abstract" opposed to the latter, although this basic contradiction could not in practice be perceived in the earlier sociological situation. Hence this particular rule of action could be permitted, with things being thus, and even be required, thus slowing down change in the situation on which it depended.

If we keep in mind these assumptions — obvious enough in themselves — then we can say confidently and with adequately certain historical knowledge that in the cultural and sociological situation at the time Jesus and the early church could not in practice have considered and still less set up any female congregational leaders or presidents of the eucharistic celebration; their procedure could even have been morally required in the light of the existing concrete situation; in their concrete situation they simply did not need to observe and could not have observed a contradiction "as such" and in the abstract between their general appreciation of women (in which they dissociated themselves from the mentality of their time) and their concrete practice with the concrete rules that this implied, any more than Jesus or Paul could have been expected to notice explicitly the contradiction between their fundamental appreciation of human dignity and the acceptance of slavery as it existed at the time and, still less, to attempt expressly to oppose and to abolish this slavery.

The practical existence of a situation causing and explaining all this is not disproved by pointing to the fact that even under these conditions there were marginal phenomena which were really opposed to the cultural and sociological situation as a whole, since such unnoticed and in the last resort unnoticeable contradictions are an essential part of human existence and of the continual change in the course of history. But Judaism in Jesus' time (as is clearly noticeable still in Paul's writings) was based on a male domination so much taken for granted that it is quite impossible to think that Jesus and his apostles (and with them their Hellenistic congregations under the influence of Judaism) could have abolished or even have been permitted to abolish this male preponderance in their congregations, despite the more fundamental and more general recognition of the equal dignity and equal rights of women which they themselves were bringing about in the religious sphere and — up to a point — even within the dimension of secular society.

At the same time the fact should not be overlooked that, if its basic thesis is not assumed as a priori certain, the burden of proof evidently lies with the declaration and not with its opponents. In any case the cultural and sociological situation with regard to the position of women at the time of Jesus was such that there would have been considerable resistance (if nothing more) to the appointment of women as leaders in the congregations. At the same time the question must be considered from the standpoint of leadership in the congregation and not from that of strictly sacramental powers, if we are not a priori to interpret the primitive church quite unhistorically while overlooking the fact that there is no immediate evidence of a special power over the eucharist anywhere in the New Testament. If then in any case there are cultural and sociological reasons for not making a woman leader of the congregation, it ought to be clearly proved that these reasons are not of themselves sufficient to explain the attitude of Jesus and the apostles But the declaration makes no attempt to provide such a proof.

Moreover, if it is assumed that Jesus and the apostles had different and more substantial reasons for their action than the existing cultural and sociological situation, then it should be explained more precisely and in detail in what these other reasons consist; otherwise, their attitude would appear to be based on an arbitrary decision. But in this respect too the declaration is completely silent. The mere fact that Jesus was of the male sex is no answer here, since it is not clear that a person acting with Christ's mandate and in that sense (but not otherwise) "in the person of Christ" (*in persona Christi*) must at the same time represent Christ precisely in his *maleness.*

But if we were to appeal to the "divine order of creation" in order to find and try to develop such reasons, then it would certainly be difficult (as is evident from the mistaken arguments of the fathers of the church and the medieval theologians) to avoid appealing to an anthropology which would again threaten what the declaration recognizes as the equal dignity and equal rights of women.

It is not possible at this point to set out in detail the historical material explaining why Jesus and the apostles in their concrete cultural and sociological milieu could not (without attempting what was impossible at the time) have thought of appointing women to be, properly speaking, leaders of the congregation or to preside at the eucharist, or even why nothing of this kind could have emerged in that situation as a serious possibility; why the assumption of such an outlook on their part would be like expecting them expressly to oppose the institution of slavery at the time or at least to abolish it among Christians, merely because they were convinced of the fundamental equality and dignity of all human beings. For the historical material in general the reader must be referred to the specialist works of reference. For the nonspecialist the material (including additional literature) presented and evaluated by Haye van der Meer in his book *Women Priests in the Catholic Church?* [Fortress Press, 1973] is still adequate.

If in scrutinizing and evaluating this historical material we must differentiate between the Jewish and the Hellenistic milieu (on which the declaration insists), this distinction in the last resort is of little importance for our question, since the structure of a Hellenistic Christian community was considerably influenced by primitive Jewish Christianity and since there was serious discrimination against women also in the Hellenistic milieu; the existence of priestesses in some of the cults of pagan deities (cults which were deeply loathed anyway by Christians under the influence of Judaism) made no difference to this. What otherwise is the explanation of the fact that the fathers of the church (and also the medieval theologians) under the influence of Hellenistic society and philosophy enormously depreciated women — as the declaration itself admits, albeit somewhat tentatively — and that they brought forward largely these (and not other) reasons against the admission of women to the priesthood, if they had other and better reasons based on the gospel? Once again the historical material will not and cannot be set out here.

If however the assumptions stated above and the methodical considerations likewise merely indicated can be recognized, then the conclusion seems inescapable that the attitude of Jesus and his apostles is sufficiently explained by the cultural and sociological milieu in which they acted and had to act as they did, while their behavior did not need to have a normative significance for all times — that is, for the time when this cultural and social milieu had been substantially changed. It does not seem to be proved that the actual behavior of Jesus and the apostles implies a norm of divine revelation in the strict sense of the term. This practice (even if it existed for a long time and without being questioned) can certainly be understood as "human" tradition like other traditions in the church which were once unquestioned, had existed for a long time, and nevertheless became obsolete as a result of a sociological and cultural change.

The theologian is now faced with a declaration of the Roman magisterium, authentic but open to revision and reform, which he must treat with respect while having the right and duty to consider it critically. To some theologians at least, and perhaps to many, such a critical examination seems to show that the arguments of the declaration are not adequate. Hence all that we can say is that the discussion may and must continue on the problem at issue even after this declaration; the discussion is not yet at an end and it cannot consist merely in a defense of the basic thesis and arguments of the declaration. If this is the state of affairs, then the discussion must no longer be centered merely on the dogmatic question in the strict sense: whether in the attitude of Jesus and the apostles there is or is not implied a doctrine of revelation properly so called.

The discussion must and can be extended again to all the aspects and questions which have been more explicitly or freshly involved in the theological discussion of the last decades. These include questions about the sociological emancipation of women in theory and practice; questions about the consequences of women's sociological emancipation in the life of the church (questions which are there anyway); questions about overcoming discrimination against women in the church (a discrimination which is still far from being eliminated, even if we disregard our main theme); questions about the authentic and integral essential image of the priest, which cannot be restricted to his purely sacramental power; questions about present-day requirements for the structure of a Christian congregation and about the function of women in the church as determined by that structure; questions about the concrete methods and measures by which the discrimination against women in church and society, persisting before and after merely theoretical ideals, can be effectively overcome in life and in society and about the different requirements in different cultural groups; questions about ways and means of educating and changing the consciousness of the church as a whole, where the causes of such a change of consciousness are to be found and what are the factors preventing it, how and in what form due consideration can and must be given — in accordance with Paul's teaching — to the "weakness" of this consciousness in many members and parts of the church (a matter which is of great importance also for our main question); questions of principle finally about methods, how in fact the essential problem that occupies us here must be realistically tackled and surmounted (questions which are still far from finding a clear and generally accepted solution in detail, since we really have no clear answer, for example, to the problem of how to distinguish in principle between a "divine" tradition and a generally and long-enduring "human" tradition).

Our main problem ought to be set against the background of all the questions and of the answers to them, if we are to hope for an answer to it in the foreseeable future: an answer on which believers in the church and the magisterium in Rome can be in complete agreement in theory and practice. Despite its argumentation, theology is always, and simply cannot fail to be, historically conditioned and dependent on the prescientific milieu, on cultural and sociological preconceptions, attitudes, and experiences of life, on the ethos of a society and its life-style. These assumptions can sometimes be very variable, but cannot be changed merely by theoretical scientific reflection, but in the last resort only by life and history in freedom, action, and decision.

If in this way the total situation of women in the society and also in the church of the immediate future is everywhere further changed, if defenders and opponents of the declaration work for it, since such a common effort is possible and necessary and since the still persisting discriminations against women in the church are admitted by both sides, then the common effort can bring about that cultural and religious situation in which the problem of the declaration still remaining but at present insoluble in practice in the church can be left to await a solution acceptable to all sides. In other words, when women have acquired practically and institutionally in the church that importance which as such they ought to have, which this declaration also concedes to them in practice but which in fact they do not yet possess, then only are the vital presuppositions present for a solution satisfying to all sides of the main problem which occupied us here. Then we can and must wait patiently to see how the solution turns out.

This of course is not to say that until then a moratorium must be declared in theology. Theology ought even now to continue its reflections, since this effort too can and must help to bring about that mental and religious outlook which is a necessary presupposition of a generally accepted solution of the problem. The opponents of the Roman declaration will of course even now think and hope that a development will lead to a clarification of the church's sense of faith which will prove them right; they will regard such a development as analogous to that which led from Gregory XVI and from Pius IX's Syllabus to the pastoral constitution *Gaudium et Spes* and the Declaration on Religious Freedom at the last council. But, as we said, we can wait for all this with patience and confidence. Nevertheless, too many demands must not be imposed on this patience, for time presses and we cannot wait again for a hundred years for an analogous development without detriment to the church.

The Roman declaration says that in this question the church must remain faithful to Jesus Christ. This is of course true in principle. But what fidelity means in connection with this problem remains an open question. Consequently, the discussion must continue. Cautiously, with mutual respect, critical of bad arguments on both sides, critical of ir-relevant emotionalism expressly or tacitly influencing both sides, but also with that courage for historical change which is part of the fidelity which the church owes to its Lord.

107 • Charisms*

The church throughout her history has always been charismatic. If the official church is also the guardian and guide of the charismatic element, if *she* herself possesses the gift of discernment of spirits, then the charismatic element is not to be looked for solely in what is very rare and extraordinary; that is practically beyond the reach of such guidance and only needs it in a very indirect and general way.

It is not, of course, as if everything to do with God and his Spirit can and must be regulated and realized in the same way. There is certainly a domain which cannot be directly administered by the church, but we cannot simply identify this with the realm of the spiritual gifts and so de-grade the official church into an external, bureaucratic, administrative machine.

In the church there is much more that is charismatic than one might at first think. How many human beings in the church keep alight in the cloister the flame of prayer, adoration, and silence? Is the intensity and magnitude of this phenomenon, even when one includes all its human and mediocre and ossified elements, all the dead wood, something to be taken for granted? Or is it astonishing, a grace and a miracle?

From this point our view broadens out into the history of the charis-matic element in the church and it becomes clearer that this seldom if ever means something that in the normal outlook of a secular historian would require to be given special prominence. It is not necessarily the case either, we hasten to add, that this grace-given charismatic element must necessarily be found only within the bounds of the visible church. The idea of special spiritual gifts, at least when each individual case is viewed separately, does not include that of being an exclusive privilege.

Consequently, if we point out charismatic features in the church and the impression is formed that such things, after all, exist outside the church as well, and even outside Christianity, that is no argument against what has been said. For the Christian knows, confesses, and feels it in no way a threat to the uniqueness and necessity of his church

* *The Dynamic Element in the Church,* trans. W. J. O'Hara (New York: Herder and Herder, 1964), 62–69.

that there can be and is God's grace and the grace of Christ outside the church.

He does not prescribe to what heights that grace can raise a human being without, and before, incorporating him or her into the sacrament of grace, the church. It is not even by any means settled in theology that any instance we observe anywhere in the world of the observance of the natural moral law, even in a single act, is, in fact, only a natural act without the supernatural elevating grace of Christ, even though it is not performed by a Christian from consciously supernatural motives. It is quite possible to hold that as a matter of fact in all or nearly all cases where a genuine spiritually and morally good action is actually accomplished, it is also, in fact, more than merely such an act.

The grace of Christ surrounds human beings more than we think, and is deeper, more hidden and pervasive in its application in the depth of his being than we often imagine. It is quite conceivable that wherever an individual really affirms moral values as absolutely binding, whether expressly or merely in the actual unreflecting accomplishment of his nature, intrinsically oriented as this is beyond and above itself toward the absolute mystery of God, he possesses that attitude of authentic faith (even if only virtually), which together with love, suffices for justification and so makes possible supernatural acts that positively conduce to eternal life.

If this is taken into account, it becomes even clearer that we have no right to assign arbitrary limits to the grace of God outside the church and so make spiritual gifts and favors simply and solely an exclusive privilege of the church alone. But on the other hand this does not mean, either, that we are not permitted to see the charismatic element in the church where it really exists within her, not in the great pages that belong to general world history merely, but in hidden fidelity, unselfish kindness, sincerity of disposition and purity of heart, virile courage that does a duty without fuss; in the uncompromising profession of truth, even when it is invidious; in the inexpressible love of a soul for God; in the unshakable trust of a sinner that God's heart is greater than ours and that he is rich in mercy. All that and very much more of the same kind is by the grace of God what it really is, and what only the believer can correctly appreciate in its full profundity and endless significance, for the unbeliever underestimates it. It is the work of grace and not of the human heart, which of itself alone would be evil, cowardly, and empty.

Now are there not things of that kind everywhere in the church, over and over again? Have we any right to observe morosely that they really ought to be even greater, more splendid and more powerful? At bottom, of course, we often don't want to see and experience such greater things out of genuine love of these holy possibilities of humankind, but because we ourselves would have a more comfortable and agreeable time in life if there were even more of such divine goodness in the world. Isn't it often rather our own egoism we should blame for our being so blind to the splendid things there are, that we act as though it were all a matter of course, or of no importance?

If we had real humility and goodness we would see far more marvels of goodness in the church. But because we are selfish ourselves, we are only ready to see good, good brought about by God, where it suits our advantage, our need for esteem, or our view of the church. But this unrecognized goodness, and even charismatic goodness, is found in the church in rich abundance.

That is not altered by the fact that more is brought into God's barns than is consigned in the pages of newspapers and magazines, histories of civilization and other such human halls of fame. Can it not be charismatic goodness to be a patient nursing sister, serving, praying, and asking nothing else of life? That does not mean it is always so. Nor need one fail to recognize that even genuine virtue is rooted in temperament, social origins, custom and other premoral conditions, just as a beautiful flower grows from mold. But only a blind and malicious mind can no longer see, on account of the imperfection of all human things, or because of the facile discovery that even the most authentic moral excellence has its antecedent nonmoral conditions, that despite all that and in it all, there can be charismatic goodness and love, fidelity and courage.

Persons of that kind, who cannot thankfully admire this goodness effected by the Spirit in the church, and outside it, might inquire whether they themselves accomplish the things they refuse to think remarkable. Consider a mother's life. It is no doubt true that she has a narrow outlook, instinctive care for offspring drives her on; probably she would not have a much better time in this life if she were not so devoted a mother. That and more of the same kind may be true and in many cases is true.

But just as life on the biological level presupposes chemistry, yet is more than chemistry (even though many theorists fail to see this), so it is, proportionately speaking, in these matters. There are good mothers whose virtue is from God above, a gift of the Spirit and of his unselfish love. And there are many such gifts of the Spirit that are the charisms in the church.

The ones mentioned are only meant as isolated examples. It is in these that the life that most truly characterizes the church is accomplished, not in culture, the solution of social questions, ecclesiastical politics, the learned treatises of theologies, but in faith, hope, and love, in the longing for eternity, the patience of the cross, heartfelt joy.

Ultimately the whole church is only there so that such things may exist, so that witness may be borne to their eternal significance, so that there may always be people who really and seriously believe that these gifts here on earth and hereafter in eternity are more important than anything else.

It remains true, of course, that human beings are frequently required to do these apparently small things of eternity among apparently greater temporal matters. And it is true that what has been said must not be made a pretext and easy excuse for narrow-minded mediocrities who lack this and that quality but flatter themselves that they are citizens of heaven because they are simply second-class citizens and philistines on this earth, and who want to award the "common man" a halo that he doesn't deserve in a matter where a more aristocratic awareness of difference of level and achievement would be more authentically human.

Of course, if it were a question of writing a history of the charismatic element in the church, one would have to speak more explicitly than has so far been done here about the great spiritual gifts, about the great saints in whose creative example quite new possibilities of Christian life can be seen; about the great figures of church history who walked like true guides and shepherds before the people of God on its journey through this world of time and led it into new historical epochs, often without realizing themselves what they were doing, like Gregory the Great who himself was expecting the end of the world and yet became the father of the Middle Ages in the West.

Of the great thinkers and writers, too, who took up again the ancient Christian view of life and succeeded in so expressing it that a new age could make that Christianity its own. And the great artists who did not speak about the religion in which God became a man of this earth, but gave it visible shape, representing it in ever new forms and so actually and concretely represented something which, without such corporeal embodiment, only too easily asphyxiates in the mere depths of conscience or evaporates, as it were, into unreality in the abstractions of the mind. In other words, one would have to speak of all in the church who had a special, unique historical mission of great import for the church and through her for the world. It goes without saying that no detailed account can be given here of all these great charismata.

Now, to add another fundamental observation, these charismata are not only properties of the church's essence which only the eye of faith perceives (all the charismata are that), but they are also criteria that convince and lead to faith, by which the church is to be recognized as a work of God. This is not the place to go into the difficult question, one of the most important questions of fundamental theology, how and on what presuppositions such criteria of true belief can be recognized by human reason, which, in faith, has to perform a "reasonable obedience," *rationabile obsequium.*

What is the role and scope of reason and of deliberate reflection expressible in rational terms; what is the function of grace; how do the light of faith and rational grounds of faith mutually support one another in the actual accomplishment of faith? This general problem has a particular application here from the fact that the charismatic element in the church is not only an object of faith but by its plenitude and enduring presence and its perpetually renewed vitality, can be a motive of faith. Here we can only stress this fact.

The First Vatican Council, taking up a thesis of Cardinal Deschamps, emphasizes (Denzinger, no. 1794) that "The Church herself is a great and enduring motive of credibility and an irrefutable testimony to her divine mission by her wonderful growth, eminent holiness and inexhaustible fruitfulness in all good, and by her Catholic unity and unshakable stability." By the nature of the case this implies that the great charismata of the church in her temporal and spatial unity and totality, in which these gifts appear to the gaze of the more prejudiced as a special characteristic of hers, are not only an object of faith but also a motive of faith.

Of course the use of this motive of faith in apologetics is not perfectly easy. The matter cannot, however, be pursued here. We discern the limits of something that was emphasized earlier, that there are gifts of the Spirit even outside the one visible church. What we have said does not, however, mean that the situation of the church is simply the same as that of the Christian and non-Christian world outside the church. The eye of faith and the human mind seeking faith with the support of grace can recognize that the charismata which are found everywhere have, nevertheless, in the church their home and native air and their most intense historical development, because more than any other historical entity she proves herself to be, again and again and ever anew, the church of the great charismata.

108 • Religious Life*

It would be an absolute misunderstanding of the religious state to regard the religious life in itself as merely a means of striving after personal holiness. In the light of the evangelical counsels, the religious life

---

* *The Priesthood*, 116–17; *Theological Investigations VIII*, 159–63.

has an essentially ecclesiological function. It is an essentially apostolic state. There must be the religious life in the church, perhaps in the most diverse forms. That is to say: the state of the realization of the evangelical counsels, as lived in the social visibility of the church, must necessarily exist in the church.

This state has always existed, since the church must be able to point to those who live the evangelical counsels and thus prove before the world that she is really awaiting the coming of the Lord, that it is she who has shifted the focal point of human existence from intramundane experience into grace, into the coming of the Lord. "Come grace, let the world pass away," says the *Didache:* this is something that not only must be lived in the church, but must also belong to what is perceptibly and visibly lived in the church.

The religious state has a witnessing function of living out what is radically Christian for human beings at all times as well as for people of today. Even the most contemplative order in the church has an absolutely apostolic function of witnessing, of confessing the faith, of protesting against a submergence in earthly things, not only by praying, but through its existence and through its way of life.

The evangelical counsels of poverty, chastity, and obedience are the expression and the manifestation of a faith that is reinforced by hope and love as well. In this they are distinguished from "this worldly" goods (those of riches, power and development of the personality), though these too are capable of being integrated into and subsumed under grace (through they do not make grace manifest in any direct sense).

The evangelical counsels also represent an attitude of withdrawal as opposed to an unreserved striving for position in the world, for the world lies prostrate "in the evil" of infralapsarian sinfulness. Now since the evangelical counsels do constitute an expression and a manifestation of a faith that hopes and loves in this way, the epithets "better" and "more blessed" as applied to them in that *objective* sense which accords them a preeminence over the opposite way of life, are altogether appropriate.

The truth of this has always been acknowledged by scripture and tradition prior to any application of them to the merely individual case. In this sense, therefore, they have a relatively greater suitability as a means of exercising love for one who has been called to follow them. Objectively speaking, therefore, the evangelical counsels do have a certain general preeminence over other ways of life. But this preeminence, taken precisely in the sense intended here, does not mean that the actual fact of fulfilling them in practice really and necessarily means or guarantees that a greater love of God is achieved than is, or can be, achieved even apart from these counsels.

It does not mean that for every individual (or even for normal cases) the "means" which is better for that individual constitutes the most perfect realization of the love of God that is possible. It does not mean that one who practices the evangelical counsels is ipso facto "more perfect" than the Christian "in the world."

But it does mean that the evangelical counsels (considered as a renunciation, though admittedly such renunciation can also be present in other ways of life) constitutes an objectification and a manifestation of faith in that grace of God which belongs to the realm beyond this present world. And this objectification and manifestation *precisely as such* are not achieved in any other way of life.

If we really say that the counsels are the "objectification" of faith and love, then this easily gives rise to the misunderstanding that they alone, and not every rational activity of the Christian in this world, can be the concrete realization of faith, that only the renunciation and sacrifice entailed in the counsels are able to constitute faith as lived in the concrete, of being faith "spiritually," instead of realizing that "everything — including our worldly activities — which we do" is able to become this if only we do it in the name of Christ.

We must therefore simply shift by saying that the counsels are the sole mode in which faith achieves its objectification *and manifestation,* though when we say this what we mean is that in the counsels *alone* (in contrast to other forms of renunciation, and especially to that which consists in consciously and explicitly embracing "passion") faith arrives at a state of objectification in which it becomes manifest precisely because all forms of objectification which entail a positive assent to the world also conceal faith (where this is not thought of and practiced as a mere ideological superstructure imposed upon one's ordinary life), since even without faith they continue to be meaningful.

Since they do constitute an objectification of the faith in this way, making it manifest (and thereby bearing witness to it as well), the counsels are, of course, precisely *not* mere empty manifestations of faith which have nothing to contribute to the actual exercise of it, because their nature is such as can only be realized in the act of objectification and manifestation.

On the theory put forward here, therefore, the evangelical counsels are of their nature the historical and sociological manifestation of the faith of the church for the church and for the world. But to proceed from this (this point must straightway be added here) to a denial of the fact that the counsels also have an "ascetical" significance for the individual would be an utter misconception. Admittedly it remains true that this faith also achieves manifestation and objectification in the *freely accepted* inescapable "passion" in the life of every true Christian (not in "passion" as such, but in the "death" which we accept in "obedience" in that "passion" as in the case of Christ himself).

But it is precisely in order to inculcate this attitude of obedience that the counsels are given, to exercise the human person, by anticipation, and to prepare him for death. They are not intended to be anything more than this. And in freely accepting the element of "passion" we are, materially speaking, achieving precisely the same effect as appears in the counsels: the free acceptance of a renunciation which, from the point of view of this world, is irrational.

The statement "the evangelical counsels are the 'better way,'" therefore, is not an assertion that those who practice them have reached a higher stage of perfection. For the sole measure of the degree of perfection which the individual achieves is in all cases the depths of his love for God and his neighbor.

This statement refers rather to the fact that the counsels are "means" (an objectification and a making manifest) of faith and love (a) *relatively speaking* in their reference to the individual called to follow them. Here a contrast is established between his situation under the counsels and the situation which would be his if *he as an individual* were to refuse them; (b) *absolutely speaking* to the extent that they alone, considered as a renunciation and a practicing of the passion of Christ himself, can be said to have the character of an objectification and manifestation of faith and love (not only as preached but as assumed and lived).

Here there is a contrast between the way of life prescribed by the counsels and the other "material" for a Christianity that is lived to the full, which is capable of being integrated into this fullness of Christian life because, as having positive existence in this world, it is the material in which the Christian can express his affirmation to the world. But even when it does this, it cannot make manifest the "transcendence" of grace and of faith.

109 • Religious Life and Change*

It is a truism that religious life is changing. All religious notice it: their numbers are falling, their work load is increasing. They find themselves asking what works they must abandon as their various activities are reorganized to accommodate reduced manpower. This change, which

---

* *Religious Life Today,* 10–14.

all orders are experiencing more or less harshly as a crisis or even as a threat to their own self-consciousness as religious Christians, has to be integrated into the general change taking place in the church as a whole and often in forms which we find less than gratifying, or which horrify us, or which are uncomfortable for us, or which force us into unaccustomed paths.

The changes in religious life are only a part of the change in the church which, viewed as a whole, is necessary. Because the world changes, the church must change with it if it is to remain itself, if, that is, it is to remain the ambassador of the living God, of his gifts and his grace, because otherwise it could no longer be heard and understood. If we really belong to the church and have to share its mission and mandate, it is self-evident that in a world of rapid change, and therefore in a necessarily changing church, things cannot stay the same in religious life. Other and new forms of religious life will perhaps emerge. Orders will have to evolve a new life-style, perhaps more "individualistic" and "antiauthoritarian" and in some sense, seen from without, more secular, more consistent with the life-style of the modern person "come of age."

The fact remains that there will always be people in the church who come together, renouncing marriage, for a common work in the service of their neighbor, out of love for the crucified Jesus and in the hope of eternal life. There will always be people (because there is no other way of doing things) who organize, institutionalize, plan, put into action such a common service, in distributing the various tasks that satisfy a common aim. In other words, as long as there are Christians, there will be religious, even in a changed world, even with a changed style of religious life.

That doesn't mean that we have to dismantle the old orders. It has always been shown in the history of the church that the old orders can take on a new lease of life, even though perhaps in a changed form, side by side with recently founded orders. For example, the French Benedictines of the seventeenth and eighteenth centuries were splendid, flourishing, vital, although it could have been said that the characteristic order of that period was the Society of Jesus. The seventeenth- and eighteenth-century Dominicans enjoyed a splendid new vitality, although they were already a very old order by then.

The idea, then, that new times need new orders does not at all mean that the old orders must necessarily be so rheumatic and unadaptable that they cannot hope to keep up with the times. There must evidently be in these old orders a certain reappraisal in the light of the new requirements and the old tradition, but there is no a priori reason why such a tension should not be worked out fruitfully and successfully. The person who denies a past is not the person most suitable for a future; on the contrary, the person who tries to master the future's new challenge with an undimmed insight into his past will win the greater future.

Religious life will change, even in the "old" orders. That doesn't mean, as far as the individual is concerned, that he must be despondent when he has the impression that his own order is responding to the force of circumstances more slowly than according to his ideas it should. In any community there are bound to be those who step on the gas and those who apply the brake, and they must all possess that love for each other and for their common service in which such tensions between "traditionalists" and "progressives" are sustained. It is also part of a rational, selfless person's maturity to adapt himself, serve, love, and be faithful wherever he finds himself in a situation which he does not always find to his liking, or which he would not have thought up in his own ideas and plans for the future. The same is surely true of family life: there are older and younger people, and different tendencies. If a family is healthy and vital, it can cope with such tensions. If the younger members of a religious institution are intent only on raising the dust and the older members only on lamenting the good old days, both sides show merely that they do not have the proper spirit appropriate to an order: the spirit of selfless love.

That spirit demands that we understand, accept, and tolerate the gifts and particular abilities of others, even though we might not appreciate them at first. When Paul, in 1 Corinthians (chapter 12) and other letters, expressly instructs Christians that there is one Spirit in the church and yet many gifts and functions and members in that one church, it goes without saying that the diversity of gifts necessarily brings with it difficulties in mutual understanding. If I absolutely understood the other person in his own particular personality, I should have his gifts. In reality, however, I do not possess them, or at least not in the same way, and I must learn to coexist with him, to share with him the loving unity of the one community. Such behavior is not, of course, exclusive to the Christian: every rational, selfless, well-intentioned person needs it. If religious can't manage this love-inspired toleration in the tensions and changes of today within a religious community, it's high time to make themselves scarce in the church and in the world.

These new times, with their inevitable change even in religious life, give ample opportunity for mutual responsibility, mutual love, and in my opinion also for what we call, in somewhat emotive religious language, sharing Christ's cross. As Christians we have confessed this cross; daily we celebrate the Lord's death in the eucharist. Now there are certainly situations in human life in which we directly feel the human being's relationship to the mystery of Christ's cross. We should, however, soberly and objectively discover and accept Christ's cross in our everyday lives: where we bear with each other; where we must and should persevere without exactly knowing the outcome; where we take a stand and, as Paul says, "hope against hope"; where our associates perhaps smile at us as old-fashioned and yet cheerfully accept our service. This cross of Christ extends very "anonymously," very implicitly, very unemotionally, in a very everyday fashion, over our lives. If we can find it there, we shall also manage to endure with resignation and even cheerful hope, the change, the insecurity, the aggression suffered by a religious community today.

110 • Pastoral Care of the Laity*

On examination, the realm of free decision reveals that the impossibility of a direct care of souls is so radical that the attempt does not merely fail in practice, but becomes evidently self-contradictory. If salvation is always the fruit of a personal decision and everything outside this is not yet salvation and destiny, but at the most a lot which one merely suffers, then the attempted obtaining of the salvation of another is necessarily the obtaining of something which is not his salvation at all.

The impossibility which appears here stems both from an absence of capacity and from an absence of calling. Every influence brought to bear upon a person from outside founders powerlessly before that ultimate sanctuary wherein that which is meant to be influenced takes place. Indeed, the stronger such influence is, the more is it in danger of negating itself. It intends to be an influence in favor of liberty. The stronger it becomes, the more does liberty disappear.

Yet it becomes efficacious only if the other himself opens the door of his own responsibility, freely corresponds with the "influence," and freely introduces it into himself. Therefore, if the "influence" really enters into the ultimate decision, then it is always something dependent upon the person "influenced" himself, something already transformed by him, therefore *his* own. To exercise an influence of this kind is of course a duty, but this duty is surely ultimately nothing else than the care we take that we "do *our* duty," that "we do what we can"; as for the rest, we say, it is "his" affair and is a matter of indifference to us. So this pastoral care is not precisely care for the soul of the other (the "rest"

---

* *Theological Investigations III*, 266–72.

which is a matter of indifference to us is precisely this soul), but care to fulfill our duty: care concerning ourselves, self-care, not care of souls.

We appear then not only to be incapable of care of souls, but also not to be called to it. For though there might be such a thing as a calling to "failure," there can be no vocation to what is self-contradictory. Further, we do not appear to be called to the care of others' souls for the more profound reason that no one knows the living God in the heart of the other; each one of us is called to manifest him in an utterly unique way in his own being as fashioned by his own decisions, yet as the ideal for this purpose God is known only to each one for himself and then only at the moment of decision. For a decision is always something more than a mere application of universal laws and rules, even though it must be made in accordance with them. This being so, how could one person be called to "care for" the decision, therefore for the "soul," of another?

Is there then no such thing as care of souls? Is the soul of the other completely beyond our anxious care? Do we escape all responsibility for it, because we are not capable of, nor called to, the care of souls? Do the wonderful words about the care of souls fundamentally only mean that a human being must have a care for his own duty, for a duty does not and cannot penetrate to what is inmost in the other?

Indeed, there is a genuine care of souls, an anxiety for the soul of the other which is not merely anxiety for oneself as in duty bound to influence the other. Examining our difficulty will permit us to understand how it is possible.

We have already said that this inner inaccessibility of the human being as freely deciding his own fate does not of its nature exist for God. Consequently, if we are to exercise any care for a person, then the shortest way into his inmost sanctuary will be that which leads through the infinitely distant God; any shorter route would in fact not get us there at all. In addition to the fact already mentioned, that God is the basic ground of every human decision, two things are required to make this possible: the one charged with the care of another's soul must first find the way to God, and then the way from God to the other. This is realized in the love which is poured out in us by the Holy Spirit, whom the Father has given us through Jesus Christ. A look at the effect of such love will make it clear that it does in fact travel this double road and that in doing so it does really go "behind" the decisions of the individual cared for.

The love which proceeds from God makes it possible to comprehend the decisions of the other, in fact it is itself such comprehension. Love "knows" more deeply than knowledge itself. Knowledge always strives to get behind the object known, to "get to the bottom" of it, to resolve it into its causes, its "principles," or into the evident inner necessity of its being. Where there are no such "hidden roots," knowledge comes to a stop faced by a stranger; by itself alone it is incapable of receiving the other completely into the being of the knower, to become one with him.

And this strangeness, this absence of further roots, this bare, uncomprehended fact is essentially what is first and last. The last is always the God who has freely created me at a particular time, and has freely acted with regard to me in such or such a particular way, and who would therefore remain alien and incomprehensible to me were I to meet him face to face merely by way of knowledge. It is only in and through love that this "strange" element becomes understandable, capable of being accepted into me in a way leading to ultimate peace.

In love one can ask no further questions, because love has its own light. In love all questioning is silenced. Is love unjustified in imposing silence upon all questioning? How could it be? But if on the other hand genuine questioning can be brought to silence only by an answer, then love must carry the answer within itself; it must have its own intuition. Love is directed to the beloved precisely in his irreducible uniqueness; it is a giving of itself with its whole being (which is an eternal question) into the beloved You.

Its own absolute character overcomes the absolute relativity which makes the appearance of every You so frighteningly foreign. And just as a decision, in spite of its unique and irreducible character, is quite clear to the one making it without its being reduced to something necessary, so it will be clear also through and in love to him alone who loves the person making that decision, because his being and his questioning now repose in the beloved and have no need of asking questions; in the other everything is quite clear and comprehensible. And so love sees clearly why the beloved God has dealt in this or that way with a particular individual, with the clearness of an intuition born of loving prayer, which can never be converted into any other form in intuition.

And when God acts, in a way which is free and not subject to retrospective explanation and brings it about that a person should make his own decision, then this adoring love understands why the individual decides this way; this is an understanding which would not be possible at all directly from person to person, because our being does not permit of being directly transported into that region in the other where decisions are made.

It is of course true that genuine direct love from person to person has also the intention of embracing the beloved in his whole being, with his incalculable individuality, with his decisions, to "take him as he is." There alone does true love begin. Otherwise one is loving only one's own ideal, and the other person only as object of, or means to, its realization; in other words one is loving only oneself.

To this extent love already "understands" the beloved and his decision in an "evidence of love." It loves the fact that he "is as he is," "it would not have him otherwise." In such love the torment of the question arising from bare, irreducible factuality is resolved. But insofar as this love is directed immediately to the other person, it is, if it is not to become sinful, idolatrous love, bound to an indispensable condition; it is, therefore, almost against its nature which does not want to be bound by any condition or reservation, made relative.

Whenever mistaken or evil decision is possible (and that is possible in the case of every human being on this earth), love cannot love the other quite for better or worse, cannot simply love that "he is just like that," cannot simply accept the other "as he is." In the face of sin there is no evidence of love. The contingent fact of free will, the shaft fatal to mere knowledge, certainly goads love to its noblest deeds. But sin as a contingent fact would be its own death if it were to make the attempt at it. It is true that the intention of immediate love too tends to include in its embrace the "other in his decision." But because it can neither take away this decision from the beloved, nor in any proper sense "take care of it," nor assent to it without reservation, it fails in this ultimate attempt to embrace the other's being in his decision, it sinks back powerless in its attempt to love to the last.

And because it is never given us to know with ultimate certainty what is the *right* decision, whether in our regard or that of the other (no one knows whether he or the other is worthy before God of love or hate), this love which desires to penetrate directly into the inmost sanctuary of the other, in order to understand in its love, must necessarily and in every case fail.

It is obvious that we are only able to cast ourselves lovingly into God and to attune ourselves to the free movements of his actions toward us because he himself transports us into himself, because he himself has given us the power to love him in the ultimate secret of his reality. This we can really love immediately, presupposing the elevation of our love by God, not merely because he has given us the power to love him as the triune God, but — and this is in the present connection the decisive consideration — because his decision, his freedom is always good.

And so in the case of our love for God there is not present that alien reservation which attaches of necessity to every direct love for others. Love for God, for him who acts freely with human beings, can be unconditional. Thus there really shines in it and for it the light of its evidence. We "comprehend" God and his action, and in his action in which he concurs with human action we comprehend also the human action, and through it the person himself in his free and unique character.

Further, love can be a participation in God's care for the salvation of the other. It can be this, because it is a love of the other for God's sake. In general, to love someone "for the sake of someone else" is no love at all. Love, after all, strives to embrace the person itself of the beloved, wants to be transported into the beloved, in order that *he* may be enriched thereby. That it should be "for the sake of someone else" appears to redirect the love away from the "beloved," to reduce him to the function of a means or passageway for love in the proper sense toward a third person, to attribute to him a value only in relation to the third person, and therefore precisely not in his supreme uniqueness, as is the case with true love. This "for the sake of" may mean "as coming from" or "as directed toward" a third person. It is clear right away that love "directed toward" a third person does not sincerely love him whom it traverses on the way to the third person. For true love considers the beloved always as its "end-goal," not as its means of access (though this does not mean that it ought not always to be subordinated to a higher and more determining love). Whoever loves someone only because this love makes possible his love for someone else (by increasing it, by attesting it, by spreading it, and so on), does not love the first person in the sense of a truly genuine, personal love.

If love for a human being for the sake of someone else means to love him with a love coming from someone else, so that the first is the true end-goal of the love and the other only the region, as it were, or the standpoint from which the love proceeds, then it is impossible to understand how one person can be for another something like a "region of love." He, though being another, a stranger, would have to make it possible for the ultimate uniqueness of the beloved to be presented to the love; this uniqueness would have to have in him its reason and ultimate norm, if it is to be in a position to be loved with a love proceeding from him. But this is essentially never the case. Therefore, it is true to say that one does not genuinely love a person, if one loves him for the sake of another human being.

All this is no longer true if the "other" is God. Love for a person for the sake of God does not lead out of the beloved but into him. God is not another "alongside" the human being. He is what is most intimate, the essential kernel of the beloved being; he is within even the inmost, the least relative, the ultimate enclosure of the human person in himself. He sustains it in his unfathomable love and almighty power, to which even the sovereignty of every individual is still subject. From him one can love someone, whose inmost inaccessible center can only be reached from God. Whoever loves such a God, whoever casts his whole being into God, in love and adoration and submission (for if all love is already a humble inclining of oneself, then when directed toward God it becomes adoration and self-abandonment), is by that very fact in the innermost kernel of the loved one. He has penetrated behind that person's ultimate mystery, because he has reached where God is. He can now truly exercise the care of souls, in union with God who alone can care for souls, for he has become one spirit with him; he can now hold in the anxiously attentive hands of love the very salvation of his brother and sister, and not merely carry out a duty which he owes to himself. For he is united with God, who has power over souls.

And because this pastoral care takes place in an act of love for God, it bears all the characteristic marks of that love. That love is adoration, surrender of one's own will to God, confidence. And so the loving will directed to the salvation of the neighbor is an adoring self-surrender, confidence, prayer. It is the care of a person who in an attitude of humility implores the salvation of his brother and sister, but who also knows himself to be bound by love to him with whom everything is possible, a bond which permits a person to reach out into the most intimate secret of another. It is just because the care of souls is thus essentially prayer, that pastoral love, particularly when it softly enters into that abyss where someone is alone with the God of his heart, remains humble and pure and leaves the other alone with the living God in spite of the loving proximity with him thus discovered. And so all apostolate is in its deepest essence prayer. Therefore, even every form of contemplative life can be pastoral; and all pastoral activity, whatever its shape and form, remains prayer of love to the God of all hearts.

Now we can understand why only he who loves God can love his brother and sister, can be a pastor: because a direct love for a human being cannot penetrate efficaciously and creatively to that point where the person is in reality and properly "himself." All direct love does not reach as far as the real self, to the "soul" in the sense of the capacity to make a personal choice for salvation. For that is the true biblical sense of the word "soul," and not something like an interior room where thinking and feeling take place as opposed to the external happenings in the world. Therefore a true care of "souls" is possible only through God.

We are now in a position to say where the consecration to the care of souls is produced. Fundamentally it is baptism which consecrates us to it. Baptism is the pouring out of love for God and therefore consecration, power, and commission to pastoral care. And every sacramental increase of grace in sacramental confession and eucharist is a renewed commission to go forth and search out the innermost being of our brothers and sisters and lead them to God. Everyone who is baptized is consecrated a pastor.

111 • Mission*

It is not sufficient for Christianity to spread and grow only through contacts between people at the level of their private life, only through the example and the "witness" of the Christian life of the individual. Such growth obviously has considerable significance for the personal salvation of those who become Christians because of it, and for the creation of a climate favorable to evangelization. Beyond it, however, the church has an explicit authorization and responsibility for mission in the strict sense, that is, the conscious effort to create new churches in nations that are not yet Christian, with the intent of winning their inhabitants over to faith and baptism.

In missionary activity, the church must always respect the freedom involved in faith and in personal decision and use only those means which correspond to the nature of faith. It cannot get involved in any kind of propaganda that would play loose with freedom or with the personal appropriation of Christianity. Nor must it think of itself in its missionary activity as always giving. Where the church creates new Christian worlds, it always receives something from the concrete historical situation of the people evangelized. It is enriched not only quantitatively but also qualitatively.

The recognition of such things cannot undermine the fact that the church has the task and the obligation to become involved in an intentional way in missionary activity. This necessity does not flow exclusively or even primarily from a concern for the salvation of individuals. God's universal and effective saving will can reach even those who are not baptized and who therefore have only in the broadest sense a relationship to the church.

Mission is necessary because of the positive mandate of God and Christ. It is rooted in the incarnational structure of Christianity accord-

* With Franz Xaver Arnold, Ferdinand Klostermann, Viktor Schurr, and Leonard M. Weber, *Handbuch der Pastoraltheologie: Praktische Theologie in der Gegenwart* (Freiburg i. Br.: Herder, 1964–69), II/2, 55–57. Trans. Daniel Donovan, University of Saint Michael's College, Toronto.

ing to which the supernatural self-communication of God in the grace of the Spirit should also take historical and social form. Thus all dimensions of human existence and not just the deepest levels involved in existential decision are touched. This including of the historical and social nature of humankind gives to our final decision about salvation a greater chance, or to put it more carefully, that chance and context that corresponds to the full reality of human nature and that God in fact offers us. The details of a theological grounding of the missionary responsibility of the church can be found in papal encyclicals on the missions as well as in the decree on the missions at Vatican II (no. 7).

This necessary external mission implies a distinct function in the church's self-actualization, one that should not be confused with other and similar functions. This point is of considerable significance for pastoral theology. If the uniqueness and independence of missionary activity in the strict sense are not seen, if missionary activity simply disappears into what is called the church's mission in general, what in fact it must carry out always and everywhere, among all peoples and in every generation, then the danger exists that the "mission" within a Christian nation or within one that once was Christian will be understood as fulfilling our missionary duty. This would amount to dispensing ourselves from any obligation in regard to mission in the strict sense.

It is possible in the abstract to imagine that a people sharing the same geographical area and biological heritage with an earlier Christian people living in the same area is so little touched by Christianity that it represents a new missionary challenge and obligation. To think of a people who geographically and biologically come from a former Christian people, but who in their own concrete and present situation encounter nothing of a Christian nature, is to think in a historical and theological sense of a *new* people in regard to whom the missionary obligation naturally stands. This case, however, does not apply to the dechristianized peoples of the West nor to those who in their historical existence have originated directly from the West. Among these peoples there are of course large masses who are not baptized and whose life is not consciously formed by Christianity. In the sphere of their historical existence, however, Christianity and the church remain immediately identifiable realities which embody in a tangible way for individuals in such a people both a question about, and an offer of, salvation. The church obviously has an immense and pressing task in regard to what in some cases is widespread dechristianization. Given the newness of the circumstances, the task itself is a new one. What is required, however, is not mission in the strict sense, that is, the initial establishment of the church among a particular people as a special moment in their salvation history. The effort to rechristianize such a people cannot dispense the church from its genuinely missionary task. The missionary obligation applies as well to local churches within dechristianized peoples, to those areas that people like to call today "missionary territory."

The boundaries between the first hypothetical case of a historically and theologically *new* people requiring evangelization on the old geographical and biological ground of an earlier Christian people and the case of a people needing rechristianization, but to whose situation Christianity and the church continue to be present as historical forces, may be fluid and in the individual case impossible to determine precisely. That changes nothing in the basic distinction between, on the one hand, the mission to a people for whom the church is of no significance in its concrete historical situation and, on the other hand, pastoral activity among a people to whose historical past and present the church, prior to the faith decision of individuals, still belongs in a concrete way. The latter situation holds even when the public decision of many is in fact against Christianity. It must not be overlooked that even former Christians and "neopagans," that is, those in the traditionally Christian centers of the West who have not been baptized, are still marked to a significant degree sociologically, psychologically, and culturally by Christianity. In this they differ from the non-Christians and the nonbaptized in genuinely missionary countries (Buddhists, Hindus, etc.) who themselves, when they are no longer religious, continue to be determined sociologically, psychologically, and culturally by non-Christian religions.

112 • Mary and the Church*

The result of saving history is redemption. Now we can ask ourselves: Is the idea of a redeemed, new, sinless person, who has been incorporated into the inner life of God, only an abstract ideal? Or does it truly find its realization in us? To this we must answer that it is in no sense an unattainable goal, but has been realized in a definite case. If we ask ourselves once again what our love of God is supposed to be like, then we do not have to be satisfied with an abstract answer. In the kingdom of the living God, the ideals are not merely general postulates, but concrete persons — just as God himself is. For we find the actualized ideal of the absolutely redeemed, sinless, holy, perfect person in the Blessed Virgin and Mother of our Lord Jesus Christ.

* *Spiritual Exercises*, 262–67.

The ideal picture we have before us must naturally be determined by Christ. For this reason, it cannot be he, so it must be realized by some other person through a perfect following of him. Now the ideal of perfect openness to Christ is found concretely realized in Mary. She is the one who is perfectly redeemed. And, of course, she is perfectly redeemed in a very definite way belonging to her alone! But this way is at the same time the ideal case, the perfect fulfillment of what is and must be the law and goal of our lives through the inner structure of our existence in grace. There are many ways in which we could consider this idea which attained its historical, concrete form in Mary, and has become tangible in our flesh and blood. Here we are not going to discuss which principle of mariology is the fundamental one. But we can, nonetheless, easily arrive at the fact of Mary's perfect redemption from what the faith says about her again and again: that she is the blessed mother of our redeemer.

As the perfectly redeemed, Mary is the absolute unity — not identity! — of spirit, body and soul. In her, everything is summed up in the act of her personal surrender to God. In her, we find the perfect integration of every moment of her existence. The act of God's love is completely successful in Mary. Election by grace and openness to grace are one in her. We could even say that here God is received by the creature in the most basic way possible.

Therefore, Mary is so much the Mother of God that she both conceived the incarnate grace of God corporeally in her womb, and — because in her conception and personal act, spirit and body, belong together in inseparable unity — is the one whose faith is praised in scripture, because she responded to God with her *fiat* at that crucial point in salvation history where the efficacy of his grace asserted itself in a decisive way for all history. Mary stands at this point! She speaks her yes and conceives God; she speaks her yes in faith and in the concreteness of her earthly life. She conceives the Word, to borrow a phrase from the fathers, simultaneously in faith, heart, and womb.

Mary's perfect redemption indicates that in her the beginning and the end, both of which were established by God, are in perfect harmony. Thus she was immaculately conceived and finally assumed into heaven body and soul, that is, she went into heaven with her total human reality. Deed and destiny, which are always painfully separated in us, achieved a blessed integration in her. In us, either the deed is not done, or else destiny encounters someone who is not ready for it, so that it cannot be incorporated into his personal self-fulfillment and ultimately passes him by. But in Mary, everything is present in her *fiat*. Even in becoming the mother of the Word, she can accept the absolute disposition of God in her regard in an act of free love and free obedience.

If we find the unity of the given and the accepted in Mary, the perfectly redeemed, then that has a very special meaning for us priests. Of course we should not make Mary into a priestess or anything like that! Nevertheless, we should not forget that she does not have a haphazard function in salvation history; rather, her function is decisive for all of humankind.

All of us, says St. Paul, are built on the foundation of the apostles and prophets (Eph 2:20), and we share in the faith of our father Abraham (Rom 4:16). Each one of us, in his own historical situation, is essentially dependent on the life history of others. If that is true of the deeds that remain, as it were, anonymous, then it is especially true of those that belong to the public, official history of the people of God and as such have entered into the reflection of the church.

Thus Mary's destiny is not just her own affair: she is not the Mother of God for herself alone — in a purely biological sense or with a love that only concerns her. Her motherhood introduces the salvation of all! This means, then, that Mary belongs in a special way to the official representation of the church, even if her position is not one that could be perpetuated. That is just the point: her function is essentially unique! And she exercised her unique function in the church in perfect correspondence with her personal, interior life. There is no separation in her between her office and her subjectivity.

Despite the church's vigorous anti-Donatism, she was so clear on this point that she always took it for granted that the mother of the Lord is also the holy mother. In other words, the church proceeds in this matter from the theological axiom that, in such a case as this, office and person could not be separated. Of course this is not to say that Mary was not free, but that she was preordained for this perfect correspondence between official function and personal holiness by reason of the efficacious grace of God which alone makes a person free. Today Mary with her unity of office and personal holiness is urgently calling to us: You also should be what I am! Our celibate, singleminded service of God, Christ, the church, and men and women is really just a part of the coincidence of official position and personal realization which we have in common with Mary.

As the perfectly redeemed, Mary in her human reality also stands for the unity of individual self-fulfillment and service of others, or, we might say, the unity of personal holiness and the apostolate. In her, these mutually determine one another. She is holy because she conceives the Word as the lamb of God for the salvation of the world, because under the cross she joins her motherhood to the sacrifice of her child, and because her life is nothing but a complete self-oblation in the service of her son for the good of souls. Her individuality is, as it were, submerged in her mission; it disappears in the apostolate, but it is precisely in this way that she becomes the unique person that she is supposed to be.

In this matter also, we can learn something from Mary. A humanistic cult of personality — such as was the mode in the nineteenth century — which is really a form of egoism, does not lead positively to Christ, and is certainly very "un-Marian." This Virgin who led her miserable, poor, simple life in a remote corner of Palestine, through her selfless, self-consuming service as the handmaid of the Lord achieved a uniqueness all her own — she became, as it were, the absolutely human individuality. Nothing remained empty, nothing remained undone in her human reality. And the reason for this is that she was not concerned about herself, but thought only of others, of her son, of her duty. "Behold the handmaid of the Lord" who is totally absorbed in the Lord whom she serves. It is exactly in this way that she became the queen of heaven and earth!

It is, therefore, easy to understand that in Mary, the perfectly redeemed, grace and freedom have attained an absolute, blessed unity. All the gifts and privileges of the Blessed Virgin and Mother of our Lord should be looked at from this point of view. The same is true of her virginity, which is one of the first fruits of the New Testament. As the first representative of this virginity, Mary's special mission in the world was to represent the church of the end-time — a church completely turned over to Christ. And that is what priests and religious are supposed to do by their celibacy.

The foregoing brings us to the consideration of Mary's relationship to the church. If the pure, immaculate, and virginal church is the community of those who are following Christ, and thereby are realizing now in their own lives what Mary accomplished long ago, then this means that Mary is the prototype of the church. A Catholic, or better, "incarnational" religiosity cannot consist in some exalted act of freedom which is directed toward the transcendent God alone, and which, as it were, annihilates everything else. God descended into this world and communicated to it his own life.

But this means, then, that the creature with its plurality, peculiarity, and beauty, which is distinct from God, has become religiously meaningful. Incarnational Christianity does not permit its glimpse of God to reduce everything else to nothingness. If we want to accompany God in his descent, then we must learn how to find God in the magnificent figures of his salvation history.

Therefore, in a very special sense, we must learn how to find him in Mary! In this matter, we should have no part of the anxiety of an unchristian religiosity — unchristian because it is not incarnational. This religiosity fears that God and perhaps even Christ himself will escape its grasp if it has anything at all to do with others within the framework of religion.

If it were true that only God could be, then we should destroy ourselves so that honor could be given to God alone. But that is not the way things are! God is honored because we are here, because we praise him in the great deeds of his love — deeds by which he establishes that which is different from himself. If this is true as a general rule, if the basic religious act in Christianity can be directed to a multiplicity of realities, then it is true with regard to all the saints and in a special and unique way with regard to our relationship to Mary. We must come to realize that all things point beyond themselves to the infinity of God's love. At the same time, we must realize that we are greatly tempted to try to get to God directly and bypass his creatures. We usually ignore this tendency in ourselves, instead of overcoming it in the straightforward Catholic piety which recognizes Mary and loves her, and does not reject her praise as something out of place.

113 • The Feast of Mary's Immaculate Conception*

In the kingdom of God, the kingdom of love, all is bestowed on each in his own particular way, the whole pervades and prevails in each, and each of the mysteries of the kingdom is inexhaustible. It has only been grasped perfectly when all has been understood. The whole, however, is the inexhaustibility of the infinite mystery of God. Consequently, the mystery of the feast of the Immaculate Conception can be regarded under innumerable aspects. No one is forbidden to seek the particular aspect which leads him best and most fully into this mystery of God, so that he comes to God himself.

We wish to consider this as the feast of beginnings. We shall reflect on the beginning as such, on the beginning of the Blessed Virgin, and on our own.

A beginning is not empty nothingness, something inconsiderable, hollow indeterminacy, what is inferior and general. That is the sort of way people mostly think today, and regard everything lofty and perfect (if they are still capable of conceiving and loving such things) as a complicated amalgam of the least precious, uniformly unremarkable,

---

* *Everyday Faith*, 163–68.

"basic elements." But the true beginning of what comes to high perfection is not empty vacuity. It is the closed bud, the rich ground of a process of becoming, which possesses what it can give rise to. It is not the first and smallest portion at the beginning of a process of becoming, but the whole of the history which is beginning, in its radical ground.

For the beginning as such is God, the plenitude of all reality. And when it is said of us that we are created from "nothing," that does indeed mean that we are not God, but it does not mean that our origin was the void, an indeterminacy indifferent to everything; it means it was God. And God posits the created beginning which is not the first moment of our time but the original ground of the whole history of our freedom in time.

For that reason the beginning is posited solely by God; it is his mystery which inaccessibly rules over us. Consequently, it only reveals itself slowly in the course of our history. That is why it has to be accepted by us in its darkness and obscurity, with trust, hope, and courage. It has to be preserved by holy anamnesis in its inaccessible mystery and in what it discloses of itself in our history.

For if that beginning is the permanent ground of human existence, and supports all, and is not something which we leave behind us as past and done with, then that beginning is the purpose of life, the content of the anamnesis which in a sacred rite renders the origin present. That is why we celebrate the birthday, the baptism, and the Pasch of the Lord. These are all festivals of the beginning which is allotted to us as human beings and as Christians.

And when we look forward with hope into the future, it is the manifestation of the beginning we are watching for. It is the beginning which is approaching us in the end, in the future whose origin has been acquired through history. If we fail to attain the fulfillment, it will be because we have lost the beginning. And if the end is pure fulfillment, then the beginning must have been a pure origin from infinite love.

In the Gospel of Thomas we read, "The disciples said to Jesus, 'Tell us what our end will be like.' Jesus said, 'Have you already discovered the beginning and yet you ask about the end? Blessed is he who will stand at the beginning and will know the end and not taste death.'"

The historical Jesus certainly did not make this statement. Yet if correctly read it is true nevertheless. Yet Jesus in reality did judge the present as a falling away from the pure beginning as this was posited by God and as it was to be reestablished by himself, when he said, "In the beginning it was not so." And when Heidegger observes that origin always remains future, he expresses the same relation between beginning and fulfillment that the historical Jesus and the gnostic Jesus affirm. We must first recall this general character of a beginning when we are celebrating the feast day of a pure beginning.

If we have understood what a beginning really means, we will understand that what the church professes in regard to the Blessed Virgin's beginning is only the correct transposition into the beginning of what the church always knew about the Blessed Virgin from her later life and from her significance in sacred history for the church. This is so, however long it may have taken the church to accomplish this regress from the consequence to the origin, from what was brought about to what was projected, from future to source, until the church finally reached the definition of 1854.

God as beginning and the beginning posited by God may not be separated in Mary through the difference established by the guilt of humankind. For this difference was not permitted prior to Christ and as superior to his redemptive work, but in subordination to it. He, as the absolute and unconditional will of God for his world, even prior to the world and its sin, was the pure and primordial beginning of God's will for the finite. Guilt was only admitted because it remained enveloped within this hidden beginning which from the start was the overflowing spring of grace, even if its previously hidden plenitude was only manifested in the actual course of its flow.

Mary, however, belongs to the will of the eternal God, the absolute will of God for the incarnation of his Logos which had already taken sin into account. Mary belongs to the beginning which contains, not to the beginning which is contained. She belongs to it, of course, as a posited, not as the positing beginning, as posited in God's will for the world, for the incarnation of the Logos and through this for redemption; therefore she belongs to it as a beginning redeemed in advance. And so she belongs to God's action within which he redemptively comprises sin, because in the concrete order this action of God in the incarnation of the Logos is inseparable from her in her flesh and her obedience.

As a consequence there cannot be that difference in herself between the divinely established beginning of each human being as such and the beginning of the individual inasmuch as he remains conjoined to the guilty beginning of humanity as a whole, the deed of Adam. Her beginning is a pure, innocent and simple one, sheer grace, an element in the object of the redemption itself. God with absolute love always willed Mary as she who would say yes to his own word addressed to the world. For this absolutely unconditionally willed word of grace is only spoken absolutely if it is heard obediently and in the flesh, precisely by Mary in fact.

Because she was so willed, and because she was willed unconditionally, she was willed from and in the beginning as accepting. She

cannot in the beginning be posited in her beginning as capable of saying no. She is endowed with grace in her beginning. Purely for the
sake of Christ who is the redeemer, and therefore as an element in
what is prior to the redemption, and for the sake of which God merely
permitted guilt.

This beginning is the disposition of God alone, the moment when
God's love bestowing itself on human beings is still collected, concentrated in itself, or rather is originally immanent in itself as a love which
has already forestalled guilt and which, because of this power, permits
the weakness of guilt. Where this love posits such a created historical
beginning, there is the beginning of the Blessed Virgin.

Nevertheless, or rather, precisely in this way, this glory of a pure
beginning originating in God was a beginning which had to be experienced with sorrow. The origin meant a future of everyday life,
customary things, silence, the seven sorrows, and the death of her son
and her own death. Only then was the beginning attained by the future
retrieving the beginning. Only then was it disclosed as pure grace.

Our beginning is hidden in God. It is decided. Only when we have
arrived will we full know what our origin is. For God is mystery as such,
and what he posited when he established us in our beginning is still
the mystery of his free will hidden in his revealed word. But without
evacuating the mystery, we can say that there belongs to our beginning
the earth which God has created, the ancestors whose history God
ruled with wisdom and mercy, Jesus Christ, the church and baptism,
earth and eternity.

All is there, everything whatsoever which exists is silently concentrated in the well-spring of our own existence and all the beginning
posited by God uniquely and unrepeatedly is. With what is hard and
what is easy, delicate and harsh, with what belongs to the abyss and
what is heavenly. All is encompassed by God, his knowledge and his
love. All has to be accepted. And we advance toward it all; we experience everything, one thing after another, until future and origin
coincide.

One thing about this beginning, however, has already been said to
us by the word of God. The possibility of acceptance itself belongs to
the might of the divinely posited beginning. And if we accept, we have
accepted sheer love and happiness. For even if in our beginning the
difference between God's will and human will is interposed, even if
even in the beginning our lot is decided both by God *and* by the history
of guilt, nevertheless, precisely in our case, even this contradiction is
always merely permitted and is already encompassed by pure love
and forgiveness.

And the more that love and forgiveness which encompasses and belongs to our beginning is accepted in the pain of life and in the death which gives life, and the more this original element emerges and is allowed to manifest itself and pervade our history, the more the difference, the contradiction in the beginning is resolved and redeemed. And all the more will it be revealed that we ourselves were also implied in that pure beginning whose feast day we are celebrating.

When the beginning has found itself in the fulfillment and has been fulfilled in the freedom of accepting love, *God* will be all in all. Because then all will belong to all, the differences will of course still be there but they will have been transformed and will belong to the blessedness of unifying love, and no longer to separation. And for that reason this feast is *our* feast. For it is the feast of the freely bestowed love in which all of us are comprised, each in his place and rank.

114 • Mary's Assumption*

If we read attentively the definitions of the church's magisterium on the "immaculate conception" and on the assumption of the Blessed Virgin into heaven — that is, on the content of the two Marian feasts — we are struck, among other things, by the fact that the immaculate conception is taught as a "special privilege" of Mary; in the teaching on Mary's assumption there is at least no explicit emphasis on anything unusual about this assumption. It is in fact quite conceivable that this emphasis is lacking because the assumption does not need to be understood as a "special privilege."

Let us examine a little more closely the question raised by this feast. This sort of reflection is not a subtle exercise of theological ingenuity, but an aid to the appreciation of this feast as one of hope for our own life.

The fact that our beginning and Mary's are different is not very surprising. The beginning of a life is always the beginning appointed by God to a quite particular life with a definite character, with a mission that is each time unique and with its own nonrecurring history. There is necessarily a hidden correspondence between the beginning of a history and this history itself. If the history of the Blessed Virgin is that of her free conception in mind and body of the Word of God for all of us, then her beginning, which is proper to her alone, corresponds to this. But the consummation is the same for all. Certainly we bring the finality of our history into what we call in the Christian creed eternal life,

---

* *Opportunities for Faith*, 46–50.

and this eternal life is not a continuation of time, but the pure finality of our history in responsibility and love. But this finality comes about because God makes this existence his own. He gives himself in radical immediacy, face to face. So for Mary and for us the consummation is the same: God himself.

We cannot confess anything in regard to her assumption more glorious than what we confess as our hope for ourselves: eternal life, which God himself wants to be for us. For the hope we have for our whole person in the unity of our existence — that single existence which we explain to ourselves as a unity of body and soul — is the resurrection of the body and eternal life. In our liturgical praise of the assumption of the Blessed Virgin we speak only of the one act of God in regard to that one person, but it is something that we likewise expect for ourselves. *Ultimately,* nothing more is said of her than what God one day, we hope, will say to us. And thus all is said.

But, someone might object, is not this consummation of her whole life known to be accomplished for her "already now," while for us who are still imperfect and even for others who have died in Christ this consummation of bodily life is still to come? There is no doubt that we usually add instinctively to the content of this feast the thought: for Mary already, for the rest of those who died in Christ not yet, not until the last day. But how do things really stand? We have to admit that we don't know for certain. It is salutary, however, to reflect on this very uncertainty. Because this is perhaps a better way of entering into the mystery of the feast of Mary's assumption than by simply celebrating it point by point in pious rhymes.

First of all, the definition of the assumption of the Blessed Virgin does not forbid reflection also on the consummated beatitude of all who are finally saved, as already achieved in "body and soul" and not merely in the soul. Nor can we say for certain that the presence of someone's corpse in the grave is a clear proof of the fact that this person has not yet found that consummation which we call bodily resurrection.

Theologians are agreed, or are coming more and more to agree, that the heavenly consummation of the one whole person — that is, "body and soul" — can be conceived as independent of the fate of his earthly-physical materiality. The body as understood in the "resurrection of the body" which we believe is the final consummation of all who are saved, the "spiritual body" which we receive according to Paul, is our own, even though it is not materially identical with the continually changing matter which we discard at death.

From this standpoint, then, there is no compelling reason to distinguish between the "points of time" at which our bodily consummation and that of Mary take place. If today more than formerly we rightly stress the unity of the corporal-personal human being in the variety of his dimensions, then it is more difficult than it used to be to assign the consummation "in regard to the soul" and that "in regard to the body" to different points of time, with an interval of time between them.

In addition, we know that the eternity of redeemed life with God, for which we hope, cannot be conceived as continuing time added on as a linear continuation to our earthly life, but is the dissolution of that time; it may be impossible to "imagine" eternity as timeless consummation, but it is just that and not ever-continuing time.

Modern physics too confirms this attitude as it becomes more and more clear how *cautiously* we have to apply our conceptual models of successive time to reality as such. In the light of this it is again difficult to say of someone who has reached perfection in his personal life that he is "still waiting" for his bodily consummation, for in a certain sense at least it is inconceivable that the completed life of those who are finally saved and are now in the supratemporal eternity of God can be kept apart by further stretches of time from the event of consummation in death.

On the other hand, we shall also be careful to avoid premature con-clusions by claiming that we know positively and certainly that what we venture to say of Mary and what we expect for all holds "already now" for all who are fallen asleep in Christ. There are also good rea-sons, despite all skepticism in regard to a time factor beyond the line of death, for maintaining a difference between Mary and the rest of the redeemed. In its most basic utterance Christian faith knows of one bodily consummation which cannot be postponed to a still unreal fu-ture: the resurrection of Jesus. And in the light of this it is clear to faith that a consummation already accomplished "in body and soul" cannot be a contradiction in itself.

And the same faith takes absolutely seriously the history which still continues, embracing *all,* including Jesus Christ: that is, a story whose end remains significant also for those who themselves have already reached their consummation. And in this light a "not yet" for those who have "already" reached their personal consummation cannot without more ado be declared meaningless. We simply don't succeed (it is evidently impossible also in the lower dimensions of reality) in uniting in a higher synthesis and thus balancing off against each other the concepts and models of time and the concepts of eternal finality.

The pointed question we have just raised finally remains unan-swered. But the very fact of raising it has revealed how close the mystery of this feast is to our hope for ourselves. We profess our faith through this feast in the unity of the human person, who is one whole. We profess our faith in the permanent validity of history as flesh and blood; we profess our hope and love for the earth, which is not merely the parade ground or theater for our spiritual life, to be abandoned as soon as finality supervenes, and which perhaps itself, even though radically transformed, enters equally with the person's spirit into the glory of the eternal God.

We acknowledge the dignity of the body, which is not merely a tool to be used and thrown away, but the historical, concrete reality and revelation of the free person who is realized in it and works within it for the finality of its freedom. And this profession of faith is not expressed in ideological propositions and principles. It is a profession of faith in the historically concrete reality of a particular human being and thus can always contain more, and in more concrete form, than can be discovered by reflection on what is stated in it.

This feast tells us that those whom God loves are redeemed, are saved, are finally themselves; they are so with their concrete history, with their whole bodily nature in which alone a person is truly himself. He is not a "ghost," not a "soul" but a human being completely saved. Everything remains. We can't imagine it. Of course not. All talk about the soul in bliss, the glorified body, the glory of heaven, amount to the unvarnished, blind statement of faith: this person is not lost. *He* is what he has become, raised up in the implacable obviousness and absoluteness of the living God, raised up in the transcendent, ineffable mystery we call God.

We can't say more than this. We don't try to paint a picture, we don't imagine anything. Everything has gone through the harsh transformation which we call death. What else could we say except that death is not the last word — or rather that it is our last word, but not God's.

The church ventures to say the word about the eternal, timeless validity of Mary. Why should she not say this of her, the mother of the Lord, if, according to scripture Mary must be called blessed by all generations? How could the church let the living history of this virgin and mother, the achievement of her faith, fall into the abyss of death where nothing any longer matters? The faith that we profess in regard to her, we profess as hope for ourselves in that blessed indifference of the believer for which time, Chronos — who devours his own children — belongs, as Paul says, to the powers which still rule and yet are already dethroned by him who died and rose again. And thus, even if there is the difference we mentioned between a "now already" of the Blessed Virgin and the "not yet" of the others, faith and hope have already leaped across it as a part of that "little while" of which Jesus speaks in his farewell discourses in John.

What we say then about this Marian feast is really the faith we always profess for ourselves: I believe in the resurrection of the body and eternal life for myself and for all. If we seize and grasp this profession of faith, confidently letting it fall into the mystery which is God, which God is for us, then in our hope we have also understood the meaning of the assumption of Mary into heaven.

115 • Does Mary Divide the Denominations?*

Is the Catholic teaching about Mary the mother of the Lord an obstacle to Christian unity? At first glance one would have to say yes. Protestant Christianity is fairly unanimous in rejecting at least individual elements of this teaching as incompatible with its own fundamental understanding of the Christian message. For this reason (and for many others) it refuses to confess the same faith as the Catholic church. This simple observation, then, is our first answer to the question and it must, as such, stand.

But it is not the whole answer. To think, for example, that mariology is the first and most important dogmatic reason for the separation is wrong. Apart from criticism by the reformers of concrete forms of Marian devotion, mariology was not a focus of controversy at the time of the Reformation. And yet a division of Christendom did take place.

The new Catholic dogmas about Mary defined since the Reformation (the immaculate conception and the assumption) could, if understood more profoundly, be intelligible and acceptable to those Protestants who continue to confess the mariology of their founders. Such a deepening of mariology, it should be added, is both possible and necessary within Catholic theology. Naturally the very fact that "new" dogmas are proclaimed in the Catholic church at all represents an offense to Protestants. But that again is an issue that did not first become a point of contention between the churches in regard to mariology.

There is another thing, too, that cannot be overlooked in regard to our ecumenical conversations about dogmatic issues. If we are serious and realistic in what we are doing, we cannot act today as if our ecumenical discussions needed to deal only with the questions that divided Christians at the time of the Reformation. Many of the theological affirmations taught in the confessional documents of the Reformation period are anything but self-evident in the actual theology of many

* *Kritisches Wort: Aktuelle Probleme in Kirche und Welt* (Freiburg i. Br.: Herder, 1972), 34–37. Trans. Daniel Donovan, University of Saint Michael's College, Toronto.

contemporary Protestant communities. Today a new consensus would have to be established about much more fundamental doctrines than those about justification, the relation of scripture and tradition, the number of the sacraments, and the precise constitution of the church. One could say that inner Protestant doctrinal differences go much deeper than those between Protestants who maintain the classical Reformation confessions and Catholics for whom the dogmas of the ancient church continue to be binding.

An ecumenical dialogue that pursues the unity of contemporary Christians must not overlook this situation. Even if we were to be united in mariology (and if we really could be united in it, given the lack of inner Protestant unity about God and Christ), we would still be very far from dogmatic agreement about basic questions of Christianity. Mariology is thus not the central theme of ecumenical dialogue.

This does not mean, however, that mariology can be eliminated from the dialogues. The teaching about Mary at Vatican II did not eliminate all the points of difference that have developed among Christian denominations in regard to mariology. The history of chapter 8 of the Constitution on the church reveals that people were conscious of their ecumenical responsibility in drafting it. Much that Catholic "maximalists" in mariology wanted to have said remained unsaid. The teaching about an office of mediation of the Blessed Virgin Mary was formulated so carefully, that a Catholic theologian can hardly imagine that understanding and agreement about what is entailed here will not slowly be achieved with those Protestants who believe in the divine sonship of Jesus and in his role in mediating salvation, and who at the same time do not forget that in the body of Christ, which is the church, we do not live and work out our salvation by ourselves. Through the grace of God each of us has meaning for everyone else, each stands before God for others by means of prayer and a life lived in that Spirit, whom the Lord alone bestows on us.

Beyond that there is still much work for Catholic theology in terms of a deepening of the understanding of the Marian dogmas in such a way as to make clear to Protestant laity and theologians that they are a development of and conclusion from our common faith in the Lord and in his saving grace. Is such an effort hopeless when today Protestants are rethinking what *they* in fact mean and do not mean when they talk of "original sin," from which we believe that Mary was preserved through Christ's redemption, or when they ask themselves whether everyone who in faith dies in Christ already "now" receives that fulfillment which we affirm of Mary, when we ourselves are not sure that it has been granted only to her?

There is need for a certain deepening in popular Catholic devotion until it is able to testify in all clarity that Catholics place all their hope in life and death in the grace of God in Christ, with whom everything in the history of salvation is not simply to be identified but from whom everything comes. If Protestants hold fast to their ancient confession that Mary "is rightly named and truly is the mother of God" (Formula of Concord) and also "prays for the church" (Apology of the Augsburg Confession), then with God's grace even the dialogue about mariology among separated Christians is not without hope.

116 • The Marian Dogmas and Protestant Theology*

As far as the first of the Marian dogmas is concerned, I venture to suggest that the possibility of an orthodox, more extensive development of the dogma of original sin may make it easier to prove than by an appeal to revelation in the wide sense and thus to remove also the offensive and incredible features that Protestant Christians see in it.

If we want to elucidate the dogma of original sin today with reference to *all* human beings *and* at the same time equally clearly and unmistakably to grasp by faith the fact that every Adamite human being, even in an infralapsarian state, always and from the very beginning comes within the scope of God's supernaturally beneficent salvific will (a salvific will that does not merely imply an intention on God's part, but is a supernatural existential of the offer of grace presented always and everywhere), then original sinfulness is not simply a state chronologically prior to the offer of grace to freedom: it is "dialectically" coexistent with the offer of salvation and grace as a determination of the human being, who is always and everywhere in his situation of freedom descended simultaneously from both Adam and Christ and freely ratifies one situation of freedom or the other.

If it is recalled that Mary also is redeemed by Christ — that is, she is in need of redemption and this need is among the permanent existentials of her existence — then the normal infralapsarian human being and Mary are not really distinguished because of a difference in a period of time at the beginning of existence, but because Mary receives the offer of grace to her freedom in virtue of her predestination to be the mother of Jesus and consequently as an offer efficaciously prevailing and as such also perceptible in salvation history.

---

* *Theological Investigations XVIII*, 50–51.

A Protestant theology of pure grace, efficacious as such, should not really find this distinction offensive. The dogma of the immaculate conception does not necessarily imply that the beginning of grace for her is different in a temporal sense from what it is for us, who likewise do not receive grace for salvation as a permanent existential of our freedom for the first time only in baptism.

It might be almost easier to achieve an agreement with Protestant theology on the second Marian dogma. For the content of the doctrine of the assumption does not imply that Mary's "bodily" assumption into heaven is a privilege granted (apart from Jesus) to her alone. It was obvious, for instance, to the fathers of the church that the Old Testament patriarchs in limbo at the time of Christ's resurrection entered bodily into their eternal bliss.

If today, as against a platonizing interpretation of the "separation of body and soul" at death, we may certainly hold that every human being acquires his risen body at death, "at that very moment" (insofar as terms relating to time make sense in this respect), a view often maintained in Protestant theology and quite legitimate with the aid of a little justifiable demythologizing, then this dogma does not refer to something granted to Mary alone, but to what belongs generally to all who are saved, while appropriate to her in a special way in virtue of her function in salvation history and consequently more clearly understood in the church's sense of faith than it is in other human beings. It can therefore be said that even in regard to these two Marian dogmas there need be no insuperable point of controversy, if the open questions undoubtedly involved also in these dogmas are clearly recognized.

117 • The Roman Catholic Church*

We are and we shall remain also in the future the *Roman* Catholic church. This in itself is obvious, but it needs to be stated clearly today, in view of a widespread theoretical and practical allergy to Rome. To stress this does not mean that we are supporters of the movement for "Pope and Church," but only that the relationship of Christianity and the church to Rome is absolutely necessary for us Catholics and not merely the result of historical or sociological accidents.

Criticism and a critical attitude in principle toward the church be-long to the essence of Christianity and of the Catholic faith itself. The

---

* *The Shape of the Church to Come,* trans. Edward Quinn (New York: Seabury Press, 1974), 52–55.

pope's concrete function in the church is also a historical factor and its history is still obviously always open toward the future. Often enough individual popes in the past 150 years have provided and still provide today an occasion for criticism even of the institution itself and of what is claimed to be normal practice. The Petrine ministry, for us a matter of faith, may be conceived and required by the situation of the modern world in a very different concrete shape. But all this by no means implies that we have a right to contradict in theory or practice the conception of the Petrine ministry taught by the First and Second Vatican councils.

Paul's opposition to Peter, described in the Epistle to the Galatians, certainly has still a meaning for us today. The style of papal devotion as it developed, particularly in the nineteenth century, may rightly seem to many to belong to a vanished age. The tiara has been abolished and now particularly we have the right, even for binding dogmatic reasons, to reject the claim of the newspaper, *Civiltà cattolica*, that our own faith and our own religious life flow from the pope. We assign to the papacy a quite definite function in the church, which is nothing like that of the head of a totalitarian state. This function is sustained and embraced by the greater spirit and life of the church; it is sustained in its binding force for ourselves by our primal faith in Jesus Christ and his church, which is greater than the papacy. The pope's universal function in regard to the whole church can be described only to a limited degree and analogously in terms of juridical categories borrowed from a secular society and which hold even there only in a way that is very much historically conditioned.

A great deal which is possible but not dogmatically stringent, which is historically conditioned and changeable, and which as such still holds today in the papacy's concrete function, permits us to hope rightly for a further change. Such hopes can be very emphatically asserted, even though they do not authorize any revolution in the church, not even in regard to this fundamentally changeable factor, and must not lead to a disruption of the historical continuity and function of the papacy: thus they must always take the form of a hope (ultimately eschatologically substantiated) that changes will come about through the papacy itself and not against it. None of this alters the dogmatic fact that the papacy belongs to the binding content of our faith itself, in its proper place within the hierarchy of truths and in our own Christian life. This holds absolutely.

However justified we may be in our critical reservations in regard to the concrete form of the papacy, these should not prevent us from approaching it, even in this concreteness, with *that* unemotional, realistic understanding with which the concrete form of Christianity itself, in all its dimensions and areas, has to be lovingly and impartially accepted at any particular time, although we know that this concrete shape is not simply identical with the essence of Christianity but is historically changeable. An irritable and embittered allergy to this concrete shape of the papacy is profoundly uncatholic. Today we can boldly but also patiently and effectively face the concrete shape of the papacy in a critical spirit without succumbing to this sort of irritable allergy toward it.

Just as in secular society there is or must be not only social criticism, but also a genuine and impartial, deliberate acceptance of the state, so there should be an analogous approach to the papacy. Its critics should not only or primarily be on the lookout for real or supposed encroachments of this supreme ministry in the church, and trying to ward them off, but ought to reflect constructively on how this Petrine ministry presumably could and should undertake *new* tasks of a *positive* character in a number of directions in a church which is preparing today to be really a world-church and is facing a unified world with tasks which can be fulfilled only by a worldwide church that is *institutionally* one.

If the worldwide movement of Marxist socialism proclaims a "democratic centralism" to be the structure of the social order, we can always take into account the fact that this concept can be and is interpreted in a variety of ways. We can insist that the church is not a secular reality, but has quite a different nature. But the church cannot be a debating society: it must be able to make decisions binding on all within it. Such a demand cannot be a priori contrary to the dignity of the human being, if — as people today are never tired of impressing upon us — he is indeed a social being. And then a supreme point at which all reflections and democratic discussions are turned into universally binding decisions cannot be without meaning.

It might certainly be desirable for decision-making processes in the church to take place with the active cooperation of as many people as possible and to be clearly visible to all. We must certainly insist that they are in accordance with the facts and that even the preference of a majority as such is itself one of the facts to be taken into account.

But we should not act as if all such decision-making processes, after sufficient reflection, could be broken down into rationally demonstrable processes, understood by all; as if individual and personal factors, which cannot be completely analyzed, played no part at all in them; as if a community decision were not in fact the decision of a few of its representatives.

Hence a "monarchical" head (in a sense which certainly requires precise definition) is certainly appropriate even in the church and is really inevitable: it does not need to be defended by paternalistic ideologies. This inevitability is better protected against dangers when it is not concealed, not suppressed, but when safeguards for its appropriate and visible exercise are built into its permanent function ("by human law" [iure humano] and in a way that corresponds to the diversity of the social situation and to special fields for which decisions have to be made).

In this respect there is certainly much that must be improved and renewed in the *concrete* structure of the supreme office in the church if it is really to be efficient and visible to the extent necessary today. But it is precisely today that we should see positively the need of an efficient supreme headship of the church and not think that the more it is restricted in practice, the more we are corresponding to the demands of the time. We should also appreciate the fact that *no* juridical structure can a priori exclude mistaken decisions and abuses. We should appreciate the fact that we simply cannot as Christians and Catholics have an impartial attitude to such an office unless it implies also a hope — which cannot be secured by laws and institutions — in the Spirit in the church.

118 • Toward Ecumenical Dialogue*

The ultimate basis of ecumenical theology is that unity, apprehended hope, which consists in a belief in justifying grace, a belief which, even though in its theological formulation and its explication in creedal form it is still in process of being arrived at, is nevertheless already in existence as one and the same belief in both of the parties involved in ecumenical theology.

Now what is meant by this thesis in *more precise* terms? First, it must be unreservedly conceded that for ecumenical dialogue and ecumenical theology in the form in which it appears today a liberal humanism, with its defense of freedom of opinion and faith within a pluralistic society, has been, and still is, the occasion and the context without which the pursuit of ecumenical theology as it in fact exists today is inconceivable. The historical necessity for this liberalism, for the relationship which the separated Christians of today have achieved with one another, does not need to be denied, and must not be glossed over. But we cannot get into this further here.

This liberalism, however, is hardly the true ground and ultimate reason of the ability which the separated parties have of conducting a

---

* *Theological Investigations XI*, 33–40.

dialogue today. So we must not confuse the essential basis for a given phenomenon with the historical situation in which such an essential basis becomes effective. Now what is the true and effective basis for ecumenical dialogue, such that it is constitutive of its essential nature? It is to this question that the thesis formulated above is attempting to supply an answer.

When we conduct an ecumenical dialogue, or pursue ecumenical theology with one another despite the fact of our being divided among many churches, then the ultimate necessary condition which we presuppose for this is that each of us recognizes the others as Christians. But what does this mean in precise and genuinely theological terms? Certainly it does not merely mean that we accept and acknowledge the fact that the other partner to the dialogue regards himself as a Christian. Nor does it merely mean that we mutually credit one another with the fact of all having validly been baptized — provided we are thinking of baptism here first and foremost in its empirical reality as an external fact of cult. Nor does it merely mean that in spite of all the differences between us with regard to the creed we can establish as a matter of empirical fact that there is agreement between us on certain of our tenets, in the sense, for instance, that is implied in the basic formula of the World Council of Churches.

What it means, rather, is that we are convinced as a matter of hope, if not of knowledge at the explicit and theoretical level, that the partners to the dialogue on either side live in the grace of God, that they are truly justified by the holy Pneuma of God and are sharers in the divine nature.

Now there have been ages in which this conviction, in which we mutually recognize in hope the real and triumphant presence of God's grace in one another, has not been felt with the force of a self-evident truth. When, for instance, Augustine upholds the validity of baptism among "heretics" against Cyprian and the Donatists, and even outside the "Catholic" sphere, he is certainly not including in this doctrine of his the conviction that this baptism actually communicates to the baptized individual an effective forgiveness of his sins and the sanctifying Spirit of God.

Probably, indeed, right down to the age of the Enlightenment, the prevailing opinion on both sides has been that in the case of the heretic (and both parties have mutually regarded each other as such) it is to be presumed that his heresy must be accounted as guilt, and therefore in controversial discussions each side must presume that the other has not lived in God's grace. It may be that it was not until the eighteenth century that this question was the subject of any close thought. Distinctions may have been drawn between the educated and uneducated, and there may have been a tendency to attribute "good faith" to the latter more than to the former. It may be that the interpretation of one's opponent from the other confession, as depicted above, may not always and everywhere have been raised to the level of an explicit thesis.

Nevertheless, human beings lived and acted upon the basic feeling that their opponents could not be living in God's grace as justified and sanctified when, nevertheless, with regard to the faith that is saving, and without which (according to the Epistle to the Hebrews) the person cannot be pleasing to God, they deviated in certain vital points from one's own convictions of faith, points which one regarded either as at least belonging absolutely to one's own faith or even (as in the case of the *sola fide* ["by faith alone"] doctrine) as the heart and center of that faith.

Today, no doubt, the situation is different. This is a point which I do not really need to substantiate where Protestant Christians are concerned, especially since, if I were to do so, I should have to raise the question of whether this attribution of a state of justification to my partner in the dialogue, who is confessionally separated from me, derived from a liberal and relativistic interpretation of my own creed, or whether it exists side by side with, and is to be regarded as reconcilable with, the conviction of the absolute truth and universal claims of my own creed. But for all this I believe that the Protestant partner to the dialogue will not only credit the Catholic one in some sense with "good faith" and a genuine conviction at the human level, but also accept that the grace of Christ permeates the innermost roots of his being. And conversely the Catholic will do the same.

The Second Vatican Council explicitly teaches that the Protestant Christian, too, is one who has received grace and justification provided he has not in any way sinfully denied God. The council recognizes just as unequivocally that such an interior state of grace on the part of the Protestant Christian can obviously be present even in those cases in which he decisively rejects specific elements in the teaching of the Roman Catholic church, following in this the claim of his own conscience with regard to truth, since according to his belief they are irreconcilable with true Christianity.

This conviction may be utterly obvious from the standpoint of a mere tolerant humanism. But in those cases in which the individual concerned is at the same time convinced of the salvific meaning of his own specific creed, a creed that differs decisively from that of another (and this applies at least to the manner in which Roman Catholic believers think of their faith), this conviction is anything but self-evident, and it is only very gradually, and with great efforts, that it has been brought to maturity in this church's understanding of her own faith, to the point where it has been given clear expression in the Second Vatican Council. Nevertheless this conviction does now exist on the Catholic side as well.

At this stage we do not need to discuss in any direct sense the question of how the significance of the Catholic creed, salvific and necessary to salvation as it is according to the Catholic understanding of faith, can be reconciled with the simultaneous conviction that one who does not share this faith still does have salvation. The question that we have to ask here is simply what this conviction implies on both sides with regard to the possibility of ecumenical dialogue and ecumenical theology, and to this question the thesis formulated above does supply an answer.

This dialogue is possible because, despite the differences in our respective creeds in terms of objective formulation and verbal expression (in other words, despite the differences of faith which exist between us in this sense), there is, nevertheless, a unity of faith such that we not only seek it but actually mutually concede it as already present and given in one another, because each of us is aware of the other as believing, hoping, and loving in the power of the Spirit of God possessing us, without whom there can be no belief and with whom there can be no unbelief.

This statement naturally forces us to a decision as to what true faith really means. In this we must neither overlook nor neglect the importance of the differences between the forms of words in which our respective creeds are expressed. At the same time, however, each side must credit the other with the presence of the divine Spirit of unity, together with the truth of God, enlightenment and faith. Each of us must recognize in the other the interior witness of the Holy Spirit.

And if we do this, then a distinction of the kind we are suggesting here becomes inevitable if we are not simply to allow two contradictory positions to exist side by side. That which we Catholics call sanctifying grace, and that which Protestant theology calls justification and sanctification may still have as many different interpretations placed upon it as there are different theologies.

Nevertheless, it still remains in any case an act of God wrought upon us in his grace which truly alters us, transforming us from sinners to justified persons, regardless of how we may interpret this sanctifying event of justification in more precise terms, whatever concepts we may use to express it, and however different the provenance of these concepts may be. Now precisely upon the Protestant understanding of grace, and at the same time on any truly rational Catholic ontology of grace, the reality involved here cannot be conceived of as though it had nothing to do with "faith," or as though it could coexist with a mere state of unbelief.

Thus if each of us credits the other with justifying grace, then we also credit one another with a real and true faith, and one which we may certainly not regard as merely empty in terms of the formative impact which it has upon our lives in the concrete, in other words, as mere credulity. Now if we credit one another mutually with true faith in this way, and if at the same time we take due cognizance of the very radical differences between the interpretations of faith put forward by the various churches to the extent that this faith is objectified in conceptual and verbal terms, then there must be a faith with which we mutually credit one another as true, and yet which is different from this faith that is given objective expression in concepts and words.

This conclusion cannot be evaded merely by saying that even at the level of conceptual and verbal objectification of the content of faith there are, after all, certain fundamental points which all hold in common, which thereby ensure that there shall be one and the same faith common to all, despite other secondary points of faith on which these Christians differ. For in the first place it is in fact questionable whether such common principles really are to be found held in common by all Christians.

It is questionable whether if there are such, there is sufficient common understanding of what they mean — over and above the mere verbal formulations which are common to all — and whether they have not been so much altered by the further theological statements which have been made and which are opposed to one another that it is no longer possible to speak of any real or effective unity of mind with regard to these more fundamental principles. And finally it may be questioned whether even in those cases in which — as with the Catholics — other points of faith are adhered to with the absolute assent of faith even though they are disputed by other confessions, these do not so intrinsically influence and modify those other points too which seem to be held in common (at least supposing that they are held with this absolute assent of faith) that we can no longer speak of any real fundamentally common mind with regard to the Christian creed.

The questionableness of all these points is such that one is certainly forced to conclude that the oneness of mind that is postulated with regard to one and same true faith cannot consist — or at least cannot consist exclusively — in agreeing upon certain fundamental Christian principles (as, for instance, after the pattern of the basic formula of the World Council of Churches).

The postulate arrived at in this way of one and the same true faith held in common by all (despite the fact that the Christians involved differ from one another in the verbal expressions of their faith in their creed) is not an entity of which the person is incapable of forming any idea merely on the grounds that manifestly it must be something that exists beneath and beyond any dogmatic principles which can be formulated in conceptual terms.

When we Christians, projecting our ideas beyond the confessional boundaries, credit one another with the presence of the Holy Spirit of grace, then manifestly what we are saying is, after all, that the ultimate and most interior *testimonium spiritus* is present in all, or at least must be presumed to be so present, that all of us are endowed with the *illustratio et inspiratio* of the Spirit (concepts with which tradition throws light upon the movements of grace), with the wordless groanings of the Spirit and utterances of Abba within the depths of our hearts, with the anointing of the Spirit spoken of by John which instructs us — all this is present even though this innermost reality of the Spirit and faith is objectified and interpreted differently in terms of words and ideas between the individual confessions.

Thus we still accept that in any anthropology of the human being as spiritual and free which is capable of looking rather deeper into the person, a difference always prevails (and one which can never adequately be overcome or transcended) between two factors in the human person's consciousness of himself: on the one hand, an ultimate self-possession of the subject as free, that is, a presence to himself which is never consciously explicated, a self-understanding on the individual's part which is never fully reflected upon; on the other, a person's objectified awareness of himself, his subjectivity and his capacity for free decision as objectified to himself.

Now if this is true, then the postulate we have put forward on theological grounds of a true faith held in common between separated Christians through and beyond that faith which can be objectified in concepts and words does not signify something of which the person himself is totally incapable of forming any idea. All of us "know" in the Spirit of God something more simple, more true, and more real than that which we are capable of knowing and expressing in the dimension of our theological concepts.

At this point we must, of course, pass over the question of why faith in the form in which it is objectified in conceptual terms is not rendered meaningless by a true faith of this kind, present in the midst of our lives in the power of the Spirit of God himself, yet preconceptual in form. This faith which we hold in common at the heart and center of our lives through the grace of God is the same true faith in all and incapable of deceiving. And it constitutes the true basis and the ultimate prior condition for ecumenical dialogue and an ecumenical theology.

Once we recognize it as the basis and prior condition for such dialogue and theology in this sense then, even when one or both parties to the ecumenical dialogue have given their absolute assent of faith to the particular propositions of faith which they uphold, the ecumenical dialogue can never be the sort of discussion in which one or both sides seek to communicate purely *ab externo* to the other parties to the discussion, at any given time, some doctrinal point which those other parties have so far simply failed to recognize or which is rejected as an erroneous belief.

Ecumenical discussion consists rather in the attempt through dialogue to render intelligible to the other parties the fact that what is being expressed to them in conceptual terms is simply a more correct, a fuller and a more precise expression of something which they have already apprehended as their own faith through the Spirit in the ultimate depths of their lives as already justified, and which they have laid hold of as their own truth.

On this basis an answer can also be given to the question of why an ecumenical dialogue is still possible even without any liberalizing prior assumptions, that is, even when an absolute assent of faith has been given to a controversial proposition of faith on the part of one or both parties. Even under these conditions ecumenical dialogue can be carried on as open to further decisions and results.

For even an absolute assent of faith on the part of one party to an article of belief that is controversial can and must presuppose the difference we have indicated between faith that is absolutely basic on the one hand and faith as objectified in words and concepts on the other. Such an absolute assent of faith, therefore, is perfectly compatible with the recognition that even a true objectification of the faith that is absolute and basic never adequately or fully expresses this, so that it is always open to further and fuller expression.

For this reason precisely this growing understanding of ourselves and of our own faith as objectified in concepts (even when these concepts are correct) can be promoted in an open dialogue by our partner in the discussion even though heterodox. Even when an absolute assent of faith has been given, this need not mean that the party to the dialogue must either be able to indoctrinate his partner through the propositions which he firmly upholds without any alteration, or else, if he cannot succeed in this, the dialogue must again and again be broken off without result, or be degraded to the level of a mere mutual interchange of information between the two sides with regard to their respective beliefs. Even one entering into dialogue when he has already given his absolute assent of faith to controversial articles of this kind can in a true sense learn from his partner in the discussion and thus conduct a dialogue that is open and that can yield fresh insights and results.

119 • Theses for the Unity of the Churches*

What short answer can we give when we are asked whether a unity of faith and church could be achieved in the foreseeable future among the large Christian churches? A difficult question, which most Christians probably answer with no. But we say yes, under the following conditions — which seem to us to be realizable in a relatively short time, if one perceives that this union is such a radical obligation coming from Jesus that one has the courage to postpone a number of rather significant scruples. These then, are the conditions we mean, although it may be that we have forgotten a few.

(1) The fundamental truths of Christianity, as they are expressed in holy scripture, in the Apostles' Creed, and in that of Nicaea and Constantinople are binding on all partner churches of the one church to be. (2) Beyond that, a realistic principle of faith should apply: Nothing may be rejected decisively and confessionally in one partner church which is binding dogma in another partner church. Furthermore, beyond thesis one no explicit and positive confession in one partner church is imposed as dogma obligatory for another partner church. This is left to a broader consensus in the future. This applies especially to authentic but undefined doctrinal decrees of the Roman church, particularly with regard to ethical questions. According to this principle only that would be done which is already practice in every church today.

(3) In this one church of Jesus Christ, composed of the uniting churches, there are regional partner churches which can, to a large extent, maintain their existing structures. These partner churches can also continue to exist in the same territory, since this is not impossible in the context of Catholic ecclesiology or the practice of the Roman church, as, for example, in Palestine. (4a) All partner churches acknowledge the meaning and right of the Petrine service of the Roman pope to be the

---

*Karl Rahner and Heinrich Fries, *Unity of the Churches: An Actual Possibility*, trans. Ruth C. L. Gritsch and Eric W. Gritsch (Ramsey, N.J.: Paulist Press, 1985), 7–10.

concrete guarantor of the unity of the church in truth and love. (4b) The pope, for his part, explicitly commits himself to acknowledge and to respect the thus agreed upon independence of the partner churches. He declares (by human right, iure humano) that he will make use of his highest teaching authority (ex cathedra), granted to him in conformity with Catholic principles by the First Vatican Council, only in a manner that conforms juridically or in substance to a general council of the whole church, just as his previous ex cathedra decisions have been issued in agreement and close contact with the whole Catholic episcopate.

(5) All partner churches, in accordance with ancient tradition, have bishops at the head of their larger subdivisions. The election of a bishop in these partner churches need not be done according to the normally valid manner in the Roman Catholic church. (The new Roman Canon Law also mentions ways of appointing a bishop other than through the pope's free choice. See can. 377, par. 1.) (6) The partner churches live in mutual fraternal exchange of all aspects of their life, so that the previous history and experience of the churches separated earlier can become effective in the life of the other partner churches. (7) Without prejudice to the judgment of another church concerning the theological legitimacy of the existing ministerial office in the separated churches all partner churches commit themselves henceforth to conduct ordinations with prayer and the laying on of hands, so that acknowledging them will present no difficulty for the Roman Catholic partner church either. (8) There is pulpit and altar fellowship between the individual partner churches.

We do not know whether we have forgotten any conditions and presuppositions for a faith and church unity which one side or another might consider irrevocable and equally fundamental. But we do think that the conditions listed can be accepted in principle by all the churches — including the Roman Catholic church — given the state of theology in all the confessions. Of course the fulfillment of these conditions would still require many reflections and many individual agreements on all sides.

But if one wants to transcend the verbal assertions of all the large Christian confessions that, in accordance with Jesus' commandment, demand the unity of the Christian churches, then in our opinion one should finally determine more exactly, more concretely, and in joint reflection, those conditions under which each existing church considers a speedy unity possible. When establishing such conditions each church would have the duty and responsibility — derived from the commandment of Jesus — to expand its own conditions no more than is clearly commanded by its own religious conviction of what is important to salvation. This should be done with real courage and some perhaps weighty doubts should be left aside.

Each historical tradition and custom contains, besides its good moments, a moment of inertia which prevents a society, and therefore also a church, from moving quickly into the future which God has intended for it and requires of it. We think that all the churches act with too much tactical caution in the quest for actual unity. They do not really come out courageously with declarations as to what the conditions are under which they are really prepared to unite with other churches, even with sacrifice. Each church waits for the other church to take the initiative and to express very clearly what it could truly not relinquish without in its own religious conscience incurring guilt before God. Nor do they express what does not belong thereto and can, therefore, be relinquished in order to fulfill Jesus' commandment.

We ourselves are pessimistic with regard to the question of whether the officials of all these churches can bring about unity in the near future, even though we have no right to deny all of them their good intentions. But we are convinced — and to that extent optimistic — that there is an objective possibility today for creating a satisfactory and speedy church unity.

120 • Dangers for the Church*

The greatest dangers are those that are not noticed. So it is in the church. It is always threatened with dangers, the worst of which come from within. Those from without only really become dangerous when and because they encounter a weakness within. The promise that the gates of the underworld will never overwhelm the church is not a promise about any kind of obvious and "empirical" strength and safety, but rather the promise of God's strength in the midst of the weak and threatened human beings who make up the church. When people feel assured and comforted because "nothing can happen" to the church, it always turns out that nothing does happen to it, because it is in God's hand, but something does happen to those who in laziness or cowardice rely on it.

Dangers to the church are often unnoticed; a feeling for contemporary life and culture, for example, is taken for granted everywhere including in the hearts and instincts of good Christians and that even

* *Gefahren im heutigen Katholizismus* (Einsiedeln: Johannes Verlag, 1955), 7–8. Trans. Daniel Donovan, University of Saint Michael's College, Toronto.

before the mind can examine it in the light of dogmatic teaching, a feeling or spirit that once there continues to work as a hidden essence even after one has protested against it. (Rationalism, for example, was fought with a form of rationalism, for, as they say, enemies are to be beaten with their own weapons.) *Such* dangers can only really be banished by saints and prophets. Only they are able to overcome the spirit of the age with the ever new (and yet ancient) Holy Spirit, "not with persuasive words of human wisdom but with a demonstration of Spirit and power" (1 Cor 2:4). They banish such a spirit not by disputing with it (as unavoidable as this also is in the household of the church) but by bringing and showing forth the ancient Holy Spirit of the church so that it becomes clear that he is the living Spirit of tomorrow. (How small and modest and without pretension are always the beginnings here, how old-fashioned and outdated they often seem!) In the battle against these dangers we others always use the weapons of human wisdom. We necessarily dispute back and forth and try to immunize people without being able to lead them out of the land where the sickness is endemic. We fight with the weapons of our opponents and can thank our lucky stars when we have not wounded ourselves more than the enemy. We fight for God's truth, we really do, but at the same time unnoticed and against our will we defend our own error which comes from yesterday against the error of today. And when we finish our task, we realize with shame that we are God's useless servants. But we can console ourselves with the thought that even the efforts of servants and poor sinners in the church are God's will, presupposed that we at least notice that it is not we who save his church but rather God who saves us in it.

121 • Trust within the Church*

I would like to put before you a few modest reflections on trust within the church. We are not talking about trusting the church. To do so would involve a very great danger of ideologically hypostasizing the church: it would not mean trusting any concrete individual and therefore it would be easy and would not hurt any of us. What I mean is trust *within* the church, trust given to concrete human beings in the church. Lay theologians too — if their study of theology has been more than a sublime scholarly-theoretical curiosity — in the course of their

---

Opportunities for Faith, 199–203.

life will enter into the church's mission in some shape or form, will have to do with the church, that is, with concrete individuals in the church and particularly with those who hold office.

That is why our trust is called for. Not merely that, but among many other things of course: faith, courage, honesty, firmness of character, willingness to serve, and many other things which must govern relations between human beings if these relations are to be truly human and Christian. But, as we said, trust too, trust in those with whom we cooperate in the service of the church's mission, trust also in the office-holders, although of course this is not to deny that the lay-theologian in the exercise of his mission also shares in the one office in the church.

What is meant by trust? I don't want to give a definition drawn from philosophical or theological ethics. But I think that trust has to do with granting someone else a prior claim on our own life and action: we open ourselves out to the other person and up to a point place ourselves at his disposal, without being absolutely sure of the trustworthiness of the other. Trust means surrendering oneself to another without an ultimate reassurance. If we are already absolutely certain that the other person is reliable, does not disappoint us, does not overtax us, does not demand more than he is permitted to demand, does not exploit us, pays back what he has been given, gives as much as he has received, we are not trusting the other, we are not entrusting ourselves to him, but (if we may put it in this way) we are trusting in our own knowledge of the other, we are not relying on the other, but on ourselves.

In trust we venture out to the other, forsake ourselves and our own security, and advance toward the other. Trust always means trusting in advance without security; it is essentially the risk of being disappointed, exploited, and of having our own uprightness turned (intentionally or unintentionally) into a weapon against ourselves. The situation is the same as that of love: this trust is a form of love. In both cases it is a question not of a deal, of give and take, not of a shrewd compromise between two egoisms, not of a calculation which we already know to be correct, but of the risk of having to give more than we receive, of knowing that what we give freely will be coolly taken for granted, of faith in the victory of truth and goodness even though this seems to be refuted a thousand times in life, of hope that love's utopia is the true future which is really coming, of love which succeeds in achieving the improbable, of getting a person away from himself. Trust is the gift of ourselves in advance, in the venture of believing and hoping, without previous cover.

I will not dwell on the fact that people cannot live in close contact with one another without this trust, that it is something without which a person is not a Christian. To make this clear would in fact be the most important thing to be said about trust. But it would take too long.

I would rather give a more concrete explanation of the way in which trust means giving the other person a start. I don't think I need in this respect to make especially explicit every time the "application" to people who cooperate with us in our service in the church's mission or who hold office.

This trust as given in advance means first of all quite simply that we approach the other person taking it ultimately for granted that he cannot a priori be considered as more stupid or less upright and straightforward than we consider ourselves to be, as intelligent and upright people. Theoretically this is simply obvious. In practice, however, it is cruelly hard, if only because in the individual case we do find in fact that the other is at least more stupid; nor is this always an illusion. It is cruelly hard particularly since we are much more egoistic, more full of our own importance, more self-confident than we are able or willing to admit. If our opinion is charged with the whole weight of our feeling as individuals and if the other person does not agree with us or even makes a demand on us in the light of this opinion, it really is difficult not to regard him as stupid or malicious.

Recently I was deeply shocked to read in the newspaper *Die Zeit,* how a former priest had charged the pope with bad faith, simply because he did not agree with the encyclical on celibacy. Mostly we don't make it so clear. But often enough we act in a similar way. Where an opinion touches ourselves in our own existence, we consider our own alone to be true and the opposite explicable only as the result of stupidity or malice. And if we look for reasons for our own opinion, we can easily find a thousand. As soon as we consider the arguments on the other side, the slightest emotional load is enough to blow the fuse in our head.

This trust of the other person in the church, if it is really given in advance, therefore implies self-criticism. In Mao Tse-tung's catechism self-criticism is one of the most important catchwords. Criticism in the church today is written in large letters. Not entirely without reasons. But in the catechism of our heart the word "self-criticism" should be written larger than we write it. We really could not but be shocked if we were to ask ourselves whether we know as much against ourselves as we bring forward against others, whether we are as critical of ourselves as of others. For we are convinced (not expressly and formally, but in the way our egoism normally functions) that we are more intelligent and upright than others, and in fact from the very start. We are not self-critical.

It is, however, only when we have a naturally, completely unneurotic, almost serene and obvious self-critical attitude toward ourselves, which we maintain without having to pride ourselves on it, that we cease to be egoists and become singleminded human beings and Christians. We gain a wonderful, serene freedom from ourselves when we no longer need to make ourselves the criterion of truth, when we can laugh at ourselves, when self-critical behavior has become natural to us.

My father, who lectured in a teachers' training college, once reproved a student for giving an answer which he was supposed to have given himself in a previous lecture. When the student therefore defended himself, my father said: "You don't have to repeat all the nonsense that I've said." Of course he had not said it, but neither was he self-assured. Many decades ago I had a professor who smiled at a student as he entered the lecture-hall and said: "Don't yawn. I haven't said anything yet." Self-critical freedom from oneself is necessary. It is because we — we Germans particularly — are not self-critical that we are so intolerant, so humorless, so pigheaded and fanatical. Self-criticism is the presupposition of being able to give our trust in advance to the other person, in the church too, convinced that it is not so certain that we are right, that it is the other perhaps who is right.

Only a person who is willing to serve can give his trust in advance. We are bound to have our own convictions, our own ideas, our own plans. But we should keep them fluid, in a self-critical spirit; we should be more expansive in our convictions, ready to make distinctions, more patiently wise: which does not mean that we want nothing more, can no longer say no, that we forgive everything because we understand everything. This self-critical growth in our convictions and decisions, if it is to be achieved within the church, presupposes the will to serve. We find ourselves only if we forget ourselves in the service of a cause: of the cause of human beings, which is greater than ourselves.

This shifting of the Archimedean point away from ourselves, without which we never really rise above ourselves in order truly to find ourselves, is possible only if there is a real source of authority in our life really pressing us, which we have not manipulated in advance in the light of our own taste and judgment, to which we have conceded the disposal of ourselves. Otherwise we just fluctuate within the circle of our own subjective whims. We must serve something else in order to become free, something greater, to which we have conceded freely but really a true power of determination over ourselves.

We must be willing to serve, we must be willing to receive orders which have not already been refashioned simply by the subjectivity of our own private sphere. Only if we succeed in this do we become free from the most deeply hidden self-alienation: that which confuses the most subjectivistic ego with the true ego which is attained only by conquering ourselves, ultimately by reaching God, not merely by a cheap ideologizing of our own subjectivity but by really exposing ourselves to another, by serving. It is by being willing to do this that we give our trust in advance. For this trust implies a willingness to listen without having completely examined already what is being said.

Someone who gives his trust in advance will often be disappointed. He will not rarely find that his trust remains unrewarded, is perhaps exploited, taken for granted, and wasted. Often he will not know (and in the last resort there is no formal prescription for this) how he can unite what is precisely his own responsibility and his own firm conviction with self-critical skepticism toward his own opinion and with the will for service without reservation, how he can be trusting without being gullible or naive. He will constantly be faced with the apparently insoluble task which was also faced by Jesus, of whom it was said that he trusted himself to no one, because he knew what was in the human heart, and who in summing up his life said that he was giving himself up to human beings and for human beings unto death. But none of this means that trust is not possible in the church, but only that this trust too is a miracle of God's grace, the folly of the cross, the Christian's self-denial, the imitation of the crucified, the faith that unarmed, foolish-seeming love will be victorious.

122 • A Servant Church*

The church ought to be a church concerned not with itself, but with people and all people. This was said at the Second Vatican Council and has been said often enough since then. But this requirement is still far from deciding the attitude of churchgoing Christians and the church. A social group which is constantly harried and nevertheless will not and cannot give way is inevitably under a great temptation to think mainly of itself and its continued existence. This is also the situation with us.

If the church cares about people — and thank God it does to an extent which should by no means be concealed from the non-churchgoing public who certainly do no more — this care is conceived in an odd sort of way and presented as an apology for the church itself it becomes too easily a means to the end. But the church with all its institutions is itself a means for human beings and they are its end.

---

* *The Shape of the Church to Come*, 61–63.

Officeholders and clerics particularly are liable to become ecclesiological introverts. They think of the church not of people. They want to see the church free, but not human beings. Under National Socialism, for instance, we thought considerably more about ourselves and about upholding what belonged to the church and its institutions than about the fate of the Jews. This may be understandable; but it was not very Christian or very Catholic if we appreciate the true nature of the church.

This task of the church to exist for human beings and not for herself is not merely directed to making people Christians in the sense of churchgoing people. A task understood in this way would really be legitimate only if it were at the same time a matter of winning people who would themselves help to sustain the church's mission to exist for everybody. If the church is indeed the sacrament of salvation for a world where in fact most people are saved without the church's institutionalized means (however much these are willed and authorized by God); if in spite of her mission the church cannot maintain that there is no salvation nor slow healing of the world without her visible manifestation; then to gain new churchgoing Christians means not so much or primarily saving those who would otherwise be lost but acquiring witnesses as signs making clear for all the grace of God effective throughout the world.

The wish to bring people into the church therefore must be a determination to make these churchgoing Christians serve everyone, even those who are ready to accept their services but nevertheless despise and oppose them; the poor too, the old, the sick, those who have come down in the world, the people on the edge of society, all those who have no power themselves and can bring no increase of power to the church.

The church has to stand up for justice and freedom for the dignity of the human being even when it is to her own detriment, even when an alliance — perhaps tacit — with the ruling powers would at first sight seem beneficial to her. Certainly none of us would deny this in theory. But since we are a church of sinners, we certainly cannot say that we would never in practice betray this essential mission of the church. We are constantly failing in this respect in the life of the church and, indeed, quite certainly even when it comes to official decisions, even in her concrete institutionalized forms which of course are themselves marked by the sin of egoism, of the quest for power, of a shortsighted wish for self-assertion.

If we are convinced that much injustice and tyranny prevail in a sinful world, if we really are or might be convinced that sin also characterizes social structures and is not merely something that happens to private individuals and is characteristic of their deeds, then we ought also really to be surprised how seldom — apart from direct and express attacks on the church — the church comes into conflict with those who hold power. This ought to make us suspicious of ourselves; it ought to make us suspicious of some of the conservatism in our midst.

We are not merely uttering pious platitudes fit only for Sunday sermons when we say that the church must not be concerned with serving others merely for the sake of proving her own claims and that she must stand by the side of the poor, the oppressed, life's failures. But does the reality correspond to this sacred principle, the principle that the church has to be there for all and therefore also for the others that she must serve, even those who attach no importance to her and regard her as a relic from a vanished age? Is this form of the "folly of the cross" very much in evidence among us? Is enough love applied in the church? Is there enough courage for stubborn confrontations and are enough power, time, and money given to unselfish service for others without calculating the advantages to the church herself?

There are of course miracles of love and unselfish service among us, and perhaps others are no better on the whole. This however does not prove that the church is wholly the unselfish servant for the welfare and salvation of the others and that we must not always be asking anxiously whether we are not fearfully introverted, concerned more for the church than for others; it does not relieve individual Christians of the obligation to protest boldly in certain circumstances, even against the officeholders of the church, when the church thinks more of herself and tries to save herself otherwise than by saving others. All this is very abstract and its practical meaning really ought to be made clearer by concrete examples. But this is simply not possible here. The brevity of these hints should not lead us to think that the matter is not of the greatest importance.

123 • The Church as a Tiny Flock*

The church of the future will be a "tiny flock," that is, a group with a particular world view within a pluralistic society. To say this is not to proclaim social pluralism as an absolute ideal. Such an apparently tolerant and liberal pluralism can mask the intention of establishing and maintaining as alone viable particular societal structures together with their injustices. The declaration that theoretically everything has

---

*Handbuch der Pastoraltheologie IV, 751–53. Trans. Daniel Donovan, University of Saint Michael's College, Toronto.

equal rights can rob what is not yet established of the distinctiveness and the power it needs to assert itself.

Talk about the church as a tiny flock is obviously not intended to suggest a goal for the church nor should it undermine its missionary impetus to win the maximum number of believers and to be present in public life in the strongest way possible. It will of course have to do these things in ways that respect the rules of a pluralistic society. The phrase clearly implies that the church of the future will continue to be in a realistic sense a world-church, present in all peoples and cultures, although of course at different levels of intensity. As a sober prognosis of what might be called an inevitable development in the history of salvation, but which implies no "should" nor offers any dispensation from missionary responsibility, the phrase about the tiny flock is true and has considerable significance for missionary strategy. It says that we have to realize that in the future the world will become even in a religious sense (and often through guilt and sin) more secular, that societies and states that identify themselves as a whole and institutionally with Christianity and its conception of human life and with the church will no longer exist. In this sense the Constantinian era of the church in the West is at an end, nor does it have any future in other areas at a moment when world history has become one. We in Europe (and analogously in North and South America) are in a transition period between the Constantinian era, a symbiosis of society as a whole and church, on the one hand, and a time in which Christianity and the church will have to live on their own in a secular society, on the other. The church does not have the obligation always and everywhere to hasten the process of which I am speaking. It has, however, the obligation to give up positions of power in society when their defense in the long term can only harm the cause of religion and when the defense itself reflects ultimately an unadmitted lack of trust in the power of the gospel.

A sober reckoning with this future situation everywhere of the tiny flock would give the church the possibility of concentrating in specific areas its limited missionary resources rather than dissipating them. The status of the voluntary community of faith as opposed to the earlier *Volkskirche,* or culturally supported church, will certainly entail significant changes in the institutionalization of the church without in any way undermining what in its constitution is of divine law. When the actual existence and the real efficiency of ecclesial office will depend more or less exclusively on the free faith of all members of the church, psychologically and socially the relation between officeholders and "lay people" will change considerably. Because it will be obvious how each side depends on the other, clerical and anticlerical mentalities and animosities will disappear. Officeholders who will no longer have any particular social prestige in the eyes of secular society will more easily be accepted by the laity as belonging to them, as people who selflessly have placed themselves at the disposition of this community of God's people. The so-called lay person, on the other hand, will be much more clearly experienced even by officeholders as the one who builds up the church, who gives it being and real effectiveness, even in its office.

124 • A Declericalized Church*

The church should be a declericalized church. This proposition is of course open to misunderstanding and must be explained. It is obvious that there are offices in the church with definite functions and powers, however these offices may be distinguished and divided, however the functions and powers transmitted to officeholders in the concrete can or must be precisely conceived. It is also obvious in the light of the church's nature, mission, and spirit that her offices and officeholders as such have a special character that is not shared by office and officeholders in secular society. But this special feature comes to these offices and these officeholders as such precisely from the nature of the church as a Spirit-filled community of all who believe in Jesus Christ. It does not originate in a way which would simply dissociate office and officeholders from the church as the community of all Christians.

Office has a functional character in the church as society, even though this society with its functions (proclamation of the word, sacrament, leadership of the church's life as society) constitutes a sign of what is real in the church: the free Spirit, faith, hope, love, to which all socially institutional factors in office are oriented and at the same time are never identical with them. Hence the "hierarchy" (if we may use the term) in the real nature of the church is not identical with the hierarchy in the church's social structure. The situation in the church is really like that of a chess club. Those who really support the club and give it its meaning are the members to the extent that they play chess well. The hierarchy of the club leadership is necessary and appropriate if and as far as it serves the community of chess players and their "hierarchy" and does not think it is identical with the latter or that it can play chess better simply in virtue of its function.

So too office is to be respected in the church; but those who love,

---

* *The Shape of the Church to Come,* 56–60.

who are unselfish, who have a prophetic gift in the church constitute the real church and are far from being always identical with the office-holders. It is of course part of the Catholic faith that the Spirit of God in the church is able to prevent an absolute schism between those who simply possess the Spirit and those who hold office, and therefore the latter also in virtue of their social function — but only in the last resort — enjoy a certain gift of the Spirit.

As soon as these obvious dogmatic truths are lived and practiced impartially and taken for granted by officeholders and other Christians, then we have what we call a declericalized church: that is, a church in which the officeholders too, in joyous humility, allow for the fact that the Spirit breathes where it will and that it has not arranged an exclusive and permanent tenancy with them. They recognize that the charismatic element which can never be completely regulated is just as necessary as office to the church: that office is never simply identical with the Spirit and can never replace it; that office too is really effectively credible in the sight of people only when the presence of the Spirit is evident and not merely when formal mission and authority are invoked, however legitimate these may be.

If we also remember (and this must be specially considered at greater length later) that the church of the future must grow in its reality quite differently from the past, from below, from groups of those who have come to believe as a result of their own free personal decision, then what is meant here by declericalization may become clearer. Office will exist in a church growing from below in this way, really and not merely theoretically emerging from the free decision of faith on the part of individuals, since there cannot be a society at all without office.

It can then rightly be said that this office rests on the mission from Christ and not merely on the social combination of individual believers, even though it is also true that this mission from above is included in God's gracious will to all persons to which the church owes her nature and existence. But this official authority will be really effective in the future in virtue of the obedience of faith which believers give to Jesus Christ and his message. It will no longer be effective in virtue of powers over society belonging to office in advance of this obedience of faith as it is today but to a constantly diminishing extent.

In this sense the authority of office will be an authority of freedom. In practice, officeholders in the future will have as much effective au-thority — not merely a theoretical claim to authority — as is conceded to them freely by believers through their faith. The assumption of an authority in the church will always have to consist in an appeal to the free act of faith of each individual and must be authorized in the light of this act in order to be effective at all; in the concrete the officeholder's appeal to his authority will be a proclamation of *faith*.

For it is only through this faith that authority becomes really effective; the church is a declericalized church in which the believers gladly concede to the officeholders in free obedience the special functions in a society — and thus also in the church — which cannot be exercised by all at the same time.

It is true that these official powers in the church are conferred by a special rite which we call the sacrament of holy orders and, when they are conferred, the officeholders are also assured by God of the help of that Spirit who is with the church; but this in no way alters the declericalized conception of office in the church. In the future questions or doubts about office will no longer be effectively dismissed by appealing to the formal authority of office but only by furnishing proof of a genuinely Christian spirit on the part of the officeholder himself. He will gain recognition for his office by being genuinely human and a Spirit-filled Christian, one whom the Spirit has freed for unselfish service in the exercise of his social function in the church.

We might ask now what conclusions are to be drawn from this declericalization for the officeholders' way of life in the concrete. The life-style especially of the higher clergy even today sometimes conforms too much to that of the "managers" in secular society. All the ceremony which distinguishes the officeholder, even in the most ordinary circumstances, from the mass of the people and other Christians, and which has nothing to do with the exercise of his office and stresses his dignity where it is out of place, might well disappear. In the very exercise of office there could certainly be much greater objectivity in judging and deciding, and particularly for outsiders the attempt to be objective could be made more clearly visible.

There is no point in being secretive. An appeal to "experience" becomes suspect when experience appears to have been conditioned from the beginning by clerical prejudices. If advisers have been consulted, we ought to be allowed to know who they were. Office loses none of its authority or dignity if the decision and the reasons for it are made public at the same time. The more secular from the nature of the case is the object of a decision, so much the more relevant are *those* reasons which can be understood, even by someone who is not well versed in theology.

There must be more courage to reverse and withdraw decisions without a false and ultimately unchristian concern for prestige and also to admit it openly if these decisions have turned out to be objectively mistaken or — humanly speaking — unjust. Reaction to criticism of decisions must be relaxed and open to enlightenment, not every time taking the form of asserting that the matter has been considered so thoroughly that the decision made is beyond all criticism.

In matters also which are dogmatically and constitutionally by no means immutable, we should remember that the simple wish of a majority in the church quite legitimately counts even in advance as part of the objective substantiation of a decision. A decision to be based merely on the weight of custom must not be decked out with ideological arguments produced for the occasion by smart theologians or church functionaries: these might seem very profound but they really convince only those who have already been convinced for a long time for other reasons of what is now propped up by subtle theological or legal arguments. The danger of self-delusion through such subsequent ideological substructures is very great in the church and it is a typical feature of false clericalism.

No damage is done to office or officeholders if the latter honestly admit uncertainties, doubts, the need of experiment and further reflection without knowing the outcome and don't behave as if they had a direct hot line to heaven to obtain an answer to each and every question in the church. The formal authority of an office, even when the officeholder exercises it legitimately, does not relieve him of the duty, in the light of the question before him and within really contemporary horizons of understanding, of effectively winning a genuine assent on the part of those affected by his decision.

It seems to me that Roman decrees in particular do not sufficiently take account of this principle and therefore in such enactments too much weight is laid on Rome's formal authority. Particularly in moral theological doctrinal decisions, it cannot be claimed on the one hand that they relate to natural law, which is in principle intelligible to everyone, while on the other hand invoking the merely formal teaching authority without any adequate attempt to expound convincingly and vividly in the language of the present time the intrinsic arguments derived from the nature of the case. Many other similar and proximate and remote conclusions could be drawn from a correctly understood declericalization of office in the church. But this may suffice for the moment.

125 • Democratization of the Church*

In the church of the future there will be more of a democratic mentality, more democratic institutions and democratic procedures than there have been up to now. Such a development is possible because what has been dogmatically defined in the area of ecclesiology leaves room for it, as a number of facts from the history of the church and especially from its earliest periods make clear.

The involvement of lay people in the life of the church, in the appointment of officeholders and in the development of canon law was not always as restricted as it has been in the immediate past. Recent practice has been rashly interpreted as being directly reflective of the fact that office and mission in the church come not from below but from Christ. The expectation of democratization in the church, the details of which can be set aside for the moment, does not presuppose any naive glorification of democracy in general. It arises much more from the basic affirmation of faith that the dignity and radical equality of all the baptized are more fundamental for the church than the necessary differentiation of functions and their distribution among various persons of whom not each has every power.

The expectation is based in the second place on the simple fact, repeatedly born out in history, that the relations and structures of secular society have had, have, and indeed must have an impact on specific constitutional arrangements within the church. If a patriarchal and feudal period of society has come to an end, this too must inevitably have implications for the church.

The expectation is related in the third place to the fact that an individual group in a pluralistic society which is dependent upon the free will of its members can take on a different structure much more easily than would be possible in the case where societal structures and power relations exist before and independent of the personal will of individual members. This "democratization" is not to be a simply copy of democracy as it exists or should exist in secular society. For that, the differences between church and society are too great.

Democracy in the church means simply, in the first place, that lay people should have as active and responsible a part in its life and decisions as possible. It means more precisely that their active participation should be institutionalized in canon law. For all practical purposes active participation and coresponsibility will only be accepted when they

---

*Handbuch der Pastoraltheologie IV, 753–54. Trans. Daniel Donovan, University of Saint Michael's College, Toronto.

are grounded in law and do not depend from moment to moment on the goodwill of officeholders.

Such democratization can take on a variety of concrete forms. It might mean an involvement in the appointment of officeholders, an active voice in determining specific forms of church life, the participation of the laity in the development of a new code of canon law, an authentic and guaranteed cooperation in the creation of public opinion in the church, and so on. That the rules of church administration and the exercise of teaching authority should in the future be more humane, more just, more concerned about protecting the individual from the arbitrariness of office and in this sense more democratic, goes without saying.

A conscious and determined effort will have to be made in order slowly to create the human and canonical presuppositions required for such a democratization. It is, for example, a difficult problem to determine what conditions lay people must meet before one can seriously grant them the right to democratic collaboration. Such a role cannot be given to someone who is only a Catholic in name. How to distinguish, however, between those who are truly Christian and those who are only nominally so is a difficult, although not an impossible, question.

126 • A Letter from the Pope in the Year 2020*

Even if I do not impute to any of my predecessors, or at least to my immediate predecessors, a lack of humility and modesty, it seems to me that today a pope [in the year 2020] may, even publicly, make this critical self-evaluation more clearly than it used to be done. Important people in the history of both the world and the church used to have the idea that their legitimate authority would be jeopardized, if they let their "subjects" see that they too were only human beings who committed blunders. It is only after their death that church historians were allowed to discover faults, mistakes, or backwardness in a pope.

But if I am convinced that even as pope I remain a human being who will commit faults, perhaps even serious ones, why would I not be allowed to admit this even during my lifetime? Is the mentality of people who really matter not such today that authority does not suffer damage,

* *Theological Investigations XXII*, trans. Joseph Donceel, S.J. (New York: Crossroad Publishing Company, 1991), 195–96.

but rather profits, when its bearer openly admits the limitations of a poor and sinful human being, and is not afraid to acknowledge them? For the time being at least, I am willing to listen to public discussions in my presence, eventually to learn from others, and to admit that I have learned.

Even as pope I would like to continue to learn. Let people notice that a pope can err, make mistakes, be poorly informed, and choose the wrong kind of assistants. All of this is evident and I believe that no recent pope has seriously doubted it. But why must such evidence remain hidden and covered up? Peter allowed Paul to confront him to his face, and I suppose that Peter acknowledged that Paul was right. Even today a pope may allow himself something of the kind. I for one, lay claim to that right and I am willing, if necessary, to let my authority suffer a loss, which it would be my duty to accept.

I shall not be a great pope. I do not have the wherewithal. So I will not have an inferiority complex if I look quite modest compared with the great popes of the twentieth century. To me that seems providential. I have a feeling that through their grandeur these popes had an influence in the church which they probably never intended and which had its questionable side, an influence that I will try to offset with my more modest pontificate.

Is it not true? Have these great popes not involuntarily fostered a mentality in the church that overestimates the pope's proper function, as it should be according to dogma, and as it was in most of the history of the popes? Does this mentality not imply that a pope must in all respects be the greatest one in the church, a point of reference for all impulses, a teacher who is superior to all thinkers and theologians, a saint and a prophet, a man who conquers all hearts with his fascinating personality, a great leader who molds his century and makes statesmen and other great personalities pale into insignificance, a pontiff, whom all bishops respectfully approach, like petty officials before their king, in order to listen obediently to his words and orders?

I will not become such a pope and I do not consider it necessary at all. The pope has a task in the church that is strictly limited despite the universal jurisdiction and the fullness of teaching authority mentioned by the First Vatican Council. I will exercise this fullness of power, but within the limits imposed on me by the limitations of my own nature. That, and nothing more. I will not be the holiest one in the church. Before God I am less than the saints who live today in the church, those who pray in silence, those who are mystically enraptured, those who perish for their faith in the prisons of the enemies of Christ and the church, those who love unselfishly, as Teresa of Calcutta did, all the unknown and unrewarded heroes of everyday duty and abnegation.

Nobody can deny that even an Innocent III pales before Francis of Assisi, and that the popes named Pius of the last two centuries are less important than a Curé d'Ars or a St. Thérèse of Lisieux. You may say, of course, that I am comparing realities that cannot be compared. However, in the life of the church and before God's eternal tribunal, saints and great theologians, like a Thomas Aquinas or a John Henry Newman, are more important than most popes, and especially more important than I will ever be.

There are many charisms in the church, and the pope does not have all of them himself. If it is true that we can really understand only our own charisms, even a pope must tell himself that he cannot evaluate everything that lives in the church, and that God alone, and not the pope, stands where all that is good and holy in the church merges into a perfect symphony.

That is why no harm will be done if my pontificate corrects, to some extent, the mentality of those pious Christians who wrongly expect from the popes what they can receive only from saints and great minds in the church and possibly from themselves. Are there Christians, and perhaps popes, who remember that, when they pray the Our Father with impatient hope for the coming of God's eternal kingdom, they are praying also for the end of the papacy? An insignificant pope too may be providential.

127 • The Church as a Critic of Society*

Precisely because of its greater distance from secular society, the church of the future will be able to and should exercise, to a more marked degree than in the past, a social-critical function. From the point of view of secular society, the church has as much right to do this in a pluralistic society as any other group functioning according to democratic procedures.

The critical function that arises out of the very nature of the church is quite different from any kind of "politicizing" activity. A political church in this sense would begin by imposing some particular political and social idea on its own members and then without any respect for pluralism or for democratic procedures would attempt to play power politics

---

*Handbuch der Pastoraltheologie IV, 756–57. Trans. Daniel Donovan, University of Saint Michael's College, Toronto.

in order to see it adopted by society at large. In such cases the idea usually bears conservative and reactionary traits.

The church has a social-critical function because Christianity is not merely a matter of the private and the personal, and because love of neighbor, without which there is no love of God, is not simply private affection between individuals but needs to become operative in the world through justice and its ever new embodiment in changing institutional forms. The eschatological hope of Christianity, moreover, always entails a relativizing and a questioning of existing social structures. It itself only becomes operative by means of such a critical function and by the creation of new innerworldly tasks and goals for society.

Consciousness of the critical function of the church, of its duty to act on behalf of the dignity of the individual and in defense of justice against institutionalized injustice, is still not very developed. This is because of the close symbiosis that existed between society and state on the one hand and the church on the other, in which secular and political society was almost instinctively seen as the "secular arm" at the service of the church. The church of the future must become much more conscious of this task. It must not protest only when state and society threaten it. It has a responsibility for the world in spite of the fact that it is not to be political in the ordinary sense of the word and in spite of its inability to develop in detail any social concept that could claim to be the right one. It must, moreover, understand and accept that there are a variety of groups within it with different political ideas, and that they all claim that their positions are inspired by the gospel.

128 • Assent to the Actual Church*

I believe that in seeking the *point of departure* for a hopeful and committed assent to the church in the concrete we can to some extent show where this lies in three ways or from three distinct aspects:

1) Human living in the concrete is not artificially developed by a process of speculation as though in a test tube. Certainly the power to speculate is a part of human nature, the capacity to experience the question of human existence, to adopt a critical standpoint toward, and to inquire into, that state in which all unquestioned we have been placed. Certainly there is nothing in this existence such that it either should or even may seem to be excluded from the outset from this pro-

---

* *Theological Investigations XII*, 147–52.

cess of critical speculation. But after all this is only one side of human existence.

We never wholly include ourselves in our critical speculation. In it we take as our starting point again and again presuppositions which we have not subjected to our critical questioning in their own right or in the same way. Constantly we find ourselves already embarked upon a course, the starting point of which already lies behind us. In our critical evaluations we proceed from certain standards and intellectual perspectives, and even though we certainly could subject these in turn to our process of critical questioning, de facto we have failed to apply this process in their case. We never really begin from zero. Indeed we are incapable of doing this because otherwise we would be standing outside our own course of history and the historical mode which is proper to us, and this is impossible for us. Even the most radical revolutionary, in his quest for an ideological critique which is unconditioned, cannot achieve this without in turn, whether he is aware of it or not, beginning from some point which he himself has not determined and upon which he has not reflected in any adequate sense.

The will to achieve a critical standpoint which is absolute, which in its concrete exercise has refused to commit itself by an act of trust to any prior assumptions, would lead only to a state of absolute immobility, to total sterility, to a radical neurosis of existence such as would incapacitate its practitioners for living. It is a fact that nothing comes from nothing. Where there is real and genuine life at the intellectual level, such as is capable of surviving and taking responsibility, there will also be an attitude of trustful and willing commitment in which that which is inevitable is accepted and accorded its due force. And for this reason anyone engaged in genuine living freely accepts, by an ultimate act of trust in life itself, the impossibility of totally comprehending life in his own speculative processes and in the process of critical inquiry precisely into this life. And this remains true even though it does not mean that any one specific factor should from the outset be excluded from this process of critical speculation.

The human person as a being endowed with critical faculties calls all things in question, and the person as finite, and as a being who exists in a specific preexisting situation which he himself has not created is himself in turn critical with regard to his own critical faculties, and for all these critical attitudes of his, in an absolutely ultimate sense he proceeds in his life from an unreserved act of trust in the fact that however true it may be that any individual factor can be destroyed, that which is prior and given would, ultimately speaking and taken as a whole, stand up to his critique even at those points at which that critique can no longer in practice be applied to it in any adequate sense.

We are speaking of a certain unity between an attitude of radical criticism at the fundamental level on the one hand, and a spirit of unreserved trust in that which is untested by criticism on the other. Now this is not something which the individual could control for himself in his practical life (different in this from theory which remains at the merely formal level). It is not something which he himself in his turn could master or bring within his control by achieving a standpoint of transcendence at some high level from which he could subject it to a concrete critique. Rather, it is something which is bestowed upon him as that incomprehensible reality of his life which is called grace, though admittedly this must also be accepted and can be refused. The actual situation is this: the concrete human life which someone lives is not created in the test tube of speculation. It is not first dissected by his critique down to the point of an absolute void, so that subsequently it can be artificially built up by speculation, criticism, and theory.

Now so far as the Catholic is concerned, one of the factors in his concrete human life is his membership in the church and his life in and with her. For him this state of belonging to the church is not some kind of minor incidental factor in his life which can even disappear without his life as a whole being thereby altered, as though it were like an individual buying a new suit or going to live in another district.

This assent to the church as she exists in the concrete has already permeated our entire life. We have prayed, supplicated for the eternity of God in his holiness. We have heard the words of eternal life from the mouth of the church, experienced the grace which she has imparted to us through her sacraments. Again and again we have been roused by her from the inertia and apathy of our everyday lives. Through her we have experienced the eternal in ourselves. Already in our lives we have lived, and in this sense uttered, an assent in the concrete to the church in the concrete. This assent has truly been made at the very center of our personal human existence.

Hence we also have the right and duty, precisely on the basis of intellectual honesty, freely and unreservedly to commit ourselves to this assent, to let it stand even though in doing so we are constantly aware of the fact that we have still not mastered all the reasons for this assent which have unconsciously asserted themselves in us or all the implications which it carries by our speculative processes; even though we are aware that this assent can be confronted again and again with fresh critical questioning, and that the relationship between the free and trustful prior decision governing our lives on the one hand and the process of critical speculation on the other is constantly shifting and constantly bringing us fresh surprises. Certainly even our relationship with the church is something that we subject again and again to critical questioning.

But we have the right and the duty, until the contrary is proved beyond all doubt (and this is something which we do not fear) to assume and to live by the fact that these critical questionings do not destroy this relationship of ours with the church, just as in other ultimate commitments and attitudes of our lives, commitments to loyalty, love, integrity without thought of reward or trust, or commitments to our neighbor, again and again through life itself and through the processes of our critical speculations we experience the fact that these commitments are under assault and yet, so long as we do not fall into a neurosis of criticism and doubt, we are aware that these basic commitments endure throughout all the purgatory of doubt and questioning.

We have already said at the outset of these remarks that we are addressing ourselves to Catholics. Now these have experienced the fact that their assent to the church is not some kind of incidental option which they have taken in their lives, but in a true sense is to be numbered among the basic attitudes which sustain those lives. But if this is true then they have the right to commit themselves to this assent in a spirit of trust, to nourish ever fresh hopes that the inner spiritual continuity of their lives will endure throughout all the manifest and painful vicissitudes in the unfolding process of their lives as spiritual beings, whether these be great or small. We cannot allow ourselves to be maneuvered into that kind of questioning which is destructive of our lives, and we would be doing this if we were suddenly to notice at some point that, after all, the ultimate grounds on which our assent to the church was based had given way as a basic reality of our personal lives and that our existence had become a bottomless abyss into which we had been cast. This is a situation in which we do not stand, and we must not allow ourselves to fall into it.

And hence, when faced with the possibility (absolutely speaking, conceivable) of a kind of doubt which of itself does not admit of any further answer in the here and now, it is meaningless to react to this with a universal doubt of the kind that negates our assent to the church. Otherwise we would be like human beings who from fear of death would even take their own lives. We must recognize the fact, therefore, that human life in the concrete cannot be constructed by any absolute process of reflection. And for this reason it must not feel itself to be called in question at the ultimate level by these particular critical questioning which may arise on individual points even if there are such.

Now the perception of this fact is the first aspect of the point of departure at which we must take our stand again and again in critically reappraising our assent to the church in the concrete in the manner that is legitimate and prescribed. The true process of critical reappraisal is itself in turn subjected to its own critique, and with regard to our experience of the realities of life in globo, which, even though we do not subject it to speculative analysis, is nonetheless genuine and sustaining, this genuine process of critical reappraisal trustfully allows this global experience the chance to endure and again and again to prove itself genuine.

2) This brings us to a second aspect of the point of departure for arriving at a correct answer to our basic question. Global decisions of life, which affect the totality of our human lives and which are therefore incapable of ever being totally subsumed under our critical speculations, should endure throughout those unresolved tensions which arise between the decisions themselves and our critical reflections upon them.

Newman pointed out long ago that a thousand difficulties of faith, such as we obviously experience, still do not constitute a doubt, of faith such as constitutes a negation of our commitment to faith. In view of the finitude of their intellectual resources in the concrete, the finitude of their knowledge and the brevity of their lifespan, neither the average Christian nor yet the learned theologian is in any position to solve for himself in any positive and clear way all the difficulties which can be raised against the convictions of faith in critical questions. We are confronted with the immense complexity of our existence, with an immense pluralism among the philosophies of life and the problems and findings of the sciences, such as cannot be mastered by any one individual. We are confronted with the multiplicity of our personal experiences of life, which can never wholly be reduced to a synthesis at the level of theory. And in view of all this it is obvious from the outset that our ultimate commitment of faith is always surrounded by an incalculable range of questions which we have not yet positively solved, mastered, or reduced to a positive synthesis within this commitment of faith in any effective sense.

But we must and can in all calmness achieve the perception that this is also something which is not for one moment to be expected, because it is impossible that this tension between question and answer can be solved in any direct and definitive manner. On the contrary, it has constantly to be endured in a spirit of confidence and patience in our lives until one day the eternal light illumines us.

Even the Catholic Christian can say: "When an individual genuinely and inculpably comes to grief as a result of this tension, when he is genuinely *incapable* of enduring it any longer, he is guiltless and hence even in these circumstances he has not lost the true substance of his faith at all." But in a spirit of self-criticism we must guard against the

danger which arises in the concrete circumstances of our lives of supposing that we have arrived at a state in which we "cannot do any
more," when in reality the point that we have arrived at is one in which
an "acquittal from guilt" of this kind is merely serving to cover up an
ultimate cowardice of life which is no longer *willing* to endure these
unreserved tensions.

In other departments of life, too, the situation that arises is in fact
this: We have enough harsh and disappointing experiences of ourselves
and our fellow men and women to have seemingly good grounds for
adopting an attitude of doubting skepticism toward humanity. Now we
can never solve such grounds as these by any process of theoretical
reasoning in such a way that they no longer represent a threat to our ultimate and basic attitude toward humanity, no longer bring it ever anew
into mortal peril, that basic attitude which consists in trust, reverence,
and love.

And yet at the same time we are aware that we must maintain this
affirmative and loving attitude toward humanity right to the end. In the
same way many temptations, questions, problems, and objections obviously arise on the personal, historical, and theoretical planes against
our assent to the church, her truth and institutions, objections which
it is not given to us to work out in any positive and direct way until
we have arrived at a complete solution to them. But the attitude of
trustfully enduring unresolved tensions even in our relationship with
the church is only one instance of a reality which is actually a factor
inherent in our lives. We cannot overcome such tensions by running
away from them.

3) This leads us on immediately to the third aspect of the right point
of departure for finding the answer to our basic question. It is only
in the act of striving for that which is greater, more enlightening, a
greater force for life, that the human person has the right to relinquish
something that belongs to his life, to surrender it. And it is only for the
sake of a greater meaningfulness that he has the right to abandon that
which has hitherto been meaningful to him as meaningless.

Perhaps this statement will not enlighten a skeptic who has allowed
mistrust, and that doubt which calls everything in question, to penetrate
into the innermost center of his life. But nevertheless this statement
is true, and without it life cannot endure. Indeed the radical skeptic
recognizes the truth of this statement even though in doing so he contradicts his own position when he achieves the courage to embrace
a skepticism which on his view is devoid of illusions as the highest
meaning of his existence. And most average human beings are quite
unaware when they adopt a skeptical attitude of this kind, of how much
in the way of meaningfulness, in the way of that which is unquestion-

ingly taken for granted and made the basis of their lives, they are still constantly allowing to remain.

But he who, as a Catholic Christian, takes this statement as the standard by which to evaluate the question of his assent to the church in the concrete can in all intellectual honesty justify this assent of his ever afresh despite all difficulties and temptations. For he can see what it will mean to depart from the truth of the church, from her essential message, from the living and protecting mystery which we call God, from the hope of eternal life, from a hopeful sharing in the death of Jesus who, in a spirit of hope and love, allowed himself to fall into this mystery of God, from the fellowship of love called the church, from the acceptance of forgiveness for the guilt of our lives — in brief, from all that which the church signifies. To depart from all this would not bring the individual concerned into a greater sphere of meaningfulness, of light, of freedom, or of hope. Instead, such a departure could only lead to one of two consequences: either an attitude of surrendering oneself to a lethal darkness of skepticism and of unworthy relativism or to the dubious attempt to live in isolation by the impoverished remnants of meaningfulness, light, and courage which still remained, without really being able to see why these remnants deserve more assent or trust than that fullness of meaningfulness which is present and living in the church.

129 • What the People Actually Believe*

First, it seems to me that the difference between what the church officially teaches and what the people actually believe does not have a merely negative value, but a theologically positive aspect as well. The fact that the *index systematicus* of Denzinger can rarely be found in the heads of ordinary Christians is not as deplorable as it may seem to many people who are tempted to identify saving faith with theological formation.

Sophisticated knowledge of something may even be a great obstacle to its personal assimilation. I suspect that today's catechisms, however modern they claim to be, still contain too many things and that they do not present the heart of the Christian message, that which must by all means be said in a striking, really intelligible way. Moreover,

---

* *Theological Investigations XXII*, 169–71.

it is that faith in the church which actually exists in heads and hearts, and not properly official church doctrine, that immediately and in itself is *the faith* that constitutes the church.

Of course we can rightly say that the often fragmentary and undifferentiated faith of the individual, and therefore also of many individuals, stands in relation to the faith of the whole church. It is within the faith of the whole church that the great and luminous totality of Christian faith is believed and practiced. One of its essential components is the faith of the saints, the heroes of faith, the mystics. But the church does not consist only of its saints. The faith of the average Christian is not just a pitiable sketch of the official faith. It is a salutary faith, borne by God's self-communication. It is really the faith that God's grace wishes to bring forth and keep alive in the church.

We may not judge this faith by its objective verbal contents. Even when its objectification in words and concepts is very poor and deficient, it is still God's action in us, constituted by the self-communication of God in the Holy Spirit. As such, it infinitely transcends the most sublime theological objectification of the faith. The *depositum fidei* ("deposit of faith") is not first and foremost a sum of statements formulated in human language.

It is God's Spirit, irrevocably communicated to humankind, activating in persons the salutary faith which they really possess. Of course the same Spirit also brings forth in this way the community of the faithful, in which the unity and fullness of Christian faith are objectified and brought to consciousness in what we perceive as the official faith of the institutional church. Nevertheless, what matters above all is the faith that really lives in the ordinary Christian. That is the faith which actually saves, in which God communicates himself to humanity, however pitiful and fragmentary its conceptualization may be.

Human transcendence, which is created by the Spirit of God, borne by God's self-communication, and enabled by God's self to aim at God's immediacy, is called faith. It always has a starting point in the world, a mediation, some individual "object" that is believed. But this mediation leading to ultimate salvation may, under God's providence, be of different kinds. It may be paltry, it may be rich, and it has its own history. It is obviously not God's intention that every individual believer should enjoy all at once the fullness of this history of mediation — not even the faithful in the church, although the church makes possible a richer and more detailed knowledge of the totality of these historical mediations.

These considerations allow us to say that the real faith of the faithful in the church has a normative significance for the official faith of the church. The latter, of course, has a normative significance for the former, a point that is rightly emphasized by the teaching of the church.

Certainly we may not say that the faith of the magisterium should be directed by that of the faithful, as discovered by an opinion poll. That would be false, not only because of the very nature of the faith but also because it is impossible to discover, by the usual canvassing methods, what the faithful believe.

The official faith of the church contains data that derive from the history of the church's faith, data that have become irreversible and are normative for the faith of the present-day church. The church possesses an authoritative magisterium that is, in principle, normative for the faith of the individual, although this magisterium, while remaining essentially the same, is itself affected by historical change in its existence and its praxis. But this does not exclude the fact that the actual faith of Christians has a normative influence on the magisterium and on the official faith of the church. However, this "normativeness" is essentially different from the one we attribute to the magisterium and its faith. These two influences *mutually* condition each other, although we must add that mutual does not mean equal.

First, it is obvious that, considered historically, the official faith of the church depends for its growth and differentiation on the growth and differentiation of the actual faith of the faithful. Among them are theologians with their work, even though this work, just like the faith of others, in the church, operates in constant dialogue with the church's official doctrine. To put it with a bit of malice: *before* the doctrine of the Council of Florence on the Trinity, theologians held a similar doctrine that had not yet received the blessing of the magisterium. The doctrine of the seven sacraments or of transubstantiation were theologoumena *before* the church's magisterium declared them defined propositions.

We should keep this in mind in looking at the last few centuries, when some popes have spoken as if the task of theologians consisted merely in defending and explaining the statements of the magisterium. If we do not want to make of theologians a special group in the church, like that of the bishops, we must say that theologians belong to the people of God. To be sure, their concern also is the traditional faith that has already been officially approved. But it is broader than that. And whatever they work at, they do as members of the people of God with its concrete "theology." That is why their theologoumena belong to the actual faith of the people of God, especially since they too may be called to order by the magisterium.

It is from these elements of the actual faith of the people of God that the church's magisterium learns and should continue to learn. While it thus keeps learning, the magisterium declares that the doctrine discovered in this way is binding because it belongs to the actual faith of the church and shares therefore in the infallibility of the believing church. It follows that the actual faith of the church has not only an actual but also a normative influence upon the church's official faith.

Distinguishing that which merely happens to be present in the consciousness of the people of God from what is binding in faith may, in the final analysis, be a prerogative of the church's magisterium. The magisterium is then considered an indispensable component of the church, as a community of faith. Yet it remains true that the faith of the people of God, as actually existing and not merely as officially approved, is a source of, and to some extent also a norm for, the official faith of the church.

Nor does it follow that there would have originally existed a believing church without a magisterium (the first apostolic "witnesses") or that there would have been a time in which these two realities would not have mutually, although differently, influenced each other.

We might also put it as follows: In the eschatologically definitive and invincible community of faith that is the church, there can be no teaching that would not be accepted by some obedient faith. That is why this obedient faith is also a necessary and rightful norm and criterion for the preaching of the faith, and not the other way around.

CHRISTIAN LIFE

130 • One Must Name the Mystery*

Our love of God and our prayer have one difficulty in common. They will succeed only if we lose the very thought of what they are doing in the thought of him for whom we are doing it. To be concerned mainly with the correct way to love or the correct way to pray, entails almost inevitable failure in the realization of either activity.

It is useful to consider these matters in retrospect by meditating on the nature of the love of God and on the nature of prayer; it is useful to attempt to describe what the act of love or the activity of prayer really entails. Yet, to some extent, such meditation destroys the very act itself, for we cannot really perform an act and at the same time be preoccupied with the mechanics of our doing it. We succeed in prayer and in love only when we lose ourselves in both, and are no longer aware of *how* we are praying or in *what manner* we are loving.

Our age is particularly given to introspection and the analysis of motive and action, with the result that we are often deprived of the power to act through sheer preoccupation with how the act is to be done. In the spiritual sphere we become entangled in our own speculative thoughts about God and about the modes of our prayer, instead of entering into union with God through meditation and love. We lose our zest for the object of the activity in our zeal for the activity itself.

Thus we become tangled with the very means to activity, and we cannot act. Our age is imprisoned in its own subjectivity. The modern tendency is to call on even the most exalted moments of the human spirit to stand and unfold themselves, declare their identity, state what they are and how they "work." The modern mind is fearful of mistaking the image and the symbol for the reality, of mistaking for pure spiritual currency what is in reality the cleverly deceptive coinage of baser cravings.

All this creates a closed circle of sterile questioning in which human beings imprison themselves. Instead of leading persons to reach out for the desired object, this kind of self-questioning leads only to further self-questioning and to a sterility in which there is no answer and no activity.

Today we tend to judge our thoughts and feelings in themselves, and not by reference to the exalted nature of the object toward which

---

* *On Prayer*, 31–34.

they tend. This is a wrong attitude, because it leads to feelings of disillusionment in which our activities cease to have any real significance for us. Thus disillusioned, we are inclined to avoid altogether such acts as deliberate raising of mind and heart to God in prayer and love.

God becomes for us the ineffable, the incomprehensible; and we live out our years in his sight, dumb in mind and heart. He sees our good works on earth, our "little nameless unremembered acts of kindness" toward our neighbor, our fundamental decency, and the patience with which we bear the weight of "all this unintelligible world."

We live, as it were, with our backs to God, knowing indeed that he is watching us, but never turning to speak to him because we fear the very act of prayer. Hence the cult of a religion so prevalent today, which could be described as anonymous morality: *I don't pray and that sort of thing, but I am as decent a person as the next,* is the way this cult is usually worded. Those who still "pray and that sort of thing" are regarded as naive, unanalytical, incapable of realizing that they are confusing God with their own thoughts and feelings *about* God. The proper attitude is, of course, to live decently and avoid the dangers of self-deception in all this praying and churchgoing. The contemporary person has come to regard prayer and expression of one's love of God as at best redundant, and at worst mawkish and effeminate.

Let us examine more closely this fear of "direct" religion. On analysis, it is found to be an aspect of the modern fear of introspection: the fear of being caught up in a circle of subjectivity which sets off from the self and returns to the self, its only fruits being inner loneliness and a sense of futility. This fear freezes the springs of prayer, because prayer is regarded as something which inevitably leads *inward* to the self, whereas the tendency is rather to reach *outward* away from the self.

Prayer is indeed such a "reaching out" to the infinity of God, and has a significance far beyond the limitations of this earthly life. It is because the contemporary human being tends to suspect everything reaching beyond the narrow sweep of the five senses and of human reason, that he shrinks from the supernatural except perhaps to the extent of passive belief.

The great masters of the spiritual life have emphasized that the objective relationship existing between God and human beings demands a positive attitude in which people look up to God in faith, worship, hope, and love, rather than adopt a remote, negative attitude in which they worship God indirectly through something other than God.

All things lead to the direct worship of God himself. Though incomprehensible and above all his works, God can be known through his works. He has spoken to us in the person of his Son, and it was in human words that the Son spoke to us of the Father. God has poured forth his

Spirit into our hearts, but we know this only through the words of the Son. Therefore we may, and indeed we must, lift up our minds to God himself, praise him in our hearts, worship him explicitly and publicly, honor him, take courage to speak to him and to call him "Father."

All our activities take their meaning from him. What our minds can know of him, we love in him, but mind and heart reach out to seize on the unknown, the incomprehensible, the infinite. A thirst for the infinite has been made part of the very essence of the human soul; and hence St. Augustine's famous words: "You have made us for yourself, O Lord, and our heart is restless until it rests in you."

While we remain on earth, we see things "through a glass, in a dark manner," as St. Paul puts it, and the Spirit of God given to us remains a hidden God. That this is so, however, does not dispense us from the duty of faith, for it is through faith that our thirst for the eternal finds its expression. Through faith, a person dares to reach away from himself toward a glory which as yet he can but glimpse, until that faith is swallowed up in the eternal light wherein he meets his God face to face.

If God is regarded as the unknown factor which, being beyond the range of our practical life, can be ignored or at most accepted passively as one might accept the presence of an onlooker, then we can never experience a nearness to God, and our vague religion will pale, to all intent and purposes, into atheism. We must invoke the mystery of God, ponder it, live with it, learn to love it, so that, even though it remains a mystery, it becomes a reality in our life.

131 • Prayer as the Fundamental Act of Human Existence*

There are realities in human life which, because they concern and actualize the whole human being, cannot be constructed and understood from a point outside themselves. There is no extrinsic point for the realization of the whole person from which this realization could be determined and constructed as by an independent system of coordination in such a way that it could be understood before it happened.

The reality of love, loyalty, trust, hope, anguish, and so on, can be grasped in its potentiality and significance only in the actual performance of such fundamental events of human existence. These events

---

* *Christian at the Crossroads*, 48–49.

cannot and could not be properly investigated synthetically from without. If they apparently are, they have fallen short of their essence. One can discover and talk about events like these only as already occurring realities, and then either accept them as offers to one's freedom or brush them aside and let them die. This is true of prayer, because if it exists at all and is to have a meaning, prayer is just such a total, fundamental act of human existence embracing that existence as a whole and bringing it, in a movement of trust and love, to that mystery whom we call God.

Prayer too, then, can be grasped as possible and meaningful only in its execution. It too must be experienced as something that in a true sense has already been given to us; only thus can it be accepted (or by the same token thrust aside and condemned to extinction). We can never speak about prayer, then, unless we include some reference to the fact that it has already been given to us in the depths of our existence, to the fact of this hidden entreaty of the Spirit of God, as Paul calls it, to which we must join our own voices in the activity of our freedom.

In earlier times, when God was a self-evident reality in the public consciousness of society, it was easy to explain what prayer meant and consequently easy to bring a person to an appreciation of its essence and necessity almost rationally, as if one were approaching prayer from some extrinsic standpoint.

Today, however, when, despite our faith, which we have and of course defend, we find ourselves asking, with what sometimes amounts to anguish, what exactly is meant by this word "God," where this God, whose presence in a world interpreted by the exact sciences with their methodical atheism is not exactly self-evident, is in fact to be found, then prayer (in the widest sense of that word) becomes itself the place in which we meet God; God has ceased to be the self-evident point of departure which would make the essence and necessity of prayer intelligible, as it were, extrinsically. Prayer — and in prayer God — must be its own justification and its own advertisement.

132 • Pray Daily Life!*

Happy is the individual who in his daily life returns again and again to prayer. Moreover, there is a higher aim to be achieved in the conse-

---

* *On Prayer*, 52–55.

cration of everyday life by prayer. Those who return again and again to prayer will never be completely overcome by everyday life; but the suffering of one's spiritual life from the cares of the world is not yet quite conquered.

Even though we frequently pray in our daily life, this life itself seems to remain what it always was — a consistent, grey monotony. Our soul seems to continue its weary way on the road followed endlessly by the multitude with its innumerable trifles, its gossip and pretense, its curiosity and vanity. Our soul seems to remain in the marketplace where, from all quarters, the hawkers congregate to sell the petty goods of the world, and where in stultifying restlessness people, including ourselves wander about offering their trifles.

Our soul in daily life seems to be in a gigantic barn into which cartload after cartload is brought, day by day, until it is filled to overflowing with mundane things. There is no end in sight. One day after the other, we go on in this way to the hour of our death, when all the goods and chattel which we called our life, will be swept away.

What will we be then and what will remain of us, whose life was nothing but the business of the day, idle talk and vain pretense? What will be the outcome of our life when at the last judgment the true essence of our hollow life and of the many days and long years that have remained empty, will be relentlessly revealed? Will anything remain beyond those few moments in which the grace of love or of an honest prayer to God shyly found a corner of our life otherwise filled with ephemeral rubbish?

It is of supreme importance to escape from this empty routine. Through the humdrum of our daily life we must find our way to him who alone is necessary, to him who alone is the Lord. Our everyday life must become a hymn of praise, indeed it must become in itself prayer. It is obvious that we cannot pray directly all the time. We cannot escape from daily routine, because it will go with us wherever we go. Everyday life is our life, and our everyday heart, our weary mind and our meagre love which abases all that is great, will ever remain with us.

Thus we have to keep to the highway of our everyday life, its cares and duties. Nor must this routine be purely of intention. God must be sought and found in the things of our world. By regarding our daily duties as something performed for the honor and glory of God we can convert what was hitherto soul-killing monotony to a living worship of God in all our actions. Everyday life must become itself our prayer.

But it can become prayer only through unselfishness and love. If we are willing and understanding disciples, we cannot find a better means of growing in spirituality than through our everyday life. There are the long monotonous hours of work, for which often no recognition is given, the continuous and painful struggle which receives little reward, the weariness and the sacrifices of old age, disappointment and failure, adversity and misunderstanding.

There are the many wishes denied to us, the many small humiliations, the almost inevitable opinionatedness of old age and the equally frequent inconsiderateness of youth. There are such things as physical discomfort, the inclemency of the elements, the friction of human contacts. Through these and a thousand other trials in which everyday life abounds, a person can learn to become calm and unselfish, if he only understands these taskmasters, mundane and yet providential. He must willingly accept them, rather than try to ward them off. Such vicissitudes must be borne without complaint as a matter of course. They must be accepted as incidental to the normal course of life.

In this way, we can use everyday life to fight our selfishness, slowly but certainly, since the evidence showered upon us by God in daily life is always certain and sure. In this way, the love of God will grow of itself in our hearts, a love both calm and chaste. It is human beings themselves who prevent the growth of this love.

In everyday life we can mortify ourselves without vanity and without ostentation. Nobody will notice our efforts, and we ourselves will be scarcely aware of our mortification, yet through the myriad occupations of our daily life one defense after another will be thrown down, behind each of which our selfishness had entrenched itself. At last, when we have ceased to put up new defenses, when we have learnt to accept our precarious human situation and rely on the grace of God, we will notice suddenly and almost cheerfully, that those defenses were quite unnecessary.

We will realize that it need not mean misfortune, if life deprives us of this or that joy hitherto regarded as indispensable. We need not despair when we fall or when our plans do not work out. Through everyday life we are taught that we become rich in giving, that we advance spiritually through holy resignation, that we are blessed in sacrifice, and that we find love when we give love to others. Thus an individual becomes unselfish and free. This freedom makes us worthy of the supreme love of the ever free and infinite God, who first loved us.

It is of supreme importance that we should achieve this conquest of our everyday life, because otherwise we allow ourselves to be dragged down to its level. Nothing can free us so much as this conquest. If we succeed, the love thus engendered will suffuse all the things of this world with the infinity of God, through a holy desire to exalt all the humdrum activities of daily life unto a hymn of praise to the glory of God. The cross of everyday life is the only means by which our selfishness can die, because in order to be utterly destroyed our selfishness must be ceaselessly crucified. This fruit of that cross will be a love born from the death of our selfishness. Thus, through love, fidelity, faith, preparedness, and surrender to God, our everyday actions are transformed into lived prayer.

Our life remains what it was, difficult, monotonous and unspectacular. It must remain what it is, for only in this way can it serve the love of God. Only in this way will it redeem us from ourselves. Through the sanctification of our everyday life, our desires, our reluctances, our stubbornness and our assertiveness must be purified. Bitterness must cease to taste bitter. Routine must lose its monotony. Disappointment must cease to be sterile.

Everyday life must train us to kindness patience, peacefulness, and understanding, to meekness and gentleness, to forbearance and endurance. In this way, everyday life becomes in itself *prayer*. All our interests are unified and exalted by the love of God; our scattered alms are given a specific direction toward God; our external life becomes the expression of our love of God. Thus our life takes on a new meaning in the light of our eternal destiny.

Make everyday life your prayer. Pray for this great art of Christian living, as difficult to master as it is essentially simple in itself. Pray in everyday life, and so make everyday life your prayer. The sorrowful and fleeting days of our life, passed in monotony and banality, in commonplace pursuits and in toil, will merge with the day of God, the great day that has no evening. Let us pray daily for the coming of that day, so that in us the words of St. Paul may be fulfilled: "And I am sure that he who began a good work in you will bring it to completion at the day of Jesus Christ" (Phil 1:6).

133 • The Prayer of Petition I*

Yes, the prayer of petition is quite a problem. Its practice is now almost exclusively confined to ordinary people. It is found only where a "primitive religiosity" holds sway, which — in the opinion of the more sophisticated — has not quite grasped the fact that we cannot ask anything of God, since he is in the ultimate analysis an inexorable fate.

These others, the clever ones, who do not form part of this folk with rosaries, pilgrimages, processions, and so on, become "primitive" only when they have their backs to the wall. Then they will pray (species A);

* *Theological Investigations III*, 209–14.

or, if they cannot bring themselves to do it even then (species B), they give way (quite rightly and quite logically) to despair. Should they unexpectedly get away with it (their life, their money, their health, and so on), then they will again give up praying (species A), or give themselves over to existentialist nihilism (species B).

It is therefore from a Christian point of view quite right and just that, in the judgments of history, the "sophisticated," the "intellectuals," should have more prospect of making bitter acquaintance with the (allegedly) inexorable march of events than the little people who do not think it entirely superfluous and unintellectual to pray for their daily bread and other such earthly needs.

But seriously: Do we or do we not believe in the flesh of the eternal Word of God? If so, then the true God must be capable of very human feelings and the earth with all that happens on it cannot be quite so unimportant to him. It is true that events here below may not always proceed very smoothly and peaceably (after all, that God did die on the cross), but what goes on among us cannot be utterly unimportant.

And if it is true that God is the Lord of the world, and that he has taught us the Our Father with its petition for our daily bread and deliverance from evil, we must clearly assume that the prayer of petition addressed to this anthropomorphic and mighty God is a real power in this world.

And here we can safely leave to one side all that the theologians have elaborated about the compatibility of the prayer of petition with the sovereignty of God, his absolute freedom and his changelessness. Even if one did not think or suspect that the theologians in these speculations were thinking a little too much in terms of the time Before Christ and were not quite aware of the fact — naturally only in this particular speculation — that the Word of God became flesh, and that therefore he through whom everything comes into being has become very approachable and easily moved, this in any case is true and certain: there is a prayer of petition which speaks to God and is not a mere exorcism of one's own heart, but boldly and explicitly ventures to ask him for bread, peace, restraint of his enemies, health, the spread of his kingdom on earth, and a host of such earthly and highly problematic things.

That such prayer combines a great measure of "self-will" (for one presents to him one's *own* desires) with a supreme degree of submissiveness (for one *prays* to him whom one cannot compel, persuade, or charm, but only beg), that here there is a mingling and an incomprehensible fusion of the greatest boldness with the deepest humility, of life with death, this makes the prayer of petition in one respect not the lowest but the highest, the most divinely human form of prayer.

Why else is the Lord's Prayer not a hymn but a sevenfold petition?

There should be more stubborn and humble, more insistent and urgent supplication among Christians — supplication even for those things which appear to *us,* shortsighted though we be, of importance, even for that realization of God's kingdom, such as we are necessarily led to imagine it. For the prayer of petition, robust and straightforward, is a power in the world and in its history, in heaven and on earth.

Ultimately even the unbeliever would have to concede this, although theoretically he will deny it. For in practice he admits it. Let us imagine, for example, that a tyrant knew that all his subjects without exception intended to fall on their knees and beg God to free them from his tyranny, and that they had solemnly assured the tyrant they would do nothing more to this end than pray. Would he for all that allow them to do it? He would try to prevent it. It is true he does not believe in the power of the one to whom the prayer is addressed, but he believes in the power of the prayer, although this prayer itself only has power if there is faith in the power of the one addressed.

On this point one could introduce a kind of transcendental deduction of the truth of prayer. That prayer exists is a fact. It is an unavoidable fact. It is efficacious. It is only efficacious where there is faith in the power of the one to whom it is addressed and not merely in the power of prayer. Can there be a phenomenon which rests in principle (and not just in individual cases) on an illusion, while at the same time it is real and efficacious? No, for such a proposition negates itself, because (among other reasons) it could also be applied to the affirmation of this proposition itself. For every proposition presupposes that the attainment of a truth in a phenomenon of knowledge is not from the beginning an illusion.

Everyone who admits this, and everyone must admit it, cannot justify either logically or existentially the fundamental and universal denial of that which is the condition of the efficacy of prayer, namely, faith in the power (and therefore in the reality) of the one to whom the prayer is directed.

And now, let us imagine for a moment that Christians were convinced of the need for prayer, no longer in a general and notional way, but in a really concrete and practical way, so that their conviction took on flesh and blood, as it were, and issued in action. Let us imagine they were convinced that this prayer must be at once very heavenly and very earthly: that is, it must understand the needs of earth in a very heavenly way, precisely *insofar as* in them the kingdom of God is to be realized; and it must be understood, the kingdom of God in a very earthly way, insofar as it means here and now the church in our time, conversion, moral discipline, reverence for the name of God and of Christ in public life, active Christianity, and so on.

Let us suppose for a moment that the Christians of today, those interested in their religion, in particular the more educated among them, were not merely to talk about the mystical body of Christ and discuss its theology but were to live this truth; that is to say, suppose it were actually to be borne in upon them with fear and trembling that we have to bear one another's burdens and that all of us are accountable before the judgment seat of God for the eternal destiny of one another.

Let us multiply these delightful hypotheses and these blessed dreams (one more or less hardly matters): suppose everyone were convinced, because he is very humble and therefore very realistic, that such attitudes cannot be allowed to remain only a distant ideal, permitting us to enjoy a spiritual pleasure at our best moments when we delight to feast upon our own sublime thoughts, but that they have to be put into practice, that they must be taken up anew each day, and that we have to allow ourselves to be reminded by *others* that we have need of certain gestures, certain usages, certain actions, in which these attitudes are already preformed and embodied; for they cannot be expected to well up out of the depths of the heart everyday with power so fresh as to eliminate the need for such preformed and preestablished practices.

Further, suppose everyone were convinced that prayer has to penetrate the whole of life, that we must pray at all times, that is to say, that our will interceding with God in Christ for the welfare of all has to be a formative power in our daily life, that the prayer of the member of Christ interceding for the whole church has to be transformed into a penitential life, into patience, love, fasting, almsgiving, and into courageous and joyful renunciation, which is able calmly to pass by many an "enjoyment" and pleasure of life. Further still: suppose everyone were convinced that those who wield ecclesiastical authority are not just the supervisors of an immense apparatus, of an ecclesiastical bureaucratic administration, but the fathers of our souls, whose words direct us in a manner at once paternal and fraternal even in matters beyond obligation.

If all this were to become true, and it would be wonderful if it were to become true, what would happen? Many things, naturally. But here we have only to follow out the consequences in a particular direction. And these look like this: Christians would pray for the whole church, that God might give her peace, might unite her and preserve her, might protect her against all the powers and forces of darkness, might make it possible for her children to glorify God in a peace such as the world cannot give.

They would pray for the pope, the bishops and priests (oh, they have such need of it), for all seekers after truth, for the whole of separated and divided Christendom, for Jews and Gentiles, for the poor and the sick, for refugees and prisoners. They would pray everyday. They would understand their whole lives as being related to the bearing of others' burdens and to the care of those souls for whose actions and ultimate destiny they will one day have to render account.

They would, in every pain of body and distress of heart and mind, declare like the apostle with serene courage: "And in my flesh I complete what is lacking in Christ's afflictions for the sake of his body, that is, the church" (Col 1:24). They would no longer be content to pray in a merely general way for the kingdom of God and its coming. Their heart would be as large as the world, and would yet be mindful of the most minute details affecting humanity and the church in the drama of salvation between light and darkness: the refugees in Korea, the priests of God in the prisons and camps behind the Iron Curtain, the importance of the cinema for the education and the corruption of the masses, the frequented and the deserted paths of Christian charitable relief, the silent despair of the lonely, who have lost God and humanity, and thousand upon thousand of other such things. They would gladly suffer themselves to be reminded by others of this or that intention. They would take up with a heart filled with self-forgetting love "intentions" proposed for their prayers like the "Let us pray, dearly beloved, for . . . " of the priest in the prayers of petition of the Good Friday liturgy.

Such prayer would generate a power sufficient to transform their lives: their piety would become less egoistic and introverted. They would no longer be resentful if they themselves have to drink of that chalice of bitterness out of which all must drink the redemption of their being. They would then spontaneously begin also to *do* their part for God and his kingdom: by witnessing to their faith, by helping their neighbor (one must first have sought him with the heart, that is in prayer, and then one's feet will also find him) and those far distant (in the missions), and so on.

They would gradually begin to feel something of that exquisite impulse of love to consume itself in service and obedience for others, until it has entirely spent and emptied itself. And perhaps they would go on from this to acquire some understanding of the heart of the Lord, of the mystery of that love which wells up out of the impenetrable depths — out of what is called the heart — of him who is the Word of God in the flesh: inexhaustible, judging and redeeming, pouring itself out in fruitless generosity and so drawing everything gloriously to itself.

They would then (still more slowly, almost timidly and humbly) dare to hope that something of the love of this heart, which moves the sun and the other stars throughout the universe, might seize and transform the meditations and aspirations of their own heart, which, alas, is of itself only inclined to evil; they would perhaps at the dawn of each day with recollected heart dedicate themselves, their life and the newly given day to this love (or at least attempt to do so; for the thing is of course not accomplished with the mere formula of such a dedication).

Would it not be good if there were many more such Christians to continue this apostolate of intercession, who at every hour of the eternal Good Friday of this world (since the Son of God is crucified continually in all his members, and together with him both those who say "remember me . . ." and those who fail to utter this word) hear to some degree the rousing call, "Let us pray," bend the knee and pray for all the estates of the church and all her needs, and who, when they hear the "Let us rise," go forth into life with a heart which has been filled with prayer of this kind?

134 • The Prayer of Petition II*

Normal Christian petitionary prayer is sometimes called hypocrisy, evidently on the ground that a modern person cannot seriously imagine changing God's mind (if he exists), getting him to revise his plans, so that (as someone once suggested) the weather would be different in Tibet if pious South Tyroleans with their processions were transplanted there.

But do Christians think of their petitionary prayer in this way, and must they think of it in this way? To give an honest answer to this question we must certainly admit that in religion as it is practiced there is usually an element of magic, conjuring, the frantic effort of the poor creature to avert something which it doesn't want to happen at any price by invoking God.

It would be wrong to deny these ingredients in religion as it exists, though in among them genuine religion may nevertheless be practiced, even if it is not "chemically pure." This sort of religion is still a thousand times better than the triviality of the average man or woman who anxiously tries to avoid all experiences which come from the unfathomable depths of his or her existence — and these are religious experiences.

But what happens in true petitionary prayer when it is part of genuine religion? Human beings face the incomprehensible plan of their existence, which they accept as at once incomprehensible and yet as originating in the wisdom and love of God; however it may turn out,

---

* Karl Rahner and Karl-Heinz Weger, *Our Christian Faith: Answers for the Future*, trans. Francis McDonagh (New York: Crossroad Publishing Company, 1981), 63–64, 67–68.

whether it brings life or death, people then have a sense of themselves, with their own identity and vital impulses, as willed by God, without wanting to produce or force an intelligible synthesis between their vital impulses and the plan of their existence.

And so they say yes to the incomprehensibility of God and to their own will to live, without wanting to know how the two fit together. The unity of the two, which is not something that we can create, is petitionary prayer, since it is only prayer if it says radically, "Your will, not mine," and it would not be petitionary prayer if it did not dare to ask God for something which we had thought of ourselves. Petitionary prayer is thus simply actualizing the incomprehensibility of human existence which, down to the last fiber, comes from God alone and goes out to him, yet is such that it can hold its own before God and not be destroyed.

Why should we be suspicious of petitionary prayer if it is in fact simply the actualization of the incomprehensibility of the creature before God? It is not an attempt to change God's mind and yet it has a meaning. And this meaning does not need to be saved by the explanation that God has foreseen petitionary prayer and included it in his plans for the world and so already made a causal connection between the answer and the prayer. Nor does the meaning of petitionary prayer need to be made plausible by an appeal to an atomistic indeterminism and chance which give God freedom of movement without infringing on the laws of nature. With or without such accidents or indeterminism, the world as a whole and in all its particulars is the expression of the incomprehensible control of God and as such is accepted in petitionary prayer as meaningful.

Why should it be a perfect example of the "immunization strategy" when a theologian says that God always answers a really genuine prayer, even if possibly in a way different from what the petitioner had imagined? If the answer to any prayer were an empirically determinable datum to be measured by the intentions of the prayer, if this sort of appeal to God, looking for this sort of answer, could still be called prayer, then certainly immunization strategy to justify prayer would be the right description.

But suppose that prayer, in spite of the creature's cry for help which it contains, is in advance an absolute surrender to the incomprehensible God, to his incomprehensible, if good, dispositions and only so can be called prayer. Suppose that prayer of this sort is regarded as meaningful as a test case of faith. In these circumstances the remark that God answers prayer in accordance with his incomprehensible wisdom and love is not an a posteriori move in an apologia for petitionary prayer, but in fact the primary and most important statement about its true nature. It has nothing at all to do with an immunization strategy.

Of course one must be able to realize that the unconditional surrender of a human being to the incomprehensible will of God who saves and liberates, in other words, prayer as the test case of faith in the true God, is meaningful, indeed is the only thing which reconciles the ultimate meaningfulness of existence and its incomprehensibility. If we look at prayer, and in particular petitionary prayer, in this way, then the only question is where and when it can be given a real place in the ordinary dreary lives of men and women. It is perfectly possible in principle to be a Christian and a person who prays even if one has no desire to pray before every snack.

135 • Love of God*

What is the love of God, and how can we attain it so as to learn how to pray? We are told that this love shows itself in particular through the observance of the commandments. This is indeed true; but it is not the whole truth. The love of God must precede and be the motive of such observance. Many efforts have been made to describe the love of God in the human soul. It is true, of course, that those who know how to talk about the love of God do not necessarily possess a greater measure of it. It remains nonetheless true, however, that when we hear others speak of the love of God, we come to realize how lacking we are in this love.

In speaking about the divine mysteries, even holy scripture had to fall back on thoughts and images drawn from human life. We may begin, therefore, from our human experience of human love. When one person loves another with a pure and unselfish love, that love gives some idea of the love we must bear to God, except that our love of God must be deeper, more unselfish, more unconditional, because it is directed toward God himself.

The word *love* covers a variety of human relationships so that it is necessary to determine what one means by the term. The love we speak of here is certainly not the narrow and selfish idea of sexual lust. Even in cases where it does not degrade itself to promiscuity or excessive indulgence, sexuality falls short of the perfection of the ideal *love* in the context: *love of God.* On the other hand, the love of which we speak must not be confused with a feeling of benevolence which, even though it may perhaps be unselfish, is fundamentally supine. For this love is something essentially positive, passionate, arising from the very

* *On Prayer*, 34–39.

recesses of the soul of a human being, shattering his egoism, surging upward from the dust of its nothingness to its glory in the worshiping of the infinite. Through such love, we lose ourselves in our union with one immeasurably greater than ourselves, who has become the sole meaning of life for us.

Unselfishness is the essential quality of love, wherein the soul rejoices at the very existence of the beloved. It is a radiant release from the self, experienced when an individual learns to break through the imprisoning walls of his own egoism and give himself to another. Beforehand, his life was a miserable one, cribbed and confined: now it has taken on "an ampler ether, a diviner air" by escaping from its own self-shackles through giving itself to another. In complete forgetfulness of self, this love clings to the beloved. The happiness of the beloved is the happiness of him who loves. To love in this manner is to have escaped from the prison of selfishness without being trapped into another prison. For this love of one person for another not only reveals the value of the beloved person, but opens up vistas of the mysterious and radiant wonders of the whole creation. In fact, this exchange of pure and unselfish love between two persons becomes the reflection and symbol of that love which embraces all things — the love of God.

But this love between two persons can lead to happiness or to misery. The secret of its happiness lies in the recognition by both parties that through this love a greater love must be born. Their love for one another must meet in and be exalted by the greater love. Again, the essence of human love is the realization that in giving oneself, one has received in return the gift of another. This gives a greater sense of security than when lived within oneself; for it is not good for a person to be alone. From the union of two loving hearts arise that thoughtful serving of one another and that unselfishness and fidelity which are at once the safeguards and the hallmarks of love.

Let us endeavor to love God in this fundamental way. Let us seek him, the almighty and holy one, before whom we are as dust. Forgetting ourselves, surrendering to him our whole being, uniting ourselves to him with every fiber of our souls, let us fling ourselves wide to God; and we shall know that bliss, at once yearning and sweet, which pervades us when we give to him our whole being and our whole world.

My Lord and my God! To you we may surrender ourselves entirely. Through you, what is hard in us becomes tender, and in our pure worship of you, we may reveal what we keep hidden from all. We can open our hearts freely to you, whispering to you what we are and what we do, our successes and our failures, our sorrows, and our joys. In yielding ourselves entirely to you, we have no fear of being deceived. We lay our most precious treasures at your feet, and we know that our loving enthusiasm in doing so will not turn to the disillusion and bitterness of a betrayed love.

This love cries out to God in the depths of our hearts. All the powers of the soul well up to meet him, and there is no ebb. God becomes the center of our life nearer to us than we are to ourselves, loved with a greater love than we bear to ourselves, loved unselfishly for his own sake. It is stained through with the inspired knowledge that it is he who has first loved us. God never falls to answer the call of love rising to him from the shadows of this valley of tears, because this love is utterly unselfish, faithful and gentle, seeking nothing but a return of love.

It loves God rather than merely loving the reward which is promised to that love; for in the love itself, it is rewarded. Trials do not daunt it, nor is it quenched by the waters of sorrow. It is something quiet and hidden, at once bold and timorous, always marked with reverence for the divine mysteries, familiarity never breeding an absence of awe and wonder. It is not the love of a human person, but the love of God; and therefore the infinite greatness of the object of love will be reflected in the reverence, humility, and burning ardor of the lover. For the love of God is holy and sublime — and eternal.

This love is the true love of God, the infinite one, who dwells in our hearts in a mysterious manner that we cannot understand. It is the love of the holy one, who alone is worthy of adoration. We love him with whom we are to come face to face in life everlasting, him who is our creator and our Lord, the eternal Father, Son, and Holy Ghost — three divine persons in one God.

We love him who first loved us, who gave us existence and life, in whom we live and move and have our being, who loves us even when we have turned our backs on him. He is patient, faithful, and wise; he is the God of our hearts and the God who is our portion forever.

Infinity lies between his immensity and our nothingness, but this very infinity is a challenge to our love inasmuch as it emphasizes how much our whole life is dependent upon his adorable providence. In awe and worship, we entrust our life into the hands of this beloved God. The more radiant his divine beauty and love, the more that love exceeds any conception we can have of love. By grace, the divine becomes more living and real in us, so that thereby God becomes to us father and mother, brother and sister, our hearts growing more intimately united with his divine heart.

Love is the soul's answer to the inscrutability of God's judgments and ways: the less able the soul finds itself to understand God, the more urgently its love reaches out toward him. Overwhelmed by our utter nothingness in the face of God, we pray the more fervently: "My God, I love you" — words which are the highest expression of love that anyone can offer. In the mystery of the love he bears toward an infinite God, a human being realizes what is most exalted in his nature.

But we must not misunderstand the nature of this love. True, it burns with the sacred fire of selflessness and self-oblation which is characteristic of all human love — be it only the fire where love turns to pain through its own yearning. While this is so, however, the fire of the love of God has a higher nature, because its power is not *in itself* but derives from the fact that it is a flame of love rising to *God.* Hence it is that this love becomes true Christian love only when sanctified by grace.

Several considerations flow from this. The love of God is indeed the highest exaltation of human nature; but it must be constantly preserved, through being continually sanctified, from degenerating into a mere expression of one's own presumptuous ability to become like unto God through one's own paltry resources. Nor should it become an expression of burning impatience to win God by our own efforts — to seize him, as it were, by sheer power of will.

The true love of God can exist only in a heart which is humbled by the unattainable majesty and unapproachable holiness of the everlasting God. To be redeemed from ourselves, we must humble ourselves in adoration of the almighty. We must control our thirst for that grace of sensible devotion which makes us experience the *nearness* of God: this must be left entirely in his hands, since what matters to us is only the doing of his holy will. The fire of our longing for God is pure only when it is kindled in us by the will of God. The love of God demands perseverance and self-restraint; and this is possible only by the grace of him who, dwelling eternally in the bosom of his Father, yet "emptied himself" to serve that Father in silent obedience in a sinful world.

The greatest and purest upsurge of human love falls short of that love which God wishes to receive from us. The divine paradox here is that we must love God with a love implanted in us by God; for this love, like everything we have received, and even like that beatific vision which we hope for in everlasting life, is a free gift of God, beyond our power to achieve or to merit by our own unaided efforts.

Between us and God is the gulf between nothingness and infinity. If our love reaches God across that abyss, it is solely because, through his Holy Spirit, God has cast into our hearts his own supreme love, in which our sinfulness and our nothingness have been swallowed up. "God has first loved us." Love has stooped to our nothingness and kindled itself in us. We were unworthy of this love, and it is only through this love that we can offer our love to God.

Or what is our love, but, as it were, a frightened surrender to that divine love that has been cast into our hearts as the fire which Christ said he had come "to cast upon the earth" with the desire that it "should be enkindled?" All our efforts to love would fail hopelessly, were they not mysteriously transformed, freely lifted to a higher plane above the reach of human effort, by divine love, through which we attain to that true love worthy of God and of redeemed creatures destined to enjoy the beatific vision. This true love of God becomes a living reality in us when we bear in mind that it is rooted in, and is the free gift of, God's love for us. Therefore our prayer of love must be: "You, O Lord, love me. Grant me the grace to open my heart to that love, that I may love you."

136 • Baptism and Confirmation*

To make sense, the individual sacraments have to be considered on the one hand from the perspective of the church as the basic sacrament, and on the other hand they have to be incorporated into the history of an individual life. Here they become manifest as the sacramental manifestation of the Christian life of grace in the *existentielly fundamental moments* of human life. Hence there is first of all a complex of sacraments of initiation: baptism and confirmation.

In *baptism* a person becomes a Christian and a member of the church. It is the first sacrament of the forgiveness of sins, of the communication of the glory of God's grace and of God's nature, and of the reception of the interior and permanent capacity to believe, to hope and to love God and neighbor. But this interior, permanent, and individual reception of grace by a person who was a sinner and becomes justified takes place in baptism by the fact that by this initiation rite he is received into the socially and hierarchically constituted people of God, into the community of those who believe and profess God's salvation in Christ. In baptism God gives a person grace for his own individual salvation by making him a member of the *church*. Membership in the church and belonging to the church is the first and most immediate effect of this sacrament of initiation which every Christian receives, and which for every Christian is the foundation of his Christian existence in any and every aspect which this life possesses, and this includes hierarchical, sacramental, and supreme powers. For no other sacrament can be validly received by the unbaptized, nor can they possess any juridical power in the church.

A person receives grace for his own salvation in baptism insofar as

---

*Foundations of Christian Faith, 415–17.

he becomes a member of the church in baptism. But this statement may not be made innocuous by being taken to mean that the church membership which is conferred in baptism exists only in order that the other and remaining elements of his individual justification and sanctification can be bestowed upon the baptized, and for no other purpose. That this is completely false is shown just by the fact that in emergency cases this merely individual justification and sanctification can be acquired by means of faith and love alone and without the sacrament, and that this situation certainly occurs for many unbaptized people.

Prior to this individual salvific effect, therefore, baptism must have a positive content and significance for the individual which have to be more than this individual salvific effect. Membership in the church is not only a means for the purpose of attaining individual salvation, but rather it receives its own meaning from baptism. This meaning follows from the meaning and the function of the church as such.

The meaning and the purpose of the church is not merely and exclusively to make it possible and to make it easier for the sum of many individuals to find their individual salvation. For it could indeed be regarded as useful and important for this purpose, but not as unconditionally necessary; this purpose is often achieved without any tangible intervention of the church, however much this salvation is oriented toward the church by God's command and by his obligatory will that the sacrament be received. But in the concrete there is one thing which is not possible without the church: that the grace of God in Christ be present in the world as an event, as an ongoing event with historical tangibility and with incarnational corporeality.

Anyone who receives grace in baptism by being incorporated into the church as the historical and social corporeality of the grace of Christ in the world necessarily receives along with the grace of the church a share in, and the mandate and capacity for participating in, this function of the church to be the historical tangibility of God's grace in the world. He receives the mandate really to appropriate this function by a personal decision and to exercise it throughout his entire life. He is appointed by baptism to be a messenger of the word, a witness to the truth, and a representative of the grace of Christ in the world.

But how then can a difference be established between *baptism* and *confirmation?* First of all, in spite of the legitimate separation of baptism and confirmation which was sanctioned by the Council of Trent (cf. Denzinger, nos. 1601 and 1628), the tradition of the church testifies that these two sacraments belong together as the single Christian initiation. In them the church offers Christ and initiates a person into Christ in a historical way and not just in the depths of existence. Indeed it does this in a final and definitive way so that, by the very nature of this first and definitive initiation into human and Christian existence, these two sacraments cannot be repeated. Both sacraments, then, belong together in the single Christian initiation: they are distinguished to some extent inasmuch as a more negative and a more positive aspect can be distinguished in a process which, although it is extended in time, is ultimately one.

In *baptism* a person dies into the death of Christ in a sacramental, social, and tangible way in time and space. He is incorporated into the church with an appeal to and in the name of the trinitarian God: in the name of the Father who calls, and of the Son who is the word of the Father to humankind, and of the Holy Spirit in whom this offer of the Father in the Son really comes to men and women to sanctify and to redeem.

Confirmation is the positive aspect of one and the same process, and it also emphasizes the social and functional aspect of the baptized insofar as he is empowered by the communication of the Holy Spirit. It is the sacrament of giving witness to the faith, of charismatic fullness, of the mission of one sealed with the Spirit to give witness to the world so that it will become subject to the Lordship of God. It is the sacrament of being strengthened in the faith against the powers and forces of this world, the powers of untruth and of disbelief, and of the demonic hubris to want to redeem oneself.

The grace of confirmation, then, is in a correct sense the grace of the church for its mission to the world and for proclaiming the world's transfiguration. God and his call and the distribution of the charisms of the Spirit decide which functions of this grace are shared more directly by an individual as his special mission. These charisms are nothing else but more pronounced directions in the unfolding of one and the same Spirit whom all received in confirmation.

137 • Original Sin*

A universal, permanent and ineradicable codetermination of the situation of every individual's freedom by guilt, and then of course of every society's too, is conceivable only if this ineradicable codetermination of the situation of freedom by guilt is also *original,* that is, is already imbedded in the origin of this history to the extent that this

---

* *Foundations of Christian Faith,* 110–14.

origin of the single history of the human race is to be understood as established by human beings. The universality and the ineradicable nature of the codetermination of the situation of freedom by guilt in the single history of the human race implies an original determination of this human situation by guilt already present at the beginning. It implies an "original sin."

"Original sin" does not mean of course that the original, personal act of freedom at the very origin of history has been transmitted to subsequent generations in its moral quality. The notion that the personal deed of "Adam" or of the first group of people is imputed to us in such a way that it has been transmitted on to us biologically, as it were, has absolutely nothing to do with the Christian dogma of original sin.

We arrive at the knowledge, the experience and the meaning of what original sin is, in the first place, from a religious-existential interpretation of our own situation, from ourselves. We say first of all: we are people who must inevitably exercise our own freedom subjectively in a situation which is codetermined by objectifications of guilt, and indeed in such a way that this codetermination belongs to our situation permanently and inescapably. This can be clarified by a very banal example: when someone buys a banana, he does not reflect upon the fact that its price is tied to many presuppositions. To them belongs, under certain circumstances, the pitiful lot of banana pickers, which in turn is codetermined by social injustice, exploitation, or a centuries-old commercial policy. This person himself now participates in this situation of guilt to his own advantage. Where does this person's personal responsibility in taking advantage of such a situation codetermined by guilt end, and where does it begin? These are difficult and obscure questions.

In order to arrive at a real understanding of original sin, we begin with the fact that the situation of our own freedom bears the stamp of the guilt of others in a way which cannot be eradicated. But this means that the universality and the inescapability of this codetermination by guilt is inconceivable if it were not present at the very beginning of humankind's history of freedom. For if it were not present, hence if this determination of our situation by guilt were only a particular event, then the radical nature of this recognition of a universal and ineradicable codetermination of the situation of our freedom by guilt could not be maintained. We have to understand this codetermination of the situation of human freedom by guilt as imbedded in the origin of history itself. The universality and ineradicable nature of the codetermination of the situation of freedom by guilt in the single history of the human race implies in this sense an "original sin" as it is called by its traditional name.

"Original sin" in the Christian sense in no way implies that the original, personal act of freedom of the first person or persons is transmitted to us as our moral quality. In "original sin" the sin of Adam is not imputed to us. Personal guilt from an original act of freedom cannot be transmitted, for it is the existentiell no* of personal transcendence toward God or against him. And by its very nature this cannot be transmitted, just as the formal freedom of a subject cannot be transmitted. This freedom is precisely the point where a person is unique and no one can take his place, where he cannot be analyzed away, as it were, either forward or backward or into his environment, and in this way escape responsibility for himself. For Catholic theology, therefore, "original sin" in no way means that the moral quality of the actions of the first person or persons is transmitted to us, whether this be through a juridical imputation by God or through some kind of biological heredity, however conceived.

In this connection it is obvious that when the word "sin" is used for the personal, evil decision of a subject, and when on the other hand it is applied to a sinful situation which derives from the decision of another, it is being used only in an analogous sense, and not in a univocal sense. Now we could ask in a critical way why the church's theology and preaching use a word which can be so easily misunderstood. We would have to answer, first of all, that what is permanent and valid about the dogma of original sin, and its existentiell meaning could certainly be expressed without this word. On the other hand, however, we have to take account of the fact that there is and has to be a certain amount of standardization in the terminology of theology and preaching, that the history of the formulation of this experience of faith did in fact take this course, and that this word is there and cannot be abolished privately and arbitrarily by some individual.

In preaching and in catechesis, therefore, we should not begin immediately with this word, which then has to be modified with a great deal of effort afterward. We should rather acquire enough theology so that, starting with experience and with a description of the existentiell human situation, we can talk about the *matter itself* without using this word. Only at the end would we have to indicate that this very actual reality of one's own life and one's own situation is called "original sin" in ecclesiastical language.

Then it would be clear from the beginning that with regard to freedom, responsibility, the possibility of expiation and the modes of expiation, and the conceivability of the consequences of guilt which we call punishment, in all of these respects in any case "original sin" is essentially different from what we mean when we speak of personal

---

* For the distinction between "existentiell" and "existential," see footnote 59, p. 34, in the Introduction. —Translation editor.

guilt and sin, and understand them as possible or as actual from the perspective of the transcendental experience of freedom in ourselves.

The nature of original sin must be understood correctly and only from an understanding of the effect which the guilt of a particular person or particular persons has on the situation of other persons' freedom. For given the unity of the human race, the fact that a human being is in the world and in history, and finally the necessity that every original situation of freedom be mediated in the world, there is necessarily such an effect.

Presupposing this basic structure of an act of freedom as being in the world and as codetermining the situation of others' freedom, what is specific about the Christian doctrine of original sin consists in two things:

1. The determination of *our own* situation by guilt is an element within the history of the freedom of the human race, an element which is imbedded in its beginning, because otherwise the universality of this determination of the situation of freedom and of the history of the freedom of all persons by guilt is not explained.

2. The *depths* of this determination by guilt, which determines the *realm* of freedom and not freedom as such immediately, must be measured by the theological essence of the sin in which this codetermination of the human situation by guilt has its origins.

If this personal guilt at the beginning of the history of the human race is a rejection of God's absolute offer of himself in an absolute self-communication of his divine life (and we shall be treating this in detail later), then the consequences as a determination of our situation by guilt are different than they would be if it had merely been the free rejection of a divine law within the horizon of God himself. This divine self-communication, which is called the grace of justification, is what is most radical and most deep in the existential situation of human freedom. As divine grace it lies prior to freedom as the condition of possibility for freedom's *concrete* action. *Self*-communication of the absolutely *holy* God designates a quality sanctifying the human person prior to his free and good decision. Therefore the *loss* of such a sanctifying self-communication assumes the character of something which *should not be,* and is not merely a diminishing of the possibilities of freedom as can otherwise be the case in the instance of a "hereditary defect."

Since there is such a loss for the human race as the "descendants of Adam" in the situation of its freedom, we can and must speak of an original *sin,* although merely in an analogous sense of course, even though we are dealing with an element in the *situation* of freedom and not in the freedom of an individual as such. How this individual responds to this situation codetermined by a guilty act at the beginning of the history of the human race is a matter for his freedom to decide, however threatening and pernicious this situation is, and especially that freedom which is exercised vis-à-vis God's offer of himself. In spite of the guilt at the beginning of the human race, God's offer of himself always remains valid because of Christ and in view of him, although it is no longer present because of "Adam" and from "Adam," and hence no longer from a guiltless beginning of the human race. Even in this situation codetermined by guilt, it remains just as radical an existential in the situation of human freedom as what we call "original sin."

An understanding of what "original sin" means, then, is based on two factors. First of all, it is based on the universality of the determination by guilt of *every* person's situation, and this factor includes the original nature of this determination by guilt in the history of the human race, for this is implied in the universality. Second, it is based on the reflective insight, deepening with the history of revelation and salvation, into the nature of the relationship between God and human beings. This factor includes the specific nature of the conditions of possibility for this relationship which are implied in the relationship, and also the special depths of guilt if and when there is guilt, and, if there is guilt, what kind of guilt is implied by a rejection of the sanctifying offer of himself which God makes to human beings.

Both the fact and the nature of what we call "original sin," therefore, can be arrived at from the individual's experience of himself in the history of salvation insofar as this history has reached its culmination in Christ. From this perspective it is also clear that the biblical teaching about original sin in the Old and New Testaments indicates phases of development which are clearly different from each other. The universality of the consequences of sin could not develop into a knowledge of original sin until reflective knowledge about immediacy to God was radicalized in the instance of a positive relationship to him. The biblical story about the sin of the first person or first persons in no way has to be understood as a historical, eyewitness report. The portrayal of the sin of the first man and woman is rather an aetiological inference from the experience of the human person's existentiell situation in the history of salvation to what must have happened "at the beginning" if the present situation of freedom actually is the way it is experienced, and if it is accepted as it is.

If this is the case, then it is also clear that with regard to the visual representation of these events in the primeval beginnings of the human race, everything which cannot be arrived at by this aetiological inference from the present situation to its origins belongs to the mode of representation and the mode of expression, but not to the content of the assertion. The assertion might be couched in the form of a myth, since this is a completely legitimate mode of representation for the human person's ultimate experiences, nor can it be replaced radically by some other mode of expression. Even the most abstract metaphysics and philosophy of religion must work with visual images which are nothing else but abbreviated and faded elements of mythology.

Original sin, therefore, expresses nothing else but the historical origin of the present, universal and ineradicable situation of our freedom as codetermined by guilt, and insofar as this situation has a history in which, because of the universal determination of this history by guilt, God's self-communication in grace comes to human beings not from "Adam," not from the beginning of the human race, but from the goal of this history, from the Godman Jesus Christ.

138 • Sin and Guilt*

A certain type of false, vulgar Catholicism is always in danger of considering sin a mere contingent event: an event in our life that occurs once in a while; an event that, if a person does not go to confession or do some other uncommon thing, God for some strange reason holds against us, even though our sinful deed took place a long time ago. On the other hand, the Protestant is always in danger of considering sin a constitutive element of the essence of the human being.

Now the truth lies between these two positions. We say this not only from theoretical reasons, but also because in this matter it is easy to see how difficult it is for a person to see himself as a sinner — even during prayer. Sin is not a metaphysical state of finiteness, of being at the end of the line, of falling off from the absolute demand of love. (This is more or less the Protestant position, which goes on to draw the conclusion that the human person is always and necessarily a sinner. However, anyone who has never run the danger of holding this view probably knows very little about sin.)

As a matter of fact, sin is not a contingent act which I performed in the past and whose effect is no longer with me. It is certainly not like breaking a window which falls into a thousand pieces, but afterward I remained personally unaffected by it. Sin determines the human being in a definite way: he has not only sinned, but he himself is a sinner. He is a sinner not only by a formal, juridical imputation of a former act, but

* *Spiritual Exercises, 35–42.*

also in an existential way, so that in looking back on our past actions, we always find ourselves to be sinners. When we have understood this, we are very close to understanding our own human existence.

Our human existence is caught between the sinfulness of all creation resulting from Adam's sin plus our own personal sinfulness on the one hand, and the redemption of Christ on the other. Therefore, it is necessary to pass a right judgment on our own sinfulness looked at from the point of view of its origin. This will reveal a makeup that tends to place suffering and misfortune before guilt. Not theoretically, but at least practically, we are tempted to think that guilt follows misfortune, and not vice versa. Actually, suffering and misfortune follow guilt, and this result is not at all a vicious circle.

In judging ourselves and the course of our lives, we are always tempted to consider our guilt as the result of bad luck, or of a lack of talent, or of exterior circumstances. By this basically false type of arguing that we use in trying to excuse ourselves before God, our conscience, our life, and the world, we manifest not our innocence, but only the way in which the unenlightened person, as yet untouched by the grace of God, considers his own guilt, that is, he will not admit it. He prefers to repress it.

The position of the unredeemed human being with regard to guilt is further characterized by the fact that he confuses guilt with fate. It is common knowledge that classic Greek tragedy does not consider guilt as the radical act of a free, responsible, human personality. Its attitude is rather that fate is something that happens to a person. Certainly he feels himself guilty in some way or other, but even more pressing is the complaint that an absolutely just and holy God must have mercy on the tragic fate of the human being.

Or, in another vein, the unredeemed person absolutizes himself, falsely makes a person out of himself to such a degree that he does not believe and does not desire that his guilt be forgiven — and it is precisely in this attitude that he commits the most serious sin. Perhaps we do not experience anything like this in our own souls. Nevertheless, there is such an attitude toward sin.

With the light of natural reason we can discover a moral philosophy. Philosophical ethics also has its theological aspect. Sin can only be known as a violation of the holy will of God the creator and Lord of the world. Therefore, there is no such thing in this world as a "philosophical sin," or, if this idea does pop up, it has nothing to do with the Christian concept of sin. A person who has this idea of sin is caught up in a primitive notion that perhaps makes it impossible for him really to commit a sin.

Nevertheless, it remains true that the real knowledge of guilt, that is, the sorrowful admission of sin, is the product of God's revelation and grace. Grace is already at work in us when we admit guilt as our own reality, or at least admit the possibility of guilt in our own lives. Grace is already at work when a person has the humility to hand himself over to the power of grace, when he tells himself that he is so dependent on the grace of God that he must possess it if he is to remain free of sin.

On the other hand, a purely natural knowledge of guilt — one that is completely independent of grace (if this is philosophically possible) — would be suppressed if God's grace and the light of revelation were not there to help us. This type of knowledge only "notices" guilt, or formulates it in such a way that it becomes a condemnation, not a liberating and saving confession. Without grace, we would not stand firm in the truth of the existence of sin for a long period of time. We would say: "Why, we can't be *that* foolish! Guilt is merely the product of our disturbed imagination and of our existential *Angst* that has objectified itself!"

God's revelation of guilt takes place especially in the apocalypse of his grace and mercy. Only in this way! Therefore, if God did not tell us about sin in the revelation of his grace, then we would either deny the existence of guilt, or else we would utterly despair. There is no neutral position between these two. Thus we can only get a clear knowledge of guilt, both of its essence and its actuality, from the cross of Jesus Christ.

What is meant here is the guilt of mortal sin which is a free act that we alone are responsible for, that we cannot blame anyone else for, that is more properly ours than any act of faith and love. We can only posit acts of faith and love if we receive them in their possibility and actuality as a gift of God in virtue of his supernaturally elevating and effective grace.

But despite all speculation, we cannot push sin off onto God, even though the philosopher is always tempted to consider the creature as a marionette of the absolute. That is precisely what the human being is not! And the sinful person is always tempted to say that fundamentally God on whom everything depends is responsible for sin. But if he takes that kind of a position with regard to sin, he has betrayed the special characteristic of his creaturehood.

Guilt is contracted through the deification of a finite reality, through the identification of my absolute worth that can only be related absolutely to God, with things that cannot be posited absolutely. In the absoluteness that has been given me from above, I desire to assert myself radically in the realm of the finite. In this deification of a finite reality, there is an attack upon the true meaning of my freedom, which is my capacity and my need for the infinite. I do not have the courage to make a leap into the infinite, to relativize everything finite, and so to surpass the finite. I remain standing on the edge of the abyss and desire to have it easier and more pleasant in this life by exhausting the possibilities of tangible things.

This attitude necessarily implies a turning away from God and his essential characteristics — his immensity, power, dominion, truth and beauty, love and holiness, and so forth. Sin is also a radical offense against the sovereign will of God. Therefore, we should not act as if the objective structure and the known essence of a thing exhaust its reality. In addition to that, there is also the element in it that is willed and freely planned by the will of God. By my sin I offend against that, too!

It is most certainly true that God wills the objective order of the nature he has established and that an offense against nature is an offense against its maker. But in the matter of sin, there is an inexplicable something left over that is also an offense against God's free will and his powerful dominion over things. This is even more the case with regard to the concrete order of our human existence, in which we are dealing directly with his person and his Holy Spirit. We are not just dealing with his law, we are also dealing with his personal self, with the God who is near! Not just with an order that he has created, but with an order to which he has supernaturally established and communicated himself.

Where sin actually takes place in this world, it offends against the infinite love of God, against the goodness that God himself is in our midst; it is an attack against the uncreated grace, against the heart of God. Our sin actually pierces God! Therefore, it is essentially the loss of grace and a falling out of the life of God.

Even though it is true that from many points of view there can be no such thing as absolute evil, still sin must be considered an *absolute nonvalue*. All other value-deficiencies can have some meaning, can be built into a larger system that brings out their meaning. A person can give up a lot of things and still nicely arrange the totality of his human existence. He can put a plus sign before an algebraic equation. But he cannot do that with sin.

If I consider sin a phase of development, if I say that it is only one of God's "tricks" so that he can throw more grace into the world, if I try to make a beginning with sin before God has said: "Your guilt is forgiven," if I should try — apart from the cross of Christ — to philosophize about a "happy fault" (*felix culpa*), then I have done away with the absolute nonvalue of sin.

And now let us tell ourselves: There is no such thing as sin! Let us summon up all our mental powers and make a few objections: There is no such thing as sin! Where does sin come from, if there is only the one, holy God who creates and sustains everything? How can sin really exist, if it is supposed to be mere negativity? How can it be so bad, if it is only a lack of value? How can it be condemned by God?

If we tell ourselves then that this falling off comes about because of our freedom, then the problem is simply posed once more: How can a freedom whose power is received from God effect such a falling off? Why is this act so bad, if it necessarily brings forth some positive good no matter how small?

From this we can see how we would not remain true to the real existence of sin, if the crucified Christ did not say to us: Sin does exist, in spite of all improbability; it is present in the world according to the testimony of your conscience in the Holy Spirit! It is here, even though it is committed in the darkness of this world and from our weakness.

We never know where we or the world with its history should be forgiven; we can never say with an absolute judgment: Here is sin, it happened right there! We cannot even say that about ourselves because we can never, with perfect reflection, grasp ourselves as agents. But we must tell ourselves: What we Christians call sin can happen in this world, has happened, and is happening right now. I, who am pleased with myself, who am so identified with myself that I must love myself, can sin. That is something frightful!

Theoretically, we never challenge this truth, but in the fulfillment of our human existence we forget it again and again. And if we do admit it existentially, then that is only because God's grace has touched us, and because the light of his mercy has penetrated into our darkness. Accordingly, then, our meditation on sin can and must begin at that place to which St. Ignatius [in his *Spiritual Exercises*] leads us: under the cross of our Lord.

139 • Venial Sin*

The presence of venial sin is obvious. In fact, it constitutes the moral disorder of our everyday life. We should take these sins, that we confess each week in an offhanded manner, very seriously. It is true that they do not realize the essence of serious sin that separates a human being from the grace of God, and in which he exercises such a total disposition over himself that he really becomes lost. But they do distract him from his eternal goal and injure him in many ways.

A few familiar phrases will suffice to bring out the harmful influence

---

* *Spiritual Exercises*, 60–62.

of venial sin on our whole life. Venial sin leads to the formation of false attitudes, and so to the corruption of character and the dulling of conscience; it lessens one's personal happiness, the state of a calm human existence that knows how to live in peace with itself. There is more. Venial sin hinders the development and growth of the life of grace, and so the personal penetration of our nature's free movement toward God; yes, in a very true sense it is an offense against God, an obscuring of the living relationship to God.

Not the least of the bad effects of venial sin is that which concerns our apostolic mission. Perhaps it is easier for many of us, looking at the matter from the point of view of our responsibility for others, to see these "mere" venial sins as factors which essentially weaken our apostolic effectiveness. A person can have more or less talent, can live in circumstances that turn the Lord's vineyard into a stone quarry in which he must nevertheless continue to labor. But very often we ourselves are responsible for the fact that our apostolic labor is much less fruitful than it should be. This means especially that we should take venial sin seriously in all of its various forms, beginning with freely chosen faults and going on to certain manifestations of our character for which we are hardly guilty, but which nevertheless show how far removed we are from that which we should be.

Some of the things we would do well to meditate on are: impatience, coarseness, uncleanliness, cheap literature, talkativeness, laughing at the faults of others, petty egoism in everyday life, petty enmities, oversensitivity, wasting time, cowardice, lack of respect for holy things, for other people, for the life of their souls; disrespectful talk about men and women, harmful spite portraying itself as a clever joke, stubbornness and obstinacy, moodiness that others must put up with, disorder in work, postponement of the unpleasant, gossip, conceit and self-praise, unjust preference for certain people that we find quite pleasant, hastiness in judging, false self-satisfaction, laziness, the tendency to give up learning anymore, the tendency to refuse to listen to others, and so forth.

The fight against venial sins must correspond with their particular nature. If a particular sin creates carelessness that can easily be overcome, if a person truly wants to overcome it and can muster the courage to demand asceticism from himself, then a particular "examination of conscience," conscientiously used, will bring quick results. But if a venial sin is deeply imbedded, if it is a spontaneous and almost reflex action of a falsely formed character, then a relatively external ascetical training is not sufficient.

In such cases, the best remedy seems to be to have a great deal of patience and to let ourselves be educated by life itself. A person must observe very carefully until he has found the critical starting point. Very often a person can only struggle indirectly against such faults, even when their symptoms are directly perceptible.

The main problem here is to discover the particular way of existence of one's own "I." No person should dare to say that he has sufficiently penetrated the meaning of his own self. Therefore, the effort to attain self-knowledge in order to reform one's character must necessarily last a long time. Normally this is a lifetime job. Certainly we should never give up. Recurring falls should not be passed off lightly.

We should, for example, be alarmed if we find that we are constantly coming into conflict with those around us — even if we discover that the others were in the wrong, or if we feel that everything we touch turns into a failure, or if we suffer in any other way that does not seem to be normal. In this regard, people often reproach themselves for things that hardly approach a venial sin. But this can still be a secondary symptom pointing to something more deep-seated.

Sometimes venial sins that we most frequently and seriously repent of are the least relevant to what we are; on the other hand, certain things that we theoretically admit without suffering from them can be our real but repressed faults. At best, a person can attempt a radical diagnosis of these secondary results. Usually it is not a good idea to attempt this alone, but in cooperation with and under the direction of a good spiritual director. For these particular types of "disorders of life" come within the sphere of psychopathology. Much more could be said here that must be passed up. At any rate, a person should not minimize the importance of personal defects. Nevertheless, at times these defects must just be accepted and suffered through, since there is such a thing as a truly Christian suffering at the hands of one's own defects. And finally, venial sins should not remain unnoticed, since they lead ultimately to serious conflicts and to serious sins.

140 • Morality without Moralizing*

The church should be one which defends morality boldly and unambiguously, without moralizing. Quite certainly the message of Christianity includes a complex of moral principles. This proposition is correct, independently of the question whether and to what extent moral norms are part of the deposit of revelation or stem from the

---

* *The Shape of the Church to Come*, 64–70.

largely historically conditioned and changeable situation of the human person and society, receiving a higher motivation and urgency from the human being's orientation by grace to the immediacy of God in eternal life only insofar as they are relevant at a particular time. A part of the courage to preach this gospel message, in season or out of season, is also the determination resolutely and unambiguously to stand up for this complex of moral principles.

If, however, we put forward this undoubtedly basic and still very relevant principle, we must honestly add that it is not always so easy and clear to say how these concrete questions of human morality are to be answered both in the light of the Christian message and with regard to the present situation. Whether it is congenial or uncongenial, in spite of all complaints that we are rendering many people in the church insecure in their moral conscience, it must be said that there are not a few concrete principles and patterns of behavior which formerly — and quite rightly in the circumstances — counted as binding, concrete expressions of the ultimate Christian moral principles, but today are not necessarily binding always and in every case; that perhaps, on the other hand, some moral imperatives ought now to be defended very concretely, much more clearly and boldly than they are in fact defended, since they were not and could not have been formerly so explicit in the church's moral consciousness.

Moral consciousness has in fact a history and this history is not merely something added externally to the human person, while most of the moral principles proclaimed by the church can be derived from his essential nature; it is rather an intrinsic factor in the human being's concrete nature, which has a history of its own. Without detriment to the individual's ultimate, essential consistency, which however can never be filtered off adequately and in chemical purity from the concrete and always historical nature, this concrete human nature has itself a real history and is subject to an internal and social mutation. Such a change, however, can render no longer binding many a feature of the concrete moral norms which were formerly and quite rightly proclaimed as binding, because they corresponded to the human person's concrete nature at the time; and it can also give an immediate relevance to norms which hitherto had no actual binding force and did not exist in the church's moral consciousness.

Connected if not identified with this is the fact that Christian morality is to a very considerable extent an "end morality" [something intended for its own sake, as contrasted with "means"]. In the individual and social sphere it is certainly possible to play fast and loose with the term by questioning, in the light of this end morality, the binding force of a moral principle which is directly relevant. But, in principle and in the last resort, Christian morality is an end morality, since every Christian is bound in principle by an *absolute* obligation ("under pain of mortal sin") to a *perfect* love of God and neighbor in thought and deed and yet (as distinct from a Protestant view of the human person's radical sinfulness, involving him in a constant state of guilt) it cannot be said that this absolute obligation binds us at every moment to the most perfect realization then possible in a concrete deed. The human being is therefore also permitted and simultaneously required to remain open to a further evolution of his own reality and to a higher actualization of his moral consciousness. This holds of the individual in his own particular sphere and of the individual in a society in the process of a moral evolution; it holds likewise of a particular society and of humankind as a whole.

This, of course, is not the place to apply such reflections and principles to particular moral questions. But what has been merely suggested here must be thought out, more deeply studied, and boldly applied to particular questions of Christian morality when the church sets out to proclaim moral norms today. If she does not do this adequately, the proclamation will sound old-fashioned and unrealistic; the church will be reproached — and not necessarily or always wrongly — not for proclaiming the moral principles flowing from human nature and sustained by the basic Christian ethos, but for defending patterns of behavior which belong to a past epoch of human history and are not noticed as such by the church's officeholders, simply because they, too, in their outlook belong to a passing or past age. Examples from recent times which are no longer disputed today even by the most conservative moral theologians can easily be listed.

This is not to dispute the possibility in principle that the church herself, through deciding for a line of conduct which is itself again an element in the human being's concrete nature — and therefore binding — can take an active part in shaping the concrete history of moral consciousness, not merely noticing that this history has in fact happened or drawing conclusions from a history which she has not helped to shape. This sort of thing, however, is not possible through a merely pedantic, ineffective insistence on concrete moral principles, but only through a deed and its appropriate proclamation which really change the historical situation, the concrete nature of the human person and the total moral consciousness of society.

If we say that the church must be a moral institution without moralizing, this does not relieve her of the obligation of standing up unambiguously and boldly for the Christian message, even in its moral demands. We are moralizing if we expound norms of behavior peevishly and pedantically, full of moral indignation at a world without morals, without really tracing them back to that innermost experience of human nature, which is the source of the so-called principles of natural law and which alone gives them binding force; we are moralizing if moral principles are not traced back to that innermost core of the Christian message which is the message of the living Spirit, the message of freedom from merely external law, the message of love which is no longer subject to any law when it prevails.

This holds particularly today. We have first and last to announce to the contemporary person the innermost blessed, liberating mystery which we call God, redeeming him from fear, from the self-estrangement of his existence. We must show the modern human being at least the beginning of the way that leads him credibly and concretely into the liberty of God. Where someone has not had an initial experience of God and of his Spirit, liberating him from his deepest fears and from guilt, there is no point in announcing the moral norms of Christianity to him. He would not be able to understand them at best; they might seem to him to be the source of still more radical constraints and still deeper fears. If a person is not really genuinely and personally in the presence of God (and this cannot be achieved by a little externally indoctrinating talk about God), he may perhaps understand that offenses against certain moral norms relating to the concrete nature of the individual and of society are inappropriate; but he cannot understand and realize just what Christianity means by sin and guilt in God's sight.

When we consider this, we may well think that the church's proclamation contains too much moralizing. Truly Christian morality has the human being in view, defends him and his open history, arises from the center of his being: a center indeed where the Spirit of God is alive, making his demands from within. Christian morality therefore must not create the impression that it is a matter of God's arbitrary legislation, imposing restraints on the person, that it is a law coming upon him merely from outside and might well — from the person's standpoint — be different. When the modern person gets the impression that the church's morality is a matter of inculcating laws which are not the concrete expression of the impulse of the Spirit liberating us from within, it is evident that we are moralizing and not really proclaiming Christian morality as it must be proclaimed.

Protests against moralizing morality are not merely negative; in the last resort they have positive implications. It is a fact that the human being and his environment, insofar as they can and should be made subject to his knowledge and control, have become much more complex and unfathomable than formerly. Because they were formerly more simple, at least insofar as they were under the person's control at all, because they were also much more stable and unchangeable, it was possible to assert relatively simple and stable norms of behavior, by which an individual could come to terms with himself and his environment.

The consequences of what a person might do had already been often tested and could be sufficiently clearly foreseen; it was therefore possible to provide very clear moral norms of behavior, which were relatively simple to manage. This does not alter the fact that these norms were always difficult for human beings and demanded moral effort for their observation. Today these human realities are both much more complex and at the same time left to human control to a greater extent; they include elements which formerly simply did not exist as objects on which the human person could exercise his freedom and thus did not demand any moral norms. This very much more complex world, however, is for that reason much more difficult to understand and therefore no longer so easily provides simple and manageable norms for human beings and for the church.

The church too, therefore, in many fields of human life, is often helpless when asked not for quite general and abstract, but for concrete and directly applicable norms. If nevertheless she acts or were to act as if she possessed always and everywhere and for all cases such directly applicable norms, she would simply destroy her credibility by her terrifyingly naive attitude to life. But if, as a result, the church is told to stop handing out these prescriptions, costing nothing, by petty clerics living remote from real life, from society, and from modern culture, and to leave such decisions to the conscience of the individual, this demand too may often be crude and overhasty; the term "conscience" may be used to cover subjective arbitrariness and whims, which have nothing to do with a self-critical conscience responsible before God and really fearing the possibility of genuine sin.

In spite of all this, in principle and rightly understood, such a demand is very often true. Rightly understood, it does not mean the retreat of Christianity and the church from the field of morals, but a very important change of emphasis in Christian proclamation: consciences must be formed, not primarily by way of casuistic instruction, going into more and more concrete details, but by being roused and trained for autonomous and responsible decisions in the concrete, complex situations of human life which are no longer completely solvable down to the last detail, in fields never considered by the older morality, precisely because they were then unknown and even now cannot be adequately mastered by a rational casuistry. Where this sort of thing was not possible in the past, probabilism might be brought in to show that a particular course of action was morally indifferent.

Today we see that there are many things which cannot be covered at all by moral theory or casuistry and nevertheless may be matters of conscience of the greatest moment. Here evidently we have a form of moral decision which was not considered at all adequately in traditional moral theology. Unfortunately we cannot discuss this further here. Such a logic of existential decision, on which people formerly reflected only with reference to very secondary decisions of conscience — as, for instance, the choice of a vocation to the priesthood — is an urgent desideratum for a real training of conscience, which today can no longer be accomplished merely by purifying the relevant moral norms.

If the effort of moral theology and preaching were to be directed on these lines, there would be less need to moralize and yet, in consciences and in the world, there would be more genuine morality. The moral decisions even of Christians would then indeed presumably continue to fall materially into many individual questions; but, in spite of their diversity, they would be sustained by a responsibility before God and before the dignity of the human being in justice and love, and there would presumably be more harmony in matters that are really decisive for his enduring substance and his dignity than there is when we moralize and thus cease to be credible, wanting to save morality by an ever more exact and detailed casuistry supposedly universally applicable.

Such a nonmoralizing morality, however, must not suggest that all life's concrete problems would be solved simply by invoking God. They are not solved in this way. Concrete moral problems are frequently intramundane, factual problems, in face of which a Christian is mostly as helpless as other people. Even an appeal to God and his gospel does not produce concrete answers to such concrete problems as the population explosion, hunger in the world, the structure of a future society offering more freedom and justice. When someone has a genuine relationship to God, freed from an ultimate existential dread, he can reflect with a more open mind and freer heart on such problems and look more hopefully for solutions; but this is still a long way from actually finding the solutions which really meet the case.

It is indeed true that today, as in former times, simply appealing to God may involve the danger of reducing religion to the "opium of the people" (not that this slogan can be regarded as a legitimate argument against religion or faith). God does not relieve us of our secular problems; he does not spare us our helplessness. In the church, therefore, we should not act as if he did. In the last resort, even the appeal to God forces us into a radical helplessness. For he is the incomprehensible mystery which forbids us to regard any sort of brightness of our

own in our life as the light of eternity. We come to terms with this final helplessness only by surrendering ourselves in hope and love to
this incomprehensible God, in a holy "agnosticism" of capitulation to
him who never guaranteed that all our calculations would work out
smoothly if only we got on well with him.

141 • Existential Ethics*

Insofar as a person's moral behavior is not merely an "instance"
of a general, essential moral norm but the realization of himself in
his unique individuality, and this fact can and must be systematically
investigated, an existential ethics can and must exist. The realization
of a person falls within the scope of existential ethics insofar as it is
possible to, and incumbent upon, him in a manner intimated to himself
alone and is and is not adequately covered by general norms.

To this extent existential ethics remains a necessary complement to
"essential ethics," but not a substitute for it as situation ethics maintains.
The general moral norms worked out in the latter must be "applied" to
each particular situation in which the agent finds himself; and by this
situation we must understand that historical point of transition created
by the unique personality of the individual, his personal relationships,
his position in his own career, and the kind of thought about general
morals of which he is capable and from which his concrete moral
action follows.

In this "application" to the individual's situation, the "thou" plays
the part of generality in the concrete form (community), for its part
positively determining the situation of the agent, insofar as it is not
only affected by the agent's activity but itself provokes and modifies
this latter by concrete demands and restraints. Of course this "thou"
is not to be misconceived in an individualistic sense, but depends on
larger social contexts. Within and behind the situation of the individual,
even as determined by the demands of the "thou," a concrete call of
God is legitimately presented to the individual concerned; and this call
engages at once the agent in his moral behavior, whose self-realization
this call demands and bends in a particular direction, and the general
moral law reflecting God's fundamental plan for human beings, society,
and their environment, which is meant to be given effect through the
activity of the individual and can only be given effect by that means.

---

*With Herbert Vorgrimler, *Dictionary of Theology*, 2d edition (New York: Crossroad
Publishing Company, 1981), 162–63.

142 • Penance and the Anointing of the Sick*

If the new life which becomes concrete in quite definite basic notions is always the threatened life of a sinner, and if to this extent and in this respect God's word of forgiveness has to be offered to people time and time again, then we have the sacrament of *penance*. And we also have the complement to this sacrament in the situation in which the threatened nature of our salvation as well as our sinfulness in grace becomes most manifest: the sacrament of the *anointing of the sick*.

We view the human person as a being who possesses responsibility in freedom and as one entangled in the guilt of his social world of other persons. If we really understand what guilt means as a possibility or as a terrible reality in our lives, and if we have experienced how hopeless real guilt before God is, just from our own human perspective, then we long to hear the word of forgiveness from God. This word is never experienced as something to be taken for granted, but rather as a miracle of his grace and of his love. Forgiveness is the greatest and the most incomprehensible miracle of God's love because God communicates himself in it, and does this to a person who, in something which only appears to be a mere banality of everyday life, has managed to do the monstrous thing of saying no to God.

God's word of forgiveness is not only the consequence, but also and ultimately the presupposition of the conversion in which a guilty person turns to God and surrenders himself in faith, trust, and contrition, and it can be heard in the depths of conscience. For as the ground upon which conversion is based, this word of forgiveness dwells within the trusting and loving return of a person to God, the return in which this person repents and does homage to the merciful love of God. Throughout the length and breadth of the history of the human race this quiet word of forgiveness often has to be enough by itself.

But what usually occurs in such a hidden and inarticulated way in the history of human conscience, namely, the grace of God which offers everyone salvation and forgiveness, has its own history in time and space. And God's word of forgiveness to humankind which becomes concrete in time and space has found its climax and its ultimate historical irrevocability in Jesus Christ, the crucified and risen one. He entered into solidarity with sinners in love, and he accepted God's word of forgiveness for us in the final act of his faith, hope, and love, and in the midst of the darkness of his death, the death in which he expe-

---

* *Foundations of Christian Faith*, 421–24.

rienced the darkness of our guilt. This word of God's forgiveness in Jesus Christ, in whom the unconditional nature of this word has also become historically irrevocable, remains present in the community of those who believe in this forgiveness, in the church. The church is the basic sacrament of this word of God's forgiveness.

This single word of forgiveness which the church is, and which remains a living presence of power and efficacy in the church, is articulated in a variety of ways which correspond to human nature. It is present in the preaching of the church as a basic message to everyone: "I believe in...the forgiveness of sins," says the Apostles' Creed. In a fundamental way which remains normative for the whole history of the individual person, the church's word of forgiveness is addressed to this person by the church in the sacrament of baptism.

This word of forgiveness continues to live and to be efficacious in the prayer of the church. In this prayer the church asks with confidence again and again for God's mercy for itself, the church of sinners, and for every individual. Hence it accompanies the ever new and ever to-be-deepened conversion of each person which does not reach its fulfillment and its definitive victory until death. This word of forgiveness, which always builds upon the word which was spoken in baptism, is addressed again to the individual by the church in a special way if and when this person, who also remains a sinner after baptism and can fall into new and serious sin, repents and confesses his serious guilt or the poverty of his life to the church in its representative, or if in certain circumstances he brings them before God and his Christ in the common confession of a community. When this word of God's forgiveness is addressed to an individual baptized person upon the confession of his guilt by a representative of the church who has been expressly designated for this, we call this event of God's word of forgiveness the reception of the sacrament of penance.

Insofar as this efficacious word of forgiveness is addressed precisely to an already baptized member of the church upon his confession of sin, it has a definite characteristic: by his serious or "small" sins the baptized Christian as a member of the church has also placed himself in contradiction to the essence of the holy community to which he belongs, that is, to the church whose existence and life is supposed to be a sign of the fact that God's grace as love for God and human beings is victorious in the world.

Hence by its word of forgiveness the church also forgives the injustice which a person's sin does to the church. Indeed we may say that by the word of God's forgiveness which is entrusted to it, the church forgives sin *by* forgiving a person the injustice done to itself, just as it communicates the Holy Spirit of the church to a person in baptism *by* incorporating him into itself as the body of Christ. Because the church's word of forgiveness is addressed to an individual's concrete situation of guilt as the word of Christ and with an ultimate and essential involvement of the church, and because it is not merely a word about God's forgiveness, but rather is the *event* of this forgiveness, this word really is a sacrament.

The situation of *sickness* also belongs to the decisive situations of a person's life which are part of the history of his *salvation,* situations which at first might appear very secular. They are situations which force him to a decision about how he freely wants to understand the totality and the real meaning of his life, whether as absurdity, or as the dark mystery in which incomprehensible love draws close to him. When we speak of sickness in this context, we mean those serious illnesses which are the harbingers signaling the approach of death, even if there can be hope of recovery. They make very obvious the intrinsically threatened nature of the individual's life and his deterioration into death, and both of these push a person back into the most inexorable loneliness where he has to come to terms with himself and with God all by himself.

As we have already mentioned frequently, the responsibility of every person for himself, for his freedom, for his own unfathomable self which he cannot make completely reflective — all of this belongs to the very essence of the human being, and it may not be taken from him. But this is one side of human existence. In his abiding loneliness a person is not alone. God is with him. But there also surrounds him the holy community of believers, of those who love and pray, of those who in life try to exercise the obedience of death, and who in life try to gaze upon *the* dying one in faith. And because this holy community which is called the church always lives from out of the death of its Lord, the dying who always die alone are not abandoned by their brothers and sisters.

We cannot develop any further here the salvation history and ecclesiological dimensions of this, but if we accept this experience of faith in all of its depths, then we ourselves want the community of those who have willingly surrendered in faith to this mystery with Jesus, the man who was completely obedient, we want this community or the church to appear visibly at the sickbed. We want this so that the mysterious course of divine life might not only circulate freely within us, but also so that it might become incarnate in the tangibility of our lives, and hence so that grace might become more deeply imbedded in us through its very manifestation, and might permeate our life and our death more fully with its salvific power.

This word, which brings hidden grace to a corporeal and quite incarnational manifestation, is spoken by the church through its designated representative. It allows not only grace and the interior acceptance of it which takes place in the one who receives the word, but also the grace of the *holy* church which is filled with God's Spirit to become a tangible "event." In this word grace becomes manifest and takes place *by* becoming corporeal. In this sense the manifestation is the cause of grace, and of course the converse is also true: the unity between what manifests itself and its manifestation is ultimately irresolvable.

If this word of grace, which in certain circumstances becomes clearer and more tangible through further gestures such as anointing and the laying on of hands, is addressed to a definite person in a decisive situation of his life by the church in an ultimate involvement of its own essence — which as a whole and as the "primordial sacrament" is the historical presence of God's grace — and hence if the church knows that here it is creatively speaking the efficacious word of God's grace, then it is saying and doing something which we call a sacrament; it is speaking the irrevocable word of God's grace by God's mandate. This word does not only speak "about" grace, but rather it allows this grace to become event. One of the seven sacramental words of this kind which the church recognizes is the prayer of faith over and the anointing of a sick person whose sickness is a situation of grace and of salvation in an urgent way.

Therefore this sickness calls out for this word of the church which makes grace corporeal and efficacious. In this word the hidden grace of the church and of its member's critical situation is expressed tangibly at least as an offer, and it works its salvific effect. To this extent it is only received by a person who believes and who is longing for forgiveness.

143 • The Eucharist*

The sacrament of the eucharist should not simply be counted among the seven sacraments. However much it involves the individual and brings him time and time again into the community with Christ, it is nevertheless the sacrament of the church as such in a very radical sense. It is precisely the institution of the Lord's Supper which is of decisive importance for the founding of the church and for the self-understanding of Jesus as the mediator of salvation.

Because of the importance and the special nature of the eucharist

---

* *Foundations of Christian Faith*, 424–27.

within the framework of the sacraments, we feel the need to mention here a few things from biblical theology. However, we can only give a brief sketch of this material. The reality which is designated by the term "eucharist" has its foundation in the Last Supper of Jesus (cf. especially Lk 22:14–23 and 1 Cor 11:23–26). There, according to his own words, Jesus gives his "body" and his "blood" to be eaten and drunk under the appearance of receiving bread and wine. The content and meaning of this action follow from the situation and from the concepts which are employed. The idea of death is of decisive importance: Jesus accepts his fate consciously and connects it with the central content of his preaching. Moreover, Jesus understands this meal in an eschatological way as an anticipation of the joy of the final and definitive banquet. Finally, at this meal with Jesus the idea of community is constitutive, that is, the union of Jesus with his friends and the foundation of the community of these friends among themselves.

From the concepts which are employed there results the following: according to the Semitic usage "body" designates the corporeal tangibility of the person of Jesus; in addition to the word over the bread Jesus is said to be the servant of God in an absolute sense (cf. Is 53:4–12); but the blood is clarified more precisely as being poured out in order to establish the new covenant with God (cf. Is 42:6; 49:8). This characterizes Jesus as dying a bloody death. The gifts, therefore, are identical with Jesus, the servant of God who accepts a violent death in free obedience, and thereby establishes the new covenant. The identity between the eucharistic food of the church and the body and blood of Jesus is defined quite exactly in the First Epistle to the Corinthians: it is the body which was offered by Jesus at the Last Supper. It is the crucified body of Jesus, and hence in eating it the death of Jesus is proclaimed as salvific and is made efficacious. It is the flesh and blood of the exalted one, and by eating it an individual is incorporated into the community of the one pneumatic body of Jesus Christ. The permanence of this food in the church, and as *the* food of the church, follows from the command to remember him which is connected immediately with the words of institution, "Do this in memory of me." In the mandate to continue to do "this" there is an assurance that the total reality of Christ is always present and efficacious wherever the Lord's Supper is celebrated legitimately by the disciples of Jesus.

At the same time the bloody sacrifice of Jesus Christ on the cross becomes present in the repetition of the Lord's Supper which Jesus himself wanted, because it is the flesh and blood of the *suffering* and *dying* servant of God *as* sacrificed and poured out for "many" which become present, and according to the institution of Jesus himself it is only as such that they can become present; and also because this

presence of the one sacrifice of Jesus Christ is found in a liturgical, sacrificial action of the church. The eucharistic celebration of the church,
therefore, is always a real meal insofar as the body and blood of Jesus
Christ are really present there as food, and at the same time it is a real
sacrifice insofar as the *one* sacrifice of Jesus continues to be efficacious
in history, and continues to be made efficacious in the celebration of
the eucharist by the liturgical act of representation in a church which is
essentially historical. Hence these two realities in the one celebration
of the eucharist cannot be completely separated in theological reflection. Moreover, the incarnation, resurrection, and exaltation of Jesus
also become present.

In the context of our reflections we do not have to present
the historical development of the eucharist in dogma and theology,
for example, with regard to the questions about real presence and
transubstantiation.

In the celebration and reception of the eucharist the church and
the individual believer really give "thanks," which is what "eucharist"
means, and they do this in the fullest possible and specifically "ecclesial" way, which is only possible for the church of Jesus Christ. But at
the same time this is imposed upon the church as a basic law by really
"having" Jesus Christ himself in her midst and by really accepting him
as food — although she does this in the courageous reality of faith — the
church "says," that is, she realizes and actualizes her thankful response
to God's offer of grace, namely, his self-communication.

Therefore this self-communication is the most intense self-
communication because it is "formulated" in flesh and blood by the
life of Jesus which has always been loved and has been definitively
accepted. The "effect" of the eucharist, then, is not only to be understood as an individual effect which takes place in the individual, the
effect through which the individual receives his personal participation
in the life of Jesus Christ, and also receives the grace to live out this
participation in a "Christian life" in the strictest sense, that is, the very
life of Jesus Christ in love, obedience, and gratitude to the Father, a
life which represents forgiveness and patience. But this effect is also
and especially a social and ecclesiological effect: in the eucharist the
gratuitous and irrevocable salvific will of God for all human beings becomes present, tangible, and visible *in* this world insofar as through the
eucharist the tangible and visible community of believers is fashioned
into *that* sign which does not only point to some possible grace and
salvific will of God, but rather *is* the tangibility and the permanence of
this grace and this salvation.

It is obvious, therefore, that, insofar as the eucharist is the sacrament of the most radical and most real presence of the Lord in this

celebration in the form of a meal, the eucharist is also the fullest actualization of the essence of the church. For the church neither is nor wants to be anything else but the presence of Christ in time and space. And insofar as everyone participates in the same meal of Christ, who is the giver and the gift at the same time, the eucharist is also the sign, the manifestation and the most real actualization of the church insofar as the church is and makes manifest the ultimate unity of all peoples in the Spirit, a unity which has been founded by God in grace.

144 • The Meal of Pilgrims*

The meal of those who are pilgrims to eternal life: How exactly this meal suits our needs! We are still traveling as pilgrims, never settled, always moving on, in the provisional. Consequently we walk among shadows and symbols in the darkness of faith. That is an unavoidable lot and its pain is salutary and should not surprise us. The highest is, after all, furthest away and remains a prize promised only to voluntary fidelity in what is provisional. Yet we should like to have this highest at once, even now although, or rather precisely because, we are wandering in search of it.

For how could we go on pilgrimage if we were not already aware of the powers of eternity in us? How could we hope, if what we hope for were *only* far away? One can only seek God with God, and we should not seek if we had not yet already found, if he himself did not permit himself to be found by us day by day. And so the promise and the possession must both be true: way and goal are simultaneously present; God is with us, hidden under the veil of his own creatures.

If therefore the holy banquet of eternity is prepared for us here in time, it is in a way which the sober humility of pilgrims such as we may expect: simple and ordinary, hidden under the signs of commonplace, everyday earthly life, under which the real meaning has to be believed and firmly held in hope and love.

And so the Lord has prepared this meal: for the senses a sign, in appearance a little bread and wine, such as usually nourish our bodies and cheer our spirits. But when at his command, by his power and with his words *the* commemoration of his last meal is celebrated, and this latter is truly brought into our own present moment, then the inner truth

---

* *Everyday Faith*, 85–89.

and reality of these signs is himself in his flesh and blood. He becomes the bread of limitless strength and the wine of inexpressible joy. He himself makes his body a sign for us in our time of what he wishes to be for us in his Spirit: God giving his own life to his poor creature. He becomes for us now as we receive the bread of the altars, what he is in himself: the earthly reality by which God's eternity has entered into the narrow limits of our finitude.

A person's head bends over what looks like an ordinary piece of bread — over what in fact merely looks like a semblance of real bread — his hand reaches for a cup such as usually contains merely the drink of this earthly life, and then there happens what is the innermost goal of *everything* that happens. God and the believing heart each from their own side break through all the sinister walls which at other times so infinitely separate them.

They meet in him who is both, in whom such a unity already occurred definitively and corporeally, in the Lord, who in one person is the eternal Word from on high and the son of the earth from the Virgin's womb. We hold the body of this earth which was born and was sacrificed in pain; we penetrate once more into the depth of what he suffered long ago, when we hold what he took from us. And we are abidingly where we and he have remained, in the center with God. Sacred banquet in which Christ is received, the memory of his passion is renewed, the soul is filled with grace and the earnest of future glory is bestowed.

Yet we commonplace people make this mystery of eternal life in this dying time so commonplace! Look how the priest performs his sublime office — morosely, impelled by objective duty, as though he were carrying out some duty of this world and not the liturgy in which the light and blessedness of heaven are contained. Consider the narrow and barren hearts into which the Lord descends and which at best do not know what to say to him except the few selfish desires which make up their everyday round.

Alas, we Christians. In this sacrament we receive both the pure blessedness of heaven and the refined transfigured essence of the bittersweet fruit of this earth. We receive it, to be sure, as though wrapped in the hard shell of custom but nevertheless in all truth. And we receive it as though nothing were happening. Weary and lazy we take the same heart back home from the table of God into the narrow rooms of our lives where we are more at home than in God's upper room. We offer the Son in sacrifice and want to refuse our hearts. We play the divine game of the liturgy and we are not in earnest about it. We have perhaps a good will but it has so little power over the dull heaviness of our heart.

But perhaps even this belongs to the sign, when God is already hastening toward his creature even here in time, and when even now the banquet of eternal life is celebrated in advance. If the supper of eternal life is prepared in the narrow houses of time, it is not surprising that the needy come to it, and that their small minds and meagre hearts do not yet realize at all what is to be theirs. It is understandable that we are rather disturbed and feel our strength overtaxed and, as it were, almost driven to irritated reserve by such lavishness on God's part. For it is after all still grace, his blessed grace, if we come at all, if we do after all have supper at his table, if we only come, if we only drag ourselves to him, we who are dreary, bent, weary and burdened.

He welcomes us even if he does not find in our eyes radiant joy at his presence. For he has of course descended into all the abysses of this earth; it does not offend him to have to enter the dull narrowness of our hearts, or if only a small spark of love and goodwill glimmer there. In the patience which God has with us weaklings, the highest sacrament is meant to be the sacrament of our everyday.

But because that is so, because we only come from so far away, because we make the feast a burden and an effort because it is a daily one, it is right for us at least once in the year to celebrate a feast of those feasts which we celebrate everyday. A feast to celebrate the fact that what is usual is most unusual, what is done every day is the substance of eternity, the bread of earth, God's coming among us and the beginning of the transfiguration of all earthly reality.

Let us therefore celebrate on Corpus Christi in mourning but with consolation the fact that everyday we so unfestively celebrate the mystery of the Lord, a feast of joy that despite this he is with us all days until the end. Let us keep a feast of the past which is present in the commemoration of the supper and death of the Lord which truly annuls all distance of time, a feast of the future which under the veil of the sacrament already even now has what all the future is to bring, the presence of the God of eternal love. Everyday God prepares his feast for us, the holy supper of the Lord. On the feast of Corpus Christi, we ourselves ought in some way to prepare a feast for God in warm gratitude for his giving us everyday that festive meal in which we pilgrims receive strength and joy so that here on the roads of time we may arrive home for the banquet of eternal life.

145 • The Mystery of Christian Marriage*

"This is a great mystery, and I take it to mean Christ and the church" (Eph 5:32). Catholic literature and preaching on marriage in the last few decades has untiringly quoted and expounded this remark of the apostle. But it has been and is mostly a question of simply transferring the mystery Christ-church to the mutual relation and loving unity of husband and wife. It has not been shown more precisely how in this mystery the dynamism of love on the human level and that of God's love from on high come together, how the former flows into the heart of God while the second pours into the hearts of human beings.

Even by the standards of human experience the holy and bold undertaking of beginning one united life of love and fidelity reaches out into the mystery of God. For a person to dispose of himself entirely in the fundamental freedom of his human reality, and to dare to entrust himself, his heart, life, lot, and eternal dignity as a person to another human being and thereby commit himself to what is, after all, ultimately the mysteriously new, unknown and unfathomable mystery of another person, is something which can only be done in the highest venture of love and trust. And viewed from outside, it may often take place in a way which makes it seem an everyday and quite commonplace business.

Nevertheless, it is in reality what it appears to the lovers to be: the always unique wonder of love. And that borders on God. For it comprises the whole person and his whole destiny. Anything of that kind, however, deliberately performed, always means coming into God's presence, whether people realize this or not. It always involves the perhaps unmentioned, silent partner, encompassing all, saving and blessing, whom we call God. For such an undertaking has no limits, points to the limitless and unconditional, and is only possible in the boundless scope of the spiritual person, which is oriented toward God. In truly personal love there is always an unconditional element implied which points beyond the contingency of the lovers themselves. If they truly love, they continually develop above and beyond themselves. They enter into a dynamism which has no longer any assignable finite goal.

There is ultimately only one name for that endlessly distant reality which such love silently evokes — God. He is the guarantor of eternal love. He is the guardian of the dignity of the person who in love gives and entrusts himself to another fallible and limited human being. He is the fulfillment of the eternal promise which love implies but which it could

---

* *Everyday Faith*, 154–59.

not itself fulfill if it had itself to provide such ultimate fulfillment. He is the unfathomable depth (in grace) of the other human being without which in the long run every human being would become tedious and empty in the other's eyes. He is the endless expanse in which we find room to lighten the burdens which we do not want to impose on another, although they would crush us if we carried them alone. He stands as true forgiveness for both, behind and above every act of forgiveness without which no love in the long run can live. He is in person that sacred fidelity which we must love if we are to be able to be always faithful. In a word, he is the very love from which all other love derives and to which all other love must be open if it is not to be a venture which does not realize what it implies, and lead to disaster through its own infinity.

Only in its sacramental mystery, however, does God's hidden partnership in marriage come to full realization and become clearly known to us. From the message of faith we know that matrimony reaches up into the mystery of God in an even more radical sense than we can surmise even from the unconditional character of human love. Marriage is a sacrament, the church tells us. We take that so much as a matter of course. But we have to understand what that means if we are to appreciate the almost strangely disturbing boldness with which the highest is affirmed of such an apparently commonplace human business.

Marriage between Christians is a sacrament. It therefore confers grace. Grace, however, does not only mean God's help for married people to be loving and faithful, patient, sturdy, unselfish, bearing one another's burdens. Grace does not mean only God's help to fulfill tasks and duties which everyone recognizes as belonging to this world and, at least in theory, accepts.

Grace means more. It means divine life, the strength of eternity, a participation, earnest, seal and anointing, beginning and ground of that life which, caught up into the life of God himself, is worthy of being lived a whole eternity. Grace ultimately means God himself who wishes to lavish himself without intermediary on his spiritual creature with the infinite plenitude of his life and inexpressible glory.

It is true that all this is still hidden under the veils of faith and hope, that it is all still incomprehensible and obscure; it may not yet have emerged from the deepest depths of our mind into the flatness of our dull everyday experience. But it all exists nevertheless, and by the slight word "grace" we mean precisely all this, which God has effected in the innermost but to us still inaccessible center of our being, as the seed of the life of eternity, of freedom final in its blessedness.

We say that the sacrament of matrimony increases this grace which is not simply a daily divine help to morally right action. That means, therefore, that when Christians marry, when a sign of indissoluble love is established in this world, which is a symbol of Christ's redemptive love for his church, grace occurs, that is, divine life occurs. If it is not prevented by the mortal guilt of the lovers, a new dynamism begins which can carry them deeper into the life of God. New depths of divine glory are opened out in that region of the spirit in which God himself communicates himself to it as the life of the soul. There the love which unites the human person with his God grows to more delicate tenderness and stronger fidelity. There the one mystery of all human life occurs even more profoundly and vitally, more strongly and unconditionally than before: the finding of God in the immediate presence of his own communication to the inner person.

That is the really consumingly bold and divine thing that is affirmed when it is said that marriage is a sacrament. It is affirmed that marriage is not only a communion of love between two human beings but, while remaining such, is also a communion of grace with God himself. No doubt that does not occur without regard to the individual and his freedom or without his interior consent. There is no doubt, therefore, that the lovers only experience this reality in proportion as they open their hearts to it in faith and love.

But God wills this grace to occur, and therefore this meeting with God himself in grace can and must occur even here and now. Consequently, marriage is really a mystery of God, a part of the liturgy in which the mysteries of eternity become present in a sacred rite which bestows salvation.

The liturgy of conjugal consent leads into the celebration of the holy sacrifice. That is as it should be. The grace of matrimony is the grace of Christ. Consequently it comes from the source of all grace, the pierced heart of the redeemer who, on the altar of the cross, gave himself for the church, his bride, by allowing himself to fall into the boundless darkness of death, confident that in this way he was committing his soul into the hands of his Father by giving it with holy generosity for the salvation of all.

All grace comes from the pierced heart of Christ, and so therefore does the grace of matrimony, without which no marriage can be good and blessed. Consequently, the grace of marriage too bears the stamp of its origin. It is the grace of sacrificial love, the grace of forgiving, enduring, excusing, unselfish love which hides its pain. It is the grace of a love which is true to death, fruitful for life and in death, the grace of that love which Paul praises, which is kind, which believes all things, bears all things, hopes all things, endures all things, which never ends, without which all else is nothing. When, therefore, in a sacred festival before the holy altar of God we link the celebration of such a marriage with the celebration of the highest act of Christ's sacrificial love for his church, what we are doing is itself a prayer and opens the hearts of human beings to such love.

"He who calls you is faithful, and he will do it," says Paul (Eph 5:24) regarding our development as Christians. Now a sacrament is indeed a part of this Christian development. And so, trusting to the power of grace and of the divine promise, we can also apply this saying to the loving community of the married couple. To have received the sacrament of matrimony is to have been called by God to share God's own love by love for one's partner. And it is he himself who comes to the help of the weak and effects the divine accomplishment of human married love.

Husband and wife must therefore give themselves to him, to the blessed power of his grace, which flows from the heart of the dying Lord, in order to give their conjugal devotion that depth and purity which its very nature calls for and demands.

146 • The Sobriety of Christian Life*

It has been said, therefore, that anyone who wants to do what is right and obligatory merely for supernatural motives will do and achieve very little. Inclination and love for something — and also that motivation which is inherent in things themselves, and this even in the premoral sphere (such as in hunger and thirst, fear, the urge to imitate, the impulses belonging to the realm of the corporeal and the sexual, and the like) — are in general necessary also for the higher achievements of the moral order. For they exist because God has willed them, and this is why they make sense. Since, moreover, they are elements of the one whole person, these things also have a purpose for the whole and hence also for the "higher" person.

Hence, just because it is false to say that the higher is simply a suspicious sublimation of the lower — just because it is false to say that the spiritual and moral achievements of the human being are merely more complicated variations of one's primitive desire — it is not necessary to deny that even the highest achievements and motivations have, and may have, their substructure. There is no harm in admitting that one may possibly pray better, in certain cases, after a cup of tea than without it.

If, therefore, such motives are not in any sense to be excluded, and if

---

* *Theological Investigations III*, 124–28.

very often they cannot be excluded, what then is the position regarding the necessary purification of motives and the proper, practicing cultivation of good and perfect intentions? One might say, of course, that urge and motivation must be kept apart. A motive is not an urge: the former is what is morally proposed in a free manner, the latter belongs to the morally still indifferent stratum of psychophysical vitality.

One might then say on the basis of this distinction that the morality of an action can be determined only according to the motives. If what is consciously and freely envisaged is in a certain measure striven for and attained by the force of the impulse, then this nevertheless does not destroy the motive and the moral quality of the action. This may be very true in theory, but it does not help us much in practice. One can eat, "simply because one enjoys it" (and this without thereby overeating and making oneself sick). The question remains, therefore, as to what is the real motive in my particular case. We have already seen that the real motives (motives even in the terminology just suggested) need not necessarily be reflex and objects of consciousness.

It can be seen that this purification can basically be undertaken only indirectly. Indeed, one might say that it *is* undertaken in us: it is a chance which life — or, better, divine grace and providence — must and does offer us if we are vigilant and faithful. For we cannot simply cut out motives and impulses just as we wish. We can do this to a certain extent; by directing our attention, we are able to alter the real state of the motives and impulses. What can be done in this respect should be done. But even where this is not possible, or where it does not lead to any clear-cut and complete success, we can still do something.

We can try to strengthen our true and desired motives by prayer and contemplation, by reflecting on them and by giving ourselves up to them, by the repeated practice of directing our attention to them. But this teaches us — to begin with — only to be vigilant and careful, to be prepared to act as far as possible out of these thus cultivated and more deeply rooted motives, even when other impulses fail, impulses which are either, morally speaking, indifferent or even dangerous, or at any rate not those really meant (that is, from the core of the spiritual person). For precisely this is to be expected in many if not all cases; and this is the chance which we have said we must expect and that life would offer to us so that our motives may be purified and our intentions perfected.

This chance has something dangerous and bitter about it; suddenly we notice that certain impulses cease: "healthy" ambition, the instinctive joy we feel in being with people, a joy which arises out of loving sympathy, the "desire to know," and a thousand other possible impulses which we ourselves cannot and should not cut off. The more someone has always taken the trouble to do justice objectively to the demands made on him by the objective structure of his external actions — the more, in other words, he has an inner motivation in the sense given above and not merely the motivation which happens to have been applied to a task from without — the more often he will notice that to a greater or lesser extent there are situations in which (to put it crudely) he "does not feel like it," but when it is nevertheless objectively demanded that the thing should be done even without feeling like it, that is, more strictly, with purified motives. Life itself has then purified the complex of motives and urges, presupposing of course that one does not now fail to do what one has always done up until now.

Of course in such a case one would then also have to ask oneself seriously whether the "official" motives were in fact the real motives before, and not merely a facade behind which lay hidden premoral or even immoral but basically freely accepted urges. We do not need to worry that such urges may be shut off by ourselves. For the moral attitudes and achievements demanded of us are structured in accordance with the objective moral motives, and the impulses springing from an ontologically and ethically lower stratum of the human being do not and cannot in the long run suffice of themselves for these higher achievements, no matter how useful they may be as the "initial fuse" and however much they remain always necessary to some extent as the underlying basis for as long as we live in the body (after all, one can completely undermine even the most heroic virtue, as far as its external appearance or the external achievement is concerned, by "injections" and similar means).

Life itself and the reality involved regulate all this. Someone may notice, for instance, that he — as managing director — is always very kind to his charming female secretary, and he may suspect that there is a certain latent sexual urge behind this in itself praiseworthy attitude (since he finds it much more difficult to be kind to others; even a St. Dominic seems to have noticed this). It is not necessary for such a person to make a special effort to fight against this accompanying feeling (provided only that it does not induce him to do things which are against the law of God). In any case, how would he go about this? Such an attempt would either lead merely to the opposite attitude or would make it more difficult for him to be polite (if it were to succeed). But it is difficult enough for us to deal with the burdensome things in life. Life in its wisdom goes on by itself, so that our managing director will not be polite for very long *merely* for this somewhat suspicious reason. Meanwhile he should have learned to be polite in spite of it all.

If one works thus in the formation of outlook and in the cultivation of good intentions from the inner nature of the objective achievement, if one tries to cultivate the true and really intended motives so that they will be strong enough when they have to suffice on their own on some occasion, if life is given a chance to educate us by keeping ourselves open to this education by using the methods just mentioned, then it would seem to be superfluous and harmful for a normal person to devote great efforts to an exaggerated reflection and "depth psychology" with regard to the world of his motives. It is true that we only know a very little about what is in us. We would be greatly shocked if we knew by what problematic urges our so praiseworthy actions are often supported. But of what use would it be if we did know all this?

Hidden behind this psychoanalytical, distrustful self-analysis and unmasking of self, there would again be urges which we would not yet have uncovered, which would themselves have to be traced (so that we might know where we stand) and which would again be just as problematical as the ones already unmasked.

No, this is not the way. In the long run, the only thing to result from such an unmasking of self (as carried on in many of our modern novels) would be a moral cynicism which thinks that it can see through everything as being hollow and base sensuality. One imagines oneself to be honest and forgets to make distinctions. One loses one's insight into the fact that the real moral motives of a spiritual, personal kind do not cease to be independent, significant — indeed, to be the deciding factor for the moral judgment of one's action — simply by our showing that they are not the only thing in our actions and that they very often (or to a certain extent, always) require other urges and powers in order to assert themselves. It is better to try to purify and refine one's motives by looking away from oneself to things and by letting oneself be occupied by life, others and their needs.

Then one can always say to oneself (when someone, worried by such distrust of himself, asks whether he is in the state of grace): if I do my duty, if the external manifestation of my actions corresponds for a fairly long period to the objective exigencies of life, if my neighbor can be fairly satisfied with me, if, in short, my (external) actions are just, if I try at least in all this not to be a pharisee but to know and realize in my life that we are unprofitable servants even after having done everything demanded of us, if there remains an honest bit of dissatisfaction with myself and I am (really) prepared to let others tell me things — then I need not worry myself sick about the ultimate motives of my actions.

Life is not arranged in such a devilishly malevolent fashion that the most nasty motives hide themselves for a long time behind an always good and — even to the attentive observer — faultless facade. This is not to say that everything will then be completely certain and above every genuinely Christian suspicion about oneself, and that then we do not need to pray anymore: Lord, be merciful to me, a poor sinner. But we will then have done what we can reasonably be expected to do; to do more would really be less and would be an attempt to gain more independent certainty vis-à-vis God (even if it be merely the certainty of having unmasked oneself completely and unconditionally, whereby one merely robs God of the glory of being stronger and greater in us by his grace than even our own heart). In other words, there is an indivisible (although not mathematically determinable) yet real limit to the formation of motives and to anxiety about good intentions.

147 • Calm Readiness for God*

Indifference — the calm readiness for every command of God, the equanimity from the knowledge that God is always greater than everything we experience of him — is a kind of removal or distance away from things that make true vision possible and is required for a proper decision. As pilgrims and strangers on this earth, we must choose and decide — we who have here no lasting city and who see things as only temporary and in certain respects as not so important. Certainly our free decisions never take place in a state of absolute reflection or under the influence of a comprehensive knowledge that would perfectly illumine this particular decision. Often we have already chosen before we begin to decide. We cannot indicate the point up to which we were undecided and at which we reached our decision. The unencompassable and the unreflective always exercise a certain influence on our decisions. From this arises the possibility of prejudices or predecisions, which, of course, can themselves be the result of former decisions.

This brings us to the real subject. The very possibility of the influence of previously held views (for example, "That would be stupid!" or, "That cannot possibly be for me!") points up the fact that by our very nature we are not indifferent when it comes to making a free decision. Indifferent is what we must become. But this does not come about through goodwill alone, or by saying that I am indifferent; for indifference is something that must enter into the nerves and the very marrow of the bones. Nor is indifference the mere resolution not to let oneself be carried along by the crowd; it demands, rather, the existential distance from things that is self-appropriated in such a way that it even frees the will to reject its own previous prejudices. Even the attitude of

* *Spiritual Exercises*, 23–26.

accepting everything that happens in silence — which in itself is very difficult — is less than what is demanded here. The *Spiritual Exercises* of St. Ignatius of Loyola propose an *active indifference* in virtue of which we are to act in such a way that both the use and nonuse of things can and must be our own responsibility.

This active indifference is surrounded and protected by the human being's humble handing over of himself to God's good pleasure. God levels out in the only proper way the differences in the reality of our human existence, even those that we ourselves may not level out. And, finally, we lose everything in death. In death, despite our great freedom, we do not have control of ourselves, but can only endure, and say: "Into your hands I commend my spirit." In death, we must let the incomprehensible dispose of us in such a way that we believe that this disposition is the work of an infinite love, and is preserving our spiritual human existence from meaninglessness.

This distance from things is a goal that must always be rewon again and again. We are never at a perfect distance from the world — a distance so perfect that it cannot be questioned. We love things, we have confidence in them because of the immediate relationship to our own corporeality, we have tasted them in sweetness and in sorrow, we have absorbed them in love or in fear. Therefore, we need the courage to undertake ever new beginnings, and we need the power to break loose from that which holds us.

The number of things about which we must make ourselves indifferent is very great, and their natures very diverse, but I cannot remove myself from God, nor may I write off the personal value of my fellow human beings. Even though my relationship to things must be determined in accordance with sound morality, still I cannot make my absolute decision on the basis of morality alone. Above and beyond universally valid morality, this decision must form my own irreducible history by also proceeding from God's will for me.

If we consider all this, then it seems that we can never attain this kind of indifference by ourselves and permanently. If we could truly attain this indifference to all created things over which our freedom has some control, then we should know for sure that we love God, that we have his grace, and that we can leave "fear and trembling" behind us once and for all.

On the other hand, we may not let ourselves become obdurate in a complete doubt: that would also be, but in a negative direction, the self-presumption of the creature. Therefore, the only thing that remains is to place our choice completely in the hands of God. In any event, we are called on to free ourselves from our own prejudices and predecisions in accordance with the grace given us, so that we can quietly and peacefully say to ourselves: According to God's will, I have desired and striven for what is right.

The true essence of indifference is its "elevation" into the decision to do "more." Indifference is distance from things with the goal of willing them *or* leaving them. Therefore, it must change itself into nonindifference. For example, when I have chosen a way of life, I may no longer be hesitant about it. Indifference does not exist for its own sake, but for the choice of "what is more conducive to the end." It is freedom for decision, which is really no longer mine, but God's: I am seeking his will in the "choice" [made during the Ignatian Spiritual Exercises]. From this point of view, indifference appears as the distance from things that must be determined from God and not from human beings; it appears as human freedom — that freedom that the person does not want to keep selfishly for himself, but wants to leave to God so that he can decide.

In this way, then, the *Tantum-quantum* of indifference must be surpassed by the "what is more conducive to the end" of the decision that I leave to God to demand. We must not let ourselves be deceived in this regard by an excessively heroic attitude. Essentially, what I am saying is that we have here no lasting city, that God is the always greater one, that he will respond to us if we remain supple and do not direct ourselves in one way and one way only. We should protect ourselves from that inner hardening that can be observed sometimes in the so-called "patent ascetics." We should remain elastic — always ready for that call of God that will lead us to higher things. The more we love God, the more we will experience his ever greater distance from us, and the more we will want to be in awe at the holy absoluteness of his demands. What we have to do in the depths of our souls is to utter a clear yes to that which is, not to that which is made by us, that is, to God and his immeasurable love.

148 • Christian Flight from the World*

What is the ultimate reason for Christian flight from the world, which has achieved expression in monasticism and also in Ignatian piety as a piety of the cross?

The living personal God has spoken to human beings in Christianity, that is, in Jesus Christ. With that, a frightening reality has entered into

---

* *Theological Investigations III*, 283–87.

the life of the human person, which renders impossible any attempt on the part of a human existence attuned to a world closed in upon itself to enter into God. Certainly it is possible to come to a knowledge of God from his creation, from the world. But this knowledge has a peculiarly double character.

On the one hand, we acknowledge God as the ground of the world, as the guarantor of its being, as the ultimate background of everything we meet as human and world in its own reality. Thus we have knowledge of God insofar as he is able to appear to us in the mirror of the world, so that it almost seems as though the world were the raison d'être of God, at least of the God who shows himself and insofar as he can show himself in the world, of the God, that is to say, whom alone we meet as philosophers.

On the other hand, in our seeking for God in metaphysics, at the same time as the fact that he appears to us as the ground of the world and the world as the meaning of God, we come to know him as the free, personal, in himself eternal being and thereby as the God beyond the whole world and all finitude, so that the world does not properly express what he is and may be as the personal and free and eternal being. The world does not reveal to us the raison d'être of God.

But with that the human metaphysical question of God has already terminated in an essential failure: it is faced with a free person closed in himself, the God who covers himself in silence, the *theos sigon*, as Origen once called him. And what this infinite God is in himself, and how this free personal God wants perhaps, as is possible, to deal with us, this question which for all its obscurity is yet decisive for our existence cannot be illuminated by the natural light of reason. Whether he wants to meet us immediately and personally, whether he wants to remain silent, what he will say to us if he does want to speak — all this is an essential mystery for all metaphysics, for every impetus of the human person's desire to know which originates in world. So in itself all metaphysics would have to conclude in an eternally watchful readiness of the human person to keep an ear cocked in case this distant, silent he should will to speak, in a readiness for the perhaps possible possibility of a revelation.

But will the human person be able to endure this ecstasy of his being, this remaining on the look-out, to see whether perhaps God will come? Will he not rather succumb to the ever-present temptation of making the world the finally valid revelation of God, of so making God the raison d'être of the world that the world becomes the raison d'être of God? Was there ever a philosophy in all history outside Christianity which did not yield to that temptation, beginning with the Greeks right up to Hegel?

For all of this philosophy was God not always ultimately the *anima mundi* ("world soul"), the God who can live only in the world itself as its inner radiance, as its secret luster of absoluteness? And is not this original sin in the history of philosophy in the field of knowledge only an expression of that which happens constantly over and over again existentially in the life of the unredeemed human being: to allow God to be only what the world is, to make God in the image of the human person, to conceive piety as consideration for the world? All idolatry is nothing else than the concrete expression of that existential standpoint of the human person based on the belief that God is nothing other than the primeval unity of those powers which hold sway throughout this world and govern its fate.

And even the most spiritual of philosophies in a Hegel still worships — so it would seem — an idol: absolute Spirit, finding itself in the human person and in the development of his being. The God according to our desires, according to our image and likeness, would be a God who had nothing else to do but let people increase and multiply, to bless them when they make the earth subject to them, who would be nothing but what we could know of him by natural means, who would therefore be nothing but the horizon remaining always in the distance, in which is unfolded the finite infinitude of the person in accordance with his own proper law; he would be nothing but the divinity of the world. And it is then a matter of no consequence whether this God in our image bears the features of Apollo or of Dionysus.

But God is more than that. And as this more-than-the-world he has broken in upon human existence and has shattered the world, that which theology calls nature. He has revealed himself in Jesus Christ. This revelation has taken place in the dual unity of a communication of supernatural being and of the word. And the ultimate meaning of this revelation is a calling of the human being out of this world into the life of God, who leads his personal life as the being exalted above the whole world, as the tripersonal God, in inaccessible light.

God is thereby bringing himself immediately face to face with the human person with a demand and a call which flings the individual out of the course preestablished by nature, which he would have followed within the horizons of the world. This gives rise to a transcendence of the human being's mission and destination, which must necessarily be felt as somehow constantly standing in opposition to nature and the world in which the temptation to round themselves off in themselves is essentially inherent, the temptation to seek completion, before God, it is true, as the ultimate ground and background, but yet essentially in themselves.

"Nature," that is, everything finite which does not arise from, and in, immediate encounter with God as free and revealing himself in word, has ever as something rounded and completed in itself in a true sense the tendency to rest in itself, to defend and perfect the closed harmony of its immanent system. If God as revealing himself comes face to face with such a nature, then there arises the most immediate possibility that he might issue commands to humankind which are not at the same time the voice of nature, are not the "laws of nature."

And if God calls the human person in this command of his revealing word to a supernatural, supramundane life, as has in fact happened in the revelation of Christ, then this command must always necessarily be a breaking-up of the groundedness in which the world seeks to rest in itself, and so it becomes a degradation, by which the world — even the good world, the world insofar as it is the will and law of God — is condemned to a provisional status, a thing of second rank, subject to a criterion which is no longer intrinsic or proper to it.

In this way, however, a sacrifice of the world, a renunciation, a flight from the world, an abandonment of its goods and values becomes possible, which goes essentially further than one that would be thinkable in any meaningful way if these goods and values in a merely natural order constituted the highest fulfillment of the existential task demanded of the human being. Indeed, such flight from the world is in this case not only meaningful, but also, at least to a certain degree, necessary. The obscurity of Christian faith is the essential and decisive beginning of it.

A flight from the world of this kind becomes necessary because the need to take into account the possibility of a free act of revelation on the part of the personal God, which is a fundamental constitutive character of a finite spirit in any hypothesis, is transformed by the actual fact of such a revelation into the duty of living existentially the need of obedience vis-à-vis the God of revelation. But if we leave aside the acceptance without contradiction of the communication of supernatural life which takes place in revelation, the only thinkable human response coming, as it were, from below to the God of revelation calling from far beyond the world is a sacrifice of the world to a degree which goes beyond any which is meaningful in an intramundane even though theonomous ethics.

For the human being can only confess existentially that God has moved the center of his human existence out of the world, if he negates his intramundane existence in its immanent signification by a "flight from the world." Thus all Christian mortification has from the beginning progressed beyond the struggling self-mastery of pure ethics — of course not by excluding it — it is already, as the primitive Christian *Didache* prays, *allowing the world to pass by* in order that grace may enter. Christianity is consequently in essence "flight from the world," because it is the commitment to the personal God who freely reveals himself in Christ, the God of grace which is not the fulfillment of the immanent craving of the world for its completion, even though it brings this completion of the world about eschatologically in a supereminent way. All adherence to the cross, which is proper to both monastic and Ignatian piety, is only a realistic putting into practice of such an essentially Christian flight from the world.

149 • Christian Joy in the World*

In order to penetrate the meaning of this joy in the world, let us begin once more with what we have said about the theological signification of Christian flight from the world in general. The "flight from the world" which belongs essentially to Christian existence appeared to us as the commitment to God, insofar as he is, as the being beyond the world, the inner center and goal of our Christian existence; as the existential reaccomplishment of the shifting of the center of our being into the triune God, a shifting already accomplished by the God of grace revealing himself.

But this existential commitment can only be itself if it really acknowledges the God of *free* grace. And this means that it must, at the same time as it asserts the center of our lives to be beyond the world, also acknowledge that this new center of our existence is bestowed exclusively by the free grace of God, and therefore not by the sacrificing flight from the world itself.

In this way, however, it becomes evident that Christian flight from the world is to be distinguished not merely from an ethics which is immanent to the world, even though guaranteed by its theonomy, and its demands for renunciation, insofar as it is a flight from the world in opposition to a mere domination of the world and of oneself; the Christian "flight from the world" is distinct also from every extra-Christian denial of the world which may perhaps be found in Orphic, neoplatonic, or Buddhist asceticism and mysticism.

For all these forms of flight from the world do ultimately regard the renunciation and annihilation which is begun by human beings, as it were, from below, as being *the* means which of itself and with nothing further compels the awareness of the absolute. All such annihilation is consequently only a way fundamentally parallel to, though leading

---

* *Theological Investigations III*, 288–90.

in the opposite direction from, the way to an immanent divinization of the world. Renunciation, flight from the world, is for such non-Christian mysticism of annihilation in itself already the conquest of God.

But Christianity acknowledges the free grace of God, that is, a divine life in the person which is first and last dependent upon the free personal decision of God's love. Accordingly, Christianity is aware of the fact that not simply dying, renunciation, flight from the world of themselves can achieve possession of the absolute, knows that asceticism of this kind is not the way in which admittance could be *forced* by the *human being* into the inner life of God. The Christian knows that his flight from the world is only an answering gesture, though a necessary one, when faced with the God who freely reveals and opens himself, who gives himself to us out of a voluntary love.

Since, however, the grace of God is in this sense free, the Christian knows, even in loving the foolishness of the cross above everything, that the free God can bless and allow to become a step forward into his presence even those actions of human beings which do not of themselves already bear such a significance, as does the dying flight from the world, which is meaningful only where it is a dying into the new life of God. Provided that the individual has once submitted himself in faith to the claim of God revealing himself, God can accept in grace also his service of the world, which is, after all his creation, as a way to himself who is beyond the world, so that one encounters the absolute God not only in a radical opposition to the world, but also *in* the world.

Once a human being has placed himself under the cross and has died with Christ, once he has entered into the obscurity of faith and the ecstasy of love for the distant God, then, to express it in the technical language of theology, every act which is good in itself, therefore also one which is already meaningful within the world, can be supernaturally elevated by grace in such a way that its aim and its meaning extend beyond the significance it has within the world, beyond the *ordo legis naturae* ("order of the natural law") and into the life of God.

This fact removes from Christian flight from the world that hubris which would otherwise be inherent in it as the exclusive way to God. In his flight from the world the Christian must acknowledge that one can also reach through the world this same God who is beyond it, to find whom the Christian abandoned the world to go its own way. Whoever remains a virgin for God's sake must recognize that marriage is a sacrament; whoever lives the "contemplative life" of flight from the world will only do this in a Christian way if he is vitally aware that God has also blessed the "active life" of work within the world and has raised it to the level of divine life.

It is only upon these deep foundations that there is built the Ignatian affirmation of the world. That there is such a thing which can be designated by this title has always been seen, even though it has seldom been grasped in its true essence. Adaptation, the acceptance of the demand upon time, the fostering of culture, love for the sciences, acceptance of the humanism and individualism of the Renaissance, the cheerful brightness of baroque, the avoidance of the external forms of monasticism, all this and much besides has been regarded — and rightly — as a sign of Jesuit affirmation of the world.

But one has really grasped this phenomenon only when one is able to explain it as arising from *one* spirit: how this one spirit inspired those possessed of it in the seventeenth and eighteenth centuries both to build baroque churches with their joyous exuberance of a shining transfiguration of the world *and* at the same time to offer themselves for the distant missions in order to die agonizingly for Christ in the boiling caldrons of Japan or the bamboo cages of Tonkin.

Ignatius approaches the world from God. Not the other way around. Because he has delivered himself in the lowliness of an adoring self-surrender to the God beyond the whole world and to his will, for this reason and for this reason alone he is prepared to obey his word even when, out of the silent desert of his daring flight into God, he is, as it were, sent back into the world, which he had found the courage to abandon in the foolishness of the cross.

150 • Grace and Dying with Christ*

Grace consists fundamentally in God's self-communication to enable the human being in freedom by faith, hope, and love to accept the immediacy to God that is offered to him. Since and insofar as grace makes God purely and simply the immediate goal, content, and condition of the possibility of an immediate relationship to God, grace and its free acceptance always imply a self-abandonment, a self-transcendence above all finite realities (among which the human subject of freedom itself must primarily be counted) toward the incomprehensibility of God as blessed fulfillment, attainable only "ecstatically."

In that sense, in every act sustained by grace toward God's immediacy there is an element of self-surrendering, "renouncing," becoming free which is also explained in scripture by the assertion that faith, hope,

---

* *Theological Investigations XVIII*, 254–56.

and love "remain" (1 Cor 13:13), that is, they are also elements of the eschatological consummation, among which particularly in hope (but also in the vision of God's incomprehensibility and in love) the peculiar character of a self-abandoning getting away from self is plainly evident.

This character of a "renunciation" does not of course remove the possibility of a blessed consummation, since the human being as creature (which he remains even in a supernatural consummation) finds himself only when he radically submits to God's disposal, seized and overpowered by God and not an autonomous subject; when, in other words, he summons up courage (again by God's act of grace), embracing and surrendering his whole existence to believe, hope, and love, that he finds himself only when he loses himself to God.

But as long as freedom continues in the present world and this realization of its nature has not yet become blessed and obvious factuality, but still remains an overtaxing task which may not be accomplished, as long as freedom still coming to be is situational, there are undoubtedly situations in which the element of renunciation in every realization of grace becomes clearly present as task, manifestation, and import of this realization of grace.

Certainly we may not adopt a more or less tragic attitude, assuming that grace and its realization are present only when and insofar as "renunciation" (to the point of extinction) is imposed on us. This is contradicted by the fact that the bliss of eternal life is the supreme act of the grace of Christ, that the positivity of the finite and not only its negativity has a positive relationship to God, that a positive relationship to reality distinct as such from God can certainly be an internal element of the individual's relationship by grace to God. But experience of the human being and the event of the cross of Christ as redemption in death, as such, show that at least in practice the situation in which the element of renunciation (present as such in every act directed toward God as grace-given goal) appears in a particularly harsh form and to immediate experience as exclusive, is the situation preferred for the event of grace in the present order of salvation.

Insofar as Christian teaching sees the peculiarity of this situation of renunciation as "infralapsarian," as consequence of sin and thus of the freedom of sinful persons and of God as "permitting" sin, the situation is not made absolute as if we knew and could say that it could not be otherwise and that, to use gnostic terminology, it arises solely from the mysteriousness of God himself; but on the other hand this situation of renunciation is explained and maintained as the universal and inescapable situation of our self-realization toward the immediacy of God.

This renunciation as present in the very nature of grace and inescapably required of us in our infralapsarian situation reaches in death its unsurpassable culmination. Since in death as an event affecting all humanity, the human person is deprived of everything and thus even of himself, since in death the actual success of the act of freedom in which as a justified person he accepts and approves this self-withdrawal in death remains hidden, in our infralapsarian situation (in which the subject cannot realize itself in integrity and cannot grasp the effect of this realization in final bliss) death is the culmination of the grace of Christ crucified and thus a dying with Christ.

At the same time it cannot be overlooked that part of this renunciation in death is to accept in self-denying freedom the fact that this concealed and concealing death in particular need not have been, that "essentially" things could have been different, so that death now contains within itself the acceptance of its own not derivable and not "ideologizable" facticity.

None of this of course means that dying and death are the mode of realization only of an "abstract" renunciation. This self-abandonment radicalized in death is in fact an aspect of the realization of grace as faith, hope, and love. Dying can be an act of *faith*, since it thwarts any recourse by the human being to a categorial justification of faith or (if that is perhaps an exaggeration) since this justification of faith in terms of fundamental theology in the light of the individual's intramundane rationality proves to be something that simply cannot produce faith as such.

Dying is *love* of God insofar as this renunciation in freedom required in death is brought about as the effect of a love in which God himself is loved for his own sake and consequently the person never recovers himself. The acceptance of death can certainly be seen also as an act of love of *neighbor*, insofar as the historical subject then leaves the mundane sphere of freedom and the stage of history free for others.

This of course does not mean that the human being's dying can be seen only in *this* respect as an act of love of neighbor. If we are obliged in love to bear witness to our neighbor by our whole life of grace, of God's freedom and the hope of eternal life, this is true also of the witness of love that we must bear by our dying. "Both during his whole life and also and even more at the time of his death," says Ignatius of Loyola, "each one ... ought to strive earnestly that through him God our Lord may be glorified and served and his fellowmen may be edified, at least by the example of his patience and fortitude along with his living faith, hope, and love of the eternal goods which Christ our Lord merited and acquired for us by those altogether incomparable sufferings of his temporal life and death" (*Constitutions,* no. 95).

Christian tradition, beginning with scripture, has always seen *mar-*

tyrdom, a death freely endured and accepted to bear witness to the faith as the most perfect way in which a Christian can die with Christ. And rightly so. For in a martyr's death the universal essential constituents of Christian death are most clearly manifested: the indisposability of death, death as free act, death as testimony of faith for others. The secret yearning for martyrdom, which is constantly attested in the course of the history of Christianity, is rooted in the hope that dying with Christ, which is part of every death in grace, is assured most securely by this kind of death.

151 • To the Greater Glory of God*

Anyone who says that he wills to live, act, suffer, and the like, to the greater glory of God thereby asserts first and foremost that he resolves to adopt an attitude of absolute self-surrender to the sovereign will of God, and believes that he has taken up this attitude. The first element in such an attitude, therefore, is obedience to God, and that "indifference" or detachment which is necessary for this as it can be formulated on the basis of the *Spiritual Exercises* of St. Ignatius of Loyola knows that when he does it he is honoring God, his disposition of things, his position as supreme Lord.

But anyone who explains that in this way he is being fundamentally obedient to God who reveals himself in his glory, and anyone who supposes that in speaking of the greater glory of God there are inevitably matters which must be tested, selected, and then put into practice on the basis of this, and that in such testing, choosing, and acting the glory of God, or even the greater glory of God, is achieved — anyone who thinks this, I say, must not overlook the fact that dispositions have already been made to which he is himself subject.

This is the second element. When the Ignatian Exercises are made or given, when plans for life are projected and subjects for choice are put to the test, when we examine what we must do, then all too often we overlook the fact that we are already subject to preexisting arrangements, that we are very far indeed from being simply those who make the arrangements. If we enunciate a maxim which is intended to govern our actions, then we must at the same time admit that we are quite unable to take this maxim alone as the sole adequate principle by which we shape our lives.

---

* *Theological Investigations VII,* 34–43.

Any principle such as that of "everything to the greater glory of God" necessarily entails an attitude which is theologically a priori, and in dealing with such principles we must see that this a priori attitude must from the outset necessarily be supplemented and limited by an existential a posteriori. Someone who is sick cannot start questioning whether an activity which presupposes good health would not be for the greater glory of God, in his case. When we set out to direct our lives to the greater glory of God, the demands of God himself are not the sole considerations from which we start.

In certain ways our lives have already been arranged for us beforehand. There is much that is totally excluded from the sphere of our choice. Freedom in the creature is already subject to preexisting conditions. Human freedom to act in history — and this applies to his striving for salvation too — always takes the form of an obedient fitting in with situations which we can do nothing to alter. Indeed it always means accepting the fact that we have been made to fit in necessarily and inevitably with a given concrete situation.

There is a certain priority of the actual over the merely possible, and this element of the concrete and the factual in us, in our life, in the span of life allotted to us, in our temperament, our hereditary traits, and the like, as it were, the woof which runs across the warp of the a priori principle "to the greater glory of God."

To put it better: this state of being fitted in with things as they are must from the outset be taken into our calculations if we are rightly to understand the maxim with which we are concerned. We are very far from being simply those who can arrange things for the greater glory of God. Rather God has — perhaps before any such decision on our part was possible — already made his own arrangements for us to act for his lesser glory. Now if we were to try to defend the principle simply by saying that humbly submitting one's self to this will of God is precisely acting for his greater glory, then it is true that, formally speaking, we would be saving the principle from being overthrown, but in fact this would do nothing to alter the situation. It can be seen, then, that when the individual inquires what he, as the disposer of things, can do for the greater glory of God, he is, even as he asks, already subject to dispositions superimposed upon him from without.

Now a maxim which is to be comprehensive enough to include both these factors must also implicitly express the fact that there is a certain fluidity in this state of being subject to superimposed conditions; that the obedience involved here has a special element in it, an element of changeableness, of being subject to the vicissitudes of history.

To put it another way, and thereby to sum up the first three elements once more: in this statement, "I will lead my life to the greater glory of God," the person says: "I await a command from God, and ask in all openness what this command is to consist in." Second, he says: "In the most essential matters the command has already been issued. Whether I like it or not it has already been imposed upon me, so that I am very far from being in all respects the one who is summoned or the one who is questioned. The field available to me to choose from for the greater glory of God is already restricted from the outset." And third, he says: "This state of being called by God, whether the call has already taken specific shape or whether it still remains open and general, is subject to change. Now I am healthy; tomorrow I am sick. Now I must do this, tomorrow that."

The human person's state of being subject to prior dispositions on God's part has a certain intrinsic fluidity in it. Obedience does not in the least imply that we have to work out a plan on the grand scale once and for all by some abstract principle. Rather, in essence it implies that obedience must take place in the historical vicissitudes of our human existence, ever new, ever unanticipated and incalculable as these are. *Ad majorem Dei gloriam* ("to the greater glory of God"), therefore, does not by any means imply — at any rate in any adequate sense — that the human being can map out the course of his life once and for all on the a priori principle of the greater glory of God. It means that in essence he is not so much the author of projects as the one who has been "projected," one whom God has already made dispositions for, and who is always only partially in a position to make fresh dispositions on his own account.

He who knows that God has already made arrangements for him, and that from time to time he must respond in all obedience to fresh arrangements imposed upon him by God, and must take these upon himself as they come upon him in a concrete historical situation (one, therefore, which cannot a priori be mapped out), such a one can ipso facto accept the vicissitudes to which he is subject.

This "letting things fall upon one" is an essentially Christian attitude. For only that freedom which, in spite of its power to dispose of things, and its capacity, so to say, a priori to map out the course of life, recognizes that it is a creaturely freedom, that is, a freedom subject to conditions superimposed from without, is a genuinely Christian freedom.

And only the life which lets itself unfold in an uncalculating manner, stage by stage, here below, is a truly Christian life, evincing the humility appropriate to a creature, trust in God, recognition that one alone knows what is adequate as the formula of our life and its reality, namely, God and not ourselves. This acceptance of the fact that our life is arranged by God, and this obedient acceptance of the fact that our life is unforeseeable and subject to the vicissitudes of history, is an essential element in Christian life.

For all this the human being is capable — and here we touch upon the fourth element — of perceiving, realizing, taking into his calculations in an extremely impressive way, the fact that this state of being subject to prior dispositions and the changeableness of such dispositions is under the greater, broader power of God to dispose of things — and at the same time in the individual's own power. The human person is essentially the one who must simultaneously plan and live from day to day. The one who plans out his life and his activities beforehand, and yet must still accept what comes to him.

If it be objected to this that planning consists precisely in the fact that the individual does accept what God sends to him, then we must reply that strictly speaking, this is not planning at all. For when God sends some fate to us, then we are no longer in a position to raise the question: Is it to the greater or lesser glory of God? Instead we have quite simply to accept it. In other words, in the concept of "greater glory of God" the explicit, reflective conscious planning of life really is included, even though the person is, and necessarily must be, the one who submits to being disposed of, who accepts and who, in a certain sense, is not capable of planning.

It is in this explicit, conscious, and constant awareness of the person's own further openness to the possibility of having conditions imposed upon him either by God or by the human being himself that what is definitive in the fourth element involved in the "greater glory of God" really consists. In this saying we must realize what it means when it says "*to* the greater glory of God." The "greater glory of God" is not so much that which is actually done, but rather that toward which our acts are oriented in order, as it were, that they may attain to it as their ultimate goal.

Let us now examine this fourth element somewhat more closely. First, what constitutes it is not found in everyone or in all cases. This brings us back once more to the problem which was already adumbrated in the introductory remarks. It might be said that either the "greater glory of God" expresses something essential to Christianity as such, in which case it must always have been there from the first, and must be present in every Christian and in every Christian life, or it says something which does not belong to Christian existence as such, in which case it follows ipso facto that it is a matter of indifference — every bit as much, for instance, as whether Ignatius wore a woolen or a linen garment.

But to say this would, as we have seen, be precisely to interpret the facts wrongly. There are factors which are essential to Christianity, which in a certain sense must always have been present wherever Christianity is found and yet which, even allowing for this, we have not always been used to adverting to so explicitly as real and vital factors present in our lives.

Now the fourth element which we are considering is numbered among these real factors. Another way of expressing this state of affairs might be to say that the actual subjectivity of the subject here becomes the theme of the subject's investigations instead of being merely the mode in which his self-explication is realized in the concrete. This is something which is typical of the new age. The Christian recognizes that what he is actually doing in the here and now, the conditions to which he is subject in the here and now, fall essentially short of what he is actually capable of in terms of the fullness of Christian existence.

As a result of this realization he constantly orients his individual decision in the here and now toward the boundless range of other possibilities open to the Christian and will thus learn to regard himself as the subject not only of what he actually does in the concrete but also of what he is capable of over and above this. In this way he can assume possession of himself as a subject in this sense on his own account. Only on the basis of this attitude can he truly ask what in the here and now is or is not "to the greater glory of God."

But just as it is not until modernity that this sense of the self as subject is arrived at, so this saying "to the greater glory of God," intended in the same sense and with the same depths of meaning, is likewise only arrived at in modernity, and in fact only from Ignatius onward. This "selfhood" of the subject was not always a theme of investigation for the subject himself in the sense in which it has come to be so in modernity. And therefore the wider range of possibilities over and above the conditions actually prevailing in the concrete here and now and ordained by God was not always a theme of investigation for the Christian considered as subject in this sense.

But in order to avoid any misunderstandings on this point, we must straight away add: modernity is very far from being the age of un-Christianity, though it is constantly being accused of this. This subjectivism is, in the last analysis, nothing else than the outcome of Christianity itself. It is true that we have become accustomed to regarding modernity more or less as a falling away from Christianity; and in fact this is correct to the extent that in modernity many individuals have fallen away from Christianity, and many legitimate developments both on the human and the Christian plane have emerged initially outside the church's orbit.

Nevertheless the modern age, in spite of its interest in the subjective, in spite of Descartes, Kant, German idealism, and modern existentialist philosophy, is, in the last analysis, something which is there because Christianity is there. It has been thrown up by Christianity to provide opportunities for self-reflection and for the necessary unfolding of Christianity itself in terms of self-reflection.

When, therefore, we say that Ignatius's formula, *Ad majorem Dei gloriam,* does not become possible until modernity, this does not mean: "Sad to say," St. Ignatius could only have lived in modernity, and he has done or seen something in modernity which is not evil, but which, in the last analysis, would have been more or less superfluous in earlier ages. No, modernity is an age which Christianity itself has ushered in in order to realize itself by way of self-reflection.

This fourth element has, furthermore, a critical function to perform in relation to the actual concrete process of taking the decision. First, an example may help to throw light on this point. In the life of St. Francis of Assisi St. Bonaventure relates that St. Francis had the gift of tears, and in his mystical meditations melted, as it were, into tears to such an extent that a doctor drew his attention to the fact that if he wept so excessively he would become blind. To this St. Francis of Assisi replied: "What does it matter if I lose my eyes, seeing that these are things which I have in common with the flies?" When St. Ignatius had his attention drawn to the same danger, he sought to stem his mystical flow of tears.

Now we can describe neither the one nor the other procedure as "the more Christian or the more holy." Moreover, because, when all is said and done, we do not understand such a mystical gift, we should not interpret Ignatius's response based on reasons which too easily allow us to understand why Ignatius could have so responded.

For someone who really can weep tears of mystical ecstasy — for such a one the reply of St. Francis of Assisi is really the obvious one. Of course if God had taken away this gift of tears from St. Francis, he would have submitted to this, and would have been content with it. But in the actual moment in which God, so to say, bestows himself upon him in this manner he looks neither to left nor right but uses to the full this gift of God's grace, this ordination of God — uses it, as it were, without reflecting upon it and, in a certain sense one might almost say, naively.

In Ignatius's case it is quite otherwise. Here the subject is alive to himself in a much more intense and radical manner. Having become aware of all these factors, he, so to say, draws back from them in a special way for which there is no precedent, withdraws himself in a certain measure from these concrete circumstances in which his own existence is realized, objectifies them to himself and asks: "Now is this really and definitely the best course? It is certainly good — but is it to the greater glory of God?" The realization of existence in the concrete — even when it is willed by God, perhaps when it is actually commanded by him, and at least when it is ordained and allowed by him — is explicitly measured against a higher standard, and inevitably in doing this the subject stands back from this concrete mode of his own existence.

Not everyone does this, and indeed not everyone needs to do it. Not every saint has done it in this sense. In fact we cannot do it ourselves in all circumstances. This is not because, as Ignatius himself will say, many situations are simply as they are and cannot be altered, so that they are not subject to our choice at all, but rather because an attitude of absolute reflection upon one's self, an absolute transcendence of the self reflecting upon itself in relation to what can be chosen or altered, would once more be the measure of a freedom and a possibility of decision which does not belong to the creature.

Everyone who has pastoral experience will have encountered this again and again in his life. Again and again he will find people who in their devotion have become neurotic from a reflection upon themselves which is excessive, because again and again they direct everything into the empty space of other, greater, ever-changing possibilities, and then want to make a fresh choice "for the greater glory of God" for every step they take on the basis of this attitude. People such as these forfeit a certain trustfulness, a certain immunity from the dictates of their own temperament and their own impulses.

But this does not for one moment alter the fact that this fourth element does involve a critical function with regard to the concrete situation which already confronts us or the decision directly demanded of us in the here and now. To this extent the typical attitude of choice is implicitly contained in this saying, "to the greater glory of God," together with all that St. Ignatius's *Spiritual Exercises* has to say about "the three classes of men," "the three degrees of humility," and the like.

It might be objected to this that every Christian must freely work out and so choose his own salvation. And if he chooses rightly he has brought to bear the right principles of choice, with which, naturally, he must in some measure be acquainted, for the purpose. All this may be true, but nevertheless this peculiar attitude of choice, this withdrawal of one's self to an absolute point in order from *there* to reflect and to test what is to be done, does exist. And this existential structure involved in the act of choice does exist in the case of St. Ignatius in a degree which the moral theologians right to the present day have probably not yet sufficiently grasped.

Again and again it seems to be presupposed that the third kind of choice, the process of rational checking, or the element of the rational in the two other modes of choice and stages of choice in the *Spiritual Exercises* and in the Christian life is absolutely *the* decisive factor.

Now this is not true. On the contrary, Ignatius is the first — is, indeed, almost unique in this among the theologians — to have developed in his Exercises a logical structure of choice which is indeed applied in the practice of these Exercises to the extent that they are carried out because it *must* be applied.

And yet no one has really penetrated beyond the theological and metaphysical principles and presuppositions behind this structure of choice. Ignatius does, in fact, envisage a Christian who — and this is something which carries immense dangers with it — as person, as "self" in modernity takes up a transcendent vantage point from which to consider, test, and choose what is and what can be to the greater glory of God. And this is precisely what lies behind saying *Ad majorem Dei gloriam.*

This in turn throws light on a further point, namely, the significance which this saying has for an existential ethics of the present day. It is precisely not true that everything can be rationally deduced. It is not true that the individual in his individuality, in his decision, is simply the individual instance of more general, more abstract principles. We can realize how difficult and obscure these questions are by considering, for instance, the difficulties raised by the theories of J. Lahitton with regard to the recognition of priestly vocation. One may be quite ready to accept that this theory has its importance as a practical rule of thumb for ecclesiastical superiors in judging of a man with regard to his possible vocation to the priesthood.

But if these principles are understood as having a theoretical, metaphysical, existential, or ontological value, Lahitton's theory is basically false. What would be the use of the whole process of choice formulated by St. Ignatius, with all these subtle rules, and so on, concerning "consolation without previous cause," and the like, if, from the aspect of metaphysics or existential theology (or however we may wish to express it) the situation were such as that which Lahitton envisages for certain cases in which the presence of a priestly vocation has to be discerned.

In such cases, indeed, one would only need to say: "Dear friend, if you are a normal, balanced man, then you only need to have the right motives and your vocation is established. You can depend upon it that it is there. You have passed the entrance examination. You are an intelligent man who shows with ample probability that he can observe celibacy, and you yourself know whether you have the right motives." And if the subject then replied: "Obviously I don't want to be a rich man, nor do I seek for any special comfort in life. I want to do something for the good God," then one would only have to fall on his neck and say: "You have a vocation!"

One has only to compare with this the complex, intricate "apparatus" for testing a vocation which St. Ignatius sets forth in the Exercises to realize that the saint had a quite different idea of the existential decision and the process of arriving at it than that implied by such rationalism. For Ignatius there really is something like an existential and ethical attitude on the part of the human being, which precisely implies an openness to that which lies beyond the data which can be calculated and deduced on the rational, abstract, and essentialist plane.

And this existential and ethical attitude finds expression both in his Exercises and also, in brief, summary form, in the saying *Ad majorem Dei gloriam.* Now if one reflects that this "greater glory of God," if it is in fact to be made effective at all, is ultimately a gift of God and must necessarily be so, then one realizes what really is implied in this saying: an openness to the direct personal love of God, which is no longer arrived at through intermediate causes, and, in fact, the end of legalism and the freedom of children of God in the Pneuma of Christ.

It is here that what is proper to God's own sovereign disposition of his creatures comes, in a certain sense, into force; a disposing of things which is no longer mediated through worldly causes or through the church's official direction, a disposing of things which really can and must be called "the better" precisely because it is itself the freedom of God in his sovereign act of disposing.

And it is only when someone knows himself to be called, and is open to this sovereign act of disposing on God's part that he is truly in the New Testament. This does not, of course, mean that it is only with this attitude proper to modernity and subjective in a good sense, which is characteristic of Ignatius, that Christianity began. But something specifically Christian here becomes explicit and actual for the first time so that it can be seen and apprehended as such.

152 • The Unity of Love of God and Neighbor*

This theme is already found, of course, in scripture. There it is said that there are two commandments of which the second, Jesus Christ says, is like the first. One commandment of love of God and neighbor. Paul says that this love is the bond of perfection; he is speaking of love of neighbor when he says that anyone who has it has fulfilled the law as

---

* *Everyday Faith,* 106–17.

such. And he says that this love is the genuine, better way. At the same time he warns us that this love and external outward help, though they belong together, are not the same. For if I were to give away all I have to the poor and delivered my body to be burned, but had not charity, I should be nothing.

He does not mean that some feeling or interior disposition is everything. For that interior disposition has to find expression in the activity of life, in the real practice of love, otherwise it is all empty talk and for all our feelings we should be nothing but sounding brass and tinkling cymbal. And yet we see what very radical significance Paul attributes to the innermost nature of this love of neighbor, when he says that it is the fulfillment of the law, the bond of perfection.

All this, however, is far from self-evident and a matter of course. If I may so express it, though this would certainly be paradoxical and exaggerated, it almost looks as though Paul were not thinking of God at all, but were actually working out an atheistic ethics of Christianity.

How is the law fulfilled if I have loved my neighbor? How is this love not merely a part, but the bond of perfection? How is it that on this love the whole of the law and the prophets depends? — the Lord says this. For in that case surely the love of neighbor would itself have to contain everything else, including precisely what is everything, what is ultimate and decisive: that God must be loved.

If for the moment we leave John out of account, scripture does not actually tell us how it is that there are not merely two commandments similar to one another, perhaps equally important and linked in some way, but that one is contained in the other. We might perhaps understand quite well that we only love God if we also love our neighbor. But with Paul it is clearly the case that if we love our neighbor we already love God.

How is that possible? John in his first letter perhaps takes us a little farther by asking how we can love the God whom we do not see if we do not love the brother whom we do see. Of course it may be said that that is a simple and obvious argument which really amounts to nothing more than: If you do not love neighbor whom you have concretely and practically there in your life, how little you will succeed in loving the invisible God who is so remote from your immediate circle. But clearly John means even more, for in the fourth chapter of the First Letter of John we find the remarkable statement that God abides in us. And clearly this also contributes to make it possible that we already love God if we really love our neighbor with absolutely genuine personal commitment.

And so this thesis — to express it in theoretical, pedagogical terms — amounts to this: love of God and love of the neighbor are mutually inclusive; when a human being acts with real unselfishness, commits himself absolutely with real renunciation of his freedom in relation to the other human partner, and thus really performs what is meant by love of neighbor, he already loves God. And this is so even if he does not explicitly know this, or tell himself it is so, even if he would not make God as such in explicit concepts a motive for love of his neighbor. The thesis means that by really loving his neighbor, the human person, as it were, falls or penetrates into the ultimate realities of created reality and, even if he does not explicitly say so, is really mysteriously concerned in this love with the God of his eternal, supernatural salvation. How is it possible to maintain such a thesis?

In the first place we may refer to scholastic theology. This speaks of three theological virtues, that is, three modes of human activity in which, supported by the Holy Spirit, by the Spirit of God in the depths of his own heart, the human being is concerned no longer simply with the realities of the world but directly with God. Three fundamental modes of the human person's ultimate orientation toward the God of eternal life himself in his own glory and independence of the world, so that we all become really and directly the partners of God himself. Faith, hope, and love are the fundamental human acts, in which he has dealings with God, the triune God of eternal life. And these three alone, as Paul says, remain.

Now theology says that by this divine fundamental power of charity, in which faith and hope are already comprised and integrated, neighbor also can and must be loved. If we as Christians really love our neighbor in a way conducive to salvation, we are not merely fulfilling one or other of God's commandments which we fulfill with his help. There actually takes place that ultimate, and really the only, eternal occurrence in our life, in which an individual truly comes directly to God himself.

When we love our neighbor in supernatural love of God, there takes place, and strictly speaking nowhere else, salvation, justification, divine life, eternity. There is no doubt in Catholic theology that there is such a divine virtue in which the person finds his neighbor in the ultimate depth of his own being. And once again, it is not merely a question of the fact that because one loves God one regards the rest of his creatures with a certain goodwill and avoids transgressing the precepts of the beloved God in regard to these other human creatures. In genuine supernatural love of neighbor, love of God is accomplished by the power of God himself.

Now it might be thought that by saying this in accordance with Catholic theology, we have already reached the point aimed at. Yet that is not quite the case. Of course, when someone loves his neighbor's very self with the consciousness of faith and from the motive of divine love of God himself, it is clear from what has been said that *caritas,* the divine virtue of love of God, is accomplished. Catholic theology has been in agreement on this for centuries as a matter of course, and expounds it more or less as we have just briefly indicated. I should like, however, to try to carry the radical character of this thesis somewhat further.

I should like to say that where a person really abandons himself and loves his neighbor with absolute selflessness, he has already come to the silent, inexpressible mystery of God and that such an act is already based on that divine self-communication which we call grace and which gives the act of which it is the ground its saving meaning and importance for eternity.

We may raise the question from quite a different angle. We meet many people who are not professedly Christians and do not even wish to be. Let us assume that such a person were really to love with ultimate radical selflessness his neighbor, the brother or sister whom he sees. Then what has actually happened? Only a very good deed worthy of recognition but to which ultimately the most important thing is lacking? Or is there already present there an ultimate relation to God which ought indeed to develop and, as it were, receive its name, which still has to be measured and named in its ultimate, inexpressible but real dimensions in relation to God, but which is nevertheless already there?

This is precisely what I mean when I say that the love of God, charity, is always and everywhere present in that ultimate, genuine, radical love of neighbor in which a person really engages himself and the ultimate strength of his being and gives himself. Not, of course, because the natural structure of such an act necessarily entails this, but because we live under the universal saving will of God. We live in a world which always and everywhere is directed by the secret grace of God toward the eternal life of God, always and everywhere where someone does not expressly shut himself off by really culpable unbelief from this innermost supernatural, grace-given dynamism of the world.

Now an act of love of neighbor is not simply one moral action among others, but basically it is the fundamental act of human moral reality, of the person himself. Knowing is immanent presence to self, and freedom is ultimately free, personal, deliberately final and definitive disposition over oneself.

Both of these, however, can only take place in loving communication with a personal partner. For the human being, as a spiritual, personal subject, the world is primarily the human world around him. We do not simply live in an environment in which every imaginable kind of thing exists. That world has an inner structure deriving from the human subject and from the reality which the individual encounters.

Ultimately it is a communication by love with another human person. The whole world of things with which we have to deal, even in economic life, society, and so on, is fundamentally only the material, the condition and the consequence of loving communication with other persons.

The human being disposes over himself in radical freedom productive of eternal consequences, and this self-disposal in the last resort is simply either the loving openness in regard to the human partner or a final self-closing in egoism, which throws the person into the damning, deadly isolation of the lost. This fundamental act is of course only possible because the human being is dynamically oriented toward the absolute of reality, that is, because in fact in a nonexplicit, unanalyzed way he has to do with God. For we do not begin to have something to do with God only when we explicitly invoke him, or when we expressly name and profess this mystery toward which we are always moving and which alone bestows the possibility of spiritual freedom and love.

Always and everywhere in the activity of knowing and most certainly in that of love, we have to do with God in an implicit way. And if a human being in the fundamental act which actualizes his human reality adopts an attitude of love toward his neighbor, then this fundamental act of his life, through the universal divinizing saving will of God which is everywhere at work even outside the church, is supported by God's Holy Spirit and, his grace and at least implicitly and tacitly but really, is at the same time an act of charity, of the love of God.

In a more precise description of what love of neighbor means, we should of course have to show how in reality it always approaches the mystery of God even if it does not expressly wish or intend to. If we are silent, if we forgive, if without reward we give ourselves wholeheartedly and are detached from ourselves, we are reaching out into a limitlessness which exceeds any assignable bounds and which is nameless. We are reaching out toward the holy mystery which pervades and is the ground of our life. We are dealing with God. And something of this kind happens necessarily and always in the act of loving freedom of real, radical personal communication with one's neighbor. Consequently, in the present order of God's saving will this is always based on God's grace; it is charity.

Whenever a human being in real personal freedom opens his heart to his neighbor, he has already by that very fact done more than simply loved that neighbor, because all that was already encompassed by the grace of God. He has loved his neighbor and in his neighbor he has already loved God. Because he cannot meet his neighbor with love except through the fact that the dynamism of his spiritual freedom supported by the grace of God is already itself always a dynamism toward the unutterable holy mystery which we call God.

This does not mean that love between human beings, just as it is usually found, is equated with the Christian's explicit love in faith and hope. All we are saying is that genuine love of God is already exercised in it. But this must of course become conscious. It must be such that the goal toward which this love always tends is expressly invoked, named, known, honored in explicit faith, explicit hope, and explicit love. The human love which in its innermost nature is already by God's grace a love of God, must also become explicit love for God who is named, explicitly invoked, religiously sought.

This inner dynamism of development is implanted in all love by the grace of God. It has the duty to develop into the explicit specifically Christian character of divine charity. Conversely, it is true for the same reason that this explicit love of God, of the God who is named, although he is not seen, is already intrinsically present in the love of the brother or sister whom we do see. Now it is a fact that there are many people who are redeemed, justified, and sanctified by God's grace, although they do not know this.

It is also the case that what we as Christians believe, hope, and thankfully proclaim of ourselves, is something which is present as an offer in all human beings through God's supernatural, free, unmerited grace. In fact, of course, it can also be present as accepted even though many think they are not Christians and not believers. In the depth of their being they can nevertheless be so, and particularly if they really succeed wholeheartedly and with utter unselfishness in loving the brother or sister whom they see. Whether they do this, we of course do not know.

We actually do not know it about ourselves either. We of course endeavor in our activity and our lives to love God and our neighbor and both in one. God's judgment alone will decide whether we really summon up this ultimate strength by the efficacious grace of God or whether all that we do is ultimately merely a specious facade behind which a profound, unacknowledged egoism prevails. But we have begun to endeavor to love God in deed and truth, by trying to love the neighbor. All that we experience thereby — disappointment, toil, fret — is fundamentally only the way in which we try to contrive to turn from ourselves to the person of our neighbor and to God.

That is difficult. It is the ultimate reality and the hardest task of our lives. We can be deceived about it time and time again. But if we have turned in love from self to our neighbor, we have come to God, not by our strength but by God's grace. God who, as John says, had loved us so that we might love our neighbor, has truly laid hold of us, has torn us, as it were, from self and has given us what in conjunction constitutes our eternity, a personal union with others in which we are also united to God.

It is possible to view the same thing once again from an entirely different angle.

Jesus says to us, "As you did it to one of the least of these my brethren, you did it to me." How often we have heard this statement and used it in pious, edifying talk. But suppose we ask ourselves how Jesus could really say that. Is it not really just a juridical fiction: I give you credit for it, as though you had done to me personally what you have done to the least of these other human beings? No, this saying of Jesus is not a legal fiction, a moral make-believe, a kind of compensation. It is truly the case that we meet the incarnate Word of God in the other human being, because God himself really is in this other. If we love him, if we do not, as it were, culpably impede the dynamism of this love and fundamentally turn it back toward ourselves, then there occurs precisely the divine descent into human flesh, so that God is in the place where we are and gazes at us in a human being.

This divine descent continues through us and it then happens that we, because God loves us, love our neighbor and have already loved God by the very fact of loving our neighbor. For, of course, we cannot achieve this love at all except on the basis of that divine love for us which in fact made itself our brother or sister. The christological side, if I may so call it, of our brotherly love would have to be taken really seriously and really realized in life. Where the other human being confronts me, there Christ really is, asking me whether I will love him, the incarnate Word of God, and if I say yes, he replies that he is in the least of his brethren.

One theological aspect may be added in clarification. If we are to take the Christianity of the incarnation seriously, it will still be the case in eternity that the incarnate Word of God in his humanity is eternally for us the mediator, the gate, bridge, God's actual concrete form, when we see him face to face. Jesus' humanity is not a barrier between us and the immediate presence of the God of grace. Nor is it something which served to mediate only in time, then to be abolished, as it were. We shall always be dealing with the God who himself became man. To all eternity there is no theology that is not anthropology.

Is it not the case that we Christians have perhaps still not sufficiently understood our faith, that the various dogmatic affirmations of our faith, though we profess and accept them, nevertheless lie much too far apart, that we have the impression of living in an endlessly complicated world of propositions, dogmas, and precepts? In reality, however, the truth is that God is man — and consequently love of God is love of the human person and vice versa.

The only condition is that we allow the innermost specific movement of this human love to come to its ultimate radical goal and essential fulfillment. Then where this happens, everything is already present — the whole of Christianity, for there is ultimately only one commandment, just as for the Christian there is only one God, he who in the eternal Word became flesh and dwelt among us and who remains not only yesterday and today, but forever.

Ultimately we know nothing of God if we know nothing of the human person, of him whom God himself assumed as his own reality and in whom also the ultimate mystery, the ultimate depth of all humanity is comprised. We can ultimately only express the deepest thing about ourselves if we say that we are the reality which God could and has made most entirely his own. Only if we say that, only if we spring, as it were, from anthropology into theology, have we understood what we ourselves are.

And consequently we have only understood ourselves in the activity of our life (and that is the only way we understand ourselves) if we are people who love, if we are human beings who in unselfish love have found other human beings and not, of course, merely here and there in some festive hour, but in the brutal, grey, everyday course of our life. There we find God. And we may certainly say that all prayer, worship, law, and institutions of the church are only secondary means for us to do one thing: to love God and neighbor. And we cannot love God unless we love him in our neighbor. Where we do that we have already fulfilled the law, thrown the bond of perfection round our whole life, taken the better way which Paul has shown us.

Only if we understand that there is a real ultimate unity between love of God and love of neighbor, do we really understand what Christianity is and what a divinely simple thing it is after all. What is divinely simple has, of course, to be expounded, and our whole catechism with all that it contains is the true and genuine exposition, the articulation, the verbal expression of what at bottom we have already grasped if we love our neighbor.

I finally return to what I tried to suggest at the beginning. How as witnesses to the truth and love of God are we to convince people that what we profess in faith actually exists? God seems remote. But there is one thing we can do, love unselfishly and try to tell people that when they do this they have already begun to love God. We can repeatedly exemplify and demonstrate to them the one possible convincing starting point for the whole of Christianity: love of neighbor. If we do that we have done what our life must do and we have borne the first and last fundamental testimony to Christianity.

We will still have to say very much more about Christianity in the pulpit and in teaching, and the like. But if this whole message does not begin with the profession by action and life that we are determined to love our neighbor unselfishly, all we say remains unintelligible. The very first key word capable of convincing anyone today is missing. If we wish to become messengers of God and his love, we must quite simply do one thing: love our neighbor, in our life, in care for him, in patience, forgiveness, toleration. Then we have not only begun to practice authentic Christianity, but we already have it whole and entire in germ and kernel. Out of that it can develop in us and bear witness to God's love in Christ Jesus for us, so that people may believe that God exists because they have experienced his love in the love which those who are his bear toward their fellow men and women.

153 • Internal Threat to the Faith*

In addition to external dangers to faith, there is the much more significant internal threat that arises out of faith itself. Those who radically and honestly raise the ultimately unavoidable *question* about the meaning of life, provided of course that they do not grasp on to some illusory or inadequate answer, find their ordinary everyday existence shattered. What was self-evident becomes questionable. What until now was not thought about or reflected on, taboos like serious guilt, the voice of conscience, or death as the "end," can no longer be repressed or declared irrelevant. The experience of a "threat" of this kind belongs to the basic phenomena of human existence; it is something that a "mature atheist" (Milan Machovec) can experience in his or her own life.

Believers, going, as they do, beyond themselves and their own narrow opinions and finding the meaning of life in the infinite God, experience this sense of the abyss and of groundlessness in human life in a particularly intense way. They are also aware of their own weakness and of what it means to fall back into themselves and their egoism; they understand middle-class smugness and blindness in the face of the inescapable puzzles of existence. They readily admit *this threat* to faith. They experience the free decision of faith as an ever new risk, the

---

* *Kritisches Wort,* 138–39. Trans. Daniel Donovan, University of Saint Michael's College, Toronto.

risk of finding in God a clear, comprehensive and radically demanding conviction about the meaning of life. Christians know that only God can protect believers from being overwhelmed by this "threat." And so they admit the possibility and the fact that a person can doubt, deny and lose his or her faith. That, however, does not lessen faith's own existential sureness and firmness. Both belong to its essence. The acceptance of this characteristic of it could be called knowledge about the threat that is always a part of it, a threat to which Christians courageously and truly expose themselves.

154 • The Christian in the World*

"The Christian in the World" — an inexhaustible topic, upon which only a very few stammering remarks can hesitatingly be offered! For the "world," as envisaged for the purposes of this discussion, is incomprehensible and indescribable. It is the world of a human race that is growing gigantically and at a terrifying rate; a world which has developed into a unified compositum made up of originally distinct cultures and peoples, so that today everyone has become everyone else's neighbor and the history and destiny of every nation has become the history and destiny of all the others as well.

It is a world of rationality, of technical achievement, of atomic power, of automation, of the "A B C weapons," of the media of mass communication, of nomadic wanderlust, of militant ideologies on the grand scale, of mass hysteria, of propaganda, of the artificial manipulation of human needs, of organized enjoyment; a world which, the more it is subjected to rational planning, the more incalculable it becomes; a world which is no longer something ready given by nature to provide a secure habitation for the human being, but which constitutes, rather, the material for the person's own creative planning; a world the tempo of which is accelerated by the person himself.

But it is also a world which, after all, never ceases to belong inalienably to what is permanent and immutable in the human person's nature: his love, his all-transcending questioning, his longing, his loneliness, his demand for happiness and eternity. It is a world of unfathomable anguish and of death; a world that is at once terrifying and familiar to us, and which, in spite of all, we love. It is our world, our fate that we accept, for we know no other besides it. It is in this bewildering

---

* *Theological Investigations VII*, 89–92.

world that we live. We must see it as it really is. Let us therefore ask in all honesty: What part does the Christian play in this world?

I believe that the first point to be recognized is this: the Christian shares this world of today, just as it is, with all other human beings in a spirit of brotherhood. He does not flee from it. He is willing neither to live in a ghetto, nor to take refuge in history. He neither takes flight into a romantic past, nor does he confine himself to one particular small group in society, in which alone he can feel happy. He accepts the world in its worldliness. He has no intention whatever of changing it back into the vanished world of the Middle Ages, in which religion exercised a direct influence upon all departments of life. He makes no pretense of knowing of some prescription, ready-made or, even, better than the non-Christians, for each and every problem that arises merely on the grounds that he knows that this world is encompassed by the power and compassion of the incomprehensible mystery that he calls God, and upon whom he dares to call as Father.

He knows as well as anyone else that his world has been caught up in a movement the effects of which in terms of concrete living in the world no one sees clearly, since all calculations serve only to increase the element of the incalculable. The Christian accepts this world as it is: a world of human power, and at the same time of human anxiety and utter impotence. He neither idolizes it in terms of ideological dreams of utopia, nor yet does he condemn it. It exists; and the Christian, true realist that he is or that he should be, accepts it without question as the sphere of his existence, his responsibility, and his proving. He can afford to be a hopeful realist because, even while remaining loyal to this world and its tasks, he is journeying toward the future that is absolute, which God himself has ordained for him, and which is coming to meet him through and beyond all the victories and defeats of this world and its history.

The second point is this: the Christian recognizes the diaspora in which he has to live today, wherever he may be, as the setting of his Christian life as something in which an ultimately positive significance is to be found. When I use the term "diaspora," I am using it in the biblical sense in which it is currently employed, not in the sense ascribed to it until recently, in which it designated the situation of a Catholic minority in the midst of a majority of Protestants. This nineteenth-century idea may still have a certain validity in the field of pastoral care, and still point to certain needs which have to be fulfilled. But this meaning is more and more receding into the background, and the term is being applied more and more to a fresh phenomenon, which we now have to examine.

This is the society which is based on a multiplicity of ideologies:

the society which, taken as a whole, and from the point of view of its constitution, its special patterns and its culture, bears the stamp of other influences besides the purely Christian one. In this society Christians, whether Catholic or Protestant, live, provided they are true Christians, in common as brothers and sisters in the diaspora.

It is the diaspora in this sense, in which non-Christian liberal humanism, militant atheism, and the atrophy of religion are everywhere apparent, that is referred to when we use the term "diaspora" here; the diaspora which all Christians have in common, in comparison with which the differences between the various Christian confessions seem not indeed unimportant, but historically speaking secondary.

This diaspora must be seen by the Christian of today as the divinely ordained "situation" of his own Christianity. It is the setting in which his free and personal act of faith is posited, a faith which cannot be overthrown in favor of any social ethic, the situation of free decision, of personal responsibility, of personal avowal of one's faith. And all this gives a fresh application to the old adage that Christians are not born but made. This is the situation which had to arise as a necessity of saving history.

Christians know that, on the one hand, if their own theological expectations of the future are to be fulfilled, they will always exist as the creed that is under attack, and on the other that when all kinds of far from homogeneous cultures are permitted to exist, each in its own sphere, as parts of one and the same world history, an attack on any one of them will only come from without, from those who do not belong to that particular culture.

We Christians accept this situation. Certainly, in common with all other citizens we want to have the right to cooperate in the sphere of public life. Certainly we also demand that in cases in which, in spite of all variations within the community, the unified political system makes it quite unavoidable for all to have one and the same form, the Christian history of our people and the fact that the great majority of the people want to be Christians even now shall be respected. We demand in the name of freedom and tolerance that he who, in effect, gives the casting vote shall not be the one who is most radical in denying Christianity. But we Christians have no interest in maintaining Christian facades behind which no true Christianity is alive, and which serve only to compromise and to discredit such true Christianity.

On the other hand it does not seem fair to us either that non-Christians, while secretly conforming to the ancient heritage of Christian culture in their private lives, nevertheless believe that they must attack Christianity in public. We Christians are not to be numbered among those who suppose that their beliefs and their conception of the world can only be rendered attractive if our faith enjoys the special protection of the state. But we do not, on that account, need to suppose that the prevailing political system must be constructed according to rationalist formulas out of a few abstract principles of freedom and equality, and that it must eliminate every element of Christianity which has contributed in the course of history to the makeup of this political system.

We accept the situation of a society made up of a multiplicity of cultures, in which Christianity exists as a diaspora. But it is to the society so constituted that we ourselves precisely belong, the masses of our own people together with the heritage of a tradition that has lasted more than a thousand years. This is no mere ballast, but rather genuine riches, carrying with it responsibilities for the future. We recognize that we must genuinely accept this situation. In other words, we must be prepared to be critical of ourselves, and to maintain a constant awareness of the fact that on our own principles we ourselves in turn have to accord to others their due meed of freedom even when they use this freedom to come to decisions which run counter to Christianity itself.

But while recognizing this, let us add in all honesty in our dialogue with non-Christians that the formal rules of the game of democracy are not sufficient of themselves to make it possible for all to live together in peace and freedom. For a society or state to exist it is indispensable that there shall be a single common basis of ultimate moral convictions, whether this be the natural law or whatever we may like to call it, or whether the state itself has a code of laws already drawn up in the concrete and conditioned by its own past history.

Furthermore, where necessary this common basis in moral law can and must be defended by the power and authority of the society and state itself. It is not easy to accord due value to all these principles at the same time, and so to arrive at a firm conclusion as to what is right for us today. We are quite ready to enter into discussion, are anxious for a fair and open dialogue with all, and are even ready to entertain reasonable compromises.

On the other hand we refuse to be intimidated when we are stigmatized as bigots, narrow-minded reactionaries, or intolerant, merely on the grounds that we hold that Christian ideas too must be allowed to exert their due influence in the sphere of political life. We have only to compare our position with that of that false liberalism which maintains that political life can and must undergo an ideological process of sterilization, and that creeds and conscience should only be allowed a voice in the churches or the clubs of the humanist society.

Is not this too an ideology, and a bad one at that? Since every fresh claim to freedom on the part of one involves an alteration in, and a restriction of the sphere of freedom hitherto enjoyed by another even before his consent has been obtained, no one member can be allowed an absolutely unrestricted sphere of personal freedom. Hence, too, not all authority is ipso facto and of its very nature hostile to the very essence of freedom. Such authority may be exercised to ensure that all have a reasonable share of freedom in the one sphere of freedom that is available, and to guarantee and maintain a due share for each individual.

We Christians are guilty — unhappily this is all too obvious — of sins of our own. For this reason it is difficult to say which of two sins is the more widespread among us: the sin entailed in a reactionary clinging to Christian forms and customs in the political sphere when these have become obsolete, or the sin of being too cowardly to stand up for what is genuine and new. Perhaps the situation is even such that both sins are often committed at once, and by the same individual Christians — even, it may be, those who occupy high offices and dignities.

However this may be, we Christians are willing to accept unreservedly the situation of our diaspora in a pluralistic society, and in doing so to guard against the error of taking refuge in the ghetto of a reactionary defense of the traditional for its own sake, or in the comfortable cowardice of renouncing all claims to influence the course of political life.

155 • The Missionary Task of the Christian*

Christians have to learn to cope with their minority situation and to find a positive relationship to it. They need to recognize that faith involves both grace and personal decision and that therefore being in the minority, far from being a situation that ought not exist, is in fact a social manifestation of something pertaining to the very nature of faith. It is part of that "ought" in which faith has to be lived.

Believers should know that the unbelievers around them are or can be anonymous Christians, that is, that through God's universal will of salvation, justifying grace is always offered to them. This offer includes what might be called a "transcendental revelation." Often mediated through *Christian* elements in the culture in which unbelievers share,

---

Handbuch der Pastoraltheologie III, 672–78. Trans. Daniel Donovan, University of Saint Michael's College, Toronto.

this offer can be and often is freely accepted even when its Christian and ecclesial explication and objectification in dogma and ritual is rejected, and the person in this sense remains an unbeliever and perhaps even an atheist. Christians need to know and to experience existentially that because of the "anonymous" Christianity in unbelievers, because of this offer of grace on the one hand and its possible acceptance on the other, the "categorial" conflict between Christians and unbelievers is already transcended. Christians have to get used to the fact that their belonging to the church, their baptism, creedal confession and cult is not finally the affirmation of something in contradiction to unbelievers but is rather a bringing to historical and social visibility of the inner reality of their being. This is certainly offered to their freedom and may well have already been freely accepted. What we are talking about is the yes of God to unbelievers and their possible but secret yes to God.

The "categorial" contradiction between believers and unbelievers remains and is both painful and an impetus to "mission." The pain of believers is from a certain point of view intensified because of their faith in, and hope for, a deeper unity between themselves and those who appear as "unbelievers" but are in fact "anonymous Christians." This pain can be understood as a testing of faith and hope and as a sharing in the cross which effects salvation for Christians and "unbelievers" alike. In this way the pain will be protected from a fanatical and impatient desire to proselytize, a desire rooted in an inability to accept the fact that one's "world view" is not affirmed by another. It will also be saved from that skeptical relativism which too lightly and in a cowardly way lets people pursue happiness as they want and from the temptation to retreat into a human and social ghetto in order to protect oneself from the "evil world" and its unbelief.

The lay apostolate in a minority situation means more than the special responsibility that this situation entails in regard to the preservation and strengthening of one's own faith, and more, too, than dialogue and collaboration with "unbelievers" in the secular sphere. It also involves a missionary outreach in the hope that these "unbelievers" might become Christians.

It probably cannot be denied that this specifically religious and missionary outreach to unbelievers is very much in the background of the consciousness of lay people, with the possible exception of the attitude of parents to children. The reason why this is so is probably that their consciousness is marked more by the experience of the *Volkskirche*, a culturally supported church, than of a community church, a church of individuals who have freely chosen to be Christian. (This is reinforced by their experience of the stable coexistence of different Christian churches.) Hence the powerful and almost self-evident impression that we become Christian (and Catholics) because we are born into a Christian (and Catholic) family and are baptized as children. A missionary effort to convert unbelievers in the diaspora can thus hardly even occur to lay people as either a real possibility or an obligation. The laity, moreover, do not think of themselves as qualified for such activity. They experience their religion as dependent on social circumstances and as something that is so complex that only the "professional," the priest, seems to be in a position actively to communicate it to others. On the other hand, the Christianity of believers appears to be so tied up with prepersonal social realities that it strikes non-Christians and unbelievers as a historical accident and not as a personal decision that might provoke them to ask whether they ought to make that decision their own.

The task of evangelizing unbelievers can only be undertaken by those lay persons who themselves have an authentic church experience, who are part of a living eucharistic community in which people have accepted Christianity by a personal decision. They must themselves have appropriated it in a personal and original way and not just (more or less) be carrying it on as a tradition and as a part of their own social conditioning. Here again one can see the importance of adult formation and of building up the community in terms of its adult members. To achieve this there will need to be a "reduction" of the dispersed and manifold forms of faith to their kernel and foundation in terms of which alone lay people will be able personally to appropriate it, put it into practice, and strengthen it. There will be a need to distinguish the essence of what is Christian, that is, the orientation of human beings to the absolute and yet self-communicating mystery of God mediated historically in Jesus Christ. In cases of conflict, pastoral planning will have to focus on building up real communities of faith rather than on maintaining the *Volkskirche*. It is only when these conditions are met that there will be lay missionaries in any significant number.

The condition for, and the heart of, a missionary outreach on the part of the laity to unbelievers is and remains "the witness of their life," their presence and work in secular society. This will become visible and tangible primarily and principally in what they do in peaceful collaboration and competition with other members of society in their own life, their family, their profession, their participation in public life, in everything, in other words, that can be thought of under the concept of the lay apostolate, whether as exercised by individuals or organized communally and institutionally. A genuine understanding of the relation between nature and grace knows that in the concrete order of salvation the furtherance of what is human, of what corresponds morally and objectively to reality as it is, is a manifestation of, and witness for, that grace which finds its clearest historical formulation and embodiment in organized Christianity. This is particularly the case when Christians are religiously motivated in accepting their task and responsibility in the world. It is true even apart from the question how far religious motivation in this area makes Christian activity materially different from that of unbelievers. Their practice, their constantly renewed hope, their objectivity and selflessness, their unconditional and unrewarded fidelity to conscience, and so on, can provoke unbelievers to wonder about the ultimate motives and attitudes out of which the actions of Christians flow. Thus their secular life itself becomes a witness for Christ and for his grace.

Given all the justified emphasis on the fact that the "presence" and the life of the laity in the world can attract people to Christianity and given even that this is the primary form of their religious apostolate, there can be no doubt that they also can and must become explicitly missionary by talking about, and inviting people to, faith. Everything, naturally, that can be said of ecclesial office in this regard is to be said analogously of the laity. Mission must begin with an indirect preparation of the milieu; it must wait with patience and tact for the right moment, and it remains bound to the realistic possibilities that are open to it given one's talent, time, sphere of influence, preparation, and so on. That, however, does not do away with the fundamental responsibility of the laity for evangelization among unbelievers, even when the "location" of their mission, in distinction to that of official ministry, is their "place" in the world. This flows from the simple fact that human life can only flourish in dialogue and social interaction and that a part of all genuine human communication is the word, the word not only in which facts are communicated but in which people share themselves with one another. Such sharing cannot in principle and a priori disregard the first and last unity that exists among human beings, that unity which is the fulfillment of all other unity among them, unity with and in God in the grace of Christ. To put it differently: since Christian love of neighbor, which is rooted in grace, seeks to unite people at the deepest level of their existence, it cannot in principle refuse the neighbor help in achieving salvation, the fulfillment of human existence. A fundamental denial of a genuine missionary obligation of the laity would be a clerical misunderstanding of the church. It would suggest that only clerics are active subjects within it. The "mission and expansion" of the early church was carried out above all by lay Christians.

The way in which an explicit lay mission is to be carried out among unbelievers can be very different depending on the situation of those involved. One could imagine, and in fact there exist, institutionalized forms of lay missionary work, as, for example, the Legion of Mary.

Such forms have the advantage that everything done with planning and team work has. In our case they also have the disadvantage that they do not easily or at all facilitate the development of that intimate, long-standing kind of human contact that is ordinarily the condition for a "conversion." The most normal and for lay people the most natural way to become involved in missionary activity presupposes the kind of human relationship that is fostered by personal, professional, family and neighborly encounters between people. If anything of a genuinely missionary nature is to take place at this level, there will have to be a profound Christian conviction and an explicitly missionary intention on the part of the Christian. Believers will have to overcome the false shyness of so many today and allow others to see into the more intimate areas of their private life. Thus they will be able to give witness to what at the deepest level moves them and is the source of their happiness.

Conviction about an "anonymous Christianity" is important in this context. With it people will present Christianity to their "unbelieving" neighbors not so much as a contradiction coming from outside to the convictions they hold, but rather as the blossoming of what already through God's grace is at work in them in the seriousness and responsibility of their moral life and in their efforts to deal with the ultimate and unavoidable questions of existence. With such a conviction lay people can more easily find the courage needed for explicit evangelization. It comes across less as a polemical and apologetical contradiction to the other's world view and more as a friendly conversation which bears witness to the hope that already touches the other when he or she in honest courage holds fast in spite of everything that seems to oppose it to a final meaning of life. Presupposed here, too, is that Christians not appear to their "unbelieving neighbors" as disappointed with life, as uneducated and uninterested in the great issues of the world, as people whose religion thus inevitably appears as an analgesic, as an "opium" against the shortcomings of life. Christians may and should reveal themselves as people who face the mystery of existence and of death and all the other great questions with which one cannot cope on one's own, and yet who feel no need to repress them as if there were no hope.

It would be helpful if lay Christians tried to develop for themselves and also for others whatever specific entries to the larger questions of meaning can be found in their own particular scientific or professional areas. They will thus be able to speak of their faith more naturally and without giving the impression that it is an added and somewhat arbitrary hobby alongside the rest of their life. In order that the way they talk about Christianity not sound too "churchy" and in the bad sense "pastoral," it is essential that their own understanding of it be a personal one and not just something that they have rather superficially learned from others. For this it has to be focused on the real essence of Christianity, on that which people in a state of skeptical hopelessness might reject, but in opposition to which they can offer really nothing positive of comparable significance.

Everything said here should also help believers to be steadfast and yet natural among "unbelieving relatives." Today believers often live in the extended as well as in the nuclear family in a minority situation. People need to be educated to deal with such situations.

156 • Christianity and Literature*

There is an intrinsic connection between a really great Christianity and really great writing. Certainly they are not to be identified one with another. Great writing is achieved only in those cases in which a person achieves a radical self-confrontation, in which he realizes what he himself is.

But even when he does this he can indeed become ensnared in guilt, perversity, self-hatred, and even demonic pride. He can confront himself as a sinner, and identify himself with this, yet even in this case he would still stand to a greater degree in that blessed peril which consists in encountering God than the narrow-minded and superficial bourgeois, who right from the first anxiously evades the imponderable factors in existence, fleeing from them into that attitude of superficiality in which there is admittedly no encounter with doubt, but no encounter with God either.

Therefore, for those who are still only approaching maturity the question of what sort of reading matter is suitable for their education can be a serious problem in itself. But the mature Christian must be fully and unreservedly free to explore all writings that are truly great, bringing to them an attitude of reverence and sympathetic love, even when this may entail pain for him.

He will do this because such writings contain a message about the human being either as redeemed or else in need of redemption and capable of receiving it. And in any case such writing will give us a deeper insight into the truth than if we simply adopt that attitude of superficiality which has only too often and for too long been regarded as appropriate for so-called good Christians, an attitude, namely, in

---

* *Theological Investigations VIII*, 119–21.

which the human person is regarded as the two-legged animal which has become somewhat craftier than the other animals and therefore less predictable than they.

The further an individual is led by the message of great writing into the immeasurable depths upon which his existence is founded, the more he is compelled by such writing to face up to the hidden depths which a person can find within himself, depths which are dark and obscure, and which are buried in that twilight of ambiguity in which the person can no longer say with any ultimate certainty whether he is in a state of grace or one of radical desolation. It is no accident, but rather inherent in the nature of the case, that the great creative writings of humankind are obscure, and for the most part leave us with the unanswered question of whether it is the mystery of grace or that of perdition which takes place and which is described in their pages.

How indeed could it be otherwise? Creative or imaginative writing must be concerned with the concrete, and not try to manipulate abstract principles like puppets in a dance. But that which is individual and concrete is a mystery which will only be unveiled by that unique judgment which belongs to God alone, yet which the creative writer makes present in his writing as a mystery. It is not in the least necessary, therefore, that his writing should have that simplicity and clarity of structure which many bad teachers would so much like it to have in their anxiety to protect the minds of their pupils from any harm.

If we are not Manichees, then as Christians we recognize that a sin that is truly great is terrible indeed because it is a sin and because it is so great, but that the only possible way in which it can come to be so great is that in it much of the greatness of humanity itself is realized and revealed. For evil as such is nothing.

Moreover we know that God allows sin to exist in this world, and to be great and powerful, and yet that for this very reason it is not so easy to confine ourselves to the saints when we seek to find examples in the concrete of the greatness of humanity. Moreover we recall Paul's instruction that we Christians must not withdraw ourselves from the world, but actually can and must, in a certain sense, have fellowship (though admittedly a different kind of fellowship from that which we have with our brethren in the faith) with unbelievers and the unchaste (1 Cor 5:9–13).

And in view of all this we Christians are not only not forbidden but positively commanded to take seriously into consideration and to familiarize ourselves with that creative writing which genuinely is such, even if it is not in conformity with the moral standards of Christianity, though admittedly here we have to distinguish this genuine creative writing from that which conveys a message of sheer unbelief and immorality under the pretense of being creative writing. And in all this we must not judge those who do not share our Christian belief.

There is such a thing as a Christianity that is anonymous. There are those who merely think that they are not Christians when in reality they are so in God's sight and under his grace. Thus it is possible for the individual to be raised to a level of human living which is already imbued with grace, even though he does not realize it, and even though he supposes that he is still at the purely human level.

We Christians are in a better position to understand this than one who is actually in the state to which we refer. We lay down as part of the teaching of our faith that even human morality at the "this-worldly" level has need of the grace of God in order to be able to maintain itself in its fullness or for any length of time. It is our belief, therefore, precisely as Christians that to achieve this supreme level of human living, wherever it manifests itself in its genuine form, and even when it is found outside the limits of professed and acknowledged Christianity, is a gift of God's grace and a fruit of the redemption itself even though the individual who has attained to this level is not himself yet aware of it. Why should we not love this exalted level of human living when we find it in such an individual? For we could actually be despising the grace of God itself if we were to remain indifferent to it.

157 • Faith and Culture*

Faith demands responsibility before God also for the culture which is and remains secular. At first sight this statement seems to be valid for all time. But we should remember that a specifically secular culture exists only today, and that Christianity does not claim to design this culture directly according to the principles of the faith, let alone of the teaching office of the church.

Hence there is the acute danger that the believer will no longer consider this secular culture as his religious responsibility before God, but will regard it as something that interests him as a human being, but no longer affects him as a Christian. The Second Vatican Council, too, recognizes the danger (*Gaudium et Spes*, nos. 43ff.) that Christians are only seeking "heavenly things" and think that earthly matters do not concern them and have no bearing on their salvation, because these things have become exclusively secular and human.

---

* *Grace in Freedom*, 71–77.

But the council says: "The Christian who neglects his temporal duties neglects his duties toward his neighbor and even God, and jeopardizes his eternal salvation." Now the words about the temporal duties should be read within the context of the council statements about the relative autonomy of the secular culture (no. 59), for only thus will the sentence just quoted receive its full weight. For precisely that culture which cannot be materially given by faith and the church is nevertheless the earthly duty that determines our eternal salvation. In lonely responsibility the Christian is confronted with these secular cultural activities, and these, though not only these, are his Christian vocation and mission.

Unified mass culture is a Christian concern. The council document does not regard culture as the preserve of a small elite of individuals or nations who would have a monopoly on its development. It speaks quite simply of a "mass culture"; it favors the cultural development of all peoples and nations. True, it desires that most legitimate civilizations should be preserved, yet it approves of the development of "a more universal form of human culture . . . one which will promote and express the unity of the human race" (no. 54) and favors a powerful international organization which, despite the United Nations, does not yet exist (no. 84).

The council wants both sexes to cooperate responsibly in this culture, and men and women of all social classes as well as all nations, whether rich or poor, to have as active a share in it as possible through education, means of communication, tourism, and so forth. The council fathers knew, of course, that there would always be differences of social status, talent, and national character, but in their view great genuine culture does not presuppose the existence of a large number of human beings who are poor, socially weak, and exploited.

For them culture is not aristocratic, and they do not favor the existence of those who, themselves without culture, make possible the culture of others. This almost socialist (to use an inexact term) characteristic of the council's idea of culture is certainly in a sense contemporary, because in former times such a program could not have been realized. Nevertheless, in the last analysis this tendency is determined by the Christian view of the human person as a creature and child of God destined for eternity. For precisely this reason every human being has the right, in principle, to share in the economic and cultural possessions of humankind. In the opinion of the council the poor have been promised the kingdom of heaven not in order that others, whether individuals or nations, should alone be and remain rich.

Mass culture is not ultimately a goal to be welcomed with enthusiasm. It is fundamentally a very sober program lacking the charm of many contrasts; indeed it may be regarded as "leveling down." But such a program is a demand of contemporary Christianity, while we are not going to prejudge the sociological justification of the mostly pejorative term "mass." The Christian faith decisively helps the individual to overcome the difficulties of the cultural situation of our time.

The council document says quite freely that it is impossible to guarantee food and peaceful existence to the immense and fast-growing population of our globe without more socialization, powerful international organizations, and public intervention in the economies of individual states as well as of humankind as a whole.

This greater socialization is not necessarily a good thing in itself, it is simply a necessity. It certainly involves also, though not only, new ties, very real dangers of the manipulation of the human being by others, new restrictions, growing technologically planned uniformity, an ever-increasing fragmentation of human work. All this is not necessarily compensated by greater freedom; but it is inevitably part of the guilt, which the individual ought not to have incurred, but which is now part of his life. Thus so-called progress will also ever increase or at least alter the burden of existence.

Faith can help to bear the burden which contemporary mass culture imposes on us. This does not mean that faith could be manipulated into becoming such a help. But if we unreservedly believe in God, accepting our responsibility to him and hoping in eternal life, this faith will also help us to bear the narrowness and boredom of our life, which has today become worse rather than better. This faith helps us to carry on, without despairing and trying to make up for the grayness of our present world by escaping into the idolatry of superficial pleasures. Sobriety and resigned acceptance of the inevitable are certainly virtues of the contemporary person and his humanism. But they either do not suffice without being founded on faith, or they are already filled unconsciously with what the Christian calls faith.

According to the council Christians have the duty to impregnate the structures of secular life with their eschatological hope (Dogmatic Constitution on the Church, no. 35, and the Pastoral Constitution on the Church in the Modern World, no. 38). This is an important statement about culture and the Christian's relation to it, for this "secular life" is actually identical with what we call culture.

Now this certainly does not mean that Christians could cause and help to establish their eschatological hope, which is the kingdom of God and ultimately God himself by their cultural activities. The fulfillment of this hope which God himself freely gives to human history is his own deed and grace. Yet, though the absolute future is not in human hands, precisely its hopeful expectation becomes the driving power in human cultural activities: the Christian hopes through creating culture and vice versa.

He fashions the future of the world by hoping for the absolute future. Or, to express it more cautiously: he ought to have this hope and thus also do cultural work. This includes a statement about an essential element of hope itself. This hope for eternity is realized in the constant transformation of the structures of secular life. Leaving aside the fact that "revolution" is a very vague and many-sided term, we might say:

Here Christian hope is declared to be the ground of an always revolutionary attitude of the Christian to the world. If Christianity be rightly understood and if Christians understand themselves correctly, things are exactly the opposite of what most Christians and non-Christians imagine: hope in the absolute future of God who is himself the eschatological salvation does not justify a fossilized conservatism which anxiously prefers the safe present to an unknown future; it is not a tranquilizing "opium for the people" in present sorrow; it is, on the contrary, the authoritative call to an ever-renewed, confident exodus from the present into the future, even in this world.

Indeed, the historical person does not realize even the ultimate transcendental structures of his nature in the abstract "interiority" of his own spirit, but in communication with the world and his surroundings. And true "practice" in radical opposition to theory is not the mere execution of something planned and hence merely theoretical, but opening oneself to and risking the unplanned, so that the true possibility of what is risked appears only in this practice.

True practice implies that the necessary and justifiable planning which manipulates the material world by technology, the human world by socialization and thus the human being himself, does not depreciate the insistent area of the unplanned. It does not reduce it to a defined residue merely waiting to be worked out. It rather increases the area in question and displays it more clearly as the result of praxis itself, since the human person, as he breaks down the unforeseen data, builds up his own unforeseeable product.

Hence in the practical risk of the unforeseen inner-worldly future the human being realizes his eschatological hope by looking away from himself to the absolute which is not in his power. It is therefore true that a person must impress his hope on the structures of the world. This, of course, does not mean precisely that certain permanent structures of his secular world could ever be the permanent objectification of his eschatological hope.

On the contrary. Every structure of secular life both present and to come is called into question by hope, because this is the anticipation of what is not in our power, and the historical and social act of hope is realized in this calling into question, though not entirely. For the Christian also accepts the passing away of the "form of this world" in his individual life, in death and the renunciation that anticipates death, and realizes his hope even in them.

This is anything but wild revolt. For the spirit of revolt either elevates the immediate future of the world into an absolute and thus is the opposite of hope, namely, a form of pride, or else it does not hope for anything, but denies everything because it is not permanent, and thus is despair. But constant criticism also of the secular structures is one of the forms of Christian hope. For it does not hold on to anything in this life as if without it the person would fall into an absolute void; and at the moment when he is becoming more clearly than before the master of his world it orders him not only to let go what is taken away from him, but also actively to surrender what, in view of the infinite future of hope, he realizes to be transitory and thus replaceable even in time.

It is strange that we Christians who must take the radical risk of hope in an absolute future should have acquired the reputation, among others as well as among ourselves, that our principal virtue is the will to preserve the existing order. In fact, however, Christians as the pilgrim people of God have been given the absolute command to hope, and this includes that they must always abandon also fossilized social structures.

Theoretical faith simply cannot deduce how the Christian is to realize this hope through the ever-renewed leaving behind of all things and how the Christian is to hold fast, because this hope also unmasks specious temporal futures, which give only the appearance of being the absolute future. This concrete imperative is not the result of the applied theory of the faith, just as little as faith as such changes the general promise into a special one which is grasped only by primeval hope. But this hope commands individual Christians as well as Christendom to risk these ever new decisions between the defense of the present and the exodus into the unforeseeable future.

And hope can do this, for it has already done the greater thing. Through it the human person has abandoned himself into the eternal absolute over which he has no power. And in the power of this greater hope he also possesses the lesser hope, which is the courage to change the secular structures of his life, as the council says. The greater hope is realized in the lesser, and eternal life in the creation of ever new forms of culture.

158 • A Prayer to the Lord Who Is Present*

Lord Jesus Christ, you are present here in this holy sacrament. But this is not the only way that you dwell among us. You also live within us. Ever since we were incorporated by baptism into your mystical body, which is the church, you live within us by your Holy Spirit. He has anointed us and sealed us. And so you are the life of our life, the life of our spirit, the life of our heart. In the strength and life-giving power of your Holy Spirit, who proceeds from the Father through you, you have taken hold of the most hidden depths of our soul, the innermost center of our being. You have transformed and glorified it; you have made it holy and divine.

It is no longer we who live, but you who live in us. We no longer belong to ourselves. We belong to you. You are the law of our life, the interior strength of our being and our actions, the hidden light of our spirit, the flame that burns in the depths of our heart, the holy splendor of our whole being. We have been transfigured by the eternal light of God himself.

You exist and live in us; you share your own being and life with us through your presence as uncreated grace; you give us the power through created grace to receive you and the one, trinitarian God, and thus to live your life, the life of God. For these reasons we are really and truly sons and daughters of your eternal Father. By the grace of your incomprehensible love, we are really your brothers and sisters, coheirs with you of the glory of your Father, that glory which the Father communicates to you as God in his eternal act of generation. He also bestows that glory on your human soul by grace, just as he bestows it on us. And so we are really filled with that eternal love which proceeds from you and from the Father as the person of the Holy Spirit.

You live in us so very much, O Jesus, that even your presence in the sacrament is only the means by which you declare, communicate, increase, and strengthen your presence in us by grace. Your presence in the sacrament will last only until the end of time, but your presence within us will remain forever. As soon as the veil of faith that hides it falls away, your presence will rise up from those depths of our heart which are hidden from us now, and will then become our eternal life.

But since you live within us, our life is subject to the law of your life, even down to what are seemingly the smallest details of our life in the

---

* *Watch and Pray with Me,* trans. William V. Dych, S.J. (New York: Herder and Herder, 1966), 25–31.

world. Our life is a continuation of your life. When we were baptized, a new chapter in your life began; our baptismal certificate is a page from the history of your life. So we must fashion ourselves after your image, you who are the firstborn of many brothers. We must even "put you on." Since you live within us, your image must become more and more manifest in us.

God's hidden grace in your human soul made your earthly life a pure expression and revelation of itself in the world of earthly phenomena. So too must this same grace — your grace — make our lives, all that we do and suffer, a revelation of grace, and thus make our earthly life conformed to your earthly and heavenly life. You wanted to live your life in every age, in every situation, among all peoples and generations. Since you could not do this within the narrow, created confines of your own earthly life, you take hold of our lives by your grace and by your Holy Spirit. He comes to us through your pierced heart to try to make our lives like yours. In this way, O Jesus, your life lives on in ever new forms and expressions always and everywhere until the end of time.

But if your life is to express itself anew in our lives by your grace and by your Holy Spirit, then this is true even of your suffering, of your blessed passion. For this is the decisive event in your life. In baptism we were baptized into your death, as the apostle says. Since we are the children of God, filled with your Spirit, and coheirs with you, we must suffer with you and thus win a share in your glory. The apostle says that we bear always your suffering in our body, so that your life might become manifest in our mortal flesh. Since you are the crucified, it is as the crucified that you must manifest yourself in us. You continue to suffer in the members of your mystical body until the end of time.

Not until the last tear has been shed, the last pain suffered, and the last death-agony endured will your suffering, O Jesus, really be finished. If your cross does not weigh also upon me, I cannot be your disciple. If your suffering does not become my portion also, I must admit that the spirit and the law of your earthly life are not dwelling and working in me. And then I would not belong to you. I would be far from you, who are my true and eternal life.

You want to continue your sufferings in me for my own salvation and that of the whole world, and for the glory of your Father. By my sufferings and agony, you want to fill up what is wanting in your sufferings for your body, which is the church. And so I shall receive in my life again and again a share in your agony in the Garden of Olives, a very small share, but nevertheless a real one. My "holy hours," those hours when I honor your agony in the Garden of Olives, will be made in the truest sense not during the peaceful hours of these pious devotions here in church.

My real "holy hours" are those hours when sufferings of body and soul come to overwhelm me. Those hours when God hands me the chalice of suffering. Those hours when I weep for my sins. Those hours when I call out to your Father, O Jesus, and do not seem to be heard. Those hours when faith becomes agonizingly difficult, hope seems to be giving way to despair, and love seems to have died in my heart. They are the real "holy hours" in my life, those hours when your grace working in my heart draws me mysteriously into your agony in the garden. When those hours come upon me, O Lord, have mercy on me.

When your agony in the Garden of Olives overshadows my life, stand at my side. Give me then the grace to realize that those holy hours of yours are a grace, that they are hours of your life, of your agony in the Garden of Olives. And let me understand at that moment that in the final analysis they come upon me not through blind chance, not through the wickedness of human beings, not through tragic fate. They come rather as the grace to share in your destiny, which was to suffer in the Garden of Olives.

Give me then the grace to say yes, yes to even the most bitter hours, yes to everything, for everything that happens in those hours, even what results from my own guilt, is the will of him who is eternal love. May he be blest forever. Give me in those hours the grace to pray, even if the heavens appear leaden and closed, even if the deathly silence of God falls upon me like a tomb, even if all the stars of my life flicker out, even if faith and love seem to have died in my heart, even if my lips stammer out words of prayer which ring as lies in my lifeless heart.

In those hours your grace is still within me, and may it transform the chilling despair that seeks to destroy my heart into an act of faith in the reality of your love. In those hours may the annihilating weakness of a soul in its death-agony, a soul with nothing left to cling to, become a cry to your Father in heaven. In those moments — let me say it while I kneel before you — let everything merge into and be embraced by your agony unto death in the Garden of Olives.

Have mercy on us, O Jesus, when the angel of our lives hands us the chalice as he handed it to you. Have mercy on us at that moment, but not by taking the chalice away from us. Anyone who belongs to you must drink it with you as you drank it. Rather, have mercy on us by being with us, not to make us feel strong during those hours, but that your strength might be victorious in our weakness.

Have mercy on us, we pray you. During your agony in the Garden of Olives you saw before you all who would ever suffer through such hours in the garden, and this sight gave comfort to your heart. Grant that we might belong to the number of those who were your consolation in that hour. This is the mercy that we ask of you.

HOPE IN GOD

159 • Utopia and Reality*

Do we Christians not say: There exists an infinite, absolute, eternal God, who is distinct from the world and for whom we are intended; the history of our freedom terminates inexorably in the very immediacy of this God, whom we hope to meet as our redeeming, forgiving, liberating judgment. At the same time, however, Christian faith does not overlook the fact that this God dwells in inaccessible light, that even in face-to-face vision, God remains for all eternity unfathomable in his nature and in the decisions of his freedom. That is precisely why Christian faith exhorts us to take seriously the world and our tasks in it, with all their humdrum, apparently ephemeral, trifles.

Our faith tells us that we are responsible before God for this world and our tasks in it, insofar as they depend on the freedom with which we are entrusted. As Paul says, this is the way we must work out our salvation in fear and trembling. For our innermost existence in freedom, as it is inexorably imposed upon us, God is not just a random, or even doubtful, factor at the edge of our existence, one we might discreetly and somewhat skeptically ignore. God is the reality that suffuses everything, orders everything, attracts everything toward himself and away from us. And precisely as this incomprehensible reality, God renders all other realities around us questionable, relative, and imbued with their own incomprehensibility.

Are we Christians not the people who call this utopia, which we cannot control either in thought or in action, God, whom we consider the true and genuine reality? Are we Christians not the people who consider heaven not only an additional boon that one might (and why not?) welcome at the end but as an integral part of our earthly reckoning and of our "real" life? Of course one should proclaim a gospel that loves the earth. Of course it is impossible to take the tasks of this earth, if correctly understood, seriously enough; of course one should praise the beauty of the earth, the greatness of humanity, the splendor of love.

But it remains true that the God for whom we are headed, for whom we exist, to whom we will have to render an account, is totally other, totally different from the "real" realities with which our experience is concerned. And this God may not be reduced to being the mere splendor with which we exalt our own reality, or try at least to render it

---

* *Theological Investigations XXII*, 30–31, 35–36.

somewhat more cheerful. As Christians we are deeply convinced that we exist for God. In his sovereign absolute majesty God is not just an additional item that must balance the budget of our life.

Only when we have decided to adore God in his absolute sovereignty, only when we even try to love God with a boldness that seems to be wholly beyond our power, only when in awed silence we capitulate before his incomprehensibility and welcome this capitulation of our knowledge and our life as the beginning of our deepest freedom and our eternal salvation, only then do we start to be Christians.

Are we then not the people of a holy utopia and not the people of a so-called realism? Are we not convinced that by thinking and living in this way we grasp genuine reality, whereas we consider and treat what we call reality as merely a stage, something provisional, even something that is secretly already suffused with and saved by the so-called utopia.

And so the theme of Christian existence between utopia and reality confronts us with the inexorable question: Are we successful in our attempts to consider and to treat as the genuine reality, a remote utopia which seems at first very unreal, very difficult to measure and hard to handle, compared to which the obvious solid reality becomes unreal? Do we Christians have the courage to reverse the standards with which we measure what we consider to be the real? Do we have the courage to feel that we are, as the Bible says, pilgrims and aliens in a world that at most allows one to speak of God only at the graveside or from the pulpit, and that finds it embarrassing to talk about God anywhere else?

Is all of this too weighty for the idealist, too utopian for the realist? Are God and faith in eternal life part of our everyday life, or is this reality only an object of pious devotion on Sundays, whereas our everyday morality does not really differ from that of an atheist? Let there be no doubt about it: The "between" of the duality "utopia and reality" truly means that we must turn upside down the standards with which we judge reality and that the appeal of the so-called utopia should be for us the most solid reality.

For Christians, perplexity in life is, in the final analysis, nothing but the concrete dawning of the sacred mystery that we call God. Our perplexity should ultimately not astonish us. Wherever we can, we should get rid of it, try to clear it up. But even if we fight it bravely and resolutely, we will not overcome it. It lingers, it overpowers individuals in their lives. The only question is whether we take it as the unveiling of the basic absurdity of life *or* as the concrete dawning of the mystery that we accept as our saving, forgiving, fulfilling, and absolute future. This is ultimately the only alternative, from which we cannot run away.

However, an attitude that pretends to be a quiet hope of eternal life may in reality be the veil hiding a so-called realistic way of life that is satisfied in false moderation with the scanty happiness of the present life. And the passionate, seemingly desperate protest against the absurdity of our existence may be the way in which a fundamental hope may be realized, a hope that finds what it is looking for nowhere on earth, a hope for infinite fulfillment.

Although we may still hear the last echoes of a triumphant human-ism that claims to have reached the limits of its self-made fulfillment, today we are assailed by a feeling that we have lost our way, a feel-ing that all our beautiful ideals are quickly becoming threadbare. Dissonant voices urge us to do a thousand things at once; hope-lessness is spreading so inexorably that all ideals, old and new, all programs for the future, which still have a following, look pitiful and lack impact.

In this situation we Christians are not allowed to give up, we must continue to do what our times and everyday life expect from us. We do not even have the right to hope for an end to earthly progress in our history and society. We Christians know that ultimately we should not and cannot choose at our liking the time for the history of our salvation. That is why as human beings and as Christians we have no reason to pretend to be very cheerful nowadays. It seems to me that, if we are honest, we must say that we are living in a wintry season, wintry in both society and church.

Undoubtedly we always have good reasons to demand more from ourselves than we can actually accomplish. But we do not have to ask too much from ourselves, nor from politicians, nor from church leaders. We do not have to act as if, with a little more courage and good will, our individual and collective situation would be changed into one of sheer pleasure and joy. Demanding too much would show that we are putting our hope not in God, but in ourselves.

If the global situation that we are living through, which looks like a harsh winter, is imposed on us, then, having done what we are able with resignation and patience, we have the right to accept the situa-tion as the mysterious dawning of the eternal mystery of God, the end we can and must reach. Christians should not try to avoid failure, dis-appointment, and adversity by means of strange ideological nostrums that are for sale in society and in the church. They can, with faith, hope, and charity, accept these adversities as the nearing of the incompre-hensible God. The more frightful, the more hopeless everything looks, the more certain is God's arrival.

160 • Christian Pessimism*

Our existence is one of radical perplexity. We have neither the right nor the possibility to ignore this situation or to believe that we can abolish it in any dimension of our experience. I need not point out, or bemoan in detail, the daily experiences that make us perplexed.

In the beginning of scripture God tells us that we must rule over nature and her powers. When we do it we start misusing them. We invent all kinds of social systems, and every one of them turns without fail into an occasion of injustice and abuse of power. We claim that we are looking for peace among all peoples, and we get ready for war in order to find peace. The whole of human history is a perpetual swinging back and forth between individualism and collectivism, and humanity has never succeeded in discovering a permanent and universally acceptable compromise between these basic demands of human nature.

What matters here however is to understand that, for a Christian anthropology, this perplexity in human existence is not merely a transitory stage that, with patience and creative imagination, might eventually be removed from human existence. It is a permanent existential of humanity in history and, although it keeps assuming new forms, it can never be wholly overcome in history. This is an essential feature of a Christian pessimism. It does not matter here whether we explain this pessimism through the fact that we are creatures, and finite creatures at that, or through an appeal to original sin, or by making our ineradicable sinfulness an argument for pessimism.

Of course we cannot say that human finitude and historicity alone explain the fact that history cannot follow its course without friction and without blind alleys. Nor can this Christian pessimism be justified merely by the fact that it is impossible fully to harmonize all human knowledge with its many disparate sources, or to build a fully harmonious praxis on the basis of such disparate knowledge. We might also mention that we can never fully understand the meaning of suffering and death.

Yet in spite of all this, the Christian interpretation of human existence says that, within history, it is never possible wholly and definitively to overcome the riddles of human existence and history, which we experience so clearly and so painfully. Such a hope is excluded by the Christian conviction that we arrive at God's definitive realm only by passing through death, which itself is the ultimate and all-embracing enigma of human existence. It is true that Christian hope has the right

---

* *Theological Investigations XXII*, 156–62.

and the duty to project, in the empirical space of our human existence, an image and a promise of a definitive existence. But ultimately this is only the manner in which we practice *faith* in *the consummation* that God alone gives, that God's self is.

People are afraid of this pessimism. They do not accept it. They repress it. That is why it is the first task of Christian preaching to speak up for it. We used to say that the Christian message must convince people of their sinfulness, which they refuse to acknowledge. Undoubtedly this continues to be a task of Christianity and of the church. And today we may rightly emphasize it, because we are still to a great extent living in a period of euphoric belief in progress. That belief is still far from dead, although our recent experiences have led us to be more pessimistic about the human situation. But we take it for granted that better times lie ahead and that our precarious situation will be easy to correct. Preaching Christian pessimism is quite legitimate, because the Christian message is convinced that a great part of human suffering is caused by sin, so that, in the final analysis, to admit sin is the same as to admit suffering.

I wonder whether the church is sufficiently opposed to the repression of Christian pessimism. We were quite upset when the Nazis reproached Christianity for speaking of a "valley of tears." Although I took part in the elaboration of *Gaudium et Spes* at the council, I would not deny that its undertone is too euphoric in its evaluation of humanity and the human condition. What it says may be true, but it produces the overall impression that it is enough to observe its norms, and everything will more or less turn out well.

It does not insist enough on the fact that all human endeavors, with all their sagacity and goodwill, often end up in blind alleys; that in questions of morality, when we really face the whole of reality, we get lost in obscurities which no moral formula can wholly remove. In short, as scripture says, the world is in a bad way and it will stay that way, even if, as we are obliged to do, we fight against evil to the death. The council wishes to get rid of triumphalism, but some of it has lingered on. The idea that, if only the unbelieving world were to accept the living church and her message, it would find salvation and happiness, is subconsciously present and continues to be voiced frequently in declarations of the magisterium. That the church herself is a church of sinners, that even her true and salutary doctrines lead to riddles, that the church too, in the final analysis, does not know exactly, clearly, and convincingly how we should go about it, is not the most clearly voiced conviction of the living church.

In 2 Corinthians 4:8, Paul says: "We are afflicted in every way, but not crushed; perplexed, but not driven to despair." The apostle's two dialectically opposed expressions not only tell us that, even as Christians, we will never grow out of our perplexities in this world, that we must see them and bear them, but also that in spite of them we are "not driven to despair." It is true that as Christians we put our trust in God, and that we are freed and consoled in all our needs and fears by the Holy Spirit. It is for this reason that Christianity is the message of joy, courage, and unshakable confidence. All of this means that, as Christians, we have the sacred duty, for which we will be held accountable before God, to fight for this very history of ours joyfully, courageously, confidently. We also have the duty to bring about a foretaste of God's eternal reign through our solidarity, unselfishness, willingness to share, and love of peace.

Yet it seems to me that we have not yet mastered the problem of the two existentials put together by Paul. How can we be perplexed pessimists, how can we admit that we are lost in existence, how can we acknowledge that this situation is at present irremediable yet, in Paul's words, "not be driven to despair?" Do these two attitudes not cancel each other out? Are there only two possibilities open to Christians? Do Christians simply capitulate before the insuperable darkness of existence and honestly admit that they are capitulating? Or do they simply ignore their perplexity and become right away persons who have victoriously overcome the hopelessness of life? Is it possible for Christians neither simply to despair nor overlook in a false optimism the bitter hopelessness of their existence? It seems to me that it is not easy to answer these questions theoretically. Yet the questions and their answers are of the greatest importance for Christian life, even if they occur only in the more or less unconscious praxis of life, and even if the very question about this Christian perplexity falls under the law of this same perplexity. This situation makes it impossible to give clear answers to the questions.

The coexistence of these two existentials, which are not necessarily mutually exclusive, is evidently based on the fundamental difference between a knowledge that all persons can attain by their own powers and the knowledge that believers alone receive from God and God's grace. Because these two ways of knowing, and the truths known through each one of them, are incompatible, the two existentials may coexist in human life. Christians may feel the hopelessness of their existence, accept it without illusion, and, for these very reasons, be free, cheerful, and (in a certain sense) persons who have already arrived.

Christians, helped by God's grace, let themselves fall into the abyss of God's incomprehensibility and discover that this ultimate and permanent mystery of God's incomprehensibility is itself true fulfillment, freedom, and forgiving salvation. They experience their radical fall into the abyss of divinity as their deepest perplexity. They continue to experience this darkness, always more intensely and more bitterly, in a certain sense, until the dreadful absurdity of death. They see that this experience of darkness is confirmed by the fate of Jesus. At the same time, in a mysterious paradox, they feel that this very experience is sent to them by God and is the experience of the arrival of God near them. The perplexity and the fact that it is lifted by God's grace are not really two successive stages of human existence. God's grace does not totally remove the perplexity of existence. The lifting, the not driven to despair, accepted and filled with grace, is the real truth of the perplexity itself.

For if it is true that we shall one day see God as he is, immediately, face to face, and if he is seen there precisely *as* the ineffable, unfathomable mystery that can be accepted and endured only in love, that is, in a total yielding up of self, then fulfillment for Christians is the height of human perplexity. Compared to it, all our riddles, our ignorance, our disappointments are but forerunners and first installments of the perplexity that consists in losing ourselves entirely through love in the mystery that is God. In the bliss of accepting the infinite mystery, that is, in absolute perplexity, all our partial perplexities, bewilderments, and disappointments disappear. The reverse is also true. As we expect and accept this end of our existence, our present perplexities are not removed, but encompassed. We are liberated, because they no longer dominate us. They have become the occasion and the mediation of our welcoming of the unfathomable mystery, which gives itself to us and causes us to accept it in love.

While we are thus freed from every enslaving power and domination, the world remains what it is: the task, the challenge, the battlefield, with its victories and its defeats, as they succeed and overlap each other. We are unable to control them completely; we must accept them with their own perplexities. Within the ultimate freedom and even serenity of those for whom night and day, defeat and victory, are encompassed by the reality of God who is for us, nothing seems to have changed. We remain the "perplexed." And even the fact that we are more than saved and liberated "perplexed" remains mysteriously hidden from us (often or forever, I do not know). But even then the fact remains that our perplexity is redeemed.

161 • The Advent Person*

Christianity is faith in the future, in a blessed, infinite future, which is the unveiled presence of the infinite God as our eternal life. Of course there are people for whom this future is too distant and therefore faith in it appears to be too illusory. Nevertheless the true Christian looks toward the future and he is a genuine Christian only if he loves the future more than the present, if he does not misuse God and his eternal life in order to glorify and defend a present situation. For him the present is the provisional, something to be conquered, the transitory, not his lasting home. He lives on this infinite future in his criticism of the present.

If then the Christian's basic attitude is given a formal expression, it cannot be described as conservative. For he cannot regard heaven as a reward for conserving the present and at the same time consider the restlessness of time, the continual decay of every present moment, and calculated dissociation from earthly things as signs that the world and he himself are still really on the way, making these things the criterion as to whether he really wants to be on the way and whether he accepts the constant alternation of interior and exterior life as material for faith in the future still to come.

If, however, the Christian is a person of the future, by contrast with other people of the future, he is not a utopian. Of course Christians and, perhaps, the church too in the concrete have often been reactionary in recent centuries. Old ideas, old social orders, cultural forms, old positions in scholarship were defended as if Christianity stood or fell with them. People therefore fought against phases of the future which came nevertheless, had to come or at least could come, and which anyway were no worse than the times to which they had been accustomed and which they then defended as something that could not be abandoned. None of this can easily be excused.

This reactionary-conservative stance did, however, imply something more: the rejection of an intramundane utopianism. The Christian is awaiting the real future, the future that is the consummation of God's deed, of the coming of his kingdom, of his grace, not the mere fruit of intramundane history which the human being himself makes and controls. And therefore he cannot be a fanatic in pursuit of his own objectives in the world.

Once again, however, since the Christian was recruited too frequently from certain classes which sociologically are inevitably conservative, he was often lazy and easy-going, conservatively attached

---

Opportunities for Faith, 21–24.

to the existing order, because he knew as a Christian that tomorrow (as also today) sin, suffering and death, futility and decay will rule. Formerly he certainly assumed too quickly that he knew the limits of what was possible to human beings in this world and that the programs planned by others were the expression of impious pride; when he appealed to the unchangeable natural law, he too often confused its perpetual character with the time-conditioned form to which he was accustomed.

Even so, the Christian is less of a public danger than the non-Christian seeking an intramundane utopia. For the latter wants to experience the consummation of the redeeming future while he is still in this world: he must therefore force it to come, he must hate people who prevent this future, he is necessarily impatient, he cannot enjoy the present since for him it is nothing more than the raw material of the future; he is a fanatic for plans and programs and must sacrifice the present and its human beings to these.

The present has meaning for him only insofar as it contains creative possibilities for the future. A person who thinks and feels like this, who simply cannot find in a "contemplative" way what is permanent and meaningful in the present, who can value recreation only as a means of gathering strength for work and work itself merely as drudgery for the future, such a one is a utopian. The Christian as an individual of the divinely effected advent of the eternal future cannot support him in this, although both — Christian and utopian — are persons of the future.

Now this is odd. Faith in Advent is a better presupposition even for an intramundane future than the antifaith of the utopian who wants to produce the definitive future himself. There are many reasons for this. The human being of Advent really has an absolutely infinite future before him, which already exists, although it has not finally reached him: he calls it God. The person of Advent believes that no one escapes *this* future, even if he lived in the Stone Age or will not himself experience the end-stage of history, the absolutely classless society of communism.

The person of the advent of God is already aware of the future within the present: he calls it grace, love, and God's Holy Spirit. He has no need therefore to sacrifice the present to the future, but for the same reason he does not need to explain the present as the permanent, as the consummation never to be surpassed. He will see intramundane recessions as signs that we have no lasting home here and will welcome all the immense advances of the intramundane future — which certainly exist — as promise and test of the eternal future of God, which they will never overtake.

Someone who must not make the present or the early future into an absolute does not get attached to the present, since he does not feel that he is banished from paradise when he has to leave it; nor does he think that we necessarily have to solve economic problems with blood and tears in order to bring about that future already saturating everything here, of which no one any longer says what it really involves and why this involvement is supposed to be so blessed, although it still takes place in space and time, between birth and death.

The person of the advent of God then can meet the future with composure: he worships neither the gods of the present nor those of the future. He proceeds toward his future perhaps more slowly than the person of utopia. And why not? He cannot and will not spare his descendants the task also of becoming aware of the finiteness and the transitoriness of this earthly life and nevertheless bearing it and plucking from the tree of this present time the fruits of eternity, which is no longer time and is offered only to those who are willing to die.

It is not true then that advent-expectation of God's eternity is bound to make us lazy and rigidly conservative. In fact, only a person who believes in this advent of God can voluntarily leave this present behind; and he alone resolutely practices during his life the total renunciation of death. Someone who does not act in this way may call himself a Christian, but he is not really one. But why should someone who is so disposed, who is resigned to leaving all things, why should he find more pleasure in the present than in the future? Why should he stubbornly defend what he wants to forsake anyway, at the latest in voluntarily accepted death?

Only the person of the advent of God is down to earth. He knows that all the answers which human beings produce only raise new questions and that every new order carries within it the area of its own death, if only because it is finite and therefore has possibilities alongside it which it does not itself realize.

There are two churches in the world (their frontiers do not necessarily coincide with the frontiers of religion and those of the Iron Curtain): the church of God's advent and the church of the human person's utopia. Some, of course, who possess the membership card of the one party belong in their innermost attitude to the other. For in the church of the utopians there are people who love the person of today, and not only of tomorrow, and acknowledge in him an absolute significance; and in the advent church there are people who see the church mainly as the preacher of a "better world" here below.

162 • The Real Future*

In the attempts which contemporary theologians are making to describe how the future provides scope for the preaching of the Christian message, one factor which is somewhat lacking is any concrete evaluation of the "future" as a phenomenon. Perhaps a theologian should allow his hearers to feel more of the perplexity and embarrassment into which he falls as soon as this word is mentioned.

For what is it, this future? I suppose that faced with this question we should immediately emphasize that the future does not consist (or at least that it does not consist exclusively) of that which is foreseen in the concrete and which will actually be in existence by tomorrow, since our concrete plans for it are already laid and the means for accomplishing it are already to hand, so that all that we still need in order to bring it to reality is a little more time. Properly speaking, all this already belongs to our present.

One of the characteristics of futurity is that it is mysterious, that for the most part we are unaware of it — indeed that we actually suppress the awareness of it in ourselves. And the concrete future which has already been determined by us as depicted above, only partakes of the nature of true futurity to the extent that it is threatened by uncertainties: the question of whether our plans may not yet be thwarted by some alien factor or another, whether we shall not be prevented from experiencing tomorrow in the same way as we experience today by the factor of our death — for instance, through heart-failure.

Hence evolutionary ideas cannot be taken as a starting point either for our understanding of the future. For in that case it would in fact precisely be something which we already possessed in our designs and within our abilities, namely, that so-called natural order which simply represents a further actualization of possibilities which we already possess and of which, in principle, we are already aware, even though we need a little more time in order to bring them to reality: just a little more patience, it is already coming!

On this view there is a certain pride in our attitude, for we think that our relationship to the future is such that it is already present to us so long as the "reality" turns out as we have foreseen in our designs and estimates, whether of a theoretical or practical kind. On this showing the future reality is, properly speaking, formed and determined so as to fit in with the plan as it exists in the present. It serves only to confirm the presence of the all-penetrating spirit and the rightness of its calculations. The only interest it still possesses is that it serves as a proof

---

* *Theological Investigations X*, 235–41.

of the fact that we have not made any mistakes in our estimates or in our plans.

I cannot avoid the impression that in the attitudes of enthusiasm with which both Western theorists and Marxists view the future there is a constant temptation to confuse the real future with this "tomorrow which is already here today," and which is based on evolutionary or technical theory or on a combination of both; a temptation, therefore, to call this combination of plans plus time in the sense of being a pure formal and empty interval the "future," and thereby distorting the true relationship which human beings bear to the real future, and suppressing the real meaning of future altogether.

I have nothing against planning; nothing against that enthusiasm with which we greet the fact that ultimately speaking the human person is no longer merely subject to the play of external forces over which he has no control, but is, himself the manipulator; that the human being imposes his own existence no longer merely at the theoretical level but at the practical level as well, and that he possesses a futurology; that the human person already knows what he wants his future to be, and how he intends to ensure that it shall be this; that the human person can no longer be surprised; that he can calculate correctly and foresee; that he imposes his own will as formed by him today upon tomorrow and, on the basis of what actually is, knows what this same reality is destined to become tomorrow.

It is remarkable that all this is already an accomplished fact; that the human being, with his cunning, and yet tormented by the factor of blind chance, has actually managed to catch the approaching event as his prey in the meshes of his own will; managed already in the present to build those paths by which his children are destined to travel — though admittedly here there is one point precisely that still remains vexing, namely, that it is our children and not we ourselves who are to travel by these ways. Nevertheless at the same time we have become extremely well informed on our own account. Yet still even this is precisely not the future.

But in that case what is the future? Precisely that mysterious element in that which we are accustomed to call the future, and which, nevertheless we have deprived of its true nature and turned into a part of the present by anticipating it through our plans and the abilities we have acquired, though we certainly recognize the rights which belong to him who is farseeing and able. The future is that to which we ourselves cannot reach out, but which rather comes to us of itself — when it decides to — and with which we have to deal, strangely, precisely on *these* terms.

The future is that which does not evolve, that which is not planned, that which is not under our control. It is all this, and it is this precisely in its incomprehensibility and its infinitude. The future is that which silently lies in wait, and which, when it springs out upon us, rips up the nets of all our plans, the false "future" which we ourselves have constructed, so as to make that which we have planned or foreseen a present fact.

The true future is that which is uncontrollable, that which is, and which remains in control calmly and silently, incalculably and yet patiently giving *us* the time we need because it itself needs none, for it never comes too late. It is that which cannot be controlled or calculated, which again and again wells up and breaks through the most precise calculations of the future, makes room for them and yet at the same time always makes them provisional and doubtful of accomplishment.

It is that which cannot be calculated or controlled, and which has the effect (this is something of which we are convinced, however strange it may be) that in this human history to which we are subject we are never finished with working out the so-called future, and trying to draw it down into the present. It is that which cannot be controlled or calculated, and that in which we cannot intervene. It does not depend for its life on any power of ours, but rather has power of itself. It can of itself make its own impact in that which we experience — but precisely as future. In relation to it we are able to be that which we have to be in order for it to impose itself. But precisely in virtue of this very necessity it confines us to those limitations in virtue of which we ourselves are precisely *not* it, but of our very nature always have before us the element of the uncontrollable in it as the alien factor in our lives.

We cannot escape from the necessity of having to deal with the future precisely because it is not subject to our control. It can be suppressed and forgotten as the specter which makes fools of us, which the sensible person looks down upon; as our shadow which we cast before us (admittedly it may be asked why that which is sheer nothingness does not swallow up this shadow too and thereby free us from it). But even so this future is there: as the silent expanse, empty so far as we are concerned, within which alone we can trace out our narrow courses of life.

It is there as the mystery which we must always take into our calculations in raising those questions which we answer to ourselves. It is there as that which empowers us freely to exercise the power given to us, for this power of ours can only achieve that which we have determined within the sphere of that which we ourselves have precisely not achieved. For we would not be able to begin to achieve it at all unless it was already open to be achieved by us.

When we have made some moment of pleasure for ourselves, we can command it to stay with us, and it makes no difference whether it punishes us for this by remaining and "freezing," or whether it strikes us dead by departing from us. We are always guilty when we command it to remain. For of its nature it exists in order to die, in order that by its coming and its departure from us the future, with its incomprehensibility and uncontrollability, may be there and may manifest itself and conceal itself at the same time in all the instabilities of this present as constituted by that which we have decided for ourselves.

We have constantly to come to terms with the true future, even when we are embittered enough, ill-disposed enough, cynical enough or culpably naive enough to seek to achieve a state in which we are untroubled by it. Its silence becomes so loud that we believe we are deafened when death begins to impinge upon our awareness and our senses, when the glory of our past achievements is suddenly transformed before our eyes into the boundary beyond which we cannot pass, yet without our being able to forget that glory, and when that which we grasp at so greedily escapes from us once more by turning out to be that which is not, after all, what we seek in the depths of our being.

Now there is a certain attitude of trust which we may discover within ourselves — discover it not merely because it is there (whether accepted or denied) but because it is manifested in us as part and parcel of our conscious presentation of ourselves. This attitude of which I am speaking is one in which we trust that this incomprehensible and ineffable future is not merely that which was and which remains the eternal that preexists us, and which serves to show us the limitations to which we are subject, but is rather intended to be and to become the future precisely as *arriving* for us without ceasing thereby to be in itself the nameless mystery.

Now supposing that we did in fact have this attitude of trust, what in that case would properly speaking be taking place in this life? What would be taking place in this event in which the attitude of trust and the future itself, considered as arriving for us, neither could nor should any longer be distinguished from one another, but where there would be a self-commitment in trust (or trust would be ventured upon) as the still-unfolding event of this future precisely in its aspect of arriving, and in this sense as a hope in the future?

Apparently nothing. The world would continue to go on just as it would in any case. We would make plans and ourselves construct the future which would be the present of today and perhaps of tomorrow — but always as lost in the infinitude of the true future. But yet at the same time everything would be different. But before we raise the question of the reasons for this difference, this "would be" must be corrected. Perhaps it *is* different, not merely "would be" different.

For in fact, to put it at its lowest, it might be the case that we actually *have* this attitude of trust which consists in hope in the true sense; that we are actually making it real and effective, and that all that we still lack is the courage openly to declare that we have it. It would be perfectly possible for someone to be quite incapable of drawing any clear distinction between one who really has this attitude of trust and one who has not. It could even be the case that it is actually achieved, and yet that we can only become consciously aware of the fact that it has been achieved at that stage at which we no longer need to speak about it.

The achievement of trust in its fullness in this sense is especially apparent in death, where the individual himself is silent, and where it is not we but the truth that begins to speak. There where this trust is present and where our hope on behalf of ourselves and others also is of *this* kind, there that which is hoped for actually takes place even when this trust has not yet arrived at the stage of reflecting upon itself and being recognized for what it is.

We must no longer ask, therefore, what in fact "would be the case" *if* such a hope was attained. Rather, we already have this attitude of trust and hope, and with this attitude no longer ask what "would be the case." We have already long passed the stage of wishing to ask this question. The assumption involved here includes the supposition that with regard to this attitude of trust we are quite incapable of establishing any way of testing or comparing what is and what might be or perhaps is, in the case of a specific individual. Only with this proviso do we ask what would be or is if someone either has, or could have this trust, that the absolute future is that which is actually breaking in upon him.

What does it mean, therefore, for a person to have this trust in the absolute future considered as that which is radically breaking in upon his own life?

First, the world of the future that we construct for ourselves still remains. It would in fact not exist at all if there were no reference to the absolute future, whether this is present as that which is actually coming to meet us or as that which repels us. This absolute future is present as presiding over us in some way or other in that it is made over to us as the "material" of the future we construct with all its variations between good and bad fortune. The existence of this — as the presence of the future in the temporal sense — is to this extent precious and indispensable.

Admittedly from this aspect it must not be interpreted as a future which can be constructed merely in technical terms. It also includes invariably the event of the love which proceeds from the "thou" to the "thou," which constitutes, in a manner quite different from the future which can be constructed at the technical level, that which provides a foothold for the future which cannot be controlled.

But at the same time this absolute future gives the future which we construct for ourselves its place in the real and effective openness of true human history. There is no future which can be constructed, no plan which would not open outward and forward into that which has not been foreseen and which no system can provide for. Every humanism with a predetermined content is relative. It can become other than it is and contains no promise within itself of any abiding permanence.

The human being is never aware of himself as the being who is open to the mysterious and absolute future in such a way that he could devise any adequate plans for himself. All ideals which he formulates in the concrete remain, when their true nature is not misunderstood, bounded by the "ideal" of the question which is kept open. The one who exposes himself to the mystery of the absolute future is the one who knows least of all about himself and who defends this awareness of his nonawareness as the ultimate achievement of life and as the ultimate truth which is proper to himself.

There are, then, two attitudes to be considered here: first, the attitude in which we take with absolute seriousness the future which we can construct, considering this as the medium of the absolute future; second, the factor in this future which can be constructed which makes its contents relative and conditional.

It is this latter factor that distinguishes it from the future that is absolute. Now through both of these factors taken together, the person who has this trust calmly and quietly faces the vicissitudes of the future which can be constructed with an attitude of ultimate freedom, without falling into any kind of stoic apathy. He actively engages himself in his lot, taking this as his absolute duty, and endures with composure any correction which may be imposed upon him by that which is outside his own personal control. For this too is in its turn the onset of the future that is absolute, provided only it is accepted without reserve.

The true future, the ultimate which itself cannot be constructed, takes place quite simply. It comes to meet us. It is intended to be imparted to us as the incomprehensible mystery. We are those who precisely experience the impact of it as a lightning flash in the hope that our darkness may be the blinding effect of its very brilliance; that it is not striking us dead, but rather imparting to us a healing that is eternal. And if anyone supposes that he has no experience whatever of this, he must say that even so he does experience it and is not aware of it, provided only that he accepts his own life unconditionally.

But because he is immersed in human history, the human being can always keep watch to see whether he finds in his history anyone in relation to whom he can entertain this trust for him and so for himself also, in such a way that he attains to that attitude in all its purity in which he submits to the breaking in upon his own life of the absolute future. It is this precisely that is also a promise for us.

163 • The Christian Understanding of Death*

The primary factor to which the Christian understanding of death directs our attention is the universality of death. This first point seems platitudinous, and simply to reiterate a fact recognized by all as a matter of natural and common experience. However, there is more to it than this. The message of faith on this point is actually addressed, in the first instance to each one of us as *individuals* as a truth which expresses the ultimate significance of the existence of each one of us taken as a whole, a truth which we must accept and opt for as an act of our own personal freedom.

Viewed in this light this initial point is not so self-evident. Certainly we are aware that "one" has to die. But this is far from implying that "I" personally have really understood that *I* have to die, that I myself am already on the way to this death, that all my life through I am advancing inexorably and undeviatingly toward this moment of my death.

It is far from implying that I constantly take the recognition of this fact as my starting point in directing the course of my life, that I never suppress it and never act as though I myself were not already a dying person. But it is this that the message of faith concerning the universality of death is intended to convey to me first and foremost as the most basic truth of my personal life. And further, if this assertion of the universality of death were based, even from the Christian point of view, merely upon the fact that at the biological and physiological level all previous experience bears it out, then indeed it might be possible to regard it as a principle which has only been valid up to the present, but which can now be abrogated.

---

* *Theological Investigations VII*, 286–92.

On this view it would have the same degree of validity as the statement that "Many die of the pestilence," a statement which was indeed true formerly, but which is not so now. It might even be possible to imagine that one day medicine will actually find a way of doing away with the "unpleasantness" (as it has been called) of having to die on the grounds that, strictly speaking, biologists are unable to explain why a cell or a group of cells should not continue to survive indefinitely.

But in contrast to this the Christian assertion of the necessity of death has an absolute validity. This is because it is based not merely upon biological considerations, but on human nature as a whole. There is a factor in the human being, in his very nature and in the way in which he was originally fashioned, which makes it impossible for him ever to escape from or do away with the necessity of dying, that makes it absolutely certain that he will always die.

Death is not merely something that is "appropriate" to the human being in the sense that it is appropriate to a precious artifact not to be broken because to break it would be an outrage to its very nature and the purpose for which it was designed. On the contrary, the human person is subject to death as a necessity of his innermost nature. It is on deeper grounds than merely biological ones that human nature inherently and inexorably tends toward death as its inevitable goal.

The deepest and most ultimate reason for the connection with and orientation to death which is most intimately inherent in the human being, which makes him mortal and in virtue of this fact renders all persons now and forever subject to death in the truest sense, is the freedom of the spirit. It is this, ultimately speaking, that makes the person mortal, and mortality in the biological sense is only the manifestation and the realization in the concrete of this mortality, which has its origin and basis in the freedom with which the person is endowed as spiritual.

How then can this be the case? Freedom is not the power constantly to change one's course of action, but rather the power to decide that which is to be final and definitive in one's life, that which cannot be superseded or replaced, the power to bring into being from one's own resources that which must be, and must not pass away, the summons to a decision that is irrevocable. If freedom were capable of achieving only that which could subsequently be abolished by a further free decision, then freedom would be nothing more than power over that which is purely neutral and indecisive, that which is always open to subsequent revision, a miserable sort of freedom, condemned, as it were, to proceed in futile circles without any final resting place, ultimately meaningless.

If, therefore, the human being *is* personal freedom, then it follows that he is one who uses the resources of his own innermost nature to form himself by his own free act, for by the exercise of this freedom of his he can definitively determine the shape of his life as a whole, and decide what his ultimate end is to be, the ultimate realization of his own nature, beyond all possibility of revision.

Now the physical side of the human person's nature, in which he actively works out the shape of his life as person and brings it to its consummation, is so constituted that it sets him in the dimension of that which is constantly open to further development. It follows from this that while it can be the dimension in which freedom is exercised in becoming, it cannot be that in which the fullness of freedom is achieved, the dimension of that consummation to which freedom finally and definitively attains.

Freedom enters into the dimension of becoming and of openness to further development only in order to achieve its own consummation. To this extent it is exercised at this physical level of the person's being only in order to pass beyond it and transcend it, and so to attain to its definitive goal. The free individual is willing to accept the limitations of mortality only in order that the exercise of his freedom on this plane may enable him to attain to that true immortality which lies beyond, and which consists not in an unending evolution in time but in the achieved finality of eternity itself — in that, therefore, which is beyond time.

At its deepest level the exercise of free decision bears upon death itself. It must do so because, in order to arrive at its own final perfection it must will death as that which puts an end to the mere prolongation of temporal existence. It is only on the surface of our awareness that we shrink from death. At its deepest level this awareness of ours craves for that which is imperfect and incomplete in us to be brought to an end in order that it may be finally perfected. Indeed if anyone told us that our present state would last forever, we would regard this in itself as tantamount to being damned, for it would mean that every fleeting and transitory moment of our existence was ipso facto deprived of its true value, a value which consists in the fact that each of these moments provides us with the possibility of making a decision of final and permanent validity. For the outcome of the free act is always something which endures.

Of course Christianity recognizes a special kind of perfection to be attained through the exercise of freedom, one that goes beyond that which death brings, namely, that state of perfection in grace which the first man was offered the possibility of attaining in paradise. In this situation of primeval blessedness, too, the human person would not simply have enjoyed an indefinite prolongation of his earthly life; here too his freedom would have defined some state of final perfection which would have been achieved by some radical transformation of the physical side of his human nature as realized in the concrete.

But in paradise the physical side of the one who had attained to the state of paradisal perfection would have undergone an extremely radical change. It would have been raised to a state of glorification in which it was no longer subject to constant change and flux, unfolding itself in an unending series of transformations. At the same time, however, the primordial person would not have relinquished the physical side of his nature as we have to relinquish it now in order to achieve our own perfection. To that extent this necessity of death to which we are subject is a sign of the guilt in Adam of the whole race, a manifestation of the sinfulness of all.

But even this does not derogate from the fact that death precisely *as* that which perfects us and raises us above the continuous flow of time, as the incursion of that finality which is posited once and for all in freedom, is on a higher level than the mere process of becoming which we now call life. The one death which comes to all is natural and in harmony with our natures inasmuch as it is the birth of that finality aimed at in freedom which is the ultimate object of the human person's will at its most basic and fundamental.

Death is "unnatural" in its immediate effect upon the physical side, which is an essential part of human nature, inasmuch as in death this cannot at once be transformed and raised in glory to that state of final perfection for which the human being's life, taken as a single and continuous whole, is designed. Instead, at first this physical side of our nature simply falls away from us as something which we have to transcend and get beyond, and is relinquished as though it were of no permanent significance.

Thus from our consideration of the universality of death, inasmuch as this is an article of faith, we have been brought spontaneously and inevitably face to face with quite different and far deeper factors which are essentially inherent in death. Death is the breaking in of finality upon mere transience — that finality which is the concretization of freedom come to its maturity.

But when we make this assertion we intend it as the Christian answer both to the materialist teaching that at death the human being ceases totally to exist, and to the teaching of the transmigration of souls, which implicitly denies the unique and final value of this earthly life and its importance as providing the opportunity for absolute decision (in reality this latter doctrine recognizes only the miserable fate of being condemned to the eternal cycle of birth and death). But while all this is true as far as it goes, a further point must straight away be added to it: this act of freedom which ultimately determines what the human person's final state is to be comes to its fullness, as we have seen, in death. For that very reason it constitutes the absolute climax of the process of enfeeblement and deprivation of power in the person.

The freedom which is exercised on the physical plane is, in fact, that freedom by which the human being lays himself open to intervention from without, submits to control by another power or powers. The physical side of human nature constitutes the sphere in which the interplay takes place of action from within himself and passion as imposed from without. As a physical being endowed with freedom the human person has to take cognizance of the fact that he occupies an intermediary position. He is neither wholly self-directing nor wholly subject to control by another, but halfway between these two.

The mysterious interplay between action and passion in the exercise of human freedom appears above all in the fact that it is precisely at the very point at which the human being freely achieves his own perfection that he is, at the same time, most wholly subject to control by another. The ultimate act of freedom, in which he decides his own fate totally and irrevocably, is the act in which he either *willingly accepts or definitively rebels against* his own utter impotence, in which he is utterly subject to the control of a mystery which cannot be expressed — that mystery which we call God.

In death the person is totally withdrawn from himself. Every power, down to the last vestige of a possibility, of autonomously controlling his own destiny is taken away from him. Thus the exercise of his freedom taken as a whole is summed up at this point in one single decision: whether he yields everything up or whether everything is taken from him by force, whether he responds to this radical deprivation of all power by uttering his assent in faith and hope to the nameless mystery which we call God, or whether even at this point he seeks to cling to his own autonomy, protests against this fall into helplessness, and, because of his disbelief, supposes that he is falling into the abyss of nothingness when in reality he is falling into the unfathomable depths of God.

On the basis of this it is possible for us to realize that death can be either an act of faith or a mortal sin. In order rightly to understand this, we must consider (and perhaps it would have been clearer to make this point right from the first) that the actual act of dying does not necessarily occur at that point in time in the physical order at which doctors suppose it to take place, and at which it is considered to take place in the popular estimation when people speak of the final departure and of death as coming at the end of life. In reality we *are* dying all our lives through, right up to the final point in the process of dying. Every moment of life is a stage on the way to this final goal, a stage which already carries this end within itself and derives its significance from it, just as when one sees a shot fired one can already estimate, even as it is traveling, where the impact will fall.

Life, therefore, is in a true sense a process of dying, and what we are accustomed to call death is the final point in this lifelong process. Dying takes place throughout life itself, and death when it comes is only the ultimate and definitive completion of the process. Now this death in life or living death, as it may be called, can become one of two things: it can be made into an enduring act of faith in the fact that our lives and destinies are being directed and controlled by another and that this direction is right; the willing acceptance of our destiny, the ultimate act of self-commitment to that destiny, a renunciation which we make in anticipation of our final end because in the end we must renounce all things; also because we believe that it is only by this poverty entailed in freely accepting our own destiny that we can free ourselves for the hand of God in his unfathomable power and grace to dispose of us as he wills.

Alternatively this death in the midst of life can become an act of desperately clinging by sheer force to that which is destined to fall away from us, a protest, whether silent or expressed, against this death in life, the despair of one who is avid for life and who imagines that he has to sin and so to obtain his happiness by force. The death that is accomplished in life, therefore, must be really the act of that loving and trustful faith which gives a person courage to allow himself to be taken up by another. Otherwise it will become the mortal sin which consists in the pride of seeking one's own absolute autonomy, anxiety (*Angst*), and despair all in one.

Now in both modes of dying there are, whether we realize it or not, others who have gone before us. We are not the first to die, but are rather the successors of these, caught up in a struggle between life and death which takes place on a more comprehensive scale. Certainly each individual dies his "own death." Certainly each individual is unique in the inexorable solitude of his own death because each individual life, despite the opposite impression of a meaningless existence *en masse*, in which many — all too many — are involved, is unique and unrepeatable in its free moral decision.

But even though this death is personal and unique to the individual in this sense, still it is the death which has been ushered into this world of the embodied spirit (a death, therefore, which only the superficial will equate with the death of animals) by the rebellion of the first man. And at the same time it is the death which the Son of Man freely takes upon himself.

Our death is modeled upon the death of both of these. For it was precisely the death of Adam that the Son of Man willed to die in order to redeem this death. And because it is never possible for us to say of ourselves with complete certainty which exercise of life we commit ourselves to with the ultimate decision of our free will, we cannot ultimately know either whether it is possible for us to say which of the two deaths we are dying, the death of perdition or the death of Adam, which has been redeemed; in other words, whether the death of Christ imports life for us or judgment, whether it is the death of despair that we are dying or the death of faith. Both modes of dying are *concealed beneath the surface* in the everyday process of dying.

Death affects every aspect of our personal lives and being. It constitutes the transition between the sort of being that is becoming and the sort of being that is final completion, from the freedom which has been given up to the achieved finality which is at the same time the moment of radical enfeeblement. To the extent that we regard ourselves from the point of view of this world, to the extent that we are those who are quitting it and not those who are coming into it, to this extent we are, so to say, losing possession of ourselves. And for all these reasons we have no clear vision of what this definitive and final state of death will mean for us. In dying we strive to attain to the incomprehensible. It is not immediately clear in the here and now what the fruit of life which we are bringing to maturity will one day be worth.

But it is precisely because death is concealed from us in this sense that it is (to reiterate) the situation par excellence in which we can make the most radical and absolute option possible between faith and despair, between the death of Christ and the death of Adam. The dying person passes into a state of silence and solitude which engulfs everything in its own stillness. It is a state to which he has been drawing ever closer throughout his life, the situation in which he is faced with a question, an option to be taken, in which a decision is demanded of him, the situation either of the faith that redeems or of the despair that kills. The fact that death is concealed from us in this way makes it possible for us to choose either of these alternatives.

164 • The Intermediate State*

Theological propositions which concern the human being when his final destiny has been personally decided at his death and yet he has not been perfected in every aspect, because the world to which

---

* *Dictionary of Theology*, 247–48.

the dead person still belongs pursues its course, are said to deal with the "intermediate state." This obscure situation is usually explained by saying that as to his "soul" the dead person is "already" enjoying the beatific vision or is already in hell or purgatory and that he will undergo his resurrection "in the body" only "later."

These statements are correct. But we must also bear in mind that given the substantial unity of the human being, which takes ontological precedence over the pluralism of his constituent principles, a statement about the body is also one about the soul and vice versa; that the dead person can neither be thought of as wholly departed nor yet as subject to space and time in the same way as those still living.

Theological propositions about the intermediate state therefore themselves hover in an inescapable duality of affirmations about the one human being who can only be rightly described at any time as both a spiritual person and an earthly being. Consequently individual and cosmic eschatology, the eschatology of the soul and that of the body, can neither be divorced nor reduced, one to the other. The doctrine of the intermediate state is based on this fundamental anthropological situation.

165 • Judgment*

The words *krinein, judicare,* and "judge" say a lot all by themselves. *Krinein* means to be separate and also to decide; *judicare* means to reveal the true situation; "judge" means to put something in right order. "Judgment" has a terrifying ambiguity for us even though we are not actually being judged. We can well say that, "It is a terrible thing to fall into the hands of the living God," if a person tries to hide himself from God as Adam did in paradise.

However, if a person dies the death of Christ, then we can well apply to the judgment the words of Jesus: "He who hears my word and believes in him who sent me has eternal life and will not come to the judgment!" And everyone who dies with Christ can say: "Father, into your hands I commend my spirit."

This judgment will only bring to light that which is "known." It will only reveal what is in our hearts, what is already present in the very depths of our being — and is present in us in such a way that we really

---

* *Spiritual Exercises,* 91–92.

become aware of ourselves through it. Nevertheless, the judgment, looked at from a human point of view, will come *very suddenly.*

In Matthew 25:37ff. we find the words of Jesus in which he lets the just and then the unjust ask the eternal judge: "Lord, when did we see you hungry...?" If we do not water down these words of the Lord, then they say that the judgment will really bring out that which is hidden from us and that which we have hidden from ourselves in the past — and this will be so with regard to the simple deeds of our daily lives (cf. Gal 5:13ff.).

This judgment will show us these deeds as that which they have always been, even though we have tried to repress their truth with superficiality or downright bad will. It will also show us our deeds as that which remains present, as the eternal face of our human existence, as that which can never disappear and is gathered together here to form a unity, even though the actual deeds were performed at different times and in different places.

When we consider this judgment, we can say with St. Paul: "But if we judged ourselves truly, we should not be judged" (1 Cor 11:31). If we separated ourselves from the lie that tries to masquerade as our true nature, if we separated ourselves from our twisted characters and from the values that we have substituted for those that God made, if we separated ourselves from this wicked world and freed ourselves for God by the practice of indifference and of the "more" of Ignatius's "Principle and Foundation" (*Spiritual Exercises,* no. 15), then we would not be judged.

166 • Purgatory*

["Purgatory" is a] term that has come into use since the Middle Ages for that purifying growth of perfection ("after" death) in all the dimensions of the human being which according to the church's teaching exists (for the defined teaching of the church, see Denzinger, nos. 838, 856ff., 1304ff., 1580, 1820, 1867), to which a person who dies in justifying grace is subject insofar as the debt of "punishment" he has incurred has not necessarily been canceled when his sins were forgiven in justification, and this debt can be paid by "expiatory suffering."

As to the detailed structure of this process, especially its connection with any place, we have no information either from scripture (which

---

* *Dictionary of Theology,* 426–27.

tells us that it is holy and wholesome to pray for the dead, 2 Mc 12:42–45), or from a detailed definition of the magisterium, so that the word "purgatory" ought not to stand in the way of a better and more accurate term for that process, especially as it causes concern from the point of view of the teaching of religion.

The following consideration may help toward an understanding of the matter. Only one who is truly perfected can be capable of the beatific vision; but such a one will be so, even as an individual before the general consummation (perfection) of the world (Denzinger, nos. 1000f.). But the interior perfecting of the human being, who matures in genuinely creaturely time, is a temporal process and on account of the many levels of the structure of human nature cannot be thought to happen by some fiat which would accomplish everything at once.

Only by phases does the human person become, through all the levels of his nature, the "one" he already "is" — by central, fundamental, personal decision (faith, contrition, love) — and by death permanently and irrevocably remains. But the execution of this fundamental decision encounters a prepersonal resistance, at the many levels of a person's being, that has been built up by earlier faults and wrong decisions. The "experience" of this resistance is "suffering" and as such is a consequence of human sin.

On the other hand, since it is distinct from the fulfillment of freedom and the self-experience of the core of the human person, it is "external" punishment. Thus that process of integration whereby after death the totality of the human person is enlisted against the resistance arising from and built up by his own sin, is real penal suffering, but suffering radically supported by the grace accepted in the basic decision, and thus issues necessarily and without fail in the perfection of human being, that is, the ultimate vision of God.

167 • Eternal Damnation?*

The question of hell cannot be disposed of by embarrassed silence. In dealing with such obscure questions one must always expect that in an attempt to answer them, which in the end one undertakes for oneself and at one's own risk, mentalities, prejudices, and unanalyzed attitudes are at work which are the very opposite of obvious and yet are felt as obvious. On the other hand, it is of course equally obvious that religious

---

* *Our Christian Faith*, 119–22.

doctrines of previous times grew up and were propounded under a variety of conditions which can equally be subjected to examination.

With these preliminaries we may say that the doctrine of the possibility that a human history of freedom may finally fail cannot be eliminated from the Christian faith during this history of freedom. Everyone must say to himself or herself: "I can be lost and only through my own freedom." However, where this freedom does not exist or not to any meaningful extent there can be no question of a possibility of such a definitive failure. This failure is not a subsequent additional punishment imposed from outside by an angry God on the real desire of a human being for freedom, but the inner nature of this very definitive decision of freedom. Like the correct, saved decision of a human being's freedom which is hidden in God, the definitiveness of freedom's no to God cannot be envisaged as time extended infinitely forward; it is the eternal definitiveness in which freedom defines itself.

A priori, therefore, hell cannot be envisaged as a period of time in which new events are freely possible and therefore pardon from God can eventually be expected. Freedom to be definitively against God is naturally the sheerest absurdity that can be imagined.

Those who conclude from this that such a situation, if it is possible at all, must arise only very rarely need fear no church anathema as long as they do not really seriously deny the possibility of such loss in which the punishment of freely chosen evil is identical with that evil. Such persons ought simply to ask themselves whether this is not a premature optimism which does not really take seriously the appalling horror of free evil in the world. Could it be engaging in a speculative trick or one of the exonerating techniques of modern psychology that too completely eliminates evil from the world, propelling the practitioners of viciousness and their victims into a common heaven in a rather inelegant assortment?

Where hell is concerned, we have one of the most basic examples of the state of our knowledge as creatures. A number of propositions must be maintained simultaneously, without its being possible to sacrifice one to the others and without its being possible to see clearly how they could be reconciled. There is a holy and infinitely good God. There is a just God. There is freedom among creatures which cannot *not* be oriented to God. There is genuine freedom even in relation to this God, and therefore there is a possibility in true freedom that can finally refuse assent to this God. How these propositions can be positively reconciled, are reconciled, is clearly not given to human beings to understand within the process of this freedom. But therefore to claim the right to deny one of a number of propositions when their absolute irreconcilability cannot be proved will also not do. How in practice these paradoxes (not contradictions) will really be solved we do not know.

In spite of the previous exhortations to modesty and caution with regard to an "optimism" which presented itself as too natural, there is nothing to prevent a Christian's hoping (not knowing) that in practice the final fate of every human being, as a result of the exercise of his or her freedom by the power of God's grace, which dwarfs and also redeems all evil, will be such that hell will not in the end exist. Christians must have this hope (first for others and therefore also for themselves) if, within their histories of freedom, they seriously consider the opposite: final damnation. In having to consider this, Christians are doubtless doing something essential to Christian existence.

On the one hand no human beings may release themselves from the responsibility of freedom by pushing it off on to other causes outside themselves; on the other hand they may not regard this transferable individual responsibility as so autonomous that it cannot be seen as embraced by God's more powerful freedom and his mercy. Both of these together, though they cannot be transcended for us now in a higher synthesis, belong to Christian existence.

If we live in this sober hope, there is no need for us today to make any theoretical judgment about whether or to what extent the possibility of a human being's being finally lost really occurs. Certainly, in view of the cross of Christ, it is false and un-Christian to act as though hell was in fact the normal outcome of world history. Augustine was still able to think in that way. If it is impossible today, that is not in the end the result of our easy modern optimism; what has happened is that the consciousness of the church has slowly become aware that in the history of a human being's freedom God in the end has the last word and that this has taken place in the cross of Christ.

To be honest, we must also admit that the emphasis in the New Testament statements on eschatology do not simplify and invariably reflect what ought to be the main elements in such eschatological statements if they took their cue from the cross of Jesus, in which God's victorious mercy becomes visible and irreversible in its triumph over evil in the world. The New Testament also has a legitimate history of interpretation, as can be seen, not only in eschatology, but also in the case of many other ideas. We need have no qualms about reading the New Testament portrayal of the existence of a present or future hell as composed in the style of eschatological threatening discourses, the point of which is to illustrate the seriousness of the situation of human freedom here and now. They are not in their real content reports brought back by a visitor to the next world or the future. If these eschatological statements of the New Testament are properly read, they do not lose their seriousness and their ineradicable importance, but gain in credibility today.

Eschatological preaching today is certainly in danger of dying out; too little is said about eternity, about the way our history of freedom becomes final, or about God's judgment. But we cannot escape this danger by simply and solely repeating the old vivid eschatological threats of the scriptures or by acting (when preaching about the cross of Christ) as though it meant establishment of a mere possibility of salvation which exists as one possibility alongside the other of being damned.

However, God, acting in the world as a whole, does not merely leave the possibility of repentance and forgiveness in the realm of creaturely freedom, but in fact brings about this repentance (in and through human freedom) through the power of his love, then we have precisely what the preaching of the cross and resurrection of Jesus says. This is something totally different from the pale doctrine of the two ways facing human freedom, a doctrine which seems to have been the basic pattern of Christian preaching for many centuries now. The proclamation of the cross is the preaching of God's victory over our guilt in and through our responsible freedom, not the moralistic preaching that our freedom is faced with two possibilities of which we have to choose one.

168 • Eternity in Time*

When we look closely at this life of ours it is of its very nature not the sort of life in which the human being wants to go on *indefinitely* taking part in activities on this plane. Of its very nature it strives to reach a conclusion to its present mode of existence. Time becomes an illusion if it involves self-consciousness as with us and is incapable of attaining its fulfillment. If it were capable of being extended indefinitely it would become hell in the sense that it would be a meaningless void.

No moment would have any value because it would always be possible to postpone and put off everything endlessly to a future that was infinite and so never made actual. Nothing would ever be too late for us (there would always be enough), and on this hypothesis everything would fall into the void of absolute indifference, where it would have no value. When, therefore, someone departs this life nothing could be

---

* *Theological Investigations VII*, 160–64.

easier to understand (If he did not do so one would have to put him to death by force).

But when the dying person departs, cannot that element which is absolutely proper to him as person survive unchanged and elevated above the "space-time" dimension of the merely physical precisely because it was all along something more than the mere interplay of the "elements" of physics and biochemistry, because it was capable of love, faithfulness, and perhaps too sheer baseness and similar qualities; because while it *comes to be* in this dimension of space and time, nevertheless it does not achieve its final fulfillment *in* this dimension. (In other words, it no longer remains behind on that plane on which those who do actually remain behind do continue to exist.)

We should not understand the existence upon which we enter at death as a mere "continuation" of temporal existence in that peculiarly indefinite and limitless state in which it is always open to fresh content, and is therefore, strictly speaking, a mere empty void. If this is the sense in which we think of human existence, then death puts an end to it for the *whole* person. Anyone who thinks that the immortality of the soul means simply that it "goes on" in time beyond death, so that after death a new period of time opens up before it, will admittedly involve himself in difficulties which are insuperable both in the realm of ideas and in accounting for the real and objective achievement of the human being's true final state which does take place in death.

But let us consider the case of one who supposes that "with death everything is over." The arguments by which he justifies this position are that since the period allotted to an individual human being began at a specific point in time it must also end at a specific point, so that the total extent of the individual's existence really does not extend beyond his death. A further and final argument in justification of such a position might be as follows: Let us imagine time as evolving endlessly in its own course into an indefinite future, while its content undergoes an infinite series of permutations.

This would imply that anything old is constantly annulled. Now properly speaking, this is quite unrealizable in fact, and would be more terrible than any hell. Anyone who takes up this position is being led astray by the limitations of his own imagination as it bears upon our human experience of time, every bit as much as he who conceives of the human soul "lasting on."

In reality "eternity" is present *in* time and emerges from it, as it were, as a ripened fruit growing out of it. Eternity does not really emerge "after" the allotted span of human life; rather it completely removes the individual concerned from time, in that it itself becomes disengaged from *that* time, a limited span of which was allotted to the individual concerned in order that he might exercise freedom in working his way toward his final and definitive state.

Eternity is not a way of expressing pure time which lasts inconceivably long. Rather, it is the mode appropriate to that spirituality and freedom which is brought to its fullness in time, and for this reason eternity can only be understood on the basis of a right understanding of time. A time which does not, as it were, act as a starting point for the spirit and for freedom does not in any sense give birth to eternity. (Such, for instance, is the time proper to animals.)

The final and definitive state of a human being, therefore, is something that pertains to the dimension of spirituality and freedom in his mode of being, something that is achieved by the exercise of these attributes. As such, it transcends time, and must be detached from it in our minds. Yet because, almost in spite of ourselves, we do find ourselves envisaging it as an infinite prolongation of time, we do fall into intellectual embarrassments.

Just as with modern physics, we must learn to think in terms that are abstract and nonimaginative, and in this sense "demythologized." Then we shall be able to say: "Through death (not *after* it) the definitive fullness of human existence, achieved by the exercise of freedom in time, is *present* (not 'begins to take place')." What has come to be, what was formerly subject to temporal conditions, now *is*. It exists as something that has been freed from its former temporal limitations. And this state of liberation came about in virtue of the fact that the human being is spiritual and free, and in order that the elements of freedom and spirituality in the person might have final and definitive validity.

Is it not possible, therefore, that what we call our life is in fact simply the brief flash of a process by which something comes to be (in freedom and responsibility), which *is* — is in a definitive sense because it belongs to the dimension of things which "are" in this special sense (and which are not merely in a constant process of becoming)? And does it not follow from this that the process of becoming ceases when the state of being begins, and that the only reason why we do not notice this is that we ourselves are still involved in this process of becoming?

It is really quite impossible to confine reality to the level of those things the existence of which even the most stupid and superficial of human beings are neither able nor anxious to contest. It is quite certain that reality extends beyond this level. Just as scientific systems have been evolved in order to establish that, even in the sphere of the material world, the objectively real extends beyond the immediately observable to the human senses, so too there are experiences for the achievement of which, while no systems have been evolved, still a more highly developed spirituality is required.

And these experiences put us in touch with eternity in that dimension in which it is no longer conceived of as a further prolongation of time stretching away "on the other side of" our present lives, but is rooted rather in the time of freedom and responsibility as in the sphere proper to its own development, and from there emerges into life in its fullness, in which time is totally abolished.

Anyone who has had to make a morally right decision in a matter of life and death (involving love, faithfulness, sacrifice, and so forth), and has made it radically and without any ulterior inducements, so that he gains absolutely no advantage whatever from it except the intrinsic goodness which he has recognized as involved in the actual decision itself, has already experienced in this decision that dimension of eternity of which we are speaking here.

And when he goes on from this retrospectively to reflect upon the decision he has taken, and tries to translate this experience into theory, he may arrive at a false interpretation, even to the point of doubting or denying the reality of "eternal life," and in that case it is regrettable because it is false and, above all, because it entails the danger of enfeebling or totally calling in question moral decisions of this kind. But it does not for one moment alter the actual experience itself.

It is not necessary here to draw speculative distinctions among the factors involved in this experience, between those factors which belong to the spiritual and immortal nature of the human person, which even as a sinner he cannot evade, and what is to be ascribed to that grace or support which is bestowed by God in his eternity, and which for the Christian interpretation of existence attains its climax, its absolute validity, and its manifestation in Jesus Christ, in his criminal's death on the cross and in the victory which he won there.

But what are we to say of the individual who of his own resources chooses to doubt the validity of his own experience on the grounds that to him, so petty and abject as he is, it is not sufficiently clear, or on the grounds that, in that deep sense of mistrust concerning the very meaning of existence from which we sinners all suffer painfully because we are cowards, it seems to him "too good to be true?" Such a person as this must hold firm to human experience itself as found in the experience of him who has risen.

169 • Hope of Eternal Life*

The Christian has the hope of eternal life. Such a statement is easy to make. Not only because it is far from being all that clear whether the individual Christian in concrete practice really does hope, really does hope for this eternal life, or merely uses this hope which we assert to exist as a facade and an analgesic so as to conceal an ultimate despair, this being the real truth of that Christian's existence. It is not only that to a person who is critical of himself and on his guard against his own deep-rooted egoism the word "hope" all too easily comes to sound like some facile consolation, although in its true sense it implies the most radical exercise of the human spirit when subject to the most bitter pain, and even though hope is present only in him who first and foremost hopes on behalf of *others* — hopes in the responsibility he takes for them, hopes in that love for him whom we call God, and in the face of whom even authentic hope must in its turn forget its own nature.

Over and above this, and on a theological understanding, the word "hope" in relation to eternal life involves a great gnoseological obscurity. Its significance is very far from having been reflected on in a really adequate sense in the traditional standard theology of the seminaries. Willy-nilly the mental picture of hope which we entertain is such that that which is hoped for is something of which we already have a neutral knowledge even beforehand as in principle possible. From this the individual who entertains the hope then has to go on to a further stage because of specific difficulties in attaining the known object in the particular case envisaged, and actually *hope* for it.

But in this view of hope we are ipso facto failing to realize its true nature in a radically theological sense. We are confusing that which is hoped for, that which is only present at all in hope, with that which is planned, that which is undertaken as the outcome of neutral speculation, that which, under certain predetermined conditions and according to certain specific methods, we have to bring to reality in the concrete. On this showing we are no longer in any real position to speak of the "hope against all hope," of a hope such that it is only *within* it that that which is hoped for can be discerned at all, of a hope which constitutes the basic dimension of the Christian understanding of existence as such. Instead we have, right from the outset, missed the real theological nature of this hope, and degraded it to a more or less accurate calculation of chances which are entertained even by one who has no hope in the real sense in striving to achieve a still conceivable goal.

---

* *Theological Investigations XIII*, 176–84.

Theological hope, on the other hand — to speak in wholly general terms — is the free and trustful commitment of love to the "impossible," that is, to that which can no longer be constructed from materials already present to the individual himself and at his disposal. It is called the expectation of that which is absolute gift, the giver of which withdraws himself into an unnameable incomprehensibility and can only be encountered in himself by actively engaging in such hope. This is called building on that which is without foundation, self-commitment to that which is beyond one's power to control.

Christian hope never for one moment conceals or denies this character which it has. It freely exposes itself to the charge of being "irrational." It merely declares that it continuously discovers at the basis of existence that an offering is being made at this level of the power freely to commit oneself in such hope, even if it is possible to reject this offer or to suppose that one has rejected it. It says only, in an attitude that is "inoffensive" and at the same time one of ultimate decision, that it cannot forbid itself to conceive of the incomprehensible, because that incomprehensible is precisely and inescapably present in existence and Christian hope cannot see why it should not also be spoken of, seeing that in fact it is spoken of by the very ones who condemn such statements or obstinately persist in holding that such statements cannot have any meaning because we cannot represent the reality concerned to ourselves or have any *comprehensive* knowledge of it.

Christian hope does indeed hold that, in the words of Anselm of Canterbury, it can "rationally consider the irrational" (*rationabiliter irrationalia cogitare*), because the recognition of the incomprehensible itself constitutes in its turn a prerogative and a function of reason, which must be unprejudiced in its encounter with reality as it is in itself. Nevertheless this hope also constitutes its own light. It carries its own authentication within itself, and is not the mere outcome of a rational insight which — itself not involving hope — would on this theory generate and release hope.

On the contrary, it is a primordial exercise of human freedom which commits itself to the unity of that which it cannot synthesize by its own power, the unity which it no longer comprehends, and yet recognizes as valid. It commits itself to the unification of that which has been divided, a unification which cannot be achieved by ourselves in some higher unity which we ourselves perceive and possess as something that we recognize within ourselves. Hope is itself a unique and underived mode of knowledge in which the creative element and the element which accepts from without in an ultimate passivity constitute a paradoxical unity, because that which is hoped for is present to us only within the hope itself, and is otherwise not even present as really comprehensible.

At the same time it is also that which constitutes pure gift, and which is received as such.

We might go on to say much more about the nature of Christian hope in general. One point which should of course be emphasized is that the word "Christian" as applied to it is not intended to have an exclusive sense such that it could only be engaged in by the kind of individual who considers himself a Christian in an explicit sense and as a matter of Christian and social indoctrination from without. We might go on to develop the gnoseological significance of hope in more precise terms, its place in the sphere of practical reason which does not merely follow speculative reason as its simple outcome and as something to be achieved of the human being's freedom. We might go on to inquire the extent to which it belongs to a subject endowed with intellect and freedom as a matter of transcendental necessity or, over and above this, how far it is sustained (albeit unconsciously) by that which we call Christian grace, in which the goal, namely, God himself, sustains the movement even as it reaches out toward this selfsame goal. But these and many other matters cannot be treated of any further at the moment.

We shall shortly have to speak of death and the process of dying which actually leads to death. We shall have to say that it constitutes the one situation for this hope, and that in which it is at its most radical, or, to put it better, that it can constitute this. But before going on to explain this, we must first say something about death itself. It is precisely to the extent that in his death the Christian has to be he who hopes that it is both possible and necessary for him not to conceal from himself the comfortless absurdity of death. One day he will actually suffer it, and for this reason he should accord it its full significance in his theology of death too, as well as he can.

Precisely from the point of view of a Christian theology it would be a failure to recognize the reality of death if we sought to approach it from an attitude of anthropological dichotomy by supposing that death affects only the so-called human body, while the so-called soul, at least if it boldly resolves upon an attitude of stoic transcendence, will be able to view the fate of its former partner, called the body, unaffected and undismayed as from above.

Of course we do have to draw a distinction within the single individual between a number of different elements and dimensions. We must do this if we wish to avoid stupidly joining the *terribles simplicateurs* of anthropology. But however true this may be, still the human person is *one* in being and act, and death is something that affects the whole person.

At this point the human being in all that he is has arrived at a conclusion. It may be questioned whether this conclusion constitutes the consummation or the termination of him, but in any case in death he arrives at a radical conclusion, one which, on any showing, he cannot bring under his own power. Some may, in all calmness, describe this conclusion as absurd and an arch-contradiction. So it is, if only because we may in all calmness say that death is a contradiction to positive *and* to negative thinking. For the absolute conclusion as such provides neither thinking of a positive kind with any subject-matter, nor yet thinking of a negative kind, seeing that this latter is in all cases capable of operating only from the basis of a positive subject-matter, and its shift away from this is only partial.

Even as the object of thought, death is, in relation to the individual existence of each person, as incomprehensible as absolute nothingness in relationship to the sum total of reality. Death as a conclusion is the absolute powerlessness of the person, in which we certainly also become too powerless to conceive of death or of God. But the dying individual, who of his freedom possesses his own life, nevertheless inescapably confronts death with a demand that it must constitute the sum total of his life as an act of freedom in which the whole of life is gathered up.

For the very nature of freedom and its claim to the absolute dignity of responsibility and of love belonging to it cannot give its assent to a mere empty draining away of life. If there is anything that is of concern to a human being, it is death. And it is precisely this that radically repels him. We can say in all calmness that to think about death is as impossible as the thought *of* death, because, in contrast to all other objects of thought, whether possible or actual, one's own death (incidentally, just as God himself) is something that we cannot comprehend in our thoughts, bring under our power, and so manipulate, and hence one who, in his thinking, seeks always to bring that which he is thinking about under his control will be thwarted in the case of death.

It is, and remains, a fact that from all the points of view already mentioned and many more besides, death is the absurd arch-contradiction of existence. If it were not both possible and necessary for the Christian, too, to experience it as such, how could the Christian assert and recognize that death is the manifestation of sin, of that no to the absolute truth and love which dwell in God, which is at once free and overthrows freedom?

In this connection it must be said that we, presumably different in this from animals, cannot refrain from thinking about death, that we cannot "pigeonhole" the fact of death. That the opinion of Epicurus to the effect that death does not concern us so long as we are alive, and, when we are dead, cannot be of concern to anyone, simply does not correspond to the reality of human existence, because in fact this advice in itself, and in the very act of consigning death to oblivion, gives it a place in life and so betrays the impossibility of putting the advice into practice.

Death is not merely any kind of occurrence within our life, or coming at its conclusion. Rather, whether we suppress it or admit it, it is that in virtue of which we are continually discovering the nature of our own existence as finite and so mortal through that supreme apprehension in which we transcend everything assignable to categories within the space-time dimension. Among other factors, this one is of constant concern to us: the absurd arch-contradiction of our life. This is something more than a mere quality or attribute of death belonging to it to the extent that we seek to set ourselves apart from it as those who live. Rather it is something that we ourselves are.

We shall now attempt to show that this situation of death constitutes precisely the true and necessary situation of Christian hope. And the first point to emphasize is that the state of hopelessness or (in order to avoid unnecessary verbal conflicts) the radical inescapability of this situation of death constitutes precisely the prior condition which makes hope in the strictly theological sense possible. In other words, it is something which the Christian is least of all in a position to conceal from himself.

Hope, in contrast to foresight, with its function of planning and controlling, is possible from the outset only in a situation in which we really are radically at the end; where the possibility of acting for ourselves is really and finally closed to us; where we can find absolutely no further resources whatever within ourselves by which to achieve a higher synthesis between a state of radical powerlessness and the supreme exercise of freedom in death; where we become those who are utterly delivered up to forces from without; where even the possibility of a heroic attitude of faith or a stoic *apatheia,* or even a wild protest against the absurdity of existence, is withdrawn from us; where we are deprived of even the innermost and ultimate subjectivity of our existence in its absolute depths. This is the situation of Christian hope.

Of course it is open to us to object straightway at this point that if death constitutes the ultimate state of absolute and dreary powerlessness, while Christian hope must still be conceived of as an *activity* on the part of the human being, then there is no longer any place or any possibility of existence even for Christian hope. Certainly as a matter of sober logic we must assign Christian hope to a place during *life,* and, as far as it goes, in the process of *dying,* and not assign it to that point of absolute void which we have to understand death to be.

But if we have to do with death even in life, the question both can and must be posed of *what attitude* we are to take, can take, or ought to take, toward this absolute null point. And it is precisely here that the answer of Christianity comes: hope in eternal life — though admittedly in that sense which we have previously sought to give to the phrase eternal life in order to prevent misunderstandings of it.

Of course on a radical view of it this hope does view God and eternal life as one and the same, and the exercise of this hope does not draw upon a reason unthreatened by death or a knowledge of God already acquired from some other source such that from it an innocuous reduplication of the real Christian hope could easily be constructed. Real Christian hope, faced with death, hopes in fact precisely while recognizing to the full the powerlessness of the human being either in thinking or willing when confronted with the absurd arch-contradiction of existence.

And what it hopes for is a unity, a reconciliation of the contradictory elements, a meaning for existence, an eternal validity for love as freely entered into, an assent to absolute truth, so that all this that is hoped for is truly *hoped* for, that is, is neither to be manipulated by one's own autonomous thinking, nor controlled by one's own autonomous power. All is hope, even the act of thinking in one who can still only think about the meaning of death, and is no longer in a position to think "through" it comprehensively.

To hope for this, however, since it is and remains hope which cannot be authenticated from any other source, but only in itself, could not be simply an exercise of sheer arbitrary choice, as if someone might hope here and now to become emperor of China tomorrow. This hope draws its life from that finality, as from an element inherent in itself, one of which we have already spoken briefly, that finality with which the individual freely decides for himself what is to constitute the good that he aims at, his personal love, his radical responsibility beyond any considerations of reward.

The nature of this moral act is such that unless we are to deny the fact that it is demanded of us in an absolute sense, it cannot be regarded as radically transitory. It itself would surrender its absolute character if it were to recognize the death of itself as its appropriate end and as an element inherent in its own nature. In fact even one who feels death to be the radical and absurd arch-contradiction of existence does also concede this in principle. For what could prompt him to feel that death was so contradictory if in the act of dying *everything* were, of its very nature, to seek out the finality of finalities and to accept it as appropriate to itself.

It might be said that in the very moment in which someone does what is proper to himself, the act of greatness, the total commitment, the act of love or duty in the most radical sense, he should of course not think of this as sheer finality, and should not thereby himself destroy himself in an attitude of ultimate cynicism, the only alternative being that he should, despite all, perform the supreme act open to the person in an attitude of incomprehensible, indeed absurd, heroism in response to this absurd finality.

But if someone were to say this, then we should have to reply along these lines: in a moment of this kind of a free act of love, radical loyalty, and the like, there is one reason why the human being cannot think of the nothingness, in a temporal sense, inherent in this act that is proper to his own nature, namely, that it is *precisely* not subject to time. A further question might be what place there can still be for a protest against the absurdity of the nothingness of existence once we take up the following position: the moment we seek to be honest and truthful we have to accept this same nothingness as having a legitimate place in existence seeing that it is an intrinsic element in that which is proper to it.

On this showing we ought to identify ourselves with Paul and ask why the maxim "Let us eat and drink, for tomorrow we die" (1 Cor 15:32) is in that case so meaningless or unworthy, if after all it can be claimed to have the value of sober truth. And if in reply someone made the further rejoinder that it is, after all, precisely the greatness and glory of human existence to maintain this protest against absurdity in the midst and in view of the absurdity inherent in human existence itself, and to practice love without recompense, loyalty, and so on, then such heroism under protest of its very nature excludes at least this finality which renders all meaningless. And then we should have to ask why at least this which is most deeply proper to oneself, namely, our protest against the absurdity of being delivered over to death, cannot allow the truth to be borne in upon us as it really is. How too can it be that it is only the appearance of a definitive finality that we encounter, seeing that everything carries within itself from the outset the marks of that death which brings an end to all as the genuine truth?

All this should not be taken to mean that hope should be generated and built up through some factor which, in the last analysis, is exterior to itself. The very fact that this which is eternally valid is present in and with the absurdity of the experience of death is in itself enough to show that this is not what is meant. But hope is offered a choice. It *must* choose precisely because that which is valid in this sense on the one hand and death on the other cannot be reconciled on the basis of human nature itself.

And hope opts for that which is offered to it as the eternally valid in the midst of an existence in process of dying. It chooses the eternally valid, rejects death as the final and definitive factor, and gives the name of God to that power which is not its own, yet which removes, by reconciliation, the absurd arch-contradiction present in existence through death. This hope is exercised on behalf of all human beings, for all persons are loved in it and it is not confined merely to the hoping subject himself.

And hence the subject of this hope hopes too concerning his fellow human beings, who suppose that the only realistic interpretation they are able to come to about themselves is that they are the hopeless, that they too, beneath and beyond this supposed hopelessness, are the hope*ful*. How could hope think otherwise? In fact it experiences these fellow human beings as those who love and those who are radically loyal and selfless, and it refuses to interpret all this as a mere ideological facade in a world made up only of an egoistic and merciless struggle for existence, an existence which for all ends in the void of death.

But if hope discovers itself afresh in the love and loyalty which it encounters in others — because in this hope is brought to its fullness in its protest against the absurdity of a life that is dedicated to death — then it will be giving no offence and doing no injustice to him who supposes that he has, in a spirit of defiant honesty, to interpret existence in a sense that is hopeless. For why should it not be the case that for some individuals their concrete situation is such that the only way in which it is possible for them to achieve a radical acceptance of death in which nothing is veiled (and this, after all, is the condition of true Christian hope) is for them to abandon themselves to the darkness of death even though it brings them despair? Why should it not be the case that many who die can only cry aloud with the dying Jesus: "My God, why have you forsaken me?" and in the midst of this abandonment that other word rises up silently in their innermost depths: "Father, into your hands I commend my spirit"?

If even we Christians are in constant danger of using the words which, properly speaking, only Christian hope as such should pronounce, as a false consolation, which can never form any true basis for hope but represents an attempt to cover over the darkness and terror of death, why should it not be possible even for such as these to entertain Christian hope unwittingly in the very depths of their souls? The borderline between real and final despair on the one hand, and illusion with regard to death on the other, is difficult to draw. We could here adapt a saying of Jesus so as to run like this: With human beings it is impossible, but in the power of God it is possible to draw this borderline, so that the individual finds his strength neither in despair nor in the illusion of self-sufficiency, but rather, believing and loving in hope, commits himself to the incomprehensible mystery which comes to him and takes effect upon him in death. We call this mystery the God of hope (Rom 15:13).

170 • The Beatific Vision*

In scripture [the beatific vision may be understood to refer to] the perfection of the personal creature as a whole, more precisely, it is that direct and, so far as the creature is capable of it, perfect contemplation of himself (1 Cor 13:12; 1 Jn 3:2), which God gratuitously imparts to the pure of heart as beneficiaries of his promise (Mt 5:8). By this, scripture does not mean intellectual knowledge alone, but the experience of God's nearness and an absorption in his glory which is grounded in our possession of the Spirit and our conformity with Christ.

Theology declares that the vision of God is essential to the glory the human being has been promised, but in comparison with scripture, theology often unduly stresses the intellectual aspect. It is the defined teaching of the church that an intuitive vision of the divine essence independent of any created mediating species is granted the souls of those who have been perfected by death (and purgatory), even "before" the resurrection of the body (Denzinger, nos.1000ff., 1304ff., 1314ff.). The church has condemned (Denzinger, no. 895) the opinions that every rational nature is in itself blessed and that the soul does not need the light of glory in order to be capable of the beatific vision. It is indirectly defined that God remains incomprehensible even in the beatific vision (Denzinger, no. 3001).

Traditionally it is possible to conceive a temporal difference between the realization of a person in the spiritual and personal dimension, and fulfillment in the physical dimension, but ultimately it is inconclusive. Since scripture always intends the single complete fulfillment of a human being, the realization of human physicality should be included in the full notion of the beatific vision.

If it be asked what the nature and prerequisites of the beatific vision are, the reply will depend on certain fundamental conceptions of the nature of knowledge in general. The primal notion of knowledge is not

---

* *Dictionary of Theology*, 42–43.

an "intentional" reaching-out of the subject to an object, not "objectivity" in the sense that the knower emerges from his very self in order to fasten upon something else, but primarily the presence of the entity to itself, its inner clarity to and for itself because its being is of a certain grade, namely, immaterial; its state of being reflected upon itself. In this sense the beatific vision must perfectly actualize the human person's being: the highest fulfillment of his nature is a transparency to the absolute God himself.

Empirical knowledge of other things is based on an adequation of the subject's being to that of the object through the "species." It is an entitative reality both of the knower and the known, whereby the knower and the known truly become "a single thing." Knower and known are not made one by knowledge, but the knower knows the object because the two are entitatively one. The ontological prerequisite for the beatific vision is a "relationship" between the creature and God which is above all categories and does not depend on an intrinsic though accidental modification of the creature by God's creative power (because nothing finite and created can mediate the direct vision of God).

It involves a quasi-formal causality of God himself with respect to the created mind, with the result that in the beatific vision the reality of the mind as a knower is the being of God himself. This new "relationship" of God to the creature — which cannot be classified in the category of efficient causality, as a production of something external to the cause, but must rather be conceived as a formal causality, a taking up into the source — is a supernatural mystery in the strict sense. It is only in the intuitive beatific vision that God's utter incomprehensibility is contemplated in itself with all its radicality; there is the vision of that very infinity which alone makes God God and thereby the object of true beatitude.

We ought not to construe this formal divine causality acting upon the human mind too narrowly, as exclusively affecting the intellect; for according to scripture it is the human being's heart that sees God. That final grace which disposes the mind to receive the formal causality of God's being, theologians call the *lumen gloriae*, the light of glory: that created grace which is absolutely necessary for the beatific vision and the seed of which is already present in the person by grace, and can grow because created grace is capable of growth.

171 • Heaven*

Theology uses the term "heaven" in two senses that must be distinguished from each other.

1) As a figure of speech in the Old Testament and the New Testament heaven means the upper region above the earth, in accordance with the cosmography of the ancient world with its various levels, the uppermost of which is quite figuratively conceived as God's dwelling place. The Old Testament itself "demythologizes" this idea when it says that heaven and earth cannot contain God (1 Kgs 8:27; Jer 23:24). In later Judaism heaven is also pictured as the abode of those who are saved: paradise was in heaven, the "heavenly Jerusalem" will be there.

The New Testament likewise says metaphorically that Christians are to strive for the things that are "above" (Col 3:1); our true country is there (Phil 3:20; Heb 13:14). Heaven is also a circumlocution for the name of God; the "kingdom of heaven" therefore does not mean that the New Testament transfers God's eschatological kingdom to the next world, since that kingdom is characterized by a glorious transformation of all creation into a new heaven and a new earth.

2) In theology heaven can be a metaphor for the fullness of salvation enjoyed by those who are finally saved in God. Whether this heaven can be called a "place" depends on the manner in which matter is likewise finally saved in God; but apart from the fact (the resurrection of the flesh) nothing on the subject has been revealed. In no circumstances may this heaven be conceived as a place existing outside time "at" or "in" which one arrives.

This follows from the essentially christological structure of heaven: heaven based on Jesus Christ's conquest of death and exaltation (ascension), which are the preconditions for the ability of creatures to enter the life of God himself. This abiding of personal creatures in the presence of God essentially means the gathering of humankind into the definitive body of Jesus Christ, into the "whole Christ," to commune with God who is made (and remains) *man*. Hence it is that we shall "see one another again," that the human relationships of this world continue in heaven. This union of the human being with God and with his fellows means no loss or absorption of individuality; rather the closer the human person approaches to God the more his individuality is liberated and fortified.

This is clear from the language of theology, which defines the essential nature of heaven and beatitude in God as the beatific vision of God (thus the Thomists) or as utter personal love between God and his

---

* *Dictionary of Theology*, 204–5.

creature (thus the Scotists). Taken together, these two views show how beatitude can be differently conceived without ceasing to be beatitude: the individual who is finally saved by God's grace alone (which is what theology means by saying that the human being must necessarily be transformed by the "light of glory" in order to be capable of heaven) remains conditioned by what he has done and what he has become in history, and it is in this historical measure and "mold" that God wholly fills and loves him.

Although heaven is based on the entry of Jesus Christ into his glory, which is the abiding validity in God of his sacred humanity and the admission to this beatitude of those who have died after him, and at the same time inaugurates a new relation between the world and Jesus and those who dwell with him, yet it must be borne in mind that "heaven" is still growing, since salvation is only complete when everything is saved (the world, history, and human beings), so that salvation is only consummated in the consummation of all things in the parousia, the judgment, and the resurrection of the flesh.

172 • Resurrection of the Flesh*

And so when we Christians profess our belief in the "resurrection of the flesh," what then do we really mean by it? What is the least we mean by it?

"Flesh" means the whole human being in his proper embodied reality. "Resurrection" means, therefore, the termination and perfection of the *whole* person before God, which gives him "eternal life." The human person is a many-sided being which in (and despite) its unity stretches, as it were, through several very different dimensions — through matter and spirit, nature and person, action and passion, and so on. And so it is not surprising that the process of the person's perfecting and the entrance into this perfection is not in itself a simple and identical quantity in every respect. And it is not surprising that the "moment" of completion of such a stratified being is not simply the same for every one of these dimensions.

Hence, as the church's consciousness in faith has come to comprehend ever more clearly — instructed as it has been by the beginnings of such a comprehension in the scriptures — the continuing reality of the personal spirit can already reach the direct communion with God by

---

* *Theological Investigations II*, 210–16.

the event and moment which, looked at from its intramundane side, we experience as death. Insofar as this union with God constitutes the innermost being of blessed completion, "heaven" and "eternal happiness" can already be given with death (Denzinger, no. 530).

Nevertheless, the deceased remains "united" with the reality, fate and hence the temporal events of the world, however little we are able to "picture" to ourselves such a continuing belonging-to-the-world and however few immediately comprehensible statements on this matter are contained in the scriptures. We must simply try to realize clearly and soberly that a spiritual union with God cannot be regarded as something which grows in inverse proportion to the belonging to the *material* world, but that these are two quite disparate matters in themselves.

Thus basically, for instance, there can be vision of God before death, and "separation from the body" for the soul in death does not by a long way need to mean ipso facto a greater nearness to God. Remoteness-from-the-world and nearness-to-God are not interchangeable notions, however much we are accustomed to think in such a framework. The deceased remain therefore (despite the beatific vision) united with the fate of the world.

This world in its totality has a beginning and a history; it goes on toward a point which is not the end of its existence but the end of its unfinished and continually self-propagating history. It is true, we may not succeed in representing to ourselves concretely *how* it will be possible at some time to separate its continued existence in itself, on the one hand, and its transition into the unknown (to our prevision), on the other hand; it may be impossible to imagine how the former continues while the latter ceases. We may not be able to say what the then remaining world will be like (all attempts to picture this to oneself never get beyond the image).

And yet, for all that, this final state of the world as a whole, which will come at a certain point but has not come as yet, is more *conceivable* for us today than it was perhaps for earlier generations and especially for the ancients. For to them this world of their experience gave the impression of being something eternal; change and transitoriness was only a happening in the lowest stratum of all in this "eternal" world of "eternal" laws, which was enveloped by the quietly reposing serenity of celestial spheres; for them (even for the Christians), beatitude could, therefore, only mean leaving the sphere of the transitory for the blessed heavenly spheres intended for this "migration" in the framework of saving history; the history of salvation took place in the "heaven"-enveloped world, but was not the development itself of heaven.

We today are becoming more clearly aware of the developmental character of our world as a whole, in spite of the ultimate uncertainty of the natural sciences and the extremely profound problems of a "harmonization" of theological data and our natural knowledge of the world. We have come to realize the senselessness of trying to retrace the existence of the world into the infinite; the world itself, practically down to the last detail — and not merely the revolutions of its stars — is temporal.

If we allow the "becoming," time and history to be really temporal and do not in the end turn them again into a false eternity, then we may say (very carefully): it does not contradict the nature of the world that this open, self-propagating history has a beginning and an end. Who can say how far this end is the very "running-itself-to-death" of the course of the world itself (which is happening in accordance with its eternal laws), how far a halt is called by the creative and restraining word of God, how far both of these things ultimately come to the same thing!

We know at any rate from the testimony of God that this history of the world will come to an end, and that this end will not be a sheer cessation, a "being-no-longer" of the world itself, but the participation in the perfection of the spirit. For this spirit is assigned a beginning, but in relation to God. And hence its beginning is not the beginning of the end, but the beginning of a development in freedom toward freely achieved completion, which does not let the becoming end up in nothingness, but transforms it into the state of finality.

Furthermore, the deepest conviction of Christianity and of idealism is true: the personal spirit is the meaning of the whole reality of the world and, in spite of all its biological-physical insignificance, it is *not merely* a strange guest in a world which, standing ultimately untouched and indifferent opposite this spirit, carries on its own history; the personal spirit, precisely as human spirit, is a material, mundane, incarnate — indeed *intra*-mundane spirit. And so the end of the world is participation in the perfection of the spirit: the world remains, beyond its previous history, as the connatural surrounding of the achieved spirit which has found its finality in fellowship with God and achieves its own history and that of the world at the same point.

If this is so, however, it is necessary to consider what exact form this history of spiritual persons has taken and is taking: it is a history which, as the history of humankind, has taken place (consciously or veiled to itself) with, for and against the person of the one who — right through death and resurrection — possessed the life of God and the history of a human reality at one and the same time: Jesus Christ, our Lord.

The end of the world is, therefore, the perfection and total achievement of saving history which had already come into full operation and gained its decisive victory in Jesus Christ and in his resurrection. In this sense his coming takes place at this consummation in power and glory: his victory made manifest, the breaking through into experience, and the becoming manifest for experience too, of the fact that the world as a whole flows into his resurrection and into the transfiguration of his body.

His second coming is not an event which is enacted in a localized manner on the stage of an *un*-changed world which occupies a determined point in space in this world of our experience (how could everyone see it otherwise, for instance?); his second coming takes place at the moment of the perfecting of the world into the reality which he already possesses now, in such a way that he, the Godman, will be revealed to all reality and, within it, to every one of its parts in its own way, as the innermost secret and center of all the world and of all history.

This is the context into which we must fit what we call the resurrection of the flesh in the strict sense. The history — which has remained within the framework of the world — of those who by their lives have already effected their personal finality, reaches its real completion and explicit expression together with the consummation of the world. These human beings now become achieved as totalities with soul and body, and their perfection, already begun in death, becomes itself perfected, tangible in the world, embodied. We cannot really imagine the "how" of this bodily consummation. But we can say in our faith together with God's revelation: I believe that we will one day be the living, the complete and achieved ones, in the whole expanse and in all the dimensions of our existence; I believe that what we call the material in us and in the world surrounding us (without really being able to say what it is basically, what belongs to its essence and what only to its temporary form and appearance) is not simply identical with what is unreal and mere appearance, with what has been cast off once and for all and which passes away before the final state of the human being.

If, however, the material world is not simply an objective illusion, and is not merely some sort of material which must be taken off and on, which the history of souls gets practice in freedom until it has achieved its end, but is a part of the true reality itself, then the material world does for that very reason enter into the consummation in accordance with the divine promise, and it too can participate in the state of finality and completion.

When we look at the risen Christ, taking into consideration the experience the apostles had with him, we may also get some idea of what the perfected condition of the body is like in which the created spirit achieves itself. Only, in doing this, we must not forget that what the apostles, being themselves as yet unachieved, were able to experience of this consummation, is a somewhat broken, translated experience, and that even then it still remains obscure how the perfected appears to the perfected. In the last analysis, therefore, we can merely say in St. Paul's language of paradox: it will be a spiritual body (1 Cor 15:44), that is, a true bodily nature which, however, is pure expression of the spirit become one with God's Spirit and its bodily existence, and is no longer its restricting and abasing element and its emptiness. It will be a bodily nature which does not cancel again the freedom from the earthly here-and-now gained with death, but will, on the contrary, bring it out in its pure form.

If (and insofar as) we cannot think of the physical nature and concreteness of the risen and real person (even in accordance with what was experienced with regard to the risen Christ) in any other way than together with a definite spatial and local determination, then we must think of heaven as a place and not merely as a "state." Insofar as there are already human beings (the risen Lord, our Lady, and no doubt others: cf. Mt 27:52) who possess a glorified bodily nature, *this* place does already exist as a result, even if not as the presupposition (as the ancients thought), of this transformation of the incarnate human spirit.

When we remember the intrinsic finiteness of our own physical spatiality, which is not a presupposition but an inner moment of nonglorified matter and the result of its history, we will not find it impossible to conceive (not: "to imagine") that this spatiality and the heavenly "kind of space" are in themselves essentially different and incommensurable quantities.

This, however, means then that, on the one hand, it is a priori senseless to ask where heaven is (if by this "where" we are to understand a location in *our* physical-spatial world), and that, on the other hand, it remains nevertheless possible to hold fast most "realistically" to the conception of the bodily existence of the glorified, including their spatial determination and location. We do not need to accommodate those in heaven in the physical world system of our experience. Since we are, however, learning in physics nowadays more than ever to think abstractly, there will be less of an obstacle in this than before to our taking the existence of those in heaven very seriously in a nonpictorial way. Once the history of the cosmos and of the spiritual world has come to its complete end, everything will be transformed. It will then be equally correct to call the one new reality a new heaven or a new earth.

The complete, all-embracing solution is always the most difficult, because it must reconcile everything. It is most difficult for such a solution to penetrate the narrow limits of our mind which demand concise and synoptical solutions. And so it is also with regard to the question about the end. Anyone who disposes of the earthly world and dismisses the perfected human being from this earth for good, spiritualistically or existentially or in whatever other way, directing him into a beatitude of (supposedly) pure spirits, stultifies and betrays the true reality of the human person, the child of this earth.

Whoever lets the human being perish, ground to pieces in the cruel mill of nature, does not know what spirit and person are, and does not know how much more real, in spite of all their apparent weakness, the spirit and the person are than all the matter and energy of physics. Whoever does not believe that both of them, once reconciled, can come to the one completion, denies in the last analysis that the one God has created spirit and matter in one act for one end.

The Christian, however, is the one with the complete solution. This solution is the most difficult, the least synoptical. The belief for this solution and the courage for such a solution he draws from the word of God alone. But God's word testifies to the resurrection of the flesh. For the Word himself became flesh. He did not assume something unreal but something created. But whatever is created by God is never something merely negative, is never the veil of maya. Whatever has been created by God, assumed by Christ and transfigured by his death and resurrection, is also destined to finality and consummation in us.

173 • Christian Optimism*

[How do I see the future of the world, the church, my own life?] Let me begin with my own future. It boils down more or less to the hope of a "noble peace," as a Protestant hymn says, for yet a few more years. It is a hope that can deceive. But then, even beyond all these earthly possibilities, hopes, and the like that I possess with a certain trembling and uneasiness, I have the hope of the absolute future, God himself. I would say that beyond all possible material, biological, or even humanly attainable spiritual evolution, I have the hope of eternal life.

I have this hope, even if I cannot actually imagine what eternal life will really be like. I know through the good news of the Christian message and I know from Jesus Christ that the absolute, everlasting, holy, eternally good God has promised himself to me as my future. And because of that, I have a good hope, an unconditional hope that is still

_____
*I Remember: An Autobiographical Interview, trans. Harvey D. Egan, S.J. (New York: Crossroad Publishing Company, 1985), 110–11.

subject to temptation as long as I am here on earth and have negative experiences with life, with society, with people, and so on. That is self-evident. But until death's door I'll hold doggedly fast, if I may say so, to the belief that there is an eternal light that will illumine me.

And I hold the same for the earthly future of one's own people or of the world as a whole. I'm all for the courageous struggle for a better economy, for a better social future, and I believe that the person who is really convinced of this must take responsibility for this social obligation before the judgment seat of God. When all is said and done, believers cannot and must not allow people who do not believe in this absolute future to get the better of them.

I would say that if the world is destroyed by atomic weapons or slips further and further into economic misery, that would be all too horrible and frightful. And everyone is obliged before God's eternal judgment to do everything in his or her power to prevent such things from occurring. One day we must give a reckoning for this. But if a people or even humanity were to fall into the abyss, then I would still be firmly convinced — and I hope to keep this conviction — that even such an abyss always ultimately ends in the arms of an eternally good, eternally powerful God.

174 • Prayer for Hope*

We ask you, God of grace and eternal life, to increase and strengthen hope in us. Give us this virtue of the strong, this power of the confident, this courage of the unshakable. Make us always have a longing for you, the infinite plenitude of being. Make us always build on you and your fidelity, always hold fast without despondency to your might. Make us to be of this mind and produce this attitude in us by your Holy Spirit. Then, our Lord and God, we shall have the virtue of hope. Then we can courageously set about the task of our life again and again. Then we shall be animated by the joyful confidence that we are not working in vain. Then we shall do our work in the knowledge that in us and through us and, where our powers fail, without us, you the almighty according to your good pleasure are working to your honor and our salvation. Strengthen your hope in us.

The hope of eternity, however, eternal God, is your only-begotten Son. He possesses your infinite nature from eternity to eternity, because

---

* *Everyday Faith*, 207–11.

you have communicated it to him and ever communicate it, in eternal generation. He therefore possesses all that we hope and desire. He is wisdom and power, beauty and goodness, life and glory, he is all in all. And he, this Son to whom you have given all, has become ours. He became man. Your eternal Word, God of glory, became man, became like one of us, humbled himself and took human form, a human body, a human soul, a human life, a human lot even in its most terrible possibilities. Your Son, heavenly Father, truly became man.

We kneel in adoration. For who can measure this incomprehensible love of yours? You have loved the world so much that people take offense at your love and call the affirmation of the incarnation of your Son folly and madness. But we believe in the incomprehensibility, the overwhelming audacity of your love. And because we believe, we can exult in blessed hope: Christ in us is the hope of glory. For if you give us your Son, what can there be you have held back, what can there be which you have refused us? If we possess your Son to whom you have given everything, your own substance, what could still be lacking to us? And he is truly ours.

For he is the son of Mary, who is our sister in Adam, he is a child of Adam's family, of the same race as we are, one in substance and origin with man. And if we human beings in your plans and according to your will as creator are all to form a great community of descent and destiny, and if your Son is to belong to this one great community, then we, precisely we poor children of Eve, share the race and lot of your own Son. We are brothers and sisters of the only-begotten, the brethren of your Son, coheirs of his glory. We share in his grace, in his Spirit, in his life, in his destiny through cross and glorification, in his eternal glory.

It is no longer *we* who live our life but Christ our brother lives his life in us and through us. We are ready, Father of Jesus Christ and our Father, to share in the life of your Son. Dispose of our life, make it conformable to the life of your Son. He wills to continue his own life in us until the end of time, he wills to reveal in us and in our life the glory, the greatness, beauty and the blessed power of his life. What meets us in life is not chance, is not blind fate but is a part of the life of your Son. The joy we shall receive as Christ's joy, success as his success, pain as his pain, sorrow as his sorrow, work as his work, death as a sharing in his death.

In one respect we ask especially for your grace. Make us share in Jesus' prayer. He is the great worshiper of God in spirit and in truth, he is the mediator through whom alone our prayer can reach to the throne of grace. We wish to pray in him, united with his prayer. May he, with whom we are united in his Spirit, teach us to pray. May he teach us to pray as he himself prayed, to pray at all times and not to slacken, to pray perseveringly, confidently, humbly, in spirit and in truth, with true love of our neighbor without which no prayer is pleasing to you. May he teach us to pray for what he prayed: that your name may be hallowed, your will be done, your kingdom come to us, for only if we first pray in that way for your honor will you also hear us if we pray for ourselves, our earthly well-being and earthly cares. Give us the spirit of prayer, of recollection, of union with God.

Lord accept my poor heart. It is often so far from you. It is like a waste land without water, lost in the innumerable things and trifles that fill my everyday life. Only you, Lord, can focus my heart on you, who are the center of all hearts and the Lord of every soul. Only you can give the spirit of prayer, only your grace is capable of granting me to find you through the multiplicity of things and the distraction of mind of everyday routine, you the one thing necessary, the one thing in which my heart can rest.

May your Spirit come to the help of my weakness, and when we do not know what we should ask, may he intercede for us with inexpressible sighs, and you who know the hearts of human beings will hear what your Spirit interceding for us desires in us.

Finally, however, I ask you for the hardest and most difficult, for the grace to recognize the cross of your Son in all the suffering of my life, to adore your holy and inscrutable will in it, to follow your Son on his way to the cross as long as it may please you. Make me sensitive in what concerns your honor and not merely for my own well-being, and then I also will be able to carry many a cross as atonement for my sins. Do not let me be embittered by suffering but mature, patient, selfless, gentle, and filled with longing for that land where there is no pain and for that day when you will wipe all tears from the eyes of those who have loved you and in sorrow have believed in your love and in darkness have believed in your light.

Let my pain be a profession of my faith in your promises, a profession of my hope in your goodness and fidelity, a profession of my love, that I love you more than myself, that I love you for your own sake even without reward. May the cross of my Lord be my model, my power, my consolation, the solution of all obscure questions, the light of every darkness. Grant that we may glory in the cross of our Lord Jesus Christ, grant us to become so mature in true Christian being and life that we no longer regard the cross as a misfortune and incomprehensible meaninglessness but as a sign of your election, as the secret, sure sign that we are yours forever.

For it is a faithful saying that if we die with him we shall also live with him, and if we endure with him we shall also reign with him. Father, we will to share everything with your Son, his life, his divine glory, and therefore his suffering and his death. Only with the cross, give the strength to bear it. Cause us to experience in the cross its blessing also. Give us the cross which your wisdom knows is for our salvation and not our ruin.

Son of the Father, Christ who lives in us, you are our hope of glory. Live in us, bring our life under the laws of your life, make our life like to yours. Live in me, pray in me, suffer in me, more I do not ask. For if I have you I am rich; those who find you have found the power and the victory of their life. Amen.

Selected Bibliography

Comprehensive lists of Karl Rahner's works can be found in the following: Roman Bleistein and Elmar Klinger, eds., *Biographie Karl Rahner 1924–1969*, with an introduction by Herbert Vorgrimler; Roman Bleistein, ed., *Bibliographie Karl Rahner 1969–1974* (Freiburg i. Br.: Herder, 1974); Paul Imhof and Heinrich Treziak, eds., "Bibliographie Karl Rahner 1974–1979," *Wagnis Theologie: Erfahrung mit der Theologie Karl Rahners*, ed. Herbert Vorgrimler (Freiburg i. Br.: Herder, 1979), 579–97; and Paul Imhof and Elisabeth Meuser, eds., "Bibliographie Karl Rahner 1979–1984," in *Glaube in Prozess: Christsein nach dem II. Vatikanum*, ed. Elmar Klinger and Klaus Wittstadt (Freiburg i. Br.: Herder, 1984), 854–71.

Secondary literature on Karl Rahner can be found in the following: Andrew Tallon, "Rahner Studies, 1939–1989, Part I," *Theology Digest* 36, no. 4 (Winter 1989): 321–46; Andrew Tallon, "Rahner Studies, 1974–1989, Part II," *Theology Digest* 37, no. 1 (Spring 1990): 17–41; Albert Raffelt, ed., "Karl Rahner: Bibliographie der Sekundärliteratur 1979–1983," in *Glaube in Prozess*, 873–75.

The Heythrop Journal 25, no. 3 (July 1984): 319–65 offers excellent English primary and secondary bibliographies on Rahner arranged according to topics.

I. WORKS BY KARL RAHNER

A. Select Basic Books

Allow Yourself to be Forgiven: Penance Today. Trans. Salvator Attanasio. Denville, N.J.: Dimension Books, 1975.

Belief Today. Trans. M. H. Heelan, Rosaleen and Ray Ockenden, and William Whitman. New York: Sheed and Ward, 1967.

Biblical Homilies. Trans. Desmond Forristal and Richard Strachan. New York: Herder and Herder, 1966.

Christian at the Crossroads. Trans. Verdant Green. New York: Seabury Press, 1975.

The Christian Commitment: Essays in Pastoral Theology. Trans. Cecily Hastings. New York: Sheed and Ward, 1963.

663

Christian in the Market Place. Trans. Cecily Hastings. New York: Sheed and Ward, 1966.

The Church after the Council. Trans. Davis C. Herron and Rodeline Albrecht. New York: Herder and Herder, 1966.

Do You Believe in God? Trans. Richard Strachan. New York: Paulist Press, 1969.

Confirmation Today: A New Baptism in the Spirit. Trans. Salvator Attanasio. Denville, N.J.: Dimension Books, 1975.

Encounters with Silence. Trans. James M. Demske. Westminster, Md.: Newman Press, 1960.

The Eternal Year. Trans. John Shea. Baltimore: Helicon Press, 1964.

Everyday Faith. Trans. William J. O'Hara. New York: Herder and Herder, 1968.

Faith in a Wintry Season: Conversations and Interviews with Karl Rahner in the Last Years of his Life. Ed. Paul Imhof and Hubert Biallowons. Trans. ed. Harvey D. Egan. New York: Crossroad: 1990.

Foundations of Christian Faith: An Introduction to the Idea of Christianity. Trans. William V. Dych. New York: Seabury Press, 1978.

Grace in Freedom. Trans. Hilda Graf. New York: Herder and Herder, 1969.

Hearers of the Word. Trans. Michael Richards. New York: Herder and Herder, 1969.

I Remember: An Autobiographical Interview. Trans. Harvey D. Egan. New York: Crossroad, 1985.

Karl Rahner in Dialogue: Conversations and Interviews 1965–1982. Ed. Paul Imhof and Hubert Biallowons. Trans. ed. Harvey D. Egan. New York: Crossroad, 1986.

Leading a Christian Life. Trans. Salvator Attanasio, Dorothy White, and James Quigley. Denville, N.J.: Dimension Books, 1970.

Love of Jesus and the Love of Neighbor. Trans. Robert Barr. New York: Crossroad, 1983.

Mary, Mother of the Lord. Trans. W. J. O'Hara. New York: Herder and Herder, 1963.

Mediations on Freedom and the Spirit. Trans. Rosaleen Ockenden, David Smith, and Cecily Bennett. New York: Seabury Press, 1978.

Mediations on Hope and Love. Trans. Verdant Green. New York: Seabury Press, 1977.

Mediations on the Sacraments. Trans. Dorothy White, Salvator Attanasio, James M. Quigley. New York: Seabury Press, 1977.

Nature and Grace: Dilemmas in the Modern Church. Trans. Dinah Wharton. New York: Sheed and Ward, 1964.

Opportunities for Faith: Elements of a Modern Spirituality. Trans. Edward Quinn. New York: Seabury Press, 1974.

On Prayer. New York: Paulist Deus Books, 1968.

Prayers for a Lifetime. New York: Crossroad, 1984.

The Priesthood. Trans. Edward Quinn. New York: Seabury Press, 1973.

The Religious Life Today. Trans. Verdant Green. New York: Seabury Press, 1976.

Servants of the Lord. Trans. Richard Strachan. New York: Herder and Herder, 1968.

The Shape of the Church to Come. Trans. Edward Quinn. New York: Seabury Press, 1974.

Spirit in the World. Trans. William V. Dych. New York: Herder and Herder, 1968.

Spiritual Exercises. Trans. Kenneth Baker. New York: Herder and Herder, 1965.

Theological Investigations. 23 volumes. *I–VI* published in Baltimore by Helicon Press; vols. *VII–X* in New York by Herder and Herder; vols. *XI–XVI* in New York by Seabury Press; vols. *XXVII–XXIII* in New York by Crossroad. Hereafter volume numbers appear immediately after the volume title with the abbreviation *TI*.

 God, Christ, Mary and Grace, TI I. Trans. Cornelius Ernst, 1961.

 Man in the Church, TI II. Trans. Karl H. Kruger, 1963.

 The Theology of the Spiritual Life, TI III. Trans. Karl H. Kruger and Boniface Kruger, 1967.

 More Recent Writings, TI IV. Trans. Kevin Smyth, 1966.

 Later Writings, TI V. Trans. Karl Kruger, 1966.

 Concerning Vatican Council II, TI VI. Trans. Karl H. Kruger and Boniface Kruger, 1969.

 Further Theology of the Spiritual Life 1, TI VII. Trans. David Bourke, 1971.

 Further Theology of the Spiritual Life 2, TI VIII. Trans. David Bourke, 1971.

 Writings of 1965–1967 I, TI IX. Trans. Graham Harrison, 1972.

 Writings of 1965–1967 II, TI X. Trans. David Bourke, 1974.

 Confrontations 1, TI XI. Trans. David Bourke, 1974.

 Confrontations 2, TI XII. Trans. David Bourke, 1974.

 Theology, Anthropology, Christology, TI XIII. Trans. David Bourke, 1975.

 Ecclesiology, Questions in the Church, The Church in the World, TI XIV. Trans. David Bourke, 1976.

 Penance in the Early Church, TI XV. Trans. Lionel Swain, 1982.

 Experience of the Spirit: Source of Theology, TI XVI. Trans. David Moreland, 1979.

 Jesus, Man, and the Church, TI XVII. Trans. Margaret Kohl, 1981.

 God and Revelation, TI XVIII. Trans. Edward Quinn, 1983.

Faith and Ministry, TI XIX. Trans. Edward Quinn, 1983.

Concern for the Church, TI XX. Trans. Edward Quinn, 1981.

Science and Theology, TI XXI. Trans. Hugh Riley, 1988.

Humane Society and the Future of the Church, TI XXII. Trans. Joseph Donceel, 1991.

Final Writings, TI XXIII. Trans. Joseph Donceel and Hugh Riley, 1992.

Theology for Renewal: Bishops, Priests, Laity. Trans. Cecily Hastings and Richard Strachan. New York: Sheed and Ward, 1964.

Theology of Pastoral Action. Trans. W. J. O'Hara. New York: Herder and Herder, 1968.

The Trinity. Trans. Joseph Donceel. New York: Herder and Herder, 1970.

Watch and Pray with Me. Trans. William V. Dych. New York: Herder and Herder, 1966.

B. Select Edited Books and Collaborations

Ed. *Concilium: Theology in the Age of Renewal.* New York: Paulist Press, 1965–69. Vol. 3, *The Pastoral Mission of the Church* (1965). Vol. 13, *Rethinking the Church's Mission* (1966). Vol. 23, *The Pastoral Approach to Atheism* (1967). Vol. 33, *The Renewal of Preaching* (1968).

Ed. *Encyclopedia of Theology: The Concise Sacramentum Mundi.* Trans. John Griffiths, Francis McDonagh, and David Smith. New York: Seabury Press, 1975. Rahner himself contributed over 80 of the articles.

Ed. *The Teaching of the Catholic Church: As Contained in Her Documents.* Trans. Geoffrey Stevens. Originally prepared by Joseph Neuner and Heinrich Roos. Staten Island, N.Y.: Alba House, 1967.

With Heinrich Fries. *Unity of the Churches: An Actual Possibility.* Trans. Ruth C. L. Gritsch and Eric W. Gritsch. Ramsey, N.J.: Paulist Press, 1985.

With Angelus Häussling. *The Celebration of the Eucharist.* Trans. W. J. O'Hara. New York: Herder and Herder, 1968.

With Paul Imhof and Helmuth Nils Loose. *Ignatius of Loyola.* Historical introduction by Paul Imhof, S.J., color photographs by Helmuth Nils Loose, trans. Rosaleen Ockenden. Cleveland: Collins, 1979. See especially, Karl Rahner, "Ignatius of Loyola Speaks to a Modern Jesuit," 9–38.

With Pinchas Lapide. *Encountering Jesus — Encountering Judaism: A Dialogue.* Trans. Davis Perkins. New York: Crossroad, 1987.

With Karl Lehmann. *Kerygma and Dogma.* Trans. William Glen-Doepel and ed. Thomas O'Meara. New York: Herder and Herder, 1969.

With Johann B. Metz. *The Courage to Pray.* Trans. Sarah O'Brien Twohig. New York: Crossroad, 1981.

With Heinrich Schlier, eds. *Quaestiones Disputatae.* New York: Herder and Herder, 1961–67. The volume numbers in the German and English series sometimes differ and in this listing appear immediately after the volume title with the abbreviation *Q.D.*

    Inspiration in the Bible, Q.D. 1. Trans. Charles Henkey, 1961.

    On the Theology of Death, Q.D. 2. Trans. Charles Henkey, 1961.

    With Joseph Ratzinger. *The Episcopate and the Primacy, Q.D. 4.* Trans. Kenneth Baker et al., 1962.

    Church and the Sacraments, Q.D. 9. Trans. William J. O'Hara, 1963.

    Visions and Prophecies, Q.D. 10. Trans. Charles Henkey and Richard Strachan, 1963.

    On Heresy, Q.D. 11. Trans. William J. O'Hara, 1964.

    Dynamic Element in the Church, Q.D. 12. Trans. William J. O'Hara, 1964.

    Hominization: The Evolutionary Origin of Man as a Theological Problem, Q.D. 13. Trans. William J. O'Hara, 1965.

    With Joseph Ratzinger. *Revelation and Tradition, Q.D. 17.* Trans. William J. O'Hara, 1966.

    The Christian of the Future, Q.D. 18. Trans. William J. O'Hara, 1967.

With Wilhelm Thüsing. *A New Christology.* Trans. Verdant Green and David Smith. New York: Seabury Press, 1980.

Et al., eds. *Sacramentum Mundi: An Encyclopedia of Theology,* vols. 1–6. Trans. William J. O'Hara et al. New York: Herder and Herder, 1968–70.

With Karl Heinz Weger. *Our Christian Faith: Answer for the Future.* Trans. Francis McDonagh. New York: Crossroad, 1981.

With Herbert Vorgrimler. *Theological Dictionary.* New Revised Edition. Trans. Richard Strachan, David Smith, Robert Newell, and Sarah O'Brien Twohig. New York: Crossroad, 1981.

C. Anthologies

Lehmann, Karl and Albert Raffelt, eds. *The Practice of Faith: A Handbook of Contemporary Spirituality.* New York: Crossroad, 1983.

McCool, Gerald A., ed. *A Rahner Reader.* New York: Seabury Press, 1975.

II. SELECT SECONDARY LITERATURE

America, 31 October 1970: Special Issue on *Karl Rahner.*

Bacik, James J. *Apologetics and the Eclipse of Mystery. Mystagogy According to Karl Rahner.* Notre Dame, Ind.: University of Notre Dame Press, 1980.

Buckley, James J. "Karl Rahner as a Dogmatic Theologian," *The Thomist* 47, no. 3 (1983): 364–94.

Carr, Ann. *The Theological Method of Karl Rahner.* Missoula, Mont.: Scholars Press, 1977.

Fahey, Michael A. "1904–1984, Karl Rahner, Theologian." *Proceedings of the Thirty-Ninth Annual Convention,* 84–98. The Catholic Theological Society of America, Washington, D.C., 1984.

Kelly, William J., ed., *Theology and Discovery: Essays in Honor of Karl Rahner, S.J.* Milwaukee, Wis.: Marquette University Press, 1980.

Kress, Robert. *A Rahner Handbook.* Atlanta: John Knox Press, 1982.

O'Donovan, Leo. *A World of Grace: An Introduction to the Themes and Foundations of Karl Rahner's Theology.* New York: Seabury Press, 1980.

Vass, George. *A Theologian in Search of a Philosophy: Understanding Karl Rahner.* Westminster, Md.: Christian Classics, 1985.

―――. *The Mystery of Man and the Foundations of a Theological System: Understanding Karl Rahner.* Westminster, Md.: Christian Classics, 1985.

Vorgrimler, Herbert. *Karl Rahner: His Life, Thought, and Works.* Trans. Edward Quinn. Glen Rock, N.J.: Paulist Deus Books, 1966.

―――. *Understanding Karl Rahner: An Introduction to His Life and Thought.* Trans. John Bowden. New York: Crossroad, 1986.

Weger, Karl-Heinz. *Karl Rahner: An Introduction to His Theology.* Trans. D. Smith. New York: Seabury Press, 1980.

Wong, Joseph H. P. *Logos-Symbol in the Christology of Karl Rahner.* Rome: Libreria Ateneo Salesiano, 1984.